Understanding Culture's Influence on Behavior

Second Edition

Richard Brislin
University of Hawaii

Harcourt College Publishers

Fort Worth   Philadelphia   San Diego   New York   Orlando   Austin   San Antonio
Toronto   Montreal   London   Sydney   Tokyo

Publisher	Earl McPeek
Executive Editor	Carol Wada
Associate Acquisitions Editor	Lisa Hensley
Market Strategist	Kathleen Sharp
Developmental Editor	Christine Abshire
Project Editor	Elaine Richards
Art Director	Carol Kincaid
Production Manager	Andrea Archer

Cover image: Joel Nakamura

ISBN: 0-15-508340-6
Library of Congress Catalog Card Number: 99-61920

Copyright © 2000, 1993 by Harcourt, Inc.

Address for Domestic Orders
Harcourt College Publishers, 6277 Sea Harbor Drive, Orlando, FL 32887-6777
800-782-4479

Address for International Orders
International Customer Service
Harcourt, Inc., 6277 Sea Harbor Drive, Orlando, FL 32887-6777
407-345-3800
(fax) 407-345-4060
(e-mail) hbintl@harcourtbrace.com

Address for Editorial Correspondence
Harcourt College Publishers, 301 Commerce Street, Suite 3700, Fort Worth, TX 76102
Web Site Address
http://www.harcourtcollege.com

Harcourt College Publishers will provide complimentary supplements or supplement packages to those adopters qualified under our adoption policy. Please contact your sales representative to learn how you qualify. If as an adopter or potential user you receive supplements you do not need, please return them to your sales representative or send them to: Attn: Returns Department, Troy Warehouse, 465 South Lincoln Drive, Troy, MO 63379.

Printed in the United States of America

0 1 2 3 4 5 6 7 8   0 3 9   9 8 7 6 5 4 3 2

Harcourt College Publishers

PREFACE

Understanding Culture's Influence on Behavior, Second Edition, for college juniors and seniors enrolled in courses dealing with culture's impact on human behavior, was written with two very basic assumptions. The first is that people all over the world will continue to increase their contact with members of diverse cultures. The second is that research in cross-cultural studies can provide helpful guidelines for people as they interact in a fast-changing world marked by increasing intercultural contact.

The text is designed to stimulate students' insights into their own cultures, the cultures of others, and how culture influences human behavior. This text may prove useful in courses such as cross-cultural psychology, intercultural communication, multicultural education, international human resources development, and international management. Many professors feel that students should be introduced to issues of cultural diversity as soon as possible, so *Understanding Culture's Influence on Behavior* may also prove useful for students taking a first course in the study of human behavior.

The reasons for the increase in intercultural contacts are many. People continue to emigrate in hopes of a chance to better themselves. Students take advantage of educational opportunities in other parts of the world. Jet travel allows easy access to most parts of the globe. People increasingly look for opportunities to actively learn about other cultures while on vacation. In business, the days of unilateral international trade policies are over, which means that more people from different countries must communicate effectively to establish joint manufacturing agreements and international marketing plans. As more countries seek political independence (e.g., within the former U.S.S.R.), growing numbers of highly trained people are needed to establish workable diplomatic contacts.

Cross-cultural research also can facilitate the interaction of people from culturally diverse groups within the same country. In many parts of the world, members of minority groups are refusing to become part of a homogenous melting pot. Instead, they are insisting that their cultures be respected and that professionals in various fields be sufficiently knowledgeable to take cultural differences into account. For example, parents want teachers to understand cultural differences that might affect their children's progress in school. Members of minority groups seeking medical help demand that physicians and nurses be sensitive to and knowledgeable about culturally influenced behaviors that affect health care delivery. When people seek jobs or places to live, legal requirements in many countries prohibit discrimination on the basis of gender, ethnicity, race, or religion.

In some cases, this means that people who might once have been members of a powerful majority group will be interacting with culturally different others even if they view these interactions as undesirable. One of the aims of this book is to teach people to examine their cultural outlooks. For some, however, the study of culture and cultural differences can be an especially difficult task. Even when they know that intercultural contact will be part of their futures, they may have had little previous experience with cultural differences. They may have grown up in neighborhoods where people were from very homogenous backgrounds. Even if they attended schools with a culturally diverse student body, social norms may have dictated that "different people shouldn't mix" and that "people should stick to their own." In addition, they may have only rarely had opportunities to examine the influence of their own cultures on their lives, because such thinking is a rather abstract exercise when it occurs in the absence of experiences with people from different cultures. Included among the benefits of being challenged and stimulated by cultural differences is a greater acceptance of the reality of increased intercultural contact.

CRITICAL INCIDENTS

In preparing this text, I have tried to keep in mind that it can be a difficult task to introduce culture and cultural differences. One helpful approach is to ask students to read and analyze various "critical incidents," and for each chapter I have written several to help clarify important concepts. Critical incidents present readers with real situations with which they can empathize; people in the incidents are making decisions about their romantic relationships, about their jobs, about their education, and about behaviors that can prevent later health problems. All of the incidents involve the influence of culture and demand an understanding of cultural differences. People from different cultures are trying to interact and to understand each other, but something goes wrong! Why were the results of the interaction so disappointing? All of the critical incidents introduce concepts developed by cross-cultural researchers that help when analyzing and understanding the differences. They introduce students to the importance of the role these concepts play in critical incidents similar to those in their own lives. With this introduction as background, cross-cultural concepts are then more fully explained through discussions of various research studies, the basic "building blocks" of our knowledge about culture's influence on human behavior. The combination of concepts useful in thinking about one's own behavior and the analysis of research studies assists in fulfilling two goals: (1) to encourage students to gain new insights into their own lives; and, at the same time, (2) to become exposed to sophisticated research studies.

RESEARCH AREAS

Another way of introducing the importance of culture and cultural differences is the selection of research areas with which students already have some familiarity, given their participation in their own cultures. For example, all readers have some memories of their own socialization experiences, during which they may have made mistakes but learned about their own cultural norms as a result (chapter 4). All have gone to school (chapter 5), have been tempted to act in a prejudicial manner and/or have been the target of discrimination (chapter 6), and have been expected to interact with others who are different, perhaps in terms of social status within their cultures (chapter 7). Most readers will have worked for wages and are either currently working or will be doing so in the near future (chapter 8). All readers have had interactions with members of the opposite sex and have undoubtedly wondered about differences among the males and females whom they have known (chapter 9). All readers desire the benefits of good health and are concerned with behaviors that can prevent health problems (chapter 10). By beginning with their existing knowledge of and interest in these topic areas, information on how culture affects people's socialization, formal education, choices about work, and so forth, can be integrated into the discussions. Ideally, students will gain further insights into their own cultures by comparing their experiences with those that are common among people in other countries.

CROSS-CULTURAL VS. INTERCULTURAL RESEARCH

When terms are used carefully, researchers often distinguish between two types of studies. "Cross-cultural research" is the broadest term, and it refers to studies dealing with how culture influences human behavior. One approach to cross-cultural research is to carry out parallel studies, or studies of similar concepts in different cultures. For example (and discussed more fully in chapter 5), Tobin, Wu, and Davidson (1989) studied preschools in Taiwan, Japan, and the United States, with special attention given to how very young children are expected to change as a result of preschool experiences. The documentation of differing expectations yields important and interesting findings. For example, American children are expected to learn to speak up for themselves; the Taiwanese and Japanese children are expected to fit into a group and to downplay individual demands.

"Intercultural research" refers to studies of people from different cultures coming into contact and interacting frequently, often in face-to-face relationships. If American children were living in Japan and were attending preschools there (a few case studies of this were discussed by Tobin and his colleagues), then investigators have the opportunity to formulate an intercultural research project. They might examine, for instance, the behaviors of Japanese teachers who are unaccustomed to American children who, in their own country, would be expected to make individual choices about preferred school activities. Studies of intercultural contact make the role of culture especially clear since, often, people are behaving very appropriately from the point of view of norms in their own cultures. When well-meaning people have difficulties interacting in intercultural settings, examinations of the cultural backgrounds of the people involved often lead to good explanations for the reasons. Both cross-cultural and intercultural research studies will be discussed in this text.

In my own teaching, I have found that students often find intercultural studies most interesting since they can often imagine themselves as participants in the types of interaction studied. For example, they can imagine themselves as schoolchildren faced with very different cultural expectations. With their interest stimulated, they then enjoy reading the cross-cultural studies that have investigated the role cultural factors play in decisions about important topics such as schooling, mate choice, work, and health.

THIS EDITION

The first edition of this book was published in 1993. In preparing this second edition, I benefited from the suggestions of students, colleagues, professors who have used the text, and consultants commissioned by the publisher. There are significant changes.

- Each chapter has an introductory section that emphasizes important points readers should note as they study the text.
- Material has been added on various approaches to cross-cultural research, including developments that flourished in the 1990s which became known as "cultural research" and "indigenous approaches."
- Research citations have been updated throughout the book.
- In each chapter, there have been additions of at least one body of recent research covered in detail so that readers can understand how a set of research questions was formulated and investigated. As with the first edition, these research areas were chosen with a combination of importance and inherent interest in mind. Examples are cultural influences on how time is used (chapter 1), studies in the universality of certain personality traits (chapter 2), adolescence (chapter 4), trust among people from different cultural backgrounds (chapter 8), and the prevention and treatment of sexually transmitted diseases (chapter 9).

SUPPLEMENTS TO THE TEXT

I was very pleased when Dr. Ted Singelis agreed to prepare a student manual to accompany this text. Dr. Singelis and I worked together on a daily basis for five years, and we maintain frequent contact now that we work at different institutions. Dr. Singelis and I agree that, whenever possible, the study of cross-cultural and intercultural research is aided when students can participate in active exercises designed around important concepts covered in traditional texts. Each of the chapters in the student manual contains an active exercise, and we hope that movement between exercises and textual material will assist student learning, interest, and motivation to do further reading.

ACKNOWLEDGMENTS

Many people offered assistance by reviewing chapters, suggesting important research studies for inclusion, testing out chapters in their own teaching, suggesting ideas for how material might best be presented, and offering encouragement when stumbling blocks were encountered. These people include John Adamopoulous, Deborah Best, D. P. S. Bhawuk, Michael Bond, Ayse Carden, Jan Fried, Ge Gao, Sharon Gorman, Geert Hofstede, Eve Howard, Lane Kelley, Shari Koga, Walt Lonner, Roy Malpass, Steven Moles, Janek Pandey, Anita Rosenfield, Karen Schmidt, Larry Smith, Pirongrong Ramasoota, Ted Singelis, Cookie Stephan, Walter Stephen, Harry Triandis, Kim Turner, Mary Wang, Wei-zhong Wang, Tu Weiming, Ann Marie Yamada, and Tomoko Yoshida-Isogai. First drafts of several chapters were written while I held a visiting appointment at Arizona State University, and I am grateful for the support of faculty and staff there. Logistical, financial, and moral support were provided by the staff of the Center for International Business Research (CIBER), College of Business Administration, University of Hawaii. I am especially grateful for the support offered by the CIBER director, Dr. Shirley Daniel. Daniel Romano and Julie Haiyan Chao conceived the drawings that were later developed into the sketches and figures found throughout the text. All of these people greeted this text writing project with enthusiasm, and I hope that our shared excitement about the study of culture's influence on behavior will be conveyed to readers.

The following professors reviewed the manuscript of the second edition, and I am grateful for their input: John Adamoupoulos, Grand Valley State University; Robert A. Howard, California State University, Chico; Ferdinand Jones, Brown University; Mary G. Klinger, Empire State College–SUNY; Walt Lonner, Western Washington University; Steve Lopez, University of California, Los Angeles; Fathali Massoud Moghadamm, Georgetown University; Debra Reece, Bethal College; Marshall Segall, Syracuse University; and Carolyn Simmons, University of North Carolina.

I would also like to thank the members of the team at Harcourt College Publishers for helping to bring this book to its completion: Carol Wada, executive editor; Lisa Hensley, associate acquisitions editor; Kathleen Sharp, market strategist, Christine Abshire, developmental editor; Elaine Richards, project editor; Andrea Archer, production manager; Carol Kincaid, art director; Kevin Meade, illustrator; Kay Kaylor, copy editor; Beth Alvarez, proofreader; and Leoni McVey, indexer.

—*Richard Brislin*

CONTENTS IN BRIEF

CONTENTS IN DETAIL

Chapter 5
Formal Educational Experiences   154

Chapter 6
Intergroup Relations: Cultures in Contact   195

Chapter 7

Interacting Successfully With People From Other Cultures   237

Chapter 8

Culture's Effects on the Work World   278

Chapter 9
Culture and Gender   322

C H A P T E R 1

CONCEPTUALIZING CULTURE AND ITS IMPACT

CHAPTER OVERVIEW

Assume a friend tells you she will introduce you to a third person tomorrow. What information would you want to have so that you can plan for the introduction? Although your awareness of the person's age, gender, and social status will be valuable, many scholars feel that knowledge of the third person's cultural background will provide the most helpful information.

This chapter will begin to investigate the importance of people's culture to understanding their behavior. A definition of culture will be discussed, with special attention to features such as shared values among people who communicate in the same language, transmission from generation to generation, and guidance concerning choices among behaviors in a variety of social settings. An example will be referred to several times: Does cultural guidance encourage or discourage the maintenance of cordial relations after the breakup of a marriage or a romance? The distinction between two approaches to research, cross-cultural studies and cultural studies, will be reviewed. Although hard and fast distinctions between the two do not exist, cross-cultural researchers are more likely to identify important concepts and to study them in detail. They often do this by comparing concepts, such as relations between men and women, in different cultures. In contrast, cultural researchers are more likely to examine concepts in the exact cultural contexts where they are meaningful to people. Their research on relations between men and women would be likely to focus on reasons for typical behaviors, given a specific culture's history, present, and predicted future. Both types of research can lead to important insights about human behavior.

Discussions about definitions of culture and approaches to research can be made clearer with analysis of specific examples. Levine (1997) studied people's use of time in 31 different cultures. He moved back and forth between the cross-cultural and the cultural approaches. Concepts investigated included the importance of punctuality and the amount of time necessary to buy products. Results were compared to important human concerns such as heart disease. This and another example, the importance of culture to understanding the centralization of power contrasted with the diffusion of power, are discussed in this chapter. These discussions also introduce concerns to be examined in more detail in later chapters: heart disease in chapter 10, which covers culture and health, and power in chapter 8, which covers culture and work.

CULTURE'S INFLUENCE: AN EXAMPLE

Stan was first attracted to Rogelia when he heard her tell a joke about Imelda Marcos's shoes. Rogelia had never met anyone with the confidence and "take charge" attitude Stan possessed.

Stan was 23 years old, having moved to the Philippines after completing his education in Ohio. He hadn't traveled very much prior to accepting a job in the Philippines as an agricultural specialist, and most of his friends had been from his same American middle-class background. He had taken courses in tropical agriculture and wanted to see for himself if the recommendations made in the books could be put to use. Rogelia was from a rural village. She moved from the village to Manila, where she met Stan, because of scholarships for academic achievement at the secondary school level. She finished her degree program at the University of the Philippines and was now teaching at a good private high school.

Stan and Rogelia started dating, and their emotional feelings toward each other intensified. After about six months, however, problems began to occur in the relationship. Rogelia's parents were not happy she was dating an American. Stan felt that Rogelia's friends disapproved of the relationship and that they were not particularly friendly toward him. Stan and Rogelia then agreed to stop dating, realizing the romantic relationship was not working.

A few weeks after this agreement, Stan called Rogelia and asked her to go to a movie. Stan mentioned that he wanted to continue the friendship. Puzzled by the call, Rogelia refused, letting it be known that she didn't want to see Stan again under any circumstances. Stan was quite puzzled and was very hurt by Rogelia's coolness.

This anecdote involves behaviors influenced by people's cultures. The culture Rogelia has grown up in has given her guidance on specific behaviors: People who were once in a romantic relationship rarely have any contact after that relationship ends. Filipinos believe that maintaining friendly relationships causes jealousy among the people's eventual marriage partners, and it interferes with the loyalty expected toward the married couple's extended families. The culture Stan has grown up in does not give such explicit guidance. Stan, rather, is in the realm of individual differences. Some Americans maintain close relationships with former romantic partners and some do not. Some want to keep up friendly relationships, and their current spouses even encourage this. Others feel that maintaining such relationships will be too emotionally painful and that it is best to cease contact. Some Americans decide one way and some the other: No widely shared set of guidelines exists, and the concept of "widely shared" is central to an understanding of culture. This point will be reiterated throughout this chapter.

A major difficulty in discussions of culture is that people rarely have the opportunity to examine the influence of their own cultural background on their behavior. Stan and Rogelia, for instance, have no way of knowing how the other is interpreting the reasons for their misunderstandings. Coming from backgrounds (Ohio and the rural Philippines) where most people were similar to them, they never have been stimulated to examine culture-based reasons for problems. They are forced to think about such possibilities only because their cultures have come into contact.

As with all of the examples discussed throughout this book, I hope many of the issues raised will encourage readers to think about the influence of culture on their own lives. In this example, the behaviors are not unique only to Filipinos or to Filipino Americans. The issue of maintaining contact with former romantic partners is controversial in any culture that emphasizes the extended family and maintains norms that encourage people to frown on divorce. Within the United States, for example, Hispanics (Marin & Marin, 1991) who maintain the traditional value of close family ties would identify with Rogelia's preferences. They would not be as comfortable as Anglo Americans are about maintaining close ties with former romantic partners. They may have been exposed to this guidance for behavior in aphorisms such as "Embers that once burned can become hot again."

Note that the term "traditional" was used. If people move away from the part of the world they were socialized in (to be discussed more fully in chapter 4), they will be exposed to cultural differences that challenge their attitudes and values. Many challenges stem from people's desire to move from the world's rural areas to highly industrialized cities. Such moves force people to make adjustments in their lives, and one potential change is that *traditional* family ties weaken as people are exposed to the impersonal norms of the big city (Triandis, 1995; Yang, 1988). Some Hispanics have made such a move, have been exposed to values that challenge their traditions, and then have decided they prefer the more modern values. Examples are Mexicans who have moved to big cities in the United States and who consequently come into day-to-day contact with Anglo American culture. These Hispanics are more likely to identify with Stan's preferences. They would agree that relationships involving past romantic partners can be maintained and that these continuing friendships do not necessarily pose a threat to current romances. They even may be able to give reasons, such as "In big cities where it is hard to get to know people, this person can be part of my network and useful for my career development." For Hispanics, then, it is important to know the amount of exposure they have had to nontraditional values, because both culture and cultural contact can have an impact on their behavior.

Such contact will become more frequent around the world, and it will be one of the major influences on life in the 21st century. Businesspeople will continue to accept international assignments. Investments across national boundaries will bring additional business-oriented contact (Adler, 1997). The increasing desire for democracy in eastern Europe and Asia will bring visits by political experts who give instruction in such modern democratic practices as appealing to the electorate through the mass media (Warner, 1990). High-quality advanced education will continue to be a product students will seek out even if it is in countries other than their own (Martin & Harrell, 1996; Paige, 1990). Within large countries, minority groups (e.g.,

African Americans, Hispanics, and Native Americans in the United States) are refusing to become part of a melting pot and are demanding respect for their cultural backgrounds. Neighborhoods, schools, businesses, and the delivery of social services will all see the increased effects of legal demands that insure the rights of previously rejected ethnic groups (Cushner, 1990). All of these facts demand sensitivity to the nature of people's cultures and to cultural differences. Given its complexity, the concept "culture" needs to be the focus of a detailed examination.

I would like to examine culture in four steps:

1. Suggesting a short definition as a starting point
2. Moving to some examples of how the term *culture* is used in everday writings and conversations
3. Discussing various aspects of "culture" at length
4. Ending with a working definition many researchers have found useful

CULTURE: PINNING DOWN AN AMORPHOUS CONCEPT

For beginning this discussion, the following definition is useful: *Culture* refers to shared values and concepts among people who most often speak the same language and live in proximity to each other. These values and concepts are transmitted for generations, and they provide guidance for everyday behaviors. As will be discovered in the rest of this chapter, great complexity can be added to this definition when analyses of cultural change, people's selections among cultural elements, and individual differences are added.

People use *culture* and related terms in their everyday conversations, but I fear the concept is not well understood. I have heard statements such as the following when people are contemplating overseas business ventures, planning a vacation in another country, or preparing classes for students from very diverse backgrounds:

- When doing business with the Japanese, Americans must keep in mind the cultural differences in how meetings are carried out and how contracts are negotiated.
- Don't just go to well-trod tourist spots! Mix with the people and experience their culture.
- The students you will teach probably will not have the same middle-class background as yourself. They will likely be from different cultures. When you are making lesson plans and making decisions concerning how best to present material to students, this important fact must be remembered constantly.

These statements are all correct but contain a potential stumbling block. The concepts "culture" and "cultural differences" are used in ways that may not be very helpful. The danger in the frequent use of the term *culture* is that it contains so much information about values, ideals, concepts, and expected behaviors that the term is not terribly useful in analyzing any one specific aspect. It is the specific aspects of culture that are helpful in analyzing human behavior. In the prior examples, the specific aspects of Japanese business practices, nontourist activities, and children's expectations about what will happen during the school day will guide decisions about behavior. In the example of Rogelia's behavior toward Stan, the specific guidance concerns continuing relationships with former romantic partners.

To pin down the amorphous concept "culture," it is useful to examine its features in a checklist. The features then can be analyzed with a possible aspect of one's own culture in mind. Put another way, various "candidates" can be put forward, with consideration focusing on whether or not they are part of, or features of, one's culture. For example, a candidate for consideration might be "continuing relationships with past romantic partners." To preview a conclusion I will make after this list is considered, the more checklist features a candidate has that qualify as "an important aspect of my life," the more likely the candidate is actually culturally influenced. Readers might list a few values, ideals, and assumptions about life that they consider personally important. Examples of candidates might be "standing on my own two feet," "education as a way of advancing myself in life," "respect for elders," "the right to own handguns," or "respect for the rights of women." Then, the list of a culture's features can be consulted. The more points on the checklist the candidate passes in the reader's judgment, the more likely the candidate is part of the reader's culture. If the candidate passes only a few of the features or checklist-generated questions, then it is probably determined by factors other than culture, such as people's personalities or their idiosyncratic preferences that are not widely enough shared to be considered part of their culture.

The following sections discuss the checklist's 12 features of culture. The checklist starts with widely shared views about how life should be lived.

Assumptions About Life

Culture consists of ideals, values, and assumptions about life that people widely share and that guide specific behaviors. Yet these are invisible elements. Assumptions, values, and ideals are not immediately obvious. Instead, they are stored in people's minds and consequently are hard for outsiders to see. Because these components are part of almost all anthropological definitions of culture (Kroeber & Kluckhohn, 1952), it is important to consider them carefully. Assumptions, ideals, and values are stored in people's minds; they can be called on when necessary for guiding specific behaviors. The value of "personal cleanliness," for example, guides widely practiced behaviors such as taking a daily bath or shower. Often, when a value is not threatened, no visible behaviors will cause people to think about the value. People don't think much about "cleanliness" if everyone they know is careful about their personal hygiene. But when the value comes into question in some way, behaviors to protect it can be expected if the value is culturally determined.

I was once a member of a club that had not held an election of officers in 50 years. Instead, a committee would present a slate of candidates to the membership, and the club members would approve the slate by voice vote. One year, a group of newcomers nominated a candidate for president after the committee chair presented the suggested slate. Without blinking an eye, the committee chairperson asked each candidate to give a short speech outlining goals for the club and called for pieces

The time spent watching television can substitute for the sense of community one gets from

of paper so that members could vote. The vote took place. The committee's candidate happened to win, but the new candidate won 2 years later. The point to consider here is that the committee chair possessed the cultural value "election through the democratic process," even though relevant behaviors hadn't been used in that club in 50 years. Because of his long-term participation in organizations within his culture outside of this one club, the chairperson could summon behaviors associated with the value "democracy." He called for speeches and for pieces of paper so that club members could vote by secret ballot. The value of democracy, shared by all club members, was retained. This value was invisible at first because it was contained in members' brains, hidden from outsiders who might have visited the club that election day. But when needed, that important value led to visible behaviors.

The Person-Made Part of the Environment

Another key aspect of culture is that it is created by people. Whenever a candidate for a cultural value is considered, aspects of it that are clearly formulated by people

frequent conversations with friends.

should come to mind. First emphasized by Herskovits (1948), the "person-made" aspects of culture can be contrasted with the environmental givens people face. Are typhoons in Hawaii part of its culture? Is the cold weather during Minnesota winters part of the culture people are exposed to? Should the hot and humid weather commonly experienced during summers be considered part of the culture that influences the lives of children born and raised in Alabama or Mississippi? The best answer to each question is no. These aspects of climate are part of the environment people face and are not person made. However, people's *responses* to the environment that surrounds them are part of their culture. In many Pacific island societies, houses are made of inexpensive and readily available materials so that they can be replaced at minimal cost should a typhoon destroy them. In Minnesota, person-made norms about the proper response to snow are so widely known that they are part of psychological personality tests to measure well-socialized individuals. The California Personality Inventory (Gough, 1969) contains the item "Every family owes it to the city to keep its lawn mowed in summer and sidewalks shoveled in winter." If people answer "agree," this contributes to their score on a scale that measures the internalization of a cultural norm that involves concern for others. Norms for proper behavior are excellent examples of person-made aspects of people's environment—in short, their culture.

An interesting example shows how person-made responses to environment influence a variety of other human behaviors. Writing in the *Encyclopedia of Southern Culture*, Arsenault (1989) argues that the introduction of air-conditioning had an impact on the cultural value of "southern hospitality." Prior to about 1950, people in the South would respond to hot and humid summers by sitting out on their porches and chatting with neighbors and passersby on the sidewalk. After the introduction of air-conditioning and its widespread adoption in the mid- and late 1950s (a good example of a person-made intervention to make life more comfortable), people would sit in their own living rooms and read, watch television, or chat with immediate family members. The southern sense of a wider community and knowledge about the goings-on in the lives of neighbors became noticeably diminished. Person-made interventions (air-conditioning and also television) had an impact on a cultural value.

Transmission Generation to Generation

Cultural values exist for long periods in a society. Examples of these values can be found in a culture's oral or written literatures. To look at this point from the opposite direction, cultural values cannot be introduced quickly. It usually takes years for people to become familiar enough with a new value or ideal for it to be considered part of their culture.

If values considered central to a society have existed for many years, these must be transmitted from one generation to another. Children must learn the values from various elders who are responsibile for making sure the children grow up as acceptable community members. These elders include the children's parents, teachers, and noteworthy community figures such as politicians, physicians, and religious leaders. Interestingly, often some adults in a community can be considered negative models who do not behave according to the culture's values. These are the adults who have not made the transition from childhood to acceptable and respected community members. Examples are criminals, derelicts, the habitually unemployed, and harmless but odd figures who in the past may have been known as "village idiots."

Parents often point to successful adults as the types of people children can become if they adopt culturally acceptable behaviors, whether these are doing one's homework in the United States or helping adults with cultivating bananas in a Pacific island society. Examples of successful adults are lawyers, college professors, and physicians in the United States and chiefs in Pacific island societies. Approaching their responsibility in another way, adults often point to negative models to convey feelings about unacceptable behaviors, such as laziness or a lack of success in career development. When my father was young, a man lived in the community who wore a hook on his deformed arm. His family name was Jackson, and "Hook" Jackson had the job of cleaning up after horse-drawn carriages passing through the streets. Teachers and parents used Hook as a negative model: "If you don't do your homework (or stop fighting or help out around the house with your chores), you'll end up just like Hook Jackson!" Hook passed into a better life by the time of my own childhood, but his activities became part of my family's oral tradition. By telling me stories about Hook and other community characters, my father clearly communicated his thoughts about acceptable and unacceptable career choices and the proper preparation (during childhood) for adult responsibilities. Guidance on behavior considered proper in a culture is often contained in stories elders share with children (Howard, 1991; Rothbaum & Xu, 1995).

Experiences During Childhood

If cultural values and ideals are transmitted generation to generation, then there must be childhood experiences that lead to the learning and eventual internalization of the values. Put another way, if people write down a candidate for a cultural value, they should be able to think of experiences during their childhood that helped them to learn that value.

Most readers socialized in North America and Europe will agree with the ideal that "it is wise to develop good public speaking skills" because they are so important in a variety of careers. Given this ideal, childhood experiences related to the development of good public speaking skills must occur. Most people in such cultures remember childhood experiences (often uncomfortable) surrounding their first public speaking endeavors. They remember their nervousness, their stumblings, and their anxieties. Often, they remember physical symptoms such as excessive sweating, an increased heart rate, and nausea. It takes a great deal of time to develop good public speaking skills, and employees, for example, become truly comfortable with their supervisor's request to "prepare a speech" only after a number of formal courses in high school and college and much practice.

At times, memorable childhood public speaking experiences can lead to specific behaviors associated with them that people practice as adults. When I was 13 or 14 years old, I was in charge of preparations for a Boy Scout hike through a national forest. Later, I was asked to talk about the hike in front of the church group that sponsored the Boy Scout troop. I described everything that went wrong: inadequate food, inadequate cold weather gear, and problems associated with transportation to and from the national forest where the hike started and ended. My father was in the audience and later took me aside. He said, "Richard, don't ever make excuses when you give a public presentation. People don't want to hear about all these troubles. If there are problems, discuss the positive lessons learned and make jokes about the difficulties." My father was not being overly critical or unkind. He was carefully grooming me to become an adequate public speaker, realizing that this skill is useful in many adult careers. My memory of this experience reminds me of what not to do when I make speeches.

Interestingly, I later learned that clear cultural differences exist in what is considered good public speaking. In Japan and many other Asian countries, speakers often begin with apologies. "Thank you for taking the time and trouble to come. Please forgive this inadequate speech, and please forgive me for preparing it so poorly. You know much more about the subject matter than I do." This difference has led to a cross-cultural joke that people knowledgeable about both styles frequently share. Note how I mentioned the role of humor in public presentations as part of my father's advice. A Japanese businessperson was visiting a *Fortune* 500 company in New York. He was asked to give a speech. He began, "I realize that Americans often begin by making a joke. In Japan, we frequently begin with an apology. I'll compromise by apologizing for not having a joke."

Culture Is Not Widely Discussed

Readers might engage in this short exercise. Assume immigrants to your community (from either Mexico, Southeast Asia, or Russia) asked the question "What should I know about your culture so that we can understand each other better?" Readers might list three answers to the question.

My guess is that this will prove a difficult exercise. One reason is that people do not frequently ask this or a similar question when they are in the company of others who share the same culture. In other words, people do not frequently talk about their own culture or the influence that culture has on their behavior. These mildly non-commonsense assertions may sound strange. On the one hand, I am writing an entire book about the importance of culture in people's lives. On the other hand, I am arguing that people don't talk about it very much.

The explanation for this seeming contradiction is that culture is widely shared. Because cultural values and ideals are widely known within a society, people have little need to discuss them. Most North Americans and many Europeans will agree that "voting in a democratic manner" is a cultural value. Yet adults who were socialized into familiarity with this value do not find the need to discuss it with any frequency or in much detail. The value is discussed instead in countries where democracy is a developing value (Romania, Nepal, Russia) and where political activists are demanding it (China, Cuba). Arguments pro and con are lengthy and intense because not all people in these countries are familiar with all aspects of democracy. In North America, with a long tradition of democratic political processes, extensive discussions of democracy itself are unnecessary, except when such values are threatened.

Returning to the example of good public speaking, I have been on selection committees for college and university faculty members. As part of the interview process, candidates frequently give a public presentation. When committee members consider the merits of the various candidates, they do not extensively discuss public speaking skills. They are very familiar with the need for these skills, and they recently have seen demonstrations of their presence or absence. Consequently, they do not have to spend much time discussing the quality of candidates' speaking skills. Yet, public speaking skills can play an important role in the committee members' recommendations. When cultural values and ideals are involved, the length of discussion time devoted to an issue does not necessarily indicate its importance.

Other important implications stem from the fact culture is not frequently discussed. One is that people are poorly prepared to discuss their culture with interested visitors and with people wishing to learn from one another's experiences. To return to the example of voting in democratic elections, many well-educated Americans cannot give terribly helpful answers to Russians, Romanians, and Chinese dissidents who ask basic questions about democracy. After a few generalizations such as "voting on the first Tuesday in November" and "candidates selected by two and sometimes a few more major political parties," people become inarticulate. The reason is that democracy in America is taken for granted and consequently people seldom have to discuss it as a cultural value. Therefore, people don't have practice discussing the nature of democracy for interested outsiders. They *are* practiced at discussing issues disagreed on within their own culture. Examples are the qualities of well-known candidates seeking elected office (in contrast to the value of the democratic elections themselves) and the best ways to encourage unregistered voters to become interested in voting (in contrast to the importance of voting as central to democracy). Other examples are the controversial issues people in a culture disagree about, such as women's right to an abortion, the wisdom of owning handguns kept at home, and the right of very old people and ill people to enlist the assistance of others if they want to take their own lives. Put another way, people in a culture do not widely share views on these controversial issues. As discussed previously, the concept of culture as "widely shared" in a society or community is central to its understanding (Triandis, Kurowski, Tecktiel, & Chan, 1993).

Well-Meaning Clashes

Another set of issues people are poorly prepared to interpret and to discuss are the well-meaning clashes that often occur when people from different cultural backgrounds interact in face-to-face encounters. "Well-meaning clashes" describes problematic encounters when such people are behaving properly and in a socially skilled manner according to their culture's norms. If the people were interacting with others from their own culture, few problems would likely occur because the people involved would share many of the same values and even might remember similar childhood experiences that led to the development of their good manners. But in an interaction with someone who does not share the same cultural background, a clash can develop if the behaviors considered proper and socially skilled in one culture are considered improper or even inappropriate in the other. The term *well-meaning* is used because no one in these interactions is trying to be difficult or unpleasant. All the people involved are trying to be well mannered and polite. But because the different cultural backgrounds of people lead them to different behaviors considered "well-mannered," clashes often develop. These clashes are difficult to untangle in discussions and explanations because the people involved have had little experience investigating their culture's guidance concerning polite behavior. By the time people reach adulthood, they are supposed to know what good manners are. Why should they discuss them all the time? Given people's inexperience, however, their explanations to smooth over well-meaning clashes are frequently so poorly done that ill feelings remain among the people involved.

Well-meaning clashes are impactful and memorable. If those involved have opportunities to examine the reasons for clashes, some of the most effective learning about culture's importance can occur. Because the clashes are personally impactful, people want to know why they happened. When they hear that an understanding of their culture is needed for good interpretation, they become interested in their cultural background, perhaps for the first time. Realizing the possibility that the interpretation of cultural clashes can be a good educational approach, Cushner and

Brislin (1996) created 110 short incidents that describe problematic interactions among people from different cultural backgrounds.

Readers of the incidents are asked to explain the difficulties the people encountered. Here is one of the 110 incidents, called "Informal gatherings of people."

> After a year in the United States, Fumio, from Japan, seemed to be adjusting well to his graduate-level studies. He had cordial relations with his professors, interacted frequently with other graduate students at mid-day coffee breaks, and was content with his housing arrangements in the graduate student dormitory. Fumio's statistical knowledge was so good that professors recommended that certain American students should consult him for help in this area. He seemed to be excluded, however, from at least one type of activity in which many other of the American graduate students participated. This was the informal gathering of students at the local pub (bar) at about 5:00 on Friday afternoons. People did not stop and invite him to these gatherings. Since he was not invited, Fumio felt uncomfortable about simply showing up at the pub. Fumio wondered if the lack of an invitation should be interpreted as a sign that he was offending the American students in some way.
>
> What is a good analysis of the situation involving the lack of invitations to the pub gatherings? (p. 202).

Readers then are asked to make choices among a variety of alternative explanations, and more than one can contribute to an understanding of the clash. Here are several possibilities (adapted from Brislin & Cushner, 1996, p. 202):

1. The Americans were rude by not inviting Fumio, a guest in their country.

2. The pub gatherings are meant to be an activity for people who are very familiar with each other to relax on an informal basis.

3. Japanese rarely drink beer. Realizing this, the Americans did not invite Fumio.

4. The Americans resented that Fumio knew more statistics than they did, and this made the Americans feel inferior because they had to ask Fumio for help.

5. Pub gatherings on Friday afternoons, like this one, are largely based on pairings of specific men with specific women. Since Fumio had no girlfriend, he was not invited.

This well-meaning clash can be analyzed in terms of what is considered well-mannered behavior toward guests. Fumio was acting from his socialization into Japanese culture, which includes the guideline that guests should be invited places. American businesspeople in Japan frequently comment on the number of social gatherings they are invited to (Ramsey & Birk, 1983). In fact, the social gatherings are so frequent that they can become a drain on the American's energy. "They expect me to go to three nightclubs on a Wednesday night, staying out until 2:00 A.M., and then be fresh for an 8:30 A.M. meeting the next day. And I'm still feeling jet lag from my trip. How do they do it night after night?" One explanation for this Japanese pattern of after-work socializing is that it is a substitute for lawyers. Americans ask lawyers to protect their interests in business negotiations. The Japanese ask Americans to social gatherings to see if their potential business partners are honest, reliable, and socially sensitive people who can be trusted (Johnson, Cullen, Sakano, & Takenouchi, 1996) if agreements to cooperate are signed. The Japanese approach may have greater cost effectiveness. It is less expensive to entertain potential partners (even at Tokyo's exorbitant costs at bars and restaurants) than to pay lawyers their $250-plus dollars per hour if deals go sour.

This rather long explanation is necessary to introduce Fumio's point of view. He was accustomed to the practice of inviting visitors to social gatherings. Consequently, he quite reasonably expected that if Americans wanted him to attend a gathering in their country, they would invite him. The Americans, on the other hand, were unconsciously making very fine distinctions within the category "types of social gatherings." For the Friday afternoon pub gatherings, a key word was *informality*. People who worked in the organization just showed up! They rarely wrote invitations nor even gave carefully worded oral reminders of the gatherings. After drinks were ordered at the pub, people sat around telling humorous stories and complaining about their superiors. Thus they let off steam, relaxing with people they knew well. Since everybody knew one another, they did not have to be spend time and energy on introductions of newcomers, on making good first impressions, and on searching for conversation topics everyone could contribute to.

Fumio was at several disadvantages regarding this type of social gathering. He didn't know the custom of simply showing up at a pub whether invited or not. If he did show up, he may have felt uncomfortable because he could not participate smoothly in joke telling (more about this point later). He may have sensed he was a damper on the merrymaking if people did not try to find conversation topics he could contribute to. Or, he may have found that the people tried so hard to find topics that they were obviously straining themselves and were thus taking away from their own enjoyment. (Further discussions of interactions across cultural boundaries occur in chapters 6 and 7; see also Landis & Bhagat, 1996; Stephan, 1985.)

The clash here, then, was between two sets of expectations people brought from their cultural backgrounds: "guests are invited" versus "people just show up." Was the clash well meaning? Were the people involved trying to be decent according to their culture's guidelines? Here, the behavior of the Americans should come under scrutiny. Were they being rude (alternative explanation number 1, given earlier), thus demonstrating an absence of intended well meaning? As with the analysis of many intercultural encounters, the answer lies in fine distinctions (Bond, 1995; Foa & Chemers, 1967). Were the Americans being rude, insensitive, or unthinking? A case can be made for the latter. Returning to the point that culture is taken for granted and not discussed, the Americans might not have thought much about the necessity of issuing an invitation to Fumio. They might have unthinkingly felt that if Fumio wanted to come, he would just show up. One of the very difficult issues when analyzing behaviors culture influences is that because they are so accepted and taken for granted, people don't think about the need to explain the behaviors to outsiders.

The incident involving Fumio and the American students also allows me to review a difficult point introduced earlier in the analysis of Rogelia and Stan's difficulty. The distinction between cultural variables and individual differences is not easy to make, yet it is critical to the study of culture and behavior. Recall that one of the alternatives that might help when analyzing Fumio's difficulties (number 4 in list) centered on the possibility of jealousy. The Americans may have resented Fumio's superior knowledge of statistics and may have avoided him due to their jealousy. This alternative is an example of an "individual differences" explanation. Undoubtedly a few individuals would be jealous if a colleague like Fumio came to their organization. Yet other individuals would be happy to have Fumio around because they can ask him for help on difficult problems. The certainty of a jealous reaction is not so widespread that it can be considered part of American culture. Rather, a few people might be jealous, a few might be happy to know a person who can help them, a few might be proud of Fumio because he brings positive attention to the organization as a whole, and a few will dislike statistics so much that they don't care one way or the other. People react in a variety of ways, so feelings toward Fumio clearly differ individually and would not be widespread. Knowledge about or participation in after-work gatherings, however, is widely enough shared to be considered part of American culture. The exact place for the gatherings differs according to people's occupations: bars serving plenty of beer for laborers, colorful but mildly seedy pubs near college campuses for legal-age students, and cocktail lounges for young urban professionals, to generalize. The similarity is that all are after-work gatherings where people "just show up," and this is an aspect of the culture.

The concept of "the well-meaning clash" is extremely important to the study of culture and to intercultural relations, especially when intercultural interactions are frequent in the business world, on college campuses, and in people's neighborhoods. An interesting phenomenon I have observed is that for many people, the path to an interest in culture's effects on behavior is through their intercultural interactions. People meet individuals from other cultures, have interactions, and find some of the interactions puzzling. Given that they want to understand the others (keep in mind that all the individuals involved are well meaning), they often develop an interest in culture and cultural differences so that they can explore their bewilderment. Without the original intercultural interactions, however, they might be no more motivated to study culture than they would any other topic represented in a list of university courses.

Julie Nikulina Compton (1998) uses the following example in her presentations on well-meaning clashes. A woman named Mary was from Toronto in Canada. She accepted a visiting assignment in Moscow at a newly opened branch of her multinational organization. A coworker named Nadia helped her make her adjustment to Moscow. For a couple of weeks, Mary was very dependent on Nadia for information on apartments, where to buy food, how to prepare for the upcoming Moscow winter, how to start a social life, and so forth. After about a month, Nadia had an out-of-office assignment in St. Petersburg and returned to Moscow after about three weeks. In the interim, Mary had to fend for herself and found that she did all right on her own.

On the morning of Nadia's return, Mary greeted Nadia in the hall. Nadia returned the greeting, told Mary a little about St. Petersburg, and then both went to their own offices to start their day's work. At about 2:00 P.M., Mary walked to a colleague's office, saw Nadia, and said "hello," but Nadia walked away without saying anything. Mary wondered if she had done something wrong, perhaps not showing enough interest in Nadia's trip to St. Petersburg.

The cultural difference here involves norms in everyday social interactions. In Canada, as in some other countries, people greet each other every time they see each other during a given day. The greeting does not have to take much time, but the norm is that the presence of a familiar person should be recognized. In Russia, and likewise in some other countries, the norm is that people have to be greeted only once. After that one time, an acknowledgment does not have to occur if a familiar person enters one's social space. After hearing this anecdote, citizens of Hungary, Greece, and the Czech Republic have talked about the same norm: "Once is enough." Some continue with "We are busy people—the norm that once is enough makes sense, or else people would waste a lot of time addressing someone they already know and whom they have already recognized."

Another point to make about well-meaning clashes is that a knowledge of culture helps people interpret events and deal with ill feelings. If a person from Canada or the United States knows the "once is enough" norm, they will not feel insulted when people seem to ignore them over the course of a day.

Culture Allows People to Fill In the Blanks

If specific values and behaviors are culturally influenced, people should be able to expand on the issues involved when given a short sketch that captures a few key elements (Higgins & Bargh, 1987). Consider the example of Fumio again. Alternative explanation number 5 suggests that these Friday afternoon gatherings are based on pairings of specific men and specific women. Knowledgeable people discount this explanation for the reasons already discussed: People just show up after work , and Friday is a work day. But if later asked, "What if the gathering were on a Saturday night? Is it more likely attendance would involve pairings of specific men and specific women?" many Americans will answer yes. To use the language introduced here, they could fill in the blanks when given a description of some basic social encounters culture influences. Returning to the earlier example of the club that had not held elections in 50 years, most people whose culture includes a long history of democratic participation could predict what the chairperson would do when faced with an unexpected nomination from the floor. Given this basic sketch, such people can predict that speeches, passing out of ballots, secret voting, ballot counting, announcement of the winner, and a gracious acceptance speech by the winner will occur.

Another example may be helpful. I might tell others, "We have a distinguished visitor who will give a talk to our organization at 3:00 P.M., and we will have a short reception at 4:00 P.M. We expect 20 people. Can someone plan a reception for a budget of $100?" If a person is familiar with American culture, he or she can "fill in the blanks" and plan a decent reception. Will it include vintage French wines and caviar? Not on a $100 budget! Filling in the blanks here means the person probably will reserve a room that can hold 30 comfortably (in case a few more than expected show up), will make sure a high-status executive is present who can give a short speech thanking the visitor, and will order pastries, coffee, and a fruit punch.

When considering the "filling in the blanks" test of a candidate for a cultural value or practice, people will be wise to place themselves in the position of an outsider to their culture. To use the three examples, will an outsider socialized in another culture know the distinction between Friday and Saturday night gatherings, know how to proceed according to democratic election practices, and know what is reasonable to do for $100 when planning a reception? The answer is clearly no. The detailed knowledge people can bring to a short sketch of behaviors influenced by their culture can be startling when they consider the sketch carefully. To reiterate a point, such knowledge is taken for granted among people within a culture, and they find little need to talk about it in great detail. This leaves people ill prepared to present this detailed knowledge to others, for instance, to a newly arrived colleague from India who volunteers to organize the $100 reception.

This discussion of details associated with cultural practices allows me to fulfill a promise I made earlier: I will discuss the cultural aspect of humor. As implied in the discussion of well-meaning clashes, one of the best ways to gain insights into one's culture is to talk with outsiders who are trying to adapt to and understand it. Once a friendly relationship is established with long-term visitors to a culture (e.g., with foreign students or with businesspeople setting up international joint ventures), good conversations can be held concerning cultural differences. The question "What do you find puzzling or difficult in this country (or community or organization)?" frequently yields interesting answers. One often-heard response is that long-term visitors (sometimes called *sojourners*) find it difficult to participate in at least one major type of informal interaction with people from the host culture. These interactions involve the sharing of jokes and funny stories. Keep in mind that such interactions are frequent: during coffee breaks at work, at informal lunches with coworkers, during the after-work gatherings already discussed, as part of weekend social activities, and so forth. Sojourners complain they don't understand the jokes and can't tell any that others will find funny. As a result, the sojourners feel out of place and also conclude they are a damper on the other people's good times.

One reason the jokes are hard to understand is that people often have to understand and combine extensive details to get the joke. Much humor is based on the joining and twisting together of two categories. Ordinarily, these two categories are not combined in everyday thinking and talking. The discovery of how the joke combines the two categories in a unique manner is how to get the joke's point. For example, Jay Leno tells his audience that a rat was discovered living in the basement of the U.S. Senate. However, the senators won't be bringing in an exterminator because they always look after their own. The reason this story is humorous is that rarely combined categories, what rodent exterminators do and what U.S. senators do, are twisted together. Discovering the point behind the twisting is intellectually satisfying and pleasurable, and the discovery is one reason for the resulting laughter. In this example, to understand the joke people must know about the long history of wheelings and dealings, some venturing into the unethical and dishonest, of U.S. senators. Outsiders might be unaware of America's traditional ambivalence between respect and distrust of its elected officials.

Another example of a humorous story, this time involving even more detailed knowledge of the categories involved, may make this point clearer. A man wanting a career as a nightclub entertainer taught a dog how to talk. The man and his dog went to a prestigious booking agent who asked the man to put on a demonstration of the dog's skills.

The man asked the dog, "What's the top of a house called?"

Dog: Roof!
Man: What's the texture of sandpaper?
Dog: Rough!
Man: What do you do for the home team at the football game?
Dog: Root!
Man: Who was the greatest baseball player ever?
Dog: Ruth!

At this point the booking agent threw the man and his dog out of his office. Outside, on the street, the dog told the man, "I told you that the best baseball player was Joe DiMaggio!"

Imagine the predicament of sojourners from Germany who hear this story at the water cooler during an informal break where they work. They have to know an incredible amount of knowledge: First, the onomatopoeic quality of the words *rough* and *root* and a dog's barking sound. In other languages, as an aside, the word for a dog's bark is another but quite different approximation of what they hear as the barking sound. Sojourners have to know that real arguments occur among baseball fans about who was the better player, given that they both had immense talent: George Herman "Babe" Ruth or Joe DiMaggio. Then, the sojourners have to see how the categories "similar sounds to a dog's bark" and "great baseball players" were twisted together. It is little wonder they find informal gatherings that involve the telling of humorous stories so troublesome. The major point for discussions of culture's influences on behavior, to reiterate, is that culture presents detailed knowledge and this knowledge is taken for granted. Outsiders, not socialized into familiarity with topics such as American baseball and familiarity with a collection of disparate English words, will be unable to participate fully in cultural practices that demand detailed knowledge. The sojourners cannot "fill in blanks" when given the basic sketches that are the core of most humorous stories.

Cultural Values Remain Despite Mistakes

If a value is strongly influenced by culture, it remains in force even when it is subject to obvious mistakes, blunders, and exceptions. Let's look at another candidate for a cultural value in the United States: a free press whose members can pursue the truth (and later report openly in the newspapers or on television) as they see fit. Most readers will agree this is an American cultural value. Some who have had courses in journalism could make arguments that a free and vigorous press, even though it is often bothersome and even abrasive, is preferable to alternatives such as government-controlled media. But do mistakes occur in the practices of a free press? Certainly! The press is far more likely to pursue stories with an obvious visual or attention-grabbing aspect. It is more "newsworthy" to cover the one embezzler as he is carted off to jail (with his hat in front of his face) than it is to cover the 1,000 people in the same organization who show up at work day after day. It is easier to do stories about powerless people (e.g., the homeless, victims at the scene of airplane accidents) than to do stories on the powerful who have layers of assistants and secretaries well trained in the art of saying no graciously. When deciding on what stories to pursue, reporters too often have to take into account possible repercussions stemming from coverage of the rich or powerful. Most reporters I have talked to point to stories their editors killed because the editors wanted to avoid negative consequences (loss in advertising revenue, loss of political support for upcoming planned mergers with other newspapers or TV stations). In contrast, reporters are sometimes so vigorous in their quest for news that they blow minor stories out of proportion and taint the reputations of honest people somehow peripherally associated with the stories.

Despite these admitted difficulties and blunders, does the cultural value of a "free press" remain? I believe it does. Even though large numbers of exceptions can be named, people are likely to conclude that the value remains part of American culture. In Japan, a candidate for a cultural value might be "respect for people who teach our country's students ages 5 to 18." Do exceptions exist? Certainly! Japan has incompetent teachers, as true of all professions. Some parents quietly and secretly maneuver so that their children are not assigned to the teachers they respect the least. These exceptions, however, do not interfere with the basic Japanese value of respect toward teachers (Stevenson, Azuma, & Hakuta, 1986).

The concept that values remain despite mistakes also can be addressed by looking at examples that probably do not "pass the test." One already has been introduced. Is "respect for teachers of students ages 5 to 18" a cultural value in the United States? I believe here too many slipups exist and consequently a "yes" answer is inappropriate. Too many mothers and fathers tell their brightest sons and daughters, "You can do so much better than to become a high school teacher!" Too many college professors and physicians quickly move on to others at a cocktail party when they find out the person next to them is an elementary school teacher. I could point to ideals and argue (rightly, in my opinion) that few professions are more important than the one that guides and educates young U.S. citizens, but too many everyday challenges to this ideal exist to make it part of American culture. Is "equal rights for women" a cultural value? It may be in the future, but too many exceptions exist for a yes answer today (Pratto, Stallworth, Sidanius, & Siers, 1997). In too many marriages women contribute to the household income and do far more than 50% of the housework (Biernat & Wortman, 1991). Too many women have to put careers on hold given the demands of childbirth and child rearing, about which American business, industry, and academia show little concern. In the cases of respect for teaching and equal rights for women, the test of "remaining despite slipups" yields the conclusion that these are not part of American culture.

Emotional Reactions When Observing Violations

People find violations of culturally influenced values and practices emotionally arousing. They do not respond, "Oh, isn't that an interesting exception to what our culture practices!" Rather, they respond in a much more emotional manner. They might become obviously angry or upset if the social setting permits such reactions. If they have to mask their feelings for one reason or another, their emotional reactions will be less visible, such as increased heart rate, sweating, heavier breathing, increased blood pressure, and stomach churning (Pines, 1994). For example, even if people raised in a Christian religion have not seen the inside of a church for a long time, they will become upset if religious objects are the targets of disrespect. The value of "respect for the religion of my childhood" yields an emotional reaction if they see others use a Bible to press leaves or to prop up their feet. Returning to other examples introduced in this chapter, emotional reactions will arise if a club president does not hold democratic elections for his or her successor when a sizable percentage of the membership requests such procedures. Despite widespread disappointment and even disgust with the efforts of television and newspaper reporters, the vast majority of Americans would become visibly upset if the government placed restrictions on a free press. Some of the candidates for cultural values do not pass this "makes people react emotionally" test. I believe many readers would not become visibly upset if they overheard one college student try to persuade another to abandon plans for a career in elementary school education.

Acceptance and Rejection Over Time

People can reject a cultural value at one point in their lives and accept it at other times. The clearest example may be participation in democratic elections. Less than 50% of eligible voters participate on any one election day. At first glance, this would seem to indicate that democratic elections are not widespread enough to be considered cultural. The key point here is that the nonvoters can participate on another election day during another point in their lives. If compelling candidates are competing for the same office or if important issues are under consideration, people who didn't vote previously may leave their homes and participate in the electoral process. In addition to giving up their right to participate in elections, some young people seem to reject their culture's values altogether. They abandon contact with their families, join communes, protest intensely against government policies, dress in a manner likely to offend a society's well-mannered citizens, and so forth. These same rebellious people, however, have been exposed to their culture's values and have participated in the childhood experiences that educate them about their culture. At a later point in their adulthood they can reenter their culture, put on attractive work clothes, change their hairstyle, and seek employment. Most readers probably know a few people who were extremely rebellious during their youth but who now are vice presidents of large organizations or who are full professors at colleges and universities.

Another example of reaccepting values that is interesting to consider is "the right to a trial before a jury, with rights the Constitution guarantees." It is extremely easy to become irritated and disgusted with these values when society's "sleazeballs" who are clearly guilty get off because the evidence against them was gathered through unconstitutional means. These same values, however, become important and cherished when people's loved ones (or the people themselves) are accused of a crime.

The Difficulty of Fast Change

When changes in cultural values are considered, people are likely to feel that "this will be extremely difficult and time consuming." This reaction applies both to existing cultural values that might be changed and to existing values that people may want to make cultural. U.S. citizens may decide they want to encourage their best and brightest students to enter the teaching profession so that they can educate children ages 5 to 18. This goal demands that the American culture begins to give teachers more status and respect. Will greater respect for the teaching profession become part of U.S. culture in the near future? I don't believe so. Assuming that America's leaders decide to make it a value (itself a problematic step in the process), it will take several generations for the value to be considered widespread. Salaries will have to be increased. Career counselors will have to recommend the teaching profession. Obviously bright and able people will have to enter the profession and become positive role models for the next generation. None of these steps will happen quickly or easily.

American society has seen the challenging of cultural assumptions during the 20th century, but these challenges have involved incredible amounts of effort. Whenever American history is discussed, the term *race* is almost always covered. Most psychologists now consider the term scientifically meaningless and only use it when analyzing concepts (sometimes called *constructions*) laypeople use in their thinking about others. Looking back on America's history, I can make a fair conclusion that a value was placed on the separation of races. As late as the 1920s and 1930s, most Americans agreed with the sentiment that "it is best to keep the Black and White races as distant from each other as possible." This value was clearly visible in society's segregated schools, churches, and neighborhoods (Brophy, 1989). It was seen in the designation of occupations that were considered suitable for Whites and Blacks. It was seen in laws ("Jim Crow") that set firm standards of who could and could not use public accommodations such as swimming pools, rest rooms, and restaurants. Cultural values have certainly been challenged since the 1940s by the set of efforts collectively called the Civil Rights movement (Williams, 1987). But simply pointing out that the efforts have been undertaken "since the 1940s" is a reminder of how long it takes to change cultural values and how much effort has been invested. Many readers could make convincing arguments that the value of racial equality is still not part of American culture after more than 50 years of intense effort (e.g., Ferdman & Brody, 1996; Gaertner & Dovidio, 1986). Too many exceptions still exist (violent racial incidents, de facto neighborhood segregation, less-than-adequate housing and inner-city schools) for "racial equality" to be considered part of American culture.

Summarizable in Sharp Contrasts

Some cultural differences can be summarized in sharp contrasts that differentiate behavior in one society compared to another. Some of the most important and early analyses on the difficulties of understanding others' cultures were written by Edward Hall (1959, 1966, 1976; see also Levine, 1997). One of the reasons his contributions are widely cited and used stems from his great skill at pointing to sharp contrasts that summarize large numbers of specific behaviors that are puzzling to people. Three of his analyses (covered in the three books just cited, respectively) are people's use of time, the spatial orientation they adopt when interacting with others, and the distinction between high and low context.

Punctuality is probably the clearest example involving the time dimension. When meetings are scheduled to start at 10:00 A.M. in a North American organization, attendees can expect the meeting to start either promptly or at 10:10 A.M. at the latest. At 10:12 A.M., it is considered quite proper for someone to say, "Perhaps we should start. Some people have 11 o'clock appointments." This sort of scheduling is not possible in other parts of the world, notably Latin America and many Asian countries. Meetings scheduled for 10:00 A.M. may start by 11:15 A.M., but then again they may not. Complaints about the lack of punctuality and the difficulties of keeping an efficient schedule are common in the "war stories" of North American businesspeople who travel to South America. There are many reasons for this cultural difference in the importance of punctuality. One is the priority people put on the requests for their time. In North America, businesspeople on their way to a meeting at 11:00 A.M. may be interrupted by a coworker needing help, for example, on a stock market analysis. In such cases it is proper to say, "I have an 11 o'clock. Can we chat about it after lunch, say 1:30?" In other parts of the world, the needs of the person making the last-minute request for assistance are as important as the needs of the person waiting for the previously scheduled meeting. Given the cultural appropriateness of treating the two individuals equally at the moment, the businesspeople try to help both by giving assistance to one immediately, realizing the other will understand and will be willing to wait. The preference to offer immediate help reflects a concern with "event time" in contrast to "clock time" (Levine, 1997). Events take a certain amount of time. When one event is completed (e.g., helping someone), the next event can start (e.g., keeping the appointment). "Clock time" involves greater attention to the formal appointment. Many Hispanic Americans and Filipino Americans retain a preference for event time and consequently are sometimes labeled as "not punctual."

The spatial orientation people choose when interacting with each other is also the subject matter of "war stories." In North America, how close together do two people stand if they meet each other at an informal reception? The answer is approximately the length of a tall man's arm: 3 feet. If the distance is closer than 3 feet, then one or more of the two people may become uncomfortable. If one person is a man and the other a woman, the conclusion may be that sexual advances are involved. If the people are of the same gender, sexual advances are still a possibility, and another is that one of the people will be judged as "pushy." In other parts of the world, including Latin America, the distance new acquaintances adopt is closer: 2 to 2½ feet is more appropriate. The possibility of intercultural difficulties should be immediately clear. If an attractive North American man meets an attractive Latin American woman, the distance they adopt might be 2 feet from each other. The woman might say to herself, "This is a prim and proper distance for me." The man might conclude, "She is interested in me personally. Perhaps I can ask her out for a date!"

Conclusions about people's intentions also can be made if the distance is more than people find comfortable. In North America, if two people adopt a distance of 4 feet or more, it is easy to conclude they have cool feelings toward each other. Sometimes this conclusion is correct, but exceptions happen. Specialists working with the Deaf, on hearing about cultural differences in people's spatial orientation, sometimes apply the concepts to a problem they have observed. When a hearing individual interacts with a Deaf individual who uses American sign language, the latter seems to prefer a distance of about 4 feet. The hearing individual often concludes that the Deaf individual does not want to have much future interaction: The adopted distance is interpreted as a polite signal that further development of a relationship is not desired.

The other person, however, has adopted the most comfortable distance. Deaf people need a 4-foot distance to express themselves using their sign language (Moore & Levitan, 1993; Siple, 1994). Some signs involve movements of the hands away from the body. If they stood closer than 4 feet, they would sometimes strike the other person with their hands! A major theme to be covered and reviewed throughout this book is that if these cultural factors are understood, people from very different backgrounds will make fewer negative judgments about one another.

I should mention here another aspect of this culture. When the physiological aspects of deafness are discussed, such as reception of sound waves within the inner ear, Deaf people suggest using the usual small *d* in *deaf*. When people speak about culture as it is discussed thoughout this book (shared patterns of behavior, transmission for generations, etc.), Deaf people strongly recommend using a capital *D* in *Deaf*.

A third sharp contrast involves behavior in cultures called "high context" and "low context." In high-context cultures, the rules, norms, and guidelines for various types of social encounters are very clear. Everyone well socialized into the culture knows exactly how to behave in a variety of situations. At meetings in an organization, who is the first to speak? When people meet for the first time, how do they know when they have introduced a conversational topic someone does not want to pursue? How do people indicate a need for privacy? Who takes credit for successful outcomes accomplished through team effort? In high-context cultures, everyone knows the answers. In low-context cultures, each of these questions leads to negotiations of one sort or another. Since no rules exist, people have to invest much time and energy to formulate ad hoc solutions. A good example of the difference can be seen during a large organization's meetings in Japan compared to the United States (Christopher, 1983). How does a person best introduce a new plan for future business ventures? In Japan, people know the rules. The person visits the offices of all the individuals who might be affected by the proposal. After these one-on-one meetings, the concerns of others are integrated into a final draft. This draft is also cleared with the people affected. Then, during a formal meeting of company executives, the new proposal is put on the table. In actuality, this step is a formality because by this time everyone present knows a great deal about the proposal. They then approve the proposal by consensus, rarely taking a formal voice vote (Cushner & Brislin, 1996). This is high-context behavior: Everyone knows what to do!

Compared to Japan, the United States is considered a low-context culture. Americans have many ways to accomplish their goals, and they feel constrained if too many rules exist (Hofstede, 1980, 1991). For example, people can introduce proposals in a number of ways in organizations. They can follow the typically Japanese route as outlined. Or, they can introduce proposals at meetings even if the people present have not heard about the ideas involved. Or, they can ask a highly respected executive to introduce a proposal and in so doing communicate a willingness to share the credit for any eventual successes. Americans have other, clever ways to introduce proposals if they feel negative reactions might kill efforts at early planning stages. A person might "leak" the proposal to a newspaper reporter. The story appears in the press, the sources of and reasons for negative reactions become clear, and the person then addresses those people and their reactions in future efforts (Brislin, 1991). The important point for this discussion is that the exact guidelines for behavior are not clear: The behavior is low context.

Another example that may make the distinction clear involves a cultural change within the United States (and many other highly industrialized nations) over the past 60 or 70 years. During the early part of this century, marriage was high context. People knew what to do: The man would be the breadwinner, and the woman would stay home and raise children and have dinner on the table when the man came home. People didn't have to spend time and energy on questions such as how to arrange for day care, where to live, and who makes the major decisions involving the family. If they had, the answers would have been, respectively, that day care is a strange concept because the woman stays home with the children, the family lives where the man obtains the best job possible, and the man makes the decisions. When problems arose, my mother tells me, the support groups for all the people involved had one basic message: Keep the marriage together! Everybody knew these facts—it was high context. Currently, the answers and the goals are not as clear. To experience challenges and positive self-identities, many women seek work outside the home. If a couple decides to have children, day care becomes a topic for consideration. Couples have to negotiate where they will live—will it be where the man or where the woman gets the best job? Decisions about important issues are reached after discussion and negotiation. If problems arise, a number of available and acceptable solutions exist, and keeping the marriage together is one of many. The answers to questions and guidelines for behavior are not at all clear—marriage is low context. The absence of guidelines and widely accepted norms is undoubtedly a reason for the high divorce rates in the world's most industrialized nations.

DEFINITIONS, CROSS-CULTURAL STUDIES, AND CULTURAL STUDIES

When I am asked for a definition of culture and am given a reasonable amount of time (e.g., a one-hour presentation), I use this list of 12 indicators as the outline of my definition, as explanations of complex points, and as examples to make points clear to any audience I happen to address. However, I realize such an approach leads to too long a definition for many purposes. When introducing their studies of culture's influence on behavior, researchers have to choose a more concise definition among the hundreds proposed (Dorfman, 1996). I have found this shorter definition useful (Triandis, Kurowski, Tecktiel, & Chan, 1993, p. 219): Culture is "a set of human made objective and subjective elements that in the past have (a) increased the probability of survival, (b) resulted in satisfaction for the participants in a ecological niche, and thus (c) become shared among those who communicate with each other because they had a common language and lived the same time-place." To this I would add that the objective and subjective elements are passed on for generations (indicator 4 of the 12) and cause emotional reactions in people when they are ignored, disrespected, or omitted in situations where they are expected (indicator 9).

Culture defined

It is always useful to examine definitions as they apply to specific examples. Let's return to the interaction between Stan and Rogelia and to the reasons, all involving culture and cultural differences, that led to their misunderstanding. The definition starts with objective and subjective elements. Examples of objective elements for the couple would be the movies they went to or the food they ate on dates and any gifts they might have exchanged. Subjective elements include the symbolism attached to such acts as maintaining a friendship after the romantic breakup, which Stan wanted. In Rogelia's culture, this is considered unwise and consequently is avoided. This avoidance is one of many cultural aspects that contribute to survival. In the Philippines, survival is based on contributing to and benefiting from strong emotional bonds with one's family. Today's newspapers and magazines report about young, very well educated Filipino women accepting jobs as domestics in other countries. When asked why, they answer that they want to send money home to their families. In the Philippines, a major contributor to the gross national product is repatriated wages its citizens send from other countries to family members. If Rogelia were to invest resources in maintaining a relationship with Stan, this could take away from her commitment to her family, especially because the family never approved of Stan. Ideas such as "don't maintain friendships after romantic relationships break up" are shared by people speaking the same language and living in the same area. They are passed on for generations, possibly captured in family stories about such people as the unhappy cousin who *did* maintain this type of friendship and in adages about once-burning embers never dying out. These cultural elements become emotionally charged, as can be seen in Rogelia's original reaction to Stan's request to go to a movie (after the romantic breakup). She was puzzled and she told Stan she did not want to see him under any circumstances.

I have to add that my treatment of the definition of culture, while capturing concepts many researchers share, is by no means universally accepted in its entirety. As long as individual researchers, when reporting the results of specific studies, are clear with their definitions, progress in understanding culture's effects on behavior can be made. As Dorfman points out (1996, p. 279), "Since many definitions of culture are valid, . . . researchers need not become overly concerned with choosing the most appropriate definition. . . . But it is important not to use the term carelessly (Roberts, 1970)."

Cross-Cultural and Cultural Research

In addition to the absence of total agreement about a definition of culture, researchers also disagree about the best general approach to documenting culture's effects on behavior. The details of the disagreements have received extensive treatments (Berry, 1997; Greenfield, 1997a, 1997b; Miller, 1997; Rogoff, 1990; Segall, Lonner, & Berry, 1998), and only some of the basic issues can be reviewed here.

Researchers attracted to the approaches known as "cross-cultural psychology" and "cultural psychology" have in common a desire to understand the central role culture plays in people's lives. Researchers who find cross-cultural studies a useful approach (e.g., Berry, 1997; Lonner & Berry, 1986; Poortinga, 1997) believe that important concepts can be identified and then compared in different cultures. Critical findings might include new insights into both the concepts and the cultures in a study. Returning again to Stan and Rogelia's story, cross-cultural researchers might hear about this misunderstanding and design a study to compare relationships between men and women in the United States, the Philippines, and other cultures. They might ask questions (as was done by Buss et al., 1990, and by Hatfield & Sprecher, 1995) such as what traits are desired in a romantic partner, how important it is to feel that one is "in love," how important it is to be chaste prior to marriage, and whether or not a person feels comfortable maintaining relations with former romantic partners. Findings from various cultures would be compared and conclusions drawn, such as the conclusion that men consider chastity in women more important in some countries (e.g., Iran) than in others (e.g., United States).

Researchers who prefer the approach now known as "cultural psychology" (Greenfield, 1997a, 1997b; Miller, 1997; Rogoff, 1990) are noticeably less enthusiastic about identifying concepts and about removing those concepts from their day-to-day existence in cultures and from their surrounding context and then comparing them with similarly removed versions of the concepts from other cultures. Cultural psychologists argue that important concepts about human behavior have meaning only within a culture and that separating a concept from its cultural context is not a good approach to research. As Poortinga (1997) points out,

> The cultural approach is relativistic; it emphasizes the study of unique events or unique constellations of events [as they occur within any one culture]. Thus the domain of research of the culturalist schools tends to differ from that of the [cross-culturalists]; there is less emphasis on behavior as observed by experts and more on the meaning that behavior has for the behaving person and the intentions this person has with an act of behavior. (p. 354)

If cultural researchers were asked to comment on the study of relationships between men and women, they likely would bring up a number of important points. They would ask whether or not a person's attitudes about relationships between men and women can be separated from their cultural context. They would point out that chastity has extensive implications in a country such as Iran. Chastity there is associated with family honor, and brothers have the obligation to insure the chastity of their sisters. In some countries, marriages are arranged, and the groom's family can demand a medical test to demonstrate chastity. In some countries, women are never alone with a man other than their husband, father, or brother. The question about love is inappropriate because marital choice is a parental decision and love is something a couple develops after marriage. To cultural researchers, removing concepts from this rich constellation of contexts and meanings and investigating them through a disembodied set of questions about "chastity" and "love" are unwise approaches to research.

Another argument cultural researchers make is that, contrary to the hard-science assumptions investigators draw from, total objectivity in research is almost impossible (Miller, 1997). Without the most stringent, careful safeguards, cross-cultural researchers may impose their own definitions of good/bad and intelligent/unintelligent or up-to-date/quaint on their questionnaires, experiments, or other means of gathering information. To their credit, the cultural researchers also give this warning to themselves: No matter the approach to research, it is very difficult to keep one's own attitudes out of a research project. In the example study, it is difficult for researchers to eliminate their own attitudes about the importance of love in marriage, about arranged marriages, and about the limitations placed on the movement of women in some cultures.

A Cross-Cultural Study: Time

Often, the best researchers can do is to describe their backgrounds and to list any potential biases they might have. I will do this, but before I do, I would like to review a study that allows more detailed analysis of the differing approaches of cross-cultural and cultural researchers. Robert Levine (1997) has been long interested in the relation between people's cultural background and their use of time. Having done his share of traveling, he made an observation others share: The pace of life in some cultures is faster than in others. People in some cultures seem to be in a hurry, rushing through the events of their day by moving quickly from one task to another. They look at their watches frequently and worry about their punctuality. People in other cultures seem to move much more slowly through their days. Their walking speed from one place to another seems genuinely slow, they do not seem concerned with their watches, and punctuality does not seem a priority.

Levine designed a cross-cultural research study to determine if indeed differences in the pace of life exist, and he also related information about the pace of life to other important concepts. For example, he compared information on pace of life to the amount of coronary heart disease in a culture, investigating the possibility that a hurried pace of life would lead to stress, which would in turn lead to coronary heart disease. So how can pace of life be measured? Levine decided to collect information on three aspects of people's lives in 31 different countries. The first was the amount of time it takes people to walk 60 feet in pedestrian areas within a city. The second was the amount of time it took postal clerks to take a bank note from a customer, to sell a stamp, and to calculate and give proper change (after the person had stood in a line and it was his or her turn at the clerk's desk or window); and the third was the accuracy of public clocks (comparing the time on different clocks to the official standard within a country). Results included the following: Switzerland had the fastest pace of life. In general, highly industrialized nations with strong economies and high family incomes had a fast pace of life. These fast, industrialized, economically successful countries tended to be in Europe, with the notable exceptions of Hong Kong and Japan. The United States, and more specifically New York City, did not live up to their reputations as fast paced. If grades were applied, the United States would get a C using an old-fashioned distribution: The United States scored 16th out of 31 countries. Levine's findings agreed with the images of countries with a slow pace of life: Countries in Latin and South America, such as El Salvador, Brazil, and Mexico, were among the slowest. Countries with a climate commonly described as "hot" had a slow pace of life. These included the Latin and South American countries, as well as Jordan, Syria, and Indonesia.

With one striking exception, Japan, countries with a fast pace of life had higher incidences of coronary heart disease. Findings such as this one have contributed to the medical conclusion that coronary heart disease has a strong lifestyle component (Taylor, 1991; Taylor, Repette, & Seeman, 1997) and that people should learn to relax, to deal with stress, and to avoid certain behaviors common in fast-paced countries (e.g., eating in fast-food restaurants, with their high-fat offerings). The findings for Japan exemplify a benefit of research such as Levine's: Information from a specific country that does not agree with general trends can stimulate further analysis and possibly important findings. Levine (1997) reviewed a number of possibilities for the Japan findings, including a diet much lower in fat. One of the explanations he finds possible is that the Japanese do so much in groups that they always have social support available to them and the presence of such support provides a buffer against health risks such as stress. More will be said about the importance of groups in some cultures in the next chapter as part of the discussion about individualism and collectivism.

The actual day-to-day work on a complex research project such as Levine's are never as tidy as a summary (such as mine) would suggest. In reality, Levine and his colleagues had to make difficult decisions about research methods and had to cope with unexpected events. One reason the data for New York City may have led to the conclusion of "average pace" is that people had to spend time dodging taxis as well as one another. People were slowed by both roaming entertainers and street muggings. In the post office, the clerk felt the need to stop work and make sarcastic comments to fellow workers about the number of stamps requested. This slowed down the delivery of the stamp to the customer, who happened to be Levine himself. In India, postal clerks did not feel they had to carry change, so the study had to be abandoned there. In Japan, postal clerks were so polite that they often wrapped the stamp in a nice package, demonstrating great attention to customer service but slowing down the delivery of the stamp. Data were gathered in 36 American cities. In parts of California, it was hard to find places where people walk from one place to another because people use their cars so frequently. Levine (1997, p. 150) admitted a temptation to go to California health clubs and to time people as they walked on their treadmills or stairmasters.

Possible Critical Comments From Cultural Researchers

Researchers more sympathetic to the cultural approach are likely to have a number of criticisms of Levine's study, and these are important to constantly have in mind. Cultural researchers probably would point out that Levine measured time and then removed it from its cultural surroundings, but time has meaning only within a cultural setting. People demonstrate their reactions to time within a culture, and time can't be properly removed from its cultural context. For example, forcing a measure of time as a certain number of seconds at the Japanese post office removes the event from its cultural surroundings. Because of such removal, the most interesting aspects of the meaning of time have been lost. If attentiveness to the customer and additional services such as wrapping the stamp are part of the Japanese postal worker's use of time, then this additional meaning has been lost by placing an amount of seconds in a table for later statistical analysis. Similarly with the data from New York: Time for sarcasm, stopping for or walking around entertainers, and street muggings need to be included in New Yorkers' use of time. These aspects of New Yorkers' use of time happen to be amusing, but they are also important, and much information is lost when a measure of seconds is added to the same table as the data from Japan. Cultural researchers also would ask if Levine imposed any of his own ideas about time in his choice of measures. Perhaps other measures, within any one culture, are much more important for an understanding of time in *that* culture.

Some Convergence

Poortinga (1997) uses the term *convergence* when he points to topics cross-cultural and cultural researchers can agree on, find mutually beneficial, or find useful complementarities for. I believe both approaches are necessary and valuable. Beginning with the excellent advice that researchers and writers should reveal aspects of themselves that might lead to biases, I am probably more identified with the cross-cultural than the cultural approach. The first book I coauthored was titled *Cross-Cultural Research Methods* (Brislin, Lonner, & Thorndike, 1973), and I have been on the editorial board of the *Journal of Cross-Cultural Psychology* since 1971. However, three of the contributions of which I am most proud are much closer to the cultural approach (all will be discussed in different chapters of this book). These research reports deal with the complexities of intercultural encounters (Brislin, 1981), with understanding power and the complex contexts that influence how power is displayed and used (Brislin, 1991), and with preparing people for the multiple challenges of living in a culture other than their own (Cushner & Brislin, 1996).

Both types of research are useful and important (Segall, Lonner, & Berry, 1998). Comparing data in different cultures, as Levine (1997) did, allows researchers to see relations among concepts that would be very difficult to see without such direct comparisons. As was previously mentioned, Levine found a relationship between pace of life and coronary heart disease. An exception, Japan, encourages researchers to examine reasons, and Levine argued that social support possibly provides a buffer. Levine also related the pace of life to happiness. Perhaps going against a common-sense argument, Levine found that people are happiest in countries with a fast pace of life. A possible sequence of influences (again difficult to determine without the cross-cultural data) is that a fast pace of life is one contributor to a successful economy, a successful economy leads to high family incomes, and high family incomes contribute to happiness.

The approach cultural researchers take, with their attention to examining behavior in its cultural context, is also important. Some researchers, for example, would be far more interested in examining the pace of life in a specific culture. They might start with Levine's observations of California and study the complex and contextualized reasons people don't walk in their neighborhoods but drive to a health club, pay their dues, and then walk on a treadmill. Each type of research can complement the other. To borrow a metaphor from art, cross-cultural research can provide the broad brush strokes of a painting, and cultural research can provide the fine brush strokes and detail. Both are necessary, and both types of research will be reviewed throughout this book.

Now that I have some gray hair and lines in my face, perhaps I can add some observations that might be akin to wisdom. Many times, people choose to emphasize either cross-cultural or cultural research based on their temperament. Some researchers enjoy the quest of identifying concepts and, after methodological steps to insure cultural compatibility (some are reviewed in chapter 3), then making comparisons in different cultures to test hypotheses. Other researchers find much more enjoyment examining a culture's features, but without separating the features from people's behavior. Because the only way people react to these features is within a cultural context, any separation of behavior and culture is problematic. Not only the temperament of researchers but also what they enjoy doing with their professional lives often influence their research choices. Another piece of wisdom is that important topics, such as people's reactions to time, attract research of both types. Indeed, I cannot think of an important research topic in the study of culture and behavior that has been investigated with only one of the approaches. Much of Levine's (1997) book, for instance, deals with his cross-cultural data, but he also puts the data into its cultural context by integrating other people's research, personal experiences, interview results, other scholars' comments on his research, treatments of exceptions to trends, and so forth.

The distinction between the two approaches might become even clearer if I can draw parallels with experiences most readers have encountered. This distinction is between using measures removed from their context (common in cross-cultural research) and attention to behavior in context (central to the cultural approach). All U.S. high school students have taken tests such as the Scholastic Aptitude Test (SAT), and people have used these test scores to make decisions about the test takers. The test scores' use has been pulled from the contexts of the scholastic aptitude they are meant to measure: family experiences, visits to libraries and museums, experiences with teachers. These test scores have been entered into data sets with those of many other people and have become part of research studies with titles such as "Trends since 1960 in the SAT scores of high school students." I hope these students also have had the experience of long, detailed discussions with teachers, counselors, parents, or other mentors about specific aspects of their scholastic aptitude and how these might relate to their school or career choices. Here, the contexts of their aptitude (or behaviors) were much more likely to be included. For another example, most people have visited physicians and have complained about headaches, fatigue, and runny noses. If the visits occur during flu season, physicians are likely to take a limited set of measures: the date symptoms were first felt, body temperature, blood pressure, reports of runny noses and headaches, and reports concerning energy level. The total context is not considered: The physicians probably would not be interested in whether patients' parents in another city have the flu or in the pressures on coworkers covering for the patients. If the symptoms indicate a flu, then the physicians prescribe action according to this diagnosis. Patients may be quite happy with this approach if they know they have the flu, simply want a prescription drug, and prefer to get out of the clinic or hospital as quickly as possible. Patients probably would not consider the possibility that this information could be entered out of context into a data set along with reports from other people. The data could be examined if researchers were interested in a study of when flu symptoms first appear, and their reported severity, in different years.

If the symptoms do not lead to such a clear diagnosis, however, physicians are far more likely to ask about complex contexts and to add information from contexts available to them. Physicians would ask about life experiences, multiple symptoms, family history, recent travel, and stresses patients are experiencing. They would integrate this information with other complex data gathered from medical tests and the contributions of specialists. In this example, patients would be pleased to have so much time and attention because they don't know what ails them and would agree with the physicians that complex information in its cultural surroundings should be gathered.

Note that both approaches are important and that one is not necessarily better in any absolute sense than the other. Both are appropriate for certain circumstances, and both need to be understood. This theme, incidentally, previews one I will return to many times in this book. Cultural differences should not always lead to the conclusion they are better or worse in comparisons. Before making such conclusions, people should understand the cultures and behaviors thoroughly. For example, judgments of better or worse or superiority or inferiority for cultural differences in socialization (chapter 4), education (chapter 5), or workplace attitudes (chapter 8) should not be made without a thorough understanding of the cultures and behaviors involved. I am presenting this position now in case it represents a bias on my part. A good way to begin such an understanding of cultures and behaviors is to review the checklist of culture's features, because this activity forces an examination of behavior in its cultural context.

REVIEWING THE CHECKLIST OF CULTURE'S FEATURES

As explained earlier, when people ask themselves whether or not certain ideals or expected behaviors are part of their culture, they first can consider them as possible culturally influenced candidates. Then, they can proceed down the checklist and ask whether or not the candidate passes the test implied in each checklist entry. The more entries that pass, the higher the probability the candidate is part of the culture.

To review, the 12 features of culture to consider follow:

1. Culture consists of ideals, values, and assumptions about life that guide specific behaviors.
2. Culture consists of the aspects of the environment that people make.
3. Culture is transmitted generation to generation, with the responsibility given to parents, teachers, religious leaders, and other respected elders in a community.
4. The fact summarized in feature 3 means that people in a community will remember culturally related childhood experiences.
5. Aspects of one's culture are not frequently discussed by adults. Since culture is widely shared and accepted, people have little reason to discuss it frequently.
6. Culture can become clearest in well-meaning clashes. This term refers to interactions among people from very different backgrounds. They may behave in proper ways according to their socialization, but a clash occurs when the people from different cultures interact.
7. Culture allows people to "fill in the blanks" when they are presented with a basic sketch of familiar behaviors.
8. Cultural values remain despite mistakes. Even though people can list exceptions, the cultural value is seen as a constant influence that continues to guide specific behaviors.

9. People have emotional reactions when cultural values are violated or when culture's expected behaviors are ignored.

10. A culture's values can be accepted and rejected at different times in a person's life. Common examples involve rebellious adolescents and young adults who accept a culture's expectations after having their own children.

11. When changes in cultural values are contemplated, the reaction that "this will be difficult and time consuming" is likely.

12. When people compare proper and expected behavior across cultures, some observations are summarizable in sharp contrasts. Examples are the treatment of time, the spatial orientations people adopt, and the clarity (high context versus low context) of the rules and norms for certain complex behaviors.

EXAMPLE OF A CANDIDATE: THE DIFFUSION OF POWER

One important use of the checklist of cultural features is that it can encourage examination of behaviors people have not thought about much. Feature number 5 suggests that culture is widely accepted and taken for granted. Because it is taken for granted, people do not have the opportunity to examine very basic aspects of their lives. One such important but rarely examined value, in my opinion, is the diffusion of power in the United States. No one person or group of people has a monopoly on power. Rather, power is spread throughout diffuse and sometimes competing groups. Further, without thinking about it too much, Americans are happy with this state of affairs (Brislin, 1991). Here I will consider the candidate "diffusion of power" in light of the 12-point checklist.

The cultural value that power should be diffuse affects a large number of specific behaviors. Consider the introduction and possible acceptance of proposals for new legislation. The number of people who become involved in the United States is massive (Smith, 1988): members of the legislative branch of government, the country's or state's chief executive, lobby groups, the press, influential community leaders, possibly the judiciary, and so forth. Yes, the fact so many people have to give their input is frustrating to those who want to see a certain piece of legislation implemented quickly. The inefficiency and time demands, however, are a protection against tyrants (Crick, 1982). If the system to implement legislation was so efficient that new laws could be passed and enforced quickly, then tyrants could use the system to introduce their own venal agenda. The quick passage of housing legislation to help the homeless seems desirable. The quick passage of legislation to dictate that all schoolchildren must read a set of politically oriented books is not. To protect against megalomaniacs who would abuse a system that allows quick passage of laws, the cultural value of power diffusion has been widely accepted (even if not frequently examined in detail).

The specific behaviors that the value "diffusion of power" guides, then, are the involvement of many people who must invest much time pursuing their goals (feature 1 in the checklist). Many specific "person-made aspects" stemming from power's diffuseness have been incorporated into American culture (feature 2). Just one is the important role of people, such as legislators, who can form coalitions among members of competing factions. Such people can communicate effectively with all factions and can be trusted by large numbers of people within each group. They are extremely valuable to the workings of a democracy: Without them factions would dissipate their energies complaining about one another. Governments in newly developing democracies in eastern Europe and within the former U.S.S.R. will be dependent on people able to communicate with feisty individuals from the multiple parties created since the rejection of communism.

Americans transmit diffusion-of-power information from generation to generation (feature 3). Respected leaders pass on their wisdom to younger people in a process commonly called "mentoring." Much of mentoring involves what might be called the "unwritten rules of power," or how people really use selected strategies to maneuver around competing factions (Kipnis, 1984). Childhood experiences related to diffusing power are remembered (feature 4). Many parents tell their children, "Don't make enemies today, or these people won't be around to help you tomorrow." When applied later to achieving power-related goals in one's organization, the advice is, "Don't reject or ignore people who you think might become enemies today. If people become enemies, they are not available to contribute their talents to coalitions you want tomorrow."

Because it is assumed people should know about power diffusion and the necessity of maneuvering among factions, this aspect of American culture is not frequently discussed (feature 5). I have seen intelligent 30-year-olds kept out of powerful decision-making groups because they make too many enemies. The leaders realize the young adults will hurt the group more than help it if they irritate others who might assist the group in attaining its goals. But because the 30-year-olds should know this aspect of their culture, nobody tells them why they are not invited to important group meetings.

Differing approaches to power lead to impactful clashes (feature 6). Consider people from a culture that has long had only one political party and one type of government they can discuss. If these people travel to a country such as the United States with its several political parties and open debate about the best form of government, they are completely unprepared to defend their political views. They never have had the experience of participating in a vigorous discussion seriously considering alternative views. They become upset and even emotionally distraught (feature 9) when asked simple questions about possible shortcomings in their government's approach to power. This contributes to the well-meaning clash.

Examples of "filling in the blanks" (feature 7) can be the exact behaviors necessary to deal with power's diffuseness. If the phrase "form coalitions" is mentioned, sophisticated Americans can fill in the exact steps needed to form them (Brislin, 1991). For example, people first should identify the interests of various factions to determine if they have enough similarities to form a coalition. Once they establish the coalition's goals, it is wise to ask, "What powerful people will be helped or hurt by the proposals formulated to achieve these goals?" Then, the group can enlist the assistance of those who will be helped and make modifications to the proposals to satisfy or at least to neutralize the opposition. The important point to consider here is that explicit instruction about the necessity of such steps is unnecessary among sophisticated Americans. Given the basic sketch about the need to form coalitions among members of competing factions, they can fill in the blanks and engage in the necessary specific behaviors.

The use of power in the United States leads to many mistakes (feature 8). Occasionally people try to monopolize power and are unwilling to share decision making with others. They do not form coalitions. Rather, they try to dictate their whims. If they have money, a high position within their organization, or the ability to punish others who do not do their bidding, they can succeed for a time. But, eventually, they are likely to lose power and to become uninfluential and sometimes pathetic figures within U.S. society. A few moments of thought should bring to mind people in national politics who fit this description: The members of Richard Nixon's inner circle are prime examples. Readers can probably think of others who worked in smaller arenas, such as universities, business organizations, or local government bureaucracies. The temporary successes of these people are slipups despite the cultural value that power should be diffuse. These mistakes do not destroy the value.

Acceptance and rejection over time (feature 10) is common when power in the United States is considered. Many young adults complain that power's necessities such as coalition formation lead to practices such as backroom deals. Later, they find they can't think of an alternative. If they want certain proposals implemented, they will need help. In return for the help, powerful people will expect favors. When people are forging coalitions, if an alternative exists to the maxim "if you scratch my back, I'll scratch yours," I am unaware of it. Yet, as seen within the former U.S.S.R., it takes a great deal of time for people to learn the necessary behaviors that accompany a democracy's diffuseness of power (feature 11).

As mentioned earlier, countries in eastern Europe need years to develop leaders comfortable with democracy. Part of power's diffuseness is that an electorate can remove power holders from office. This means leaders have to remain attractive to voters, which was unnecessary under previous totalitarian governments. Amusing stories will continue to be written (e.g., Warner, 1990) about eastern European leaders learning to make political television commercials, to talk in 10-second sound bites, and to stage attractive media events to draw attention to themselves. Such behaviors, of course, are in sharp contrast (feature 12) to the "we dictate; you accept" relationship of government leaders to their citizenry.

I believe that the value that power should be diffuse passes the test: When the 12 features are considered, they indicate that the value is part of American culture. At this point, the concept of cultural values should be clearer; widely accepted ideals of how a society should work guide the choices of specific behaviors. Another way to examine how culture works is to consider theoretical developments that social and behavioral scientists (educators, psychologists, communication researchers, anthropologists, etc.) have contributed. These theoretical ideas help to answer the question "What are some of the major ways cultures differ?" A few of these ideas involve sharp contrasts (feature 12) and consequently can be understood if behaviors commonly found in U.S. culture are compared with behaviors found in other cultures that differ significantly. Some of the theoretical contributions may seem overly abstract and unhelpful at first glance, but if care is devoted to their understanding, rich dividends will be repaid. Several such theoretical contributions, useful toward understanding the arguments made in the rest of the book, are covered in chapter 2.

CHAPTER 2

THEORETICAL CONCEPTS FOR UNDERSTANDING CULTURE

CHAPTER OVERVIEW

People's experiences in their culture have major effects on their behaviors. As will be discussed in future chapters, these behaviors occur in many social settings: family environments, schools, workplaces, and health care organizations. To continue the treatment of culture's influence on these and other aspects of our lives, I have chosen several broad and theoretical concepts for discussion. A major reason for their inclusion here is that these concepts are often discussed with research studies of any topic. Understanding these concepts, then, prepares people for the analysis of many highly focused research studies that investigate specific behaviors in specific social situations.

Almost all readers are encountering this book as part of a formal educational or training experience. As people continue to learn about culture and cultural differences, various changes may occur. These are reviewed in this chapter, and readers may want to compare their own views of personal change and development with those researchers identify. One of the changes is that people often become less ethnocentric. The term *ethnocentrism* refers to the natural tendency to believe that one's own culture is the most important and has the most reasonable guidelines for behavior. As individuals learn about other cultures and how different behaviors meet a culture's demands, ethnocentric viewpoints become untenable.

When people observe others behaving in unexpected ways, they are likely to make attributions about those behaviors. *Attributions* refers to judgments about the causes of behavior, and these are often incorrect if observers are unaware of the behavioral guidelines of other cultures. As people learn more, they can make *isomorphic* attributions, that is, make the same explanations for behavior as people socialized in the other culture do. Once people can make isomorphic attributions, other potential difficulties diminish. For example, they become less prone to problems disconfirmed expectations bring. Often, problems occur not because of actual events but because the events differed from those people expected.

Research has shown a major source of cultural differences that demands special attention. This is the set of differences due to a culture's emphasis on individualism or on collectivism. In individualistic cultures, members emphasize their own goals, attitudes, and values. In collectivist cultures, members emphasize their membership in groups and can integrate their goals with those of others. In addition to this cultural distinction, it is also important to understand differences among people *within* a culture. Culture offers guidance for behavior, and people combine this guidance with other influences drawn from their personalities. A model of personality, based on five general traits, will be reviewed in this chapter. It has been found useful for examining human behavior in many parts of the world.

IDENTIFYING GENERAL CONCEPTS USEFUL FOR ANALYZING SPECIFIC CULTURAL DIFFERENCES

The analysis of culture's influence on behavior is not an easy task. Just one reason is that so many specific cultural differences are found around the world that the challenge of understanding even a small percentage of them seems impossible. One approach to this problem is to set aside (but not ignore) the quest for specific details and instead to aim at the discovery of concepts that underlie specific differences. In chapter 1, for instance, cultural differences about the proper way to behave at business meetings were discussed. Many specific differences could have been listed, but these would soon tax the patience and memories of readers. The approach chosen was to discuss a concept at a higher level of generalization that should put specific differences in a helpful perspective. That more general concept was high versus low context: well-accepted rules versus ad hoc negotiations among individuals.

I believe several such general concepts, if understood, assist in the analysis of numerous behaviors in many areas of life: the school, the workplace, the family, and so forth. Indeed, important behaviors in these areas will be the subject of later chapters. To meet the joint goals of (a) continuing the discussion of culture and cultural differences and of (b) introducing concepts relevant to future chapters, I would like to discuss six topics in this chapter. These follow:

1. The changes that can be expected from good cultural education and training programs

2. Ethnocentrism

3. Attributions, or people's judgments about the causes of behaviors they observe

4. People's disconfirmed expectancies during their intercultural interactions

5. Individualism versus collectivism in people's cultural background

6. Similarities and differences in personality in various cultures

DOCUMENTED OUTCOMES OF TRAINING AND EDUCATION PROGRAMS

Formal programs with goals of educating and training people to better understand culture and cultural differences will be reviewed in chapters 6 and 7. The goals of these programs are to prepare people to live and work effectively with individuals from other cultural backgrounds and to increase people's understanding of culture and cultural differences (Landis & Bhagat, 1996; Landis & Brislin, 1983). Research on the outcomes of successful programs can be profitably reviewed here, because their accumulated findings define the general concept of "greater sophistication about culture and cultural differences." Put in a slightly different way, these outcomes pinpoint the types of sophistication people in such programs can expect to develop. The program outcomes can be conveniently grouped in three categories: changes in people's thinking, changes in people's emotions, and changes in people's behaviors. This list represents a compilation of findings from a large number of studies (e.g., Befus, 1988; Blake, Heslin, & Curtis, 1996; Brislin, Landis, & Brandt, 1983; Brislin & Yoshida, 1994; Cui & Van Den Berg, 1991; Cushner, 1989; Hammer, 1989).

Changes in People's Thinking

Greater sophistication in people's thinking involves movement toward complexity. After moving from simple to complex thinking about culture, people are not satisfied with quick, facile, and inadequate explanations of behavior they observe or read about. Instead, they search for a more complex picture that involves multiple points of view and multiple possible explanations. When reading about developments in eastern Europe, for example, they want to know about political and economic factors, possible changes in people's everyday lives, implications for the movement of people across national borders, the role of rarely discussed differences among various factions within countries, the possible roles world powers such as the United States, Russia, and Japan can play, and so forth.

Given this ability to think in complex terms, people are less willing to use stereotypes when discussing other cultures. *Stereotypes* are generalizations about a group or class of people that do not allow for individual differences. Examples can be heard in everyday conversation: "Blacks want . . ."; "Republicans can never . . ."; "People in Russia are moving toward democracy because . . ." These generalizations ignore real and important differences among the positions Blacks, Republicans, and Russian citizens take. Based on their knowledge that good education and training programs dealing with culture can lead to less stereotyping, some researchers have adopted an interesting measure in their evaluation studies. They have presented the graduates of their programs with a list of groups (e.g., Hispanics, Poles) and have asked them to match the groups with various descriptive adjectives (e.g., *ambitious, aloof, fun loving*). If graduates refuse to do the task and instead scrawl "this is a silly test that does nothing more than stereotype the groups," then the researchers conclude that their education and training programs had a positive outcome.

When people think with more complexity and refuse to stereotype, this usually leads to appreciation from members of other cultures. Individuals do not want to be stereotyped; they appreciate people who take the time and energy to learn another culture's complexities so that fine distinctions can be made. Another outcome of good education and training programs is that their graduates can accurately explain the reasons for complex problems and dilemmas found in other cultures. Further, they can explain the reasons in terms and arguments people in the other culture consider acceptable (Triandis, 1977; Triandis, Kurowski, & Gelfand, 1994). If the graduates can make arguments in this manner, they are not imposing positions that are familiar only in their own culture. Rather, they are taking the trouble to explain issues using analyses members of the other culture consider sophisticated.

Given this increased sophistication, people become more skilled at interpreting and responding to the sorts of problematic intercultural encounters discussed so far in this book. Recall in chapter 1 that various well-meaning clashes were discussed: opposite views on relationship breakups, feeling left out of social gatherings, irritation when a scheduled meeting does not start on time, and so forth. Skilled people can identify the problem sources and can suggest reasonable ways to deal with the difficulties (Cushner, 1989). One term for this skill is *means-ends thinking*. People can imagine reasonable end points, such as increased understanding or interpreting difficulties in cultural terms when appropriate. They also can identify effective means to reach the ends, such as well-timed private conversations with the individuals involved in the difficulties. Skilled people also have learned to identify the reasons for difficulties in their own lives. When asked to examine puzzling episodes that involve others from quite different backgrounds, they can analyze the encounters with increased sensitivity, understanding, and knowledge about cultural differences.

Changes in People's Emotions

Numerous factors cause the study of culture and cultural differences to be emotionally impactful. People put a great deal of time and effort into becoming well-socialized members of their own culture. They develop a worldview that makes sense to them. When they discover that members of other cultures have a different view, some of their fundamental assumptions about life are challenged. Most Americans believe it is best if they choose their own spouse after a period of dating various people. It is quite disconcerting for them to study the tradition of arranged marriages common in many Asian countries. They are further upset after learning that good arguments exist for arranged marriages. Parents often know many of the eligible candidates for marriage within their own and neighboring communities. They certainly know their own children and are deeply concerned about their welfare. They also know what it takes to keep a marriage going after the fun and exuberance of the honeymoon period. Parents know the challenges of life after people reach their 30th and 40th birthdays. Why shouldn't they pick spouses for their children?

A related point to constantly consider is that intercultural interactions are anxiety arousing. When they are discussed, the meaning of *intercultural interactions* is precise: face-to-face encounters among people from different cultural backgrounds. Examples are meetings between international students and host-country citizens on a university campus and business negotiations between delegations from mainland China and the United States. Various researchers have argued that any intercultural interaction can cause anxiety (Barna, 1983; Gudykunst, Guzley, & Hammer, 1996; Weldon, Carlston, Rissman, Slobodin, & Triandis, 1975). Assume a student from Korea enters the room of an American professor of Caucasian ancestry. Compared with interactions between similar people (Korean student with Korean professor, Caucasian American student with the American professor), more anxiety will arise. If the participants' physiological responses could be monitored, the intercultural interactions would lead to increased heart rates, increased sweating, elevated blood pressure, and perhaps stomach churning. One reason for anxiety is that the participants don't have clear guidelines about how to behave. What is a proper request of a college professor? What sorts of things might this student ask that the professor couldn't handle? Such thoughts are more likely to run through people's minds if they are from different cultural backgrounds (Chick, 1990).

Good education and training programs that deal with culture and cultural differences lead to decreases in anxiety in intercultural interactions. People become more comfortable with the cultural differences they might have to confront, and they experience a decrease in the feelings of uncertainty that so commonly lead to anxiety (Gudykunst, Guzley, & Hammer, 1996). Other emotions from these interactions switch from burdened to pleasurable feelings. People begin to enjoy interacting with culturally different others both in the workplace and during their free time. They look forward to the challenges intercultural contact can bring, such as expansions of preconceived views and alternative ways of looking at complex issues. They also begin to view others as different from a stereotyped mass vaguely known as "them" or "those people over there" (Amir, 1969; Scarberry, Ratcliff, Lord, Lanicek, & Desforges, 1997). The others become known as individuals with names, goals, and problems much like everyone else: worries about their children's future, coping with the cost of living, and frustration with the traffic! It is far more difficult to feel negatively about individuals one has met in positive circumstances (such as a good educational program) than to feel negatively about a bunch of others one has never seen.

With this set of positive feelings toward people previously considered as "those others," a deep understanding of cultural relativity is possible (Broaddus, 1986). *Cultural relativity* refers to an awareness that different cultures have different ways of meeting life's demands. Different cultures have various guidelines about important decisions such as choosing a marriage partner (as discussed earlier), raising children, taking care of the infirm elderly, and so forth. If people consider these guidelines in terms of the other culture's values, they are thinking with cultural relativity. The opposite of cultural relativity, of course, is the imposition of one's values learned in one's community. If arranged marriages are frowned on simply because they seem unfamiliar to the point of bizarreness, then such a judgment is an imposition rather than an example of culturally relative analysis.

Many students become acquainted with the concept of cultural relativity in their studies of psychology, anthropology, education, and other disciplines. Some students learn the concept well enough to write a short essay on midterm and final exams so that they receive a good grade. The difference between this type of learning and a deep understanding of cultural relativity involves people's emotions. People who understand cultural relativity realize the importance of culture and how seemingly strange behaviors can be analyzed only if they understand many other aspects of the culture. They are unwilling to make judgments based on the one set of values they know from their own cultural background. Further, they become emotionally upset if they do make such nonculturally relative judgments (Devine, 1995, 1996; Devine, Monteith, Zuwerink, & Elliot, 1991).

A related emotional reaction is that sophisticated people can admit to themselves that they are not yet ready to understand unfamiliar behaviors. When encountering difficulties in other cultures they are unprepared for, they are willing to suspend their judgment and to await further information. The exact term for this desirable reaction is *tolerance for ambiguity*. People in these situations do feel emotional arousal from their inability to engage in appropriate behaviors. They know they are in a state of ambiguity: They do not understand the unfamiliar behaviors around them and do not know how to behave appropriately themselves. But they can tolerate this emotional arousal, knowing that if they suspend judgment and search for additional information, they will be able to engage in culturally appropriate thinking and behavior.

Changes in People's Behavior

When people think about or have emotional reactions toward other cultures, the results are often invisible to observers. In contrast, behaviors are visible. Some of the most memorable difficulties in intercultural encounters are caused by contradictions among people's thinking, emotions, and behaviors. People might *say* they can engage in culturally relative thinking and will not become emotionally upset when faced with challenges to their preconceived views. However, they might become obviously uncomfortable when faced with such difficulties, and they might engage in such visible behaviors as angry outbursts, sullenness, or withdrawal from conversations (Crosby, Bromley, & Saxe, 1980).

Good intercultural training and education programs decrease the number of such negative behaviors (Gudykunst et al., 1996). Rather, people engage in behaviors much more indicative of positive relationships, and these behaviors are clearly visible to outside observers. For example, people do not tense their bodies when culturally different others approach them. Rather, they are relaxed and can engage in the informal, pleasant banter that is part of the workday at constructive organizations. People from these programs report that they feel comfortable interacting with culturally different people and feel they are successful in encouraging a positive tone in the workplace. It is important to note that these reports are not just the product of overactive imaginations. Individuals from other cultures also report that the people in question are engaging in positive behaviors. For instance, if the training or educational program is meant to prepare Whites to interact more effectively with Blacks in the workplace (Randolph, Landis, & Tseng, 1977), Blacks have positive reactions about the behavior of Whites. Blacks report greater ease in everyday communication, sense that the Whites have respect for the behaviors Blacks exhibit, and feel that all the people in the workplace are willing to help each other. The distinction between Whites reporting positive behaviors and Blacks having the same reaction is important. Everyone has met individuals who feel they are positive influences in the workplace but are, in reality, very much disliked. After good training and education programs, the reports of positive behaviors are mutual.

In studies of intercultural education and training, an interesting and important finding has been documented several times (O'Brien & Plooj, 1977; Weldon et al., 1975; see also Crocker, Major, & Steele, 1998). The finding combines information from the previous discussion of anxiety with this current discussion of behavior. One way to measure changes in behavior is to have graduates of education and training programs interact with people from very different cultures. After the training program ends, graduates are invited to a reception and are told that culturally diverse people will attend. In addition to the graduates, a second group, consisting of people who have not participated in education and training programs, also attends. For convenience, let's call the people "graduates" and "nongraduates." Finally, the numerous culturally diverse people (from countries other than those of the graduates) attending the reception take on the task of rating the intercultural sophistication of the attendees. These raters are unaware of who is a graduate and who is not, so their ratings are not influenced by such knowledge. The raters keep in mind such factors as which people seem at ease interacting with culturally different others, who is good at keeping up conversations on topics of mutual interest, who shows respect for people from other cultures, who avoids stereotyping people, and so forth. The results of various studies (Landis, Brislin, & Hulgus, 1985; O'Brien & Plooj, 1977; Weldon et al, 1975) have shown that nongraduates were rated as more interculturally sensitive and sophisticated than graduates.

The last sentence is not a misprint, and at first glance it might seem a disappointing finding that hardly stands as a beacon in the dark for the creation of education and training programs. The key (as just introduced) is the relationship between anxiety and behavior. The receptions with culturally diverse people were held immediately after the programs ended. The anxiety of graduates had increased because, probably for the first time, they had become aware that their behavior can have an impact on culturally different others. A point made in every good program is that behaviors appropriate in one culture are sometimes inappropriate in another (leading to the sorts of well-meaning clashes discussed in chapter 1). Consider the plight of the graduates, then, at the postprogram reception. They were thinking to themselves, "I have learned about cultural sensitivity and how my behavior can be misinterpreted by well-meaning people from other cultures. I'll have to be careful about how I behave at the reception." When interacting with the culturally diverse others, then, they were tense, anxious, and ill at ease. Or, they may have tried so hard to be culturally sensitive that their efforts came across as clumsy. The culturally diverse raters sensed these difficulties and reported to the researchers that the graduates, at best, stumbled through the reception. In contrast, the nongraduates were blissfully unaware of the impact of their own cultural background on their behavior. They undoubtedly interacted with the culturally diverse raters in their normal style. While not especially culturally sensitive, the nongraduates were more pleasant to be with than the uptight graduates.

This interesting set of research findings has a positive side. After a period of time during which graduates could calm themselves, the culturally diverse people at the reception rated them as more sophisticated. For instance, if the reception was held the day after the program ended, graduates interacted well with the people from different cultures. Graduates need time to think about their new knowledge of the importance of culture and cultural differences. They need time to recover from the anxiety caused by their awareness that their behavior has an impact on culturally diverse others. These findings have led to a recommendation for education and training programs. Administrators should schedule time at the end of programs to allow participants to work through their anxiety. A session of about two hours for openly discussing the nature of anxiety and for practicing recommended behaviors is very valuable.

Once the initial anxiety that stems from increased cultural awareness has dissipated, people can engage in the sorts of behaviors recommended during their program. Some behaviors already have been discussed in chapter 1: sensitivity to the spatial orientation adopted when interacting with others; making a point to include visitors in informal social gatherings; and engaging in modest versus forthright introductory remarks during public lectures. Research has shown (Brislin & Yoshida, 1994; O'Brien, Fiedler, & Hewlett, 1971) that good cultural programs can increase job performance *when* job-related behaviors are both teachable *and* central to good job performance in other cultures. The emphasis on "when" plus "and" are important because it is all too easy to overpromise the positive effects of good programs. The research project that led to the conclusion about teachable and performance-related behaviors is an interesting one to review.

The research (O'Brien et al., 1971) involved young American volunteers doing health-related projects in Honduras. One of the projects contained the job requirement that volunteers give inoculations to Honduran citizens so that diseases might be prevented. A culturally based difficulty, however, is that Honduras has values centering on respect for elders, and most Americans are not familiar with these values. In the United States, a young person can have expertise in an area and use it during interactions with elders. As part of these interactions, young people can direct the behavior of elders when the expertise is relevant. For example, 25-year-old X-ray technicians can tell 75-year-old patients where to go, what clothes to remove, how to stand or lie down for the X-rays, and so forth. Such behaviors are expected and even encouraged in American culture.

In Honduras, elders expect much more deference from younger people. Elders direct the efforts of the young and do not react comfortably when a community's youth tells them what to do. So how do young American volunteers give inoculations to older people in Honduras? This question may have several answers, but the one chosen centered on the manner the inoculations were given. As part of their training, the volunteers were instructed to give the inoculations in a calm and respectful manner and to combine this with a demeanor as if they had been giving inoculations for years. This calm, respectful, and confident attitude did not allow the elders opportunities to conclude that their cultural values were being violated. If the volunteers had been slow and nervous instead, the elders would have had reason to think about possible violations of cultural practices. Often, signals in the well-meaning clashes already discussed can lead to negative conclusions. Examples are nonverbal signs that a person is upset, changes in voice tone, slipups when trying to pronounce easy words, and so forth. The communication of calmness, confidence, knowledge, and respect (Chaika, 1989) gives people little reason to think about anything but receiving the inoculation and returning to their daily activities.

Medical volunteers who successfully graduated from a cultural orientation program performed more effectively during their assignment in Honduras. They were more productive in their jobs, as shown by records of the number of inoculations they administered. Note that the behaviors involved, a respectful and confident demeanor in the presence of older adults, have a cultural component and are teachable. As part of their training, volunteers could practice these behaviors. A good recommendation for the sorts of programs considered in this chapter is to search out such teachable behaviors. Here's an anecdote: I was once the beneficiary of this type of behavior-based education. I was about to travel to Japan for a lecture tour. A good friend, who was very knowledgeable about Japan, took the time to rehearse me in a number of very specific behaviors. These included having business cards printed, giving them out during initial encounters shortly after shaking hands or bowing, presenting and receiving the cards with both hands, preparing physically for the multiple long evenings out hosts will offer as part of their normal hospitality, giving modest initial remarks during my lecture, thanking people for taking the trouble to come to a lecture that could be better given by audience members, and welcoming attendees to the reception that followed the lecture. Without this preparation that involved teachable behaviors relevant to my task and considered important in the other culture, my lecture tour would have been a total failure.

When considering the introduction of new behaviors, it is important to keep in mind that some behaviors are far more difficult to introduce than others. People might ask themselves four questions:

1. *Am I familiar with this behavior?* If people are not familiar, they may have to search out opportunities to practice the new behaviors. In the study of the American volunteers in Honduras, opportunities to practice were provided during training sessions. Before my trip to Japan, my friend showed me how to present my business card (with two hands, accompanied by a slight bow).

2. *Do I know why I should perform this behavior?* While not always possible, at times people can learn why certain behaviors are appropriate in certain cultures. Before my first trip to Japan, I was told that demonstrating modesty about one's accomplishments is a sign that one wants to fit into a group and not stand out as an individual and that this is a desirable quality in Japan. In the United States, it is desirable for international students to contribute in their smaller classes because this is a way to forge a place in their professors' minds.

3. *What is my comfort level with these behaviors?* Even after opportunities to practice, people may not feel comfortable using new behaviors every day. At times, the new behaviors will interfere with people's beliefs about ethics. For example, training can give businesspeople practice in the exchange of gifts with potential overseas partners, but giving large gifts may make people feel as if they are engaging in bribes. International students may want to speak up in class, but they may be so uncomfortable doing so that they remain silent. A fourth question should be asked in such cases.

4. *Are substitute behaviors available?* If one behavior is ethically troublesome or thoroughly uncomfortable, an acceptable substitute may exist. The substitute

The rules for exchanging name cards in Japan are formal and involve using both hands.

often will follow from a knowledge of why certain behaviors are expected (question 2). If professors need to know about students' individual contributions, perhaps the students can e-mail their ideas. If expensive gifts are seen as symbols that a good business relationship is developing, perhaps other symbols (e.g., difficult to obtain, personalized, but inexpensive gifts) can be substituted.

Summary: The Benefits

I believe the list of benefits that can stem from good education and training programs is impressive. The changes in people's thinking include the willingness to entertain more complex viewpoints, the rejection of stereotypes, and the ability to understand problematic encounters in a manner similar to individuals in other cultures. The changes in people's emotions include decreases in anxiety intercultural encounters bring, an acceptance of the fact observed differences cannot be interpreted in isolation and solely from one's own viewpoint (i.e., cultural relativity), and a willingness to tolerate ambiguity while searching for good explanations of observed differences. Changes in people's behavior include greater ease when interacting with culturally diverse others, positive responses from the others about people's anxiety-free and respectful interactions, and the ability to engage in specific culturally sensitive behaviors, which can be introduced and rehearsed during good training and education programs.

CONCEPTS CENTRAL TO GOOD PROGRAMS

These benefits, then, are the results of efforts to increase people's sophistication about culture and cultural differences. What material for education and training programs would help people obtain these benefits? I believe the answer to this question is the same as the answer to another: What important concepts permeate virtually all attempts to understand culture and cultural differences as they apply to people's everyday lives? Certain concepts are covered in good educational programs and assist people greatly in understanding the role of culture in focused discussions about specific social settings. These settings will be discussed in future chapters: the home, school, workplace, and so forth. Covering a few central concepts in this chapter, then, allows me to continue the discussion of education and training programs as well as to introduce material central to later chapters. These concepts are ethnocentrism, attributions, disconfirmed expectancies, individualism and collectivism, and similarities and differences in people's personalities. The links among these five concepts, which now probably seem like a random collection, will be clarified toward the end of this chapter. Understanding these theoretical concepts allows very practical insights into everyday human behavior, and I will try to point out these applications.

Ethnocentrism

When people make ethnocentric judgments about culturally diverse others, they impose the standards they are familiar with given their own socialization (Adler, 1997; Allport, 1954; Hsiao-Ying, 1995; Keller, 1997). The roots of the word *ethnocentrism* give other insights into its meaning. "Centrism" refers to the center of one's judgments, and "ethno" refers to one's ethnic or cultural group. Ethnocentric judgments, then, are based on feelings that one's group is the center of what is reasonable and proper in life. Further, the term implies that others can be judged according to one central set of standards. An implication of this judgment is that one group is clearly better, even superior, than the other because its members practice sensible and correct behaviors. Again, the group considered better or superior is the one to which the person making ethnocentric judgments belongs.

Other overly dogmatic and overly focused views about life also have the suffix "ism" attached to them. In fact, these views are sometimes called "the isms." They include racism, sexism, and, less frequently, classicism and ageism. Their commonality with ethnocentrism is that all these views about life have a strong component that puts people into favored and inferior categories (more on these topics will be presented in chapter 6). Once people are put into an inferior category, disparaging remarks about them are easy to make. Further, the group that considers itself superior can think of justifications when it denies opportunities to the other group. Examples of racism abound in most societies. In the United States, the White majority in the past has justified and protected its privileged position by viewing the Black minority as inferior. If Blacks are considered inferior, then substandard schools and inadequate job training programs can be defended. The view is, "They can't benefit from anything better." Similar arguments are made when members of one gender (most often men) deny opportunities to the other. For years, women were denied entrance to medical schools because they were not considered capable of meeting the profession's demands. Another argument was that if women were given medical training, they eventually would leave the profession to have children and a lot of money would be wasted. When similar arguments are made to deny opportunities to people with a less than privileged social class background or to people who have reached a certain age, the vile practice of "decisions according to isms" is continued. Children of working-class parents might be denied opportunities for executive-level training programs because they are seen as having inadequate communication skills compared to peers from the middle and upper class. People who have reached 60 or 65 years of age might be automatically retired from their jobs in favor of younger people. In all these cases people from one favored group, whether it is based on their skin color, gender, class background, or age, view another group as inferior and as unworthy of equal treatment.

Discussions of ethnocentrism are made more complex when its admitted advantages are considered (Damen, 1987; Keller, 1997). If people view their own group as central to their lives and as possessing proper behavioral standards, they are likely to aid their group members when troubles arise. In times of war, the rallying of ethnocentric feelings makes a country's military forces more dedicated to the defeat of the (inferior) enemy. Undoubtedly, at times in the historical past ethnocentric feelings did not play a great part in people's everyday lives. People might not have traveled 50 miles from where they were born. Given natural barriers such as mountains and rivers, they might have never met others who were clearly different in terms of skin color, language, and customs. If they did, their natural ethnocentric viewpoints and lack of familiarity with culturally different others must have combined to make interactions defensive and often hostile.

People's natural ethnocentric feelings that include the positive feature of looking after one's own group and protecting against what might be hostile outsiders do not suit us well in today's world. Many reasons combine to challenge the usefulness that ethnocentrism might have once yielded. Some of these reasons were reviewed in chapter 1: air travel, international investments, the spread of democracy, the movement of students and workers across national boundaries, and the insistence of culturally diverse people that they not become indistinguishable contributions to a melting pot. How can people overcome their natural ethnocentric tendencies and begin to think in broader, culturally relative terms? The answer is to use the skill that separates us from other primates: People can think about their behavior (Seligman, 1998). They can become aware of the disadvantages of ethnocentric thinking, intercept themselves when putting culturally diverse others at a disadvantage, and switch to a more tolerant and culturally relative position (Devine, 1996; Schneider, 1991). An important conceptual tool for this switch in thinking is an understanding of how people make attributions about behavior.

Attributions

When people observe behaviors that differ from what they expect in their normal, everyday routines, they make judgments and draw conclusions so that they can make sense out of their observations. *Attributions* refer to judgments about the causes of behavior (Ehrenhaus, 1983; Gudykunst & Nishida, 1989; Jones, 1979; Si, Rethorst, & Willimczik, 1995). Internal questions center on why people are behaving as they do, what reasons they have for their choices, who might be influencing them, how they came to the point when they made certain choices about their behavior, and so forth. Consider the most basic case: Two people meet, and the interaction clearly does not go well. The people strain to find something to talk about, stumble in their attempts to put each other at ease, and leave the interaction in a clumsy manner. This is what might have happened if Stan and Rogelia, whose romance was discussed in chapter 1, accidentally met each other during intermission at a concert they were both attending with others. It is important to note they will make at least four types of attributions:

1. Stan will make attributions about Rogelia's behavior.
2. Rogelia will make attributions about Stan's behavior.
3. Stan will make attributions about his own behavior.
4. Rogelia will make attributions about her own behavior.

The attribution types summarized as numbers 3 and 4 are sometimes ignored. They should not be because people clearly think about their own behavior. "How am I doing? Am I acting confident? Am I making myself clear?" An important issue in intercultural interaction, I believe (Brislin, 1981), is that for at least two reasons people's attributions risk being more problematic than if the people were from very similar cultural backgrounds. One is the increased level of people's anxiety, as previously discussed. When anxious, people are not as careful and clear in their thinking. In the example, Stan and Rogelia are not in good positions to reflect clearly, especially about their own behavior (attribution types 3 and 4). The other reason is that people are less familiar with the other culture than they are with their own. Consequently, they have less access to the reasons behind the other person's attributions. In the example under consideration, Stan may not know that Rogelia is unfamiliar with the possibility that former romantic partners might maintain warm friendships. Not knowing that this possibility is part of Stan's thinking, Rogelia may think Stan is acting extraordinarily rude by pursuing any sort of interaction.

Stan and Rogelia, then, are making quite different attributions. Neither person disagrees about the behaviors involved (that Stan continues to seek out Rogelia's company), but they do disagree on the attributions about these behaviors. Stan feels he is friendly and that Rogelia has withdrawn her friendship. Rogelia feels she is behaving properly according to her upbringing and that Stan is acting rudely. A major

Four types of attributions are possible when two people meet. Each person makes attributions about the other (1 and 2), and they make attributions about themselves (3 and 4).

intervention into problems such as these is to search for opportunities to make isomorphic attributions (Triandis, 1977; Triandis et al., 1994). This somewhat technical term is frequently heard in discussions among specialists in cross-cultural research (e.g., Bhawuk, 1990; Cushner & Brislin, 1996; Gudykunst & Nishida, 1989). As noted earlier, it refers to the ability to make the same attribution as the other person in the interaction. Isomorphic attributions can be a goal in any interaction; all readers surely have been in conversations where they were badly misunderstood by someone well known to them. Readers have surely thought, "I wish that other person could see the issue from my point of view!" And this is the key to isomorphic attributions: understanding the other person's judgments about the causes of problematic interactions. Making isomorphic attributions does not necessarily involve agreeing with the other person's judgments, but it does involve understanding the basis of his or her views.

Making isomorphic attributions about the behaviors of others who people know well is difficult enough. Complexity is added in intercultural encounters because people usually are unaware of how cultural factors may be influencing the other people's behaviors. Whenever a misunderstanding occurs, people have a strong tendency to interpret it in personal terms: "The other is making decisions that deal with me and that are specifically targeted at my feelings" (Cushner & Brislin, 1996). Without the types of educational programs discussed earlier or extensive intercultural experiences when people work through problematic encounters, this tendency to interpret problems in personal terms continues. Often, the quest to make isomorphic attributions will move people's analysis of problems away from personally directed reasons to explanations involving culture and cultural differences. If Stan and Rogelia have the opportunity to learn about each other's culture, they more likely will make isomorphic attributions. Stan will learn that Rogelia is unfamiliar with maintaining past romantic relationships. Rogelia will learn that Stan simply wants to keep the friendship and is not acting rudely according to his culture's values. Neither Stan nor Rogelia has to agree that the other has a reasonable viewpoint. Recall from the discussion of culture's features in chapter 1 that familiar values and behaviors cause emotional reactions when they are violated. Stan and Rogelia will not quickly become comfortable with each other's viewpoint. But they can learn to understand each other's attributions and then become more tolerant of behaviors that once seemed strange and ill mannered.

A lack of understanding of the reasons for observed behaviors is the root of many intercultural difficulties. At times, people make attributions about an entire cultural group based on limited knowledge of a few members. This has been called the "ultimate attribution error" (Aronson, Wilson, & Akert, 1999; Pettigrew, 1997). For example, attributions about Jewish people often include the conclusion that they are overly concerned with making money. People who make this ultimate attribution about an entire group do not realize that, historically in Europe, the business of lending money was one of the few occupations Jewish people were allowed to enter (Aronson et al., 1999). Similarly, many people describe African Americans as "musical" or as "having rhythm." They do not consider the possibility that at one time entertainment was one of the few professions African Americans were allowed to enter so that they could make a living and provide food and shelter for their families.

Often, the movement away from such attribution errors is stimulated by intense interpersonal relationships that cut across cultural boundaries (Pettigrew, 1997). One of my friends is in an intercultural marriage (this type of marriage is discussed in Romano, 1997). He was socialized in Palestine, and his wife was socialized in Wisconsin. One of the reasons for the marriage's success, he feels, is that he and his wife explain cultural differences when misunderstandings and disagreements occur. In one disagreement, my friend sided with his father in a family argument about where to send his children (his father's grandchildren) to school. He later confided to his wife, "I agree with you, but I sided with my father." His wife said, "How could you do that?" My friend replied, "He's an old man and, as you know, has a terminal cancer. He won't be with us much longer. My cultural background says that I should respect him and honor his wisdom. I also have to make his last years comfortable. That's why I sided with him." His wife might not agree with this viewpoint, but she can learn to understand how culture gives guidance for such behaviors.

I have mentioned a few reasons for the greater likelihood of making incorrect attributions in intercultural encounters. The encounters are anxiety arousing; many encounters are unfamiliar and consequently demand explanations; and so much about the other culture is unknown that people try out explanations of observed behaviors simply to fill the uncomfortable void that uncertainty and ambiguity always bring. Another feature of intercultural encounters is that they are often very memorable, impactful, and sometimes very vivid. People have a strong tendency to overinterpret the effects of vivid and impactful events they are directly involved in (Sherman, Judd, & Park, 1989). These events overwhelm other, often less colorful, evidence that might assist people in making isomorphic attributions. An example should make this point clear.

Assume that a highly respected book gives information on overseas job opportunities. Interested in gaining international experience, Jack consults the guide and discovers that Japan has many opportunities. The guide reports that respondents in a survey of 300 Americans living in large Japanese cities feel that well-qualified Americans with good job searching and interviewing skills can find employment in Japan. This is especially true for Americans seeking positions as English-language teachers in Japan's schools or in the training division of Japanese companies. Jack is impressed, applies for a passport and visa, and tells his friends of his plans. One friend, Sharon, expresses surprise. "My cousin went to Japan looking for work. He couldn't find a job and was very disappointed. He spent all his savings traveling and living there for a while, and he had go come back to America when his money ran out. Are you sure you want to go to Japan?"

What will Jack do? The strong tendency would be to put the most weight on Sharon's comments. Her comments were delivered in a memorable, impactful manner. Her recollections of her cousin's experiences were presented in vivid, emotional language. Jack became deeply involved in the conversation with Sharon and began to sympathize with the cousin's plight. Sharon's comments were much more attention grabbing than the information in the guidebook Jack read. From the standpoint of careful decision making, Jack should examine 301 pieces of information: the reports by the surveyed people in the guidebook and the experiences of Sharon's cousin (Kahneman & Tversky, 1984). But because Sharon's report is so much more colorful than the rather dull information in the guide, Jack likely will give it far more weight than it deserves. The strong tendency would be to accept the personalized report and to ignore the survey results from the 300 people. This tendency would be so strong that Jack might not even think very much about why Sharon's cousin is an exception. Maybe the cousin interviews poorly, perhaps he showed little respect for the Japanese he met (discussed in chapter 8), and so forth.

The only way to stop making attributions based on limited or faulty information is to become aware of the underlying reasons people think the way they do. Then, they can stop and ask themselves, "Am I making an attribution based on easily available, personalized, and colorful information? Might I seek other, perhaps duller, information before coming to any conclusions?" This same search for additional information is the recommended action to nullify the other factors leading to potentially faulty attributions in intercultural encounters (Adler, 1997). If people ask themselves questions such as the following and behave according to the answers, they are likely to succeed more in their intercultural interactions: "Am I too anxious, too upset to make good attributions? Am I tempted to make more attributions than I should because so much new is going on in my life? Am I unaware of certain aspects of the other people's cultural background that, if better understood, would help me to make better attributions?"

Disconfirmed Expectancies

If people make incorrect attributions, they also may behave incorrectly before they find out their attributions are wrong. Put another way, people might experience a puzzling intercultural encounter. They make an attribution, follow up their thinking with seemingly appropriate behaviors, and only later discover that both the attribution and behaviors were faulty. This discovery involves an added set of emotional reactions.

The additional emotional reactions stem from *disconfirmed expectancies*. Such reactions are a guaranteed part of any extensive intercultural interactions (Cushner & Brislin, 1996). People make decisions about what to expect when crossing cultural boundaries, and they also (with every good intention) make decisions about their behavior. A major reason for people's decisions about their behavior is that they feel that it will bring positive results, such as a good impression on others (Bandura, 1986). When they find that their expectations are disconfirmed, they become very upset.

Most often, the degree of emotional upset is based on the difference between expectation and reality. Readers may find the following mental exercise helpful. Think of an upsetting past event that led to an intense emotional reaction. With the benefit of hindsight, was it the event that caused the upset, or was it the *difference* between the event and what was expected in that social situation? I believe many readers will conclude that, in retrospect, the event was not all that bad and was not all that difficult to handle. The intense emotional reaction was due to the fact the event differed so much from expectations. If expectations had been more accurate, the difference between reality and expectations would have been smaller, and consequently the event would have involved less emotional trauma. Many educational programs that prepare people to live and work in other cultures cover the issue of disconfirmed expectancies. One specific exercise is to ask participants to list their expectations. Often, people list unrealistic goals (Katz, 1977), such as making 10 or 12 friends in the other culture within three months. The program leader then can engage the participants in discussions that lead to reformulated expectations more likely to align with reality.

Disconfirmed expectancies are certain to occur in intercultural encounters. Some colleagues and I had an interesting experience. We prepared a set of educational materials designed to help prepare people to live in other cultures or to work extensively with culturally diverse people in their own country (Brislin, Cushner, Cherrie, & Yong, 1986; Cushner & Brislin, 1996). We organized the materials around 18 thematic areas that should help people interpret any specific intercultural experience they would later encounter. Some of the 18 themes have been integrated throughout this book (e.g., attributions, ethnocentrism), and others will be covered later in this chapter (e.g., individualism and collectivism) or in other chapters. To best present the

18 themes, we decided to make them part of 100 critical incidents or short vignettes of the type already presented (Stan and Rogelia's difficulties with their relationship; Fumio's feelings that he is being ignored). We felt these short vignettes would bring life to the 18 themes because the stories involve the sorts of problems and issues with which readers can sympathize. One of these 18 themes is disconfirmed expectancies. After the book containing the 18 themes and 100 critical incidents (110 incidents in the second edition) was published, we were asked to give workshops for people anticipating extensive intercultural interactions: overseas businesspeople, university professors wishing to internationalize the curriculum at their schools, counselors working with a culturally diverse clientele, adolescents about to spend a year attending high school in another country, and so forth. We found that people appreciated talking about disconfirmed expectancies as one of the 18 themes or concepts that would help them understand their future interactions. But we also found that disconfirmed expectations permeated virtually all of the 100 critical incidents we prepared (a point also made by Bhawuk, 1990). Put another way, it is extremely difficult to write incidents that capture experiences people are likely to have without including disconfirmed expectancies as part of the reason for the problems reported.

To borrow from psychologists' research on abilities (e.g., Anastasi, 1988; Vrij & Winkel, 1994), disconfirmed expectancies is a general factor found in large numbers of situations. Just as, as many psychologists argue, intelligence has a general component used for large numbers of specific tasks (e.g., arithmetic, vocabulary learning, writing), disconfirmed expectancies seem to be a component of virtually all memorable and impactful intercultural experiences.

If this is true, then people should have a set of tools that are useful when they find that their expectations have been disconfirmed. As needed for insight into the ways people make attributions, the tools involve using more sophisticated thought processes. A good tool is to "talk down" the disconfirmed expectancies (Brewin, 1996; Meichenbaum, 1977; Seligman, 1989) encountered during intercultural experiences. Talking down means putting the experience into a proper perspective so that it does not permeate all of one's thinking. Rather than the person interpreting the experience as a sign of failure, which eventually can lead to a sense of helplessness and to depression, talking down involves focusing on the experience and moving beyond it only after very careful thought.

Assume the experience involves a clearly unsuccessful job interview in another country. The three steps in the talking-down process follow:

1. *Make thoughts specific.* Rather than interpreting the incident in global, general terms such as "I am making a terrible adjustment in this country," the person should focus thoughts on the specifics. Further, care should be taken not to move beyond the specifics until after extensive thinking. A more specific focus would be, "I didn't do very well in this interview, but this doesn't mean I'll do poorly in all interviews." Focusing on specifics makes change possible, because it is far easier to change specific behaviors (e.g., interviewing style) than highly general behaviors that suggest few opportunities for direct intervention (e.g., adjustment to another culture). Indeed, change is central to the second step in the talking-down process.

2. *Make the issue involved changeable.* If step number 1 is taken, then people can focus on a specific issue or behavior. The next step is to focus on the issue's changeable aspects. For the unsuccessful job interview issue, changeable aspects the disappointed candidate might focus on could include manner of dress, how to keep up a conversation with a Japanese interviewer, or methods of showing respect for others during the conversation. One possible cultural difference (Pascale & Athos, 1981) is that American job candidates might be anxious to communicate their qualifications. Consequently, they might discuss their education and job experience during the first 15 minutes of their interview. This might be quite proper behavior if they were interviewing in a big city within the United States. But the Japanese interviewer may prefer casual conversation on seemingly unimportant matters—what Americans call small talk. The interviewer may want to obtain a "feel" for candidates: Are they trustworthy, are they respectful, and do they seem to have the social skills needed to fit into the Japanese organization and to cooperate with others? If candidates begin to talk about themselves too quickly, they may be seen as boorish. The key to the discussion here is that American candidates have a specific focus they can view as changeable. They can change their behavior by engaging in the pleasant, friendly small talk the Japanese host prefers.

3. *Focus on possible external aspects.* When people experience failure in a social situation, they might conclude, "It is my fault! Something is wrong with me!" When people think in this way (Carson, 1989; Seligman, 1989, 1998), they are focusing on possible internal aspects of their experiences—aspects that involve their abilities, their social skills, or their personalities. In reality, the event often involves external aspects that have little to do with a particular person experiencing failure. Regarding the example, a 5-minute glance at any good book in organizational behavior (e.g., Landy, 1989; Robbins, 1998) will reveal that interviews are a notoriously unreliable method of selecting people for jobs in an organization. Interviews have so many factors external to the job applicant, such as the number of openings at any one time or the interviewer's idiosyncrasies, that the interviewee's focus on internal factors can be both incorrect and damaging. Another external reason, very common in my observations, is that the organization already has committed the job opening to someone but has to go through the charade of multiple interviews to satisfy legal requirements. A better reaction than a knee-jerk focus on internal factors is to say (to oneself) something like, "I didn't get this job offer, but it could be for many reasons that have nothing to do with me. I'll just keep scheduling interviews until I get a good mix of genuine job openings and an interviewer who appreciates what I have to offer."

However, an overemphasis on external thinking is dangerous, because it can take attention away from internal factors that should be addressed. If the job candidate is not showing respect for the interviewer or is not engaging in the preferred small talk, a total focus on external factors would mean the candidate is excluding appropriate behavior modifications. The recommendation to consider external factors is meant to help people broaden their thinking so that they are not overwhelmed by internals thoughts such as "It's all my fault!"

When the three steps are followed, people are less likely to feel helpless and to become depressed if their expectations of an intercultural experience don't match reality (Seligman, 1989, 1998). Rather, they can think about ways to move from their temporary failure into new situations (or new mental views of their situations) that can lead to greater chances of success. Part of this thinking in people's intercultural encounters should include the self-directed question "Should I be considering the cultural background of the other people?" As discussed in chapter 1, this can be a difficult question because many people are unaccustomed to thinking in terms of culture and cultural differences. One approach to more sophisticated thinking is to examine the conceptual tools cross-cultural researchers have developed to summarize and to organize cultural differences they have studied. One such tool centers on the individualistic contrasted with the collectivistic background of people in different cultures. This distinction helps people understand many specific cultural differences and intercultural interactions.

Individualism and Collectivism

Numerous researchers have argued that one of the most important factors in a culture is the relative emphasis it places on individualism and collectivism (Hofstede, 1980; Kagitcibasi, 1997; Triandis, 1990, 1995; Triandis, Brislin, & Hui, 1988). Although no culture totally ignores individualistic or collectivistic goals, cultures differ significantly on which of these factors they consider more critical. In individualistic cultures, people set and work toward their own goals. When a conflict arises between an individual's goals and those of a valued group (e.g., family, coworkers), the individual considers his or her goals more important. Given this emphasis on a person's own goals, the words *individual* and *individualized* are constantly used in the culture. Americans, for example, hear the terms in elementary schools ("the individual learning style of each child"), in the workplace ("the individual's career development"), and in the family ("each child develops an individual identity"). Aphorisms and advice related to individualism are frequently heard: "Stand on your own two feet," "Learn to blow your own horn because no one will do it for you," and "Take the initiative—don't wait for someone else to throw something your way." Other signs of cultural individualism include parental beliefs that part of their task is to prepare children to leave the home (perhaps at age 18 when they go to college) so that they can have their own separate and successful lives. Many parents in individualistic cultures are proud to say that they will have enough financial resources at age 65 or 70 so that they will not have to depend on their adult children.

In collectivist cultures, people are more likely to downplay their own goals in favor of goals a valued group sets. That group is most often their extended family (Georgas et al., 1997), but it also can be organizational or religious. People in such cultures obtain much of their identity as members of their collective. When asked to complete statements that start with the phrase "I am . . . ," members of collective cultures (hereafter called collectivists) are much more likely than individualists to list membership in a group (Bochner & Hesketh, 1994; Triandis et al., 1988). They might list membership in a family, a religion, or an organization. Individualists, in contrast, are much more likely to list trait labels that imply how they are distinct from other people. They will list aspects of their personalities such as "hard working," "intelligent," or "athletic."

Generalizations about where individualism and collectivism are found must be made cautiously because exceptions always will exist, but a few remarks may help. Individualism is commonly found in North America and western Europe and in countries strongly influenced by these areas, such as Australia and New Zealand. Collectivism is common in Asia, Africa, Central and South America, and small Pacific island societies. As might be expected, in a worldwide survey of work-related values in more than 50 countries, the United States is the most individualistic nation (Hofstede, 1980, 1991).

The differences in how people describe themselves has implications for their everyday behaviors. In Japan, a collectivist country, people have to mention the organization they belong to when talking to someone else who is not already familiar with them. The organization is mentioned first: "Hello, this is Mitsubishi company's Fumio Yoshida. May I please talk to . . . ?" When I first went to Japan, an experienced colleague wisely advised: "Have business cards printed with your organization prominently indicated. If you don't, people will not know who you are!" This advice means people often have two sets of cards, one for Japan and one for their own country. In the United States, people often have cards that emphasize individual features, such as books written, unique talents, and hobbies. The organization they work for is sometimes not mentioned.

A few of the key differences between individualists and collectivists can be summarized in pictorial form (Figure 1). Both types feel a sense of self separate from others. All adults know they have a face they cannot see except in a mirror, learn (sometimes to their horror) that the voice quality they hear when they speak is not what others hear, and realize only the self can take certain steps in life (e.g., eating well, entering a marriage). The differences between individualists and collectivists involve the amount of psychological distance from, or the importance of emotional closeness (Kagitcibasi, 1997) with, other people.

Moving from the bottom to the top of Figure 1, note that individualists and collectivists do not differ in terms of closeness to nuclear family members: a spouse, parents, children. The caveat has to be added, however, that this statement is true only when members of the nuclear family are getting along well. Surely all readers have known nuclear families whose members have engaged in bitter, hostile actions against one another. The differences between individualists and collectivists emerge in relations with people beyond the nuclear family.

Individualists keep a comfortable psychological or emotional distance between themselves and group members. With the extended family, they might have good relations with some uncles and cousins but merely cordial (sometimes called "Christmas Card") relations with other kinfolk. Collectivists keep a much closer relationship between the self and another collective, often the extended family. The collective becomes the place where people find their identity as human beings. Collectivists identify themselves as better depicted in the bottom drawing in Figure 1. Or, they identify with a modification of the picture that has the self surrounded by a group. Collectivists feel comfortable with this constant psychological presence of their group. Individualists report they would feel stifled if they were steadily surrounded

The Relation of the Self to Others in Individualist and Collectivist Cultures   **FIGURE 1**

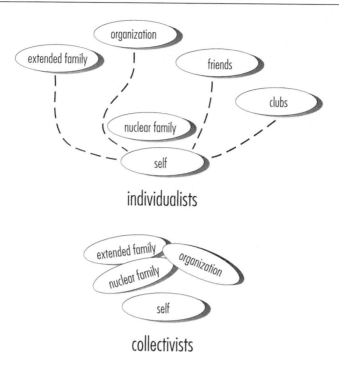

by others. Too many people's opinions would have to be considered before an individualist could pursue his or her goals. Individualists find that clearing their plans with others interferes too much with their desire to "do their own thing."

Placing an individualist and a collectivist in a similar dilemma may clarify some key differences. Assume a 40-year-old woman lives in the same city as her 78-year-old mother. The two live in separate houses, but the daughter can check in on her mother two or three times a week. The daughter is an only child, and her father has passed away. The mother is in reasonably good health for a 78-year-old but is beginning to experience the problems many elderly people face: mild arthritis, poor vision, slow recovery from respiratory infections, and so forth. The mother has an active social life in her church, in a bridge club, and as part of volunteer work at the local hospital. Then the daughter receives a job offer in a city 1,000 miles away. It is exactly the sort of job she has long desired: a high salary, challenging work, excellent working conditions, intelligent and pleasant coworkers, and good opportunities for future promotions. What will the daughter do: stay near her mother to take care of her or move 1,000 miles away to take the job?

A collectivist is more likely to turn the job down to stay with her mother. Her identity as a human being is much more closely tied to her family, and she is likely to feel responsible for her mother's happiness during her mother's old age. By turning the job down, she is demonstrating a collectivist's key value: downplaying her own goals (i.e., her own ambitions) in favor of the group's goals (i.e., her nuclear family member's happiness). An individualist is more likely to take the job in the city 1,000 miles away. Her sense of identity is more closely linked to the pursuit of her own goals, ambitions, and preferences. She is more likely to follow through in her desire for a better job, leaving the care of her mother to others (e.g., a nursing home or a retirement community). Even some possible compromises involve downplaying the mother's preferences. If the daughter takes the mother with her to the new city, the mother has to leave her friends and active social life behind her.

It is important to note that these generalizations will not fit all cases. In collectivist societies, some people in the same situation will make the move to the new city; in individualist societies, some people will stay and take care of their mothers. The generalizations about individualists and collectivists (this one and others to be made in later paragraphs) refer to trends for large numbers of people. If 100 cases were studied in collectivist and individualist societies, a majority of collectivists would behave in a manner that emphasized their group's goals, and a majority of individualists would behave in a manner that emphasized their personal goals. This concept of "trends for large numbers of people" is important to keep in mind whenever culture and cultural differences are discussed.

Understanding some basic comparisons of individualism and collectivism allows insights into seemingly unrelated behaviors. Three topics will be discussed here: social skills, the distribution of rewards for group effort, and advice for people moving from one culture to another (more details can be found in Hsu, 1981; Triandis et al., 1988).

Social Skills

Considering effective social skills allows a review of the concept "ethnocentrism." Judgments about "effective" or "proper" behaviors only can be made fairly if people have detailed knowledge about culture and cultural differences. If, for example, people judge those from another culture as "lacking in social skills," they are undoubtedly making an ethnocentric judgment based on their own culture's standards.

Proper social skills for individualists and collectivists follow from the length of the imaginary lines (see Figure 1) linking the self to others. Take individualists and their relationship to organizations that might offer them employment. Who is expected to make the move along the line from the self to the organization? The answer, of course, is that the individualists are expected to make this move. They cannot expect others to assure them of entry to organizations with good jobs. Instead, they have to depend on themselves. In doing so, they must summon a set of behaviors known as social skills (Singleton, Spurgeon, & Stammers, 1980), although a more proper label is "social skills useful in individualist cultures." These include meeting people quickly, putting them at ease, finding conversational topics others can readily discuss, being interesting so that the others will remember interactions six months later, and so forth. These skills are useful because they allow people to obtain information from others central to the pursuit of individual goals (Brislin, 1991).

For instance, assume individualists are at an informal party. If they can meet others quickly and put them at ease, they may find that someone has a good link to an organization where they seek employment. The other person may be able to share the names and phone numbers of the key people involved in hiring decisions. The same social skills of quickly meeting others and finding interesting conversational topics are also useful if a job interview is scheduled. Public speaking is an example of another important social skill. If a person can give a dynamic, interesting, and memorable speech at a public gathering, audience members may later remember the speaker if they are asked to recommend people who can fill job openings in their organizations. As discussed in chapter 1, my father realized the importance of good public speaking skills and encouraged me to develop them.

This example from my interactions with my father reminds me of a recent incident involving my son. He was 12 years old and wanted to attend a school dance. But this meant he would miss the last hour of Little League baseball practice. I approached his coaches, prepared to argue for a long time about his desire. But I was surprised when the head coach immediately said, "Sure, the dance is important. It's good that he wants to go." As discussed in chapter 1, people cannot always discuss their culture using explicit terms. Rather, they have a general understanding that allows them to consider alternatives and to choose those that make good sense. The head coach may not have said my son would be "developing social skills useful in an individualist culture," but he approved missing baseball because he realized that going to dances is also important.

Similar social skills as those discussed aid in the movement from the self to other groups: to clubs, to churches, to opportunities to make new friends. This movement is especially important in a highly mobile society such as the United States, where numerous people move to new communities each year. They must summon their social skills to establish new relationships that lead to various benefits: information about the best jobs, about opportunities for creating deep friendships, about possible romantic partners, and so forth.

Social skills that put a premium on movement away from the self to others are not as important in collective societies. Consider the bottom half of Figure 1. When the person labeled "self" needs a job, who arranges opportunities to meet potential employers? The answer is "a high-status member of the collective." If a person wants an accounting job in a large organization, then someone in the collective who is a member of that organization is asked for help. Alternatively, someone who knows an influential executive in the organization initiates the task of identifying job possibilities for the job seeker. Other than letting collective members know employment is desired, the job seeker is not expected to take as active a role as the individualist described previously. One collectivist from India explained to me, "The person seeking a job is rather like a member of the audience watching a play in which others talk about a person. The strange part [to an individualist] is that the person being talked about is me!"

Another example comes from one of my students' experiences. He was a tennis player recruited out of his hometown in Mexico on an athletic scholarship. Because he was a student in my course, he could make distinctions between expectations in individualist and collectivist cultures. He told me that during the last month of his senior year, he had difficulty keeping up conversations with friends. When graduation is scheduled for June 1, what do college seniors talk about when they see each other in early May? After greetings, they often talk about their experiences with job interviews. My student reported he couldn't participate in these discussions. It was not his task to arrange job interviews: That was a task for his parents, uncles, and aunts back in Mexico. If he were to take a career step such as accepting an invitation to join the professional tennis tour, he would have to discuss this with extended family members after graduation. His comment was, "After exchanges of 'hello, how are you,' I don't have much to say."

Social skills that allow people to meet strangers quickly and to put others at their ease are not as important in collective societies. Important collective social skills are loyalty to the group, cooperation, contributing to the group without expecting immediate reciprocity, and public modesty about one's abilities (Triandis, 1995). Loyalty and cooperation are expected because these qualities insure the collective's survival and effectiveness. Loyalty is eventually repaid when a given person needs the collective's assistance, as in the employment search example. Modesty is needed for a number of reasons. One is so that the person can defer to the high-status members of the collective who have the most favors to grant. In exchange for deference, thereby having their high status reinforced, influential members of the collective share their resources. Another reason is that too much immodesty can interfere with the collective's smooth functioning. If people "blow their own horns" about their abilities, this can cause envy, jealousy, and strain for the collective. If people who are obviously self-confident about their abilities constantly put themselves forward (as they do in individualist societies), then they are investing their energies into self-promotion rather than into the collective's welfare. Many collective societies have a saying (or its equivalent) that "the nail that sticks up gets hammered down" (Damen, 1987).

Distributing Rewards for Group Efforts

When people work together on a group project, it is sometimes difficult to decide how the benefits of the work will be distributed. Assume four people have worked on a joint project within their organization. Two of the four clearly did more work than the others. They worked overtime, read more on topics related to the project, and so forth. As a result of the group's success, the organization's president decides to present the group members with a $10,000 bonus above their salaries. How is the money to be distributed among the four people? Several distribution patterns are possible. In the pattern known as "equality," each person receives the same amount of money: $2,500. In the pattern knows as "equity," each person receives an amount corresponding to his or her contributions (A. Fiske, 1991; Hui & Luk, 1997; Leung & Iwawaki, 1988). Assume an outside observer studies the contributions of the four people in the group (A, B, C, and D) and makes conclusions about their efforts. Assume further that the conclusions (accepted by the four people) are that A contributed 35% of the effort, B contributed 30%, C contributed 25%, and D contributed 10%. In an equitable distribution pattern, the four people would receive $3,500, $3,000, $2,500, and $1,000, respectively.

An equitable distribution of rewards is preferred in individualistic societies. People who invest time and effort in a project want their contributions recognized and rewarded. The goal is to reward the efforts of individuals in the group rather than to insure that the group will survive into the future. The quest for individual rewards often leads to a great deal of tension when benefits are distributed. People disagree about the relative contributions of group members and feel ill treated if they do not receive as much as expected. They may become upset if coworkers who put in less time and effort receive a large percentage of the benefits. This concern with individual rewards and recognition often leads to difficulties in forming work groups in the first place. Many readers undoubtedly have had experiences similar to those in the following example. A professor wants to introduce the importance of cooperative team effort to her American students. She asks the students to form groups of three for doing a team project. One grade will be given for the final report each group submits. Some individualist students will surely say, "What happens if I end up doing more than one-third of the work or if the others don't follow through on their promises? If I work harder, how will this be recognized? I'm trying to get into a prestigious law school and can't afford a C grade."

Collectivists, in contrast, prefer an equal distribution of rewards. The goal is to keep the collective intact, and it must be constantly remembered that collectivists obtain their identity from their group memberships more than from pursuing individual goals. Collectivists feel that if the benefits were distributed unequally, even if some people put in more effort, then ill feelings would result and the group's existence would be threatened. Given that the group's well-being is important, people downplay their desires for individual recognition. If one person feels upset, he or she might think, "Some of the people did not work very hard on this group task, but they may work harder on the next one the group undertakes."

Advice for Moving From One Culture to Another

Now that individualism and collectivism are understood better, here are some specific suggestions for moving across cultural boundaries. Different advice is applicable to individualists moving to a collective society (e.g., from the United States to Japan) and to collectivists moving to an individualist society (e.g., from Argentina to Great Britain; Bhawuk, 1989, 1990; Triandis, 1995; Triandis et al., 1988).

Recall the discussion of social skills. Individualists moving to a collective society are well advised to work through a collective to obtain such goals as introductions to prestigious people or interviews for good jobs. They should contribute to the well-being of a collective and only later ask for benefits the collective might offer. If they pursue their own goals as they would in their own society, they will be seen as pushy, ill mannered, and disrespectful. In general, people should remember that members of the host culture obtain a great deal of their identity from collective membership. Nothing should be done or said that might be interpreted as an insult to the collective or to one of its members. If a person does something positive for a collective member, he or she can rest assured that other members will hear about it. Members of a collective share information among themselves far more frequently than individualists share information with their friends and acquaintances.

Once people start contributing to a collective, they should expect that rewards will be distributed equally rather than on an equity basis. In fact, the people can interpret this as a compliment. When distributing rewards equally, the collective is saying, "We realize you value your group membership, and we value your presence and your contributions. Because you are putting the collective's well-being foremost, we know you will want to accept this equal reward distribution." Individualists are also well advised to be modest about describing their abilities and accomplishments and to defer to high-status people in the collective. If the individualists contribute to the group, others in the collective will accept the task of praising their abilities.

Different advice should help collectivists moving to individualist cultures. Most collectivists will not be traveling with their group: Foreign students, overseas businesspeople, and immigrants almost always leave some collective members in the home country. Consequently, they cannot depend on their collective to provide them with key information and opportunities for goal attainment. They must adopt the sorts of behavior individualists display, such as actively meeting people graciously and finding conversational topics of mutual interest. They must develop what individualists call a *network*, that is, a circle of acquaintances who give each other assistance. Network members are different from close friends. The latter give emotional support; people in a network trade favors. For instance, one person in a network has the phone number of a clever accountant knowledgeable about income tax deductions for people living in more than one country during a given year. If a person shares this phone number, he or she can expect to have a favor returned at a later date. If people don't return favors, they are often dropped from network membership.

When preparing a set of materials useful for helping people move across cultural boundaries, Cushner and Brislin (1996) found that collectivists frequently complained about the difficulties of setting up a network. They are not accustomed to meeting people they have never seen before and behaving memorably. After individualists (correctly) have told them that parties and other informal social gatherings are good places to meet people, when they attend such events they are confused by the informal rules. At parties, people are expected to circulate, to speak with many others who are present. If they spend too much time with specific individuals, they are said to monopolize the other's time and also risk the reputation of being a bore. In contrast to the rule that people should circulate, collectivists would rather spend one or two hours with a few people so that they can get to know one another well. They feel that the movement from person to person at an individualist party leads to superficial interactions, and they are very uncomfortable with the practice. Recall Figure 1: The top drawing suggests greater comfort moving from person to person at parties. The bottom one suggests greater comfort with long conversations among two or three people.

Collectivists also have to learn to communicate their abilities and accomplishments so that individualists will know what their contributions to projects can be. Again, they will not have their group to perform this task for them. They should not brag, of course, but they must learn to talk about themselves so that they become part of other people's memories. Recall the saying common in collectivist societies: The nail that sticks up gets hammered down. Collectivists have to put this saying aside when in individualist societies. Businesspeople have to speak up at meetings and communicate their ideas; foreign students in graduate school have to present their research in seminars; and immigrants have to present their qualifications and job experiences at employment agencies and elsewhere. Explicit attention to public speaking skills (as defined by individualists) should help collectivists with any tasks that involve putting the self forward.

Once collectivists realize they do not have a group that demands the loyalty and deference they are accustomed to, they will become more comfortable with the equitable rather than the equal distribution of rewards. They will realize that rewards often follow the level of individual contributions, because individualist societies place greater emphasis on individual accomplishments and recognition than on group solidarity.

Balancing Individualism and Collectivism

Perhaps some personal observations about the balance of individualism and collectivism will help at this point. Many developments in the late 20th century will encourage greater worldwide individualism: movement across cultural boundaries, movement from rural areas to cities within various countries, increased dependence on technology, the desire of women to gain personal identity from employment rather than from (or in addition to) homemaking (discussed further in chapter 9), the worldwide demand for democratic governments, and so forth (Kagitcibasi, 1997). But individualism has its price: Other people who might lend support in times of trouble may not be present.

The lack of a supportive collective is undoubtedly one reason for difficulties found in the world's most individualistic nation, the United States. It has a very high divorce rate because concerned others are not always present when a married couple needs help. Stress-related problems such as heart disease are common (Beardsley & Pedersen, 1997), and one reason is that supportive others are not always available to help people cope with difficulties (Bond, 1991). Members of culturally diverse groups sometimes experience contradictions. Black Americans may be willing to compete and to develop the social skills necessary for success in an individualistic society, but they may find their goals thwarted because of prejudice and discrimination. The resulting stress is one reason for high blood pressure and anxiety disorders among Black Americans (Cutain, 1992). Social problems such as homelessness and inner-city poverty are embarrassments to a great nation, but one reason they exist is that individualism does not necessarily include a concern for (and the willingness to invest resources in) the unfortunate. People's happiness in the most individualistic societies, I believe, will be dependent on their ability to shift their thinking from the single-minded pursuit of their own goals to a greater concern for the welfare of others in their communities.

Personality: Similarities and Differences

Individualism and collectivism are *cultural-level* variables. They are helpful concepts that give people guidance about what to expect when moving across cultural boundaries. Of course, it is not the only cultural-level variable: More will be covered throughout this book. Nor are cultural variables all people need to know for intercultural interactions. Another major type of concept they need to know about is personality, that is, *individual* differences in how people think about and behave in a variety of social situations. Almost everybody talks about the personalities of individuals they know. When asked about someone else, a person might use terms such as *shy, lazy,* or *friendly*. These are terms that summarize an individual's tendencies

One criticism of highly individualistic societies is that people have too little concern for the intense difficulties others face.

to think and behave a certain way in multiple situations, that is, the individual's personality. People often can apply such descriptions to themselves when asked about their own personalities.

One of the benefits of cross-cultural research is that important concepts identified in one or a few cultures can be tested for their possible universality. By investigating a wide variety of cultures, researchers can examine whether or not a concept is specific to one culture or whether it is applicable to many or to all. In recent years, much research has concentrated on personality dimensions in various cultures, and this research has successfully identified five that may be universal (McCrae & Costa, 1997; Paunonen, Jackson, Trzebinski, & Fosterling, 1992; Piedmont & Chae, 1997; Salgado, 1997). Countries this research covered include the United States, Canada, Israel, Finland, Poland, Germany, Russia, Korea, Hong Kong, Japan, and the Philippines. Sometimes called "The Big Five," these dimensions are at a higher level of abstraction than many personality descriptions, yet they help integrate research on both multiple and specific personality dimensions. I am discussing these five dimensions here because this recent research suggests that people interact with others who can be described by these dimensions. These descriptions are not complete, but they provide a helpful starting point. Readers may want to consider themselves and others they know well as they think about these five dimensions.

1. *Extraversion.* People with this trait are sociable, talkative, and look forward to being with others, in contrast to introverts, who are shy, withdrawn, and reserved.

2. *Conscientiousness.* This dimension summarizes the more specific traits that mark careful, responsible, and dependable people, in contrast to people who are irresponsible and who lack self-discipline.

3. *Agreeableness.* Agreeable people are good natured, cooperative, and easy to get along with, in contrast to disagreeable people, who are irritable, uncooperative, and inflexible.

4. *Emotional stability.* Some people have noticeably more control over their emotions than others. Emotionally stable people are calm, do not get excited easily, and are secure, in contrast to others (sometimes called "neurotics") who are insecure, anxious, and become excited in many different social situations.

5. *Openness to experience.* This dimension summarizes people's approach to new experiences, especially their interest in and participation in them. Some people seek out new experiences to stimulate their imagination and intellects. Others are more narrow and simple in their interests and likely would turn down opportunities to become involved in new experiences.

Culture-Specific Demonstrations of Personality

Given this possible universal structure of personalities, culture-specific issues still play an important role in shaping people's characteristics. Recall the discussion of Levine's (1997) study of time and, more specifically, the distinction between clock time and event time. People high on the conscientiousness dimension, for example, would behave differently depending on their culture's expectations about valued goals. In a clock-time culture such as the United States or Canada, conscientious people would give much attention to writing down appointments on a calendar, to punctuality, and to investing in a watch that keeps accurate time. Further, they would expect similar behavior from others. In an event-oriented culture, conscientious people would be expected to react appropriately to unexpected demands on their time. They might have scheduled a meeting for 2:00 P.M., but they would be expected to put this aside if someone asks for their help at 1:45 P.M. If they ignored the request for help or scheduled a help session for 3:00 P.M., they could not maintain a reputation for conscientious behavior. Given this cultural factor, problems would not arise for conscientious people who schedule a 2:00 P.M. meeting and stop to help someone. They simply are starting a new event appropriate to the social surroundings.

Cultural factors also influence the intensity of people's demonstrations of these personality dimensions. In some cultures, harmony with others, decorum in public settings, and a desire to not stand out from others are preferred. In such cultures (e.g., Japan, Korea), extraverts may be hard to identify. The person who speaks up a few times during a meeting, making well-formulated suggestions in about 30 seconds with a small amount of vocal animation, may be extraverted in that culture. Identifying such a dimension requires knowing baseline rates: Is this amount of public speaking and vocal animation noticeably more than the baseline expectations from observations of many people? If it is more, then this person may be an extravert in that culture. In other cultures, such as middle-class American, people might have to speak longer and louder and use a variety of vocal mannerisms and body gestures to be considered an extravert. I teach many undergraduate and graduate students from Asia, and frequently I mention to them that I have a more difficult time making comments on their personalities than I do on their fellow students from North America. The reason is very basic: I have known North Americans all my life and know the baseline rates that mark their behavior for distinguishing different personalities.

To digress only slightly and to give another example of baseline rates, a knowledge of typical behaviors within a culture and as expressed by any one person is key to understanding individuals. People with this knowledge are known as skillful at "reading others." I have lived in Hawaii since 1972, and one aspect of life there is that people have lots of visitors. One of my friends, whom I had observed in hundreds of social encounters, does not express emotions openly. He once told me his in-laws were coming for a visit. He tried to show some enthusiasm in his voice, but I told him, "You don't seem very happy about it." He admitted this was true and that he had never gotten along terribly well with his demanding in-laws who didn't think he was good enough for their daughter. But he then asked how I knew about his feeling. I pointed out that he had some movement in his eyebrows and forehead that told me he was resigned to the visit but was not looking forward to it. Normally, he showed nothing or very little in this area of his face, a baseline rate I knew.

Additional Culture-Specific Features: Chinese Tradition

As has been emphasized, the personality dimensions the Big 5 summarize do not exhaust the possibilities for describing people accurately. In different cultures, other dimensions summarize expectations about and characteristics of people's thinking and behavior. Often, reasons for the importance of these other personality dimensions for shaping people's behavior in specific cultures can be identified.

Research among Chinese-speaking people has attempted to identify personality dimensions that capture important aspects of Chinese thinking and behavior (Cheung et al., 1996) that may be less central to personality discussions in other parts of the world. Researchers also have asked whether or not these additional dimensions provide more information than the Big 5 dimensions. Recent research indicates that a factor called "Chinese tradition" exists. It includes concepts and guidelines for behavior that have been long discussed as important in Chinese culture (Bond, 1986). The Chinese tradition factor includes an emphasis on harmony with others, and this is consistent with the previous discussion of collectivism. The factor also includes *Ren Qin*, a term that summarizes people's adherence to norms guiding various social exchanges and other types of interactions with others. "The forms of interaction involve courteous rituals, exchange of resources, reciprocity, maintaining and utilizing useful ties, and nepotism" (Cheung et al., 1996, p. 185). The Chinese tradition factor also includes an emphasis on thrift (more about thrift in chapter 8) but downplays thinking and behavior that might move away from tradition, such as modernization and flexibility.

Two behaviors this Chinese tradition factor includes are filial piety and using identifiable influence tactics (Zhang & Bond, 1998). Filial piety involves respect for one's father, but it extends to all of one's older family members and to revered grandparents who may have died. Filial piety extends to the workplace, where noticeably greater respect for older supervisors is given than in individualist countries. A Chinese student I work with recently told me that when working in Shanghai, she once asked for a morning off to meet her brother who was visiting from a far-off city. The boss pointed out that it would be a busy day and that her presence at work would be missed. The young woman accepted the decision without comment, informed her brother, and went to work. The key is that she was not upset: She had so much respect for her boss that she accepted the decision without resentment. Here is another example that implies the extension of filial piety. A student at a Chinese university has scheduled a social engagement with a same-age friend at 4:00 P.M. At about 3:00 P.M., a professor asks the student to come into his office in about an hour. It is an acceptable excuse for the student to call the friend and say, "We can't meet—the professor asked me to come in to his office." I believe that if this occurred in the United States, the friend would say something like, "You're blowing me off! What a lousy excuse! You could have told the professor you could come another time!"

Cultural Specificity: *Guanxi*   A sensitivity to Ren Qin is important in the cultivation of relationships in China known as *guanxi*. Understanding guanxi is central to understanding interpersonal influence tactics (Zhang & Bond, 1998). As analyzed by Luo and Chen (1996, pp. 293–294), "Guanxi is the word that describes the intricate, pervasive network of personal or business relations which Chinese cultivate energetically, subtly, and imaginatively. It refers to a relationship between two people or organizations containing implicit mutual obligation, assurance, and understanding and governs Chinese attitudes toward long-term social and business relationships." If people need a favor, they must have good guanxi to have a chance of obtaining the favor. For example, they must have built up relationships with influential people who might grant the favor. The term *nepotism* was previously mentioned. Given that a young person probably has a good guanxi relationship with an influential uncle, the uncle may prefer to grant a favor to his nephew than to an unknown, unrelated person. If the unknown person is well educated, is articulate, and has socially appropriate uses for the requested favor, observers who see the favor go to the nephew attribute it to nepotism.

People living and working in China should develop good guanxi. That is, they should develop relationships with many individuals for eventually exchanging favors. Without good guanxi, it is hard to accomplish very much. This can be a frustrating fact for people who come from cultures where reasonably efficient, responsive bureaucracies are common.

When in an intercultural situation, readers might ask themselves: "If I want something done that demands the involvement of bureaucrats, can I expect the bureaucrats to be responsive and efficient? For example, if I want to change my courseload at the end of a semester's first week, will any responsive bureaucrats assist me? If I want to renew my driver's license, can I go to a bureau where people expect, as part of their jobs, to help me?" The answer is not always yes in all cultures. In some cultures, bureaucrats treat people's requests as favors that should be returned—sometimes the "favor" is the payment of fees that no written guidelines cover (Francesco & Gold, 1998). People from cultures unfamiliar with such fees easily would make the attribution that "I am expected to pay a bribe." By understanding how cultures view these practices, people can learn to deal with them, such as developing guanxi in China.

If people have good guanxi with bureaucrats in China, they are far more likely to have their requests granted and they will not have to pay a fee. Of course, the people receiving the favor must be prepared to reciprocate when the bureaucrats want something at a later date. An interesting question arises: What is the difference between guanxi in China and good *networking* among people in various cultures? (I have discussed the importance of networking as part of power acquisition: Brislin, 1991.) A network refers to people who exchange favors but who do not have strong emotional relationships with one another. Their strong relationships are with close relatives or good friends. For example, I know the name of a good mechanic who charges reasonable fees. You know the name of a specialist in a branch of medicine who may be able to diagnose a strange condition my mother complains about. If we were in the same network, we would exchange these pieces of information. As another example, say I am good at statistics and you are good at team building. We might exchange these skills and work together on a research project required for a certain senior-level college course. We do not necessarily have to develop a close relationship to effectively exchange the information and skills.

Guanxi is different from networking in at least three ways (Luo & Chen, 1996). The first is that guanxi is more pervasive than networking. Given that people in some cultures can expect an efficient and responsive bureaucracy, they do not need to develop networking relationships. The need for guanxi in China applies to far more social situations than does networking. A second difference is that guanxi follows a certain ordering of behaviors: developing a relationship first and then asking for favors. Relationships are developed by spending time with people, giving them gifts, paying them compliments, doing favors for people's relatives, and so forth. After such relationships are nurtured, favors might be asked. In networking, the first interpersonal contact between people can be a request for a favor. Then, a relationship may or may not develop depending on the circumstances surrounding the favor giving. In a culture where the type of networking I am describing is common, the first interaction between people can be almost entirely concerned with a request for information or services. For example, I receive telephone calls such as the following: "Dr. Brislin, this is Jack Hall from the downtown Rotary Club. I heard that you can speak about diversity in the workplace. Can we schedule you for one of our noontime meetings?" Depending on whether or not the talk was successful and whether or not it was a positive experience for those involved, I might ask Jack for a favor at a later date. Then again, I might have little or no future interaction with Jack. The term for what Jack did when first contacting me is "cold calling." This type of contact is unthinkable in China because no relationship was established prior to the phone call.

A third difference is that guanxi is transferable to other people. Assume I have a good guanxi relationship with both a same-age Chinese colleague and a much younger professional. I can call on my relationship with this colleague and ask him or her to give time and attention to the young professional. Put another way, I can transfer my guanxi to the young professional, who then will feel comfortable contacting my colleague even though they have never met. As one of my Chinese colleagues put it, "A good guanxi relationship is like a bank check that a person can endorse so that someone else can cash it." A good networking relationship is not as transferable. In the example from the previous paragraph, if Jack and I are network members, he would make his own decision whether or not to grant favors to someone I recommend to him.

Different people will have different approaches to developing guanxi when they work in China. What do I do? I have taken my own advice and have reviewed the guidelines for adopting new behaviors when living in other cultures (pp. 42–43). I find that the approach of giving personalized gifts is acceptable to me, and it seems acceptable to my Chinese colleagues. Because my major hobby long has been playing various musical instruments and performing in a group, I know a variety of musical genres and can converse about them. When I discover a colleague's specialized musical tastes, I often can identify a hard-to-obtain compact disk (CD) that I can bring with me on a trip to China. My colleagues seem to appreciate the personal attentiveness that such a gift represents, and I don't feel as if I am engaging in bribery because CDs cost about $15 in the United States. Readers should keep in mind that this is my solution. Other people will develop different solutions given their personalities, age, status, goals, previous experience in China, knowledge of culture and cultural differences, and other considerations.

CHAPTER SUMMARY

The material in this chapter was selected and organized to answer the question "What are some useful concepts helpful for understanding virtually any treatment of culture's influence on behavior?" These concepts then can be applied to various analyses in future chapters of culture's relevance to behaviors in such areas as socialization, gender, health, and the workplace. Six broad concepts were selected. The first dealt with how people develop an understanding of culture's impact, as shown by the results of effective education and training programs. As people become more sophisticated about cultures, they will be able to work better with culturally diverse people in the sorts of settings discussed in future chapters: schools, hospitals, business and industry, and so forth. The five other concepts dealt with various challenges people will face as they (a) participate in good orientation and training programs and/or (b) experience everyday intercultural interactions. These concepts deal with overcoming one's ethnocentric attitudes, understanding how people make attributions about others' behavior as well as their own, the inevitability of disconfirmed expectancies, understanding how behaviors familiar to people from individualist and collectivist backgrounds differ, and understanding the similarities and differences in the personalities of people in other cultures.

As people develop a greater sophistication about culture's influence on behavior, their thinking, attitudes, and behavior will change. Changes in their thinking include an ability to take a more complex view of issues, decreased use of oversimplified stereotypes, and a greater understanding of culturally diverse others *from the viewpoint of those other people*. Changes in people's attitudes include a deeper understanding of the meaning of cultural relativity, the willingness to admit to themselves that they do not understand certain cultural differences and to withhold judgment about them, and decreases in the anxiety intercultural interactions bring. Changes in people's behavior include more ease and comfort when interacting with culturally diverse others and the willingness to engage in specific behaviors members of other cultures consider appropriate.

Along the route to these desirable changes, people will confront numerous important concepts. They will experience challenges to their ethnocentric feelings, or their tendency to judge others by the standards they are familiar with from their own socialization. One reason for these challenges is that people find the attributions they make about culturally diverse others simply are not working: They are not helping people achieve their goals. Attributions refer to judgments about the causes of behavior, and judgments based solely on familiar standards are likely to be inappropriate. As people become more sophisticated about other cultures, they can make more isomorphic attributions, that is, attributions that agree with interpretations of behavior *the other people make about themselves*.

While making more accurate attributions as they become less ethnocentric, people will have fewer disconfirmed expectancies. Many times, the reason for people's stress is not due solely to the difficult experiences they have to cope with during interculteral interactions. Rather, the stress is due to the differences between what was expected and what was experienced. As people have more and more intercultural encounters, they likely will develop a more realistic set of expectations about what may happen to them. One set of differing expectations comes from people's socialization in individualistic or collectivist cultures. In individualistic cultures, people learn to emphasize their personal goals. They will make mistakes in collectivist cultures if they do not attend to the goals of the collectives they have joined. In collectivist cultures, people are willing to place less priority on their own goals by deferring to those of a collective, whether it be their extended family, organization, or religious affiliation. Collectivists living in individualistic cultures have to develop various skills not previously needed. These include effective public speaking skills, describing one's abilities and accomplishments, and developing a network of people whose members exchange favors.

In addition to understanding cultural-level concepts such as individualism and collecitivism, people must be sensitive to individual differences in the personalities of others they meet. Extensive research by various investigators has identified a personality structure that may be universal. This structure consists of five dimensions people may exhibit, and it provides a good starting point for looking at personality, but people must keep in mind that culture influences many aspects of personality. One is the expression of these five traits, and another is the necessity to add culture-specific dimensions to the basic five-factor structure. The example of guanxi in China was discussed because it is related to a culture-specific factor called "Chinese tradition" and is extremely important for understanding how to achieve goals in China. Research on culture-specific factors (e.g., Zhang & Bond, 1998) should include demonstrations that predictions can be made about behavior beyond those that can be made with knowledge of the Big 5 dimensions.

When applying any of these concepts, attention must be paid to the viewpoint of people in other cultures. A theme found throughout this chapter is that the reasons for others' behaviors can be understood only if people avoid imposing their pre-existing socialized views. This central concern is also part of any good research methodology that allows the careful study of culture and cultural differences. The topic of research methods and approaches is the focus of the next chapter.

C H A P T E R 3

Some Methodological Concerns in Intercultural and Cross-Cultural Research

Chapter Overview

Imagine trying to ask questions about important matters and that the person you are questioning is someone you have known for many years. For some reason, you cannot phrase the questions so that the other person understands perfectly. Despite this, you receive answers of some limited use. Then, assume you are asking questions and that the other person is someone you don't know. Further, she or he is from another cultural background and speaks a different language. You don't seem to be receiving answers that make any sense at all. Researchers who carry out studies in other cultures commonly face the frustration stemming from this second scenario. The major focus of this chapter is how to increase communication for cross-cultural research.

First, some reasons for doing cross-cultural research are discussed. These include increasing the range of variables *beyond* those found in any one culture. For example, the impact of television viewing on behavior is an important topic for study, but a researcher would have to move beyond the United States to find people who have watched little or no television for comparison. The importance of understanding the context of behavior is emphasized in this chapter. The example of in-context and out-of-context learning is discussed. Readers now are engaging in the latter: They are reading material they later may apply in another context. When they engage in in-context learning, they receive information in social settings where they will actually use it. An example is learning to find information on the World Wide Web while sitting at a computer terminal and going online.

An important distinction in actual research is to recognize culture-common and culture-specific concepts. The former (also called *etics*) are found in all cultures, while the latter (also called *emics*) are specific to a given culture. One reason for ethnocentrism is that people view their emics as common or etic to all cultures. One way to avoid this problem is to carry out indigenous research and to examine behavior as it is explained from the viewpoint of people in other cultures. Americans, then, would not impose their emic view of a concept such as "achievement" but would examine its meanings and implications as seen by members of other cultures. Once meanings are examined, the issue of equivalence arises. What behaviors lead to the attribution that people are achieving their goals? Are these behaviors the same, similar, or quite different in various cultures? When researchers wrestle with these questions, they are dealing with the equivalence issue.

Research on translation between languages is also discussed, and methods for examining the equivalence of original and translated versions of research instruments are considered. A method called back translation is reviewed, and it is of special interest because it allows researchers to have limited control over instrument development even if they are not fluent in other languages.

To highlight important topics in the discussion of cross-cultural and indigenous research methods, two examples are examined in detail. One study investigates the life experiences of children with various disabilities in different cultures. The second study examines the perception of risks (e.g., asbestos, pesticides, ozone depletion) and of their potential harmful effects in two cultures. A theme throughout the chapter is the belief that research in unfamiliar cultures is admittedly difficult, but the benefits from examining human diversity worldwide outweigh these difficulties.

THE CHALLENGES OF RESEARCH

People's intercultural interactions can be frustrating or exciting, depending on the viewpoints they bring to these encounters. The well-meaning clashes described in chapter 1 can cause anxiety, but they also can stimulate people to examine the cultural influences on their behavior. If people move beyond the ethnocentric reaction (Adler, 1997; Keller, 1997) that "we are right and they are wrong," they may be willing to analyze their own behavior when they are misunderstood or when they cannot communicate effectively with others. These miscommunications are guaranteed to occur during extensive intercultural encounters. When people make attributions about the reasons for unfamiliar behaviors, they surely will make errors. This *could* cause people to cease seeking out intercultural interactions and, instead, to stick with others much like themselves to increase the chances of mutual understanding. In contrast, people might think about their mistakes after making attributions and use these as opportunities to examine the normal thought processes of human beings. People use the same thought processes to make attributions about culturally different others as they do to think about a wide variety of important events in their lives. Psychologists have attempted to help people cope with various problems (e.g., depression, weight control, marital difficulties) by guiding them toward more effective and realistic thought processes (e.g., Bandura, 1989; Seligman, 1998).

People familiar with these thought processes from examining their intercultural encounters will have an advantage in benefiting from such interventions.

These same frustration and excitement reactions also are possible among researchers who engage in cross-cultural and intercultural studies (Berry, Poortinga, & Pandey, 1997; Lonner & Berry, 1986; Triandis & Berry, 1980). Consider researchers in such fields as psychology, education, and communication who are deciding among various interesting and important topics to analyze. Among several possibilities, one might involve the career development of young executives in the researchers' hometown. Another might involve the cultural adjustment of some of those same executives who have accepted international assignments at their organizations' branch offices. If the researchers decide to investigate the second study area, they (I hope after careful thought) are accepting burdens beyond those of the first study area. They will not have easy access to the young executives given their assignments to other countries. The researchers probably will have to deal with translation issues if they include the important step (discussed in chapter 2) of assessing host feelings toward the contributions of the young executives. Hosts in some countries may have little familiarity with interviews or with being questioned about their reactions to colleagues, in contrast to executives in other countries who may have participated in 15 or 20 research studies during their high school and college years. When researching in countries other than their own, people often have to trust somewhat unfamiliar mail and communication systems. These systems seem to be especially prone to error exactly when the most important steps of the research process are to begin (Johnson & Tuttle, 1989).

So why do researchers accept the additional burdens that cross-cultural research demands? Some related reasons revolve around a set of clear advantages that cross-cultural research brings to the investigation of important topics. This set of advantages, in the view of many researchers who have devoted their careers to cross-cultural efforts, offsets the admitted difficulties just introduced.

SOME ADVANTAGES OF CROSS-CULTURAL RESEARCH

Virtually all cross-cultural researchers (see Berry, 1997; Segall, Dasen, Berry, & Poortinga, 1990; Triandis et al., 1980) argue that the development of concepts and theories dealing with human behavior demands that behavior in all parts of the world be investigated. This seemingly commonsense proposition is at odds with an alternative position that so much commonality exists in human behavior that researchers can investigate it in one place (e.g., the United States, western Europe) and then generalize to behavior everywhere. If the first position is accepted, then cross-cultural research brings a set of benefits that are almost impossible to achieve in research carried out within any one country.

Increased Range of Variables

Research involves the study of how one variable (more frequently called a concept) relates to others. However, it is difficult to study the effects of one variable on another if a variable has little range or if the people who participate in the study show little difference in behavior. For instance, can researchers study the effects of having a television set in the home on student achievement in school if they carry out the study only in the United States? The answer is most likely no because almost all homes in the United States have a television. Researchers would have a terribly difficult time finding homes without a television for comparing students living there with students from TV-owning homes. To study the effects of owning a television, people would have to research cultures where television is being introduced for the first time (e.g., rural Arctic villages in Canada and Alaska; Lonner, 1985). With most introductions of new technology, some people in a community adopt innovations quickly and others take a wait-and-see approach (Rogers, 1989). Researchers also could study early purchasers of television sets with people who delay their decision. To use the language of research methodology, a person can observe a range in the variable of television ownership (yes or no) only by working in certain countries.

Another example may clarify this important point about the range of variables. In the United States, could a study investigate the effects of divorce on children's attitudes? Specifically, could researchers study the attitudes toward marriage among 12-year-olds familiar with a divorce among married couples they have known? I believe the answer is no. Virtually all 12-year-olds know of marriages that have ended in divorce. It would be extremely difficult to find U.S. adolescents who do not know of a divorce within their extended family or within their communities. This would have to be researched in other countries (e.g., the Philippines) where divorce is far less common to obtain the necessary range (in this case, knowledge of divorces contrasted with no knowledge) of variables for the concept under study.

Important work using the advantage of expanded ranges has occurred in studies of personality (Church & Lonner, 1998; J. Miller, 1984; Pepitone, 1987; Shweder & Bourn, 1984). In the United States and western Europe, an extremely active research tradition involves studying personality as defined by combinations of trait labels. When people in these parts of the world describe themselves and others, they are likely to use permanent trait labels, such as "friendly," "dominant," "achievement oriented," "shy," and so forth. Most readers probably have taken personality tests and have received the results in the form of these trait labels. This manner of describing personality may not be universal, however. Perhaps the fondness for trait labels that summarize a great deal of information is a convenient aid in fast-moving, individualistic societies. As pointed out in chapter 2, individualists often move from community to community throughout their lives. They must make quick judgments when they meet others about whether or not to seek more interactions with them. Trait labels (other examples are "hardworking" or "gracious") can tremendously help newcomers make these important judgments.

People in collective societies, in contrast, are much more likely to have known each other for long periods. Especially in rural areas, collectivists have many years to become very familiar with the behavior of various family members, neighbors, and community leaders. In addition, it must be constantly remembered that collectivists obtain much more of their identity from their relationships with other people than do individualists (as discussed in chapter 2). Due to their greater concern with others, collectivists are likely to be much more attentive to subtle differences in the behaviors they observe. Some subtle differences involve different behaviors in different social situations. A person may be very kind to his or her spouse but not to people he or she supervises. Another person may be hardworking in school but rather lazy and unproductive at a job taken after graduating with a college degree. These observations about behavior involve traits in a social setting. They require more complex analyses than the simple use of a general trait such as "kind" or "hardworking." Research has shown that collectivists make complex personality judgments more frequently than individualists (J. Miller, 1984; Schweder, 1991; Shweder & Bourn, 1984; Triandis, 1995). Collectivists are more sensitive to differences in people's traits when those people interact in various social settings.

The advantage of cross-cultural research is that it adds range to the concepts under study. If only individualists were studied, researchers would run the risk of concluding that people think about personalities only in terms of traits. But the range of people participating in the study places limits on our conclusions. Individualists move so frequently within their society that the easy summary labels represented by traits provide useful shortcuts when individualists meet new people and decide whether or not to seek out more interactions in the future. The danger in the study of personality, however, is that these useful shortcuts might be mistaken for a universal description of how people think about themselves and others. If cross-cultural research includes the participation of collectivists, then range is added to the study. The increased range is the length of time people know one another and their expectations that they will have interactions with one another well into the future. This greater familiarity and increased time perspective explains why collectivists are more sensitive to differences among people in different social settings.

Interestingly, personality theorists in individualistic societies have begun to investigate personality in social settings (Funder & Colvin, 1991; Magnusson & Endler, 1977; Steel & Rentsch, 1997). They have found that they can make more accurate predictions about behavior when they have information both about people's personalities and their social situations. By adopting this approach, they are thinking about human behavior in a way similar to collectivists. This is another benefit of cross-cultural research: not only examining how people in other cultures behave on an everyday basis but also using some insights to improve theories about human behavior.

The distinction between describing people's traits as a general summary of their personalities and describing people's traits in social settings may become clearer if an example is discussed that readers probably have experienced. Consider the traits of people with whom one might form a romantic attachment. What comes to mind? "Considerate," "good looking," "fun to be with," and "exciting" all could be desirable characteristics. Note that these terms are the sorts of traits individualists tend to use to describe personalities. But are these the best ways to think about potential romantic partners? Shouldn't differences in social settings also be taken into account? For instance, most readers probably have had exciting first dates with people but disappointing later dates. One reason is that the early stages of the dating relationship and later stages involve different social settings. Different traits are given careful consideration at the two stages. For instance, people are impressed with others who are "exciting" and "physically attractive" (Buss, 1996) when they consider going out with them on a first date. As relationships develop and as people decide whether or not to become committed to each other, they attend to different traits. "Considerate," "hardworking" (so that people can hold down good jobs), and "likes children" undoubtedly receive greater prominence in people's thinking. If the people are sensitive to the fact they consider different traits at different stages of their relationships, they are showing an understanding of personality in social settings that is very common among collectivists. One reason for the practice of arranged marriages in some collective societies is that 50- and 60-year-old adults know about these different priorities. Consequently, they can choose a person who will be a good spouse over the entire marriage span, not just the "honeymoon" phase.

Many times, individualists have to learn from the "school of hard knocks" that different traits are important in different social settings. Most readers undoubtedly have heard complaints (from their own lips or those of their friends) that someone they know was exciting in early stages of a relationship but turned out to be a "real jerk" in later stages. I remember a counseling session where a colleague and I were trying to help a faltering marriage. The man complained that his wife never cooked meals and never cleaned the house. My colleague asked, "What attracted you to your wife before you were married?" The man answered, "She was fun to be with and was always ready to go to parties." The counselor then asked, "Aren't you now changing the rules? You dated because of a fun-loving personality, and now you want someone who can cook and keep house. These are very different traits!" Encouraging people to become more sophisticated in their thinking is central to various interventions meant to help them cope with life's stressors (Seligman, 1989, 1998).

Unconfounding Variables

Another very intriguing benefit of cross-cultural research is that variables that occur together in one culture sometimes can be separated in studies done in other cultures. When researchers identify two or more important variables or concepts that have an impact on human behavior, they often want to identify their relative importance. If the study were concerned with people's preferences in marital partners, for example (Buss, 1996; Buss et al., 1990), the researchers would want to make statements about the relative importance of such variables as "dependable character," "good looks," and "similar political background." If variables always occur together, however, they are said to be *confounded*. If the variables occur together in the same people, it is very difficult to separate out their relative impact on human behavior. At times, the variables can be *unconfounded* or separated if cultures can be found where they do not occur together within the personalities or life experiences of the same people.

A classic example from the work of Malinowski (1927) carried out in the Trobriand Islands is worth retelling (example also reviewed by Campbell, 1964, and Guthrie & Lonner, 1986). Malinowski had read the work of Sigmund Freud, who proposed a concept called the Oedipal complex. According to Freud, young boys have an inevitably difficult relationship with their father because they are jealous of the father's role as the mother's lover. Malinowski observed that Freud's work had a problem with confounded variables. Other variables occurred together with the father's role as mother's lover in the study. One is that the father was also the son's disciplinarian, and he could have been the target of his son's negative emotions because he administered punishment for misbehaviors. Based on Freud's observations in Vienna, Austria, no one can say which reason for the son's negative emotions was the stronger. The variables of "mother's lover" and "son's disciplinarian" were confounded.

Do any cultures keep the roles separate or unconfounded; that is, do different people have the roles of mother's lover and boy's disciplinarian? The answer is yes. In many Pacific island societies, including the Trobriands, the mother's oldest brother is responsible for disciplining his nephew when necessary. The father continues to have normal marital relations with his wife but is expected to play a less important role than the uncle in the disciplining of his sons. Who is the target of the boy's negative emotions in this society? The answer is that the boy is more likely to dislike his uncle than his father. This important work casts doubt on Freud's assumption that the Oedipal complex and its inevitable son-father tension was a universal found in all parts of the world.

The important role of the mother's brother in some Pacific island societies has led to another cross-cultural joke (another was discussed in chapter 1). Teachers from the United States were asked to accept two-year contracts in various Pacific island schools, sometimes arranged through the Peace Corps. They naturally began by introducing ideas they were familiar with, such as Parent-Teacher Associations (PTAs). They were disappointed with the attendance, especially from the children's fathers. After a few months, they discovered the important point already introduced here: The maternal uncle is responsible for the child's socialization, and this includes monitoring the child's progress in school. When the American teachers started an organization more like a UTA (Uncle-Teacher Association), they had more success.

Research on health and medicine often looks to cross-cultural research to unconfound variables (Beardsley & Pedersen, 1997; also chapter 10). Two sets of variables that are often confounded are (a) the biological heritage of people in a culture and (b) their dietary habits. If research is done within a culture where people have the same biological heritage and similar dietary practices, it is difficult to assess the relative importance of the two types of variables. These variables can be unconfounded when people from the same biological heritage accept the dietary habits of the different cultures where they live. In investigating the relative importance of biological and cultural factors on alcohol use, Sue, Zane, and Ito (1979) studied people whose biological heritage was Japanese. However, some Japanese people within their study had lived in the United States for varying lengths of time. If biological factors were of prime importance to alcohol use, all the people of Japanese heritage should have a similar pattern of alcohol use. If cultural factors were more important, the people should have differing patterns of alcohol use depending on their exposure to and active participation in American society. Sue and his colleagues argue that the latter factor is more important. People's pattern of alcohol use was predicted by the length of time they had been in America. Similar results have been shown for the effects of diet (Mukai & McCloskey, 1996). The longer people of Japanese ancestry have been exposed to a typical American diet (more meat, more fat, fewer vegetables, and more calories than in Japan), the more likely they are to have health problems typical of Americans (e.g., coronary diseases; Mukai & McClosdkey, 1996; Reed et al., 1982).

Increased Sensitivity to Context

One of the basic principles in many theories within the behavioral and social sciences is that behavior is a function of the person and the situation. To understand behavior, researchers must have extensive knowledge about the people (e.g., their personalities, their attitudes, their values) and the situations in which they find themselves. Aspects of situations (Argyle, Furnham, & Graham, 1981; Detweiler, Brislin, & McCormack, 1983; Funder & Colvin, 1991; Markus & Kitayama, 1998) include the formal and informal rules, types of challenges, publicness versus privateness of behaviors, and amount of structure. For example, consider behavior at a funeral. To predict behavior, researchers need to know about the people attending and the social situation summarized by the term *funeral*. If the funeral is highly structured and has the rule that people behave in a very solemn way, then most observations will involve people's quiet, attentive behavior. In this case, the social situation will overwhelm the aspects of the people involved (e.g., their sense of humor, their extroversion versus introversion). But imagine the funeral is an Irish wake. Here, the social situation is more like a party, and the acceptable rules allow a greater variety of behaviors. Parties have "rules" that allow some people to be very loud and energetic and others to be quieter. Some people can drink large amounts of alcohol, and others will sip ginger ale. Some will talk to five or six others over the course of the party, and others will circulate and have a few words with all those who attend. Behavior at an Irish wake, then, will be more variable than at a solemn funeral. Given that the wake's rules allow a wider variety of behaviors, knowledge of people's personalities (e.g., extraversion versus introversion, as discussed in chapter 2) and their attitudes toward alcohol use will be predictive of how they will act.

The important point that behavior is determined both by aspects of people and by the situation should be constantly kept in mind. It appears in arguments that are central to many different academic disciplines. In linguistics, for example, the point appears as part of the competence-performance distinction. This distinction, which also applies to nonlinguistic behaviors, refers to the fact people should not automatically diagnose the competencies of others from their performance in a specific situation. Very often, aspects of the situation do not allow the person to express underlying competencies. Readers have undoubtedly experienced a problem stemming from this competence-performance distinction. Hasn't everybody performed poorly on a test, resulting in others calling to question their underlying competencies? But were there problems with the testing situation making it seem unfair and unreasonable to judge competencies? The test might have been administered in a threatening situation, may have had ambiguous questions, or may have been taken on a day the test taker was ill. All of these features of the situation can interfere with a fair assessment of underlying competencies.

In an article with the interesting title "Some Issues on Which Linguists Can Agree," Hudson (1981) presented the following summary of the competence-performance distinction:

> A child's poor performance in formal, threatening, or unfamiliar situations cannot be taken as evidence of impoverished linguistic competence, but may be due to other factors such as low motivation for speaking in that situation, or unfamiliarity with the conventions for use of language in such situations. (p. 336)

Problems with mistaking people's competence from their performance and insensitivity to the situational factors people respond to are common despite Hudson's important arguments. Many people, including behavioral and social scientists who should know better, continue to make judgments about competencies from performance analyses. One reason is that most people (as discussed in chapter 1) have had extensive experience in only one culture, the one that socialized them. In the one culture, they are often insensitive to the social situations that influence behavior because the situations are so familiar. They take for granted the social situations at their schools, churches, workplaces, and homes (chapter 1). Given this degree of familiarity, people rarely have any reason to examine how situational factors might affect behavior.

When behavioral and social scientists do research within their own society, they will have this same difficulty analyzing the effects of situational factors because they are so familiar with them. It is difficult for researchers to take a step backward and to look objectively at the differing contributions of people and situations because researchers also live in such situations on an everyday basis. To use a common metaphor, it is hard for them to separate the forest (the total number of factors that influence behavior) from the trees (various people and social situations).

This long introduction has been necessary to provide the background for an argument about an advantage of cross-cultural studies. Researchers observing other societies may have an easier task separating the contributions of people from the contributions of situational variables in the behavior they observe. When doing research in other cultures, they will discover many situations new, unfamilar, and fresh to their eyes. Because the situations will not be so familiar as to be taken for granted, researchers should find it easier to examine the social settings they observe and to make suggestions about their possible impact. They then can combine these observations with analyses of person-centered concepts (some of which also may be unfamiliar and thus easier to perceive) to make more accurate predictions about behavior. Often, the identification of person-centered and situational variables will be facilitated if the performance-competence distinction is kept in mind.

An actual incident may make all these arguments clearer. (Only names have been changed to protect people's privacy.) Wiladluk was a teenager from one of the rural provinces in Thailand that is quite distant from any large city. She had learned many skills necessary for making a living in her village, such as farming, homemaking, and even some native healing practices. She had learned these skills by working closely with respected adults in her community: her father for farming skills, her mother for cooking and sewing, and the native healer for herbal remedies for various illnesses. She was clearly what her neighbors called "a clever girl," and she also was very friendly with others. These were the two reasons the native healer took a liking to her and shared knowledge of select herbs.

Wiladluk's formal schooling was spotty. Educated teachers from the big cities such as Bangkok got bored living in the provinces and either maneuvered their way out of their contracts or put minimum effort into their teaching. Still, Wiladluk learned reading and writing skills, and because she was clearly the brightest person in her classes, she received the greatest amount of attention from her teachers. When Wiladluk was 16 years old, an especially concerned teacher came to the village. He recommended that Wiladluk take the national exams for entry to Thailand's universities. He worked side by side with Wiladluk helping her to improve her academic skills so that she would do well on the formal exams (similar to the Scholastic Aptitude Test familiar to many Americans). Wiladluk did well on the tests, won a scholarship that was to pay all her expenses, and went away to a good university in one of Thailand's big cities.

At the university, Wiladluk did not do well. Her professors did not give her good grades on her essay tests, complaining that Wiladluk does not make her points clear to people who might read her essays. Wiladluk was very disappointed and was afraid she would have to return to her village with a reputation as a failure. She felt she would bring disgrace to her family because she could not take advantage of the tremendous opportunity offered to her. Assuming she is still at the university, what might be done to help Wiladluk?

Many reasons explain Wiladluk's difficulties, and researchers from countries other than Thailand but living there may bring insights different than those of Thai nationals. Because the researchers themselves are undoubtedly experiencing adjustment difficulties in Thailand, they may be able to empathize with Wiladluk's plight. Just as it is difficult to move from country to country, it is stressful to move from rural areas to big cities within a country (Brislin, 1981). Friends and family are left behind in the village, difficulties have to be overcome in the search for housing, and life in big cities is almost always experienced as more impersonal than life in villages (Berry, 1990; Kagitcibasi, 1997). If the researchers are individualists (chapter 2), they may have a clearer view of the special problems collectivists face. Thai researchers, probably socialized as collectivists, may take the expectations collectivists have for granted and may see Wiladluk's problems less clearly. In this case, Wiladluk faces a problem brought on by a basic aspect of the collective person. Her identity is obtained by reference to a group, and the group's relationship to her is central to her view of herself. If she does poorly at the university, she is not the only one who will be seen as a failure. She perceives that her entire collective will be disappointed, and this brings additional stress into her life. Note the importance of keeping the competence-performance distinction in mind here. Wiladluk clearly has many of the necessary competencies, as shown by her achievements in her village. But situational factors in the big city, such as the more impersonal lifestyle and lack of daily contact with her supportive collective, put such stress on her that she cannot express her competencies through effective performance.

MORE ON CONTEXTUAL FACTORS: LEARNING IN AND OUT OF CONTEXT

Because sensitivity to the context of human behavior cannot be overemphasized in cross-cultural research, it is useful to analyze Wiladluk's difficulties from another

In-context learning involves using new concepts immediately.

viewpoint that also involves contextual factors. When analyzing how people best learn new facts, attitudes, and skills, researchers make an important distinction between whether the new ideas are presented *in context* and whether they are presented *out of context* (Cushner, 1990). If people learn in context, this means they learn new ideas in the same situation where they are actually applied. So when Wiladluk learned farming skills while working side by side with her father and learned the uses of various herbs while sitting next to the healer (in the setting where the healer met her patients), Wiladluk is said to have been learning in context. Wiladluk made immediate links in her mind between the new ideas and possible practical applications of the ideas. Further, Wiladluk's teachers at home observed the development of her skills and made adjustments as they presented new ideas to her or decided to go over

Out-of-context learning involves the possible later use of concepts.

ideas already presented (a process analyzed by Greenfield, 1997b; Karpov & Haywood, 1998; and Rogoff, 1990). Even Wiladluk's tutor who prepared her for the university exams was working in context. He worked side by side with his student, and he made adjustments in the material he presented. Further, the new learning had a clear application in the near future: performance on the university entrance exams.

In contrast to the type of learning Wiladluk was accustomed to, the presentation of new ideas and material at the university level is out of context. Wiladluk is assigned material from texts and is expected to learn ideas professors present in a lecture format. She does not work side by side with a teacher. Rather, she reads her texts by herself and takes notes on her professor's lectures as one of hundreds of students in a lecture hall. The learning may or may not be useful or applicable in the future.

The material might be useful for taking an exam in the not-so-clear but near future, but Wiladluk cannot be sure. The learning may be useful if she returns to her village, but it also might be forgotten, remaining in her old, dust-gathering former textbooks.

In addition to the stress of adjusting to a new lifestyle at the university, then, another reason for Wiladluk's difficulties is her unfamiliarity with a different learning style. Returning to the distinction already introduced, her underlying competencies are difficult to express because she is expected to perform as a participant in an unfamiliar teacher-student learning style. As pointed out in chapter 1, observations of cross-cultural differences and of one's intercultural encounters can stimulate examinations of one's socialization. This point can be combined with the argument being made here: Observers in Thailand from other cultures might be able to diagnose Wiladluk's difficulties more readily than Thai nationals. The observers may be more able to distinguish Wiladluk's abilities from the context where she is expected to display her abilities. Because many Thai nationals were socialized in a culture that linked abilities with context, they may have a difficult time separating the two.

For example, only after I studied these cultural differences could I see the importance of out-of-context learning in the American school system. When thought about carefully, out-of-context learning is rather odd. Children go to school and learn material they might apply someday. In high school, students take geometry and may use it someday when they figure out how many square yards of carpet to buy for their newly acquired first home. Such out-of-context learning is probably a relatively recent phenomenon brought about by industrialization and the rise of cities. In the past, certainly before the printing press and the norm of literacy in technologically developed societies, most learning was in context. Children learned the knowledge, attitudes, and skills necessary for survival in their culture by observing adults' behavior in the context where the new learning could be applied. Given the presence of books and the need to instruct children apart from their parents who go to jobs in the business world, out-of-context learning became the preferred style in places called schools.

In addition to my realizing this style's importance, my cross-cultural comparisons and personal intercultural encounters also have led to an awareness of how some of my socialization experiences have prepared me for out-of-context learning. Put another way, some of my socialization experiences led to less of a distinction between home and school than Wiladluk's experiences. For instance, my mother tells me I used to put puzzles together by myself, sitting in a corner of our home and deciding how the puzzle pieces go together to make a complete picture. She would read books to me when I was 3 and 4 years old, but then I could thumb through them on my own. On finding a picture that I did not understand in a book, I could initiate conversations with my parents by asking them about the picture's content. All of these childhood experiences (recall their importance from chapter 1, p. 9) led to positive outcomes. The skills learned before I entered school—working alone on intellectual tasks, gathering information from books, and initiating conversations with adults—were very useful in my adjustment to kindergarten and the first grade.

People who never had the opportunity to develop these skills likely will experience more stress in their first extensive out-of-home encounters with a new setting and with unfamiliar adults, such as a university and its teachers (Cushner, 1994;

Heath, 1983). I would have been unable to make the distinction between skills at home and skills in schools unless I had observed schoolchildren in other cultures. My own development of person variables (skills) applicable to various settings (home and school) occurred together, and they are difficult to separate in any analysis of person-situation interactions. This example shows that, given my analyses of how people use skills in different life settings in other cultures, I then can look back on my life and apply the concepts these cross-cultural observations stimulated. As noted earlier, this ability to look with fresher eyes on one's own socialization is one of the benefits of cross-cultural research and of intercultural experiences.

GUIDANCE IN MAKING CROSS-CULTURAL OBSERVATIONS: EMICS AND ETICS

In their quest for the benefits of cross-cultural studies and analysis, researchers have developed a set of conceptual tools useful for making decisions about their research methodology. One is to make a distinction between culture-common and culture-specific concepts. *Culture-common* concepts are those that can be found among people all over the world. Many culture-common concepts have a basis in the demands people face in their desire for survival and the survival of their community. Some examples already have been discussed: socializing children to become responsible members of society; maintaining harmony among people so that disagreements do not result in violence; and dealing with the stresses encountered when cultures come into contact. Other examples of culture-common concepts are placing controls on people's sexual appetites and looking after the needs of elderly people who can no longer contribute their labors to the community (Aberle, Cohen, Davis, Levy, & Sutton, 1950; Keller, 1997; Lonner, 1980).

Culture-specific concepts are found in some societies but not others. These concepts represent a culture's unique adaptations to the demands it faces. Often, culture-specific concepts represent additions to or variants on the culture-common concepts familiar to all people. Some examples covered already include the maintenance versus severance of relations with past romantic partners, differences in responsibility for the disciplining of children (the children's father versus the uncle), and the prevalence of in-context versus out-of-context learning. Note that these culture-specific concepts represent different ways people deal with culture-common demands: bringing people together for consideration as marriage partners; socializing children to be responsible adults; and educating children in the skills needed for survival in a culture. Very often, cross-cultural research focuses on this combination of culture-common and culture-specific concepts, and both are necessary for an understanding of culture and cultural differences.

Cross-cultural researchers frequently use a shorthand pair of descriptors to summarize their arguments about their studies. Culturally common concepts are frequently called *etics*, and culturally specific concepts are frequently called *emics*. The emic-etic distinction has encouraged a rich and extensive body of literature that has sharpened the thinking of cross-cultural researchers (Berry, 1969; Brislin, 1980; Brislin, Landis, & Brandt, 1983; Headland, Pike, & Harris, 1990; Poortinga, 1997;

Poortinga & Malpass, 1986). I will make some basic points here to (a) explain key aspects of the distinction and to (b) introduce the longer treatments of emics and etics referenced above.

The basis of the two terms is interesting, and it also provides another way to explain culture-common and culture-specific concepts. The term *etic* comes from *phonetic* analysis as carried out by linguists. In a phonetic analysis, an attempt is made to develop a system that includes all meaningful sounds in all the world's languages. A meaningful sound is one that makes a difference in communication between speaker and listener, and in a phonetic analysis sounds have to make a difference in at least one of the world's languages. For instance, some languages have a glottal click sound, some have an initial "ng" sound, and some have a trilled "r" sound. People have to make these sounds clearly to be understood and to be considered a good speaker of the language. If a sound makes a difference in any of the world's languages, it should be part of a phonetic analysis.

The shorthand term *emic* is borrowed from the linguistic word *phonemic*. In a phonemic analysis, linguists document the meaningful sounds within any one language. If a language does not have a sound that speakers have to make to be understood, then that sound would not be part of a phonemic analysis. Does the English language have an initial "ng" sound? No, it does not. Does English have a glottal stop (in contrast to a glottal click)? After quick consideration people might answer no, but after a more lengthy analysis an example would be found. If English-speaking people are suddenly surprised at something that might bring them negative outcomes, they might say, "Uh-oh! This is going to be difficult!" The sound between the "uh" and "oh" is a glottal stop, and it is one of the phonemes in the English language. People must be able to articulate phonemes to be considered good speakers of a language. For example, people must be able to make the initial "th" sound (the symbol is θ) in the words *these, think*, and *through*. Some languages (and even dialects within English) do not have this sound, so those speakers might say in English something like, "I dink I will go to the baseball game tomorrow." This shows that they do not know the phonemes of standard English. Incidentally, nonnative speakers frequently complain about this "th" sound when they study the English language. The best-known phonemic distinction, given that it forms the basis of ethnic jokes, is the initial "l" versus the initial "r" sound in a word. The sentences "I have a lock" and "I have a rock" have different meanings. People have to make this phonemic distinction to be considered good English speakers. The Japanese language does not have a distinction between the initial "r" and the initial "l" sound. Native Japanese speakers have to put extra effort into making this "l-r" distinction in their English speech.

Borrowing from the meanings of phonetic and phonemic analysis, the term *etic* refers to concepts and ideas that are common across cultures. In the best cultural research, theoretical ideas are put forward to explain how various concepts relate to one another in people's thoughts, emotions, and behaviors throughout the world. Examples include guiding children into responsible adulthood and dealing with the inevitable conflicts that arise as people interfere with one another's pursuit of their goals (Leung & Wu, 1990). Emics refer to culture-specific concepts found in some societies but not others. Often, emics are the culturally specific ways cultures deal with etic concepts. For example, some cultures stress strict obedience in their socializing of children because the society is dependent on people working together and following well-known rules. Traditional agricultural societies are examples: People have to follow strict rules about when to plant crops, when to harvest them, and how to store food to prevent against a future bad crop. People cannot behave in any way they want; they have to be socialized to follow rules.

In contrast, hunting societies emphasize more independence in their socialization. Hunters usually work in small groups, because too many people would make so much noise that game would be scared away. They have to be flexible in their behavior, changing their plans and even the sites of their communities as game in a certain area becomes scarce. They have to live a more independent lifestyle than agricultural peoples, and their socialization of children emphasizes independence training (Berry, 1979). The etic, then, is that children should be able to contribute to the economy of their communities. The emics are the differing child-rearing practices adults emphasize. A combination of etics and emics is necessary for understanding children's socialization in agricultural and hunting societies.

When reviewing phonemic analysis, I gave examples of sounds that nonnative speakers of a language have difficulty learning. This aspect of "difficult to learn and to understand" is also an aspect of emics. The emics of another culture are hard to understand. The etics are easier to grasp because, by definition, they are common to people in all cultures. When living in another culture, then, people can relate to the etic, for example, of "developing relationships that may lead to marriage." The emics of another culture, however, will be unfamiliar because they are not experienced in one's own culture. Learning emics is similar to Japanese speakers learning the "l-r" distinction or English speakers learning the "r-trilled r" distinction if they study Russian. Time and effort have to be invested; behaviors will seem strange at first; and it will take time before the emics seem natural and everyday in their occurrence. For example, it will take time before someone from a collective society can maintain friendly relations with previous romantic partners and before someone from an individualistic society recognizes and understands the reasons why maintaining friendly relationships is problematic.

A common error in both cross-cultural research and people's everyday thinking is to believe that one's own etic-emic combination is true for all cultures. When such thinking occurs, it broaches the problem of ethnocentrism. If, for instance, the etic-emic combination involves raising responsible children (etic) together with the goal of encouraging independent thinking (emic), it is wrong to feel that this combination applies to all cultures. The etic part may be reasonable, but believing that one's culture's emics are part of the culturally common etic is problematic. When people think and behave in this way, they are said to be imposing an etic (Berry, 1969; Poortinga, 1997). They are forcing a point of view (an assumed etic) on another culture without looking for emic aspects. Further, they are viewing their culture's emics as part of a complex concept that they are imposing on others.

Knowing about emics and etics has practical applications. American teachers are most often socialized in a middle-class background where one emic in parent-to-child behaviors is encouraging independent thinking. Children from this type of background often do well in school because the teachers expect and reward independent thinking (Cushner, 1990, 1994; Hamilton, Blumenfeld, Akoh, & Miura, 1991; Karpov & Haywood, 1998). Examples are the students' abilities to choose topics for their class papers or books for free-reading period. If the teachers impose this emic aspect of their own socialization on their expectations for student behaviors, they will not be as effective with children socialized according to other emics (e.g., obedience and deference to authority, as described earlier).

Emics and Etics: An Example

Complex problems involving extensive cultural contact often can be analyzed using etics and emics as a starting point. Clear failures usually involve a misunderstanding of another culture's emics.

In a foreign-aid project meant to assist the economy of a developing nation in East Africa, a highly industrialized nation (the United States) attempted to improve the rangelands where cattle graze (case analyzed by Talbot, 1972). The East African tribal members had small cattle herds because their rangelands had little grass. Natural events such as fires and droughts kept the rangelands relatively barren. Each herder, however, tried to have as many cattle as possible as this was a sign of status and wealth. Multiple cattle also allowed more food for a herder's family in the form of milk and blood (a protein source).

The development team members attempted to improve the tribe's economy by instituting water irrigation projects. They were "successful" in the sense that they did indeed introduce projects that delivered more water. Grass on the rangeland became more plentiful. After a period, however, disaster struck, and the tribe faced starvation. The increased availability of water had led to increases in the amount of land where good pastures could be established. With increased food for their cattle, the tribespeople allowed their herds to multiply. Eventually, the larger number of cattle overgrazed to an extent that no more grass was available. Cattle died, so tribal members faced starvation.

Analysis of this case study can be aided with explicit attention to emics and etics. As discussed previously, complex concepts are often combinations of a common etic core plus culture-specific emics. This combination is sometimes called the *etic core* with its *emic coloring*. As noted, people must avoid viewing their own etic-emic combination as universal and imposing it on others. If this is not avoided, the extremely important step of examining the other culture's emics is forgotten.

This analysis of the rangeland development project centers on the viewpoints of the technical assistance advisers from the United States and of the herdspeople from the East African tribe. The two groups of people share some etics, by definition. Examples are that cattle demand a great deal of care; that cattle can be used as a protein source (meat for Americans, blood for the herdspeople); and the knowledge that the improved water delivery will increase the land available for pastures. In addition to these etics, however, some emics are the sources of the difficulties. I will number them because each emic in one culture can be presented in a way that contrasts with the emics of the other group.

In the United States, (1) many sources of wealth and status other than cattle exist. People can make much money selling stocks and bonds, for instance, and they can demonstrate their status by owning an expensive car or wearing trendy clothes. America has (2) a long history of conservation of resources. Most American science texts have units on the conservation of natural resources, and children who join the

Girl Scouts or Boy Scouts can earn several merit badges dealing with conservation. (I was once a merit badge counselor for the "soil and water conservation" award.) Another possible U.S. emic (3) is that big projects bring more attention to people, and are more useful in their career development, than small but efficient projects. Somehow, spending tens of millions of dollars on an irrigation project is more attention grabbing than a smaller project that helps herders raise healthier animals within their small herds.

In contrast, among the East African herders, (1) cattle are the prime sources of wealth and prestige. Consequently, opportunities to increase the number of cattle in one's herd are welcome. However, (2) the herders do not have much experience with activities summarized by the term *conservation*. Before the irrigation project, a number of factors limited the size of herds, so tribespeople rarely faced the issue of having too many cattle. Fires and drought limited the amount of grass available for grazing, and diseases occasionally decreased the size of herds. When ample water and grasslands became available, the herdspeople had far fewer limits placed on the number of cattle they could adequately raise. Without a conservation history and its important component that animal quantities must be decreased now to plan for a productive future, herders allowed their cattle to reproduce until large numbers overgrazed the grasslands. Undoubtedly, small herd increases occurred each year, but only (3) small increases noticeably improved the herdspeople's economic status. An American dairy farmer might have to add 100 cows to a herd to warrant comment from neighbors (recall the American emic of big projects bringing attention). For the East African herder, an increase of 3 or 4 per year would bring positive comments from others. But if many tribespeople increased their herds in this slow but sure manner, they eventually would have too many cattle for the available grasslands.

The difficulties stemmed in part, then, from an unwillingness or inability to understand another culture's emics. The American etic-emic combination (i.e., delivery of water with a history of conservation activities) was imposed on the herders. The East African herders admittedly shared some etics with the Americans, such as water delivery and the importance of taking good care of one's animals. However, a danger is inherent with etics: The similarities in some aspects of a complex concept can lead to a false sense of security that all the concept's aspects are the same. When this is believed, people miss the other culture's emics.

A final example may help, especially because virtually all readers will be familiar with some aspects of it. When researchers consider the concept "intelligence" across cultures, they find some etic aspects. Solving problems whose exact form has not been seen before is one etic. Intelligent people can be confronted with unfamiliar problems and suggest workable solutions. In many parts of the world, an emic aspect of intelligence is "quickness." The most intelligent people of these cultures not only solve problems, but also they do so quickly. This is an emic aspect virtually all readers have experienced. Surely they have taken timed intelligence tests (e.g., the Scholastic Aptitude Test is a variant), and all probably have said to themselves, "If I only had more time, I could have answered a lot more questions!" This emic aspect of intelligence is not universal.

A number of psychologists (Dasen, 1984; Greenfield, 1997b; Serpell, 1982; Wober, 1974) have analyzed the emics of intelligence in other cultures. The Baganda people of Uganda, for example, associate intelligence with slow, careful, and deliberate thought (Wober, 1974). They find it much more important to carefully consider many potential solutions to problems, slowly examining their memories to see how these solutions worked in other problematic situations, before sharing their thoughts with others. As Lonner (1990) points out, if Baganda leaders attended a supercharged hour-long decision-making meeting among executives in North America or western Europe, the meeting would be over before the leaders contributed. A grave mistake would be made if the Western executives made judgments about the Baganda leaders based on their own etic-emic combination: problem solving with an emphasis on time. Not all children in North American and western European classrooms have had this "quickness" emphasis. I probably did. When I presented completed puzzles to my mother (discussed earlier), she probably said, "Oh, Richard, it's wonderful that you did them so quickly!" This made me better prepared to benefit from the expectations of my elementary schoolteachers. But quickness is not universally valued, and it is not in the background of all schoolchildren in a culturally diverse country such as the United States or Canada. The wise teacher realizes that quickness is not universal and will make efforts to gradually introduce students to the emphasis on time they will face during their lives.

THE INDIGENOUS APPROACH TO RESEARCH

Some researchers examine important cultural aspects by working primarily and sometimes exclusively with emic concerns. Once these emics are identified and explained, researchers then move to discussions of etics only if their results clearly indicate the wisdom of comparisons with other cultures. This is often called the *indigenous approach* because the starting point is important concerns *within* a culture (Ho, 1998; Kim & Berry, 1993). The approach moves beyond the emic-etic distinction and views emic analysis as essential and the examination of etics as possible only after a thorough understanding of emics has been achieved. As much as possible, such researchers begin with observed behaviors and shared concepts within a culture. In addition, they attempt to understand why people behave as they do and why the people themselves consider the concepts important. Researchers avoid using questionnaires, tests, and experimental procedures developed in other cultures for fear these imported measures will not capture what is important within a culture.

Chapters 1 and 2 reviewed findings from research projects that could point to important indigenous studies. In his excellent study of time use, reviewed in chapter 1, Levine (1997) could not carry out some of his research procedures in India. One reason was that Levine wanted to present a banknote, buy a stamp, and measure how long it took a clerk to hand over the stamp and the necessary change. But Indian post office clerks do not view "carrying change" as part of their jobs, so Levine had to abandon this part of the study. Researchers interested in an indigenous approach would begin with this behavior and try to analyze it: What happens in an Indian post office? How do postal clerks' employment in this career come about? What activities are part of their jobs, in contrast to what they don't do? Answers to questions such as these give information about the work of postal workers from an indigenous perspective, not from an outsider's perspective.

In the discussion of research on personality in chapter 2, work on personality characteristics among the Chinese was reviewed (Cheung & Leung, 1998). Virtually all readers of this book have taken a personality test. Most likely, they were asked to agree or disagree when presented with adjectives or sentences that might describe them. Examples are "I am one of the first people to speak up at meetings in my workplace," or "It is important for me to have clear goals I am working toward." Such items measure traits such as "assertiveness" and "achievement." These tests can be translated and administered to people in other cultures. This would be an etic approach, because it assumes the importance of "assertiveness" and "achievement" in other cultures. But what if these are not centrally important in other cultures? The response is that such tests may miss what is important about personality to people in these other cultures.

The indigenous approach has the goal of avoiding this major problem. The approach begins with behavior and concepts in other cultures: How do people describe one another? When asked a general question, "What terms to people use when they say good and bad things about others and themselves?" what are common answers? This was the approach taken in the research on Chinese personality discussed by Cheung and Leung (1998). They found various aspects of personality that would have been missed by the importation of a personality test from another culture. Examples are filial piety, smooth participation in social exchanges known as *guanxi*, and thrift. The Chinese use these terms when talking about themselves and others. They are important to Chinese people, and the documentation of such importance is central to the indigenous approach.

Starting Points

All research projects need a starting point. If indigenous research is to deal with the importance of behaviors and concepts within a culture, how do researchers start their investigations? Many general guidelines (Kim & Berry, 1993) exist: Four will be discussed here. The starting point for one approach is for researchers living in other cultures to take careful notes about what they find interesting or striking. More formally, researchers can ask themselves, "Am I observing differences here that I cannot explain well given my experience in my own culture? Or, do the cultures have similarities that I did not expect and can't explain?" Examples have been reviewed in earlier chapters. During his travels, Levine (1997) was struck by differences in how people use time. Work on documenting the importance of guanxi in China was stimulated by the reports of many overseas businesspeople who had difficulties setting up joint ventures with Chinese counterparts. They might say, "We are proposing good, reliable, and fairly priced products, and we are ready to pay good wages. Why can't we get a hearing?" One reason is the businesspeople did not realize they must spend time and effort developing good relationships prior to introducing a business proposal.

A second and similar approach is to ask colleagues from other cultures to keep a record of what they find striking when visiting the researchers' own culture. Such a practice often allows researchers to view their own cultures with fresh ideas. As discussed in chapter 1, people often take for granted their own culture. They sometimes have difficulties thinking about the question "Why do we behave as we do in our culture?" because it is often hard to separate daily behavior from explanatory frameworks. The observations of researchers visiting the United States often lead to this response from American researchers: "You're right, of course, but I never thought about it very much." In chapter 2, I reported the insightful example about campus conversations one of my students from Mexico suggested that illustrates this approach. When other graduating seniors stopped and chatted on campus, they would ask, "How are your job interviews going?" He had difficulty responding because setting up job interviews is the responsibility of senior members of his collective, not himself. This example reminded me of a key aspect of individualism: People can set their own goals, but they must engage in individual effort to attain them. Do they want to get married? If so, then they have to find a partner—individualists rarely expect or want someone else to make the choice for them. Do they want a good job? If so, most individualists realize they will have to make efforts to secure good interviews. They cannot depend on others to the extent common in collectivist cultures.

A third starting point, related to the first two, is to ask what current explanatory frameworks miss or what behaviors seem to be underemphasized in journal articles and texts. This approach goes beyond the observations of the first two approaches because it demands a knowledge of explanatory frameworks and a familiarity with the current published literature. For example, individualism and collectivism were introduced in chapter 2. The collectivist emphasis on cooperation, harmony, and support of others long have been part of collectivism explanations (Naroll, 1983). But other observers in collectivist cultures point to many examples of nonharmonious interactions and downright public rudeness. Once, a reporter from Detroit came into my office and shouted at me because he had earlier heard me lecture on collectivism but had found what he thought were many counterexamples in Japan. Japan is a collectivist culture, but this reporter had missed one of the more difficult-to-grasp points about collectivism (Triandis, 1995). Collectivists are cooperative, harmonious, and emphasize mutual support, *but only within their in-group*. Relations with people from the same culture but outside the in-group are not guided by norms that emphasize harmony. For example, many travelers to Japan have commented on the pushing and shoving that occurs in subway stations during rush hours. People rush to secure a spot in subway cars. The subways employ husky men who push people into cars in a manner reminiscent of packing sardines in a can. People are crammed so tightly that they have difficulty breathing. And don't get these observers started on stories about the personal hygiene of some subway car riders and about opportunities to grope others' private body parts! How is such behavior explained? In the subway, there is no in-group present with whose members any one person is expected to be cooperative and harmonious. In the absence of an in-group, people are not guided by norms that expect cooperation and thus are free to behave in ways that may seem very rude to outsiders.

This point about the importance of the in-group is now part of current explanatory frameworks. For example, Triandis (1995) writes:

> Collectivists hoard information even more than individualists do and do not share
> it with outgroups. . . . Cooperation in collectivist cultures occurs only within the

ingroup; extreme competition is used with outgroups. Leonard Brezhnev was exasperated by the Soviet bureaucracy's inability to cooperate: each small face-to-face group fought all other groups. (Kaiser, 1984, p. 178)

A fourth starting point is to consider the behaviors, concepts, and practices all cultures must deal with in some manner. Then, researchers ask how these various universal issues (Lonner, 1980) are treated in a specific culture. For example, to assure survival of a culture, men and women must produce and care for children. Given this fact, researchers then look at how different cultures deal with these demands. In some cultures, marriages are arranged, and in others people choose their own mate. In some cultures, people can have multiple spouses, while in other cultures monogamy is the only acceptable practice. Because the man and woman must come from different families, all cultures face the question of giving roles to people's in-laws. In some cultures, women are expected to be extremely deferent to their mother-in-law. In other cultures, an "avoidance taboo" means people are expected to avoid contact with in-laws for the rest of their lives. The combination of universal issues and then cultural variations often leads to important research.

The list of demands that people in all cultures face varies widely and touches on many aspects of life. In many examples, the starting point is a biological fact. For instance, newborn babies are helpless, and they must be given extensive care for years. This could be the duty of the mother, a shared duty of both parents, or a responsibility of the extended family. People need food to survive, and they need ways to survive periods of food scarcity. One possibility is to have culturally respected practices of food storage, along with the strong norm that people can take from the storage area only in times of severe famine. Or, people could maintain knowledge of edible but foul-tasting plants that are not part of their everyday diet but that are housed in respected elders' memories. As another example, people become sick and need to recover so that they can continue to make contributions to their cultures. In some cultures, specialists with knowledge of healing plants address the needs of sick people. In other cultures, preventive practices have been discovered such as maintaining distance between areas where human waste is discarded and the sources of a culture's water supply.

Indigenous Research: An Example

As with all approaches to research, the steps necessary for indigenous research are best communicated with a careful examination of specific studies. Harper (1997) long has been interested in the impact of physical disabilities on the life experiences of children and adolescents. He had the opportunity to research physical disabilities in Nepal and chose the indigenous approach. His goals were to obtain information about Nepalese reactions to disabilities, from their viewpoints reflected in their communications, rather than information about other countries' perspectives on disabilities. He had two starting points. The first was based on his observations, as well as those of others, that people in various countries stigmatize individuals with disabilities and do not treat them as well as they treat individuals without disabilities. A second starting point was based on the cultural demand that young people be socialized to take various roles so that they contribute to the culture's maintenance.

Such a viewpoint leads to a value placed on young people who are clearly healthy, strong, and mentally alert. When young people have disabilities, this may be taken as a sign that the time and effort needed to socialize them into productive lives will be better spent on people without disabilities.

In Nepal, Harper (1977) collaborated with colleagues who could interview children in both Nepali and local dialects. Children from a big city (Kathmandu) were interviewed, as were children from rural villages. Children whose parents sent them to private schools, as well as children from public schools, were included in the study. A number of steps were taken in the preparation of materials shown to children to obtain their reactions to disabilities. These materials were prepared specifically for this study—none were imported from previous research in another country. For example, pictures were prepared that depicted children from the six castes whose members research participants would have had experiences with during everyday interactions. The pictures depicted children without disabilities and children with five disabilities familiar to the respondents: (a) a child with a crutch; (b) a child with a hand missing below the elbow; (c) a child who is obese, (d) a child with disfigurement of the nose and mouth, and (e) a child with a foot missing below the knee. In preparing the questions that would be asked of respondents, Harper put extensive effort into selecting terms that the interviewer and children could easily use in a smooth, nonforced manner. He prepared them in English with a view toward eventually reporting the results in this international language for scientific communication, but he was careful to use easily translatable English. This is an important step (translation is discussed later in this chapter). People have many ways to express thoughts and ask questions. Working with his colleagues, Harper chose English-language wordings that had ready equivalents in Nepalese. If a colleague were to say, "I understand your English language wording, but it would be hard to translate this into Nepalese," the methodologically wise decision would be to change the English so that it is translatable.

Respondents, ages 10 to 12, were asked to look at all the pictures. Then, they were asked to choose the picture (a) of the child they liked and of (b) the child they would like to play with. After a choice, that picture would be taken away and respondents would be asked the same questions and would choose among the remaining pictures. This procedure continued until respondents chose between the last two pictures. Respondents were also asked to give reasons, in their own words, for their choices.

For boys and girls combined, the order of preference (most frequently chosen to least frequently chosen) was the (a) child without a disability, (b) child who is obese, (c) child with a crutch, (d) child with a missing hand, (e) child with a facial disfigurement, and (f) child with a missing foot. The results showing the frequent choice of the child who is obese in preference to children with other stigmatizing features were different from results in other countries (e.g., the United States). One reason has a cultural component. In some countries with low average personal incomes and widespread poverty, obesity is seen as a sign of wealth and even high status. This reason was expressed by some of the respondents, who made comments (after looking at the picture of a child who is obese) about "strong and healthy," "there is nothing wrong," and "good looking."

When differences between boys and girls were compared, boys placed more emphasis on limitations to physical activities and girls placed more emphasis on facial features. Boys chose a child with a facial disfigurement more frequently than they chose children with a crutch or a missing foot. Girls chose a child with a missing hand or a crutch more often than they chose a child with a facial disfigurement. Reasons for this difference follow from theories dealing with gender differences (discussed in chapter 9). Men value physical activities, and their status is gained through successful participation in challenging sports events. Children with a facial disfigurement can compete successfully in such physical activities. One respondent looked at a picture and said, "He can still play even though his mouth is broken" (Harper, 1997, p. 722). Many cultures, Nepal included, provide far fewer ways for women to obtain status than for men and have far more norms dictating what women can do. One of the ways women obtain status is by being attractive to men. Consequently, girls might be more sensitive than boys to facial disfigurements that would interfere with this status-enhancing feature.

Harper concluded that rejection of people with a facial disfigurement by both genders is illogical in the sense that respondents used superficial characteristics to make negative conclusions about multiple aspects of people. He speculated that this devaluing of people might be less frequent as individuals become exposed to certain ideas common in other cultures: arguments against discrimination, added opportunities for people with various skills, moving beyond features of people that are merely skin deep, and so forth. Follow-up research could include measures of acceptance of these ideas and then determining if the respondents who accept nondiscriminatory views in the abstract are less rejecting of people with facial disfigurements. In Harper's own study, he may had an opportunity to investigate the possible link between exposure to nondiscriminatory ideas and choices among the pictures. Some of the respondents were attending Jesuit schools, and some were attending public government schools. Researchers might have examined the curriculum at the different schools. Possibly, the Jesuit schools may have placed more emphasis on tolerance and nondiscrimination. Students at these schools might have had a different pattern of choices than students at the public schools.

I chose this study for review for a number of reasons. The issues raised have an inherent interest for people. All of us have to make choices among the people we will associate with, and all of us are tempted to make these choices based on superficial features. A second reason is that I wanted to discuss some key features of the indigenous approach. As much as possible, the indigenous approach allows people in different cultures to present their viewpoint on various issues. In terms researchers who use this approach frequently use, it allows people to tell or to demonstrate their "own story." I can't point to any aspect of Harper's (1997) study that would lead to the conclusion the results are based on a Nepalese reaction to imposed and artificial measuring devices (imposed etics) researchers from other countries use. This study also has the desirable feature of contributing to theory development. Findings from this study help people understand gender differences found in various cultures and help the development of general theories that assist in explaining the importance of gender.

EQUIVALENCE OF CONCEPTS

This discussion of emics, etics, and theory development leads directly to another major concern investigators must deal with when making decisions about research methodology. The concern is about the equivalence of concepts across the cultures included in studies (Butcher, Lim, & Nezami, 1998; Van de Vijver & Leung, 1997). In general terms, questions about equivalence are put in this form: "Do the concepts being investigated, and especially the way the concepts are being measured, have the same meaning in the different cultures?" In more specific terms, researchers refer to the topic under investigation in a specific study. For example, a researcher might be interested in studying the concept "disciplining young men to control their aggressiveness" and might study this in several cultures (a topic investigated by A. Goldstein & Segall, 1983). Questions about equivalence must be raised when a concept such as "aggressiveness" is used. Is the concept equivalent in all the cultures under study?

Assume children are on a playground, and a young boy has been playing with his ball for a half hour. A slightly older and heavier boy comes along and takes the ball away. The equivalence issue arises when researchers consider possible responses the younger boy might make. When is a behavior considered "aggressive"? If the younger boy forces his ball away from the older boy, shoving him slightly in the process, is this aggressiveness or sticking up for one's rights? Cultures vary in their guidelines for labeling behavior as aggressive. To make the matter more complex, differences exist *within* a complex society such as the United States. One of the graduate students I have worked with remembers when he was 10 years old. His mother (who happened to be a well-known member of the school board) and father met with his teacher for discussion about his progress. The teacher said, "His schoolwork is fine, but I wish he would be more aggressive about asserting himself on the playground and in the classroom when other students take advantage of him." His parents replied, "We're Quakers; we are trying to raise him according to Quaker values, and so we are happy to hear that his behavior is pacifist." The rest of the parent-teacher conference proceeded in a clumsy manner after this exchange of views.

Other research examples that must be examined with the equivalence issue in mind have been introduced in this chapter. The concept "intelligent behavior" is certainly not equivalent between the United States and the Baganda of Africa if part of the meaning involves quickness in one culture and slow, deliberate thought in another. The concept "making judgments about the personalities of others" demands a careful analysis of equivalence issues (Church & Lonner, 1998). If people in individualist societies make judgments about traits that supposedly generalize across situations (recall the discussion, pp. 73–75) and if people in collectivist societies also make judgments about traits in situations, direct comparisons of the judgments would be difficult to make.

A number of approaches to dealing with the equivalence issue have been developed (Embretson, 1997; Hui & Triandis, 1985; Malpass & Poortinga, 1986; Van de Vijver & Leung, 1997). Three will be discussed here: translation equivalence, conceptual equivalence, and metric equivalence. Some researchers prefer to use the terms *culture-common* and *culture-specific* instead of *etics* and *emics* in discussions of equivalence. To prepare people for further reading of the material cited throughout this book, I will use *culture-common/etic* and *culture-specific/emic* interchangeably.

Any treatment of emics, etics, and equivalence involves measurement. Two concepts central to measurement should be reviewed here: reliability and validity. (Readers probably have been introduced to reliability and validity in other courses and texts.) Some of my examples will be based on cross-cultural research studies introduced earlier in this book.

Reliability and Validity

Reliability refers to a consistency in measurement. Issues of reliability arise in answer to this question: If people measure a concept, will other measures of the same concept yield the same or similar results? Probably the clearest examples deal with tests, and one reason is that all readers have experience with them. In chapter 1, scores on the Scholastic Aptitude Test (SAT) were discussed. If a student takes the test in September and receives a score of 600, then the student should receive a similar score when taking the test on a second occasion in October. This is called *test-retest reliability*. With long tests, researchers often compare results based on half of the questions with results based on the other half of the questions. Again using the SAT as an example, results from odd-numbered questions might be compared with results from even-numbered questions. If the scores are similar, then researchers present evidence for what is called *split-half reliability*.

The exact type of reliability a researcher chooses to emphasize follows from the type of concepts investigated in any one study. Studies based on questionnaires and tests that respondents fill out lead to the use of split-half reliability, test-retest reliability, or both. Other types of reliability, with the same emphasis on consistency of measurements, are appropriate when researchers use methods other than those based on respondents' completion of scales. For example, if people are observed and conclusions made based on the people's visible behaviors, then reliability based on multiple observers could be emphasized.

Readers might be interested in an example that did not yield high reliability. A group of researchers I knew wanted to study children's physical aggressiveness in school. Different researchers would observe children and make aggressiveness ratings. They could not conclude they had a reliable measure. The researchers were from different cultures (Nepal, Philippines, Japan, United States, Canada) and brought different assumptions to the task of rating childhood aggressiveness. For one rater, the physical contact involved when one child cuts in front of another child in a line was assertiveness but not aggressiveness. For another rater, any physical contact as a child darted from one part of the schoolroom to another was rated "aggressive." This lack of agreement led to low reliability. The slightly more technical term is that the study had low *interrater* reliability. Chapter 2 reviewed a study of intercultural communication covering some people who had been given preparatory training and some who had not (pp. 40–41). If the trained or untrained people then interacted with individuals from other cultures, raters could agree that some people are much more comfortable in these interactions than others. Put another way, the concept "communicating comfortably with culturally different individuals" can be rated in a reliable way by multiple observers.

The key to understanding reliability, then, is that if researchers conclude they successfully measured a concept, then they have additional information that their measure is consistent. That additional information may be based on people completing a test or questionnaire a second time, showing consistency on one half of the test or questionnaire compared to the other half, and the observations of multiple independent raters.

Validity involves relationships between measures of a concept and information *beyond* the measure itself (Greenberg & Baron, 1997; Landy, 1986). A phrase frequently used is that examinations of validity assess whether or not a test, questionnaire, or set of observations *measures what it is supposed to measure*. This phrase must be examined carefully, and an example makes any arguments clearer. Assume researchers have the results of a questionnaire they have administered. The questionnaire was meant to measure people's interest in high-technology communication. The assessment of validity involves gathering other, independent information that will answer these questions: Does this assessment of people's interest in high-technology communication actually accomplish this task? Does independent evidence indicate the questionnaire actually measures an interest in high technology? In other words, is the measurement valid? Independent evidence, beyond the questionnaire, would include information such as the following about the people studied: Do people own a personal computer? How much software do they own? Do they have e-mail accounts? Do they subscribe to magazines that deal with these topics? Do they watch TV shows, such as PBS's "Nova," when the topic is high-technology communication? Do other individuals contact them to ask questions about these products and TV shows? Results of the questionnaire would be compared to these independent information sets. The questionnaire would be considered valid if it identified the people with interests in high-technology communication as shown by the independent assessments of product ownership, TV shows watched, and types of conversations with others.

Choices of independent sets of information to demonstrate validity often involve clever thinking and creativity. For example, in the research discussed earlier on communicating with culturally different others, assume that observations (the original measure) were made on a university campus. Independent information to demonstrate validity might include the following about the respondents: Which students voluntarily attended the reception for international students? Which students decide to take advantage of their university's junior-year-abroad program involving studying in another country? Do the courses students choose as electives have a strong cross-cultural component (e.g., cross-cultural psychology, intercultural communication, international business, etc.)? Do students regularly talk, at length, with international students and students from diverse groups within their own country? Do they go to social gatherings with these students? Again, the original observational measure of intercultural communication effectiveness would be considered valid if it identifies students who engage in these activities involving uses of their free time, choices of university courses, and interactions with international and other culturally diverse peers.

In chapter 2, the importance of thrift as an emic aspect of personality among the Chinese was discussed. Information on validity would compare results of a written self-assessment of people's thrift with other, independent information. This additional information could include the amount of money in their bank account, the percentage of their monthly income that goes into various types of savings accounts, the amount of time they spend researching products before buying them, and the number of overdrafts from their checking account requiring penalty payments. People who score high on the written self-assessment of thrift should demonstrate their thriftiness according to these and similar independent behaviors.

Again, when choosing both the concepts to measure and the types of validity information to be gathered, researchers must keep in mind that the same behaviors do not have the same meaning in all cultures. In my list of thrift indicators, I might have included whether or not people tip for good service beyond the standard 15%. People who rarely venture beyond 15% could be considered thrifty but at the same time would avoid the reputation labels of "cheapskate" or "tightwad." This variable would not be a good indicator in a cross-cultural study because tipping is not universal. Waiters in Australia and Japan, for example, do not expect tips. In many European countries, an automatic service charge of 10% is added to bills. Such concerns arise in discussions of equivalence across cultures, and this is the next topic.

Translation Equivalence

A good start at identifying problems involving equivalence is to examine descriptions and measures of concepts as they are translated across languages. If concepts can be easily expressed in the languages of the different cultures under study, then researchers are making a first step in dealing with equivalence issues. If concepts do not translate well, researchers should not throw up their hands in frustration. Material that does not translate well can indicate emic aspects that researchers could identify to determine the meaning of concepts in different cultures. Researchers must keep in mind that the emics of other cultures are likely to be unfamiliar to outsiders, and these "outsiders" include researchers from other countries. Unfamiliar aspects of a concept might be difficult to translate because (a) no readily available terms capture those aspects, and/or (b) translators working across the various languages might be unfamiliar with the emic aspects. Rather than discard the seemingly unsuccessful attempts to translate concepts, researchers should collect them and analyze them for insights into behavior in the other cultures. These general points may become clearer with this example.

Back translation is a good place to start examinations of the equivalence issue. In this procedure, material in the researcher's language is carefully prepared. For example, the material might be a questionnaire asking about child rearing practices. A bilingual then translates the material to the target language, and a second bilingual (unfamiliar with the first bilingual's efforts) translates the material back to the original language, such as English. The two English versions then can be examined to determine what "comes through" clearly, and the assumption can be entertained (not yet proven) that the target-language version is adequate if the two English versions are equivalent (more about back translation can be found in Brislin, 1980, 1986; Butcher et al., 1998).

By studying the back-translated original-language version, researchers can gain insights into what can, and what cannot, be easily expressed in the target language. When doing research in Guam, where the native language is Chamorro, I was interested in the personality variable called "desire for social approval." If people have this desire, then they want to express themselves to others in a manner that gains approval. To do so, they often boast, deny their faults, and say positive things about themselves even when these are not strictly true. To measure this concept, Crowne and Marlowe (1964) wrote statements that identified mildly negative behaviors common to almost all people. If people who respond to the statements deny engaging in these behaviors, they are said to be desirous of social approval.

One of the statements is "I like to gossip at times." The assumption behind using statements such as this is that if people were totally honest with themselves, they would answer yes. In the Guam study (Brislin, 1970, 1986), I used back translation to develop a Chamorro language version of the statements. One bilingual translated them into Chamorro, and another independently back translated to English. Changes were made in an effort to make a second English version more easily translatable, and this was given to a third bilingual. The process continued for three rounds, and it can be summarized in a diagram:

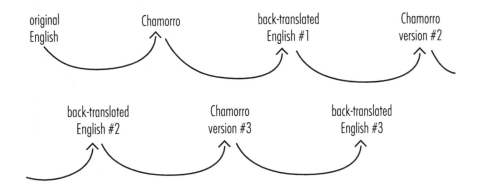

The assumption was that if the English-language materials could survive this procedure (called *decentering*), then the concepts that remained in the back-translated English version number 3 must be readily expressible in Chamorro. An additional assumption was that the Chamorro version number 3 and the English version number 3 could be "translation equivalent" and that if so, further cross-cultural research efforts would be warranted. Note that the procedure is much like the game called "rumor." Ten or more people form a circle, and one person whispers a sentence into a second person's ear. The whispered communication continues around the circle, and the last person tells the entire group what she or he heard. Often, a great deal of the original sentence is lost or changed. The material that comes through, however, is usually very clear, memorable, and easily expressible (e.g., "The temperature was over 100 degrees.").

In the study involving the Chamorro language, the item "I like to gossip at times" ended up as "Sometimes I like to talk about other people's business" in the third English back translation. Results such as these then stimulate discussions with the translators, and some of the most important findings emerge from this important step. The bilinguals told me that Chamorro had no one word for "gossip." The language demands that the speakers indicate whether they are referring to a man or to a woman who gossips. Chamorro had readily available words, however, to render a good translation of "talk about other people's business." It had a better equivalent for "sometimes" in contrast to "at times," and consequently the former was favored. In subsequent research efforts, the modified version of the original item was used (i.e., the "talk about other people's business" rather than the original "gossip" version) because the latter is translation equivalent according to this procedure. Although these differences may seem subtle, examining them does lead to new information about the culture.

The results of seeking translation equivalence for other items sometimes demanded even smaller, but no less important, changes. Another of the original items was "I have never intensely disliked someone." The third back-translated version was, "I have never really disliked anyone." The bilinguals told me that it was difficult to translate "intensely," and this is an example of the more general point (Brislin, 1986, p. 146) that adverbs frequently cause troubles. Chamorro also had a better equivalent for "anyone" than "someone." Again, the modified version based on the third back translation and the third Chamorro version were used to measure the need for social approval among English and Chamorro speakers.

This multiple translation procedure is more suitable for identifying culturally common aspects of a concept then for determining possible culturally specific (emic) aspects. If wording survives the multiple translations into and back from another language, then both the original and target languages are likely to have frequently used terms and phrases to describe the ideas contained in the material. If aspects of the concept cannot be readily translated (as with "gossip"), then these aspects will not be found in the back-translated versions. If aspects are either dropped out or added by translators following instructions to "communicate these ideas as best you can in the target language," they may be emics. For instance, when I found that "gossip" was not in the back translations, I suggested to myself that an emic may be involved. I was correct: Conversations with translators led to the realization that a distinction must be made between men and women who gossip. This is an emic aspect of the Chamorro language. Again, the recommendation for working with etics and emics in translation is to avoid frustration when material does not translate exactly in the back translations. Instead, researchers should keep a careful record of what their translators drop and add so that they can try to identify etic and emic aspects of concepts. Searching for emic aspects of concepts can be very exciting, because it is intriguing to consider unfamiliar features of human behavior. Researchers also must remember that emic aspects will be unfamiliar to some people. If the aspects were instead similar among cultures, they would be familiar to people and readily expressible in the various languages indigenous to the cultures.

At times, findings will be very dramatic. Phillips (1960, p. 32) was interested in studying family relations and chose a sentence-completion task as a method suitable for comparing responses in the United States and Thailand. He reported difficulty, however, having the following sentence stem translated into Thai: "Sometimes a good quarrel is necessary because . . ." Phillips responded to this difficulty by viewing it as an opportunity to have a conversation with his translators. After comparing notes and hearing Phillips's analysis of why this item is readily understandable to native English speakers, the Thai translators developed an important insight that helped Phillips with his study. The translators concluded that although Americans might find it conceivable that a quarrel would have some kind of cathartic effect, this aspect of the more general concept (husband-wife disagreements) is incomprehensible to Thais. Returning to the major point, difficulties in the translation procedure should not be viewed as an opportunity to throw one's hands in the air while using foul language. The procedures should be viewed as opportunities to determine culture-common aspects (based on materials that translate easily) and culture-specific aspects (based on materials lost or added during translation).

Conceptual Equivalence

Summarizing, the results of a multiple back-translation procedure can yield insights into culture-common and culture-specific concepts. The material that proceeds smoothly through the multiple steps is said to be translation equivalent. Material that does not translate well or that translators add is set aside for its possible usefulness for identifying culture-specific aspects of concepts.

Conceptual equivalence involves the assumption that most likely different aspects of a concept serve the same purpose in different cultures. An analysis that has the goal of conceptual equivalence often identifies etic aspects first and then further identifies the emic aspects related to the etic in the various cultures under study. As with many general points, explanations become clearer when specifics are examined. A few examples already introduced can be called on here. If an etic aspect of intelligence is "solving problems," then various emic aspects are related to this goal, and they are different in various cultures (Mishra, 1997). In the United States and western Europe, one such emic is "quickness." Among the Baganda of Uganda, one emic is slow and careful thought. Among the Chi-Chewa of Zambia (Serpell, 1982), one emic for intelligence in solving problems is responsibility to the community, which involves getting along well with others. All of these emics are conceptually equivalent in that they are part of the definition of intelligence in solving problems as employed by respected adults in the different cultures. Quickness, deliberate thought, and social responsibility are conceptually equivalent in the three cultures because they are used by adults who are asked the question, "Which young people in your community are considered intelligent?"

Important research involving conceptual equivalence has investigated the concepts of privacy and crowdedness. Undoubtedly, cultural differences exist in the amount of time desired for privacy. Because people in collective societies obtain much of their identity from their relations with others (chapter 2; Triandis, 1995), they are probably more likely than individualists to seek the company of in-group members. Because individualists obtain much of their identity from their unique interests, many of which can be carried out alone, they may be interested in greater amounts of privacy than collectivists. Still, privacy and the company of others probably involves a dynamic process whereby people desire some mix of the two and too much of one will lead to discomfort. Some people will demand more than others, but an interest in privacy is probably universal. How people seek and maintain privacy, though, may involve differences from culture to culture (Altman & Chemers, 1980; Werner, Brown, & Altman, 1997).

The possible universality of the need for privacy and of perceived crowding with attention to possible cultural differences in their manifestation was investigated by Nagar and Paulus (1988; see also Pandey, 1990). Based on work in the United States and India and combined with observations in Colombia, Peru, and Mexico, they identified four possible universals of perceived crowding:

1. *Spaciousness*, or the perceived amount of space possible where a person can move freely

2. *Positive or supportive relationships*, or the number of people in a social setting that a person enjoys having present

3. *Negative or disruptive relationships*, or the number of people in a social setting that a person does not enjoy having present. This aspect also includes the presence of one or a few people that actively disrupt a person's behavior in a social setting.

4. *Uncontrolled disturbances*, or irritants that a person cannot eliminate. These include noise, the presence of disruptive people, pollution, a stress-causing supervisor, and so forth.

The four aspects or factors work together, and positive aspects of one can ameliorate the negative aspects of another. Little spaciousness may exist on a crowded bus or airplane (aspect 1), but if the person has a pleasant and attractive companion who is a good conversationalist (aspect 2), the social setting may be experienced as pleasant. Likewise, negative aspects can overwhelm positive features. A person might be in a large, attractive, and beautifully furnished room, but if one disliked person is present, the setting might be experienced as both crowded and unpleasant. The various aspects have differing influences on a wide range of people's attitudes and behaviors. Reported psychological problems, such as stress, were most closely associated with the uncontrolled disturbance aspect (4). People seem less affected by a clear difficulty in a setting if they feel they can control it. A lack of control over the difficulty is more impactful than the presence of the difficulty itself. For example, an obnoxious person at a party will not necessarily cause stress; an inability to avoid this person is the more likely cause. The best predictors of a general sense of psychological well-being were a satisfaction with the amount of space and the absence of negative relationships. Cultural differences occur in the amount of space considered necessary and the exact reasons people label a relationship as negative. In Japan, for example, homes are much smaller than in the United States, and less space is needed for a person's judgment of feeling comfortable. In the United States, a person might be labeled as "disruptive" (a negative relationship) if he or she does not follow through on commitments to complete a task in an agreed period. In Latin America, that same person might be labeled as cooperative if reasons for not completing the task centered on assisting members of the in-group on their tasks.

Returning to the concept of conceptual equivalence, people have different ways of seeking to reduce the feeling of crowdedness and of seeking the company of others. In the United States and many other highly industrialized nations, people build fences around their homes. The need to be with others is satisfied through invitations to others who then join people inside their homes (or elsewhere). Because Japanese homes are small, a frequent conceptual equivalent to entertaining in the home is to entertain guests at a restaurant. Put another way, Americans in Japan might ask themselves, "How do I know when the Japanese are accepting me?" If they wait for a behavior they are most familiar with, invitations into the others' homes, they may wait a very long time because such behavior is uncommon. The equivalent to the American home visit is an invitation to a restaurant where the Japanese act as hosts and pick up the bill for dinner.

Various conceptually equivalent ways to achieve privacy also exist. Given the large homes many Americans live in, people can go off to a room to be alone. When they appear in a room many people use, such as the living room, they are signaling to others that they are available for social interaction. Pandey (1990) analyzed conceptually equivalent behavior among people crowded into Mexican slums. When people retreated to their small homes, this was a widely accepted signal in the community that they wanted privacy. Respecting this norm, others did not drop in to people's homes. People's need for social interaction was satisfied by simply leaving the house. The slums are so crowded that people will surely run into each other in the common areas outside homes. These extensive opportunities for social interaction served the need to be with others, and any sense of psychological overload due to crowded conditions could be alleviated by retreats into one's home.

Conceptual equivalence always will be an important issue in cross-cultural research and in the analysis of people's intercultural encounters. Returning to the discussion of ethnocentrism in chapter 2, a knowledge of conceptual equivalence assists in the understanding of odd and different behaviors people observe in other cultures. These different behaviors often represent conceptually equivalent ways of obtaining widely understood goals. Given the sophistication needed for a good analysis of conceptual equivalence, the imposition, simplicity, and judgmentalness involved in ethnocentrism have to disappear. As discussed, occasional periods of privacy are a universal goal, as is the desire for interaction with others. The varying uses of one's home to balance these two needs represent conceptual equivalents. If understood, they reduce the ethnocentric feeling that "this is strange" and help people behave in appropriate ways when they are involved in extensive intercultural interactions.

Metric Equivalence

A sharp contrast exists between conceptual equivalence and metric equivalence (Van de Vijver & Leung, 1997). Conceptual equivalence centers on the analysis of different behaviors serving the same general concept. The example of the behaviors quick versus slow thought serving the analysis of the intelligence concept in different cultures has been used several times. *Metric equivalence* centers on the analysis of the same concepts across cultures, and its analysis assumes that the same scale (after proper translation procedures) can be used to measure the concept everywhere. Because all readers probably have taken a version of an intelligence test, I'll use that as an example. Assume that an American woman takes a test, and the conclusion is that her intelligence quotient (IQ) is 120. A woman in Chile takes a carefully translated Spanish version of the same test, and she also scores 120. If metric equivalence is assumed, the conclusion is that the two women are equally intelligent. The assumption is that the scale, or metric, is measuring exactly the same concept (intelligence) in the two countries and that a score in one country can be directly compared with a score in another.

Explanations of metric equivalence are clearest in their *misuse*. People often assume metric equivalence exists, even when they do not use the term, rather than think about the complexities of emics, etics, and conceptual equivalencies analyzed in this chapter. Assume that high school counselors are deciding who they might encourage to take an advanced mathematics course during their senior year. If an American man has an IQ score of 130 in his folder, he might receive such encouragement. Assume that the counselors also have the file of a student who was born in Mexico and has lived in the United States for the past five years. His native language is Spanish, and he has learned English well enough to receive good grades and to occasionally find his name on the school honor roll. His folder says that his IQ score is 115. Say the counselors do not encourage him to take the advanced math course, assuming the metric equivalence of the IQ scores. They are assuming that an IQ of 130 as achieved by the American student (whose native language is English) is better than the score of 115. The counselors have made no analysis of the special problems the native speaker of Spanish faces. They have given no consideration to the fact he took the IQ test in a less familiar language and that a score of 115 under these circumstances might indicate more intelligence than the score of 130. When the counselors assume metric equivalence, they are saying the IQ test measures the same abilities of the two students. Readers may find it instructive to recall a time in their lives when they were put at a disadvantage by someone's assumption of metric equivalence. Many people have been treated badly because a number was attached to them, while someone else with a higher number was given privileges or opportunities. But given their current understanding of the complexities of research methods discussed in this chapter, people now might discover problems in the assignment of such numbers that led to unfairness.

Occasionally, people can deny metric equivalence when it should be considered. Continuing the example of school counselors and their recommendations about mathematics, assume a female student has achieved a score of 130 on an IQ test. If counselors fail to recommend that she take the mathematics course, perhaps believing the myth (analyzed by Hyde, Fennema, & Lamon, 1990) that women do noticeably less well in advanced mathematics, they are denying the possibility of metric equivalence. They are applying their mistaken myths rather than studying the research literature and finding that men and women with ability levels represented by IQ scores of 130 can rise to the expectations of good science and mathematics teachers. Given proper support and encouragement (Mayer, Sims, & Tajika, 1995), men and women both do well in advanced mathematics courses (Stevenson, Chen, & Lee, 1993).

In good cross-cultural research, claims of metric equivalence will be just one part of a scholar's claims that he or she has identified cultural differences in behavior. For example, Berry (1979; also introduced in this chapter, p. 85) did research to determine if people in cultures whose economy is based on agriculture are more conforming than people whose economy is based on hunting. The argument is that agricultural people are more conforming because they have many rules to follow: when to plant, when to harvest, how to store food to prepare against the possibility of poor crops in the future, and how to prevent raiding the storehouses whenever people wish. In contrast, hunters have to be more independent. They have to try different ways to attract game animals, must be willing to work alone in small groups (too many hunters would scare game away), and must be willing to abandon current hunting areas for other places when game is scarce.

To test this prediction, Berry showed people figures such as Figure 2. He or his research assistants asked, "Which line is the same as line A?" The questioner also mentioned that many people who already participated in the project answered that line 4 is the same. This is clearly wrong. The dependent variable in the study was the number of agriculturalists and hunters who ignored the suggested answers of others and answered in their own independent manner that line 5 is the same.

As predicted, hunters (Inuit in northern Canada) were more independent in their judgments than were agriculturalists (the Temne of Africa). The agriculturalists were more likely go conform to the suggestion that others had reported that line 4 matched the standard line. Berry is assuming metric equivalence in his claim. He is assuming that if people in one culture report that line 4 is the same as the standard, then this has the same meaning in the other culture. He is assuming that the "measure of conformity and independence" can be used to assess the same concepts in the two cultures. A key point is that Berry brought in a great deal of additional information to bolster his case. He presented the results of other measures that can be predicted from an independent versus conforming orientation; he presented details on the child-rearing practices in the two cultures; and he analyzed the agricultural and hunting tasks adults face in the two cultures. His total set of arguments were consistent, and they also agreed with the independent work of others (e.g., Barry, Bacon, & Child, 1957). His findings based on an assumption about metric equivalence fit into a large set of arguments supporting his prediction about independence and conformity.

FIGURE 2   **Task Presented to Assess Conformity or Independence**

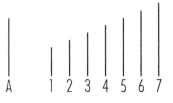

I believe that metric equivalence will often play this sort of limited but still important role. At times, a concept (or aspects of a concept) will be so similar in different cultures that the quest for a metrically equivalent scale will be worthwhile. The number of seconds it takes a clerk to help a customer is part of a metric scale, and Levine (1997) used such a scale in his studies of time discussed previously. More frequently, however, the facts that (a) human behavior in any one culture is complex and (b) complexity is added when behavior in different cultures is studied will lead to the conclusion that the assumptions behind metric equivalence are unwarranted. Instead, researchers who sought metric equivalence often will return to conceptual equivalence, searching for different behaviors that serve similar functions in different societies. Various examples of conceptual equivalence will be covered in future chapters: different approaches to assuring that society has well-educated adults (chapter 4), different expectations about what good supervisors do for their workers (chapter 8), and different approaches to interventions when people encounter stresses in their lives (chapter 9). The realization that different behaviors serve similar goals and that these differences can be interpreted only in relation to the pursuit of those goals in different cultures is one of the most important contributions cross-cultural research has made.

CHAPTER SUMMARY

Cross-cultural researchers take on additional burdens when they decide to study in cultures other than their own. They often have to work in an unfamiliar language and among people suspicious of outsiders asking questions about human behavior. When researchers travel to other countries, they must leave most of their support group behind and must experience the stresses of adjustment all people face when living in another culture.

Many researchers feel, however, that the benefits outweigh these difficulties. One advantage is that the range of variables can be increased by comparisons across cultures, such as comparing the number of people individuals feel should be consulted about important decisions. This number is usually much larger in collective than in individualist cultures (chapter 2). Variables can sometimes be unconfounded, or separated, to determine the relative contributions of each. As Beardsley and Pedersen (1997) point out, if people in a certain culture consume similar foods, the variables of the people's genetic propensity for certain diseases is confounded with their diet in terms of research possibilities. If people from such a culture become immigrants to another, the variables can be separated if the immigrants acquire the dietary habits of the new culture.

Another benefit is that researchers often can analyze the contributions of social contexts when they do research in other cultures. Much behavior is made suitable for the context people find themselves in: solemn at a Catholic funeral service, lighthearted and joking at an informal party, and sympathetic when listening to friends describe their current problems. As they grew from children to adults, researchers experienced combinations of behaviors appropriate to situations in their own culture. They often find it difficult to analyze the influences of social contexts in their home country because people within any one culture take the behaviors for granted. When observing behavior in other cultures, however, researchers discover the influences of social contexts are sometimes easier to analyze because they are fresher, less familiar, and clearer to outsiders.

An ability to analyze the contributions of social contexts can be helpful in many different attempts to understand human behavior. The experiences of schoolchildren are good examples for study. Much of the learning in school is out of context. Children learn material from the teachers' presentations and from books, and this new learning might be useful at some later date. In many parts of the world, most learning is in context: Children learn agricultural, hunting, and domestic skills by working next to their parents and other respected elders. Further, clear uses of the new learning are introduced simultaneously, and the children can apply the knowledge almost immediately. One type of learning is not better than the other; they are simply different. When children accustomed to in-context learning enter formal schools, however, stresses are added to their lives because they are unfamiliar with out-of-context instruction.

Another important conceptual tool for cross-cultural research is a sensitivity to etics and emics. An *etic* is a shorthand term to describe concepts that are common across cultures. Many of these concepts are based on the demands people all over the world must deal with: insuring a food supply, controlling people's sexual appetites, socializing children to be responsible adults, and so forth. *Emics* refer to culturally specific aspects of complex concepts, for instance, how different cultures socialize children. Emics often cause intercultural misunderstandings because, by definition, they are widely accepted by people in one culture but are unfamiliar and consequently seem "strange" to people in another. In the United States, for example, adults punish naughty children by confining them at home. This interferes with children's desire to play with their friends in different parts of their neighborhood. In Japan, adults punish naughty children by keeping them out of the home, forcing them to spend time in their neighborhood until their punishment is over. This interferes with their desire to become part of the close collective their families represent (Stevenson, Azuma, & Hakuta, 1986). The etic aspect of the two examples is that children are punished when they displease their parents. The emic aspects are the specific ways the different cultures under study punish children. One culture's emics will seem odd to people from another, and the analysis of difficulties in intercultural interactions often involves studying emic differences (Landis & Bhagat, 1996). The meaning of a concept for any one culture will be a combination of the etic core (here, punishment for misdeeds, parental disapproval) and the emic coloring (the places where children are sent).

Discussions of emics and etics are closely related to treatments of the equivalence of meaning across cultures. The starting point for most analyses of complex concepts is the knowledge that perfect equivalence does not exist. Rather, some aspects of concepts may be similar, but analyses of translation, conceptual, and metric equivalence must be made in the cultures under study.

To analyze translation equivalence, researchers study what is readily expressible in the various cultures. In the back-translation procedure, one bilingual translates original materials from one language to another, and a second bilingual translates that version back to the first language. The two original-language versions then can be compared. Material that is not easily expressible often will be dropped. Researchers then should consider the possibility that the material dropped is emic to the first culture's language. At times, some material will translate smoothly but will not necessarily be equivalent. The English term *friend* will translate readily into the Spanish *amigo*, but are the meanings of the two words equivalent? For example, are the same behaviors expected of a "friend" as an "amigo"? To answer this question, an analysis of conceptual equivalence is necessary.

When analyzing conceptual equivalence, researchers attempt to discover different behaviors that relate to the same complex concept. Intelligence is a concept that relates to the solving of unfamiliar problems, but behaviors serving this concept vary in different cultures. In some cultures, intelligence involves quick thinking and an emphasis on time. In others, intelligence involves slow and deliberate thought. The aspects of quickness and deliberateness are conceptually equivalent in that they guide people's answers to the question "Which people are considered intelligent in this culture?" The identification of conceptually equivalent behaviors is one of the most exciting possibilities in cross-cultural research. It helps researchers reduce their ethnocentric thinking because analyzing conceptual equivalence forces them to think about complex behaviors in a very different manner. If people can observe unfamiliar behaviors in other cultures and can determine that they relate to complex concepts in ways that make sense in the other cultures, then they are avoiding ethnocentric thinking. They are avoiding the imposition of their own culture's way of thinking and are instead attempting to understand culturally diverse people from the people's viewpoint.

Metric equivalence is uncommon, but understanding it assists research because it is a type of equivalence that has very clear assumptions. If metric equivalence is claimed, then researchers are asserting that the same number on a scale represents the same meaning in the cultures under study. A clear example is body temperature: A reading of 100° F indicates a slight fever. If researchers assume this number has the same meaning of "slight fever" in the cultures they are examining, then they are assuming metric equivalence. Given that human behavior is so complex and given the frequency of conceptually equivalent rather than exactly equivalent behaviors when cultures are compared, arguments for metric equivalence should be made only when researchers have extensive evidence to support their claims.

A central feature in all of the approaches to cross-cultural studies discussed in this chapter is that good researchers make intensive efforts to understand behavior from the viewpoint of the people in the cultures under study. They are not imposing their own viewpoints. In the language of this chapter, they are not imposing their emics by assuming the emics are etic, and they are not assuming that their own understanding of complex concepts are universally equivalent. This sensitivity to others and the quest to understand the cultural background of seemingly strange behaviors are good goals for all people who deal with cultural diversity. Many insights into people's cultural background can be gained by studying how children are socialized to become productive members of their society. This is the topic of the next chapter.

ADDENDUM: THE ANALYSIS OF METHODS IN A CROSS-CULTURAL INVESTIGATION

Another way to introduce some key methodological concerns in cross-cultural research is to review their use in a specific study. This discussion introduces concepts covered in book-length treatments of cross-cultural research (Berry et al., 1997; Brislin, Lonner, & Thorndike, 1973; Lonner & Berry, 1986; Triandis & Berry, 1980) and in standard methodology texts applicable to various types of research within the behavioral sciences (e.g., Dane, 1990; Grimm & Yarnold, 1995; Miller, 1991; Nachmas & Nachmas, 1987). Consequently, the concepts will be clearest to readers who are familiar with one or more of these books or whose professors have covered important concepts presented in these sources.

The study reviewed here was carried out by Kleinhesselink and Rosa (1991) and was concerned with the perception of risks, especially their harmful effects, in the United States and Japan.

The Formulation of Research Questions

Modern technology has brought comforts to many people, such as air-conditioned homes and offices, affordable automobiles, and drugs to combat disease. However, all of these technological innovations include risks that can harm people: air-conditioning demands electricity, and this requires power plants, where accidents are possible. Automobiles demand gasoline, and gasoline use leads to harmful air pollution. Drugs can prolong life, but risks (often called side effects) are associated with the use of virtually all powerful drugs, and risks increase when the same person uses two or more drugs. Because the United States and Japan are two of the world's most highly industrialized nations, it is important to determine what people think of these risks and how they organize information about risks in their minds. If health care workers and accident prevention specialists know how people organize information about risks, they have a greater chance of formulating recommendations for risk prevention (discussed in chapter 9) that people will follow.

Culture-Common and Culture-Specific Factors

Kleinhesselink and Rosa (1991) integrated their research ideas with the existing published literature by starting with the list of 81 risks and hazards Slovic, Fischhoff, and Lichtenstein (1985) developed and standardized. Examples from the list include motorcycles, oral contraceptives, asbestos, commercial aviation, crime, pesticides, fluoridation, and radiation therapy. When adapting this list used previously among U.S. respondents, the authors made a number of modifications for use in Japan. One was that more newly known risks were added that had achieved more prominence in the mass media and people's lives since the development of the original list. These included AIDS, the greenhouse effect, and ozone depletion. Risks that were significantly less familiar to people in Japan were eliminated, such as high school football and coal tar in hair dyes.

An alternative procedure could have been to retain these items and to add others that are familiar in Japan but far less familiar in the United States. These could include risks such as overtraining in high school baseball (discussed by Whiting, 1989), overwork in the office, eating blowfish (a little of its toxin leads to euphoria; a little too much causes death), and being pushed into subway cars during rush-hour commutes to work. Retaining and creating items familiar in one society but less so in another adds to the possibility of identifying culture-specific concepts. In cross-cultural research, items people reply "I don't understand this" to are not useless as long as researchers have a purpose in including such items. Here, the purpose would have been to identify culture-specific concepts as indicated by collections of items, and those concepts (as discussed previously in this chapter) are certain to be unfamiliar to people socialized in a different country.

Participants in the Study

Decisions about the type of participants the researchers ask to cooperate with them should follow directly from the formulated research questions. This may seem a commonsense assertion, but it is frequently violated. For example, intelligence tests standardized in one country are all too frequently administered in another without attention to the meaning of this procedure (issues involved analyzed by Lonner, 1990; Mishra, 1997). Why should people in Mexico, or recent Mexican American immigrants to the United States, be expected to demonstrate the abstract quality "intelligence" when administered tests that were standardized on middle-class Caucasian Americans? Too many researchers, and users of standardized tests, give insufficient attention to this question.

The responses (e.g., opinions, behaviors, statements about personality) gathered from participants should allow the researchers to perform straightforward analyses that provide clear answers to their research questions. In research investigating the role of people's self-interest in their attitudes toward government-directed interracial interaction, for example, Sears and Funk (1991) reviewed studies where self-interest was a possible factor for some participants but a remote factor for others. For example, one type of government-directed interracial interaction is forced busing, when children from a certain neighborhood are bused to another school whose administrators are trying to achieve a racial balance. Some participants in the research studies had children in public schools who might be bused. Other respondents were childless or had the funds to send their children to private schools. Comparing the attitudes of the two groups allowed the researchers to test the role people's self-interest plays. Results of this and similar studies indicate that a broader assessment of people's racial tolerance or intolerance (analyzed more fully in chapters 6 and 7) is a better predictor of the effects of governmental policies than is the assessment of people's short-term self-interest. Further, Sears and Funk argue that busing is not the only governmental policy where racial attitudes play a stronger role than self-interest. They argue that racial tolerance or intolerance plays a strong role in the acceptance or rejection of policies toward neighborhood integration, affirmative action, health insurance for the poor, and bilingual education.

Returning to the study of risks, the researchers chose samples of college students in both the United States and Japan. Student samples are much maligned because they often represent a choice based on convenience to the researchers rather than on the possibility of answering carefully formulated questions. The researchers thought about these issues and carefully defended their choice of participants.

> [M]any of the risks being assessed are the result of recent developments in science or high technology. Proper assessment of these risks, then, requires some awareness on the part of respondents, and this is more assured with college students who are generally more informed on such matters. . . .
>
> Colleges and universities are likely one setting where the impacts of changing values and attitudes are first experienced. This means, in turn, that we would expect college student samples from two advanced societies, ceteris paribus, to be more similar than samples drawn from other settings. The net effect of the expectation is a more conservative, and therefore more rigorous test, of cultural differences (Kleinhesselink & Rosa, 1991, p. 17).

The argument about conservativeness in research is important. When researchers call their tests conservative, it means they accept the fact it will be hard to discover differences—in this case, between respondents in the United States and those in Japan. College students in the two countries have some similarities. Their ages are similar and they attend classes, read newspaper stories about technological breakthroughs, worry about the dangers associated with premarital sex, and so forth. If differences are found among respondents in the two countries despite these similarities, then the researchers can claim strong support for the answers they provide to their original research questions.

Translation

The researchers used the back-translation procedure in a manner similar to the recommendations made earlier in this chapter. The English original was translated into Japanese, and this version was then back translated into English. After revisions, the procedure continued until the meanings of the English version, Japanese version, and back-translated version were equivalent as judged by (a) comparisons of the two English versions and (b) an independent review of the Japanese version by two bilinguals.

Results

Separate analyses of data gathered in the two countries indicated that people use two culturally common factors when organizing their perceptions of risks. One is the degree a risk is known or unknown, and the second is the amount of dread people feel toward the risk. Cultural differences occurred in the degree these factors played a role in the thinking of Americans and Japanese when they considered a given risk. For example, the risks associated with nuclear power (war, weapons testing, waste disposal) were rated as more known to the Japanese, and the items clustered together more for the Japanese than for the Americans. One reason, of course, is that the Japanese have firsthand experience with widespread nuclear destruction as a result of atomic bombs dropped on Hiroshima and Nagasaki in 1945. None of the results could be considered culturally specific or emic; that is, no factors guided the thinking of people in one country but not the other. One reason, as discussed previously, is that the researchers did not include individual items that identified risks in one country but that might be far less familiar in the other.

Future Research

One indicator of a good research study is that it stimulates important follow-up work. Less important studies may be printed, but others who might have used the results to formulate new and more sophisticated research questions may ignore them. One of the risk study's results was that the Japanese, compared to the American respondents, felt that the AIDS epidemic is a more familiar risk. This is a surprising finding because the number of reported cases is far lower (both in absolute numbers and as a percentage of the population) in Japan than in the United States.

So how can a risk be perceived as more familiar in one country compared to another despite far fewer reported cases? This is an important research question. Possible answers might be found in the educational system in Japan, where high school graduates read the newspapers more often than American high school graduates. Another possibility is that the Japanese mass media has done its job so effectively that the AIDS epidemic is perceived as familiar despite fewer actual cases. A more dynamic possibility is denial among American respondents. In the presence of many cases, people may find comfort in thinking that the epidemic is not so common as to be called "familiar." Still another possibility is the Japanese wariness of elements from outside their culture. The AIDS virus was introduced to Japan by outsiders who had sex, shared needles, or shared contaminated blood with Japanese nationals. The distrust of any outside factor is a familiar concept to the Japanese, whether that factor is a new idea in higher education, a new group of immigrant workers, or a new way of marketing consumer products. The Japanese familiarity with the concept "wariness toward outside influences" may have led the students to attach it to the AIDS epidemic. The key point for consideration here is that such thinking about future research questions could not occur without the results about risk perceptions Kleinhesselink and Rosa (1991) reported.

C H A P T E R 4

SOCIALIZATION

CHAPTER OVERVIEW

As part of their childhood and adolescence, many people wonder what it would be like to be a member of their friends' families. This natural curiosity serves people well when they examine family life in cultures other than their own.

Socialization refers to the experiences in which children participate so that they eventually will become productive and responsible adults. Many of these activities take place in families, so parents often are referred to as *prime socialization agents*. In cultures where extended families are common, aunts, uncles, older cousins, and grandparents also share the responsibility for socializing children. Such socialization is quite distinct from that of children in cultures with nuclear families, that is, where the typical family consists of parents and children and where contact with extended families occurs only on special occasions.

Cultures provide the settings children participate in while learning skills that are necessary for later successes in adulthood. Social class criteria such as family income, parents' occupations, and amount of formal education provide different settings and consequently encourage the development of different skills. Children from the middle class, for example, are encouraged to master social settings where intellectual curiosity is valued. Such children spend time in libraries and as entrants in science fairs. Children from the working class spend time in social settings where obedience and deference to authority are emphasized. One reason is that parents feel these skills will be useful when the children seek jobs where they will take orders from supervisors.

Complexity is added to discussions of socialization when social change is considered. The skills necessary for adult success are not the same generation to generation, as shown by children whose computer skills are far better than their parents. As families move across cultural boundaries as part of immigration, old skills from people's culture of socialization may cause stress in the new culture. Women in some

Asian countries may have been socialized to defer to men, for instance, but they become unhappy with this expectation when they earn salaries after immigration to another culture. Children always actively participate in their own socialization, and this becomes especially clear among immigrant families. Given that they attend the new culture's schools and interact with age peers in their communities, they often learn the new culture's language faster than their parents. This can cause stress in the family if it interferes with traditions of respect for elders and deference to parents.

Adolescence brings unique challenges. All cultures recognize a period of years beyond childhood but prior to the time when people are expected to assume adult responsibilities. Culture-common features of adolescence include the importance of the peer group, the need to control sexual expressiveness, and adult expectations that adolescents make various contributions. Possibly, adolescence also involves a "time-out" period when young people are tolerated if they break a culture's norms. After this period, however, adults expect young people to settle down and to accept responsibilities such as full-time jobs, marriage, and parenting.

This chapter discusses all of these socialization issues.

PREPARING FOR THE COMPLEXITIES OF ADULTHOOD

Children are born into a world, in the classic words of William James (1890), that is little more than a "blooming, buzzing confusion." The total set of experiences in which children participate so that they eventually cease to be totally confused and instead become respected members of a culture is called *socialization*. An important point to constantly keep in mind is that children can behave in many different ways and can engage in many different types of experiences (Child, 1954; Segall, Dasen, Berry, & Poortinga, 1990; Super & Harkness, 1997). An important part of socialization is that children are guided away from this total set of possible behaviors. Instead, they are encouraged to engage in the more limited set of behaviors considered acceptable and important within a culture (Spiro & Swartz, 1994). The people responsible for the socialization of children are a culture's elders. Parents are universally involved in socialization, but which other elders become involved varies across cultures. In different cultures, elders other than parents include grandparents, uncles and aunts, teachers, employers (if children engage in work for pay or apprenticeships), religious figures, coaches, and so forth. Age peers also can play an important role, especially in cultures where adult men and women work outside the home (Dong, Weisfeld, Boardway, & Shen, 1996; Sinha, 1988).

Many scholars make distinctions among types of socialization experiences (Camilleri & Malewska-Peyre, 1997). The term *enculturation* refers to the experiences that encourage children and adolescents to become respected members of a specific culture. Other types of socialization activities, to be discussed in this chapter, lead to individual differences within the broad term "becoming respected members of cultures" and to movements beyond one's culture of birth. These experiences include those associated with birth into different social classes, with social changes within a culture, and with movements across cultural boundaries, such as when people immigrate to another country. Because much of the discussion in this chapter (and later in the book) deals with dynamic cultures, with individual differences, and also with the experiences of people moving across cultures, the broader term *socialization* often will be used.

One reason socialization is often a hard topic for analysis is that all people participated in enculturation experiences without thinking about them very much. People have been so close to these and various other socialization experiences in their lives that it is difficult to take a step back to analyze them. As with many important aspects of culture that are part of people's lives, the best way to understand a concept is to examine how it influences behavior in other parts of the world. An example of the difference between "total possible behaviors" and the "fewer behaviors acceptable in a culture" is useful for understanding socialization processes. Recall the discussion of individualism and collectivism in chapter 2, and review Figure 1 on page 55. Assume you are 14 years old and are at a family gathering with grandparents, aunts, uncles, and cousins attending. One of your 8-year-old cousins is rowdy and loud and keeps running around and bumping into the furniture. What are your possible behaviors? You could discipline your cousin through physical punishment. You could shout at your cousin to stop. You could try persuasion. You could call an adult's attention to the problem. Or you could wait for an adult to become irritated enough to take action. The "fewer acceptable behaviors" are learned during socialization, and a 14-year-old considered a "responsible young person" in a given culture would be expected to behave within this more limited set of possibilities.

In collective societies, as noted earlier, people are socialized to view themselves as part of a group, and the most common group is the extended family (Georgas, et al., 1997). To keep the group functioning well, harmony is a prime value. People are expected to look after one another and to correct one another if a problem can be avoided. In a collective society, 14-year-olds are expected to take an active role in the disciplining of 8-year-old cousins. Consequently, the more active behaviors (physical punishment, shouting) from the list of possibilities are considered appropriate. In fact, if 14-year-olds do not discipline the naughty cousins, the adults might chastise them for not behaving properly. By the time children reach their 14th birthday, they would have been socialized to take this active role.

In contrast, people in individualistic cultures are socialized to be more independent of groups. They are close to a nuclear family but do not as often identify with their larger extended family. Consequently, adolescents are not expected to take an active role in disciplining their younger cousins. They would be expected to choose from the more passive set of total behaviors available to them (e.g., calling the problem to the attention of adults or simply waiting for adults to intervene). If they choose a more active behavior such as striking their cousin, they might be punished. Even the intervention of uncles can be unclear at best and inappropriate at worst. When I was a rowdy youngster, it was very unclear whether or not my uncle should intervene or whether he should wait for my father to notice the difficulties I was causing. One reason involved change. Earlier my uncle had been involved because we saw him daily. Then my parents moved, and we saw my uncle monthly. In individualistic societies, the issue of disciplining children by anyone other than the parents is complex and problematic. This is seen in elementary, junior high, and high schools, where teachers sometimes find it difficult to keep order and to engage in their main duty (the education of youth!) because of the limitations placed on what they can do with boisterous students.

Various concepts are useful for analyzing how children learn to participate in their culture and how they learn to adjust during times of social change. Five conceptual approaches are discussed in this chapter:

1. Socialization takes place in a cultural context, and cultures provide the settings with which children are expected to become familiar.

2. The social class into which a child is born affects both his outlook on life and the opportunities in life from which he might benefit.

3. Social change can affect how parents interact with their children when familiar socialization methods, remembered from the parents' own childhood, are no longer appropriate.

4. Children are active participants in their own socialization and affect the behavior of adults and peers as they attempt to learn skills valued in their culture.

5. Adolescence may be a universally recognized phenomenon with unique challenges, especially in times of cultural change toward "Westernization" and "modernization."

SOCIALIZATION INTO A CULTURAL CONTEXT

One of the most important ideas in cross-cultural analysis is that people's behavior can be understood only as it relates to the social context where people live and work (Berry, 1984; Cole & Scribner, 1974; Gauvin, 1998; Super & Harkness, 1986). Think of the example already reviewed. The behavior of the 14-year-old can be understood only in relation to a social context: whether the family at the gathering is individualist or collectivist. People can consider a given behavior (physical punishment or simply waiting for an adult's intervention) appropriate only if they understand the behavior's context. It is especially interesting to examine behaviors that are perfectly appropriate in a specific setting within one culture but absolutely boorish in a similar setting within another culture. Consider the following short example where the social setting consists of an informal dinner party at someone's home.

Kiyoshi, a Japanese executive, was visiting an automobile plant in the American Midwest and was exploring the possibility of a joint venture involving the manufacturing of a new car model. Hank, an executive at the plant, wanted to show Kiyoshi (who was traveling with his spouse) some American hospitality. So he invited Kiyoshi and his spouse to dinner at his house. After a prompt arrival at the agreed time of 6:00 P.M. and after some pleasant conversation over soft drinks ("No one drinks hard liquor any more!" Hank thought), dinner was served at 7:00 P.M. After they had cake for dessert at about 8:15 P.M., Kiyoshi and his spouse thanked Hank for his thoughtfulness and walked slowly toward the door. Hank thought something was wrong, either with himself or with Kiyoshi's manners, because he left right after dessert was served. What went wrong?

Hank and Kiyoshi were socialized into different cultures, and, as noted earlier, these two cultures give guidance in the narrowing of the range from "total possible" to "fewer appropriate" behaviors. In Hank's culture, people spend time with one another and engage in pleasant conversation after dessert. If people leave early, it is taken as an insult: "They only want our food, not our company!" In Kiyoshi's culture, remaining after dessert is served has a far different purpose. If he stayed, Kiyoshi would be communicating, "We are still hungry." Hank then would have to search his house for more food if he were behaving according to the norms of Kiyoshi's culture. The two behaviors, remaining or leaving, can be understood only in relation to their context. Here, the context is best described as "a social setting at someone's home where food is served."

In other settings, the meanings of the behaviors would be quite different. If the setting were a business meeting and if the Japanese were to stay beyond the time when the Americans thought the meeting would end, it could indicate an interest in the negotiations. The longer period might be necessary for the Japanese to understand the proposal thoroughly and to think about ways to communicate the key points both to their supervisors and to their employees. It is also important for all the Japanese at the meeting to understand the entire proposal, so some of their time would be spent explaining key points to one another. Americans in such a setting might interpret the extended meeting as a sign of discontentment and might feel they have to make concessions to maintain interest among the Japanese. For the Americans, it would be far better if they spent the time patiently explaining their proposal to their Japanese colleagues. In doing so, the Americans would be demonstrating their good will and understanding of Japanese business practices (Cushner & Brislin, 1996; Tung, 1984).

Once more, the key point is that behaviors can be understood only in relation to their social settings or cultural context. The same general behavior in Japan, remaining in the setting, can have quite different meanings depending on the purpose of the gathering. Part of socialization is the learning of such proper behavior/social-setting combinations. An interesting result of increasing intercultural contact is that virtually all people, as adults, will have to learn new combinations to interact successfully with people from other cultural backgrounds. In fact, training programs to prepare people to interact effectively in other cultures (Bhawuk, 1990; Brislin, 1989; Landis & Bhagat, 1996) frequently recommend that people learn to label the various social settings where they find themselves. Then, they can attach recommended sets of behaviors to these labels. In the prior examples, for instance, American business-people would say to themselves, "OK! I'm in a business setting. If the meeting runs long, this may be a sign of interest rather then a request for concessions. I should patiently go over all the points in the proposal, and they will appreciate this effort."

Cultures Provide Settings

The concept that behavior can be understood only as it relates to various social settings is centrally important to an understanding of behavior in different cultures. Whiting (1980) has pointed out that more attention must be given to understanding the various settings children are exposed to while developing appropriate behaviors.

In fact, she emphasizes that culture affects the way children are socialized by providing the collection of settings where they learn to behave according to the culture's norms. Consequently, understanding the differences in settings children are exposed to allows insights into cultural influences on behavior. A reasonable generalization is that in all cultures children are expected to interact side by side with their parents or another elder and to learn gradually some of the skills expected of adults (Greenfield, 1984; Rogoff, 1990; Valsiner & Lawrence, 1997). Cultural differences reside in the exact settings and in the skills necessary in those settings. In some cultures, children are exposed to the fields where crops are raised; in others, to the pastures where cattle graze; and in still others to the vast areas outside a village where game might be hunted. Just as with the concept of socialization in general, settings are often not thought about because all people have learned appropriate behaviors in many settings while not consciously aware of this fact.

Not all settings involve the exotic jungles and elaborate holiday festivities pictured in issues of *National Geographic* magazine. In many cultures, an important setting is the area just outside the home where adolescents are expected to look after their younger siblings while parents earn incomes at various work sites that are distant from their residence. In middle-class homes around the world, the side-by-side tasks parents and young children are involved in center around books and television (Cashmore & Goodnow, 1986; Lambert, Hamers, & Frasure-Smith, 1979; Tulananda & Young, 1994). Parents read to their young children and ask questions about picture content and about the various letters in words. Parents also might watch the same television shows as their children and then ask questions about the shows' content. When engaging in these activities, parents are guiding their children into behaviors appropriate in and for settings the culture defines as important. One of the settings, of course, is "the nuclear family as a center of preparation for school," a concept important in virtually all advice teachers give to parents interested in a smooth transition from the home to the early years of a child's formal schooling (Chao, 1996; Lindgren & Suter, 1985; Wright, Taylor, & Ruggiero, 1996).

SOCIAL CLASS AS A PROVIDER OF OPPORTUNITIES

Given that most adults have had at least some interactions with people much wealthier and much poorer than themselves, one of the most effective ways to discuss socialization is to examine the influence of people's birth social class (Brislin, 1988; Frable, 1997; Kagitcibasi & Berry, 1989; Thurow, 1987). A discussion of social class also permits an introduction to some interesting research that compared the relative influence of social class and culture on parents' socialization practices. Finally, the discussion allows some speculations about socialization practices around the world given the movement toward democracy that occurred in many nations during the late 1980s and early 1990s and that undoubtedly will continue into the 21st century.

Social class refers to the position of people within a society in terms of prestige, power, and influence. Within North America and western Europe, important markers include people's income, the amount of education they have attained, the prestige of the job they hold, and the reputation of the neighborhood where they live. Across a large and complex society, at least four social-class levels can be found (treatments that describe more levels are based on subdivisions of these basic four):

1. A wealthy upper class whose members can afford items their culture considers luxuries

2. A comfortable middle class whose members can afford the necessities of what their culture considers a pleasant lifestyle

3. A struggling working class whose members experience uncertainty about job stability and ownership of necessities

4. A frustrated underclass whose members are frequently if not constantly faced with unemployment and little hope of positive change

The latter two are sometimes combined and called "the lower class." These markers are useful for initiating efforts to understand social class in all parts of the world, but other indicators (culture-specific factors or emics; see chapter 3) must be added for a more complete analysis. These other markers (which vary across countries) include the status of a family name and bloodline, the names of patrons or protectors, religion, the infrequency of physical labor associated with jobs, time available for scholarly pursuits, occupational skills, social skills, and the prestige of the segment of society into which a person is born. Countries with a caste system are probably the clearest examples of the influence of birth into specific segments of society.

One aspect of people's culture is the ease versus the difficulty of moving beyond one's social status at birth. In some cultures (e.g., India: Biswas & Pandey, 1996; Sinha, 1990), people's caste is a major influence on what they are permitted to do throughout their lives. In other cultures, people can move beyond their low status level at birth and have a much wider range of opportunities available to them as long as they have the appropriate income, occupation, education, and skills they can offer employers.

In many countries, a family's income is the central influence on class standing, and other markers are associated with it in predictable ways. In North America, for example, income is influenced by the amount of education people have received (D. Gilbert & Kahl, 1982). In turn, income influences how much education parents can offer to their children. Given a certain level and type of education, people then can pursue careers in prestigious occupations, which, of course, then usually brings in high levels of income (N. Brown, 1997). People's income, in turn, influences the amount of money they can spend on housing in different neighborhoods. The various status markers are thus interrelated. When an inconsistency of some sort occurs, people can become uncomfortable because they don't know how to relate to individuals who demonstrate the inconsistency. Some people who make much money, for instance, have little formal education. They may have the income to be considered members of the upper class, but they may not have the intellectual interests or the social graces that longtime upper-class members consider proper.

Inconsistencies are also important when people analyze intercultural contacts. Many foreign students from Asia who study in the United States, Canada, or western Europe decide to remain in the country where they studied rather than return home. This contributes to the problem known as "brain drain," because their skills would be valuable in their home country. A major reason, however, is the inconsistencies they would face should they return home. They may have earned an advanced degree after four years of very hard study but might foresee a very low paying job awaiting them should they return. Or they may have been born into a low-status group, and no matter how much education they receive, they will still carry the label of that low-status group.

One of my colleagues from India (a full professor at a U.S. state university) was not born into the highest caste group. If he returned to India, he would have limitations placed on his career given his modest birth. In the United States, he has faced no such limitations. As many readers surely will agree, few people in the United States care one bit about the caste of intelligent and well-educated Indians they meet. Interestingly (and consistent with studies of brain drain: Glaser, 1978; C. Ward, 1996), my colleague remained in the United States to give more opportunities to his three children. "Their social mobility is open in the United States, based on their abilities and work. If I returned to India, they'd have the same limitations placed on them as those I would face."

Social Class and Socialization

Based on research with more than 4,000 respondents, Kohn (1977) argues that parents from different class backgrounds emphasize different values when raising their children. Middle-class parents, for example, emphasize self-control, intellectual curiosity, and consideration for others. These values can be seen in a typical American childhood event many readers undoubtedly will remember: birthday parties for 5- or 6-year-olds. Self-control is encouraged by the arrangement of events. For instance, children learn to wait to open their presents and to dig into their cake until all the guests have arrived, introductions made, and games played. The value of intellectual curiosity can be seen in the typical presents given to children: books and, now that the 20th century is ending, videotapes. Children at the party also are encouraged to ask questions of adults and to take the party as an opportunity to learn new information (e.g., new party games, new songs, new comic characters depicted in the presents given). Consideration for others is shown in attempts to encourage everyone present to become involved in activities and in parental guidance such as "lets wait for everyone to finish their ice cream before opening presents." This description might seem very culture bound, but, to preview an interesting research finding discussed more fully in the next section, these activities are very similar among middle-class people in various countries. I have been to children's birthday parties organized by parents from a number of different countries (e.g., Japan, Nepal, India, Indonesia), and the structure of the parties is very similar. Certainly, differences arise in the exact games played, in the sorts of books given as presents, and in the snacks available to children. But the commonalities of children as the center of attention, of encouragement to take into account the feelings of others, and of control of impulses are striking.

When socializing their children, working-class parents emphasize obedience, neatness, and good manners. One set of activities considered good manners is that children are expected to be quiet and almost invisible when adults are present

(D. Gilbert & Kahl, 1982). Rather than interact with adults so that they have opportunities to have questions answered, children are expected to be quiet and to entertain themselves in a room other than the one where the adults are talking. These emphases have implications when the children become adults themselves and enter the workforce (Offermann & Gowing, 1990). Children of the working class have learned to be comfortable with external standards in contrast to their internally set goals. They have learned to accept what other people consider good manners, and as young adults they have limited experience making suggestions to and requests of authority figures. In contrast, on entering the workforce, middle-class young adults have certain advantages given their experiences during socialization. They are more comfortable with self-starting and self-instigated behaviors and more easily ask questions of and make requests of their supervisors (Watkins & Regmi, 1996). The skills they learned as children during interactions with adults (asking questions, making their wishes known) are useful in the work world.

Again looking at the world of work, Kohn (1977) further concludes that middle-class children are better prepared than working-class children to accept, as young adults, managerial and professional jobs that demand intellectual curiosity and good social skills. For instance, an important social skill that good managers have is that they can understand and empathize with the needs of their employees, even if the employees are not very clear in communicating their opinions and feelings (Greenberg & Baron, 1997). Note that this important skill comes from the empathetic understanding and consideration for others that were encouraged during their middle-class socialization. In contrast, working-class children are more prepared to take as young adults wage labor jobs that involve physical effort and that are closely supervised. They accept such jobs partly due to less emphasis on intellectual curiosity in their childhood and partly due to their parents' concern for external standards and obedience to authority figures. This concern for obedience to parents and adult relatives emphasized during childhood prepares them to obey the external standards a visible supervisor in the work world sets. One way to summarize these findings is to point out that middle-class children are socialized to earn a good income by using their minds and their interpersonal skills. Working-class children are socialized to earn an income by using their hands and other physical labor.

Do possible points occur in the lives of working-class children and adolescents when interventions can increase the chances of developing skills useful in managerial and professional careers? The answer is yes, but I have to return to a basic point introduced earlier. Income is the key factor in discussions of social class. Adolescents can develop managerial skills through various community activities that occur outside the home. I'll examine what are probably the most common examples of such activities: participation in school clubs, athletic teams, and service projects for the community. While participating in these activities, adolescents can learn to set goals, to work hard toward their achievement, to bring in the viewpoints of others, to work through bureaucratic rules, to meet influential people in the community and to deal with them (Brislin, 1991), and so forth. Students from the working class, however, participate in fewer such activities than their middle-class peers (Lindgren & Suter, 1985). Family income has its impact: Working-class adolescents often have after-school jobs so that they can earn money both for family necessities and for basic needs such as acceptable clothes and a reasonable number of social activities. After-school work might be a source of possibilities for the managerial skills development discussed here. However, most jobs available to adolescents are closely supervised and do not involve the choice of activities and the self-directed movement within these activities that encourage the development of managerial skills.

Class and Culture

The effects of social class are very strong, and this point has been underemphasized in studies emanating from the United States (a point argued by Brislin, 1988, and Kagitcibasi, 1990). One reason for this underemphasis is based on cultural values. As discussed in chapter 1, a culture is defined partly by the values its people should have (even if they slip sometimes in putting those values into practice). One value in the United States is that Americans are members of a classless society. The U.S. Declaration of Independence states that "All men are created equal." This cultural value includes the belief that given access to universally available education and the possibilities people have to improve themselves through hard work, anybody who tries can move upward within society. The research findings that indicate advantages given to middle-class children are at odds with this value. These findings are uncomfortable for Americans to consider because they have so little experience discussing social class. Recall chapter 1: If people accept a value (classless society), they don't have to talk about it very much. Recent findings that indicate the effects of social class on career possibilities (Frable, 1997; Kohn, 1977), on achievement in school (Yando, Seitz, & Zigler, 1979), on performance on standardized tests (Burg & Belmont, 1990), on recovery from failure experiences (Moghaddam, Taylor, Lambert, & Schmidt, 1995), and on health (Belle, 1990; S. Taylor, Repette, & Seeman, 1997) are difficult for Americans to discuss.

Another important relationship between class and culture is that the effects of one can be much stronger than another. In two studies comparing child-rearing practices in different countries and among various ethnic groups within Australia (Cashmore & Goodnow, 1986; Lambert et al., 1979), the researchers were surprised to discover that class differences were stronger than cultural differences. In the Australian study, for example, working-class parents from both Italian and Anglo backgrounds emphasized "being neat," "having good manners," and "being obedient." Any differences that might have been attributed to the Italian versus Anglo background of the parents was eliminated or decreased when the parents' educational level was taken into account. Specifically, the least-educated parents from both Italian and Anglo backgrounds preferred neatness, manners, and obedience in their children. These findings have an important implication for future research: Studies of cultural differences in the socialization of children will be considered inadequate unless the children's social class background is taken into account.

I am no more comfortable about discussing social class differences than most Americans. Yet I believe more good than harm would come from such discussions. Without an acknowledgment of class differences, people are left with the need to find other reasons for why children from various segments of society are clearly achieving less in school and in the workplace once they reach adulthood. If the children have a different skin color, then "race" or "racial differences" are used to explain poor achievement. Of course, this leads to vicious attacks on people and leads to conclusions that some people are biologically inferior. If the focus, instead, were on the advantages and disadvantages that class brings, race would enter the discussion far less frequently. Yando, Seitz, and Zigler (1979) are three researchers who have been sensitive to this important point about class differences. In a study of 8-year-old Black and White children from different class backgrounds, these researchers found that racial differences meant little. Achievement differences were far more strongly related to social class. Regardless of whether they were Black or White, advantaged children (from homes whose parents had adequate incomes) chose harder problems when asked to make their own choices on a reading task. The advantaged children were also more confident about their abilities. Interestingly, some of the disadvantaged children (from homes with unpredictable incomes) had good intellectual skills as shown by their scores on intelligence tests. However, the fact the children came from disadvantaged homes had a stronger impact than their intellectual abilities. As the researchers summarized, "Indeed, it is striking that even the most capable disadvantaged children showed such low expectations of their abilities" (p. 88).

Even with good intellectual skills, then, the disadvantaged children were not confident that they could use their abilities for the reading task. Robert Cialdini (1990) has suggested that a metaphor can help people understand this important issue. Cialdini says that middle-class children grow up in surroundings that are like a successful farmer's fruit orchard. The children can look around and see apples, oranges, peaches, and plums growing from trees. They certainly will have to make some effort to pick the fruit and will have to learn to use tools such as ladders to perform this task, but the opportunity to harvest fruit is present. Less advantaged children, in contrast, look out of their neighborhoods and are more likely to see unhealthy and barren trees. Even if they possess the necessary abilities to harvest fruit and to learn to use the required tools, they don't see the possibilities of putting their abilities to use. Disadvantaged children are less likely to be socialized into a set of expectations that they can obtain society's benefits and rewards through their efforts (Schutte, Valerio, & Carrillo, 1996).

SOCIALIZATION, FAMILIARITY, AND CHANGE

Earlier, Whiting's (1980) insight that culture provides a collection of settings children become exposed to was discussed. An addition to this insight is that culture encourages children to become familiar with and comfortable in a number of situations so that they know how to achieve their goals. Some children in some cultures become familiar with settings where agricultural, fishing, hunting, and herding skills are valued. Other children (more in the highest than the lower socioeconomic levels) become comfortable with settings where they learn from teachers who introduce reading from books, writing on paper, and oral presentations to both adults and peers. Young women in some cultures are not encouraged to read and write but instead learn to become comfortable in domestic settings where child-rearing, cooking, cleaning, and spouse-nurturing skills are valued.

People are socialized, then, to be quite familiar with a number of social settings so that they can achieve their goals (adequate food supply, academic accomplishments, obedient children) and can be considered valued members of a culture. When a culture is stable for many years and when people wish no more than to obtain the goals available in these social settings, little discontent arises within a culture. Difficulties emerge in times of social change when people are not familiar with the new or modified settings in which they are expected to participate (Berry, 1990; Berry & Sam, 1997; Wagner, 1988). One reason for increased stress in people's lives is that, given changes in the settings they were once comfortable with, people are unfamiliar with the behaviors necessary to achieve their goals (Liebkind, 1996; Moghaddam, Ditto, & Taylor, 1990). People were not socialized into knowledge of the skills necessary in the new and modified social settings rapid social change brings.

A simple example familiar to virtually all readers should make these points clear. Unmarried men and women might meet in many settings: classrooms, laundry rooms, offices, churches, and so forth. Who usually makes the first offer of a date, the man or the woman? When I ask this question of students, they complain that today's society doesn't give much guidance. Thirty and 40 years ago, in the United States, the answer was clear: The man was expected to make the first move and was socialized to do so from the early teenage years. With the emphasis on women's rights and gender equality that has occurred over the past 25 years, the commonsense answer is that women should be able to ask men for a date should they choose to do so. But socialization hasn't caught up with social change; women were not socialized to be comfortable with this task. According to my students, one (probably one of many) solution is that a woman will ask a man to lunch, perhaps to a lunch with four or more people attending. But it is up to the man to figure out that this is a display of the woman's interest, and it is up to the man to suggest a one-on-one date with more "serious" signals, such as a weekend dinner at 8:00 P.M. in a nice French restaurant with dim lighting and an expensive wine list.

The distinction between how people were socialized to behave so that they could achieve their goals and how these socialized behaviors are less useful given recent and rapid social change is important for analyzing behaviors all over the world. I believe the world movement toward democratic governments will continue to cause the sorts of changes that will challenge the behaviors people learned in an earlier era (Brislin, 1991). Democracy requires the careful consideration of numerous candidates for leadership positions. This is uncomfortable for people who were socialized to never disagree publicly with leaders. Democracy involves respect for, or at least tolerance of, people whose opinions are different from one's own. This respect for plurality is not a universal part of people's socialization. Democracy implies respect for the contributions all sorts of people can make, whether they are minorities within a culture, women, immigrants, and so forth. Cultures where people socialized their children to make very clear distinctions between classes of people will find this aspect of democracy a challenge. This difficulty also applies to those who emphasized gender differences when permitting people to obtain such societal benefits as higher education and entry into the professions.

Sinha (1988, 1997) has analyzed social change in India and the challenges change has brought to familiar behaviors learned during socialization. It is useful to review

Children in extended families, in which aunts, uncles, and grandparents may take part in raising

his research in some detail because I believe these changes and challenges will be seen in other parts of the world into the 21st century. Sinha points out that the changes include increases in people's per capita income, food surpluses in some parts of India in contrast to the famines of past years, increases in the amount of education people receive, and recent legislation covering property rights, inheritance, women's rights , marriage and divorce, and minimum wages. These changes have altered traditional relations between powerful landowners and impoverished peasants, interactions within extended families, and the relative power of the traditional caste structure. Referring to a culture's most important institution in children's socialization, the family, Sinha (1988) points out that "conferring rights on women and making divorce laws easier have dealt a fatal blow to the traditional pattern of joint family [relations] and have even generated familial tensions" (p. 49). The total collection of changes in India are marked by their all-embracing nature, their rapidity, and the fact they unfold in a nonorderly, unpredictable sequence. In the following discussion, I

them, have very different socialization experiences than children in nuclear families.

will draw from Sinha's (1988, 1990) analysis of socialization in India. I also will integrate research and examples from other parts of the world and will ask readers to recall some of their own socialization experiences.

Move Toward Nuclear Families

Families have moved away from a structure that kept extended-family members constantly communicating with one another, sharing resources, and providing instant availablility for emotional support in times of trouble. One reason is the growth of cities and the types of jobs available in industrial economies. Rather than depending on the extended family, people can move beyond their traditional collective and find employment elsewhere. Once people earn an income through their own efforts that are clearly independent of their extended family, they are likely to become oriented toward self-interest rather than a collective interest. It is important to note that the meanings of *self-interest* and *selfishness* do not overlap totally. When applied to the move toward nuclear families, *self-interest* still refers to looking after parents (if not married), spouses, and children. The linkages that become weakened are to extended-family members such as grandparents, aunts, uncles, and cousins. Sinha (1989) discusses this move, called *nucleation*, in his own life. He remembers when he was a young man in India that he spent a great deal of time with uncles and cousins. Although still in India in the 1990s, he points out, his family consisted of himself and his spouse. He moved away from the area where his extended family lived to receive his university education. He accepted employment in a city, again away from his extended family. He had children, but they also went to the university and accepted very good jobs in various parts of the world. His grandchildren live with their parents, so Sinha and his spouse see them only during their occasional visits. Sinha, then, has experienced a move toward nucleation within a society where people traditionally experienced close collective ties among extended-family members.

When the members of a traditionally collective family are not distant from each other, in contrast to Sinha's case, nucleation can have collective features, Kagitcibasi (1988, 1997) points out. Nuclear families can be the economic unit, but they still can remain emotionally dependent on the extended family. When extended-family members are ill, want to share joyous events such as weddings or graduations, or need counseling and solace in times of personal difficulties, relatives beyond the nuclear family frequently become involved. Grandparents still can be important figures in their grandchildren's socialization. Still, the absence of daily contact takes its toll. Recall that socialization involves becoming familiar with various settings. One difficulty social change brings is that children need to be socialized into their culture (a) that has become different from what their parents experienced and (b) whose socializing events are not yet well developed. Referring to Sanua's (1980) work on the supportive environment a well-functioning family can provide, Sinha (1988) points out that in the traditional Indian family children could interact with many people. If they were having temporary difficulties with a parent, a grandparent, aunt, or uncle could provide support. It is important to point out that the parents were quite aware of and comfortable with such support, remembering times in their own childhoods when the presence of extended-family members was important. Children were not "putting something over" on their parents by seeking out others. With nucleation, however, these other people are not always present for the children. The difficulties parents and children inevitably experience with one another can intensify into severe problems if the buffers the extended family provides are absent.

Segregation of Children From Adults

The traditional Indian family socialized its children through constant interactions among extended-family members, many of whom lived under the same roof. Through observing the interactions of many adults, including observations of problem-solving behaviors that inevitably occur when people interact in close quarters, children learned the necessary skills to become respected members of their culture (Joshi & MacLean, 1997). Children also were socialized to view themselves as part of the emotional lives of their extended-family members. They were not separated from adults as frequently as children are in North America. When guests came to visit a family, for instance, children were not put in a separate room and were not expected to amuse themselves someplace other than where the adults interacted. Rather, children were integrated into the events involving the guests, and they learned about interactions with other types of people by observing and participating in family-member/guest relations.

With nucleation, children do not have this large number of adults around for learning daily lessons. Children are likely to spend time alone or with age peers and, consequently, become emotionally separated from adults at an earlier age than before. Although the separation in years past occurred when children went to school, it occurs today when adults are no longer in the house during daylight hours. Separation from the large number of extended-family adults occurs at birth after nucleation. Separation from an adult whose traditional role involved constant nurturance during infancy and early childhood can occur when the mother decides either to join the workforce or to reenter the workforce a short time after the child's birth. When mothers take jobs outside the home, they must become consciously concerned with their children's socialization. Such concern is itself an important change, given that mothers didn't have to think about socialization very much in generations past with helpful grandparents and aunts present. Another result of mothers entering the workforce is that institutions external to the family must become involved, such as day care centers. Whatever people think of day care centers, positive or negative, it is important to note that many mothers have not been socialized themselves to become familiar and comfortable with these institutions.

The Move From Nurturant to Stricter Child Rearing

Traditionally, Indian families indulged their children during the first two or three years of the children's life. Someone was always available to hold, cuddle, and talk to the baby, and body contact between caretaker and child was frequent. Breast feeding frequently extended into the child's third year, far longer than common in Europe or North America. The extensive body contact provided a great deal of security for the child. Other aspects of child rearing were traditionally nurturant. Parents felt no pressures to toilet train children at any particular age. Children learned to eat, walk, talk, and dress themselves on their own schedule, without extended-family members comparing notes about which age this cousin or that neighbor achieved these milestones.

Social change has led to a stricter style of child rearing. Rather than follow the children's preferences about times for eating, sleeping, and playing during a given day, adults are more likely to schedule these events. They give more attention to "proper" ages to wean children from their mother's breasts, to toilet train children, to have children dress themselves, and so forth. Adults present lists of "dos and don'ts" to children and expect children to distinguish acceptable from unacceptable behaviors at an earlier age than in generations past. One reason for these recent pressures is, again, the absence of multiple adult caretakers. When only the parents are present regularly, they feel less stress if they encourage strict standards (e.g., food at certain times, rather than at any time the child desires). When both parents are working, they understandably do not have the energy to jump up and down during the evening to meet the unrestrained and unscheduled needs of their children. Another factor to consider is the presence of people or institutions external to the family. When neighbors as caretakers or day care centers become involved, they strongly prefer toilet-trained children who can meet a regimented schedule of eating, playing, and napping.

Whenever social change occurs, people will disagree about whether to behave in traditional ways or to behave according to new practices they observe (Berry & Sam, 1997). Most readers will have experienced this fact. The traditional practice in many parts of the world is that husbands and wives live in the same home in the same city. Currently, with both men and women desiring important and influential careers, some dating couples are willing to consider living in different cities and participating in a "commuter" marriage. Other couples find this possibility unacceptable and have to work toward a compromise of either alternating cities or finding a city where they can both work and find acceptable (if not the most advantageous) jobs. Sinha (1988) points out that such disagreements are frequent in India, and they can have impacts on children. With respect to traditionally nurturant compared to more strict child rearing, it is easy to imagine a marriage where the husband prefers one style and the wife prefers the other. When parents disagree, however, their children have more difficulty adjusting to school and achieving scholastically (Kakkar, 1970).

Inconsistencies in Raising Children

Parental disagreements about how best to raise children lead to problems that stem from unclear, inconsistent, and sometimes contradictory standards. If the disagreement is between traditional and the still unclear and unfamiliar contemporary methods, children may be rewarded one day and punished the next when they engage in the same behaviors. One result is that children become anxious because they cannot meet these unclear and inconsistent standards.

During social changes, the sources of rewards and punishments are also unclear and inconsistent. Traditionally, Indian mothers were not expected to discipline their children. The people expected to punish children, when necessary, were fathers, elderly aunts and uncles, and sometimes grandparents. Mothers were expected to be the sources of affection, so children knew where to go when they needed positive attention. Given the absence of extended-family members, mothers have to share the disciplinarian role with fathers. Even if women prefer to act in the traditional manner (in India) of offering only love and affection, they will need to discipline their children on various occasions. Their spouses may have to work late, may be traveling on business, or may be ill. In such cases, mothers have little choice but to combine the roles of affection giver and disciplinarian, even though they are unfamiliar with ways to manage this combination. Children, then, have to adjust to mothers who offer both rewards and punishments. This becomes confusing for them if they have cousins or friends whose mothers can behave in the more traditional manner and if their mothers are uncomfortable with the task of administering both rewards and punishments.

When both parents work, the problem becomes more complex in nucleated cultures. Parents not only have less time to devote to child rearing, but also they cannot present clear sex-role models to their children. Under traditional extended-family norms in India, mothers took care of domestic tasks and fathers worked outside the home (Durodoye, 1997). When both parents work, the various duties around the home are more likely shared. Further, children quickly learn that two people, not just one, provide the family income. If this state of affairs is given only quick consideration, many readers will applaud it and will point to the fact the children have a more complex, potentially more enriched set of role models they might emulate (Moghaddam et al., 1990). Young girls in India, especially, will have more opportunities for a full life if they can move from the traditional expectation that they must be no more than wives and mothers. This eventually may be true, but currently parents are still trying to work out their income-producing and domestic duties because they are unfamiliar with this combination from their own socialization. When the parents are confused and unclear about their own appropriate behaviors, children become anxious because they do not have consistent rules to follow and clear models to emulate.

Absence of Role Models

In addition to the anxiety that stems from models who are themselves unclear about appropriate behaviors, other implications center around the adults children might emulate. Under the traditional extended-family system, children had a number of role models whom they might respect and with whom they might identify. If for some reason a young girl did not find her mother an acceptable role model, she would have aunts, older cousins, and grandmothers to consider. Currently, given nucleation, these other people are not in daily contact with the primary family, so young girls do not have the constant presence of multiple models. Gatherings of the extended family still occur, but these visits among relatives differ from the constant presence of people living under the same roof. In addition, far fewer individuals are available to tell children about the culture's mythological figures and to relate its lesson-giving folktales (Rothbaum & Xu, 1995; Vitz, 1990). Parents often are too busy and tired to take on this important task. Grandparents used to pass on such tales of history and heroism, but, as has been mentioned several times, they are absent from the children's daily lives. Their lack of exposure to such folktales and histories has its own set of implications. Children do not learn about great figures who behaved in ways the children might emulate or, in the case of villains, make a point of not emulating. Children also are less prepared for the transition to formal schooling. Teachers might expect incoming children to know some of the culture's folktales and to know about some important historical figures. Children also would have less practiced listening skills. Teachers might be disappointed and label children as "slow" if they lack such knowledge.

The Changing Status of Women

Severe limits traditionally were placed on the roles women could accept in many cultures. Wife, mother, and agricultural and domestic laborer covered much of the acceptable range of opportunities. Recently, governments have given attention to the political and legal rights of women. Written statements about these rights admittedly can be formulated more quickly than people's everyday and comfortable acceptance of the changes. But, even so, more opportunities for women are available. But as women achieve prominent positions in the various professions, this places pressures on families where women traditionally accepted a subservient role. When women bring in money to their families, they naturally want their opinion respected about how the money is to be used. But the men in these cultures are uncomfortable with this type of change (Durodoye, 1997; Kapur, 1970). Husbands like that their wives are working and bringing in money, but they are uncomfortable with the changes this brings to the traditional manner decisions are made in the family. Men also may feel the women are neglecting their domestic and child-rearing duties given their participation in the professions. Many readers are familiar with these difficulties either in their own lives or among their married acquaintances. They also are familiar with the demands expecting women to be "superwomen" who can effortlessly hold a job, raise well-behaved children, and attend to the needs of their spouses. The conflicting demands stemming from women's desire to advance in their professions, to maintain domestic harmony, and to be good mothers eventually lead to stress, tension, and anxiety (Hanassab & Tidwell, 1996; Sinha, 1988).

If the traditional extended family is no longer a reality in the lives of married couples, parents must find an alternative to the practice of leaving children with grandparents and elderly aunts. Day care centers have sprung up, but their use separates children from their parents' socialization preferences. Instead of parents offering socialization settings, children in day care centers turn to their peers. Children share socialization experiences among themselves, and in so doing learn about their culture from one another. With their attention given more to their peers, children no longer are socialized into the extremely strong ties of the traditional family. This probably leads to greater ease when the children themselves move out into society to seek further education and employment, but it means the traditional family structure is further weakened. This ease of movement from a conformity-demanding family into society can be viewed as a positive change by some, but this sort of change causes anxiety and tension until people become comfortable and familiar with its implications. One implication is that young adults become much more independent if they move away from their traditional neighborhood as they participate in peer group activities. They may become more adept at seeking opportunities where they can meet adults outside the family, at accepting new challenges, at developing their own opinions about a variety of important issues in their communities, and at discovering how to solve problems on their own. This independence may be unwelcome, however, if fathers accept the more traditional view that their children should conform to their fathers' wishes and views about important social and political events.

The Effects of Migration

Another and quite different change in people's lives has affected relationships within the family in many cultures. In the search for a better life, nuclear families move from rural to urban areas. Although the major reason for migration is the quest for better jobs for the father and (as discussed previously) possibly the mother, children accompany their parents and recently have accounted for 50% of migrants. Migration has predictable consequences, and these are seen in many urban areas around the world, not just cities in India. The extended family is left behind in the rural village, and all child-rearing responsibilities have to be assumed by the parents, who have not yet become comfortable raising their children without help from relatives. The nuclear family has to adapt to the city's unfamiliar lifestyle, with its more impersonal norms for everyday behavior (Button & Bart, 1998; Kagitcibasi, 1997; Yang, 1988), its strangers who cannot be called on in difficult times, and its unfamiliar bureaucracy needed to provide services such as education for the children and medical care. Given that newly arrived families do not yet have much money, they cannot afford good housing and often must live in shacks handmade from scraps or in rundown buildings in slum areas at best and in public areas (e.g., under bridges) at worst. In such areas, the basic necessities of life, such as water, sanitation, and protection during foul weather, are frequently absent.

The fact of migration from rural areas to the city is a frustration for planners, politicians, government officials, and concerned citizens all over the world. It is easy to wonder why people leave their rural areas and accept the squalor, poor living conditions, and uncertainty of employment in big cities. However, several important points should be kept in mind. One is that village life should not be romanticized as something that is pleasant and problem free. Villagers often have to submit to the whims of powerful and uncaring landowners. Land is often poor given the number of years it has been used and the high cost of fertilizer. The backbreaking work necessary to provide even a minimal standard of living for a family causes health difficulties and premature aging. When considering the move to a city, sometimes stimulated by news from friends and relatives who left the village in years past, people are not seeking to turn their lives around. Rather, they are seeking to improve their lives by a small but noticeable amount.

The city does have attractions that lead to the possibility of a better life. Schooling could be more available for the children, so even if the parents are unsuccessful in improving their own lives, they know its possible their children will do better given the opportunities from achieving a formal education. Both men and women can be more independent when they leave behind the landowners and traditional village leaders who often demand unquestioning deference. Despite the problems many migrants face with chronic underemployment, even part-time work can bring in more money to the family than could be earned back in the village.

Although this migration discussion has focused on developing countries such as India, people all over the world face decisions about whether to remain in a rural part of their country or to move to a big city. Readers might consider this decision as it affects their own lives. Big cities in industrialized nations such as the United States have high crime rates, poor air quality, expensive housing, and high taxes. So why do some people choose to live in them rather than in small towns? Reasons will vary, but they include prestigious jobs with high salaries, stimulus from cultural events such as operas and symphony orchestras, the excitement of living where important events are happening, and far more choices for leisure time activities. Some people do not enjoy being reminded of childhood mistakes that occurred during their socialization in small towns, and they escape these memories by welcoming the impersonal norms of big cities.

The general point, then, is that people who move to urban areas expect improvements in their lives. Especially for villagers in less industrialized nations, these changes are often accompanied by potential psychological difficulties. Migrants are forced to adjust to many new norms and values in big cities, and the new challenges they face can overwhelm their resources for coping with difficulties (Golding, Karno, & Rutter, 1990; Hsiao-Ying, 1995; Peeters, 1986). Many migrants undoubtedly expect much better treatment in the city than they actually receive. They may expect decent housing, ease in finding jobs, and adequate schools for their children. These expectations may have been fueled by letters from their relatives who painted an overly positive picture of city life so that people who remained in the village would see them as resourceful and intelligent. The difference between expectations, set up by the letters, and the reality experienced in the city is one cause of stress.

Readers might examine this distinction between expectations and reality in their own lives. If people think back about a stressful episode, they might ask themselves, "In retrospect, was the episode as stressful as I thought it was at the time? Or was the resulting stress due to the difference between what I expected and the reality I found?" For migrants to the city, others have few opportunities to intervene in the migrants' lives so that expectations can be brought closer to reality. The result is psychological disturbances, including such psychosomatic disturbances as problems with digestion, sleeplessness, headaches, back pains, and so forth. The difficulties then have negative impacts on the migrants' quest for such goals as employment and acquiring housing, compounding the problems originated by the difference between expectations and reality. City life is stressful for everyone living in less-than-ideal conditions, but it is higher for recent migrants (Thacore, 1973) who have not yet learned the necessary skills to cope with problems they have never encountered before (Biswas & Pandey, 1996).

To summarize some major points, social change brings about clear and visible changes in people's lives, such as technological innovations (television, telephones) and greater ease traveling away from the community where people were born. Also, less visible changes within people's lives can cause anxiety and stress, especially among children who are experiencing the changes themselves and who do not have clear adult role models who can provide guidance. These less visible changes include the following:

- Movement away from the extended family (Kagitcibasi, 1997)
- The segregation of children from adults
- Stricter norms for child rearing in contrast to the indulgence of children more common in the past
- Inconsistencies in child rearing due to disagreements within the family
- The absence of role models who are confident how to behave in the face of these multiple changes
- The desire of women to seek a wider variety of opportunities than were available in previous generations
- The effects of migration from rural to urban areas

The key to understanding the difficulties that arise from social changes is not the changes themselves. Rather, difficulties arise because parents cannot call on widely accepted and familiar socialization practices to raise their children to be responsible members of the culture. The parents were socialized into a different culture from the one their children are experiencing today. They remember a culture based on an extended-family structure, women who accepted limited roles, nurturant child-rearing practices, and so forth. Faced with many social changes, parents are unsure about how to raise their children, and this lack of clarity causes anxiety and stress among the children. Interventions have been developed to lessen the difficulties social changes bring, and they will be reviewed in the next chapter, which deals with various informal and formal educational programs.

Children's Involvement in Their Own Socialization

In this analysis of socialization in India (Sinha, 1988) and elsewhere, a number of points relate to a more general theme that is becoming increasingly important in cross-cultural research. This theme is that children play an active role in their own socialization. Children are not solitary learners, sitting back passively waiting for instruction from a role model and then practicing new behaviors by themselves. Rather, children actively participate in a complex social world where they constantly interact with people and, through their behavior, have an impact on exactly what happens during their interactions with others. In Sinha's analysis, this theme was touched on a number of times. For instance, when children from traditional extended families had difficulties with a parent, they could approach an aunt or grandparent for nurturance. When children were exposed to one set of relatives who behaved according to traditional role demands and to other relatives who had accepted recent social changes, they could choose models to emulate. This admittedly caused stress in their lives, and their choices could cause conflict within the nuclear family. When children do not have the constant presence of adults in their lives, given that both parents may be working, they do not sit back and wait for the occasional guidance adults might offer. Rather, the children seek out alternative socializing agents and turn to their peer group for participation in new learning experiences.

Rogoff (1990; Rogoff & Chavajay, 1995) has been especially influential in encouraging people to view children as active participants in their socialization rather than as passive recipients of information. She views socialization in a manner consistent with ideas already presented here: Children are exposed to various social settings where they learn to achieve various goals. The goals can be the acquisition of skills, such as reading, weaving, or medicinal plant uses, but they also can be of an emotional nature, such as the desire for affection and respect. If people understand the goals, together with the methods children and adults use to interact so that these goals can be obtained, then people can make real progress in understanding the complex question "How are children socialized to be respected members of a culture?"

Rogoff has been especially concerned with the cognitive development of children, so most of the examples reviewed here will deal with this aspect of socialization. She offers a framework that stresses three factors:

1. Children actively seek out and use guidance that various people can offer in the children's efforts to attain goals.

2. Children and adults participate in arrangements of activities that are uniquely designed to help children attain their goals. Some of these arrangements involve very explicit instruction ("Never play with matches!" after mothers comfort children who have burned themselves). A less frequently analyzed set of arrangements involves *tacit* instruction. This term refers to settings where adults offer instruction to children without conscious awareness that they are encouraging children to learn and without awareness of exactly how they are modifying their behavior for the young learners. Still, the arrangements are routinized because they can be observed in the behaviors of different adults interacting with different children. For example, good adult athletes simplify their instructions to children about how to use a baseball bat, tennis racquet, or hockey stick. Even the best adult coaches may not be able to tell others exactly what their thinking is when adjusting to the children's skill level. The knowledge is tacit, but it is also routinized because different adults present information to children in similar ways.

3. Cultural differences can be found in the goals adults and children have as they participate in the many activities helping children grow to adulthood. Cultures also differ in exactly how "children achieve a shared understanding with those who serve as their guides and companions through explanation, discussion, provision of expert models, joint participation, active observation, and arrangement of children's roles" (Rogoff, 1990, p. 8). Several examples taken from studies in various cultures will be discussed later, but a few remarks here may help make these concepts clearer. In some cultures, adults explain the steps necessary to complete a task in detail, and children are expected to learn these step-by-step procedures. Many readers will remember the specific steps they had to learn before their mathematics teachers allowed them to complete the solutions to complex long-division problems. In other cultures, children observe adults carry out a task as a set of interrelated behaviors that are not broken down into steps explained in words. When children feel they are ready, they work on the task until they meet a stumbling block, and then the adults intervene with guidance on how to overcome the difficulty. This guidance may involve verbal instruction, the modeling of exact behaviors, or both, depending on the methods commonly accepted in a given culture (Karpov & Haywood, 1998).

Guided Participation

A key concept Rogoff employs throughout the analyses that use this three-part framework is called "guided participation." As children learn the tasks necessary to obtain their goals, they participate in activities with people (often adults but sometimes age peers) who know more than they do about a certain knowledge area or skill. These people give various types of guidance, adjusting their behavior in various ways to meet the needs of the children who desire to learn from them. The guidance is tacit or explicit, and either children or adults take the responsibility for making arrangements so that learning can occur. Borrowing heavily from the writings of Vygotsky (1987), Rogoff emphasizes that guided participation includes the building of bridges that allow children to move from their present skill and understanding levels to higher levels. It also involves the structuring of various activities so that children can reach these higher levels, with the level of responsibility the children assume changing over time. An important underlying factor in guided participation is "intersubjectivity," or a shared understanding between learners and people who are more expert. The understanding involves such features as the degree of expertise the learner wants to achieve, the learner's skill level in relation to task mastery, and the feelings of shared success between learners and teachers when progress is made. As children interact with different experts in their communities who encourage accomplishments in various skill areas, children increase their understanding of the many problems that well-adjusted adults have to solve in their culture.

Children's Involvement in Guided Participation: Examples

As with all aspects of socialization when analyzing cultural differences, people should keep in mind the *goals* of guided participation. For example, children must learn what adults consider good manners while eating and proper behaviors related to personal cleanliness. Cultural differences in table manners and personal hygiene have been the basis for many misunderstandings when North Americans and Europeans travel to India, Indonesia, Nepal, and other countries in South Asia (Cushner & Brislin, 1996). For example, Bob, visiting friends in India who were students with him a few years ago at an American university, wants to express his appreciation for the hospitality he has received. He takes them to a nice restaurant. After ordering their food, the dinner party members give Bob a small gift, which he takes in his right hand. When the first plate of food arrives, Bob doesn't bother putting his gift down on the crowded table and accepts the plate, sets the plate down, places a little food on his dish, and then passes the plate on, all with his free hand. From the expressions on their faces, Bob realizes he has made a mistake but can't figure out exactly what he did wrong.

The difficulty arises because Indians are socialized to believe the two hands have very different functions. The right hand is the "clean" one and is for eating. The left hand is "dirty" and is used when eliminating one's solid waste. People from many other parts of the world do not make this strong distinction and, instead, switch hands for various tasks when convenient.

At what age is this distinction learned? Freed and Freed (1981) observed that children in India are expected to make this distinction about the use of their hands between 1½ and 2 years of age. If a child does not learn the difference by observing others and through everyday participation in eating and hygienic behaviors, the mother or sister intervenes. One of these socializing agents guides the child's right hand for eating while holding down the left. This intervention continues until the child behaves in the proper way. Note how guided participation is part of how the child learns the correct way to behave. The involvement of a mother or sister continues only as long as necessary. The outcome of the socializing process is impressive. Two-year-olds can tear a piece of chappati (an Indian bread) with their right hands, pick up vegetables with the chappati, and put the combination of foods in their mouths.

As previously discussed, much learning that takes place during socialization is tacit. One aspect of tacitness is that adults encourage the children to learn in situations the adults might not consciously label as good places to master important skills. Baseball coaches, for instance, almost always will point to participation in team sports as an opportunity to learn physical skills. They do not always, however, label participation in team sports as an opportunity to learn important social skills, such as cooperation in the pursuit of commonly accepted goals (Brislin, 1991). The teaching of physical skills is explicit; the teaching of social skills is often tacit. Gaskins and Lucy (1987; analyzed by Rogoff, 1990, pp. 124–126) presented an important analysis of how children learn what is important to know in their communities, not just in their own homes. In the Mayan culture in Guatemala, children can wander about their villages. They are exempt from such social norms as "don't eavesdrop" and "mind your own business." Children can observe adults working, talking, and interacting in other ways with one another. If an adult comes along and begins to observe the other adults, social norms dictate that the observer and the observed must engage in some sort of social interaction. In a sense, children are considered "nonpersons" whose presence adults do not need to acknowledge.

If Mayan mothers are confined to their homes because of such domestic duties as cooking or raising infants, they can send their children out to observe village events and to report back later. In this way, mothers keep up with current events and village gossip. The concept of guided participation applies to part of this process because of the questions the mother asks of her children. The children learn what aspects of social events are important from the content of their mothers' questions. If they can't answer a certain question after an afternoon of wandering around the village, they modify their behaviors on their next venture so that they can answer their mothers' questions the next time. The mothers' questions thus guide the children's behavior. Children learn who in the community is important, the exact places where the most eventful happenings occur, the places they are "supposed to" avoid but where they should go to get information nevertheless, and so forth.

Insights From the Work of Jean Piaget

Rogoff (1990; Rogoff & Chavajay, 1995) integrated her work on guided participation with the observations of children's cognitive development made by the Swiss psychologist Jean Piaget (1966, 1970). Space limitations prevent an extensive discussion of Piaget's many contributions (for further discussions, see Dasen, 1984; Dasen & Heron, 1981; Flavell, 1963; Ginsburg & Opper, 1969; Mishra, 1997), but a few examples provide additional insights into adult-child interactions during guided participation.

Piaget's contributions are best introduced if readers imagine participating in a psychological study that uses one of the most frequently employed tasks Piaget designed: water conservation. Imagine that a psychologist has a beaker 10 cm tall and

Five-year-olds think a tall container (with a small diameter) has more water than a shorter container with a wide diameter when both have the same amount of water.

10 cm in diameter. The beaker is full of water. The psychologist then pours the same amount of water into a much taller beaker that is 4 cm in diameter. When the beakers are placed together, which beaker has the most water? Adults, of course, have no difficulty answering that the amount of water is the same: It simply has changed its shape (i.e., the amount of water is conserved). Children of about age 5 often answer that the tall beaker has more water. Five-year-olds attend to the height that the water reaches and cannot set aside this visual cue to focus on the underlying reality that the two beakers have the same amount of water. Many 8-year-old children, however, answer in the same way as adults: The amount of water is the same; it just has changed shape. Eight-year-olds are also impressed with the height of the water in the second beaker, but they have developed a set of rules that allow them to manipulate concrete ideas (here, the amount of water they see) in their minds. If readers know children of various ages (son, daughters, nieces, nephews), they might try this short experiment. Bowls and tall drinking glasses work well in informal demonstrations if beakers are not readily available.

Piaget and his collaborators placed 5- and 8-year-olds at different stages of cognitive growth. The four stages and the approximate ages that apply follow:

1. *Sensory-motor intelligence* (birth to about 2 years old). Children learn that a physical world exists independent of their own perceptions. They learn, for instance, that an object they are familiar with has an existence even if they can't see it. During these early years, for example, children learn that the book they had been playing with still exists even if a blanket is covering it.

2. *Preoperational stage* (2 to 7 years old). Children learn that objects and events occur even when they cannot be seen or heard, but children do not possess a set of rules that allow manipulations of these objects and events in their minds. Returning to the water conservation task, they do not have a rule that allows them to judge that the amount of water is the same in both containers. Glickman (1983) argues that, "In summary, the preoperational child is the prisoner of its own immediate perceptual experience and tends to take appearance for reality" (p. 215). He also provides the interesting example of a magician who entertains a group of 4-year-olds. If the magician pulls a rabbit out of a hat, it does not impress 4-year-olds because to them rabbits might be anywhere: a hat, a cage, a zoo, or in the park. The visible evidence of the rabbit is important to 4-year-olds, not the "impossible" place it comes from.

3. *Concrete operations stage* (7 to 11 years old). Children have developed a system of rules that allows them to manipulate concrete objects such as water, clay, or even pencil marks on paper as they learn to do addition and subtraction in school. So they are accurate on the water conservation task because they can manipulate thoughts about the volume of water in their minds. And they can be impressed with magicians because they know that the originally empty hat should not have a rabbit in it.

4. *Formal operations* (11 years old and older). Children not only can manipulate ideas about concrete objects but also can manipulate ideas about abstract concepts such as people's intelligence and motivation, ethics, morals (Eckensberger & Zimba, 1997; Miller & Bersoff, 1995), and so forth. For example, assume children and adolescents are confronted with this problem: A boy tries to help his mother clean the house and accidently kicks a cupboard door, leading to the breakage of 15 cups. Another boy tries to take some cookies from a container, even though his mother told him not to eat before the big family meal. This boy accidently kicks a cupboard door, leading to the breakage of 1 cup. Which boy behaved badly and thus should be punished? Children who have reached the formal operations stage are far more likely to take into account such abstract concepts as "motive," "intent," and "explanatory factors." They focus on the less desirable motives of the boy who broke 1 cup. Young children often focus on the breakage of 15 cups and say the boy who caused this extensive damage should be punished.

Extensive cross-cultural research (Dasen & Heron, 1981; Mishra, 1997; Segall, Dasen, Berry, & Poortinga, 1990) has led to the conclusion that this sequence of stages is universal among children around the world. The exact ages for the stages can be influenced by the types of stimulation found in children's daily environment. The sons and daughters of potters, for instance (Price-Williams, Gordon, & Ramirez, 1969), sometimes reach the concrete operations stage at a relatively early age because they help their parents knead clay. They become used to the fact the amount of clay is the same whether it is a round ball or a flat pancake. Children who are exposed to ethical dilemmas in a social studies class or as part of religious study (e.g., is it acceptable for an adult to steal bread if that is the only way to feed one's starving child?) receive the type of stimulation that allows them to reach the formal operations stage at a relatively early age.

The conclusion about the universality of stages is based on careful research that examined culture-specific aspects (chapter 3) of children's experiences. In contrast, careless research has led to the conclusion that children in some cultures do not reach the higher stages. Often, this conclusion simply reflects that the researchers did not examine the typical experiences of children (e.g., pottery, other stimulation in their daily environment, religious study). Rather, they imposed unfamiliar tasks from their own culture on children. In the language of chapter 3, they imposed the emics of their culture and made incorrect conclusions about stages of cognitive development (an etic). If researchers are to make the significant conclusion that children from some cultures do not reach certain stages, they must be prepared to demonstrate that they presented children with familiar and appropriate tasks that make sense *given the children's past experiences*.

Returning to the discussion of guided participation, adults experienced at working with children undoubtedly modify their behaviors in response to the children's developmental stage. These adults rarely use Piaget's terms, but they become sensitive to the tasks children are capable of carrying out. Price-Williams and colleagues (1969) and Georgie-Hyde (1970) worked with the children of adult potters. The children were expected to help their parents, but the exact type of help depended on their developmental level. Children at the preoperational stage were expected to help their parents prepare clay but were not expected to estimate the amount of clay necessary to make a pot "quite a bit smaller than the one we made yesterday." Children at the concrete operations stage might be asked to make this estimate, but they would not be asked to suggest what new modifications might make a certain pot more useful for cooking. Children at the formal operations stage might be asked about such modifications, and they might be asked to make suggestions about new abstract designs that are consistent with the traditional ways of making pots in a certain culture.

An example of attempted guided participation that failed may make some of these points clear. My 6-year-old son was on a soccer team. One of the coaches, a very concerned man who had little experience working with children, brought a chalkboard to practice. He made abstract drawings that indicated the tasks the players should perform (fullbacks drop back to defend the goal, halfbacks kick ahead of themselves, forwards move up to receive the leading pass, and so forth). The 6-year-olds were supposed to understand the diagrams on the chalkboard and apply the lessons to their plays on the soccer field. As might be expected from a review of what children in the preoperational stage can do, coaching based on chalkboard use was unsuccessful. The children could not take the abstract arguments about proper strategy and apply it to their actual play. The coach figured this out on his own after two practices, and the chalkboard was not seen again. Instead, the coach made sure the children learned their tasks while actually practicing them on the playing field. He learned to effectively teach with guided participation. Teaching must take the existing abilities of children into account.

Children's Influence

An important point is that children can begin to influence their own socialization at a very early age (Best & Ruther, 1994). When children's behaviors cause their parents or other socializing agents to make responses that affect what the children learn, then all the people involved are participating in the guided participation process. When our daughters were very young, Susan Braunwald and I kept diaries of their language acquisition (Braunwald & Brislin, 1979a, 1979b). Braunwald was enthusiastic about the concept that children do not simply act as recipients of language and later show what they have learned in the utterances commonly called baby talk. Rather, children participate in social settings involving guided participation where they learn language along with the other important lessons about their culture. Laura is Braunwald's daughter; Cheryl is mine. All of the events described here took place in either California or Hawaii. When she was 1 year and 3 months old, Cheryl was with her mother at a bookstore. They were waiting for me to pick them up in our car. Two vagrants who had been drinking heavily were in front of the bookstore.

CHERYL: Hiya! Hiya! Hey, Hiya! *(while she waves and looks at the men)*
MOTHER: Cheryl, you'd say hello to anyone!

At that point, I arrived and all three of us left.

When she was 1 year and 6 months old, Laura was in the seat of a shopping cart in the grocery store. She was with her mother.

LAURA: Hi. *(to a strange man who passes near the cart)*
MAN: Hi, how are you?
LAURA: Fine.

Laura repeated this sequence a second time when the man was encountered again in another part of the store. (Both examples are from Braunwald & Brislin, 1979b, p. 103.)

Both children were learning the appropriate words to use when greeting people. But they were also learning some social rules: It is all right to greet some people, but not others. The process of guided participation is involved because the children's behavior affects the socializing agent's response. Cheryl began to learn that it is improper in her culture to speak to vagrants. The response she heard from her mother had a negative tone, and she was taken from the social setting so that she could no longer interact with the two men. In contrast, Laura learned that it is OK to speak to a well-dressed man who carries himself with a pleasant demeanor as long as she is in the company of her mother. Note that at 1 year and 6 months, Laura had learned an important part of an American conversational routine: The exchange continues for several rounds (as seen in Laura's response, "Fine," when asked how she is). Her mother approved of these conversations, as shown by Laura's behavior when the man was encountered again. If the social setting were different, for instance, if Laura had left her mother and run up to the man to initiate a conversation, the outcome would have been different. Laura's mother would have guided the participation into an important lesson in American culture, "Don't go running up to talk to strangers!"

One of the contributions of analyzing guided participation is that it points to learning opportunities that, whether present or absent, adults rarely examine, so it makes their implications explicit. As will be seen in the next chapter, on education, some children are guided into activities that allow them to take full advantage of the formal educational system. Other children have not been exposed to similar settings where they might have participated in the activities, and consequently they are at a disadvantage on their first day of school. Interventions are possible, but they are successful only if parents, teachers, and all concerned citizens recognize that socialization involves exposure to settings where learning takes place. Children who seem "slow" simply may not have had the same exposure as children who appear well prepared (N. Brown, 1997). If parents, teachers, and other responsible adults recognize that some children make smoother transitions across social settings than others, they are less likely to label the children as "slow" and will put resources into making the transitions proceed more smoothly. If children seem slow, they instead may be sending a message that "this transition is not smooth."

Children Send Messages to Adults

A basic point to constantly keep in mind when discussing any form of communication is that it involves a sender, a message, a means of communication (face-to-face verbal, television, etc.), and a receiver. If people accept the position that children can contribute to their socialization, this means children send out messages about their needs and desires. Parents and other adults sometimes miss these messages, and this becomes a source of stress for the children. Cushner (Cushner, McClelland, & Safford, 1996) uses this story in his public presentations and training programs for teacher trainees: A young student 10 years old (I'll call him "Bob") frequently left school about a half hour prior to the formal dismissal of all students. Teachers took note of this, his grades dropped, and he was called into the principal's office for disciplinary action. Other than this problem of leaving school early, he was a good student. Fortunately, one of his teachers asked the very intelligent question "Is Bob trying to tell us something?" After investigating, she found that Bob had figured out what days his stepfather would be likely to come home drunk. When drunk, the stepfather beat his mother. By being home at a certain time on certain days, he could distract attention from his mother, sometimes getting hit himself but at other times avoiding direct physical contact. The reason for retelling this story here is to emphasize that children sometimes give subtle messages that adults must make efforts to interpret.

THE UNIQUE CHALLENGES OF ADOLESCENCE

Many parents have observed that adolescents spend much time with friends their own age, that is, with age peers. In fact, one sign that young people are moving from childhood to adolescence is that they seem actively embarrassed to be seen with their parents. However, given previous discussions of culture-specific and culture-common concepts, many readers may ask: "Is this a feature of adolescence in general, or is it specific to a smaller number of countries or cultures?"

Many anthropologists (e.g., Schlegel, 1995a) have argued that adolescence as a life stage is most likely a universal and point to the documentation of its existence in various ethnographies gathered all over the world (Barry & Schlegel, 1991). Many languages have terms to capture a description of the age range between childhood but before adulthood. In addition to its probable universality, another generalization about adolescence is that it provides a period to prepare for adult responsibilities. Six features of adolescence with be discussed here:

- Culture's control over mating and reproduction
- The importance of the peer group
- Adolescent contributions to their communities
- The possibility that adolescence involves a time-out period prior to adulthood responsibilities
- The stresses frequently experienced during adolescence
- Parental responses to their adolescent children.

Many times, understanding social change is necessary to analyze adolescence as it is currently experienced in many cultures.

Culture's Control Over Mating

The future of any culture depends on the formation of families, procreation, and the multiyear socialization of infants. Adolescents often can produce children before they have positions within their culture that allow them to care for their children. Cultural norms, then, provide guidance that places limits on the activities of young adolescents that involve interactions with opposite-sex members. Schlegel (1995a) suggests that adults in all cultures recognize that procreation is so central to the well-being of cultures that controls are needed. No culture willingly allows adolescents to engage in sexual activity with whoever they want, whenever they want, and in whatever manner they want. Limits always exist. Within the term *limits*, the range is extreme. In some cultures, adolescent women dress so that they are minimally provocative to men, and women are subject to demands that they demonstrate virginity prior to marriage. In some cultures, premarital playfulness is OK, but it is supposed to stop short of sexual intercourse. In many cultures, once adolescents are ready to marry, the choice of a partner is seen as far too important to leave to youngsters who have not yet reached responsible adulthood. Marriages are arranged by parents and other members of the extended families, and often extensive negotiations occur between extended families. The sometimes-heard comment "People marry families, not an individual" is true in these cultures. Other cultures have accepted norms for interacting with opposite-sex members described by the term *dating* and involving, after a "dating period," personal choice of one marital partner. Many readers will say they would never consider an arranged marriage and may further argue, "I never had any limits placed on my choices of who to date." But on closer examination, they might realize adults imposed limits that focused readers' dating choices and, eventually, marital partner choices. For example, in the United States and elsewhere, adults arrange social events for adolescents, and the invitees to these events are controlled. Some adolescents are active members of churches and thus interact frequently with age peers who practice the same religion. After high school, adolescents go off to college and meet opposite-sex members who also choose college attendance rather than entry into the job market. Many adolescents, encouraged by influential adults, develop interests in specific aspects of their culture (opera, athletics, political action groups). They become so actively involved that they would find it difficult to marry someone who did not share these interests or political positions. The key point is that the decision to mate and to eventually procreate always is subject to a degree of control. That degree can be total (no premarital dating, parental choice of mate) or partial (control over the pool of people chosen for mates), but adolescents are not given complete free choice.

Peer Group Identification

When there are a number of adolescents in a community, they begin to spend large amounts of time together, often in same-sex groups. In fact, this is often a recognized mark of the move from childhood to adolescence. Time that used to be spent with parents is now spent with age peers, and opposite-sex friends from childhood join same-sex groups. Parents wistfully comment to each other that "our child is growing older" and also often comment that they seem to have less influence over their children compared to the peer group.

Various reasons have been suggested for the strength of peer group influence, which sometimes reminds observers of a force akin to strong magnets or glue. Two reasons will be reviewed here, one based on biological predispositions and one based on societal expectations, and they are not mutually exclusive. One possibility is based on facts in our evolutionary past. The life expectancy of people, thousands of years ago, was less than one third of what it is today. This meant many young teenagers were orphaned. One way for orphaned teenagers to survive might have been to bond with others so that they could look after one another, share resources, and prepare one another for adulthood. The motive to survive is extremely strong, so steps leading to survival would have become part of people's basic psychology along with the capacity to learn language, to seek rewards and to avoid punishments, and so forth.

A second possible reason for peer group influence is that the phenomenon of adolescence contributes to a major goal of child socialization. At some point, young people must break the strong bonds with their parents and establish families of their own. The strength of the break varies in different cultures, but it exists in some form everywhere. A period of interaction with age peers provides young people opportunities to move from the total dependence of early childhood to the far more independent responsibilities of adulthood. Often the adolescent peer group activities might be called "controlled rebelliousness." Young people signal their growing independence from their parents by engaging in activities their parents disapprove of to some extent. The extent can be mild to severe, but the disapproved target is recognized as such within the culture. Targets of mild disapproval can be the new terms adolescents add to the culture's language, the way they dress, the music they play or appreciate, the entertainments they frequent (e.g., professional wrestling), the changes they make in the culture's accepted forms of dance, and so forth. Targets of stronger disapproval can be drug and alcohol use, development of a tobacco habit, unsafe driving, inattention to study of required political documents the central government supplies, and premarital sex. At times, this rebelliousness can have positive consequences according to some standards. If adults in a culture are highly prejudiced toward members of a certain racial or ethnic group, the rebelling teenagers might reject these prejudices. Further, they may develop friendly relations with the racial or ethnic minority group members.

Work and Other Contributions to the Community

Even if adolescents practice some controlled rebelliousness, they make various types of contributions to their communities. These contributions also provide adolescents opportunities to develop useful skills for their adulthood. Teenage contributions can be clearly work related, and, of course, these differ from culture to culture. In less technologically developed cultures, the work can consist of activities related to farming, hunting, fishing, or the gathering of nondomesticated plants. In more technologically developed cultures, it can consist of activities often labeled as age specific, such as baby-sitting, delivering newspapers, and staffing fast-food restaurants. In many cases, these activities would not exist unless enough adolescents in a culture take responsibility for them.

The contributions also can take the form of providing entertainment for the community. In some countries, adolescents put on talent shows, make up the only large orchestra in a town, and participate in competitive team sports adults attend well. People interested in maintaining a culture's traditions sometimes bemoan the lack of adolescent contributions to these traditions given a youthful preference for more modern uses of their time. Among the Inuit in Canada, for example, time and energy that was once invested in traditional games are now displayed on special occasions that people label as "traditional" rather than the more spontaneous occasions of the past (Condon, 1995). Further, they invest time and energy in organized adolescent team sports with modern features such as aggressive competitiveness, leagues, officials, record keeping of wins and losses, and so forth. Schlegel (1995b) points out these changes have negative and positive points to consider. If negative points include the loss of traditional games and a greater tolerance for aggressiveness, then positive points include working within a bureaucracy and the development of leadership skills. If Inuit adolescents are to seek jobs within the larger Canadian bureaucracy, the development of these latter skills is useful.

Closely related to entertainment, adolescents also provide amusement for adults and the subject matter for their gossip. If adolescence is a time to prepare for adulthood, then adolescents surely will make mistakes during this preparation. They will say the wrong thing in a certain social situation, they will behave inappropriately during a ritual, and they will attempt adult behaviors but will fall short. For example, in some cultures limited male-female interactions are allowed that clearly fall short of the one-on-one date. Young men and women may try to make eye contact at a public event or may "accidentally" meet and exchange a few words. Adults keep track of who is engaging in these behaviors, which young men and women seem to be pairing off, and how skillfully they engage in these courtship rituals. Comments from an adult such as, "I was a lot more skillful than that adolescent!" are expected in these cultures. A feature of such commentary is that it contributes to the enforcement of norms. If on one of these occasions a young man and woman disappear for a long period, adults will no longer be amused. They will take disciplinary action.

A Time-Out Prior to Adulthood

Another feature of adolescence, perhaps more recent in its development and perhaps confined to highly industrialized nations, is that it allows a short time-out from the upcoming responsibilities of adulthood. Without explicitly stating their reasoning, adults in effect say, "Adulthood is stressful given the responsibilities of parenting, career development, caring for aging parents, and time demands from community groups. We'll allow teenagers to enjoy themselves a little before they have to join this pressure-cooker period known as adulthood." This acceptance of a time-out could be another reason for the tolerance shown for adolescents' mild deviations from adult norms, such as their less-than-perfect social skills.

At times, the time-out is institutionalized. In Japan, the academic expectations are very high. Teenagers must study very hard to pass a college entrance exam. Far less emphasis is placed on extracurricular activities and on the development of a "well-rounded personality" than in the United States. The strongly enforced expectation is that adolescents study hard and get good grades. One reason so many Japanese women stop working once they have children (Lebra, 1995) is that they want to help their children with their schoolwork. Adolescents go through a highly stressful "exam hell," sitting for a countrywide college placement test. Students with high test scores go to prestigious colleges, and graduation from them contributes immensely to the probability of getting a good job. This experience is so intense that a number of Japanese mothers I know have moved to the United States so that their children do not have to experience "exam hell" and its preliminary years of intense and stressful study. The mothers tell me, "I went through it, but I could never expose my own children to the intensity of that studying and formal testing system."

But once adolescents enter college, they have a relatively easy four years of study, or, in effect, an institutionalized time-out. The expectations of college students in Japan is not as high as in a good accredited college in North America. Students join clubs, go to parties, and in general relax for about four years. Then, at age 22 or 23, they seek jobs in organizations where demands on workers are intense and stressful. A colleague, Tomoko Yoshida, spent her undergraduate years at a university in Japan. She feels that a reasonable generalization is that for many Japanese adults, their most intense years of formal study ended at age 18 (Brislin & Yoshida, 1994). One of the jokes that demands quite a bit of intercultural knowledge is heard in the complaints of some Japanese students who study in the United States. They good-naturedly complain that they went to high school in Japan and then went to a demanding undergraduate college in the United States, so they never had their four years of time-out behavior!

The Stresses of Adolescence

Many adults remember their own adolescence as a relatively stressful period of their lives. Or at least they remember a number of stressful episodes they wish they could have avoided. When these people begin to look at behavior in other cultures, they ask the reasonable question "Does a culture exist where children make a transition to adulthood with no or relatively little stress or strain?" Researchers have discussed this question ever since Margaret Mead (1928) argued that teenage girls in Samoa had a relatively easy, stress-free adolescence.

A reasonable conclusion from more recent literature (Barry & Schlegel, 1991) is that adolescents all over the world experience stress. One reason stems from the purpose of adolescence. Because one of all cultures' goals is to prepare people for adulthood, researchers might ask whether adulthood has stresses. If it does, then adolescence must involve some stress so that people can learn to cope with it. Especially with creeping industrialization and modernization all over the world, adults encounter stress in their lives. They might deal with any of these questions: Who will choose a marital partner, me or my parents? How much formal schooling is best to prepare me for the world of work? Should I use traditional methods of farming, fishing, and herding or the modern methods suggested by university-trained experts? How many of my own children will I be able to support? Should I send my children to the city where they might receive more formal education or keep them in the village with me? These and a thousand other decisions can cause stress, and people might be ill prepared to deal with stress if they have an idyllic adolescence.

Recent research has examined possible culture-common and culture-specific stresses during adolescence. Bagley & Mallick (1995) administered a formal instrument known as the Adolescent Stress Scale in Hong Kong, Canada, and Great Britain. They found four culture-common sources of stress:

1. *Relationship problems*, such as poor interactions with other students in their schools. This was the strongest stress factor, and it is especially interesting given that adolescence is often marked by an extreme interest in peer group relations, as discussed earlier.

2. *Abuses at home*, and this can include physical abuse, psychological abuse in the form of perceived lack of respect from adults, and physical punishment that adolescents see as too extreme given their comparisons with the punishment others receive.

3. *Scholastic and career problems*. This type of stressor can include problems with courses and grades at school as well as problems with other forms of career preparation. As might be expected of industrialized nations, the item "examination and tests" in this category was emphasized the most in the three countries.

4. *Loneliness and social isolation.* Again, the importance of relationships appears in the test results, this time as stressful feelings from the possible effect of too many problems with others.

The study was designed to permit insights both into (a) cultural differences in the strengths of the four culture-common aspects of stress and (b) culture-specific aspects. One difference in the intensity of stress occurred among the items dealing with scholastics. Hong Kong students found tests and examinations more stressful than the others did. This is understandable given the educational system in Hong Kong. Hong Kong has few colleges and universities, so many more interested applicants exist than places for them. Test scores are taken very seriously in the admissions process, and students who do not receive good scores are denied entrance to college. This highly selective admissions policy has implications for the movement of people across national boundaries. Many students from Hong Kong who attend colleges in other countries are very intelligent but have difficulty demonstrating their academic abilities on standardized tests.

One of the study's results that is best called culture-specific is that sexual abuse of young women is found far more frequently in Canada and Great Britain than in Hong Kong. Several reasons for this are possible. One is that the crowded conditions of Hong Kong and the strength of extended families means that young women are frequently in the company of many adults. Further, young girls have influential adults (uncles, older brothers, family business partners) they can complain to if they feel a potential for abuse exists. Crowded conditions may bring problems, such as more adults to nag an adolescent about poor grades in school, but these same conditions may deter sexual abuse.

Parental Responses to Adolescents

As noted earlier, research on the socialization of children over the past 20 years has pointed to the need to examine parents' behavior, children's behavior, and the interactions between parents and children in various social settings (Chao, 1996; Joshi & MacLean, 1997; Super & Harkness, 1997). This point is especially true for the study of adolescence given the strains that can occur in parent-child relations during this critical period. Examinations of parent-child interactions are more complex than those that attempt to make conclusions about how children are socialized by looking, for example, only at the behaviors of parents. Many examples of these interactions have been presented in this book. Parents do not simply demonstrate behaviors that children should imitate. Rather, children often initiate interactions with their parents, who then can offer guidance about acceptable behaviors. Parents do not necessarily raise their children in a manner similar to the way they were socialized 20 or 30 years ago. Due to rapid social changes resulting in the absence of extended family members, the need for day care if both parents work, and the presence of children's peer groups, the more traditional socialization methods are often impossible to use. Parents do not always tell their children that certain features of their culture are important and thus should be given special attention. Instead, children discover the important cultural aspects through answering the questions their parents raise after the children report on their wanderings about the community.

Pettengill and Rohner (1985) argue that two major dimensions of parental responsiveness to their adolescents are the degree of the parents' acceptance or rejection of their children and the degree of their strictness or permissiveness in how they discipline the children. The first dimension, the degree of acceptance or rejection, involves how much warmth parents feel toward their children, and the second dimension refers to the amount of control the parents maintain over their children. Rohner (1986) has studied the effects of parental warmth and has documented the severe difficulties that rejection can cause for children.

Rejecting parents often dislike their children and resent the time and effort the socialization of children entails. They view their children as a burden, and they frequently compare them to other, seemingly better behaved children in their neighborhoods. Important indicators of rejection are parental hostility and aggression and neglect and indifference about the children's welfare. Rohner argues that parental rejection has predictable effects that are universal in nature. That is, parental rejection causes difficulties no matter where in the world it is found. Based on analyses of more than 100 societies, Rohner concludes that parental rejection leads to children becoming hostile and aggressive in their own lives. Further, they have problems managing their antisocial feelings and controlling them in schools, among their friends, and with their siblings. The children develop feelings of low self-esteem and view themselves as inadequate compared to age peers. They are emotionally unstable, develop feelings of distrust toward others, and have a difficult time establishing and maintaining close relationships. Close relationships, of course, involve emotional investment, and children of rejecting parents are less able to make this commitment to others. They have a negative worldview and are more likely to view their surroundings as the source of difficulties rather than as the source of opportunities. Finally, they are more likely to develop psychological problems that demand the intervention of professionals, such as social workers and clinical psychologists.

Returning to the point that socialization involves complex interactions between parents and children, recent research indicates that children's *expectations* of how their parents should behave also must be taken into account (Kagitcibasi & Berry, 1989; Liebkind, 1996; Pettengill & Rohner, 1985; Rohner & Pettengill, 1985). Research in Connecticut showed that among American schoolchildren, parental control was seen as a sign of overall hostility and rejection. Children were upset at their parents and thought of them as rejecting if the parents imposed large numbers of rules and regulations on the children. In sharp contrast, research in Korea and Japan showed that children viewed strict discipline as a sign that parents cared a great deal about them. Children in these two countries would be upset if parents did not maintain strict disciplinary standards. The key to understanding the cultural differences is to examine the expectations children develop based on the social settings they are exposed to in their lives. American children who view their parents as controlling are likely to have friends and classmates whose parents impose far fewer rules. Based on their interactions with these friends, children of strict parents can develop the view that they are being rejected. In contrast, the norms for strict discipline are more common in Korea and Japan (Farver, Kim, & Lee, 1995). Children there have far fewer opportunities to encounter social settings where friends and classmates expose them to standards noticeably less strict. Kagitcibasi and Berry (1989) summarized these findings by suggesting:

> In cultural contexts where strict parental discipline is prevalent and therefore perceived as normal by children, it is perceived not as rejection but as parental concern. . . . In contexts where permissive parental behavior is culturally valued, strict parental control is perceived as rejection. (p. 509)

Children often make the distinction between parental rejection and concern based on their observations of children from other families. If other parents are strict, any one child will not perceive his or her own strict parents as different. This is a classic example of cultural influence (chapter 1): The norms and values that are widely shared and practiced in a community come to be seen as normal and natural. One of the graduate students from China (Shanghai) who works with me remembers that her father regularly placed a clock on her study desk. He said, "You will study until the hands of the clock reach this point" (while indicating a time quite a few hours into the future). This student did not feel that her father was being overly strict because all her friends received similar attention from their parents.

Returning to the discussion about the potential within-family strains adolescence brings, researchers have looked at issues that occur when adolescents move across cultures. In such cases, another source of stress may arise. In addition to the already discussed typical complaints of many adolescents, further stresses may stem from the preferences of parents from one cultural background compared to the preferences of the peer group from another culture. Some of the most rapid social changes that involve important human behaviors occur in the area of children's preferences about their parents' behavior. Pettengill and Rohner (1985) asked Korean American adolescents about their parents' disciplinary practices. In all cases, the parents had been socialized in Korea and were living in the United States as permanent residents or as naturalized citizens. Approximately one half of the adolescents had been born in Korea and one half in the United States. The interesting research issue centered on the expectations of the Korean American adolescents. Keeping in mind that they are the sons and daughters of immigrants from Korea, would they view parental behavior more like age peers in Korea (where control is seen as concern for children), or would they view parental behavior more like age peers in the United States (where control is seen as rejection)? Readers might like to predict the results of the study. Pettengill and Rohner found that the Korean American adolescents viewed their parents in ways similar to those of their American age peers. The rapid change in expectations about parental behaviors is striking. "Within a single generation since their parents' immigration, the Korean-American teenagers perceive their parents' behavior, not as adolescents in Korea do, nor perhaps as their parents might expect them to" (p. 248).

These changes in expectations undoubtedly cause stress within Korean families. Where do the Korean American adolescents learn this set of expectations that differ from those of their parents? As was seen in Sinha's analysis of socialization in India, the peer group plays an important role. In addition, the teenagers are exposed to new ideas in the American educational system. For example, American students often are asked to make choices among elective courses and are encouraged to pursue their individual interests through choices among extracurricular activities. Some American teachers expect students to argue and to express disagreement with issues raised in the classroom. Students are exposed to other socializing experiences that emphasize less strict control over their behavior, such as the honor system while taking exams.

Thus children's views about how their parents discipline them cannot be understood without taking the cultural context of behavior into account. If the cultural context emphasizes loyalty to the family and filial piety, one set of expectations will be preferred. If the culture emphasizes individualism and freedom of choice, then children will favor a different set of parental behaviors. Stress within families can occur when a culture's institutions do not have consistent views about the roles of children (Cheung & Chan, 1996; Georgas et al., 1997). The Korean and Japanese parents, for instance, may expect deference to the views of the oldest male adult in the house. In contrast, the American school may expect that children formulate their own views and speak out in public, even when these views are different from those of the school's authority figures. A culture's formal educational system has strong effects on the people who participate in its many activities. These effects are discussed in the next chapter.

CHAPTER SUMMARY

Socialization refers to the total set of experiences children participate in that allows them to become productive adults, to express their individual differences, and to deal with major life changes. A culture's adults are responsible for socializing children. Parents are always involved, and other people become involved depending on the culture in which children are born: teachers, religious figures, grandparents, aunts and uncles, coaches, older siblings, and so forth. Socialization includes activities where children are guided away from certain behaviors and are strongly encouraged to engage in others. When angry, children might shout, hit somebody, plot revenge, or keep their feelings to themselves. Children learn which of these behaviors are appropriate and which are inappropriate, depending on their culture. At times, this guidance leads to behaviors considered proper in one culture but rude in another. For example, interrupting someone may be considered ill mannered in one culture but a sign of interest in what the person is saying in another culture (Carbaugh, 1990a).

Culture affects the way children are socialized by providing social settings with which members are expected to become familiar. These settings can include fields where crops are grown, pastures where cattle are grazed, or birthday parties where social skills are nurtured. Stress can occur when children are expected to move from one setting to another if the behaviors expected in the new settings are quite different. Children who are unaccustomed to seeing books around their homes, for instance, often experience stress when they start school due to their unfamiliarity with the new objects in the new settings. Other children who are accustomed to books, and to parents and older siblings reading books to them, often have a smoother transition to the new school setting.

A major influence on children's socialization is their social class when they are born. Middle-class parents in various parts of the world encourage their children to exercise self-control, to be intellectually curious, and to be considerate of others.

Children who develop these skills are likely to accept managerial and professional jobs that demand self-initiated behaviors, a respect for new ideas, and the ability to work well with others. Working-class parents are more likely to emphasize obedience, neatness, and good manners. In adulthood, working-class children are more likely to accept wage labor jobs that involve physical effort and that are subject to close supervision. Their greater comfort and familiarity with these types of jobs stems partly from their parents' downplaying of intellectual curiosity during socialization and partly from concern with obedience. Because wage labor jobs are closely supervised, children raised to be obedient are likely to be more comfortable with such jobs than their middle-class age peers.

Another reason for class differences is the expectations children develop about the world. If their parents always have brought in a satisfactory income such that the family could afford some luxuries, middle-class children grow up with a positive attitude about life's possibilities. They learn to view the world as an orchard full of fruit trees. They will have to work hard to harvest the fruit, but the opportunities for life's benefits are visible. If their parents were constantly struggling to keep ahead of their bills, in contrast, less privileged children are more likely to grow up with a more negative attitude. They may learn to view the world as a barren orchard where it does not make much difference whether they work hard or not. The fact that the social class into which a person was born provides different opportunities for development is difficult to discuss in some countries. In the United States, for example, a value reflected in the Declaration of Independence is that "All men are created equal. . . ." Given their familiarity with this value, many Americans are uncomfortable with discussions about the advantages and disadvantages birth into different social classes brings.

When a culture undergoes extensive social change, it often takes three or four generations for people to become comfortable with the new socialization settings. Parents may have been socialized in one way but find that recent social changes prevent them from socializing their children in similar ways. Sinha (1988) has pointed to seven types of changes in India that impact how children are raised, and many of these changes can be seen in other parts of the world.

1. Families have moved toward nucleation. Instead of the extended family of years past, with its collection of other adults to help parents with the demands of socializing children, the nuclear family of only parents and children has become more common.

2. In nuclear families, children are more likely to be segregated from adults. In traditional families, children had many opportunities to observe how adults interacted and how they solved problems when difficulties arose. With fewer people to observe in the nuclear family, children do not have as many opportunities to learn from large numbers of adults.

3. Given that grandparents and aunts aren't nearby to help with child rearing in nuclear families, pressures fall on the parents. In the past, someone always was available to nurture the children. Child rearing has become more strict due to the demands placed on parents in more recent years. Children cannot eat, play, and sleep when they want as in the more nurturant past. Because parents have

limited energy, they have to set schedules for activities such as eating and sleeping, leading to stricter rules affecting the child's preferences.

4. As with any set of social changes, however, some people prefer the traditional ways and some prefer more modern approaches. The mother and father may disagree about a nurturant versus strict child-rearing style, causing inconsistencies in the way they behave toward their children.

5. Given nucleation, children must learn from fewer role models. A grandparent or elderly aunt, for instance, has less of a chance to tell stories about the important historical and mythical figures in a culture. Visits from relatives become a special occasion, not a normal, everyday part of socialization.

6. Social changes often include greater rights, and more opportunities, for women. When women work outside the home and bring in money, they want their opinion respected when discussing how the money is to be spent. This demand for respect, however, may interfere with the man's expectations that he is the head of the household and makes all important decisions. When both parents work, children often turn to age peers for socializing experiences. Children are likely to become independent of their family at an earlier age than in the past if they spend large amounts of time with people outside their families.

7. Another important result of social changes is migration within or across national boundaries in the search for better employment, improved housing, and more educational opportunities for children. Often, the move is from rural to urban areas. Such moves, however, require additional demands of family members, such as adjustment to a different lifestyle and disappointments that reality in the big city did not meet the family's expectations.

All of these changes can lead to stress because parents are struggling to socialize their children into a culture with which they are not yet comfortable. The parents are not yet familiar with the new social settings that rapid change has brought. Interventions to ease the stress have been attempted, and a number of them will be reviewed in the next chapter.

Recent research, especially by Rogoff (1990; Rogoff & Chavajay, 1995), has emphasized the point that children actively participate in their socialization. Children actively explore their world, and their behavior influences how adults and peers offer socializing experiences. Much of the learning is tacit; people are not consciously aware they are participating in activities that encourage children to learn about their culture. Further, even if adults are aware they are encouraging children to learn, they cannot explain exactly how they are structuring the tasks they present to children.

Still, adults and children clearly interact in a process called guided participation. People who know about a task or skill adjust their behavior in various ways to guide children in their goals of learning about important aspects of their culture. For example, children in India and other countries in South Asia have to learn that the right hand is for eating and the left hand is for personal hygiene. If children do not learn this through everyday participation in home activities, adults or older siblings guide the children's hands. During meals, the "teachers" might hold down the left hand while guiding the right hand toward the food. A key point is that the children's behavior directs the family teachers' behavior. When children learn through simple observation, no one needs to provide the more active intervention of holding down and guiding hands. In some cultures (for instance, the Mayan culture in Guatemala), children are allowed to wander around the village and to observe the behavior of adults. They learn exactly what is important to look for when they are expected to answer their mothers' questions about community events and village gossip.

Almost all cultures recognize a unique period between childhood and adulthood. Roughly corresponding to the teenage years, the period known as adolescence has a number of functions within a culture. Given that same-sex rather than cross-sex groupings of peers are more common in this period, adolescence allows adults to control the mating of their children by imposing restrictions on where and when young men and women interact. The peer group also becomes a vehicle for breaking the strong parent-child bonds of early socialization as young people move toward the responsibilities and relative independence of adulthood. In many cultures, adolescence is recognized as a time-out period, a relatively relaxed collection of years, prior to the intense expectations of adulthood. Adolescents make contributions to the community in the form of work, entertainment, or both. They commonly experience predictable stresses, such as relationship problems, abuse, scholastic and career problems, and loneliness and social isolation. Parents can become especially confused about their adolescent children, especially if their lives include one set of standards from their own childhood and other standards imposed by industrialization, modernization, or migration from one country to another.

Parents can demonstrate varying degrees of warmth toward their children, and they can exert varying amounts of control over their children's behavior. When children perceive their parents as extremely rejecting, harmful effects result, as research in societies all over the world has documented. Children of rejecting parents become aggressive and hostile, cannot control themselves, are emotionally unstable, and are more likely to develop severe psychological difficulties. Interestingly, a key factor is the type of behavior children are socialized to expect from their parents. Rohner and Pettengill (1985) demonstrated that American schoolchildren see parental control as a sign of overall hostility and rejection. In contrast, Korean schoolchildren see control and strict discipline as signs their parents care about them. For example, Korean mothers buy clothes for their children giving no thought to asking for their children's opinions. The children see this as a positive indication that their mothers are concerned that their sons and daughters look good when going to school or attending social gatherings. The American and Korean children are exposed to different cultural values. Stricter control of children is valued in Korea, while parental permissiveness is far more common in the United States. Children internalize these values and then reflect on their parents' behavior with these values in mind.

Some of the most rapid social changes involving important human behaviors can be seen in children's behavior. When Koreans immigrate to the United States, their children learn to value the more permissive norms in one generation. Korean American children see their parents as rejecting if they are subjected to strict discipline. One place where the children are exposed to the new values is the school, and the various effects of participating in a culture's educational system will be the focus of the next chapter.

C H A P T E R 5

FORMAL EDUCATIONAL
EXPERIENCES

CHAPTER OVERVIEW

Adults passing by a school at the start of the academic year are likely to witness a heart-wrenching scene. Parents bring their very young children to school, and the children cry loudly as the parents leave. A culture's leaders must view the school as an important place if they are willing to see unhappy children year after year. Indeed important places called "schools" are in virtually all industrialized and many developing nations. Although adults cannot always discuss exactly what they expect schools to do, they have enough of a vision to fund schools, to require attendance, to support teacher training institutions, and so forth.

Predictable changes in children's cognitive abilities occur as children attend school, and these include more efficient learning strategies and changes in perception based on art lessons. School is especially beneficial for children when few discontinuities exist between their cultural background and the school's expectations. For example, an emphasis on the one student with the best grades may be appropriate in some cultures, but it is not in those where cooperation and mutual help are strong norms. Many times, proper attention to cultural factors leads to the integration of entire families into the educational experience. Parents and older siblings can become coteachers, and younger children can prepare themselves for their formal schooling by overhearing these lessons. Some children clearly benefit from school more than others. Research has asked, "Why?" The case of Asian Americans is reviewed in this chapter, and the suggestion is put forth that members of this culture view schools as "a level playing field" and view success in school as a contributor to upward mobility in society at large.

Cultures differ in what their leaders expect of schools. Visitors to schools in China, Japan, and the United States see major differences very quickly. In the United States, children are encouraged to develop their own identities and interests. In Japan, they are encouraged to develop strong ties with a group. In China, teachers feel they must correct the efforts of parents, who teachers believe spoil their children! Children's experiences in school can be understood given a knowledge of the values emphasized in their cultures. Cultures also differ in the value people place on knowledge of several languages. In some cultures, knowledge of one national language is so highly valued that the entire school curriculum is taught in this one language, even if many other languages or dialects are spoken in these cultures. In other cultures, bilingual educational programs are emphasized. Children either move from their native language to the national language (transition programs), or they are taught in more than one language throughout their schooling (maintenance programs).

Several times in this book, I make the prediction that the future will see more intercultural contact given major developments such as the globalization of economies, immigration, and increasing emphases on the appreciation of cultural diversity. A final section of this chapter considers the possibility that the college classroom can be where preparation for effective intercultural contact can occur.

Culture and Educational Institutions

As discussed in the previous chapter, children are exposed to many opportunities to learn about their culture during the socialization process. For example, while observing adult relatives argue, they learn what issues people become upset about as well as methods for resolving interpersonal difficulties. When interacting with age peers, they can learn the benefits of compromise in contrast to the difficulties that arise when everyone insists on following their preferences. When answering their mothers' questions about village gossip, they learn what issues are important to people outside their families. If children participate in organized group activities, they learn when the efforts of groups are more productive than the efforts of isolated individuals. These and many other opportunities to learn can be considered part of children's "informal education." The activities summarized by the term "formal education," in contrast, are more organized, are more predictable, and are marked by many features found in cultures all over the world. The key features are that children leave their families for a certain number of hours each day, go to a designated place in the community called "the school," and interact with specialists known as teachers. Certainly, exceptions to this generalization occur, such as parents in highly industrialized nations who petition to keep their children home with the promise that they will provide them formal education. But these exceptions should not keep people from examining one of the major institutions for socializing children in numerous cultures: the special places called schools where parents send their children (Cushner, 1990; Cushner, McClelland, & Safford, 1996; Serpell & Hatano, 1997).

Few institutions within the countries of the world have received more attention than the schools. Even when a discussion topic might appear at first glance as separate from schools, such as "intelligence," "learning," or "social change," information about a culture's schools quickly becomes relevant. A key aspect of intelligence, for instance, is how it is measured so that teachers and school administrators can best provide for children's needs (Greenfield, 1997b; Irvine & Berry, 1988). Teachers are constantly barraged by new advice from researchers about how children best learn, but the teachers must separate what is intellectually fascinating about the latest learning theory from what is truly helpful. When government decision makers are contemplating major socioeconomic changes, such as the integration of a country's ethnic groups or greater attention to industrial competitiveness in the world economy, schools are very frequently where the changes are introduced (Anderson & Bowman, 1965; Holtzman, 1997; Tobin, Wu, & Davidson, 1989a). So many socialization experiences occur in schools, and societies expect so much from them, that efforts to understand human behavior around the world would be lacking if children's formal education were given too little attention.

This chapter reviews research in seven important areas:

1. What changes in children's cognitive development occur because of their participation in their culture's formal education? This is a difficult question to answer because research must separate the effects of formal schooling from (a) children's natural cognitive development as they increase in age and (b) the effects of other socializing experiences, such as the informal education children receive from working beside adults on tasks valued in their cultures.

2. Can classrooms be made more culturally appropriate to the backgrounds of children attending schools? Do children participate in socializing experiences prior to their formal schooling that prepare them to do well in school? Do children have experiences that interfere with their schooling?

3. With some insights gained from the analysis of the questions posed in research topic number two, can educators introduce interventions so that more children can benefit from schooling? Are benefits derived from involving the entire family, not just the children themselves?

4. Do children from certain cultures benefit from schooling more than children from other cultures? In North America, children of Asian descent seem to win more academic awards and seem to go to college in higher numbers than children of European descent. Are these observations accurate, and, if so, can the reason Asian Americans do well in school be clearly explained?

5. Do leaders in different societies identify problems they feel changes in the school curricula can address? At what age are children targeted by leaders for major changes? Given that cultures have different goals and are changing in different ways, at what educational level (preschool, elementary, secondary) can large differences in curricula be found?

6. Here is a joke based on a series of questions. What is a person called who can speak two languages? A bilingual. What is a person called who can speak three languages? A trilingual. What is a person called who can speak one language? An American. In terms of languages people can handle well in daily interactions,

Americans are in a minority (Hakuta, 1986; W. Lambert, Genesee, & Holobow, 1993). Most people in the world are fluent in more than one language, whereas the vast majority of Americans are fluent only in English. The important issue that arises is whether or not Americans are at an educational disadvantage given that competence in multiple languages is so rare. Is bilingual education, where children receive instruction in more than one language, a workable policy?

7. One purpose of formal education is to prepare people for the events in their lives that will occur after their schooling is completed. Such events will surely include interactions among people from different cultural groups. Can people, especially those preparing themselves to become leaders, become better prepared for such interactions through innovative educational experiences in the college classroom?

Before turning to these issues, I find it is useful to pinpoint aspects of formal schooling that can be found all around the world. These are the etics (or culture-common factors; see chapter 3) that emics specific to a culture can be added to by researchers. Many of these characteristics of formal schooling, based on an analysis by Greenfield and Lave (1982; see also Watkins & Regmi, 1996), contrast sharply with descriptions of informal education as discussed in chapter 4.

CHARACTERISTICS OF FORMAL EDUCATION

When people observe schools anyplace in the world, they are likely to observe a number of common characteristics. Exceptions to this list will certainly occur, such as when teachers and administrators make attempts to enrich the curricula of their schools through innovative approaches. However, the characteristics are widespread enough to provide a good starting point for analyses of how schooling affects children. In addition, these characteristics are useful for describing the types of schools teachers are reacting to when they attempt innovations.

- Schools are set apart from the context of everyday life. Children leave home and travel to a special place set aside for their formal education. In contrast to informal education, with learning embedded in everyday activities such as tending the garden and looking after siblings, formal schooling occurs during designated times.
- Schooling involves specialists called teachers who are responsible for developing curricula and methodologies so that they can impart their knowledge to students. This results in a system whereby teachers decide what is to be learned. Only rarely can students designate topic areas that become part of the curricula.
- Teachers are rarely members of students' families. In many parts of the world, children are encouraged to join classrooms taught by someone from outside the family if their relatives happen to be faculty members. This contrasts sharply with settings where children learn informally by observing and working with various relatives.

- Formal education teachers are much more likely to have explicit goals and ways these goals can be reached. This contrasts with informal education's implicit goals and tacit knowledge discussed in chapter 4. For example, when students work together in groups, their teachers are more likely to have the explicit goals that the children will learn certain content areas well through peer instruction and will learn how to work well with others on complex tasks (Farver, Kim, & Lee, 1995; Johnson & Johnson, 1987; Kagan, 1990).

- Another aspect of formal education involves emphases of characteristics rather than their constant presence. When compared to informal education, schools are more likely to be an institution where cultural change is introduced or re-inforced. One reason is simply efficiency. It is far easier for a specialist in teaching to introduce new ideas to a class of 20 or more students than it is for far-flung and less organized sets of parents and relatives to introduce new material to children. It is certain, for instance, that schools in eastern Europe and Russia will introduce new curriculum materials for the study of democracy as a political system.

- Schooling is far more likely to involve the practice of verbal interchange between teachers and students, with students able to ask questions about material they do not understand well. Informal education, in contrast, is more likely to involve learning through observation of more expert people, whether those experts are older siblings, coaches, or other respected figures in the community. After a period of observation, learners try to imitate the more proficient people, probably engaging in more trial and error than well-educated teachers would permit. Returning to the characteristic about the explicitness of instruction, professional teachers are more likely to introduce tasks and goals that structure learning in a way distinct from pure trial and error.

- Teachers also are more likely to introduce general principles useful for solving a variety of problems rather than methods for solving one specific problem. If the topic is agriculture, a teacher would likely discuss the contents of good fertilizer, crop rotation practices, and irrigation systems. This contrasts with the informal education method of learning how to plant a specific crop at a specific time in a specific place. As introduced in chapter 4, the practice of teaching general principles in a classroom that might be useful later is known as out-of-context learning. One danger is that some students benefit from this type of learning while others have difficulty seeing the relevance of general principles that seem to have no immediate application. This leads to the last characteristic of formal education Greenfield and Lave (1982) suggested.

- Schools carry the danger that some of the students will be less motivated in formal educational systems than in the informal settings their culture provides. The grading system found all around the world, for instance, leads to labeling some students as "less capable," and this in turn affects their motivation. The efforts of policy makers to improve schools, as part of programs dealing with "culturally relevant curricula," "decreasing school dropouts" (called "school leavers" in some countries), and "basic life competencies" all reflect the fact that many students are not motivated to strive for success in schools (Lambert, Knight, Taylor, & Achenbach, 1996).

CHANGES FROM PARTICIPATION IN FORMAL SCHOOLS

The problem of less motivated students is discussed later in the chapter. The goal of working with such students, of course, is to increase the chances they will experience success in school. But what is success? One way to answer this question is to examine the changes that occur in students who spend large amounts of time in school making adequate if not stellar and prize-winning progress. A number of behavioral scientists deeply concerned about education have analyzed the changes schooling brings (Cushner, 1990; Rogoff, 1981; Scribner & Cole, 1981; Serpell & Hatano, 1997; Wagner, 1988). The documentation of these changes is difficult because the contributions of formal schooling must be distinguished from maturation (children can do more as they grow older) and from children's informal educational opportunities.

One way to document the effects of schooling is to carry out research in cultures where children differ in the amount of formal education they receive. In some cultures, children who do not attend school (even though they are sometimes very bright and able) can be compared with children who do. Keeping in mind the difficulties of making claims for schooling beyond other experiences in children's lives, researchers have proposed many changes in students' abilities.

Use of More Efficient Learning Strategies

When faced with tasks that involve demands on people's memory, such as learning a list of words, children who have attended school can apply strategies that allow better performance (Cole, Gay, Glick, & Sharp, 1971; Cole & Scribner, 1974). Consider the following list of words:

red	*plate*	*mother*	*sister*
knife	*cup*	*father*	*spoon*
green	*blue*	*brother*	*white*

Children are asked to study the words, the list is then taken away, and they are asked to recall the words. The children are told they can recall the words in any order they wish.

Children who have attended school (hereafter called "schooled children") are more likely to use the very efficient learning strategy known as clustering. They are more likely to cluster the words into the categories "colors," "eating implements," and "family members." Very often, schooled children are explicit about this strategy, reporting they put the words into various groups. They might not use the same labels for the word groups (for instance, they are more likely to use a phrase such as "things on the kitchen table"), but the children clearly organize the information effectively in their minds. When people cluster information, they place fewer burdens on their memories. If they memorize the names of the clusters, these names then become cues for the contents within each cluster. Without an efficient learning strategy such as clustering, the children's task is simply trying to memorize 12 words, and this is difficult and often rather boring. Based on research among the Kpelle in Liberia, Cole and his colleagues (1971) suggested schoolchildren's use of efficient learning strategies begins between the fifth and eighth grades. Students younger than this and children of any age who had not attended school did not impose any meaning (such as the names of clusters) on the words.

The exact reasons for the effects of schooling are not entirely clear. Rogoff suggested various reasons that might be called "test-wiseness" and "generalizable skills." Test-wiseness simply means that, given experience with such daily activities as following the teacher's instructions, using paper and pencils, working within time limits set for various assignments and classes, and comfortableness with outsiders (here, the researchers) who come into classrooms with new tasks, schooled children are simply more prepared to do well in learning experiments. They simply know how to take tests well, and this is their only advantage over their unschooled peers. Test-wiseness is undoubtedly a factor, and good research takes this into account by allowing unschooled children extensive amounts of time to become familiar with the test materials, to interact with experimenters, to become sensitive to any time demands, and so forth (Dasen & Heron, 1981; Katriel, 1990).

Two of the more generalizable skills Rogoff (1981) suggested are that, as part of their schooling, children learn familiarity with various ways of organizing knowledge, and they learn that many problems can be solved through the careful examination of information presented in the problem. Keep in mind that Cole and his colleagues found that children began to organize information in the fifth grade. By that time, they would have been exposed to many lessons with clearly organized information: history according to various significant events; science according to the steps involved in various experiments; mathematics according to recommended orderings of addition, subtraction, and multiplication when solving complex problems; and so forth. In mathematics, especially, children learn that the information necessary to solve "word problems" is contained in the problem's written or verbal information. Here is an example: "John has two dollars and goes to a store where carrots cost fifty cents a dozen. How many carrots can John buy?" When children learn the information is there, as long as they can find it, they are likely to apply it to the task of learning the list of words presented earlier. They might say to themselves (as children have told me after participating in research studies), "There is something in this problem that will make it easier to do as long as I can figure it out." With this attitude, they are likely to discover that the words cluster into clear groups.

Greater Field Independence

If people can extract information from its surrounding context, they are said to be *field independent*. Consider Figure 3, a type of drawing used to test for field independence called an embedded figure (Witkin, 1967). If people can look at the small figure on the left and quickly find it inside the more complex figure on the right, they are demonstrating the quality of field independence. They can extract or find information in the complex figure and are not distracted by the surrounding context or "field." They can find information independent of the field. If people are *field dependent*, they are more likely to attend to the total context for information. They are

An "Embedded Figure," a Type of Drawing That Tests for Field Independence   **FIGURE 3**

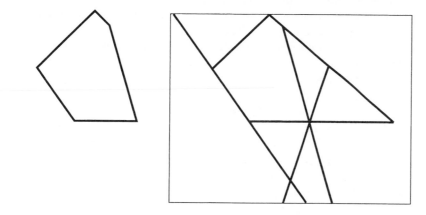

more comfortable making conclusions about the total package of information. If the total package of information (e.g., the figure on the right-hand side) demands that it be broken down into component parts, field dependent people cannot do such a task as quickly or as accurately as others.

Cross-cultural research (Berry, 1979; Mishra, 1997; Witkin, 1967) has been concerned with the important question of whether socialization into different cultures has an impact on skills such as field dependence or field independence. Suggesting that a relationship between socialization and skills does indeed exist, Berry (1979) has done research in cultures where the major subsistence activity is hunting. Berry argues that if subsistence activities demand certain skills, then people have to develop those skills or else their culture would not survive. Skills, then, can be viewed as people's adaptation to their environment. Further, adults encourage children to develop these skills. Hunting is a skill where field independence is extremely useful. Consider hunting a brown deer living in a forest where the trees are similarly colored. Or consider hunting white seals in the Arctic where the snow-covered surroundings make the seals very difficult to spot. Field independent hunters who can extract information (the vague figure of a deer or seal) from the total context have an important advantage in their quest for food.

Everyday words for the skills summarized by the terms *field independence* and *field dependence* are admittedly hard to identify. Possible approximations are *analytical* for field independence and *sensitive to context* for field dependence. Consider a meeting of 20 people expressing their various opinions about an important social issue. If asked what happened after the meeting, analytical people might focus on the views of individuals. "Person A had one opinion, person B had another, . . ." and so forth. People sensitive to context may be more able to identify a sense of the group as a whole. They might report, "I felt the group's consensus was that we should proceed in this specific way."

Although more studies are desirable before firm conclusions can be suggested, Rogoff (1981) entertained the possibility that schooling increases field independent skills. One possible reason is that many tasks children are expected to master involve breaking a problem down into component parts. Complex mathematical problems have to be broken down into simpler steps. Information has to be extracted from complex pictures, figures, and graphs. The arguments students want to make in their essays or in their public presentations have to be broken down and organized in an understandable way. These various tasks demand the sort of analytical skills the concept field independence covers.

Ideally, increases in field independence would not come at the expense of the positive features field dependent people possess. People who can summarize the "sense of the group" after hearing many individual positions have a very useful skill. Another possible benefit of field dependence is that such people are more sensitive to the needs of others (Witkin, Dyk, Faterson, Goodenough, & Karp, 1962). They have more social skills for dealing with many different types of individuals. The sensitivity to context of field dependent people extends to sensitivity to others, because these others are part of the total context individuals must deal with in their lives. Given that many of today's social issues (drugs, inadequate housing, poverty, diversity in the workplace) involve various people and their special needs, social sensitivity should be encouraged whenever possible. Further, school curricula should nurture the positive aspects of the field dependent learning style.

Use of Pictorial Information

The interpretation of drawings and photographs is based on an understanding of how three-dimensional information is depicted in two dimensions. Consider the drawing on the right in Figure 4. The drawing is presented on a two-dimensional surface. All the objects depicted have the same two dimensions of a flat surface. People learn to use certain conventions when they need to depict or to interpret the third dimension. These techniques involve positioning objects so that they are seen as further away from the viewer, or "behind the flat surface of the page." In the right-hand drawing, the converging lines represent railroad tracks extending away from the viewer. People see lines converge when they look straight ahead at similar objects in the real world, such as straight roads, long corridors, and railroad tracks extending into the distance.

Other cues in two-dimensional drawings and pictures indicate three dimensions. When objects are drawn so that they overlap, the proper interpretation is that one is in front of the other, as in real life. In the same drawing in Figure 4, one overlapping tree is supposed to be seen as closer to viewers than the other. The largest tree is supposed to be seen as even closer to viewers, because objects appear closer if they are drawn larger than the same type of objects nearby. In other words, the farthest trees in a real forest look much smaller than trees really similar in size near the viewer.

Children encounter many places where they can become familiar with the interpretation of three-dimensional cues depicted on two-dimensional surfaces. Many children from middle-class homes in different countries have access to books with lots of pictures. Even before they begin school, they become quite skilled at identifying objects, at indicating which are near and which are far away, and so forth. Schooling seems to improve this skill for children who have had experience with pictures, and it offers the opportunity to develop the skill for children who have had

Drawings Illustrating How Three-Dimensional Information Is Depicted in Two Dimensions

FIGURE 4

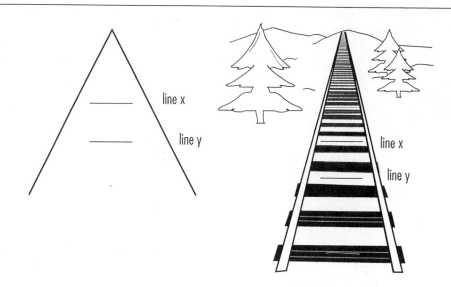

line x

line y

line x

line y

little exposure to two-dimensional drawings and pictures (Rogoff, 1981; Segall, Dasen, Berry, & Poortinga, 1990; Wagner, 1977). The reasons for the effect of schooling in this case undoubtedly include exposure to many different types of drawings and pictures and practice in interpreting them.

An especially interesting finding is that schooled children begin to make certain types of mistakes when interpreting pictures. The mistakes involve visual illusions (Russell, Deregowski, & Kinnear, 1997; Segall, Campbell, & Herskovits, 1966). Both drawings in Figure 4 are versions of the Ponzo illusion. Viewers who demonstrate susceptibility to the illusion will report the top line (line x) as longer than the bottom line (line y) when both are equal in length. Cross-cultural research has indicated that people in some cultures are more susceptible to the illusion than are people in other cultures (Brislin & Keating, 1976; Leibowitz, Brislin, Perlmutter, & Hennessey, 1969; Wagner, 1977). One explanation is based on the "ecological hypothesis." People learn to interpret cues in the physical environments where they are raised. If they had many opportunities to see objects that seem to converge in the distance, then they learn the cue that "converging lines tell me that certain objects are far away." People who are not raised in such environments are not as familiar with this cue to distance. For instance, people who live in rural communities with few buildings and roads and who see their flat farmlands extend into the horizon are not as familiar with the experience of clear lines converging in the distance. When asked to report which of the two lines is longer in different versions of the Ponzo illusion, such people are more accurate. Because they are not as familiar with the cue that converging lines indicate distance, they do not use it when viewing the Ponzo illusion.

People familiar with converging lines (e.g., people in U.S. urban areas) are more susceptible to the illusion. They use the cue that converging lines indicate distance and make the *unconscious* interpretation that "since the top line is farther away, it must be longer than the closer one because objects in the distance look smaller." The interesting effect of formal education is that schooled children become more susceptible to the illusion than their unschooled peers (Wagner, 1977). This is especially true for the more complex versions of the Ponzo illusion (e.g., the version on the right-hand side of Figure 4). The more complex version has more cues to depth and schooled children learn how to use these cues, so they become more susceptible to the illusion. For them this illusion becomes another example of using cues (or habits of inference: Segall et al., 1990, p. 75) that most of the time lead to correct decisions. After all, lines that converge in the distance usually are helpful for making decisions about the relative size of objects. In this case, however, a usually helpful cue leads to a mistake. Cross-cultural studies of other visual illusions (e.g., Deregowsi, 1980) have attempted to identify the normal, everyday perceptual cues people in different cultures learn to use. Much research has taken the view that visual illusions are not anomalies unrelated to anything else. Rather, illusions are helpful tools for the study of people's normal perceptual processes that happen to lead to mistakes in some cases.

The feature of schooling common to the three skills discussed in this section is that children benefit from specific experiences commonly found in classrooms all over the world. They learn to organize information they learned from their texts and from teacher presentations, and they apply these organizational methods to new learning tasks. Schooled children learn to pick out key information in complex problems and to apply this skill to tasks meant to measure field independence or that require it. They learn to interpret three-dimensional cues in two-dimensional pictures and use these when asked to examine visual illusions and for other purposes such as art appreciation. Some children come to school with a solid background that allows them to develop these skills readily. Others do not, but after several years some (not all, unfortunately) participate in so many classroom activities that they "catch up" to children with a better before-school background.

These observations lead to several more questions. What, exactly, is a good before-school background? If the background of children who are ready to benefit immediately from school attendance is known, will this help teachers concerned with the progress of children from other backgrounds? Are any aspects of the children's background related to cultural factors, as these have been discussed throughout this book? If so, can teachers benefit from knowledge of the cultural background of the various students in their classes? These are some of the issues discussed next.

INTEGRATING CHILDREN'S CULTURAL BACKGROUND INTO THE SCHOOL

As was discussed extensively in chapter 4, socialization into a culture involves behavior in social settings. Children become familiar with certain settings and learn to engage in appropriate behaviors so that they can achieve their goals. If they move to different settings, as in the example of families in India moving from rural to urban areas, they experience stress because they are unaware of the behaviors necessary to achieve their goals. Applying these concepts to schooling, studies have shown some children are well prepared to benefit from their formal education. Consider the three skills reviewed in the previous section: organizing information, the analytical ability to pick out key information in a complex problem, and interpreting information in pictures. Some children are socialized into settings where they are exposed to these skills by the time they are 3 or 4 years old. They are accustomed to organized play activities adults encourage. When wanting their children to play with blocks, for instance, some parents sit down on the floor with their children and begin, "First we'll clear an area, then we'll get the blocks out, then we'll build a base, . . ." Many children have puzzles of various sorts where they have to analyze how to solve problems and then use a specific approach to reach a solution. Some puzzles children have bear a similarity to the embedded-figures task. In books of games their parents buy, children look at complex figures and are asked to find the three clowns, horses, or trees. Many of these same children have books with pictures and converse with their parents about the figures in the picture, where things are in relation to each other, and so forth.

Many people take these learning opportunities for granted, but recall from chapter 1 that this is an important insight about culture. People become so familiar with their culture's everyday aspects that they don't think about them, take them for granted, and are rather impatient with others who are not as familiar with those aspects. When cultural aspects related to schooling are taken for granted, however, the great danger is that children unfamiliar with these aspects will be shortchanged. One way to deal with this issue is to ask, "What are children familiar with, given their socialization in their culture, and can these skills and social settings be integrated into the school curricula?" Important research on this question has been carried out (Cushner, 1990; Laboratory of Comparative Human Cognition, 1986; Vernon-Feagans, 1996; Vogt, Jordan, & Tharp, 1987), and some findings will be reviewed here. A good way to introduce this research, I believe, is to present findings about another aspect of middle-class American culture that (a) prepares children to benefit from school, (b) is a major part of classroom activities, and (c) is extremely easy to take for granted.

Conversational Partners

Children need to communicate with others to become competent native speakers of the language(s) of adults in their communities. Some of children's exposure to language is via their give-and-take conversations with other native speakers. The important question related to preparation for school is, "Who are these others with whom children interact?" Heath (1983) argues that there are important cultural differences in answers to this question. In the American middle class, mothers and fathers view their children as conversational partners. That is, adults converse with children, taking their viewpoint into account during the give and take of conversation. The diaries Braunwald and I kept of our daughters' language development were introduced in chapter 4. Consider these two other diary entries (Braunwald & Brislin, 1979a, p. 30).

Laura is 1 year, 5 months old. She is on the changing table, and her mother is changing her diaper. Her mother senses that Laura wants to play.

MOTHER: I'll tickle you as soon as I put on your diaper.
LAURA: Now!

Cheryl is 1 year and 2 months old. She is in the kitchen with her mother. A TV can be heard but not seen.

TV COMMERCIAL FOR A LAUNDRY DETERGENT: "Get rid of ring around the collar . . ."

Immediately after Cheryl hears the words "ring around the . . . ," she begins to turn as she does when she plays "ring-around-the-rosie."

MOTHER: Yes, that's "ring-around-the-rosie." Good girl.

The point for discussion here is that both mothers are conversing with their children and are reacting to their attempts to communicate: Laura's desire to be tickled and Cheryl's desire to play a game she knows. A number of researchers have pointed out that this adult willingness to communicate in this way with children is by no means universal (Heath, 1983; Rogoff, 1990; Vernon-Feagans, 1996; Ward, 1971). In many cultures, children are not considered appropriate conversational partners. Children hear their native language(s) spoken, but not during frequent conversations with adults. Rather, these children are much more likely to engage in conversations with age peers. Adults in such cultures consider it strange to talk with children. When they do, they do not switch to the baby talk common in the U.S. middle class when adults want to be sure they are understood. For instance, the same diary study shows me saying "Here's your wawa" when giving Cheryl the water she requested. I used her word to make sure we communicated. Even though adults in the American middle class probably never think about such verbalizations, the fact they interact with children in this manner is good preparation for the children's formal schooling. If children learn to communicate with their adult parents, they most likely can transfer this ability to communicate with their adult teachers. Children also will be prepared for their teachers' attempts to simplify language, a practice most American preschool and kindergarten teachers engage in frequently. Further, this practice prepares children for initiating behaviors, that is, for deciding what will be done rather than just reacting to the teachers' directions. Note in the two diary entries that Laura and Cheryl began the tickling and dancing activities themselves. This familiarity with the initiation of activities is useful when the children are expected to make individual and original contributions during their formal schooling, such as bringing in objects from home and describing them during "show and tell" sessions.

Integrating Children's Cultural Background: An Example

As shown in some examples so far, without much conscious awareness, the parents of the American middle class prepare their children to benefit from formal schooling. Teachers learn to expect these well-prepared students and prepare their lesson plans with the children's already-existing skills taken for granted. If the children begin their

In many, but not all, cultures, children are considered appropriate conversational partners for adults.

formal schooling without these skills, they risk not benefiting from their attendance and falling behind their better prepared peers. Realizing these facts and also realizing that some of the reasons for frictions in school are related to the children's cultural background, various researchers (reviews in Laboratory of Comparative Human Cognition, 1986; Cushner, 1990; Cushner et al., 1996) have attempted to design school curricula that take the children's culture into account. One of the most carefully documented efforts of this kind (Jordan & Tharp, 1979; Vogt et al., 1987) is the work with Hawaiian and part-Hawaiian children who attend schools in Honolulu and other parts of Hawaii as part of the Kamehameha Elementary Education Program (KEEP). As discussed earlier and as exemplified by the diary entries about children, one of the ways children are socialized is through conversation with others (Carbaugh, 1990a, 1990b; Vernon-Feagans, 1996). The KEEP researchers wanted to determine who children talk to and in what social settings they become comfortable (again recall the discussion of social settings in chapter 4), realizing that this information would be useful for understanding the children's formal schooling. Based on their research in the communities where the children lived, they documented a number of important facts. Given that both parents often have to work to cope with Hawaii's high cost of living, children are frequently given responsibility for looking after their younger siblings. One way these Hawaiians look after siblings is to involve them in games and other group activities, and these efforts are often integrated with those of friends and their siblings. Consequently, Hawaiian children participate in group activities more frequently than do children from many other cultural backgrounds (e.g., Anglos originally from the mainland United States). The Hawaiian children become accustomed to integrating their own efforts with group goals and are less insistent than others on the pursuit of their personal goals. When instruction on the game rules or procedures for the group activity are needed, children take responsibility for those younger than them. In turn, as these younger children become older, they pass their knowledge on to younger children. As a result, Hawaiian children become accustomed to the roles of both teacher and learner within their peer group.

Another group activity among Hawaiian children involves discussions of recent happenings in their lives or shared experiences within their communities. Called "talk story," children sit around and tell what has happened to them in narrative form: who did what to whom, what happened as a result, who else became involved, and so forth. Adults also engage in talk story, but it is more likely to be done with other adults so that story themes adults share (e.g., difficulties with opposite-sex members, filling out tax forms) can be discussed. In other words, people in Hawaiian communities converse with one another in a format much like storytelling. In addition to the fact that far more of this activity occurs among Hawaiians than among middle-class Anglos, a procedural difference among Hawaiians is striking to outsiders. If the story is about a shared community happening or if it is about one person's experiences that bear similarities to recent events in the lives of others, people interrupt each other. Similarly, much overlapping occurs between the verbal contributions of one person and the additions to the story by others. People who were socialized to show good manners by not interrupting others and by waiting for others to stop talking before responding find it hard at first to participate in talk story. If they use the conversational rules they learned during their socialization and wait a polite period before contributing, someone else will have already begun speaking!

Can these significant cultural differences be integrated into the formal classroom? It is important to note that the attitudes of teachers and school administrators are central to determining the answer to this question. Recall the discussion in chapter 2 about the possibility of ethnocentric judgments when cultural differences are observed. School personnel could observe Hawaiian schoolchildren and could conclude the children have deficits that make it difficult for them to learn. They might point to overlapping conversations and conclude the children are impatient and do not have an adequate attention span. They could point to the children's deference to group goals and conclude the children are not independent enough to benefit from the many choices offered to them. Instead, school personnel could observe the children and could conclude the children have been socialized in a different culture. This conclusion is neither good nor bad—it is simply a fact. The children bring a set of differences to school, and teachers and administrators have an opportunity to encourage the children to draw on these aspects of their culture during their formal schooling.

The KEEP researchers made modifications to the elementary school curricula of these communities based on cultural factors they documented. Four factors are reviewed here: Children play in groups, they defer to goals the group sets, they are accustomed both to teacher and learner roles within their groups, and they engage in talk-story conversations that involve interruptions and overlapping contributions. These factors have been integrated into the methods teachers use in the early elementary grades to encourage the development of various skills expected of schoolchildren. Methods for teaching reading provide a good example.

KEEP teachers have introduced cooperative group learning (Johnson & Johnson, 1987; Kagan, 1990; Aronson, Wilson, & Akert, 1999). Students are divided into groups, and tasks are given to the group as a whole rather than to individuals. If one student doesn't understand an aspect of the task, someone in the group who does takes the teacher's role and offers an explanation or demonstration. Given Hawaiian children's familiarity with this approach from their out-of-school play activities, they find it easy to share information in the classroom. They also find it relatively easy to relate to the group goal that "everyone is expected to learn the skill," rather than the more individualistic "some will learn it very well and will receive a gold star." For learning to read and developing reading comprehension, the familiar talk-story method was adapted for KEEP. Children read sections of the book aloud and then talk about what happened in the stories. While doing so, children also can bring in personal experiences when some aspect of the reading assignment triggers memories. Interruptions and overlapping verbal contributions are allowed. By hearing the reactions of other children and by linking story content to their own personal experiences, children develop their reading comprehension skills. They show teachers and peers that they understand story content through their frequent contributions to group discussions. If their comments are unrelated to a story, the teacher and peers can ask questions or make suggestions to bring them back to the story's theme, characters, or plot.

Evaluation studies of these classroom interventions showed very positive results. Compared to part-Hawaiian children taught in more traditional classrooms, KEEP children (who are all part-Hawaiian) scored better by scoring at grade level on standardized reading tests. These are the same reading tests given to children on the mainland United States (and that probably have been taken by a majority of this book's readers) to assess progress and to indicate areas (e.g., vocabulary, comprehension) that need improvement. Keeping in mind that the tests were designed to be compatible with the backgrounds of children in the Anglo-American middle class, reaching grade level (e.g., third graders are indeed reading and understanding third-grade material) is a significant achievement for students with different cultural backgrounds.

Long-Term Difficulties

Does this good news have a sad side? Unfortunately, the answer is yes. After the children leave KEEP and enter traditional classrooms or schools, they fall behind age peers from other cultural groups (e.g., Japanese Americans, mainland Anglos) and participate in a spiral called the "cumulative deficit phenomenon." That is, they might, for example, fall a little behind in the fifth grade. But because sixth-grade work demands the skills learned in the fifth grade, they get further behind as they proceed through junior high and later high school. These results from the KEEP research are consistent with studies that followed the progress of a project for low-income, inner-city children from Milwaukee, Wisconsin. While initial results showed positive benefits of early educational intervention programs for 4- and 6-year-old students (Garber, 1988; Heber & Garber, 1975), these benefits were not maintained when students entered junior high and high school (Prasse & McBride, 1991).

With KEEP's impressive results, why haven't programs been developed that assist children through their later school years? This question has many answers. The research program that developed the classroom interventions was very expensive, and the competition for dollars is always difficult given that the school system has other demands (e.g., after-hours day care for the children of working parents; better teacher salaries; antidrug education; organized team sports for women). The program also took many years to develop, and the original set of forward-looking administrators who recommended funding the program had moved on to other jobs by the time the program had been successfully implemented. More recently, critics have charged that Kamehameha school trustees have moved away from outreach programs such as KEEP and have moved toward serving the most elite and academically prepared Hawaiian and part-Hawaiian students. The trustees also have been severely criticized for their performance, and this led to resources being invested in lawsuits and court actions (Barayuga, 1998).

Another reason such programs have not been expanded relates to the discussion of culture in chapter 1. Recall that one aspect of culture involves the time necessary for change. If an important institution is part of a culture, as is formal schooling, it does not change quickly. The sorts of classroom activities KEEP adopted involve many changes. The teacher is no longer the sole authority figure; groups work toward tasks; and children interact with others in ways different from the well-managed classroom familiar to teachers. Many teachers are simply uncomfortable with these changes and, given that administrators no longer push for change, will fall back on the familiar past methods that are not very different from those used during their own childhood.

Researchers working on cultural differences in the classroom, then, face a problem. Even if they document the benefits of specific programs, they have absolutely no assurance that interventions sensitive to cultural differences will be adopted. Still, research must continue on this important topic. Researchers and other people willing to use the results of good cross-cultural research must remain optimistic that their suggestions will receive careful consideration. Keeping this in mind, researchers did important studies that might shed light on the problem identified in the KEEP work—that the benefits of the program introduced in the early elementary school years are not retained as children become older and enter the later grades. This research examined the role the children's families play in the children's maintenance of skills developed during their formal schooling.

WORKING WITH THE ENTIRE FAMILY

Children in the KEEP program developed solid reading skills during their early elementary school years, but they did not maintain grade-level reading skills in the upper elementary and junior high school years. One reason may be that skills learned at school are not necessarily reinforced at home. If the children are reading well but have no opportunities to use their skills outside of school, they may not feel much of a link between the time they spend in school and the time they spend with their families. Further, if parents have little understanding of what goes on in their children's schools, they may be unable to reinforce newly developed skills even though they desire to do so. Recall that KEEP involves a number of innovations. Even though the parents may be familiar with the underlying cultural practices used for developing the innovative methods (given their own socialization in Hawaii), they may be quite unfamiliar with the methods themselves. It must be remembered that the parents most likely were exposed to very traditional classroom methods during their own schooling.

Kagitcibasi (1990, 1997) has advised researchers and educators to keep in mind that children will learn best if they see clear links between what they learn in school and what they experience at home. If different skills are called for in these places, then confusion can result, which interferes with the children's subsequent learning. Kagitcibasi argues that home-based schooling has its benefits. Bringing education into the home changes several of the formal-schooling features discussed in the beginning of this chapter. Schooling no longer occurs in a special place; it takes place in the familiar surroundings of a child's home. Ideally, children taught at home will be more motivated to take part in the formal educational opportunities accompanying it given the support of their parents and other family members. Other features of formal education remain with home-based schooling. Specialists called *teachers* are still involved, the curriculum is explicit, sequences of questions and answers occur between teachers and children, and general principles are introduced. "In-between" features also exist in the sense that home-based schooling involves aspects of informal and formal education. One such feature is that trained teachers and the family members share teaching responsibilities. Another is that the general principles taught can be applied to specific tasks around the home, such as gardening, cooking, child care, and other chores.

Home-Based Schooling: Some Advantages

The great danger with formal schooling is that if children develop skills in school, there is no guarantee that they can use and improve those skills anyplace else. Family members who become involved in education are more likely to seek opportunities where the children's new skills can be used (Crozier, 1996). One reason is familiarity. They simply know about and are not threatened by the new skills children possess. Another is that family members become more confident in their own abilities. Analyzing the role of mothers, for instance, Kagitcibasi (1990) writes: "Specifically, helping the mother build self-esteem and competence, so that she can engage in cognitively oriented communication with her child, can help to foster the child's sustained cognitive development" (p. 132). Contributions to the education of parents are especially important in developing countries (such as Turkey, where Kagitcibasi lives and where she has carried out much of her research), because many adults have not had the opportunity to participate in formal educational programs of any kind.

Another advantage is that the benefits of home-based schooling are likely to generalize to other children who were not the specific targets of this intervention. These include younger siblings and neighbors. Especially in rural areas, an outsider to someone's home is likely to receive much attention. When teachers arrive in a village and begin to introduce their educational program in someone's home, many neighbor children will gather around. If the teacher can integrate them and their parents into the program, the benefits will increase not only because more people are reached but also because the added people can provide reinforcement for skills developed during the program.

Home-based schooling also permits the introduction of various interventions meant to assist children and their families. If the goal is literacy, it is a relatively easy matter to use reading materials that deal with issues such as nutrition, family planning, and health education. If researchers use their imagination, they can find opportunities to reach parents and their children if home-based schooling proves impractical because of travel distance and consequent expenses. Some communities have "feeding centers" where mothers come for nutritional supplements. Sometimes parents and their children have to wait until the nutritional specialists can help. During the waiting time, educators can involve the children in creative play activities that require the children to exercise various cognitive skills. Such efforts "can also get the mothers involved in such creative play in order to sensitize them to the importance of play for the cognitive development of their children and in order to encourage them to continue it at home" (Kagitcibasi, 1990, p. 133).

Home-Based Schooling: An Example

Working in Turkey, Kagitcibasi, Sunar, and Bekman (1989) evaluated a 4-year home-based educational program for low-income families in Istanbul. Components of the program included emphasizing the importance of frequent parent-child interactions, encouraging positive self-concepts, encouraging parents' feelings of competence, introducing various cognitive skills, and emphasizing the importance of cognitive stimulation in the home.

Recall the important but disappointing KEEP research finding that children did not retain their grade-level reading skills as they moved into the upper elementary school years. In addition to the reasons already discussed, another reason for the results may be quite subtle and difficult to identify. As children learn to read and find out information about important topics on their own, they become more autonomous and do not need to relate to their families and peer groups as often. This can be upsetting to parents who desire the quality of relatedness, which involves close ties and mutual interdependence, among family members. If parents communicate their difficulty with their children's newfound autonomy, children may sense this and cease developing the skills that seem to be taking them away from their parents' desire for relatedness.

Realizing this possibility in their own work in Turkey, Kagitcibasi and her colleagues (1989) dealt explicitly with the issue of relatedness versus autonomy. Prior to the introduction of their multiyear program, they asked mothers what they desired in their children. More than 80% of mothers expressed a desire for various types of relational behaviors, such as good behavior toward family members. Autonomy actually angered mothers. Then the program (in this case, lasting two years) was implemented in the homes. In addition to introducing various cognitive skills mothers could pass on to their children, it reinforced various relational skills, such as showing physical affection, helping, and supporting others. The goal was not to interfere with existing cultural values. However, the program introduced new concepts, such as the usefulness of autonomy when children later go to formal schools, the importance of children being able to make some of their own decisions, and the value of children being able to set their own goals and work toward them.

Follow-up studies found that mothers who participated in the program learned to value their children's autonomous behaviors. This did not interfere with their continued desire for relational behavior. Mothers also wanted their children to remain close to the family. What happened, then, is that the program encouraged an important combination of behaviors that mothers learned to appreciate. The mothers continued to stress relational behaviors while learning about and teaching the usefulness of autonomous behaviors in certain social settings (e.g., formal schools, perhaps jobs later in the children's lives) the children surely will encounter. An important point is that nothing was taken away from the children. The value of relatedness, including offering and receiving support, was retained while the benefits from the new value of autonomy were added. Such syntheses of values and skills are not uncommon (Markus & Kitayama, 1998). With bilingualism, for instance, learning another language does not necessarily interfere with a language a person already knows well (such interference is called subtractive bilingualism: Cummins, 1976; Hakuta, 1986). Instead, learning another language can be a positive aspect of people's education (Mohanty & Perregaux, 1997) and can lead to increases in cognitive skills and greater numbers of opportunities (additive bilingualism). The possibility of adding to people's abilities and not taking away strengths they already have is an important goal in educational efforts that take cultural differences into account.

In the study carried out in Turkey, mothers learned to appreciate the importance autonomy plays in formal schooling. After the full four-year program when children later attended traditional schools, participating mothers had higher expectations of their children's school achievements and hoped the children would stay in school longer. Children behaved in line with these expectations and demonstrated superior performance in school. A key concept here is expectations. Once mothers and children are exposed to a wide variety of cognitive skills, values, and supportive behaviors to reinforce school success, they learn to expect more out of their lives. They become more aware, for instance, of the role schooling plays in improving opportunities for people born into the less privileged classes within their societies. They can develop a positive view of their abilities (recall the emphases of positive self-concepts and of the benefits of autonomy included in the Turkish program) and can set their sights higher. An interesting question this analysis raised is, "Do people from some cultural groups set their sights higher than others and, if so, why?" Recent research has addressed this question.

BENEFITING FROM FORMAL EDUCATION

Many journalists, as well as researchers, have observed that Asian Americans succeed in American schools more than other ethnic group members (Goto & Abe-Kim, 1998; Hsia, 1988; "The New Whiz Kids" in *Time Magazine*, 1987; Sue & Okazaki, 1990). More specific observations, documented in careful studies, include the fact Asian Americans are more likely than other Americans to graduate from high school, attend college, and graduate from college. They receive better high school grades and are frequently the winners in such competitions as the National Merit Scholarship Program, Presidential Scholars, and the Westinghouse Science Talent Search Program.

Calling Asian American educational success "a phenomenon in search of an explanation," Sue and Okazaki (1990) analyzed a number of possible reasons. They could not find evidence for any genetic factor that would lead to the sorts of abilities that might give Asian Americans an advantage in school. They could not find evidence of an advantage from their social class background (recall the discussion of social class in chapter 4). In fact, Arbeiter (1984) provided evidence to show that the mean household income of Asian Americans is lower than that of Whites. Setting these two factors aside, Sue and Okazaki focused on two other reasons: cultural differences in the socialization of children and an innovative idea they call "relative functionalism."

Cultural factors exist at a very high level of generalization, such as values that pervade a culture, and they exist at the level of very specific behaviors, such as parent-child interactions. When people consider Asian American success in school, their appeals to cultural values include the assertion that Asians are more likely to feel that success in school is important. Asian parents point to education as a way for children to better themselves, to make a contribution to society, and to find happiness. These parents are more likely to value the formal aspects of education, such as reading, test taking, and grades, and to downplay other aspects, such as organized athletics programs, extracurricular activities, and efforts to develop "the whole person." The parents exhibit this value in more specific behaviors, such as monitoring their children's homework, expecting extra effort and achievement, making special attempts to provide a quiet place for children to study, hiring tutors when necessary, and encouraging children to try harder on a daily basis.

Insights into the behaviors and achievements of Asian Americans can be stimulated by examining research carried out in Asia. Immigrants to the United States bring many of their cultural values with them and try to find ways to maintain them. Based on research in Japan, Hess and his colleagues (1986) argue that the Japanese are likely to blame poor performance on a lack of effort. If they do not achieve at first, the way to improve is through greater effort (Mizokawa & Rychman, 1990; Yan & Gaier, 1994). Research in the United States indicates that American children are more likely than their Japanese age peers to blame something other than their own effort if they do not perform well (Hess, Chang, & McDevitt, 1987). Students who received a D grade, for example, were more likely than the Japanese to blame the test or to claim they studied the wrong material. Compared to Japanese parents, American parents are more likely to blame the teacher, the school, or the curriculum for their children's poor grades. These differing interpretations of poor performance (or attributions about behavior; see chapter 2) lead to different parent-child interactions. As already noted, the Japanese parents are more likely to encourage their children's efforts and to demand that their children work harder. Evidence also indicates that in Asia obtaining good grades is a means for obtaining status among age peers (Dong, Weisfeld, Boardway, & Shen, 1996). Because this is combined with the value placed on collectivism (chapter 2; see also Kagitcibasi, 1997), which encourages children to remain close to their parents and to show their love for their parents by pleasing them, Asian children are likely to try hard and eventually reap the benefits of higher grades.

Another cultural difference for Asian Americans was documented by Ritter and Dornbusch (1989). Compared to other ethnic group members, Asian Americans are more likely to believe that success in school has a relationship to success in life. That is, Asian Americans believe that if they do well in school, this increases their chances of achieving success outside of school. Developing this concept, Sue and Okazaki (1990) suggest a set of ideas summarized by the term "relative functionalism." The term is best explained by looking at the two component words. *Functionalism* means that people see a clear use for certain behaviors or a clear link between one set of behaviors (e.g., studying hard) and others (e.g., good grades, praise from parents). *Relative* refers to one set of social settings in contrast to another. If one set of behaviors is seen as more effective relative to others (e.g., studying harder rather than blaming the teacher), then that set of behaviors will be adopted (McInerney, Roche, McInerney, & Marsh, 1997). Sue and Okazaki argue that given prejudice and discrimination in the United States toward minority groups whose members have a different skin color and a different accent when using English, Asian Americans cannot benefit from all areas in society. Limits are placed on them in areas such as politics, athletics, entertainment, leadership in various organizations, and so forth. Realizing this, they examine various aspects of society and try to identify where they will receive fair treatment. After such a search, Asian Americans identify the area of formal education. Teachers are seen as appreciative of hard work and attentiveness, and they reward these qualities with good grades (Stenlund, 1995). Teachers are likely to give good students a "fair shake" regardless of their skin color. Asian Americans expect that relative to other parts of society, hard work in school will be functional to success in other arenas of life, such as the search for decent-paying jobs and membership in various professions. Given that they internalize the link between success in school and success in other aspects of life, they work hard and demonstrate exceptional educational achievement.

This discussion of relative functionalism applied to an entire cultural group allows a review of a difficult concept first introduced in chapter 1. This is the distinction between individual differences and cultural factors. Many individual Anglo and African Americans view education as the road to later success. I am certainly one of these. My parents made it very clear to me that financial burdens brought on by the Depression of the 1930s prevented them from going to college. If their children were to be more successful, then education was the avenue. This deeply held belief, however, is not widespread enough to be considered part of present American culture although it probably was in the early 20th century. Today, too many Americans do not see a link between education and success in life (Finn & Rock, 1997), spend as little time as possible on their schooling, and do not give sufficient attention to the education of their children. In contrast, the belief in the importance of education as leading to later success is more widespread among Asian Americans. The argument is not that all Asian Americans have this deep-seated belief. Rather, the argument is that the belief is widely enough shared to be considered part of Asian American culture. Importantly, the issue of generational differences has to be integrated here. A more precise statement of the findings is that the first few generations of Asian Americans behave according to the relative functionalism hypothesis: Success in school leads to success in other aspects of society. Sue and Okazaki (1990) point out that among members of later generations, acculturation to American society shows its effects. Asian Americans of the third and fourth generations behave much like Americans in general. Some do behave according to the relative functionalism hypothesis and some do not. What had been a cultural value, with its key component of being familiar and widespread among ethnic group members, has become an "individual differences" value. The key component of individual differences is that some people think and behave one way but many people think and behave in quite a different manner.

SCHOOLS AS SOCIALIZING AGENTS FOR THE NEEDS OF SOCIETY

The importance of success in school can be viewed as part of the cultural background of many Asian Americans. They view schooling as functional: It has uses for people in their quest for success and happiness in life. Do schools serve other uses for people and for the societies that put tax dollars into formal education? The answer is clearly yes. In many countries, the school is seen as a place where (a) desired changes in society can be introduced or reinforced and (b) problems not addressed effectively in other parts of society can be treated. Consider some examples in the United States. During the first 50 years of this century, African Americans made demands that they be integrated into society and that they be given the same rights as Anglo Americans. After a number of Supreme Court decisions, action was finally taken. What was a major site of this action? The answer, of course, is the public schools. With the Supreme Court decision of 1954 known as *Brown* v. *The Board of Education*, the concept of "separate but equal" schools was set aside and efforts were begun to integrate America's public educational system (Knappman, 1995). Government officials felt they had more control over funds for schooling than for other programs where massive integration efforts could have been undertaken. The schools became one of the major places where society tried to change itself in the area of race relations. As will be discussed in chapter 7, lessons learned from the painful efforts to integrate schools were later applied to other parts of society, such as in neighborhoods, workplaces, and private schools (Landis & Bhagat, 1996; Williams, 1987).

Other examples of responsibilities falling to the schools exist, occurring especially when society's leaders feel that problems are not being addressed effectively elsewhere. People get into too many automobile accidents. Too many drink alcohol to excess. Too few, especially if they are young, know anything about birth control. Many people get into trouble because of drug abuse, poor skills in managing their frustrations and aggressive tendencies, or a general disrespect for the country's legal system. The content of this book also is brought to the attention of schools. Not enough people know how to get along, and communicate effectively, with members of cultural groups other than their own. In all these cases, American schools are asked to add programs to their curricula so that society at large will function more smoothly. Consequently, programs dealing with driver education, alcohol and drug abuse, police-community relations, intercultural interaction training, and so forth are implemented.

The general concept here, then, is that U.S. society identifies problems and schools are asked to deal with a number of them. Is this concept found in other parts of the world? Examining schools in Japan and China, as well as the United States, Tobin, Wu, and Davidson (1989b) answered yes and found that schools deal with so-cietal problems as early as the preschool level (see also Spodek & Saracho, 1996). One of their findings allows insights into a puzzling problem many American moth-ers who reside in Japan face. Consider this example.

Margaret Blake was an executive in a fast-food chain that was exploring the pos-sibilities of introducing franchises in Japan. Accepting the assignment in Tokyo after a successful career in San Francisco, Margaret brought her 5-year-old son and placed him in a highly recommended Japanese preschool. Like many 5-year-olds, Margaret's son, named Mark, already had attended preschool in the United States. In fact, he had begun right after he was toilet trained at age 2. The preschool in San Francisco that Mark attended, in addition to offering good educational programs, also met Margaret's needs for day care. Margaret had long ago learned that Mark loved peanut butter sandwiches and also usually ate his entire lunch consisting of a sand-wich, fruit, cookies, and juice. So for his first day of Japanese preschool, Margaret prepared Mark's favorite type of lunch. Margaret took off time from work so that she could pick up Mark after his first day of school. She found that Mark was rather sullen, and on returning home he began to cry. Mark complained that the other chil-dren laughed at his sandwich, and even the teacher looked at Mark in a strange way during lunch. What is the source of the problem? (This incident is adapted from sim-ilar examples in both Tobin et al., 1989a, and Cushner & Brislin, 1996).

Integration Into a Group

In Japan, one purpose of preschool education is to encourage the child to become part of a group. Especially in Tokyo and other large cities, children frequently do not have age peers they can play with until they start school. Land is so scarce and ex-pensive in Japanese cities that people live in small apartments, and less land is set aside for playgrounds than in other highly developed nations. So even if young chil-dren do meet age peers in their apartment buildings, they have little room to play to-gether. The school becomes the place where children first learn to get along with others outside their immediate family. When they asked people in the three countries, "What are the most important things for children to learn in preschool?" Tobin, Wu, and Davidson (1989b, p. 190) gave special attention to the three most important reasons each respondent gave. Eighty percent of Japanese respondents (both men and women were questioned) indicated that they expected children to develop sympathy, empathy, and a concern for others. In comparison, 20% of the Chinese and 39% of the American respondents listed sympathy, empathy, and concern for others among their most important expectations of preschool education.

What does this have to do with Mark's lunch? In Japan, children show their concern for others by becoming part of a very disciplined, well-behaved group. Visitors to Japanese preschools are amazed to see 5-year-old children clean up after lunch, without noise and without any need for disciplinary action, after the teacher simply indicates that lunchtime is over. The concern for others and the infrequency of disciplinary problems, however, come at the expense of individual expression. Children are expected to blend together into a classroom group and not to stand out as unique (Hamilton, Blumenfeld, Akoh, & Miura, 1991; Markus & Kitayama, 1998). This has implications for dress, for styles of interacting with others, for toys, and for the lunches children bring from home. A Japanese lunch consists of a predictable collection of foods placed in a box called a *bento*. Anything other than a bento lunch is seen as overly individualistic, and 5-year-old Japanese children have had enough experience with the demands for uniformity that they find Mark's lunch unacceptable. In addition, bentos must be very carefully prepared, necessitating that mothers spend much time and effort on their children's lunches. As discussed in the previous section, Japanese culture places a great deal of emphasis on education. Japanese mothers show their concern for their children's education in many ways, and just one is lunch preparation. Such cultural differences lead to difficulties for Americans living in Japan. An American mother living in Kyoto ran into the "nothing other than a bento lunch" problem. So she learned how to make acceptable lunches. But her son came home crying. "Now what's wrong? I made you a Japanese lunch," she said. "But you didn't cut the apple slices so they look like bunny rabbits like the other mothers do," he said in tears (Tobin et al., 1989a, p. 38).

Communication Skills

One way Japanese children show a concern for, and empathy with, others is to behave in very similar ways as their age peers. This has important implications for communication skills. If people become empathetic with others in their group, members do not need to express their special needs with preciseness. When members have learned empathy and concern for one another, they sense an individual's special needs without that person stating them clearly. In Japan, communication between people is successful when the listener understands what a speaker is trying to say (M.-S. Kim, 1998; Lebra, 1976). This emphasis on the listener's responsibilities for successful communication is quite different from the emphasis in both China and the United States. In these countries, speakers are expected to make their points clearly, and examinations of communication difficulties are more likely to focus on the speaker's errors. This cultural difference shows up in answers to the earlier question about what children should learn in preschool. In China 27% of the respondents and in the United States 38% felt that communication skills were important. In Japan only 4% of the adults felt that communication skills were among the most important things for children to learn.

One reason for emphasis on the speaker's skills is that in China and the United States people must communicate with others who are very different from themselves. Readers are familiar with the differences that must be transcended in the United States. Some are due to social class background, age, amount of formal education, parental language, accents within the English language, region where socialization occurred, and so forth. Although outsiders often view people in China as the same from one place to another, this stereotype is totally inaccurate. The differences among the Chinese are vast. In terms of population, the Chinese constitute almost 20% of the world's people. In terms of area, China is twice the size of Europe. The Chinese government recognizes more than 50 official minority groups, and most have languages that are mutually unintelligible when members of these minority groups attempt to interact in face-to-face encounters. As Chang (1989) states:

> Americans typically see China as a political, economic, and sociological monolith. Nothing could be further from the truth. Although under the mandate of a central government, the people and provinces of China are as different from each other as the countries of Europe. And it has always been this way in China, for thousands of years. (p. 36)

Given vast differences within a country, its citizens cannot develop the same empathy as expected in Japan with its one national language and long history of cultural traditions shared by all people who identify themselves as Japanese. When Chinese and Americans want to communicate with others, they cannot expect so much shared culture that all listeners will understand what they want. Chinese and American speakers have the responsibility to communicate, and this is an emphasis in their education as early as the preschool level.

The Chinese make other requests of their preschools. One very important expectation has been brought on by a national policy to limit families to one child. Designed to curb population growth, the policy is at odds with a long cultural tradition of large families. Given the program's success, many adults worry about what they call the "4-2-1" syndrome (Tobin et al., 1989a, 1989b). The "1" refers to the child whose two parents and four grandparents are so attentive that the child may become spoiled and consequently not a hard-working citizen of China. When asked, "Why should a society have preschools?" 12% of Chinese adults answered "To reduce spoiling and make up for deficiencies of parents" (Tobin et al., 1989b, p. 192). This figure is much larger than the 2% of adults in both Japan and the United States who were concerned about spoiling and other parental deficiencies. Also, more concern was felt in China for preschools "starting young children on the road toward being good citizens."

America's Expectations

Adults in the United States had expectations of preschools that were different from the other two countries. Readers may want to try to guess what these expectations are, especially given the discussion in chapter 2 on individualism and collectivism. In responding to the question about what is most important for children to learn, 73% of American adults expressed a desire for children's self-reliance and self-confidence. These figures were larger than the 29% of Chinese and the 44% of Japanese who had similar concerns. Self-reliance and self-confidence include the beliefs that people can set, work toward, and achieve their own goals and can do so without total dependence on others. "I did it all by myself" is a sentence American children use when solving a puzzle, and parents and teachers are happy when the children say this to describe their efforts. Self-reliance is extremely useful in a highly individualistic society such as the United States where people must set and achieve goals without the constant presence of a supportive collective whose members can help out in times of trouble (Chao, 1996; Farver et al., 1995). Even with this emphasis on individualism, the importance of working cooperatively with others and developing a sense of identity that includes others is part of America's thinking about its schools. Tobin et al. (1989a) observe:

> American folklore celebrates the loner and the self-made [person] and looks with scorn on the "ant-colony" mentality seen as characteristic of group-oriented cultures. But some Americans worry that in the celebration of individualism the threads that bind people to one another have been stretched too thin. They are looking to government, church, and community organizations—including preschools—for direction and for a sense of shared purpose and identity. (p. 45)

The balance between individualistic and group-oriented concerns will continue to be debated in the United States well into the 21st century. When applied to formal education, the issue might be posed in a question such as this: "What aspects of American culture should be reinforced in the school and what should be changed?" One aspect of American society that many feel needs to change is the lack of appreciation given to people who are fluent in more than one language. In a conference that led to the publication of a volume on language learning, interpretation, and translation (Gerver & Sinaiko, 1978), Europeans and Americans attended and shared ideas. The relative respect given to bilinguals was captured in this thought that attendees were asked to consider. Someone says, "We will be having a meeting where attendees speak different languages. Your interpreter has just arrived." In Europe, the concept "interpreter" has a positive image of a well-educated individual who possesses a valued skill. In the United States, the image is much more likely to be of an individual who speaks English with a noticeable accent, dresses in a slightly rumpled jacket with patches on the sleeves, is probably an immigrant to America, and in general does not command much respect. Can the schools do more to encourage respect for people who are fluent in several languages? This is one of the concerns of educators who have considered the introduction of bilingual education programs.

BILINGUAL EDUCATION

Few topics related to formal schooling have been the focus of more controversy in the United States than bilingual education (Brislin & Horvath, 1997; Gersten & Woodward, 1995; Hakuta, 1986; Padila et al., 1991; Paulston, 1980). Few disagree about one fact: If children participate in a bilingual education program, they receive instruction in different subject matters (e.g., reading, history, mathematics, science) in different languages. The key words are "subject matters." Bilingual education differs from foreign language instruction because it goes beyond the typical class in French, Spanish, or German that students take for their foreign language requirement. Rather than being a separate class devoted solely to teaching a new language, bilingual education involves various classes where children learn the subject matter as dictated by the curricula established for the school as a whole. Beyond this fact, people do not agree about the goals, purposes, dangers, and advantages of bilingual education.

One of the basic disagreements centers on the expectations adults in a community have for schoolchildren. Many adults feel that instruction in any language other than English puts children at a disadvantage once they seek higher education or employment. They feel that instruction using another language involves time that should be spent using the language children need to succeed in the United States: English. Other adults feel that America has given far too little emphasis to languages other than English and that this inattention has led to a decline in America's competitiveness within a global economy. Many of these same adults also feel that if some children already know a language before coming to school (e.g., immigrants from South America or Asia), then formal educational programs should benefit from this blessing.

Maintenance and Transition Programs

At least in terms of people who write letters to newspaper columnists and who contribute to the "letters to the editor" section of periodicals, four times as many people are against bilingual education as are in favor of it (Hakuta, 1986) in the United States. Much sentiment against bilingual education will remain for decades given the deep-seated belief among many Americans that use of the English language is one of the demands of citizenship and is one of the unifying elements in a diverse society (a belief analyzed by Padila et al., 1991). Some of the negative sentiment, however, might diminish if several issues were better understood.

One issue involves the goals of different bilingual education programs. Two basic goals exist, so two different types of programs have been created (Gersten & Woodward, 1995). In a *maintenance program*, children who already speak a language besides English are encouraged to maintain it. For example, numerous children who might benefit from a maintenance program are native speakers of Spanish in the United States (Mackey & Beebe, 1977) and French in Canada (W. Lambert et al., 1993; W. Lambert & Tucker, 1972). While maintaining their original language skills, they also receive instruction in the English language and eventually use both languages in their subject matter instruction. The eventual goal of maintenance programs is to encourage the development of true bilinguals, that is, adults who are fluent in two languages.

In a *transition program*, children begin their schooling in their native language and are gradually exposed to increased instruction in English. The transition, then, involves a move from their original language to the language introduced in school.

Many transition programs have the goal of moving speakers of other languages into all-English instruction in two or three years. Contrary to popular belief, the United States has far more transition programs than maintenance programs. Educators who believe in the value of transition programs argue that certain general skills are transferable across languages (e.g., Mackey & Beebe, 1977). For instance, if children learn to read in one language, they have learned a general skill and thus can read in another language. The general skill of reading involves making sense of marks printed or written on a page, and it does not matter which language children use to develop this general skill as long as they speak and understand the language. Educators favoring transition programs argue that it makes sense to teach these general skills to children using the tools (e.g, the Spanish or French languages) the children already know. At the same time, instruction in the English language can be introduced, and children later can use their general skills when asked to read materials written in English.

Are Children Naturally Good Language Learners?

In addition to discussing the maintenance/transition distinction as a source of disagreements, Hakuta (1986) analyzed other reasons why bilingual education has been the focus of such heated arguments in the United States. An additional reason is the belief of many adults that children under about age 12 pick up languages naturally and easily. The argument goes that if speakers of other languages are put into an all-English curriculum, they simply will use their natural language acquisition abilities and learn English. Hakuta (1986) argues that the "child as natural language learner" concept is a myth. Some children do learn other languages quickly, but others find it a struggle. It also must be kept in mind that many children who are nonnative speakers of English do not have good support at home for other-language learning. Some children downplay their English language abilities for fear of distancing themselves from their parents and older siblings who may be far more fluent in Spanish, Chinese, Korean, or another language. Just as in the research by Kagitcibasi (1997) reviewed earlier indicating that some mothers become upset with the autonomy children show after school attendance, parents of children who are successful English-language learners may communicate subtle signs that they are uncomfortable with their children's progress.

Many adults who point to children's natural language learning abilities are themselves immigrants who spoke another language on their first day of school, were placed in monolingual English classrooms, and were successful. "I learned English and did OK in school. Why all this fuss about special bilingual education programs that everybody admits cost a lot of money?" Again, the distinction is between some children and all children (Goto & Abe-Kim, 1998). Many adults did indeed thrive in America's classrooms without knowing a word of English on their first day of school. But others did not, dropped out, and had far less access to the benefits of American society. It was mentioned earlier that people who write letters to the editor are against bilingual education by a four to one margin. Many of these letter writers use the "I did it—why can't others?" argument. It must be kept in mind that these people have developed the literary skills and self-confidence necessary to write letters to the editor. School dropouts are far less visible when a "pro and con" count is made of these letters.

Political Considerations

Another important reason for the heated, sometimes unpleasantly hostile, debates about bilingual education is that political considerations are involved (Paulston, 1980). Whenever many different people desire scarce resources, a system has to be developed that allows decisions about the exact people who receive the resources (Brislin, 1991; Greenberg & Baron, 1997). In authoritarian societies, a limited number of privileged people make the decisions, and the vast majority of citizens are not allowed to voice their preferences. In democratic societies, many people are allowed and are often encouraged to make recommendations about the distribution of resources. Although not always recognized as such (Crick, 1982), the system that allows people to participate in decisions about the distribution of scarce resources is called "politics." While often considered unpleasant words that polite people should avoid (Brislin, 1991), "politics" and "access to power" summarize the process people use to participate in decision making about important matters such as public education. As Crick points out, an absence of politics and a lack of power mean that people have to accept decisions others make that affect them.

The role of politics in the distribution of resources becomes clearest when specific examples are examined. Bilingual education programs can be very costly. These programs often demand the hiring of new teachers who are themselves bilingual or the hiring of bilingual aides who assist full-time teachers. The programs demand the acquisition of new books and teaching materials. With some languages, such as Spanish and French, suitable materials might be readily available after people examine schoolbooks used in Spain, Mexico, or France. With other languages, such as Laotian, Vietnamese, or any of the languages native to the Pacific islands, new materials might have to be prepared, and costs can mount quickly in any efforts to write new texts or to prepare new teaching materials. A major aspect of politics in a democratic society is that everyone who wants to contribute must have a chance to speak out. People who strongly believe in a certain position are happy to hear the speeches of supporters but become frustrated when opponents (who have the same right to speak out) disagree. To increase this frustration, bilingual education is a topic many people feel compelled to speak about without knowing much about it (Hakuta, 1986). At public forums, such as meetings of boards of education, people frequently begin by saying, "I don't know much about bilingual education, but I feel . . ."

Given its costs, people who favor other uses of public funds may feel that money invested in bilingual education will be taken away from other desirable programs. Consequently, opponents of bilingual education argue in favor of other programs and in doing so participate in the competition for scarce resources. Examples of other programs many people favor over bilingual education include special English-as-a-second-language classes (ESL), where well-trained teachers give instruction in English with sensitivity to the background of students who are native speakers of other languages. Or, preferred programs can involve very different aspects of the educational system, such as a three-year plan to raise teacher salaries, programs to encourage the best college students to enter the teaching profession, antidrug workshops, and efforts to encourage schoolchildren to engage in volunteer work within their communities. All of these programs are worthy of consideration, and bilingual education has to compete against them in the political arena.

The Effectiveness of Bilingual Education Programs

If evaluations of bilingual education programs showed that native speakers of other languages clearly benefit from them, then this information would be very useful when proponents of bilingual education compete for funds in the political arena. Unfortunately, general or blanket statements that "bilingual education is effective" cannot be made. As Hakuta (1986) concludes:

> There is a sober truth that even the ardent advocate of bilingual education would not deny. Evaluation studies of the effectiveness of bilingual education in improving either English or math scores have not been overwhelmingly in favor of bilingual education. To be sure, there are programs that have been highly effective [discussed by Padila et al., 1991], but not very many. . . . An awkward tension blankets the lack of empirical demonstration of the success of bilingual education programs. Someone promised bacon, but it's not there. (pp. 219–220)

This summary statement about the effectiveness of bilingual education programs brings up an important argument found, in various forms, in several chapters of this book. The argument is that an understanding of complex programs is more likely to occur when very specific behaviors are investigated (W. Lambert et al., 1993; Lindholm, 1991). Bilingual education programs are complex, but little is learned about them by asking the question "Does bilingual education help children?" The key phrase in the quote just given from Hakuta (1986) is, "there are programs that have been highly effective." More valuable insights into bilingual education would be forthcoming if research was done on exactly what happens in these *successful* programs. Is it the attitude of teachers? Is it a specific type of learning material that students use? Does it involve the sort of cooperative effort among students encouraged in KEEP that was discussed earlier? People do not know the answers to these questions.

The research on bilingual education, with disappointing results, has tried to answer the question "Does it work?" Critics of this research feel that more useful information would be available if the question had been "What types of bilingual education programs work for children in what age groups, from what social class backgrounds, with access to what other educational enrichments in their lives, using what specific types of learning materials, interacting with what kinds of teachers . . . ?" and so forth. Paulston (1980) also recommends that research examine other outcomes of bilingual education programs besides classroom progress in subjects such as English and mathematics. She recommends that researchers ask whether children stay in school until they graduate, whether they find employment after completing their education, whether they avoid drugs and alcohol abuse, and so forth. If bilingual education programs help speakers of other languages benefit from their schooling, its effects could well show up years later in their contributions to society.

THE UNIVERSITY CLASSROOM AND CROSS-CULTURAL EDUCATION

When reviewing the research on both KEEP and bilingual education programs, I discussed the cultural sensitivity of teachers and administrators. Whenever new ideas are to be introduced into a culture that demand an understanding of culture and cultural differences, those interested must ask whether or not enough people are prepared to work with these new ideas. Are enough people sensitive to culture and to cultural differences so that the new ideas will receive careful and fair consideration? Where might people learn such sensitivities?

The development of intercultural sensitivity (also to be discussed in chapters 6 and 7) is an important topic for a chapter on education given that many researchers and educators have pointed to the college classroom as a place where intercultural skills can be developed (Brislin, 1997; Cushner & Brislin, 1996; Goldstein, 1995; Singelis, 1998). Many of these scholars have developed classroom exercises that encourage skill development in addition to the learning of new material typical of all college courses. They also view these exercises as a substitute for or as a supplement to extensive intercultural experiences that would ideally take place in people's everyday lives. If I had the power and funds, for example, I would ask every college student to spend two years in another country so that they would be forced to develop their intercultural skills. This is clearly impossible, so various educators (e.g., 40 people contributed to a collection edited by Singelis, 1998) have suggested classroom exercises meant to capture aspects of the desired two-year intense intercultural experience. They also have given attention to covering solid course content so that students master relevant material. This latter point is especially important when professors teach courses that are prerequisite to more advanced work.

Considerations for Class Exercises

The term *exercise* is used here to mark classroom activities that encourage active student involvement in new material and that move students beyond the role of audience member for a lecture. Classroom activities only should be used, however, after careful consideration of the goals for any one course. On many college campuses, such exercises have a bad reputation because critics feel they are "fun and games" and are not a serious use of classroom time. In my own teaching, for example, I consider these issues (Brislin, 1997). What are my goals for a given class presentation? Can I cover this material effectively in a lecture format? Have I said to myself after a lecture, "Could I have covered this material more effectively if students had become actively involved in some way?" Are exercises I might use available, or should I develop a new one?

Exercises range in amount of student activity from quiet consideration of ideas to discussions with others and extend to active involvement with others that demands much movement around the classroom. Readers should keep in mind that they have been exposed to this broad use of the term *exercise* both in the critical incidents they have read and considered and in the examinations of their own experiences I have asked them to do in this book. When deciding whether to do activities that involve group interaction and extensive movement around the classroom, I keep in mind what I call the "stuffy dean" criterion. Assume I am introducing material through an exercise. Students may talk loudly and perhaps even laugh given the elation people sometimes experience once they figure out a difficult point. If a rather conservative dean who is quite convinced of the value of formal lectures happens to pass by my class, when will he or she do so? Of course, the dean will pass by exactly at the moment people are talking loudly or laughing as a reaction to the new learning. The dean may later call me in and say, "I wonder if much learning is taking place if students are simply talking and laughing." Keeping in mind my "stuffy dean" criterion, I want to be able to reply along the following lines:

> My judgment was that I could cover the material best through an active exercise, and this generated the response you observed. I would be happy to have you come in to question the students about the content of the material I presented or to give them a pop quiz so that you can be sure they have mastered it.

Example: A Framework for Understanding Acculturation

Criteria for using an exercise in the classroom, then, start with important material to be covered and proceed to questions about the best way to present the material. An excellent example of a useful exercise has been developed by Kyle Smith (1998) to communicate important points about acculturation. I chose to cover this exercise here because I have observed Smith introduce the exercise and have discussed it with him, I have observed a graduate student who worked with me (Catherine Snyder) use it, and I have used it in the classroom. Another reason for the choice of this exercise is that it allows review and integration of some key points discussed in chapters 3 and 4.

Smith wanted to introduce the concept of *acculturation*, or the process and results of extensive intercultural contact or cultural change introduced from outside influences. He found that the model Berry (1990, 1997) developed summarized numerous research findings. In Berry's approach to acculturation, a *donor culture* exerts much influence on a *recipient culture*. In the previous chapter, for example, research on Korean immigrants to the United States was reviewed. The United States would be considered the donor culture, and the Korean immigrants would be the recipients of various potential influences. Members of the recipient culture respond in one of four ways to various aspects of the donor culture. The four ways are based on two decisions:

1. Whether to retain selected aspects of one's first culture: yes or no

2. Whether to pursue relations with members of the donor or host culture: yes or no

One of the four ways for recipients to respond is *assimilation*, and the pattern of answers to the two decisions is no for Decision 1 and yes for Decision 2. Continuing with the example of immigrants, they would not seek to retain one or more aspects of their culture and would seek extensive contact and relationships with members of the donor culture. A familiar example would be job selection and career advancement. If immigrants seek jobs in the host culture and advance their careers in similar ways as hosts but do not pursue jobs that were common in their first culture, then they are assimilating this aspect of the host culture.

In an *integration* response, the answers are yes to both decisions. People seek to maintain aspects of their own culture while interacting extensively with host culture members. If immigrants, for example, put time and effort into preserving artistic traditions from their first culture but present them in host museums, auditoriums, and television shows, this would be integration of a cultural aspect.

In a *separation* response, the pattern of answers is yes for Decision 1 and no for Decision 2. People seek to maintain aspects of their culture but express no desire to associate with hosts when that cultural aspect is involved. If immigrants make a strong point of maintaining their first language but have no goal of using it in interactions with hosts, then they would be engaging in separation in this aspect of their lives. At times, the choice to engage in separation is based on perceived host reactions. Immigrants who speak Spanish in the American Southwest, for example, are proud of their language but do not use it in the company of English-speaking Anglos for fear of becoming stereotyped as "poor Mexican immigrants" (Freimanis, 1994).

In a *marginalization* response, the answers to both decisions are no. People feel no desire to maintain aspects of their first culture and have little interaction with host culture members. Ideally, examples of this response would be rare because it leads to feelings of rejection and helplessness (Berry, 1997). An example might be immigrants who receive a good education and advanced degrees in the host culture. However, this education leads members of their first culture to reject them as "elitist and not one of us anymore." Further, because of discrimination and preference for "native born" citizens, it also could lead host culture members to reject them.

Berry's model allows analysis of aspects of people's acculturation and a summary view of their predominant reaction to acculturative pressures. The combination of attention to specific aspects and overall patterns allows greater understanding of individual differences among people engaged in extensive intercultural interactions. For example, immigrants might have an overall pattern resembling assimilation if they are employed in the sorts of jobs that long have been common in the host culture, have left the religion of their parents and have joined a local church, and spend most of their leisure time with hosts. However, these people might have a specific separatist aspect to their lives if they have maintained their skills in a traditional musical or art form from their first culture but find that hosts are completely uninterested in this aspect of their lives.

Exercise Activities

Once the two decisions and four patterns of acculturation are introduced in a class, students then analyze examples of acculturation and match them to one or more of the four patterns. K. Smith once told me he introduced this matching task to complement his formal presentation of acculturation. "I could tell by the students' faces that they were interested in the material, but that they were at least a little confused with distinctions among the four patterns. I could have presented more examples in lecture format, but I thought it would be better to have them work with their own examples as much as possible," he said. The exercise offers three possibilities for student analysis of examples and consequent mastery of the material. Smith uses one or two videotapes that deal with movement across cultures. In my experience, most college audiovisual centers have several quite suitable tapes. The two Smith uses are:

- *A Clash of Cultures*, 1986, which deals with African cultures and the influence of Western, Islamic, and traditional aspects of culture
- *Return to Paradise*, 1987, which covers the influence of the West (especially North America, Europe, and Australia) on Pacific island nations in Melanesia, Polynesia, and Micronesia.

The students view portions of one of the videotapes. They then either generate examples of the four patterns of acculturation or take Smith's examples and put them in categories based on the patterns. Using the latter (probably more common) approach, students would see examples on separate cards and would sort these cards in four groups based on the four patterns (exact examples for preparation of the cards can be found in K. Smith, 1998). For example, the *Return to Paradise* tape reports that only 15% of the population in Tahiti is French but that Tahitians must learn French language and history in school. Students would place this example in the "assimilation" group of cards. Another card, again summarizing a point made in the videotape, states that Tahitians sometimes gather on a designated island to salvage neglected aspects of their culture such as songs and weaving. Students would place this in the "separation" group of cards.

Students who view *A Clash of Cultures*, would see a card that reminds them that a university in Nigeria, patterned after schools in Europe and North America, offers a science department course in traditional divination methods. They would place this in the "integration" group of cards. They also would see a card that reminds them of the discussion about the giving of gifts to powerful people. Traditionally, this was a sign of respect. Currently, it is being questioned because it might be part of "corrupt practices" in today's business world. Western businesspeople and Africans themselves have no clear answer about the "respect" versus "corruption" aspect of the practice. Consequently, students probably would put this card in the "marginalization" category.

Review of Previous Material in This Textbook.   In addition to, or instead of, viewing and reacting to one of the videotapes, students can review material previously discussed in this book. Examples would be the material on social change in India (pp. 122–133), parental response to adolescents (pp. 141–150) and bilingual education (pp. 180–184). In all of these sections, the choices and dilemmas people faced were discussed. Students would evaluate these and apply them to one of the four acculturation patterns. Here are some examples students have gathered when I have used this exercise.

In the material on social change in India, an example of assimilation would be the possibility that both parents work outside the home. However, if the man of the family wants to keep control over all family income with minimal tolerance for suggestions from the woman, this would be separation. If parents who work outside the home ask the children's grandparents, aunts, and uncles to share in child-rearing responsibilities, this would be an example of integration because elements from traditional culture and recent social changes from the West are being combined. If extended-family members do not become involved, however, certain traditional elements of culture may become marginalized. Grandparents used to tell traditional stories to children that captured lessons useful for socialization into a culture. If parents forget these stories and if grandparents are not present to tell them, then the stories may become marginalized with a label such as "terribly old-fashioned."

Much of the discussion on parental response to adolescence dealt with teenagers from Asia acculturating to urban cities in the United States. If the students want to go out on dates and go to school dances, this would be an example of assimilation. However, if they accept their parents' wishes for them to study extremely hard, to de-emphasize membership in school clubs, and to make a point of receiving high grades for their schoolwork, this could be an example of separation. Teachers often want students to formulate their own opinions and to speak up in class. If the students combine this with a nondisagreeing respect for their parents' opinions presented at the dinner table, this would be an example of integration. If parents want their children to succeed in the English-speaking high school with its set curriculum and if students become attracted to the interests of their American age peers, interests in artistic activities of their first culture easily can become marginalized.

When students discuss bilingual education in terms of the four patterns, they will conclude transition programs are clearly an example of moving students toward assimilation. Transition programs often begin with lessons in the students' first language, but then lessons increasingly use the culture's dominant language (e.g., English). Maintenance programs represent an attempt at integration. Skills in the first language are respected and developed, and skills in the country's dominant language are introduced. At times, schools do not offer bilingual programs. If leaders in a community want to encourage children's use of their first language, they sometimes start language schools that meet after school hours or on Saturdays. In many big U.S. cities, it is relatively easy to find Japanese language schools. Given that these schools are quite independent of a community's educational bureaucracy, the schools are separatist. Many immigrant children from Asia have language skills that might be maintained, but they find no encouragement to do so. Their parents sometimes emphasize English with the view that "We are in America, and learning English is the way to get ahead!" The children also may find that teachers and age peers in their schools show no appreciation of their Asian language skills. Consequently, these skills can become marginalized.

Personal Experiences.   After working with information presented on videotapes and/or in a textbook, students can suggest examples of the four acculturation patterns in their own lives. If a class is blessed with students who are recent immigrants or from diverse cultural groups, students should have few difficulties finding examples if they start with cultural elements such as language use, interests, interactions with others, and so forth. Even for classes where students come from a relatively homogenous background, examples may be possible. First, sources of diversity among them would be suggested. These can be based on gender, religion, rural versus urban background, socioeconomic class background, and so forth. Then, students might be told, "Think of the four acculturation patterns if your current life in college is viewed as the donor and dominant culture."

When I have proposed this, students have made these suggestions. Some students from rural backgrounds attending college in a big city report they find themselves assimilating. They discover that they enjoy life in the city and have no desire to return to the small town where they grew up. In contrast, some students from rural areas try to maintain their interests and skills through a type of separation. They may be psychology majors, but they make a point of taking courses in animal science or horticulture. Psychology-major friends often do not know about this additional coursework. Women who are engineering majors report examples of integration. They enjoy competing in demanding departments where most faculty and fellow students are men, but they maintain aspects of their personality (e.g., sensitivity to others, a topic to be discussed in chapter 9) that they plan to integrate into their personal leadership style. Students from economically disadvantaged backgrounds sometimes report feelings of marginalization. They aspire to a middle-class lifestyle but do not feel accepted by age peers from economically comfortable circumstances. However, given their aspirations and new interests developed through the college coursework and activities, they feel that friends from past years are uncomfortable with the changes they observe in those who "went away to college."

I agree with K. Smith (1998), who has found that after participating in this exercise, students move from a textbook knowledge of the four acculturation patterns to a deeper understanding. They gain the ability to generate examples from their own lives. Further, and this is an advantage of many good exercises (Brislin, 1997; Goldstein, 1995; Singelis, 1998), students become exposed to multiple components of the acculturation process. Students can study cognitive components and can learn *about* stress and parental strife through their reading. More active involvement, such as examining specific behaviors seen on videotape and comparing them with specific examples from their own lives, begins to introduce students to *emotional reactions* that accompany people's acculturation. It also allows students to think, again, about a theme discussed in various chapters of this book. The study of culture and behavior involves generalities, such as acculturation, but people undergoing acculturation pressures experience individual differences. The specific behaviors that are part of one person's acculturation (e.g., desire to maintain interest in horticulture as mentioned earlier) will not be the specific behaviors that are part of another person's life.

The argument that complex human behavior is best understood by examining specific aspects can be applied in many areas. Recall the analysis of the success of Asian Americans in school. Sue and Okazaki (1990) argue that general appeals to "cultural differences" for explaining their success are not helpful. Much more specific behaviors and factors have to be examined, such as the number of hours parents encourage their children to spend on their homework and the quality of school texts (Mayer, Sims, & Tajika, 1995; Stevenson, Chen, & Lee, 1993). This argument about understanding the specifics also is presented in the next chapter, concerned with prejudice and discrimination. Many readers probably have heard the recommendation "Let's just bring people from different cultural groups together so that they can get to know each other—this will reduce prejudice!" In actuality, such efforts simply can reinforce and even increase prejudice if people from the less powerful groups feel they are being ignored or exploited. Attention must be given to a very specific set of recommendations for programs to reduce prejudice, and this will be one of the topics covered in chapter 6.

CHAPTER SUMMARY

Many of the socialization experiences children participate in take place within their culture's formal school system. Further, leaders in different societies frequently identify problems that other institutions, such as the family or the judicial system, are not addressing effectively. These leaders then often assign schools the task of finding solutions to these problems, placing expectations on schools that go beyond the teaching of traditional subject matters such as reading, writing, and mathematics.

In contrast to informal education, formal schooling is set aside from everyday life, occurs in a designated place, and is organized by specialists in the teaching profession. Compared to children's other role models, teachers are far more likely to be explicit about education goals and are more likely to introduce general principles that may have specific applications in settings outside the school. The fact that formal schooling is removed from children's daily activities with their families leads to the risk that some children will not see the relevance of schooling and will not be motivated to meet the teachers' expectations.

If children succeed in school, they are more likely to develop several specific cognitive skills than are equally intelligent age peers who do not attend school (Rogoff, 1981; Serpell & Hatano, 1997). Three of these skills are the efficient organization of new knowledge; the analytical skill of extracting information from a complex figure or picture; and the more efficient analysis of pictures, especially recognizing two-dimensional cues for depicting three dimensions. These skills undoubtedly develop from the typical school experiences of (a) learning to organize efficiently the ideas teachers present rather than simply depending on rote memory and (b) learning to find the key information necessary to solve particular problems from the total information presented in written or pictorial form.

Many educators feel that some children do better in school than others because some have socialization experiences prior to their first day of school that prepare them to benefit greatly from their formal education. Some come from families who keep many books in the home and who frequently read as an activity. Some children have experiences with puzzles, some of which are very similar to the sorts of tests used to analyze children's analytical skills. An especially interesting cultural difference involves the concept "conversational partners." Who are acceptable conversational partners for adults in various cultures? In some, the answer is "only other adults." In these cultures, adults rarely sit down with children to have a long conversation involving several rounds of verbal exchanges. In other cultures, such as the middle-class United States, it is considered quite acceptable for adults to have long conversations with children, and it is a recommended practice for children's language development. Children accustomed to adults as conversational partners are far more prepared to benefit from interactions with their schoolteachers than are children unfamiliar with such interactions with adults.

The fact that some children are familiar with adults as conversational partners is an example of socialization experiences that can lead to a smooth transition into their formal education. Researchers have argued that if school officials recognize various aspects of children's cultural background, they can support interventions that lead to greater success for the children (Cushner et al., 1996; Laboratory of Comparative Human Cognition, 1986). One of the most carefully evaluated examples is the Kamehameha Elementary Education Program (KEEP) in Hawaii (Vogt et al., 1987). Research was carried out to determine children's everyday socialization experiences. One finding was that Hawaiian children take part in group activities far more than children from other cultural groups. In a group activity called talk story, children have extensive verbal exchanges with others about familiar events, or stories, in their lives. Taking advantage of these socialization experiences, the KEEP researchers designed an educational program that involves a great deal of group learning. The program to teach reading integrates talk story. Children read a story from a book and then discuss it with others in a familiar manner—many interruptions, multiple overlapping verbal contributions, and so forth. Evaluation studies showed that the program is very effective in teaching children in the early elementary school years to read at grade level. A disappointing finding is that children did not maintain their grade-level reading skills as they moved into the upper elementary and junior high school years.

One reason for this lack of skill maintenance may involve the children's families (Cushner, 1990; U. Kim, 1990; Vernon-Feagans, 1996). Skills learned in school may not be reinforced at home, not through direct interference but because family members are unfamiliar with and perhaps uncomfortable with the skills their children or siblings have developed. Realizing this strong possibility, Kagitcibasi (1990, 1997) introduced home-based schooling in her native country, Turkey. Teachers work with both children and mothers and suggest ways mothers can interact with their children so that they can encourage their cognitive growth. Evaluation studies have shown that the mothers increase their own self-esteem and become more confident of their abilities to encourage their children's development. They become more comfortable with their children's autonomy, which their children develop by solving problems on their own and depending less on the family. An especially interesting finding is that even though home-based schooling is aimed at certain children and their parents, younger siblings pick up some of the skills. This generalization to younger children results from their observations of the teachers' activities as well as from their later interactions with their more knowledgeable peers and mothers.

In some countries, an emphasis on doing well in school, together with parental encouragement about homework, reading at home, and good grades, is so widespread that researchers have looked to cultural factors. Many observers, including journalists, researchers, and businesspeople concerned with education, have argued that Asian Americans are highly successful in American schools. Attempting to identify cultural differences as factors, Ritter and Dornbusch (1989) found that Asian Americans, compared to other cultural groups in the United States, were more likely to believe that success in school had a strong relationship to success in other aspects of society, such as finding a good job and earning a high salary. Developing this idea, Sue and Okazaki (1990) argued that the hard work in school can be explained in terms of "relative functionalism." Asian Americans examine various aspects of society and ask themselves, "Where will work be reinforced? Where will prejudice be least? Where will we receive fair treatment, regardless of our skin color or accent?" After their examination, they conclude that relative to other parts of society, hard work in school will bring rewards. Hard work will be useful, or functional, in helping them to acquire the benefits society has to offer.

Does formal schooling serve other uses for people? Research on this question has led to the important conclusion mentioned in the beginning of this section that schools are often treated as places to address some of society's problems. When other parts of society cannot deal with a problem effectively, it is sometimes turned over to the schools. In the United States, schools are expected to address such problems with programs preparing people to drive automobiles safely, encouraging them to avoid drug and alcohol abuse, introducing racial integration, and teaching birth control. Society's leaders make demands of their formal educational system that apply as early as the preschool years (Spodek & Saracho, 1996). In work carried out in Japan, China, and the United States, Tobin, Wu, and Davidson (1989a, 1989b) found cultural differences in adults' expectations of preschools. In Japan, schools are expected to encourage children to become part of a group and to become empathetic with and concerned about others. In China, schools are expected to deal with the "4-2-1" problem, that is, one-child families with two parents and four grandparents who are overly attentive to the child's every wish. Adults see the schools as the places where spoiling is to cease and where children will learn to be productive and hardworking members of Chinese society. In the United States, adults expect preschools to encourage children's self-reliance and self-confidence. These skills are useful in an individualistic society where people have to set goals and work toward them without the constant presence of a collective whose members are committed to helping each other. The future of education in the United States undoubtedly will include attention to the balance between individualistic strivings for personal goals and a concern for others, such as for the less fortunate who do not have homes, skills for the job market, and strong representation by influential political leaders.

Another aspect of formal education that may receive more future attention in the United States is valuing fluency in more than one language. In a global economy, society should value bilingualism and multilingualism. Bilingual education programs are one way to give this skill attention (Hakuta, 1986). Such programs, however, have been the topic of heated, often unpleasant debate. Many opponents of bilingual education feel that one of the unifying forces in a society is that all citizens should be fluent in one language (e.g., English in the United States). They feel that attention to other languages takes time and energy away from efforts to make children fluent in English. Educators argue that people often take this position based on mistaken information. Most bilingual education programs are transitional (Gersten & Woodward, 1995), meaning that children start school in the language of their parents (e.g., Spanish, Vietnamese) but move toward all-English instruction over a period of two or three years. Programs aimed at maintenance, where children are encouraged to keep and to develop their first language while simultaneously learning English, are less common.

Proponents and opponents of bilingual education programs must enter the political arena, where many proposals for ways to improve children's schooling are considered. Many adults, just as concerned with the welfare of children as proponents of bilingual education, feel that other programs are more useful. These include instruction in English as a second language by well-trained teachers; programs to bring society's brightest college graduates into the teaching profession; efforts to increase the status of teachers by increasing their salaries and giving them more decision-making power, and so forth. All these worthy programs have to compete for such scarce resources as funding, the attention of the school boards in various communities, and the support of concerned parent groups.

Numerous people hope knowledge of more than one language will become an American cultural value, rather than continuing with the belief that "English only" language skills are sufficient. These attitudes toward language, in turn, will be influenced by how Americans view people who are different from themselves in terms of skin color, cultural values and practices, accent when using English, and so forth. Greater understanding of others can be introduced through active teaching exercises introduced in the college classroom. Given that many students may not have had previous intercultural experiences, these exercises also can provide an admittedly modest substitute for the two years of study or work abroad that professors often wish more students could experience. One exercise developed by K. Smith (1998) asks students to examine the acculturation process when people (e.g., immigrants, international students) are exposed to the values of a dominant culture. The four patterns of acculturation, from the model Berry developed (1990, 1997), follow:

- *Assimilation*: when people accept the values and everyday behaviors of the dominant culture
- *Integration*: when people maintain valued aspects of their first culture while also benefiting from active participation in the dominant culture
- *Separation*: when people seek minimal contact with the dominant culture and seek to preserve their own culture
- *Marginalization*: when people subscribe to values and behave in ways that are acceptable neither to members of their first culture nor to members of the dominant culture

All of these acculturation patterns can be found both as overall approaches to dealing with the relationships between people's first culture and the dominant culture and as approaches to selected cultural elements, such as music, dress, ways of interacting with elders, and many others. Often, the choice of an approach is strongly influenced by the attitudes of people in the dominant culture, especially their willingness to understand and to appreciate cultural differences.

To understand people's views of others who are different from themselves, people must understand issues such as stereotyping, prejudice, and discrimination. These are the topics addressed in the next chapter.

C H A P T E R 6

INTERGROUP RELATIONS: CULTURES IN CONTACT

CHAPTER OVERVIEW

Imagine people who are dating individuals from a very different cultural background. When they introduce these special individuals to their families and friends, what will reactions be? Will the individuals be rejected outright, greeted cordially but not warmly, or welcomed with enthusiasm? Will various people in the family and friendship groups have differing reactions? The types and ranges of these reactions to culturally different people will be discussed in this chapter.

Stereotypes refer to generalizations about people based on the names of groups in which the people are real or imagined members. If people who are not African American, Japanese, or Mexican think of these groups, do images immediately come to mind? If images are easily retrievable from people's memories, this means they have learned a well-established stereotype during their socialization. Stereotypes represent a way of storing information in people's minds. They become dangerous in intercultural interactions when people move beyond stereotyping and make decisions based on their stereotypes.

Prejudice refers to people's feelings toward other cultural groups. Prejudices have functions and uses for people, such as expressing values ("we are better than others") or defending self-images ("the others have more money because they cheat"). Prejudices also take various forms, ranging from hostile rejection to very subtle tokenism. They can also serve symbolic uses: people can say that they are not against another group, only what that group stands for. Examining stereotypes and prejudices at the same time leads to important implications. For example, many people know the stereotypes of other groups given that these are learned during their socialization and formal education. However, unprejudiced people try to move beyond oversimplified thinking and consciously avoid behaving according to the guidance the stereotypes provide.

If people want to improve intercultural relations in their communities, plenty of helpful guidance is available. Various studies have been done in schools, summer camps, neighborhoods, and workplaces to determine conditions that lead to positive intercultural interactions. These conditions include equal status contact, the pursuit of superordinate goals all people desire, and communications that encourage the sharing of personal information. Another recommendation for improving relations centers on candidly discussing the difficulties of improving intercultural interactions. Effective contact with this focus often occurs in special circumstances (weekend retreats, workshops) where everyone involved devotes time and energy to tolerance and to prejudice reduction. The people involved must realize, however, that they will be returning to the "real world" where not everyone shares their goals.

INTERCULTURAL CONTACT

Everyone can make with certainty three predictions about the 21st century. These are that people will continue to experience death, will continue to be taxed, and will continue to experience extensive intercultural contact. As discussed in chapter 1, an interdependent global economy, the worldwide movement toward democratic forms of government, the insistence of minority groups that their cultural heritages be recognized, and laws prohibiting overt discrimination all lead to the conclusion that people must be prepared to interact effectively with members of cultural groups other than their own. Various arguments about intercultural contact (also referred to frequently as intergroup relations: e.g., Brewer & Brown, 1998; Stephan, 1985) have been made in the first five chapters of this book. In chapter 1, the argument was made that one of the best ways to gain insights into cultural differences is to interact frequently with people from other cultures. When people are unchallenged by the presence of differences, culture becomes much like the air they breathe. They take it for granted. People think about air only when it is taken away, and they think about culture only when the familiar behaviors they learned during their socialization fail to help them achieve their goals in different social settings.

In chapter 2, various theoretical concepts were discussed. One was the difference between individualism and collectivism in people's orientation toward others in their lives. Understanding this distinction allows people to offer advice for individualists about to interact extensively in collectivist cultures and for collectivists about to interact in individualist cultures.

Chapter 3 introduced some basic ideas about cross-cultural research methods. Suggestions were made about understanding complex concepts in different cultures. One approach is to identify aspects of the concepts that are common across cultures (e.g., intelligence as socially valued) and others that are specific to different cultures (e.g., intelligence as a quality involving "quick" versus "slow and careful" thought). When people from different cultures come into contact, the culture-specific aspects of each culture must be given special attention. These will be the most puzzling and most problematic aspects for people encountering another culture for the first time.

In chapter 4, the ways people are socialized into their own culture were discussed. One of the arguments made is that people are socialized to become familiar with a number of social settings where important behaviors take place in their culture. One example is the family setting, involving many socializing agents in the traditional collective culture and fewer people in individualistic cultures. When cultural changes occur, such as the shift from a collective to an individualist lifestyle brought on by urbanization and the nucleation of families, stress can result for people unfamiliar with the new social settings where they are expected to interact.

In chapter 5, the differences between informal and formal education were discussed. Extremely impactful culture contact occurs in the institution called "the school." Children from some cultural backgrounds are far more prepared to benefit from schools than other children given that typical socialization practices (e.g., interacting as conversational partners with adults) are similar to practices children encounter in the school. Other children have far more difficulty benefiting from school attendance given that the behaviors encountered there are so different from familiar behaviors. Various interventions, such as programs to prepare teachers to understand cultural differences, efforts to integrate behaviors children are already familiar with into the school curriculum, and teaching in languages familiar to the children (e.g., through bilingual education programs) have been developed to ease the stress of cultural contact.

Other examples of extensive intercultural contact will be examined in future chapters about the workplace (chapter 8), about gender roles and gender differences (chapter 9), and about the delivery of health care services (chapter 10). The pervasiveness of intercultural contact demands that its complexity be understood. Two chapters will be devoted to this topic. This chapter draws from the work of behavioral and social scientists who have been concerned with the difficulties intergroup contact brings to the people involved and to society at large. The starting point of this chapter is that people must understand the prejudicial attitudes and discriminatory behavior of people who would prefer to avoid intergroup interaction if they could. Much of this work has been done in the context of explaining long-standing stereotypes and intense negative feelings, for example, among Anglo and African Americans in the United States. In addition to increasing understanding of the negative feelings, researchers have studied interventions that have attempted to improve intergroup relations, and the successes of such interventions have led to good advice that administrators of future intervention programs should consider. Chapter 7, although not ignoring or even setting aside the difficulties involved in encouraging intercultural contact, begins with the assumption that many people recognize that intense prejudice and discrimination are no longer acceptable (Devine, 1995; Devine, Monteith, Zuwerink, & Elliot, 1991). The chapter assumes people are willing to communicate effectively with people from other cultures in the workplace, in schools, in their neighborhoods, and so forth. Given this willingness, the questions then become, "What are the problems people will face given that intercultural contact will increase in the future? What insights from cross-cultural studies will assist us?"

This chapter on the difficulties of intergroup relations is organized into four sections:

1. Understanding stereotypes, or generalizations people make about others that ignore individual differences within the stereotyped group

2. Understanding the functions of prejudice, or why people have strong feelings about others who differ on dimensions such as skin color and cultural background

3. Understanding the forms prejudice can take, especially those that involve discrimination such that members of certain groups are put at a disadvantage

4. Understanding the types of interventions that have led to improvements in relations among people from different cultural groups

STEREOTYPES

As noted earlier, *stereotypes* refer to beliefs about a group of people that give insufficient attention to individual differences among the group's members. Whenever statements are made that "African Americans are . . . ," "Native Americans do not . . . ," or "Japanese prefer . . . ," the content is stereotypical because the claim gives no attention to the differences among individual African Americans, Native Americans, and Japanese. Stereotypes refer to beliefs about *any* group of people, so statements that describe "Democrats," "fraternity members," "career women," "full professors on this campus," or "graduating seniors" are stereotypical unless they clearly include recognition of differences within groups of people.

Much recent research on stereotypes has dealt with how people use their normal thinking skills on a daily basis. Stereotypes should not be viewed as a sign of abnormality. Rather, they reflect people's need to organize, remember, and retrieve information that might be useful as they attempt to achieve their goals and to meet life's demands. This emphasis on normal thought processes has led researchers to borrow heavily from studies by psychologists and educators who investigate cognition and cognitive processes (S. Fiske, 1998; Hilton & von Hippel, 1990; Messick & Mackie, 1989; Stephan, 1985).

One important cognitive process, part of normal human thinking, is *categorizing*. People cannot respond to every piece of information they are exposed to. The majority of readers of this chapter will not know the brand name of the lightbulbs illuminating this page. The last time they drove a car, readers did not pay attention to the manufacturer of the various automobiles they saw. Instead of this attention to detail, people form categories and then react to the categories as a unit (E. Smith, 1998). Regarding lightbulbs, people have at most three categories: sufficient illumination, burned out and in need of replacement, and insufficient illumination and in need of replacement by a brighter bulb. For automobiles while driving, people also probably have three categories: those going in the opposite direction, those going in the same direction, and those changing direction that might come close. People then respond to the categories as if all members were the same. When driving, people don't respond individually to the interesting features of each car they see, such as whether it is a classic 1957 Chevrolet, whether it has had a recent paint job, or whether it has whitewall tires. If they did, they would pay insufficient attention to their driving and get into accidents! Rather, they use a category, such as "changing direction close to me," and then react accordingly.

Categories also exist for people we know. As much as people might like to, they cannot respond individually to everyone they see on an average day. If they did, they would never get from one place to another because they would have to stop and talk with so many people. Instead, they form categories. While walking 100 yards or more during daytime hours on a college campus, for example, people place others into one of approximately four categories: (a) those not at all well known and who need no sign of recognition; (b) those known slightly for whom a nod of the head and a "hello" will do; (c) those who are better known and for whom a few more words are customary, such as "How's it going?" or "Have you finished your term paper?"; and (d) those who are very well known and for whom stopping and chatting rather extensively are expected. These four categories summarize information about others encountered (in this case, how well known they are), and they also give guidance to people for making decisions about their behavior.

Because stereotypes are categories about people (Allport, 1954; Ben-Ari, Schwarzwald, & Horiner-Levi, 1994; Brislin, 1981), they have all the features of categories, especially the organization of specific bits of information and subsequent reaction to the category as a whole. If people hold a well-formed stereotype about some ethnic or cultural group, then they may use that stereotype when they interact with any individual belonging to that group. If people meet me, for instance, knowing only that I am Irish American, they might use information from the relevant stereotype: musical, hard drinking, fun loving, Catholic background, ancestors who came to America to escape famine, quick tempered, and so forth. As with most stereotypes applied to individuals, much of this content is inaccurate about me.

Categories in general and stereotypes in particular are shortcuts to thinking. People have to make so many decisions about their behavior during a given day that they need guidance, hints, helpful rules, and so forth. Stereotypes serve this purpose. Assume an Anglo American college student meets a tall, thin African American student for the first time. The Anglo has to make a number of decisions: Should I assume a friendly demeanor or be more reserved? What should we talk about? Should I indicate that I want future interaction with this person? The Anglo wants guidance, and the stereotype of African Americans can provide some. If the stereotype includes the belief that African Americans are aloof and unfriendly toward Anglos, then this gives guidance to the decision about a friendly versus reserved demeanor. If the stereotype includes the belief that tall, thin African Americans are on campus to play basketball, this can guide the choice of a conversational topic. If the stereotype includes the belief that African Americans prefer to stick to their own group, this will influence the decision about future interactions. The key point is that attaching a stereotype to a person allows all the information in that stereotype to be brought to prominence in people's thinking on demand.

Stereotypes are found whenever people can attach a label to a certain group. Using labels can place limits on the behavior of individuals assigned the labels. In the business world, for instance, if the stereotype of women includes "inability to make tough decisions," women may not be given the types of job assignments that lead to promotion into the senior executive ranks (Morrison & Von Glinow, 1990; Pratto, Stallworth, Sidanius, & Siers, 1997). In a university or community counseling center, people might hold a stereotype that Hispanic clients are less serious about working with a counselor because they drop out after a few sessions and do not return to the center (Atkinson, Morten, & Sue, 1989; Paniagua, 1994). This stereotype can affect decisions about funding priorities during the next budget hearings when administrators present their plans for the counseling center's future.

Stereotypes as Part of a Culture

If similar stereotypes exist about some labeled group for generations within a society, they become part of the culture (Biernat, 1991; Devine & Elliot, 1995). They meet the criteria (chapter 1) of culturally influenced behavior: "widely shared," "transmitted from parents and other elders to children," and "the subject of memorable childhood experiences." Most readers probably can think back on their childhood and remember an adult saying, "If you don't behave yourself, you'll end up just like the _____!" The word that completes the sentence is the name of some downtrodden group in a community. My experience in working with Americans as well as citizens of Asian and Pacific island nations is that virtually everyone remembers adults saying such things. The only differences are the names of the groups adults used to get children to behave by eating their vegetables, completing their homework, or doing their chores.

A useful exercise for readers is to list the names of various groups in their communities. Then, write down words that describe these groups. The words can refer to traits of people in the groups, to their attitudes, or to behaviors expected of people in the groups. Then, readers can compare their lists with those others prepared. A number of features then can be examined. For a given group, are the contents of the stereotypes similar across various people who completed the exercise? What percentage of the stereotypes are positive, and what percentage are negative? Recall that stereotypes refer to descriptions of people that give insufficient attention to individual differences. Although the content of stereotypes could include terms that put the group in a favorable light, stereotypes more frequently include large amounts of very negative content. Another feature of the lists that can be examined is whether or not the stereotypes might influence various behaviors. For instance, might the stereotypes affect whether or not people will seek future interaction with one another? Might the stereotypes affect the opportunities people are offered? For example, Atkinson et al. (1989), discuss how stereotypes can affect the advice given to people from different groups:

> If Black students are seen as possessing limited intellectual potential, they may be counseled into terminal vocational school trades. Likewise, if Asian Americans are perceived as being good only in the physical sciences but poor in verbal-people professions, counselors may direct them toward a predominance of science courses. . . . Many minorities may eventually come to believe these stereotypes

about themselves. Thus, since the majority of stereotypes about minorities are negative, an inferior sense of self-esteem may develop. (p. 23)

Avoiding the Negative Consequences of Stereotypes

Given that people cannot respond to the specific traits, needs, and goals of every individual when they meet, they have to group people together and then respond according to their knowledge of that group or category. By doing so, they run the risk of stereotyping the individual and putting him or her at a disadvantage. What is the difference between making reasonable generalizations about other people and stereotyping? This question has no easy answer, and the area between "well-thought-out generalization" and "stereotype" is very gray. Over a period of 25 years, almost all meetings I have attended that have dealt with intercultural interaction and cross-cultural research have generated charges that one or another speaker stereotyped members of some cultural group. It can be argued that I have done this in earlier chapters of this book. In chapter 1, I discussed the case of women in the Philippines (and other parts of the world) who become upset when former romantic partners want to maintain cordial, friendly relations. In chapter 4, I discussed the case of people in India who move from rural to urban areas, leave behind various support groups, and experience stress when adjusting to a new lifestyle. In chapter 5, I discussed the development of reading programs that take advantage of group activities schoolchildren in Hawaii are already familiar with given their everyday behavior in their culture. When these generalizations are looked at carefully, exceptions can be found among people in the Philippines, India, and Hawaii. Some women in the Philippines are very gracious after the breakup of romances and are more than happy to maintain cordial friendships. Some Indians experience little or no stress after moving from rural to urban areas. Some children in Hawaii are not particularly familiar with the group activities that formed the basis of a new reading program. In fact, some children have to become familiar with the group activities (such as storytelling, or talk story) before they can benefit from the reading program. The attention people give to exceptions is one of the key differences between stereotypes and reasonable generalizations. When using stereotypes, people do not consciously consider individual differences. When thinking in terms of careful generalizations, many people are constantly willing to entertain the possibility of individual differences (e.g., Devine, 1995; Toupin & Son, 1991). Adler (1997) has developed a helpful checklist to help move people away from the negative consequences of stereotypes. Before it is discussed, a case study I was involved in may make some points about stereotyping clearer.

Virginia was a newly hired foreign student adviser at a large American university. She had received a college degree in biology about three years ago, served in the Peace Corps for two years, and then returned to the United States where she entered the job market. During her years in the Peace Corps, she not only participated in but also observed large amounts of intercultural contact. Voluntarily and informally, Virginia hosted a few university-sponsored study tour groups. Students on these tours received college credit for overseas travel that combined "experiencing another culture" with reading and writing assignments. After these experiences, Virginia became interested in working with students and began to search for jobs at colleges and universities after her return to the United States.

Although she hoped her job would involve developing various programs that would enrich the education of students at the university where she worked, Virginia found that much of her job involved a great deal of administrative detail. Were the visas of foreign students up to date? Were they taking the required courses that would allow them to graduate on time? Did they have adequate funds for housing, meals, and tuition? Could their spouses work in the community under the type of visa they had? For Americans contemplating a year of study abroad, could they take courses abroad whose credit would transfer back to the university, or would they have to attend school for another semester to graduate? Virginia dealt effectively with these administrative matters and occasionally found time to participate in enrichment activities, such as arranging for foreign students to serve as guest lecturers in various courses on campus and in nearby high schools. She had especially good working relations with a number of professors who asked her regularly to either give a lecture herself or to recommend one of the foreign students she knew. One of these professors was Charles Adams.

One day, Professor Adams called Virginia on the phone. "I think I have one of the students you see frequently in one of my classes," he said. "Michael—he's from Nigeria. I've got a problem! Michael turned in a term paper in which he just wrote down words from a number of books—no citations, no indication that he was using the ideas of other people. It's a plagiarism case. I have to give him an F grade, and I'm thinking of sending the information on to the dean for possible disciplinary action. Do you have any advice?"

Fortunately, Virginia had studied some books on foreign student advising that treated issues such as this one (e.g., Althen, 1995). Virginia explained that Michael came from a culture that had a different orientation toward knowledge. In Nigeria (and in many other cultures), knowledge is not attached to one person. Once somebody discovers something and writes about it, the knowledge is considered open and accessible to anyone who might use it. People feel free, then, to use passages from books (considered open knowledge) without the need to provide specific references for the exact sources of this knowledge. There is not the demand, as there is in the United States and other parts of the world, to make links between the knowledge and the developer of the knowledge through conventions such as references to books and articles, footnotes, and bibliographies. Virginia continued, "It's quite possible Michael was just behaving according to what is familiar in his culture and had no intention to cheat at all. I recommend that all this be carefully explained to him but that it not be referred to the dean." The professor accepted Virginia's recommendation. Both he and Virginia talked with Michael about what American professors consider "plagiarism." Michael understood and never had any more problems with his papers for other classes.

A few months after this incident, Virginia was asked to plan for the cross-cultural training program that would prepare next year's foreign students to benefit from the time they would be spending at the university. Remembering the stress Michael experienced when he heard he might have to see the dean about a disciplinary matter, Virginia decided to have a session on preparing term papers and theses.

Realizing that the problem has arisen on North American and European campuses often enough to be called "the foreign student plagiarism issue" (Althen, 1995; Cushner & Brislin, 1996), Virginia decided to behave according to the adage, "An ounce of prevention is worth a pound of cure." She reasoned that if foreign students learned about term paper preparation during the cross-cultural training program, they would be less likely to run into difficulties and experience debilitating stress.

Virginia proposed this to the advisory committee helping with plans for the orientation program. Several people voiced objections. "You're stereotyping foreign students. Many know all about what Americans consider plagiarism, and they'll be insulted if you talk about it with them. If you have such a session, it could be interpreted as saying that foreign students are ignorant, cheats, or both. You'll just be contributing to the stereotype that foreign students are not as good as American students." At this point, Virginia sought the advice of others (including myself) who have engaged in cross-cultural research and have developed orientation programs to prepare people for extensive intercultural contact. She received conflicting views. Some said the stress stemming from a major disciplinary action can be reduced if students are clear about what is expected of them in university classes. Consequently, a unit on plagiarism is appropriate. Others argued that such a session would label foreign students as "potential plagiarizers" and would contribute to negative stereotypes. What decision did Virginia make about the proposed unit on plagiarism for the orientation program?

Virginia decided to cover the plagiarism issue during the program, and she combined it with a treatment of the relationship between reasonable generalizations about people and stereotypes. She benefited from Adler's (1997, pp. 75–76) checklist of concepts that people should constantly keep in mind whenever they might make a decision based on stereotypes. Adler argues the following about stereotypes:

1. *Stereotypes should be consciously held.* People using stereotypes should be fully aware they are thinking about an individual based on that person's membership in some labeled group. Further, people should be very conscious that exceptions to the stereotype exist and that they even should actively look for these exceptions. By doing so, people will be far less likely to put others at a disadvantage based solely on a label that can be attached to them. For example, people who work with foreign students can present information by saying, "Many exceptions exist, so many students will have few problems in their coursework, but enough students have difficulties preparing term papers that we think some key points should be discussed."

   The danger of unconsciously held stereotypes is that people make decisions based on little or no thought. For instance, if a professor believes female students are so sensitive that they cannot accept firm feedback, he or she may give detailed suggestions about improving classroom performance only to men. Consequently, men receive far more opportunities to improve than do women. Or, if professors believe minority group members are less capable than others, they may suggest that minority students tackle far easier topics for their term papers than other students. Consequently, minority students have fewer opportunities to rise to challenges. These unconscious stereotypes are so familiar to the professors that they apply them to decisions unknowingly. The self-imposed intervention has to be self-generated thoughts such as, "I realize I might stereotype if I don't think about the different students in my classes. I must make sure women receive the same sorts of feedback as men and minority students receive suggestions about their term paper topics that challenge them."

2. *Stereotypes should be descriptive.* As much as possible, generalizations about people should describe behavior and should contain no evaluative commentary about the behavior. Further, people can actively search for complexity to move away from the oversimplified thinking that it so common in the use of stereotypes. For example, the statement can be made, "Some foreign students turn in term papers that do not meet the standards of professors in terms of how ideas are referenced and how bibliographies are prepared." This is a descriptive statement, and it allows the presentation of additional material, such as model term papers that received good grades. People can add complexity to this example by giving reasons for the different ways students in various parts of the world prepare written work, as was discussed previously when the "openness of knowledge" view was contrasted with the view that "ideas should be attached to the individuals who developed them."

3. *Stereotypes should be accurate.* Whenever possible, people should search carefully to determine whether the generalizations they make are supported by various types of evidence. Given that many people have very little contact with members of groups other than their own (Kealey, 1988, 1989; Pettigrew, 1998; Taylor, Dube, & Bellerose, 1986), pure and simple ignorance can have a major impact on intercultural relations (Stephan & Stephan, 1984). One danger in using stereotypes is that people who hear them conclude that people in the labeled group behave in a manner different from people in other groups. For example, if people hear the statement "Foreign students have run into plagiarism problems," it is easy for them to conclude (perhaps inaccurately) "Foreign students are accused of plagiarism more often than American students." If people who might make the first statement work with foreign students and have access to the information, they might compare the number of American students who have had disciplinary hearings about plagiarism with the number of foreign students who have had similar hearings. If the numbers are similar (as they are on many campuses), they can add this information to the cross-cultural orientation program for foreign students. They can say, "We've checked, and foreign students have no more problems with plagiarism than American students, but it is so stressful to anyone who is called to a disciplinary hearing that we are covering it in this orientation program." Returning to the examples of giving constructive feedback to women and suggesting research topics to minority group members, professors can add the concern for accuracy to the concern that generalizations be consciously held. After professors think about whether or not they are applying a stereotype, they can ask themselves, "What hard evidence is there that I deal with my female and minority group students differently from my Anglo and male students?"

4. *Stereotypes should be the first best guess.* Any stereotype should be viewed as only providing guidance for a first guess about the way an individual might be-

have. Then, as people make a point of discovering more information about the individual, they can move beyond the first guess with the conscious addition of new evidence and complexity (Toupin & Son, 1991), as already discussed. When people move beyond the first best guess, they often discover information that will be useful in their future interactions. Earlier, it was mentioned that Hispanic clients often do not keep their appointments at mental health clinics. If the counselors in the clinic quickly move beyond the first guess about clients being "not serious about dealing with important issues," they can examine other information, such as other demands on clients' time, transportation difficulties, the acceptability of what happens in a counseling session from clients' viewpoints, the cultural sensitivity of counselors, and so forth (Atkinson et al., 1989; Ponterotto, Casas, Suzuki, & Alexander, 1995).

5. *Stereotypes should be modifiable.* Once people show a willingness to move beyond a first best guess, they also are indicating a willingness to modify their generalization based on the additional information they find. The modifications often take the form of adding great amounts of complexity to generalizations that recognize various exceptions. The exceptions are based on differences in people's socialization experiences within a culture and on their age, education, employment history, and so forth. One of the major "messages" of cross-cultural research, but also one of the most difficult to communicate, is that often more differences exist within a culture than between two or more different cultures. For instance, more differences are likely to exist in the stress levels within a group of Indian 20-year-olds who move from rural to urban areas than between these Indians and a group of 20-year-old Americans. This fact does not negate the necessity of studying stressful life experiences. It is only a reminder that people are very complex and that simple statements are rarely very helpful. This fact about differences also can direct people to sharpen their thinking with more complex questions, such as asking why some Indians make the rural to urban move with little stress (e.g., presence of support groups in the urban area: Biswas & Pandey, 1996; Sinha, 1988) and why some 20-year-old Americans experience more stress than others. In both cases, simple stereotypes are inadequate and people must modify them in the direction of more complexity.

Moving Away From Stereotypes

In addition to modifying stereotypes to incorporate more complexity, people can make other types of changes when faced with the possibility of generalizing about members of another group. A major change people can attempt is to move from automatic processing of information to more controlled processing (Devine, 1995; Kawakami, Dion, & Dovidio, 1998). These terms need explanation prior to their application to the analysis of stereotypes.

The distinction between automatic and controlled processing of information has been found useful in many analyses of how people interact with one another and how they manage their complex lives (Petty & Wegener, 1998). *Automatic processing* involves a quick reaction to information and occurs with little or no thought, little or no contemplation, and little consideration of the information's value. Some of the clearest examples occur with television advertising. Many television advertisements do not present information people are expected to ponder in a careful manner. Rather, the ads present a series of images that are supposed to lead to automatic reactions. Some recent ads for athletic shoes, for example, present pictures of a famous athlete such as Michael Jordan superimposed on a fast-changing collection of backgrounds that include deserts, skyscrapers, and mountains. Viewers are supposed to apply their automatic processing capabilities to this advertisement and to conclude quickly that this brand of athletic shoes is modern, versatile, exciting, and fashionable. Again, supposedly, the next time viewers are in the market for athletic shoes, they will buy this brand. Incredible amounts of money are spent by companies that desire similar automatic reactions to consumer purchases of items such as tobacco products, automobiles, and cosmetics.

Controlled processing involves thoughtful and careful consideration of the information in a message. Again using the example of consumer products, people sometimes have to seek opportunities to engage in controlled processing. If people want to be careful about their purchase of running shoes, they could seek a set of independent ratings from a magazine such as *Runner's World* or *Consumer Reports*. Or, they could visit a club where runners, basketball players, or tennis players work out together. They could ask others in the club about different brands of shoes and their relative merits. From either magazine ratings or their new informants, they could discover specific information about details such as cushioning, stability of the cushioning when feet move sideways, support for the heel, and so forth. At the very least, they could carefully examine shoes while comparison shopping. If all this sounds a bit dull, it probably is because what is interesting and important for one person (who has problems with sore ankles) is not of interest to another (who has had no problems with soreness and who can search for the most economical shoe). This potential boredom from such research is one reason advertisers spend so much time and money with messages meant to elicit automatic responses in many magazine readers and television viewers.

Applied to stereotypes, automatic processing occurs when (a) people have an immediate, thought-free reaction while observing a member of another group, and (b) that reaction involves a characteristic of the other group widely shared within a culture. Any example is going to be controversial, but I must examine such examples both to explain automatic and controlled processing and to use these concepts to fight the negative consequences of stereotyping. Assume a student is on a college campus in the midwestern United States and that this college has an active athletic program sanctioned by the NCAA. The student sees an African American man who is 6 feet, 10 inches tall; lean; and well muscled. If, within a half second of seeing this person, the student thinks "basketball player," this is an example of automatic processing. Interestingly, one of the student's companions on the walk across campus is an international student from a country where basketball is not particularly popular. This second student does not know the stereotype (point *b* in this paragraph) and so does not have the automatic reaction.

Another example occurs in Hawaii where I live. I am originally from the mainland (contiguous 48 states), so sometimes I am put in the "mainland haole" stereotype, with *haole* very roughly translating as "Anglo outsider." People who have lived all their lives in Hawaii do not like to hear suggestions for improvement that start with, "When I was in Indiana, we did it this way. . . ." The stereotype of mainland haoles contains elements such as "know-it-alls, overly talkative, quick to make suggestions without knowing very much," and so forth. When I have entered a room where committee members are meeting, I am sure I have been automatically stereotyped in this manner given people's immediate facial expressions.

Controlled processing involves careful thought and reflection. It can contain thinking such as the following: "I realize I could apply a stereotype, but I should move beyond it and look at the individual and his or her viewpoint." On the walk across campus mentioned earlier, controlled processing might include the stereotypical thought about basketball, but thinking would move quickly to ideas such as, "Not all African Americans play basketball; this person might be well muscled because he works out to maintain good health, and he may be here on an academic scholarship." In the committee meeting people using controlled processing would recognize that a stereotype of Anglos from the mainland United States exists, but they would not tune out anything I say and instead would wait to see if I had a contribution to make.

In encouraging people to move beyond stereotypes, Devine (1995; Devine et al., 1991) argues that the distinction between automatic and controlled processing plays a very important role. She measured Anglos' levels of prejudice toward groups other than their own. In different studies, for example, these other groups included African Americans and gays and lesbians. Based on this independent measure, she designated some people as high in their levels of prejudice and some as low in prejudice. People high and low in prejudice did not differ in their knowledge of stereotypes. If a stereotype is commonly discussed in a culture (sometimes for generations; see chapter 1), then most members of that culture know about it. In fact, a good measure of membership in a culture is a person's knowledge of stereotypes of groups with a long history in that culture. Almost all middle-class Anglo Americans from the contiguous 48 states know the stereotypes of Japanese Americans and Hispanic Americans given these groups' long presence in the United States. But few mainland Americans have stereotypes about Samoans or Ilocanos from the Philippines given that these groups have not had a multigenerational presence on the mainland. Stereotypes of these groups do exist in Hawaii.

If people high and low in prejudice know the content of stereotypes, what makes them differ? Devine (1995) presents evidence that people differ in their endorsement of the stereotypes and in their willingness to use them in their decision making about people from the groups. Put another way, highly prejudiced people do not engage in controlled processing. They accept the immediate, automatic reaction commonly known in their culture and do not move beyond it in their thinking. People low in prejudice know the content of the stereotype but are far less likely to endorse it in their thinking. They are likely to move beyond the stereotype and to search for and to appreciate individual differences among people in other groups.

Some people recognize they stereotype too much and that they do so without sufficient thought. Without using the terms, they want very much to move from automatic to controlled processing. Devine (1995) argues that moving away from automatic processing is much like moving away from a bad habit. People have to recognize their bad habits and give attention, time, and effort to change them. For example, I have a very strong tendency to overeat and to put on weight. Undoubtedly, this has a genetic component. All my close relatives, on both sides of my family, are stout and heavy people. If I am to avoid being overweight and its subsequent ill effects on my health, I have to give the bad habit of overeating much attention. In other words, I have to engage in large amounts of controlled processing. I have to avoid desserts, practice my social skills in turning down candy brought by colleagues returning from France or Switzerland, and run or work out in the weight room even though I don't feel like it. It takes time and effort, but perhaps I can be motivated by the thought that more healthy behaviors eventually can become habitual. The argument is similar for moving beyond automatic processing when interacting with people from other cultural backgrounds. If they desire, people can break the habit of engaging in too much automatic processing. But they will have to make special efforts, such as asking and answering questions like the following: "I'm tempted to judge this other person based on skin color, but is this a superficial reaction? Am I dead wrong in my initial assessment? For example, a person who looks Hispanic and 'foreign' may have roots in Texas going back five or six generations, long before Anglos thought to move there. Should I try to get to know more about this person before making a decision that involves him (or her)?"

Current research is investigating whether or not people low in prejudice can avoid automatic processing entirely (Kawakami et al., 1998). Not enough evidence has been found yet to provide a clear answer, but I will speculate that certain people, because of major life experiences, avoid automatic processing when interacting with certain groups. Some people have intense experiences in other cultures given their roles as international students, overseas businesspeople, missionaries, members of organizations such as the Peace Corps, and so forth (more about such people in chapter 7). Given that they have to interact with another culture's members virtually every minute of every day, automatic processing no longer is useful. Rather, they have to engage in controlled processing involving issues of personality differences, variations in how these others approach various tasks, differences in skills needed for both task and social demands, and so forth. My further speculation is that this move from automatic to controlled processing becomes smooth and effortless and that people recognize this change in themselves (again, probably not using the exact terms). People's satisfaction with this move is a major reason why they claim that their long-term intercultural experiences are some of the most important events in their lives.

PREJUDICE: ITS FUNCTIONS

The difficulty with stereotypes, of course, is that very few people put the amount of care into thinking about other groups required to move from automatic to controlled processing. Rather, people are much more likely to use oversimplified stereotypes that deny individuality and uniqueness to a person just because he or she can be conveniently labeled as a member of some group. In many cultures, stereotypes of certain groups are so negative, are so pervasive, and have existed for so many generations that they can be considered part of the culture into which children are socialized. In these cases, the stereotypes become part of people's prejudicial feelings about other groups.

Prejudice refers to the emotional component of people's reactions to other groups. It involves not only a set of beliefs about others, which are captured in stereotypes, but it is also a deeply felt set of feelings about what is good and bad, right and wrong, moral and immoral, and so forth. Although prejudices can be positive, for example romantic feelings about Pacific island nations as near-utopias unaffected by the ills of civilization (Daws, 1977), they more often refer to very negative feelings about others. The word's components specify that prejudices also involve a prejudging of others based on limited knowledge and limited contact. A close relationship between negative stereotypes and prejudice exists because people have feelings (or prejudices) about various traits and beliefs (the content of the stereotypes) they believe others possess. W. Jordan (1989, p. 1119) also makes a link between the two when he argues that negative "stereotypes may be defined as the bundles of belief carried by the energy" of people's attitudes about other groups, or their prejudices.

Prejudices about other groups that differ in some way, such as by their skin color, accent, cultural practices, and social class background, are a universal aspect of human behavior (LeVine & Campbell, 1972)—found in all cultures and in all eras of recorded history. Despite vigorous attempts to change people in the direction of tolerance toward and acceptance of others (e.g., Adler, 1997; Brewer & Brown, 1998; Miller & Brewer, 1984; Stephan, 1985), prejudices have been remarkably persistent, and children continue to learn them during their socialization. A good exercise for students is to think about their socialization and to remember times when they were discouraged from developing close relations with people from certain groups and were encouraged to think negatively about them. Memories could include interventions by adults when the others were invited to a party or adults finding the others acceptable only in certain social settings (e.g., on athletic teams, but not study groups in school). If students compare their memories, they undoubtedly will find a striking number of similarities. These memories frequently include the feelings that people from certain groups are in many ways inferior. They are presumed less able to accept adult responsibilities, such as holding down good jobs. They are considered better suited for manual labor than managerial and professional white-collar jobs. The memories also might include the advice that it is usually best to keep the others at a distance—that people will benefit more from life's opportunities if they don't limit themselves by too much attachment to the other groups.

As they hear different adults giving such advice, children learn that they have clear in-groups and out-groups in their lives. A division of people into distinct in-groups and out-groups is another universal aspect of human behavior (LeVine & Campbell, 1972). *In-groups* refer to individuals a person has positive feelings about (Horenczyk & Bekerman, 1997). Further, the person interacts with these others frequently and can depend on them in times of need. These others are thought of as "similar to me," and their approval or disapproval of various behaviors are considered important. *Out-groups* refer to individuals that people keep at a distance and have far less positive feelings about for various reasons. Out-group members are often viewed as "too different" to be considered as deserving of the person's time, effort, and concern. When people are asked to describe who they are, they often list the names of their in-groups, such as their family, group of friends, coworkers, and so forth. When asked to describe who they are not, they often list the names of their out-groups.

As the term is most frequently used, *prejudice* refers to negative feelings about out-groups. The most important reason prejudicial attitudes are so resistant to change is that they serve clear functions for people. The concept of "functions" was discussed in chapter 5 when possible reasons were suggested for Asian American success in schools. The concept of "relative functionalism" also was introduced: Asian Americans view success in schools as functional for achieving success in other aspects of society, such as respect in the work world and influence in their communities. Another word for *functional* is *useful*. That is, they see hard work in school as useful for attaining many goals in life. When I say prejudices serve several functions, I mean they are useful to people. Because prejudices are so useful and because they have brought certain benefits to people (as described later), individuals who hold prejudicial attitudes are resistant to change. The concept that *attitudes* serve various functions was most fully developed by Katz (1960) and updated by Eagly and Chaiken (1998). I have applied his framework to *prejudicial attitudes* (Brislin, 1978, 1986). Prejudices serve one or more of four functions for people, and these are discussed separately here.

The Utilitarian or Adjustment Function

People hold certain prejudices because they lead to various rewards in their society and to the avoidance of punishment. The prejudices help people collect rewards, and if people collect enough rewards valued in their society, they are very likely to experience a smooth adjustment into a comfortable lifestyle. Jordan (1989) argues that the Anglo view of African Americans as inferior in abilities is long standing and is an attitude America's earliest settlers brought rather than an attitude that developed after the importation of slaves from Africa. One reason was utilitarian: By viewing slaves from Africa as inferior and not worthy of society's benefits, Anglos could exploit them as a cheap source of labor. Rather than work in the hot sun day after day, Anglos could achieve a comfortable lifestyle by forcing slaves to work long hours in the fields. If the Anglos ever experienced a challenge to their consciences about this exploitation, they could justify their behavior by arguing that African Americans would be much worse off if they didn't have Anglos to protect them and to offer them honest work. Even after slavery was eliminated, prejudicial views about African Americans continued to be useful. If Anglos who wanted jobs in the professions, such as law, medicine, or college-level teaching, kept the widespread view that African Americans were less able, this meant they would have less competition for these well-paying, high-status jobs.

Understanding the utilitarian function means understanding people's access to rewards and avoidance of punishment. In addition to providing insights into American history, as in the example of slavery and institutionalized discrimination extending over centuries, the utilitarian function can be seen in people's everyday activities. In many parts of the world, people continue to be discouraged from interacting with individuals from certain out-groups. Assume a husband and wife move into a neighborhood where prejudicial views prevail. They decide to work toward intergroup tolerance and harmony by seeking out interaction with many different people, including people the community leaders consider out-groups members. The married couple might withstand the pressure community leaders put on them to "keep things the way they have always been." But what about the couple's children? Imagine the punishments others can inflict on them: taunting in the schools, lack of invitations to parties, being ignored on the playground during recess, having their athletic talents ignored and not being given a chance for an honest tryout for the school team, and so forth. Few parents can maintain their stubborn insistence on intergroup tolerance in the face of such punishments inflicted on their children.

The Ego Defensive Function

People hold certain prejudices because they do not want to acknowledge various deficiencies in themselves. If they hold prejudices that blame out-groups for these deficiencies, people do not have to examine their own inadequacies. Certain prejudices, then, protect people's sense of self-worth. In everyday language, one person sometimes says of another, "He (or she) has a healthy ego." One way to protect or to defend one's ego is to blame difficulties on other people. Prejudices against Jewish people often have had an *ego defensive* component. Rather than examine their own skills as they relate to potential success in the business world, people find it is easier to blame Jews for banning together and making it difficult for anyone else to start new companies (Allport, 1954). After the devastation World War I brought, German leaders blamed defeat on the Jews, thus protecting themselves from examining the mistakes that led to failure.

Another ego defensive prejudice stems from people's socialization into their culture (chapter 4). People put large amounts of time and effort into learning behaviors acceptable in their culture. They come to believe they behave in a "correct and proper manner." This is another cultural universal. People believe that their culture presents its members with the "best" guidelines for meeting life's goals. These beliefs become part of people's sense of personal identity—their ego. When members of other cultures behave in ways different from these guidelines, these others are viewed negatively. Holding these negative views allows people to protect their sense of self-esteem. In addition, when people automatically dismiss different behaviors as unworthy of attention, they are not motivated to examine their own culture to identify areas where changes in behavior (e.g., conservation of resources) will yield benefits. For example, if Americans believe that their diet is the best in the world, they will not be motivated to examine diets common in cultures that have less cancer, less heart disease, less obesity, and so forth (Beardsley & Pedersen, 1997; see also chapter 10).

The Value Expressive Function

People hold certain prejudices because they want to express values they believe are correct, moral, and ethical. By viewing themselves as "right," they put forward various prejudices that communicate their positive view of themselves. The ego defensive and value defensive functions are related in an important way (S. Fiske, 1998).

When people hold ego defensive prejudices, they are protecting themselves from admissions that aspects of themselves or their culture may be inadequate. Ego defensive prejudices allow people to hide certain features about themselves from the rest of the world. In sharp contrast to hiding their attitudes and values, people who hold value expressive prejudices attempt to make them as clear as possible. For example, people who hold negative attitudes about members of a certain religious group may view themselves as standing up for the "one true religion of God." People who view people with a different skin color as inferior may view themselves as belonging to a superior race. When expressing these attitudes about religion and skin color, people are not hiding their beliefs about themselves—they are attempting to communicate that they and their beliefs are better than others.

As discussed when the utilitarian function of attitudes was introduced, one reason for the centuries-long prejudice of Anglos toward African Americans involves people's lifestyles. The prejudice began with the belief that if African Americans were viewed as inferior, then Anglos could exploit them as manual laborers and maintain a less arduous lifestyle themselves. Anglos, then, became accustomed to dominating another race and exercising power over it. One of many evils that stems from dominance is that the people wielding power begin to enjoy it, seek more of it, and come to view themselves as the only people who can use power responsibly (Brislin, 1991; Kipnis, 1976; Sidanius, Pratto, & Bobo, 1996). Another reason for the longstanding domination of Anglos over African Americans is that it reinforces the Anglos' view of themselves as superior (Jordan, 1989). Power is intoxicating; it gives pleasure to people wielding it and eventually "goes to their heads." The English historian Lord Acton was correct: "Power tends to corrupt, and absolute power corrupts absolutely." As Anglos dominated African Americans for decades to obtain their cheap labor, many eventually came to believe that such an arrangement was natural, moral, and correct. Anglo views that African Americans are fit only for manual labor came to serve their value expressive needs. By keeping African Americans submissive, Anglos could communicate clearly that they viewed themselves as worthy of their superior position in society.

The Knowledge Function

People hold certain prejudices because such attitudes allow them to organize the various pieces of information they encounter. Much overlapping occurs between prejudices that serve a knowledge function and stereotypes. The major difference for the purposes here is that discussions of stereotypes usually do not include analyses of the functions they serve for people as they make various decisions in their daily lives. As discussed previously, stereotypes are bundles of information brought to mind when people think about a group label, whether that label is "Hispanic," "African American," "working woman," "Republican," or "fraternity/sorority member." When the content of stereotypes supplies the "facts" people use when making decisions, then the stereotypes are serving the knowledge function. For example, assume parents are deciding on the school they want their children to attend and that different schools are in neighborhoods that attract students from various racial and ethnic

People who direct the behavior of others often become intoxicated with power.

groups. If parents make their decision based on their beliefs about the abilities of children from different groups, then they are using stereotypes to serve the knowledge function. Or, assume staff members in a counseling center can attend one of several conferences devoted to the special problems members of different cultural groups face. If they believe that people from some groups are more serious about working on their problems than others, they may make their decision based on stereotype-influenced "knowledge." Attitudes that serve only the knowledge function can be changed as long as people can present more accurate knowledge to those who hold the stereotypes. If educators, for instance, can demonstrate to concerned parents that there are no differences in the abilities and motivation of culturally diverse students within their community, the parents will cease to use this information in their decision.

The difficulty, however, is that attitudes rarely serve only one function. Parents making a decision about schools undoubtedly possess views about other groups that they consider "knowledge." But they also may be insecure about their own abilities as parents and may hold prejudicial views about others so that they do not have to examine themselves (ego defensive function). In addition, they may have developed the idea they belong to a group that deserves special attention from the educational system given their superior status in society (value expressive function). By maintaining such views, they make sure more time, attention, and funding are devoted to their children's education (utilitarian function). Given this complexity of functions, attempts to change attitudes by dealing only with the knowledge function are likely to fail because the three other functions go unaddressed.

PREJUDICE: ITS FORMS

In addition to the necessity of understanding the functions prejudices serve for people, it is also essential to understand the different forms prejudices take when they are expressed (Brislin, 1986a; Devine, 1995; Devine et al., 1991; Fiske, 1998; Sears & Funk, 1991). Just as programs for changing attitudes will succeed only if they deal with the various functions prejudices serve for particular people, these programs also must deal with the different ways those same people express their views about out-group members in order to succeed.

Intense Racism

Some people believe that virtually all members of certain out-groups are inferior in various ways and cannot benefit fully from society's offerings such as education, good jobs, and participation in community affairs. *Racism* centers on the belief that, given the simple fact some individuals were born into a certain out-group, those individuals are inferior on such dimensions as intelligence, morals, and an ability to interact in decent society. Other terms that end with "ism" also have the connotation that because of a fact surrounding certain people's birth, they are less capable than others. For example, *sexism* involves the belief that women are less capable than men in certain areas, such as leadership or decision making. Until very recently, many of the professions (e.g., law, medicine) discriminated against women out of the belief men were more capable of making important contributions as professionals, executives, and power holders. If individuals are denied opportunities because of their social class background (the term *classism* is occasionally used), age, or ethnic group, these prejudices can be very similar to racism and sexism. The similarity is that people are denied opportunities because of a fact they have no control over, such as the class background of their parents, the year they were born, or the ethnicity of their ancestors (Brislin, 1988).

Currently, it is unfashionable in many parts of the world to express intense racist statements in public forums such as community meetings, offices, and classrooms. Such statements are more likely to be shared among people who know their listeners well and who feel they will find an appreciative audience for their racist remarks. Discussing ways to measure various sorts of prejudicial attitudes, Ashmore (1970) presented items from different research questionnaires. Many of these statements were designed to capture the deep-seated feelings of intense racism. One such item is, "The many faults, and the general inability to get along, of (insert name of out-group), who have recently flooded our community, prove that we ought to send them back where they came from as soon as conditions permit." Another item is, "(insert name of group) can never adjust to the standard of living and civilization of our country due mainly to their innate dirtiness, laziness, and general backwardness."

The majority of people who read a book like this one that deals with understanding and appreciating cultural differences undoubtedly will cringe when encountering feelings such as those expressed in these statements. Yet intense racism continues to exist, even though it may have gone "underground" in terms of its open expression. Still, readers may underestimate the current levels of intense racism given that they normally do not interact frequently with people who hold these views. Because people of today are more hesitant to express intense views, the diagnosis of racism (and the other "isms") does not necessarily include people's frequent use of hate-filled statements. Rather, the diagnosis now centers on beliefs about inferiority. The belief in inferiority distinguishes racism from the other forms prejudice takes, and the diagnosis of these other forms involves cues much more subtle than current expressions of racist attitudes.

Symbolic Racism and Realistic Group Conflict

Certain people hold negative views about out-groups, not because they believe in their inferiority but because they feel the out-group is interfering with important aspects of their culture. The people do not dislike members of the group as individuals, and their views are quite dissimilar from those that mark intense racism. Rather, people believe the out-groups are interfering with the symbols of their culture, and these symbols can be abstract or concrete. *Abstract symbols* include (a) the belief in hard work as the backbone of society and (b) the importance of standing on one's own two feet and solving one's own problems. *Concrete symbols* include (c) the classroom as a place of learning the basics, not a place to deal with everyone's social problems, and (d) the job interview as a "level playing field" where some people should not have an advantage because they are from a minority group. *Symbolic racism* (Kinder, 1986; McConahay & Hough, 1976; Pettigrew & Meertens, 1995; Sears and Funk, 1991) centers on the attitude that minority groups are interfering with a culture's long-held values (captured by abstract and concrete symbols). For example, people might dislike welfare programs because they believe too much money is being paid to out-group members unwilling to work (symbol a) and who are unwilling to pull themselves up by the bootstraps and solve their own problems (symbol b). Or, they may dislike the busing of students to achieve school integration because they feel it takes time, attention, and money away from the school's mission to teach reading, writing, and arithmetic (symbol c). They may be against affirmative action programs in various organizations if they believe out-group members are being given unfair preferences in employment procedures that (they feel) should give equal treatment to all (symbol d) and that should focus on people's ability to work hard for the employer (symbol a again).

Symbolic racism is expressed in terms of threats to people's basic values and to the status quo they have become comfortable with in their culture. When directly questioned, people assert that out-group members are "moving too fast" and are making illegitimate demands in their quest for a place in society. For example, people express symbolic racism in their responses to questions such as these (from Mc-Conahay & Hough, 1976; the answer indicative of symbolic racism is noted at the end in parentheses):

"*Over the past few years,* (insert name of group) *have gotten more economically than they deserve.*" *(agree)*

"*People in this country should support* _____ *in their struggle against discrimination and segregation.*" *(disagree)*

"_____ *are getting too demanding in their push for equal rights.*" *(agree).*

People who hold these views do not see themselves as racists, so programs involving such people and aimed at changing extreme racist views (such programs are currently the most common type) are doomed to failure. McConahay and Hough (1976) are quite correct when they state that current programs seem incomprehensible to holders of symbolic prejudices, "and they do not understand what all the fuss is about. This enables racism to be considered 'somebody else's' problem while holders of symbolic views concentrate upon their own private lives" (p. 44).

In addition to dealing with the complexity of distinguishing intense racism from symbolic racism, a number of researchers have asked whether symbolic racism is different from what they call "realistic group conflict" (Bobo, 1983; Stephan, Ybarra, Martinez, Schwarzwald, & Tur-Kaspa, 1998; Veilleux & Tougas, 1989). Recall the discussion of bilingual education in chapter 5. Bilingual education is expensive, and its support depends on public funding. Many groups of people want to see public funding for other programs that members feel will improve education, such as increased teacher salaries, a "back to basics" emphasis on academics, repairs to buildings, and the attraction of the best and brightest college students to the teaching profession. These groups are competing for the same funds—they have a realistic conflict with other groups, because almost never does enough money exist for every group that wants its program funded. The competition for funds does not necessarily involve intense dislike of people from other groups, but it does mean groups have realistic differences they are trying to deal with as best they can. They attempt to deal with their differences in the political arena, where members from various groups make proposals in their quest for scarce resources (Brislin, 1991; Crick, 1982; Greenberg & Baron, 1997).

When applied to relationships among people from different racial, ethnic, and cultural groups, arguments about realistic group conflict look at the competition for various scarce resources. Money is the most obvious scarce resource, as discussed in the example about funding for educational programs, but others exist. Other scarce resources include classroom space for people's children in good schools, honest interviews for good jobs, homes in crime-free neighborhoods, and access to the influence that elected politicians can wield. When different groups that happen to form around racial and ethnic criteria compete for these scarce resources, the result may be realistic group conflict. Someone might think, "I want my fair share of these resources, no more and no less. In my community, people seem to be forming political groups to compete for these resources based on their race and their ethnic group. To compete on an equal footing, I'll have to do the same and join members of my group." Disagreements exist about whether taking such action represents symbolic racism ("other groups are moving too fast, so I'll have to work with my group to get our fair share") or whether it represents a realistic view that political action is more effective if individuals ban together (Bobo, 1983). Not enough evidence exists at present to make a clear choice between the two possibilities. I feel that both symbolic racism and realistic group conflict can affect intergroup relations simultaneously. A person can be quite irritated that minority group members seem pushy in their support of such policies as busing to achieve school integration (symbolic racism). That same person then can join a group of like-minded people who argue to both the school board and to the judicial system that money spent on a fleet of buses would be better invested in salary increases for teachers (realistic group conflict about the distribution of scarce resources).

Stephan and his colleagues moved beyond opinions and presented evidence that *both* symbolic racism and realistic group conflict can contribute to the quality of intergroup relations and intergroup attitudes (Stephan et al., 1998). This research group investigated prejudicial levels among Spanish citizens toward immigrants from Morocco and among Israelis toward Russian and Ethiopian immigrants. The major component of prejudice investigated was its negative affect, ranging from "no *(insert evaluative term)*" to "extreme *(insert evaluative term)*." This represented a 9-point scale (no = 0; extreme = 9), and evaluative terms inserted in these scales included *hostility, disdain*, and *hatred*. Positive terms were reverse scored, such as *affection, approval*, and *sympathy*. The researchers were careful to separate, as much as possible, political stances from their measures of symbolic prejudice so that the two would not be confounded. Measures were designed to capture emic aspects of the concepts investigated (see chapter 3) in each culture. Keep in mind that symbolic racism represents feelings about threats to a person's familiar culture and way of life. In Spain, items to measure symbolic racism included "The religion of the Moroccans is not compatible with our religion," and "Our way of life is not being modified by Moroccan immigration" (reverse scored). In Israel, because the culture is different from Spain, the symbolic threats also would be different. Items included "The Ethiopian *aliya* [a term in Israel for immigration, which connotes an ascent in status as people move from one country to another] damages Israeli culture," and "The values and beliefs of Russian immigrants regarding work are quite similar to those of most Israelis" (reverse scored).

Potential realistic group conflicts also differed in the two countries. In Spain, items were designed to measure possible realistic threats such as increased crime, loss of jobs, economic costs for social services (recall the competition for money), increased drug use, and differences in expectations about religious education. In Israel, items measured the similar potential threats of crime, job loss, and money for social services. In addition, items measured resources associated with public schooling and access to medical care.

Stephan and his colleagues (1998) found that both realistic and symbolic threats contributed to prejudicial feelings. They also found two other predictors of prejudice:

people's anxiety about interactions with immigrants (discussed in chapter 2) and threats due to the negative stereotypes of immigrants. The relative strength of the four predictors varied in the two countries. Symbolic threat was a strong predictor of prejudice in Israel when Ethiopian immigrants were considered, most likely because the Israelis saw Ethiopians as bringing a very different set of cultural norms and values to Israel. Realistic threat was a strong predictor in Spain. The Spaniards saw immigrants as taking away resources such as jobs and causing a drain on funds for social services. Symbolic threat did not contribute to prejudice as strongly in Spain, perhaps because Spaniards are very confident of their centuries-old culture and do not see a relatively small number of Moroccans as interfering with their culture. The important points are that symbolic racism can be measured separately from realistic group conflicts, that both can be predictive of prejudice, and that various predictors of prejudice can be synthesized if other concepts (e.g., numbers of immigrants) are also considered.

Reconciliations of the differing positions on symbolic racism and realistic group conflict undoubtedly require complex analyses of various attitudes people possess, not just people's overall like or dislike of other groups. Veilleux and Tougas (1989) developed a concept called "relative deprivation on behalf of others." In their studies, if people from one group felt another group's members have been deprived of certain rights, then the people were much more likely to reject views indicative of symbolic racism. For example, if men (who had good jobs) felt women were disadvantaged in the workforce in terms of hirings, salaries, and promotions, then the men were more likely to endorse policies such as affirmative action. Using the terms Veilleux suggested, if men spoke out on behalf of others and argued women were deprived relative to men, the men were willing to endorse special efforts to provide opportunities for women. Other men who felt women had not received negative treatment in the workplace were less enthusiastic about affirmative action. Regarding the men who felt women had not experienced a lack of opportunities, different observers of the men will have different conclusions influenced by their political positions. Some observers will view the men as "blind as bats," some will view them as symbolic racists, some will view them as uninformed, and some will view them as realistic.

Tokenism

Consider this short case study. George is a staff member of an organization that sponsors overseas exchange programs for high school students. For example, 16- and 17-year-old Americans are sent to France, where they live with French families, and an equal number of French teenagers are sent to the United States, where they live with American families. These programs would be impossible without families who are willing to sponsor the teenagers and to welcome them into their homes. The costs of the programs would be prohibitive if students had to pay for their own housing.

George's job involved preparing the students for life in a culture other than their own, raising funds to pay for "extras" such as trips to historically important places within the countries, and finding families with a spare bedroom they could offer to a visiting student. One week, he happened to be emphasizing the fund-raising and the "family finding" aspects of his job. George noted an interesting fact. The responses

Tokenism, such as contributing small amounts of money to out-group charity, can convince people they are unprejudiced.

he received depended on the order of these two types of requests. If adults had been asked to make a small donation to the program, they were later far less willing to have a student live with them. In contrast, if they had not been asked recently to donate money but were asked to welcome a student into their homes, they were more likely to say "Yes, a student can live with us." What might explain this relationship between people giving money and their willingness to sponsor students in their homes?

The type of prejudice known as "tokenism" may be one reason for the pattern of behavior George observed. Some people harbor negative feelings about an out-group but do not want to admit this to themselves or to others. The people definitely do not view themselves as prejudiced, and they do not perceive their behavior as discriminatory. One way they reinforce this view of themselves is to engage in behaviors affecting those out-groups that require little effort but that can be interpreted as supporting intergroup relations. By engaging in such relatively effortless behaviors, people can persuade themselves and others they are unprejudiced toward these groups and then later can refuse to perform more difficult and important intergroup behaviors. For example, Dutton (1976) found that if people gave a small amount of money to out-group members, they later were less willing to donate a large amount of their free time to a Brotherhood Week campaign that was to emphasize positive intergroup relations and goodwill. The small amount of money, then, was a *token* that allowed some people to persuade themselves they were unprejudiced about the out-groups and consequently did not have to prove themselves again by engaging in the more important, time-consuming behavior.

The analysis of tokenism is similar for George's case. By donating money, people could demonstrate they are in favor of overseas exchange programs, so they do not view themselves as unsupportive if they later refuse to accept the far greater responsibility of housing an exchange student. Knowledge of how tokenism works can be very helpful to administrators in charge of various programs that promote intercultural relationships. They should identify reasonable behaviors they can expect of volunteers, such as a sensible number of work hours, different types of hospitality, a practical amount of goods from retailers at wholesale cost, and so forth. Then, they should approach people with requests to engage in those behaviors. They should not approach people with requests for behaviors that are less demanding, such as contributing small amounts of money. If people agree to the less demanding behaviors, they often will refuse the requests originally identified as reasonable and necessary for the program's success.

Different types of tokens exist. If a few symphony musicians' physical appearance marks them as minority group members, then administrators of the more than 100-member orchestra can convince themselves their hiring practices are nondiscriminatory. If a university has a small number of female or minority faculty members, administrators may place them on committees that are very visible in the community. By pointing to the female or minority representation on these committees, administrators can persuade themselves and others they are making every attempt to involve women and minorities in university decision making. The danger for these faculty members is that the time they spend as tokens on committees takes away from their teaching and research efforts. Teaching and research are far more important for job success and career development than are committee assignments.

Arm's-Length Prejudice

Some people engage in friendly, positive behaviors toward out-group members in some social settings but treat those same out-group members with noticeably less warmth and friendliness in other settings. A colloquial term for treating people with little warmth is to say they are "held at an arm's length." The treatment difference across social settings involves the perceived intimacy of people's expected behaviors (Brislin, 1986a; Triandis, Brislin, & Hui, 1988; Triandis & Davis, 1965; Yoshida, Sauer, Tidwell, Skager, & Sorenson, 1997). Intimacy here does not refer to sexual contact. It refers to how much personal information is shared among people. In some social settings, people are not expected to share large amounts of personal information. Examples are (a) relations with casual acquaintances within the workplace, (b) interactions between a speaker and the audience at a lecture, and (c) interactions at a catered dinner party. In such settings, people are not expected to provide personal information and instead can talk about such impersonal topics as the weather, recent organization policies affecting salaries, the speaker's topic during a question/answer session, and the menu at the dinner. In these settings, people can treat out-group members in a very cordial, seemingly friendly manner. But in other settings where intimate behaviors are expected, such as (a) dating, (b) interactions during an informal dinner held at someone's home, or (c) relations between neighbors, some people will interact in a tense, sometimes hostile manner. These people are uncomfortable treating out-group members as equals in settings where everyone is expected to share some of their private thoughts.

I had read the early research about this form of prejudice (e.g., Allport, 1954; Triandis & Davis, 1965), but I did not fully understand it until I saw it in action. My wife and I were entertaining an Anglo social psychologist in our home. To make the story even more complex, this psychologist had written some very insightful, penetrating, and sensitive analyses of prejudicial attitudes. Our Chinese American neighbor unexpectedly dropped by for a visit. The visiting psychologist became noncommunicative and ultimately rude when he left the room where we were sitting and trying to keep up a conversation for everyone's participation. In my opinion, the psychologist was demonstrating arm's-length prejudice. He could handle himself well in formal encounters with out-group members, such as at a public presentation with a Chinese speaker or writing about the nature of prejudice toward out-groups. Yet he was extremely uncomfortable in informal settings where he was expected to engage in relaxed, casual conversations and where he was expected to discuss personal topics beyond such formalities as the weather. Arm's-length prejudice is hard to detect because people who engage in it seem so tolerant and even respectful of out-group members much of the time.

Real Likes and Dislikes

Some people have negative feelings about a certain out-group because the group's members engage in behaviors the people dislike. People avoid interacting with the out-group members, then, because the people want to avoid behaviors they perceive as unpleasant, unhealthy, and even immoral. For example, I sometimes ask students this question: "How many of you use the smoking habit of others as a major reason for choosing how much interaction you have with them?" As many as 50% of Americans in my colleges classes have raised their hands to indicate they use people's smoking habits as a reason to limit interaction with them. I then point out this is an issue they will have to face if they decide to live in certain other countries. Smoking is much more common in certain countries (e.g., Japan, Turkey), and they do not have policies to provide smoke-free places in restaurants and offices. People who live overseas and who really dislike the smoking habit may use this attitude when deciding how much interaction they will seek out with host nationals. Research treatments of real likes and dislikes have to include an understanding of people's everyday, normal behaviors (Hammer, Nishida, & Wiseman, 1996; Pittam, Gallois, Iwawki, & Krooneberg, 1995). People do have strong aversions to certain behaviors, and they try to avoid them. No one person is so saintly as to be tolerant and forgiving toward all who engage in behaviors she or he dislikes. Many Americans who travel overseas bring back stories about the necessity of "bribing" public officials who have such duties as extending visas or providing government forms so that people can file various requests. These stories are especially frequent among Americans who travel to countries with extensive government bureaucracies but with a policy of low salaries for the bureaucrats (e.g., India). Americans complain they have to wait incredible lengths of time to have the requests granted unless they slip some money to a government official. They view the money as a bribe, and they intensely dislike providing bribes. Avoidance of this behavior then affects the amount of contact they have with host nationals. At times, the Americans can be assisted if a knowledgeable person tells them the money should be viewed more like a tip in a restaurant they are expected to leave if service has been adequate (Cushner & Brislin, 1996). The salaries of waiters and waitresses are low, as they are for the government officials. "Tips" in both cases are viewed as part of their expected total take-home pay.

As another example, some people dislike others who complain and gripe all the time. Those who dislike this may find it difficult to interact with many Israelis. Katriel (1990) discusses the verbal ritual of "griping" in Israel. Griping is a common activity, so common that Israelis gather in what is called "griping parties," where they share complaints about Israeli politics and economics, their jobs, and their everyday problems. Katriel (1990) says she feels

> Israelis' disposition toward griping seems to be nourished by a deep sense of frustration related to the perceived inability to partake in social action and communal life in a way that would satisfy the high level of commitment and involvement [that characterized the early, visionary settlers of Israel]. . . . The prevalence of griping suggests an overwhelming, culturally sanctioned concern with the public domain, on the one hand, coupled with a marked absence of widely satisfying participation channels, on the other. (p. 104)

Katriel also points out that not all subjects are proper conversational topics in griping sessions. Proper topics involve problems somebody with responsibility and authority might address through competent actions, and improper topics involve problems fate totally determines. If visitors to Israel do not enjoy griping or listening to gripers, then their dislikes will affect the amount of interaction they have with Israelis.

The Familiar and the Unfamiliar

Even if visitors to Israel were willing to participate in griping parties, they may be unfamiliar with the widely accepted norms that guide "proper" behavior during the parties. For example, visitors may be unfamiliar with the "action possible" versus "fate" distinction for proper griping topics. Their unfamiliarity may lead to negative reactions from Israelis, and these negative reactions may affect later intercultural contact. Even more complex, and admittedly very hard to deal with, is the concept that Israelis can gripe about an issue (e.g., extremely hard-line minority political parties), but visitors cannot comment negatively about the same issue. This reaction to outsider criticism is by no means limited to Israel. Many people are quite vociferous about certain problems in their country, such as Americans who complain about inadequate policies to assist the homeless. But Americans become upset when someone from another country comments on the same inadequate policies. The visitors who comment may be avoided not because they disagreed with the Americans but because they were unfamiliar with the fact "insiders" can say things openly that "outsiders" should keep to themselves.

When analyzing the familiar and the unfamiliar as it relates to intercultural contact, people should keep in mind some of the ideas addressed in chapter 4. People who are socialized into one culture are likely to become familiar and thus comfortable with various aspects of that culture. When interacting in another culture, these people are likely to observe unfamiliar behaviors and to be challenged by new ideas. In turn, people's unfamiliarity leads to discomfort because they do not know how to engage in behaviors that are acceptable to others in the host culture (Tsai, 1995). Consequently, people are likely to seek interaction with members of their own cultural group that happen to be living nearby. Such "enclaves" of compatriots are very common, especially in large cities around the world (Kealey, 1989, 1996).

Chapter 2 had advice for people socialized in individualistic cultures who are about to live in collective cultures (and vice versa, collectivists about to interact in individualistic cultures). Unless they receive extensive preparation before living abroad (Bhawuk, 1990, 1997), they may have limited interaction with host nationals due to unfamiliarity. For instance, individualists may be offered membership in a collective but may make mistakes due to their unfamiliarity. Membership in a collective involves extensive time investment and a broad set of obligations as well as privileges. Individualists may be unprepared for these commitments. A collectivist in an individualist country could be offered business opportunities but may be unfamiliar with the necessary behaviors to obtain them, such as developing a network of contacts who help one another on an ad hoc rather than permanent or long-term basis. When people have difficulties and occasionally become frustrated with people from other cultures, the reason may not involve anything like intense racism, as discussed previously. The frustration may be due to unfamiliarity with the behaviors host culture members expect.

As discussed earlier, intercultural contact will increase in the future, so people will have to become comfortable interacting with others who exhibit unfamiliar behaviors. Some especially interesting examples involve behaviors considered familiar and proper in one culture but rude in another. The challenge here is to understand why a certain behavior is proper, and this often demands an understanding of cultural differences. A further challenge is to move from automatic to controlled processing. Rather than the automatic reaction "This is rude," a controlled analysis would include such thoughts as "This is rude according to how I was socialized in my culture, but perhaps people are behaving as they do for a reason and I should find out about it." Consider these three examples (drawn from Cushner & Brislin, 1996):

- At a party attended by many Deaf people, a room is so full of people it is hard to move from one place to another. Unable to easily go around two other people who are conversing in American Sign Language, a person who is deaf barges through them quickly without apologizing.

- At an American university, a visiting professor from Germany becomes irritated when students visit him during office hours and ask him to clarify points he made in his lectures.
- In Hawaii, newcomers from the mainland United States join in activities that many "locals" attend. When talking with locals, the newcomers can't understand why they are interrupted so often.

All three of these examples involve cultural differences that need to be understood as people become familiar them. In many cultures, stepping between two people while they are having a conversation would be considered rude. In Deaf culture, "barging through" is the most socially skilled behavior because it is the least intrusive. Picture the situation. If people are using sign language, they must be very attentive to each other to receive signs as well as the important additional information facial expressions and body language convey. They would have to stop and acknowledge a person who is trying to apologize before stepping between them. If the person barges through in a brisk manner, however, the two people signing do not have to stop their conversation. If the person moves quickly, he or she will not block the people's reception of each others' signs, facial expressions, and body language. Barging through is the most polite behavior because it is the least intrusive.

In the example of the German professor and office hours, the two cultures differ in their views about student-professor interactions. In Germany and other European countries, office hours are set aside for serious discussion of ideas that go beyond the lecture material. These discussions might be stimulated by material the professor presented in class, but they ideally deal with issues such as the material's implications, alternative explanations, future research needs, competing paradigms, and so forth. Professors from Europe often comment on this difference after they have entertained American students with their vary basic questions that often involve clarification of points made during a lecture. One reason students in the United States and Europe deal differently with office hours stems from how they are tested. In the United States, several tests often are given in each course taken, and these tests usually center on specific knowledge. In Europe, far fewer tests are given in each course, and instead students take long essay tests that ask questions demanding the integration of knowledge from multiple courses.

People who have been socialized in Hawaii, called "locals," often interrupt one another while conversing. Participants in the conversation and observers do not make the attribution that someone is "rude." Rather, the attribution is that people are interested in the discussion so they want to jump in with their contributions. If people don't engage in this conversational overlap, it could be a sign a discussion topic is not of interest to all parties. I was socialized in New England, and I specifically remember my mother telling me it is impolite to interrupt. The reason is that frequent interruptions show a lack of respect for the viewpoints of others. I have lived in Hawaii for more than 25 years and have learned to converse with this pattern of overlap. When I travel, or when I am discussing issues with a newcomer to Hawaii, I have to think carefully about the other person's potential attributions about me. My caution differs for people socialized in various cultures. Conversational overlap is more frequent in Spain, for instance, so I don't change very much from my Hawaiian pattern when I talk with Spanish visitors. Very focused attention and a norm of "don't interrupt" are common in Sweden and among Deaf culture members. I am careful to avoid interrupting with members of these groups.

What was once unfamiliar and potentially irritating, then, can become challenging and interesting when people bring a positive viewpoint to their intercultural interactions. At times, reasons for unfamiliar behaviors cannot be easily identified, but I believe the search for reasons brings enough successes that people will continue to find intercultural interactions a positive addition to their lives.

Are Some of These Behaviors Best Described as Prejudices?

Many types of behavior have been described with the label "prejudice," ranging from intense racist beliefs involving perceived inferiority to unfamiliar behaviors that people are poorly prepared for and find irritating. Is the term *prejudice* used for too many behaviors? A strong case could be made for the answer yes. Prejudice involves negative feelings about other people. For three of the forms of prejudice discussed in this section, a case can be made that people have views about out-groups that do not necessarily involve these negative feelings. In the first form, realistic group conflict, people simply may join forces with in-group members to compete for scarce resources, such as funding for a community mental health center. Out-group members may compete for the same public funds, preferring that money go to preschool education programs. Conflict occurs because not enough money may exist to fund both worthwhile projects. The two groups, however, may not harbor negative feelings about each other. They simply may recognize that they prefer different allocations of funds.

In the second form, real likes and dislikes, individuals may make a distinction between the behaviors of people and the people themselves. For example, some Americans overseas may dislike smoking, but they may realize other countries have not had extensive and well-funded public health campaigns against smoking. They may be able to set aside their attitude toward smoking and seek the stimulation interactions with people from other cultural backgrounds can bring.

The argument is similar for the third form, the familiar and the unfamiliar. Individuals may be able to distinguish unfamiliar behaviors from the people who engage in those behaviors. If they, too, desire the stimulation intercultural interactions can bring, they perhaps can find opportunities to practice the unfamiliar behaviors so that they can later interact effectively across cultural boundaries.

I believe that cases like these three occur where relations among in-groups and out-groups that involve conflict, disliked behaviors, and unfamiliar behaviors are not necessarily prejudicial. Just as often, however, attitudes can turn negative, and prejudices about out-groups develop. When, for example, people lose in the competition for scarce resources, they often develop negative views about their successful opponents. When people dislike certain behaviors, they often generalize their attitudes about the behaviors to the people who practice them. When people are unfamiliar and uncomfortable with certain behaviors, they often do not take the time and trouble to practice them so that they can interact smoothly with others. Given this continuing unfamiliarity, in-group and out-group members continue to keep their distance. Over a number of years, this "distance" becomes the norm and becomes "the way things are done around here."

This absence of interaction across boundaries between in-groups and out-groups is the major reason I have discussed the three forms of behavior as leading to or not leading to prejudice. Even though negative attitudes about out-groups may not be involved, the results of realistic conflict, dislikes, and unfamiliarity can be the same as for prejudice: Unless people make efforts to improve relations, they will not interact effectively across boundaries between in-groups and out-groups. Rather, people may keep their distance and interact far more within their in-group than with out-group members. When this pattern of behavior occurs, stereotypes develop because people do not have the extensive interactions with individual out-group members necessary to break down conclusions about a category of people (Pettigrew, 1998). For example, Anglo college students may not have the necessary interactions with African Americans on their way to law, medical, and business schools to break down the stereotype of "they are here to play basketball." Eventually, unchallenged stereotypes can affect attitudes, such as that African Americans may be great in athletics but inadequate in the classroom.

The most effective way to break down negative stereotypes and to challenge negative attitudes is to encourage carefully thought out contact among in-group and out-group members. The emphasis is on "carefully thought out," because contact itself is no guarantee of positive intergroup relations. Once again, if readers have heard somebody say, "Let's just bring people together so that they'll get to know one another, and this will reduce prejudice," then readers heard an oversimplification. Much research has been undertaken to identify the types of effective contact, and people who study the research will find some very helpful guidelines for interventions designed to improve intergroup relations.

INTERVENTIONS FOR EFFECTIVE INTERCULTURAL INTERACTION

As just noted, an extensive body of research has focused on the question "What types of contact best encourage the development of positive intergroup relations?" The shorthand term for the research has been "studies of the contact hypothesis" (Allport, 1954; Amir, 1969; Brislin, 1981; S. W. Cook, 1969; Cushner, 1990; Gudykunst & Bond, 1997; Leong & Kim, 1991; Miller & Brewer, 1986; Pettigrew, 1998; Stephan, 1985). Since Allport's highly influential book on prejudice published in 1954, researchers and practitioners have known that contact itself does not necessarily bring positive benefits. In many cases, contact simply reinforces existing prejudices. For example, people from different groups may have extensive contact in a factory where they seem to work cooperatively on the products their organization manufactures. However, if the managers are from one ethnic group and the laborers are from another, the contact may simply reinforce the existing stereotype that members of one group are fit for leadership and members of another group are happier in subservient roles.

Intervention programs that have the goal of improving intergroup relations are based on the assumption the program administrators have some control over what happens when people come into contact. That is, the program administrators must be able to intervene in ways that should improve intergroup relations according to guidelines from researchers and experienced practitioners. Several of the guidelines are especially important (longer treatments in Brislin, 1981; Pettigrew, 1998; Stephan, 1985).

Equal-Status Contact

The guideline most frequently suggested is that people participating in intergroup contact should have equal status. Members of the various groups should have equal power, should be treated equally by program administrators, and should have equal access to rewards. In efforts to desegregate schools, for example, students from various ethnic groups should receive equal amounts of attention from teachers and should have equal access to rewards such as good grades and active participation in school activities. In public housing projects, people from different groups should have equal access to the homes considered the "best," such as those with the best views or with the easiest access to shared facilities such as playgrounds. In the workplace, equal-status contact means people should have equal access to benefits such as advanced training opportunities, salary increases for meritorious work, and promotions.

In chapter 5, reasons for Asian American success in schools was reviewed. One suggested reason was based on the concept "relative functionalism." I believe that equal-status contact contributes to the explanation of exactly what relative functionalism means. Compared to other parts of society and even other aspects of school, such as athletic activities and elected student government positions, Asian Americans perceive they will experience equal-status contact in the classroom. If they perform well in their studies, they will have equal access (along with hard-working students from any ethnic group) to rewards such as teacher approval, good grades, and listings on the honor roll. Thus, Asian Americans perceive work in the classroom as functional in leading to success, and one reason for this perception is that they feel teachers will treat them equally.

In some cases, equal status in the contact situation may not go far enough. Considering African Americans in the United States, Riordan (1978) says he feels they have experienced such a long history of discrimination that special steps are needed. Riordan says he fears that an equal-status contact experience between Anglo and African Americans may not have enough impact to counter years of experience with unequal status. One suggestion for program administrators is to arrange experiences that give Anglos contact with African Americans who have higher status than the Anglos. Within the contact setting, Anglos would have to interact with African Americans who are better educated, are more articulate, and have more abilities to contribute than the Anglos if they are to work cooperatively on various projects. Riordan feels that these interactions with higher status African Americans will be more likely to offset the familiar status quo where Anglos are both more numerous and have superior positions.

I feel these concepts of equal-status and higher status contact help explain Anglo reactions to life in my home, Hawaii. Many Anglos from the mainland United States settle in Hawaii given its climate, outdoor lifestyle, clean air, and so forth. However, some stay only a few years and move back to the mainland for various reasons. Hawaii has a very high cost of living; given the number of people desirous of jobs, salaries are not very high; people find that they genuinely miss their families and old friends; and so forth. But another reason is that many Anglos come from parts of the country where they are clearly the majority and clearly hold down the most powerful and influential jobs. On the mainland, they may have interacted adequately with minority group members but more often in the sort of arm's-length manner discussed earlier. Many Anglos can be polite in formal settings but do not seek interactions with minority group members during their free time. In Hawaii, however, they inevitably will experience people from culturally diverse groups who hold powerful positions. Japanese Americans, Chinese Americans, Filipino Americans, and others hold high-level positions such as elected congresspeople, judges, chief executive officers, school principals, college professors, and so forth. Many of these positions represent much higher status than those held by Anglos who decide to settle in Hawaii. Some Anglos benefit from interactions with high-status people from culturally diverse groups and become much more tolerant and appreciative of cultural differences. Other Anglos become uncomfortable and move back to the mainland United States.

Superordinate Goals

Program administrators also can give attention to the tasks people work on during their intergroup contact. The most effective tasks are directed toward "superordinate goals" (Sherif, 1966), or goals everyone desires and that demand the efforts of everyone involved. When people work together to achieve goals all value, prejudicial attitudes have to be set aside or else people will not accomplish anything. Instead of sniping at one another, people will put their efforts into hard work if the goals they are striving for are important to them. For example, superordinate goals have been integrated into classroom activities designed to improve the learning of new material. In one type of cooperative group learning activity (Aronson & Osherow, 1980; Aronson, Wilson, & Akert, 1999), teachers divide students into four-person groups. In desegregated classrooms, teachers make a point of maximizing the cultural diversity of each group. If Anglo, Hispanic, Asian, and African Americans are represented in the classroom, they become members of culturally diverse learning groups. The teacher gives part of the lesson to each student, who has to share his or her part with the others. To achieve the superordinate goals of learning the entire lesson and achieving teacher praise and good grades, the students have to work cooperatively and have to make sure all group members have mastered the entire lesson. Research has shown that students learn as much from this approach as from traditional "teacher centered" activities such as lecturing, and the students become more tolerant of classmates from different cultural backgrounds.

Of course, programs can focus on various types of superordinate goals to improve intergroup relations. In athletics, a superordinate goal is to have a winning team, and the time and energy that might be spent on prejudicial attitudes toward teammates from minority groups or other cultures instead can be invested in the cooperative task of developing the skills necessary to compete successfully in the league. In international business activities, superordinate goals include profits and the successful acquisition of a niche in the marketplace. Great amounts of money and effort have been invested in cooperative efforts among businesspeople from such countries as Japan, the United States, and Germany. When business goals are made very clear, people become motivated to find ways to harness cultural differences in the pursuit of success (Adler, 1997; J. Johnson, Cullen, Sakano, & Takenouchi, 1996). This motivation replaces the useless complaints about businesspeople in different countries who "don't do things the way we do."

Intimate Contact

As noted earlier, when researchers and practitioners make recommendations that contact be intimate, they are not referring to sexual relations. Rather, they are referring to the sharing of personal information. Most people share much more personal information about themselves with in-group than with out-group members. Further, most people have a rather well-rehearsed set of statements about themselves they use when meeting strangers and out-group members. Typical examples of well-rehearsed, nonintimate facts are personal names, schools attended, hometown names, and perhaps a few words about hobbies. Statements about these facts reveal little about people.

In contrast, intimate statements shared with in-group members usually have much more emotional content and include thoughts about people's personal ambitions, worries, troubles, successes and failures in relationships, and so forth. The advantage of intimate contact is that it is far more likely to break down the barriers between "us" and "them." When people reveal personal information about themselves, they are more likely to be seen as individuals rather than as members of a category. Further, the sharing of personal information often leads to the discovery that others previously considered as "them" have some of the same feelings, concerns, and ambitions. Again, this leads to a breakdown of barriers between in-groups and out-groups (Pettigrew, 1998).

In one of the first studies of extensive intergroup contact, Deutsch and Collins (1951) studied the reactions of Anglo and African American residents in an integrated housing project. The project included small apartments for families together with shared facilities such as laundry rooms and playgrounds for children. Even though people may have preferred to stick with their own ethnic group, they had numerous opportunities for intergroup contact. One set of opportunities took place in laundry rooms. It was more interesting for Anglos to chat with African Americans than to stare blankly at their clothes tumbling in the dryer. Another set of opportunities occurred on the playgrounds. Four- and 5-year-olds, too young to be attached to their parents' prejudices, played together regardless of skin color. Children followed each other as they reported back to their parents at the end of playtime. Children met one another's parents, and eventually the parents learned to recognize one another, having been introduced (in effect) by their children. Parents eventually chatted while watching their children on the playground. Over time, the chats moved from topics such as the weather and the quality of the washing machines to the sharing of personal information. People learned they shared many of the same concerns: the job market in their community, the quality of schools for their children, problems in balancing the family budget, taxes, problems in the romantic liaisons of friends and relatives, and so forth. The discovery that people shared these concerns and experienced similar problems helped to break down the boundaries between in-groups and out-groups based on skin color. Ashmore (1970) argues the following in a similar manner:

> Intergroup friendship causes a redeployment of motivation with respect to the intergroup attitude. The prejudiced person wants to hang onto his [or her] prejudice; but becoming friendly with a member of an outgroup makes [the person] more amenable to information that favors tolerance. (p. 320)

The Candid Treatment of Difficulties

Enough is known about intergroup relations that program administrators can identify problems that almost inevitably will arise. My recommendation is that they give these explicit attention during the program. It is far better for people to deal with difficulties after having heard suggestions for their alleviation than it is for them to face the difficulties after the program without guidance for dealing with possible problems.

For example, people can become quite tolerant of out-group members in the contact program knowledgeable administrators arrange, but this tolerance might not transfer to others outside the program. If the contact, for example, is between Anglo and African Americans in the integrated housing project discussed earlier, the people may have become quite tolerant of out-group members who lived in the housing project. This does not assure, however, that these positive feelings will transfer to other out-group members in the community at large. In this situation, challenges have been made to people's previously existing categories (see the left-hand drawing in Figure 5). The difficulty is that people simply may develop a new and smaller category that splits off from the previous, all-encompassing category (Brewer & Brown, 1998; Brewer & Miller, 1984). This is shown in the right-hand drawing. People in the example, then, may have two categories: almost all out-group members and those few in the housing project. The larger category remains almost untouched, so people who were prejudicial are likely to treat out-group members outside the housing project in a prejudicial manner. I recommend including this problem, called "splitting," in the material presented to participants during the contact program. Administrators should point out the problem in a manner similar to this:

> Participants in programs such as this one often report that they grow to like each other. This does not mean they will show the same affection toward out-group members outside the program. We must keep in mind the possibility of splitting, or the development of a new category that contains only the out-group members met in the contact situation.

When writing about Anglo–African American relations some years ago, I referred to the splitting problem as the "Lena Horne–Harry Belafonte effect" (Brislin & Pedersen, 1976). It is easy for Anglos to like these handsome entertainers, and it

A Representation of Splitting in Intergroup Relations   **FIGURE 5**

is easy to split them off in a separate, small category. It is harder to tolerate all out-group members, who cannot all possibly be as attractive as these two celebrities. The name of the effect might have to be changed so that younger audiences understand it. Suggestions are welcome. Would perhaps the "Whitney Houston–Michael Jordan" effect capture the same concept?

Knowing about difficulties such as splitting helps administrators plan their program content. One way they can continue to challenge the large preexisting category of "all out-group members" is to make sure people have contact with many out-group members who have different abilities and characteristics. If people learn to interact with diverse out-group members, this may challenge their preexisting category so many times and in so many different ways that they no longer find the large category useful for thinking about others they might later meet.

Many other issues can be covered as part of the recommendations to prepare people for the difficulties they will face during extensive intercultural interactions. Most of these are based on the realization that many people (a) are willing to be tolerant and to seek opportunities for intercultural contact but (b) do not know enough about other cultures and ethnic groups to be comfortable during contacts with them. Further, they may find that (c) intercultural interactions involve both frustrating and irritating behaviors because they are so poorly understood. Such problems will be the focus of the next chapter.

CHAPTER SUMMARY

One prediction about the future that can be made with absolute certainty is that far more contact across cultural boundaries will occur than has in the past. Such contact will challenge people's preexisting beliefs about others, their attitudes, and their behaviors. It also will challenge administrators (e.g., school principals, employers) who must guarantee the equal treatment of individuals regardless of their skin color or cultural background.

Challenges to preexisting beliefs immediately bring up the problem of stereotypes (Bar-Tel, 1997). Whenever individuals can be grouped together or categorized in some way, then stereotypes about them become part of people's thinking. When people use stereotypes, they are ignoring individual differences among the members of the group or category. Many stereotypes are used without much thought, as when people talk about "the Republican position on taxes" or "women's ways of making decisions." In actuality, large differences can exist in the positions different Republicans take and in how different women make decisions. Even though stereotypes can involve any group or category of people, the term is most often used when it refers to people's beliefs about out-group members who have a different skin color and who are from a different ethnic or cultural background. Stereotypes provide shortcuts to thinking and allow people to make decisions without a great deal of mental effort. Assume an Anglo student has the opportunity to approach and to chat with an African American student at a campus reception. If the Anglo holds a stereotype of African Americans that includes the belief that "they don't particularly want to interact with Anglos and prefer to stick to themselves," then the Anglo student has assistance in making his or her decision about whether or not to talk to the African American student. The decision here will be to avoid contact with the African American and to seek someone the Anglo considers friendlier at the reception. One of the difficulties with such decision making is that once a person is put into a category, all the information from that category becomes available to the decision maker and is applied to that person. In the business world, a stereotype of "women executives" may be that they cannot make tough decisions. If a young woman with an advanced degree in business seeks a serious interview for an executive-level position, her individuality may be denied if she is simply put into the convenient category of "women in the business world." All of the information from the category becomes available to decision makers, and she may be denied the interview because she is seen as unable to make difficult decisions.

In this busy, stress-filled world, people seek shortcuts for thinking about the many others they might meet on a daily basis. They must form generalizations about others, because they do not have sufficient time to examine the individuality of every person they see. The goal for people who want to reduce stereotypes should be to improve the generalizations, and Adler (1997) recommends using a 5-point checklist.

1. People should be quite conscious of using stereotypes. People also should consciously look for exceptions and should ask themselves if they are making decisions based on stereotypes.

2. Generalizations about people should be descriptive and should have as little evaluative content as possible. The danger of evaluative content is that people then judge "goodness" or "badness" based on their own standards and become insensitive to cultural differences concerning these standards.

3. People should conduct careful searches of available evidence to determine if the stereotypes are accurate. What evidence exists, for instance, that African Americans do not want intergroup contact or that women cannot make tough decisions?

4. Stereotypes also should be considered only a first best guess about out-group members that will be sharpened through firsthand experiences with many different others.

5. Consequently, stereotypes will be modifiable rather than rigid and will include an important fact: Often, more differences exist among the members of one category than between the members of two categories.

All of these guidelines move people from automatic processing to controlled processing of information. Automatic processing refers to immediate reactions. Applied to stereotypes, examples would be immediate reactions when seeing members of other cultural groups. Controlled processing refers to the addition of careful thought. If people say to themselves that they are tempted to stereotype but they should move beyond this and search for more accurate information, then they are engaging in controlled processing. Devine (1995) argues that members of a culture know the stereotypes of various groups, but low-prejudice people are uncomfortable with stereotypes and engage in controlled thinking to move beyond them.

A major difficulty, of course, is that many people are not willing to interrupt their automatic processing and to put extensive effort into changing their stereotype-influenced thinking. One reason is that many stereotypes are the result of deep-seated attitudes toward out-groups, and any discussion of attitudes and feelings about out-group members immediately raises the topic of prejudice. As Jordan (1989) points out, "stereotypes may be defined as the bundles of beliefs carried by the energy" (p. 1119) of people's prejudicial attitudes. *Prejudice* refers to the emotional content of people's reactions to out-groups, and the roots of the word help explain its meaning. People prejudge out-groups based on limited information and on emotion rather than careful thought. People's prejudgments have a far greater likelihood of involving negative rather than positive feelings.

Prejudices remain, sometimes for generations within a culture, because they serve various functions or uses for people. Four functions have been suggested.

1. If a prejudice serves an *adjustment function*, it helps people to obtain rewards and to avoid punishment in their culture. It is functional, for example, for people to view certain out-group members as lazy and as unable to hold down good jobs. It means the in-group members will have less competition for good jobs given that the out-group members are never even considered for interviews.

2. If a prejudice serves an *ego defensive function*, it means people can hide negative aspects of themselves they don't want to admit publicly. Rather than admit they do not have the necessary skills for success in the business world, for instance, they might charge that certain out-group members conspire to keep all the good business opportunities to themselves. This conspiracy charge has long been part of anti-Semitic prejudices.

3. If people want to clearly communicate certain information about themselves, they may hold prejudices that serve the *value expressive function*. For example, they may want to communicate clearly that they belong to the "one true religion of God." They may communicate this by viewing other religions as wrong-headed or even evil.

4. Other prejudices serve the *knowledge function*. Attitudes serving this function help people organize what is "correct" and what is "incorrect" in their culture. For instance, assume parents are deciding which school their children will attend

next year and that they have four or five possibilities. If part of their "knowledge" is that one of the schools attracts members of a certain ethnic group and that people from this group are not terribly serious about the importance of good schools, then the parents may eliminate that school as one of the possibilities. Their prejudicial "knowledge" helps in their decision making.

Many attitudes serve several functions (Eagly & Chaiken, 1998). Children may adopt a certain prejudice (e.g., "those out-group members are not as good as us, so don't interact with them") to avoid punishment by their parents (adjustment function). They may maintain this attitude as adults so that they can use the out-group as an excuse for their own shortcomings (ego defensive) or to demonstrate clearly that they belong to a superior group (value expressive). They may use "information" about the out-group for making decisions (knowledge function). Programs aimed at changing prejudices often address only the knowledge function. For instance, they present information about successful people from the out-group, the concern out-group parents express toward their children, how admitted difficulties such as the out-group's living standard can be explained by the denial of opportunities for betterment, and so forth. Although the programs possibly are successful in challenging the knowledge function, the prejudices often remain because the other three functions are not addressed.

In addition to an understanding of its functions, an understanding of prejudice demands recognition of the various forms it takes. The most virulent form is *intense racism*. When people believe certain individuals are inferior simply because they were born to parents from an out-group, then the people are guilty of racism. Examples of racist feelings are that certain out-group members are naturally ignorant and cannot advance to a decent standard of living. The public expression of racist sentiments has become unfashionable, so the prevalence of intense racism is difficult to establish. When people believe out-group members are interfering with valued aspects of a culture, such as the importance of hard work and raising oneself by the bootstraps when faced with difficulties, they may be expressing either *symbolic racism* or may be recognizing *realistic group conflict*. Symbolic racism involves the beliefs that out-group members are getting more than they deserve and are receiving too much support in their struggle against discrimination. Recognizing realistic group conflict means various groups realize they are competing for society's scarce resources, such as public funding for their favored programs. Some groups compete for such resources by organizing around racial and ethnic affiliations. This type of behavior may not involve prejudice; it simply may involve the realization that political action is more effective when people join together.

Recent research has shown that symbolic racism and realistic group conflict can combine to contribute to the quality of intercultural interactions. Stephan and his colleagues have investigated attitudes toward immigrants in Spain and in Israel. Some long-term residents of these countries fear interference with their cultures and with their familiar ways of life (symbolic racism). In addition, they fear the negative consequences of competition for resources, such as jobs and funds for social services.

In *tokenism*, people engage in unimportant behaviors on behalf of out-groups so that they can convince themselves they are unprejudiced. Given this self-definition, they do not have to engage in more important, challenging, and time-consuming behaviors. *Arm's-length prejudice* involves people's apparent tolerance in formal situations, such as meetings in the workplace, but their rejection in more intimate settings, such as informal interactions in someone's home. The difference between the settings seems to involve the necessity of communicating personal information in the informal interactions. "Safe" topics such as the weather and business conditions can be discussed in formal settings. Informal settings call for the sharing of information usually reserved for in-group members. Although not always involving prejudicial feelings, *real likes and dislikes* and *familiar and unfamiliar behaviors* can lead to preferences for interaction with in-group members and the avoidance of out-group members. No person is so saintly as to tolerate all behaviors. For example, Americans who dislike the smoking habit will have a difficult time interacting cordially in cultures where far more people smoke than in their own country. If people are unfamiliar with certain behaviors common in a culture, such as Israel's communication rituals involving subtle rules for what are proper and improper topics in gripe sessions, they may feel unwelcome even if invited to interact with individuals from that culture. If well-meaning and unprejudiced people must engage in multiple unfamiliar behaviors, one possible reaction is irritation. These people may seek out less intercultural contact not because of prejudice but because they are uncomfortable feeling irritated frequently.

Encouraging people to understand the reasons people engage in behaviors that seem unfamiliar is one goal of formal programs created to encourage intergroup contact. Another goal is greater openness toward, and tolerance of, individuals previously rejected as out-group members. Numerous guidelines are available to administrators of such programs, whether those programs focus on schools, the workplace, neighborhoods, the military, or elsewhere (longer treatments of various guidelines can be found in Brislin, 1981; Pettigrew, 1998; and Stephan, 1985). Administrators should make efforts to insure that all people involved in the intergroup contacts have *equal status*, or equal access to the rewards and benefits of the school, workplace, or neighborhood. At times, the status of certain groups outside the contact setting will be so much lower (e.g., African Americans in the United States) that efforts should be made to expose in-group members to individual out-group members who possess very high status. Administrators also should encourage people to work toward *superordinate goals*, or goals desired by all and that need the efforts of all involved. When people work toward goals they deem important, they often set aside the energy they need to maintain prejudices and instead invest it in goal attainment. *Intimate contact* should be encouraged so that people have opportunities to share personal information. When people find that many of their concerns about life are shared by out-group members, they find it harder to maintain rigid distinctions between "us" and "them."

Still, it must be recognized that increasing intergroup tolerance always will be a difficult undertaking. Administrators should treat candidly some of these difficulties. For example, people often tolerate out-group members they meet in the contact setting, but this frequently does not transfer to individuals they meet elsewhere. One reason is that people form a category of "out-group members I had contact with" that is distinct from "out-group members in general." Administrators can address this issue by encouraging people to meet as many different out-group members as possible so that the latter's unique traits constantly challenge the all-encompassing category.

The tendency to form a separate category of favored out-group members and to distinguish this from a more general out-group category is just one example of the difficulties involved in encouraging more intercultural interaction. Even if people seek increased intercultural contact and generally are tolerant of individuals from other racial and ethnic groups, they may find that actual interactions with out-group members are often puzzling and unsuccessful. Further, they cannot figure out the reasons for the difficulties. This theme of "difficulties despite good intentions" will be examined in the next chapter.

CHAPTER 7

INTERACTING SUCCESSFULLY WITH PEOPLE FROM OTHER CULTURES

CHAPTER OVERVIEW

Increasingly, people will find themselves interacting with neighbors, coworkers, classmates, and bosses who are from different cultural backgrounds. Rather than feeling satisfied with merely getting along, some will embrace this diversity and will view it as positive and potentially enriching. The question "What leads to successful long-term intercultural interactions?" has received attention, and it can be applied to both international experiences and interactions among diverse groups within a nation. A four-part criterion of success has been developed and is discussed in this chapter. It includes positive relations, reciprocation of those relations by individuals from other cultures, task accomplishment, and stress management. The special term *culture shock* has been coined to refer to people's sense of loss, helplessness, and reactions to multiple demands on their resources, and this complex reaction almost always occurs when people move across cultural boundaries.

Some individuals adjust more quickly to the demands of intercultural interactions than others. More successful people behave flexibly, are enthusiastic about their intercultural interactions, and effectively resolve conflicts. They also can recognize differences in communication styles. Intercultural interactions involve both the content and the delivery style of multiple communications. Often, difficulties arise not because of the content but because of the styles. Various styles are reviewed in this chapter that are common in different cultures. These include directness, silence, the degree of emotional expressiveness, and the amount of warmth and openness expressed. Misunderstandings can occur when people make misattributions about style. In some cultures, a warm and open style is common when people meet for the first time. In other cultures, this same warmth and openness is reserved for people who are trusted and who have known each other many years.

Many times, people want to interact more effectively across cultural boundaries but they don't know how. As discussed throughout this book, these people might consider participating in a training program that encourages people to increase their knowledge, deal with their emotional reactions, and to practice culturally appropriate behaviors. Training can be either "culture-specific" or "culture-general." Specific training focuses on issues people from a specific background will face when interacting with individuals from another known culture. An example is college students from France about to spend a year in Mexico. General training deals with intercultural issues virtually all people will face no matter what their job is or where they will be living. One type of training is not better than the other, and most programs deal in some way with both types of training content.

MOVING BEYOND PREJUDICES AND STEREOTYPES

If people learn to understand *some* of the major difficulties of intercultural interactions, such as learning how prejudice's forms and functions discussed in chapter 6 affect interactions, they may feel ready to seek relationships with people from other cultural backgrounds. They may, however, still experience difficulties because they fail to understand cultural differences that impact the formation and maintenance of relationships. Further, because the people are very well intentioned in their pursuit of positive relationships, they may become very frustrated if their intentions cannot be translated into behaviors. They may conclude, "I tried my best, and I don't think my failures are due to my prejudices. But I just can't seem to communicate with those other people, and I'm not going to continue trying!"

These frustrations, and suggestions to alleviate them, are the focus of this chapter. Even though frustrations are common in the development of relationships across cultural boundaries (Landis & Bhagat, 1996), I feel the tone of this chapter is positive in contrast to the tone demanded in the previous chapter's discussion of stereotypes, racism, prejudice, and discrimination. I assume many readers either accept that effective and respectful intercultural relationships are necessary or they actively look to developing these relationships. I realize I am not addressing everyone's needs, because many people prefer to retain their prejudicial outlook and to interact only with individuals much like themselves. However, numerous people overcome the problems that stem from prejudices and stereotypes (chapter 6) and seek intercultural relationships. I hope the content of this chapter will assist these people.

Another way to view the relationship between this and the previous chapter is to ask, "After dealing with prejudice, do problems still remain?" The answer is yes. Many of the remaining problems stem from unexamined aspects of one's culture. Recall the presentation in chapter 1 on "well-meaning clashes." People from different backgrounds may have every good intention to interact effectively, but a clash occurs. The clash is usually based on a violation (from one or the other or both people's viewpoints) of what should happen in an interaction meant to proceed smoothly. Chapter 1 had the example of an Japanese student pursuing a graduate degree at an American university. He expected an invitation to a late Friday afternoon social gathering. The American students behaved according to their expectation that "the word will get out, and everyone who wants to come will just show up!" No one is prejudiced—no one is trying to be unpleasant—but a clash occurs. The result is that the Japanese student is frustrated in his desire to develop effective intercultural relationships. Various reasons for such well-meaning clashes will be discussed in this chapter.

When people are willing to move beyond the problems prejudicial thinking brings, they want to experience success in their efforts to develop intercultural relationships. What does success with these relationships mean?

SUCCESS WITH INTERCULTURAL INTERACTIONS

A four-part definition has been developed to analyze exactly what it means to "succeed" when engaging in extensive intercultural interactions (Bhawuk, 1990; Brislin, 1981; Brislin & Yoshida, 1994; Hammer, 1989; Hammer, Gudykunst, & Wiseman, 1978; Kealey, 1989). A person must satisfy all four parts to succeed—achieving two or three parts is not sufficient. '

1. People must feel they are having successful relationships with people from other cultures. They must show respect, seek activities of mutual interest, work cooperatively on projects, spend part of their free time with others, and so forth. In short, relationships should be warm and cordial, and people should look forward to their intercultural interactions.

   In actual research projects, this aspect of success is assessed from people's self-reports about their interactions with others. People simply tell about their interactions and label them as successful or unsuccessful. Although researchers would like to follow people around and keep careful records of their interactions, practical considerations and ethical principles (especially the invasion of people's privacy) make such research almost impossible. Given the researchers' dependence on people's self-reports, it is important to add a second part to the criteria of success.

2. Individuals in the other culture (sometimes called "hosts") must feel the interactions are warm and cordial, reflect respect, involve cooperation, and so forth. This insistence on the two parts reflects researchers' awareness of a type of person many readers probably have encountered. Some people report they have many friends and that they are gracious and cordial, but others report that those people are abrasive, are unfriendly, and should be avoided!

3. Most extensive intercultural interactions involve tasks of some kind. Foreign students want to obtain college degrees within a reasonable period; businesspeople want to start or to maintain joint ventures in other countries; diplomats want to develop treaties; technical assistance advisers want to develop projects useful to the host country; and so forth. Even if an intercultural relationship develops outside a workplace, people often cooperate on some tasks: obtaining visa extensions; filling out dreadful, unfamiliar tax forms; maneuvering through

bureaucracies if legal, government, or medical interventions are needed; and so forth.

Tasks must be accomplished in an efficient manner. As will be discussed later in this chapter and in chapter 8, which is about the workplace, task accomplishment often involves dealing with cultural differences.

4. People should experience minimal stress due to dealing with individuals from other cultures rather than from their own culture (Bochner, 1994; Hsiao-Ying, 1995). Life is stressful, so the definition cannot include the assertion that no stress should occur. If people in an organization are working to meet an upcoming deadline or if they are competing with other companies for lucrative contracts or if they have an abrasive boss, they will experience stress. The definition of success in intercultural relations suggests that additional stress should not arise because the others people interact with frequently (e.g., coworkers and boss in the examples) are from a different cultural background.

When stress becomes overwhelming in another culture, people often experience the intense emotional reaction known as "culture shock" (Bochner, 1994; Bock, 1970; Furnham & Bochner, 1986; Oberg, 1958). Stress arises when people cannot meet their everyday needs as they would in their own culture. They cannot communicate, they cannot make themselves understood, and they cannot figure out why hosts behave the way they do. The familiar ways of behaving, learned during their socialization, do not work in the other culture. As a result, they experience a sense of loss and a sense of shock that others behave so differently and seem to have such a different worldview (Greenberg, Solomon, & Pyszczynski, 1997). It is important to note that culture shock is not an indication of failure to adjust to another culture. Often, it is a signal that people are interacting with host nationals in such a way that they will surely experience differences and will encounter challenges to their worldviews. People who do not experience culture shock may be so rigid as to not see cultural differences where they clearly exist, or they may be interacting only with fellow nationals who happen to be living in the other country.

Assuming people are positively inclined toward developing intercultural relationships and want to achieve success according to the four-part definition, what should they do? Is good advice available that they should keep in mind? Can they take specific steps to increase the chances of success? To provide answers to these questions, the rest of the chapter deals with three approaches to helping people achieve success.

1. *Qualities of individuals.* One approach involves studying the qualities of people who achieve success in extensive intercultural interactions in contrast to people who do not. The "qualities" of people are various traits within their personalities, their abilities, and their attitudes (Kealey, 1996).

2. *Difficulties in face-to-face conversations.* To develop relationships with others, people have to converse about various tasks, about potential social activities, about outlooks on life, and so forth. Cultural differences in how people converse with one another can lead to irritations and to decreases in people's willingness

One reason for culture shock is that people must adjust to many differences in a short period.

to seek future conversations. If these difficulties can be identified and understood, irritations may be less intense because people know what to expect. At times, however, these difficulties are almost invisible. Just as people usually have few opportunities to examine their culture and to identify how it affects their behavior (chapter 1), people rarely have opportunities to examine how interpersonal communication affects success and failure in their interactions.

3. *Formal training programs.* People may decide they are unprepared for the difficulties they might face in future intercultural interactions. They may want to take advantage of intercultural training programs, or formal efforts to prepare people to live and work in cultures other than their own. Various types of programs are aimed at providing people with information, encouraging greater sophistication in their thinking, and preparing them for the emotional confrontations that accompany extensive intercultural interactions (Brislin & Yoshida, 1994; Landis & Bhagat, 1996).

QUALITIES OF INDIVIDUALS

Many researchers, working in different parts of the world, have identified a core set of traits that seem to distinguish people who are more and who are less successful in their intercultural interactions. For example, research has been carried out with Canadian technical assistance advisers working in Africa and Asia (Hawes & Kealey, 1981; Kealey, 1996), with U.S. Peace Corps workers in various parts of the world (J. G. Harris, 1973), with Japanese businesspeople working in the United States (Black, 1990), with Asian immigrants to North America (Berry & Sam, 1997), with students from various parts of the world pursuing college degrees in other countries (Althen, 1995; Klineberg & Hull, 1979), and with German businesspeople contemplating expansion into marketing efforts in other countries (Dichtl, Koeglmayr, & Mueller, 1990). Further, some reviews attempt to integrate these studies and others (Brislin, 1981; Kealey & Ruben, 1983; Spitzberg, 1989; Ward & Kennedy, 1993). Although all these studies and reviews do not use the same terms and although certainly not all totally agree, I believe good evidence indicates that several identifiable traits increase the chances of success in intercultural interactions. These are each presented separately here.

Cultural Flexibility

As discussed in chapter 1, the culture people are socialized in provides much guidance for choices about everyday behaviors: what and when to eat, what activities to pursue, how to talk with higher status people, and so forth. *Cultural flexibility* involves making changes in behavior to meet the demands of situations found in other cultures (Cross, 1995). Many businesspeople working in Japan, for example, have commented on a difference between Americans and Japanese (e.g., Chesanow, 1985). When negotiating with the Japanese, Americans like to get right down to business! They were socialized to believe that "time is money." They can accept about 15 minutes of small talk about the weather, their trip, and baseball, but more than that becomes unreasonable. The Japanese, in contrast, want to get to know their business counterparts. They feel the best way to do this is to have long conversations with Americans about a wide variety of topics. The Japanese are comfortable with hours and hours, and even days and days, of conversations about small-talk issues. One reason is pragmatic. The Japanese want to determine if they can trust their potential American counterparts. If business dealings are to be agreed on, they want to know that any eventual problems can be settled through their feelings of trust for their American counterparts. The Japanese do not want to settle difficulties by bringing in lawyers to hash out or litigate a settlement. Rather, the Japanese want to place a phone call and ask their American friends, "We have a problem. Can you take care of it?" The Japanese feel the best way to develop this trusting, friendly relationship is to have these long conversations for people get to know one another and for constantly demonstrating goodwill.

People working in Japan will have a greater chance of success if they possess the cultural flexibility trait. The opposite of flexibility is rigidity: Rigid people behave in a very limited set of ways and believe other ways are incorrect or even silly. Flexible people can modify their behavior to meet the host culture's demands. Overseas businesspeople in Japan demonstrate flexibility if they are willing to engage in long discussions of small-talk issues, to show they are trustworthy people who will be good friends, and to communicate clearly that they will later solve problems the way friends do. Friends do not bring in lawyers—rather, they come to each other's aid in times of need.

Analyzing the experiences of Japanese businesspeople working in the United States, Black (1990) provides a more general example of cultural flexibility. One way people reduce stress is to have hobbies. It is difficult to pursue some hobbies when working in another country when no one else is interested, when materials are not available, and so forth. Culturally flexible people can find activities that interest them. They can replace valued activities from their own culture (e.g., cricket in Great Britain) with those available in other countries (e.g., baseball in the United States). Rigid people are less able to modify and to replace valued activities, so they cannot reap the benefits enjoyable hobbies can bring.

Enthusiasm About Forming Intercultural Relationships

Some people actively want to establish close relationships with people from other cultural backgrounds (Dinges & Baldwin, 1996). Rather than simply tolerating such relationships as a necessity for task accomplishment, they look forward to the stimulation of intercultural relationships. Some people even look forward to having aspects of their own culture challenged during intercultural interactions. They realize that understanding the underlying reasons for these challenges is a excellent way to increase their learning about their own and other cultures.

People also will achieve practical results if they carry out their goals of forming intercultural relationships (Ying & Liese, 1994). Adjustment to other cultures is hastened if people have "cultural informants." When people have difficulties, cultural informants can provide information that can help alleviate problems. They can answer variants of this question: "Is something about our cultures and cultural differences causing this problem I am having?" For example, assume an American businessperson in Japan is impatient with the length of time it takes the Japanese to make decisions. If the American has developed good intercultural relationships, one or more Japanese friends may be able to take on the role of cultural informant. When questioned about decision making, the informant could point out that Japan is a more collective culture than the United States (see chapter 2). In Japan, the feelings of all group members are very important. Each person in the workplace who might be affected by the decision has to examine all the American proposals (Hijirida & Yoshikawa, 1987). Each Japanese individual makes a mark or signs off on the proposal he or she approves or makes suggestions for improvement. Because so many people have to read and sign off, much time is needed for each proposal. Interestingly, even though it may take the Japanese company a great deal of time to reach a decision, implementation might be rather fast. Because all the Japanese businesspeople involved know the content of the final proposal, have expressed their approval, and feel involved in the decision making process, they can implement plans quickly. In the United States, however, decision making may proceed quickly because so few people are involved in the process. A few high-level executives may make the decision and pass orders on to people they supervise. Implementation may take a long time because other workers resent not being consulted, do not know how to implement the part of the proposal that deals with their department, have not developed good communication links with others in the organization, and so forth.

The best cultural informants have had experiences in other cultures themselves. As discussed in chapter 1, "culture" and "cultural differences" are difficult concepts to grasp unless people have firsthand experience with them. Given such experiences, when people have to make adjustments, they learn that culture is much more than an abstraction. With this knowledge, they then can assist others in the role of cultural informant and can answer questions about adjustment to other cultures. In the example of businesspeople in Japan, the best cultural informants will be Japanese who have been overseas for one reason or another. Perhaps they had an overseas assignment for their company; perhaps they went to college in another country; or perhaps (years earlier) they participated in an overseas exchange program for adolescents sponsored by AFS International or Youth for Understanding. Whatever the exact experience, they had to adjust to another culture, encountered confrontations with their expectations, were frustrated in their desire to be understood, and so forth. With their firsthand knowledge of what is involved in adjusting to another culture combined with their knowledge of Japanese culture learned since they were children, they make good cultural informants.

Effective Conflict Resolution

No matter how well prepared people are and no matter how much help cultural informants can offer, people will encounter misunderstandings and conflicts when interacting in other cultures. One key to success in intercultural interactions is the ability to deal with conflicts such that long-term relationships are not threatened. Consider the following short case study (based on research by Saraswathi & Dutta, 1988).

Vasanthi was a foreign student from India studying at a university in the United States. She came from a family that would be considered conservative in India about the importance placed on traditional values. Consequently, even though she was 23 years old, she had little experience socializing with men outside her family. Paul, from Boston, Massachusetts, was one of her fellow students in a statistics class. Vasanthi was quite a good statistics student, so good she could offer help to others. Paul was quite grateful for all the help Vasanthi offered him, and he bought her a box of candy and a bouquet of flowers at the end of the semester. "I bought these for you," Paul told Vasanthi. "I was afraid I was going to flunk, but your help allowed me to pull a B." Obviously uncomfortable, Vasanthi accepted Paul's gifts but did not show any signs of appreciation and did not say "thank you." Paul concluded that Vasanthi was ungrateful and didn't seek out further interaction with her.

What mistakes were made in this case? Studying the experiences of Japanese businesspeople in the United States, Black (1990) found that one predictor of success was the ability to solve conflicts in a manner that was collaborative, was issue oriented, and allowed for the development of mutual understanding. Rather than conclude that Vasanthi was an ungrateful person, Paul might have asked himself, "Did cultural differences cause these difficulties?" By asking this question, Paul would move away from Vasanthi's personality as a cause of problems to an issue based on people's cultural background. Focusing on a cultural difference is far less threatening, and is far less likely to cause hurt feelings, than focusing on personalities. A focus on cultural differences also allows a collaborative effort toward dealing with the problem, because the misunderstanding is caused by the clash of two cultures and both cultures must be understood. With such a focus, people also have the opportunity to develop a mutual understanding of why they behaved as they did (Singelis & Pedersen, 1997).

In this case, many differences exist. Vasanthi had not had much practice receiving gifts from men, while Paul may have participated in many exchanges of gifts. Vasanthi did not know how to interpret Paul's gifts. Were they a romantic gesture, a sexual advance, a symbol of thanks for help received, or something else? Vasanthi may have been especially confused by the attention of American men if she was quite content to have her parents choose her eventual husband. Other possibilities are even more complex. If Paul and Vasanthi had been spending a great deal of time together studying statistics, Vasanthi may have developed warm (nonsexual) feelings toward him and may have viewed him as a member of her collective. She may have felt that Paul would always be close to her and would be one of the people she can call on in difficult times. People in the same collective don't have to say "thank you" nor expect special acknowledgment when one member helps another. They know their efforts are appreciated and that they will have many opportunities to reciprocate in the future (Triandis, 1995). What Paul interpreted as a rejection, then, may have been the exact opposite: The absence of a clear "thank you!" can be interpreted as a sign of acceptance.

When conflicts occur, the best way to resolve them is to avoid conclusions about people's personal quirks and to search for underlying issues that will not threaten people if they are raised and discussed openly. A few days after the incident, for instance, Paul might have engaged Vasanthi in a discussion of gift giving in the United

States and India. During discussion of this nonthreatening topic, they could have exchanged information that increased their chances of mutual understanding.

Willingness to Use Various Ways to Communicate

To develop intercultural relationships and to intervene effectively when conflicts arise, people must be able to communicate effectively with others. The more ways people can communicate, the better. Two ways will be discussed here: use of the host culture's language and nonverbal communication.

When people encounter settings where a different language is spoken—for example, on international assignments—various aspects of oral communication must be understood. One is the distinction between knowledge of another language and the willingness to use it. In many cases, people's knowledge of another language is good enough so that they can enter various social settings and make their ideas known. However, they do not always take advantage of these opportunities because they are afraid of making blunders. Given that they do not practice their language skills, they do not improve. Further, they do not benefit from the feedback native speakers offer when mistakes are made. The lack of fear of making mistakes is probably one reason children seem to be more effective language learners (Hakuta, 1986). Adults, who pride themselves on their hard work, success in life, and status within their societies, do not like to think of themselves as prone to blunders. They may be very reluctant to enter social settings where they might make mistakes, and mistakes are inevitable when using an unfamiliar language. Children, however, are not as concerned with protecting the self-image of "a competent and successful person." Children use their language skills in schools, on playgrounds, and in their neighborhoods. They can practice their skills, accept and benefit from the feedback they receive, listen to native speakers, and so forth. Consequently, they improve.

Returning to the problems adults face, interesting links exist among the qualities of individuals under discussion here. If people are flexible and obviously enthusiastic about developing positive intercultural relationships, they are forgiven a certain number of mistakes. That is, hosts will forgive people from other cultures who sometimes use the language incorrectly and even make social errors such as speaking out of turn, bringing up a discussion topic before others are ready, and so forth. The hosts' sense of people's overall goodwill and positive attitude toward intercultural relationships will outweigh a collection of mistakes. This aspect of intercultural contact is very similar to Hollander's (1985) concept of "idiosyncrasy credit" developed when analyzing the behavior of leaders in various organizations. If leaders work effectively on behalf of their groups most of the time, they are allowed to deviate once in a while from the group's preferences. Through their good works, they earn idiosyncrasy credit they can "cash in" when they cannot pursue a certain goal their groups want to see accomplished. Given sufficient idiosyncrasy credit, they can refuse to pursue a certain goal and still retain their positions as leaders. In intercultural encounters, overall goodwill, respect, and enthusiasm allow people to generate "credit," and their credit allows mistakes to be ignored or forgiven.

People also communicate through nonverbal means (Hall 1959, 1966; Krauss, Chen, & Chawla, 1996). The study of nonverbal communication has become a speciality that has generated much research, and only a few highlights can be described here. In general, *nonverbal communication* refers to information exchanges (or difficulties in such exchange) that do not involve oral or written language forms. Examples are gestures, body positionings, body tenseness, facial expressions, and so forth (Damen, 1987). Few of these are cultural universals except the generalization that all cultures communicate through both verbal and nonverbal means and the advice that people should not make conclusions about nonverbal behaviors without a great deal of knowledge. Understanding nonverbal interactions involves learning about many specific gestures, expressions, uses of the body, and so forth. For example, during face-to-face encounters, many Pacific islanders flash their eyebrows in an up-and-down movement when listening to another person. If the person receiving eyebrow flashes is an American woman, she may be very disconcerted if she perceives the flashes as a romantic or sexual gesture. In actuality, the eyebrow flash is merely the listener's sign to communicate the message "I am following what you are saying" and has no meaning beyond this message. The equivalents in American English are the verbal "uh-huh" and the nonverbal slight head nod, which indicate the listener is following but not necessarily agreeing with what the speaker is saying.

The distance people keep from one another is also a means of nonverbal communication. In the United States, if a man and woman meet for the first time, a typical distance they keep from each other is 2½ to 3 feet. If they stand closer than that, it can be interpreted as a sign of more than casual interest in each other. In Latin America (Hall, 1966), however, the typical distance people stand from each other while conversing is about 2 feet. This does not have a special message of "desire for more future interaction." Difficulties arise when Americans impose their interpretation of what a 2-foot distance means during interactions with Latin Americans.

A willingness to communicate, then, refers not only to spoken and written languages but also to nonverbal behaviors. People who want to establish close intercultural relationships are well advised to learn about nonverbal behaviors and to engage in as many as possible. Such behaviors can include much more touching than they are accustomed to, more bowing, longer periods of silence, different sets of gestures, greater use of the hands when speaking (Krauss et al., 1996), greater sensitivity to the way time is used (Levine, 1997), and so forth (Damen, 1987). As with spoken and written language, people are forgiven a certain number of mistakes in nonverbal behaviors if their overall enthusiasm and goodwill about intercultural relationships are high.

DIFFICULTIES IN FACE-TO-FACE CONVERSATIONS

Admittedly, the last sentence has an ambiguous term. People may be forgiven "a certain number of mistakes," but when is this number too large for effective intercultural interaction to continue? No firm answer can be suggested because the answer depends on so many factors. For instance, the answer depends on how may favors one person has done for others, how long the intercultural relationship has existed, the personalities of the people involved, a country's current political climate concerning how much intercultural interaction is desirable, and so forth. Another factor is how much people know about the style people from different cultures use to communicate. *Style* refers to factors such as how people contribute to the conversation, the actual amount of talk (versus silence) they prefer, and the degree of comfort and familiarity people communicate when introducing various topics. Analyzed by researchers such as Carbaugh (1990a, 1990b), G.-M. Chen (1995), Kochman (1981), and Philipsen (1975, 1990), communication style is one of the more difficult aspects of intercultural encounters to discuss. People are unaccustomed to examining stylistic differences as a reason for intercultural misunderstandings.

Assume two people meet, have a one-half-hour conversation, and then go their separate ways with the conclusion they don't particularly want to have any more interaction with each other. What could be the reasons? People can focus on such reasons as the lack of any common interests that could be discussed, such total disagreements on certain issues that the two would gain little through further conversations, and personality factors such as dominance (never letting anyone else speak) or abrasiveness. People are less able to focus on stylistic factors, such as expressiveness or the use of silence, as reasons for the decision to limit further contact. Further, people may have mistaken impressions if they fail to make distinctions between stylistic factors and personality factors. If they encounter a person who is very expressive when contributing to the conversation, they may mistake expressiveness for "pushiness" or even "rudeness" (Pittam, Gallois, Iwawaki, & Krooneberg, 1995; Sakamoto & Naotsuka, 1982). If they experience large amounts of silence during a conversation, they may focus on this stylistic feature but mistake it for "boredom" or "lack of interest in pursuing a relationship."

One reason for the difficulty of analyzing stylistic features is that no widely accepted language exists for talking about them, or no convenient set of terms people can easily use. People can talk about personality factors (e.g., rudeness) and about the results of conversations ("I don't want any more interaction with that person!"), but they are less able to talk about how people interact as a reason for difficulties. One reason for this lack of easy expression is that people's cultural background provides them with guidance for conversing with others. In American culture, for example, guidance includes not interrupting people, not dominating conversations, filling in silent periods with small talk, and so forth. As discussed in chapter 1 and noted throughout, people take such cultural guidance for granted, so they find it difficult to analyze cultural differences in communication style. For example, they find it difficult to consider that cultural differences may exist in the desirability of interrupting others (discussed in chapter 5), in putting ideas forward in a very vigorous and seemingly dominant way, or in the acceptability of long silent periods. However, if people learn to analyze stylistic features and learn to recognize their importance, they are likely to have far more success in developing and maintaining intercultural relationships. They will learn to accept stylistic features as the products of cultural guidance and will not automatically interpret use of these features as signs of intercultural difficulties. Four examples will be considered here: the use of silence, the importance placed on a very expressive style, the use of a warm and open style that seems to signal an interest in future interactions, and a direct style.

As part of these examples, the behaviors of people in four cultural groups will be examined: American Indians, African Americans, middle-class Anglo Americans, and the Deaf culture. As with all discussions of cultural influences on behavior, the possibility of their including unreasonable stereotypes must be kept in mind. As discussed in chapter 6, statements about cultural differences and culturally influenced behaviors must be carefully made. The four examples will describe cultural norms—specifically, behaviors frequently found in four cultures. Exceptions do exist. Behaviors of some individual American Indians, African Americans, middle-class Anglo Americans, and Deaf people are not well captured by these descriptions. Any generalization about culture and behavior provides a "first best guess" (Adler, 1997) about the differences people who engage in intercultural encounters can expect. These first guesses always should be open to modification based on specific encounters with specific people in the other culture.

Silence

The importance of stylistic features in communication can be most readily seen in actual examples of their use. Consider the following example.

John is a Native American raised on reservation lands in a rural area of Arizona. Having done well in his studies at a nearby high school, he won a scholarship to study at a university about 500 miles from his home. The scholarship was adequate to cover his basic support, such as tuition payments, board and room in the university dormitory, and books, but it did not allow "extras" such as frequent trips home. After his freshman year, he returned to his community for the first time in nine months. His parents met him at the bus station. They said nothing when they saw him. All silently got into the family car and drove home, again with no verbal communication. Stopping for groceries on the way home, John noticed a very attractive young lady who was stocking shelves. He later learned she is a Native American named Irene and that her family had recently moved into the community. At the store John looked at Irene, and Irene returned John's gaze while quickly looking up from her work, but no words were exchanged. John and his family paid for their groceries, got into their car, and continued home. With few exceptions (such as announcements about dinnertimes on various days), John and his family spoke very little to one another for the next few weeks. Are these signs that John was having difficulties either with his family or with community members?

The answer is no. John was encountering behaviors that are very common among American Indians. (The specific case studies this discussion draws from are based on interviews with Western Apaches: Basso, 1970; see also Braithwaite, 1990.) In many American Indian cultures, silence is a response to ambiguity, especially when the ambiguity involves people's role relationships and relative status. *Role* is a term that refers to expected behaviors given some sort of label people use when describing one another's positions within a society. Within a culture, behaviors are expected of such role labels as "professor," "boss," "son," "secretary," "mother," and so forth. When entering a new community, people may be uncertain about the role expectations *others* have of them (Cushner & Brislin, 1996). Silence is one of several possible responses to ambiguity guided by cultures. In other cultures (e.g., middle-class America), a frequent response when encountering ambiguity is to engage in small talk. If John and his parents were Anglo Americans, for instance, they would be likely to engage in small talk about the current weather, the names of courses John had completed in college, recent events in the community, and so forth. On seeing Irene and deciding he found her attractive, John might have engaged in such conversational openings as "Where is the cheddar cheese?" or "How long have you been working here?" For many traditional Native Americans, silence is preferred.

What are the sources of ambiguity in this case study? At least two very clear sources occurred in this story as analyzed by Basso (1970) and expanded on by Braithwaite (1990). John's parents may have feared he had changed due to his studying at the university, given that Anglo culture dictates the predominant influences there. "Uppermost is the fear that, as a result of protracted exposure to Anglo attitudes and values, the children have come to view the parents as ignorant, old-fashioned, and no longer deserving of respect" (Basso, 1970, p. 220). John's parents were unlikely to question him directly about his experiences. This would have placed John in the uncomfortable experience of being directly interrogated, and this sort of behavior is frowned on in American Indian culture. Instead, the parents just waited silently. John was expected to talk eventually. Based on the sorts of topics he chose to discuss and on the respect he showed to people with his verbal and nonverbal behavior, the parents (and others in the community) could decide whether he still valued his Indian identify or whether he had assimilated himself into Anglo culture. No pressure was placed on John to begin speaking. This would have interfered with John's choices about his behavior, and this avoidance of interference is valued in his culture.

His decision about how to communicate with Irene involved several sources of ambiguity. John did not know Irene's family, because Irene (perhaps along with both nuclear and extended family members) had only recently moved into the community. Irene's family may have higher status than John's, and this influenced John's behavior. Note how this is different from Anglo norms. During his stay at the university, even though John may be the son of a mechanic, he could approach and chat with a female classmate who is the daughter of a millionaire company president. Another source of ambiguity was that John and Irene did not know enough about each other and had not known each other long enough to have long conversations according to cultural norms. "The Western Apache draw an equation between the ease and frequency with which a young couple talks and how well they know each other. Thus, it is expected that after several months of steady companionship sweethearts will start to have lengthy conversations" (Basso, 1970, p. 219). The desirability of silence is especially encouraged in young women because American Indians equate silence with modesty. Further, if young women are overly fluent in conversations with men, this can be taken as a sign of too much experience with too many men. In extreme cases, talkativeness may be interpreted as a willingness to engage in premarital sexual relationships, a practice frowned on by elders.

Other social settings call for silence in American Indian culture. These include meeting strangers for the first time, encountering and interacting with someone who is extremely angry, or consoling someone during times of grief, for instance, following the death of a spouse. As with the other two social settings of coming home to one's family and communicating with opposite-sex members, ambiguity is involved.

People don't know what to expect of people they meet for the first time. Are they individuals who bring goodwill with them, or are they out to cheat people and then leave the community? When encountering someone who is angry, people are unsure of how the other will behave. The other may become so upset that he or she will harm others. Talk might increase the intensity of the person's behavior. It is considered best to wait silently until the person's anger is discharged or until the person walks away. While consoling a person who is experiencing grief, American Indians often feel no need for talk because the people involved know that they care deeply about one another. In addition, people who are grieving over a loved one sometimes lose control of their emotions (Basso, 1970). Rather than encourage loss of control through talk about good times remembered from the past, people consider it best to remain silent.

The value some cultures place on silence can have an impact on intercultural communication (Schoonhals, 1994). I have spoken to several Anglo Americans who have taken jobs on American Indian reservations, often in the role of teachers. On arrival at the schools where they would be teaching, these people naturally expected a few words of welcome. Instead, they encountered silence. "Practically nobody spoke to me for six months!" one person remembered. The American Indian use of silence in these cases is again a response to ambiguity. The Indians are concerned about how well intentioned these Anglo newcomers are, whether they will be "fizzlers" who leave in a few months, whether they are bleeding-heart liberals who want to bring their better way of life to the Indians, and so forth. By observing the newcomers and waiting quietly for them to display their attitudes and intentions, longtime community residents can make conclusions about whether extensive communication is advisable or not. Once a judgment is made that the newcomers are good people, verbal communication will begin.

Expressiveness in Communication Style

Another stylistic feature of face-to-face communication is people's degree of expressiveness when they convey their messages. Expressiveness can include the amount of emotion people communicate in their word choices and voice tones (Pittam et al., 1995), the amount of their body movement (Krauss et al., 1996), their intensity when communicating disagreement with others, and the amount of boasting or bragging people choose to use when describing themselves (Kochman, 1981). Consider this example (which occurred in a class I observed, so I am using the terms the people involved chose).

Harry is an Anglo American student taking a class in social psychology. The class instructor encourages considerable student participation, so she approved Harry's plan to invite two African American students to come to class when the unit on "stereotypes and prejudices" was treated. Harry invited two African American students, Darrell and Jennifer, whom he had met in the dormitory where he lives. As far as Harry could determine, Darrell and Jennifer were not particularly well acquainted.

Prior to class, Harry asked the two students to prepare a few remarks about their personal experiences with stereotypes and prejudice. Harry told the students he simply would introduce the two and then moderate any discussion and help with the question and answer part of the class session. After introducing the two students, the discussion proceeded as follows:

DARRELL: America is a racist society! Blacks are not allowed the same opportunities as Whites in education and in organizations where they seek good jobs. As a result, many live in poverty.

JENNIFER: I personally have not experienced much prejudice. Sure, some people don't like Blacks and discriminate, but this is true of any group, including ethnic groups like the Polish or the Irish, even though they are all White.

DARRELL *(with lots of emotion in his voice and with a great deal of obvious tension in his body)*:   How can you say that? If you have two applicants for a job with equal qualifications, one Black and one White, you know damn well that the White will get the job.

HARRY *(trying to keep tensions from increasing)*:   Since this is a college classroom, I think we should try to be less emotional in our contributions to the discussion.

JENNIFER *(with just as much emotion in her voice as Darrell)*:   No, let him have his say! I just think that Blacks have to stop whining and complaining about Whites and instead focus on their own behavior. I don't know any Whites forcing Black 14-year-old unmarried girls to get pregnant and have babies. Even Jesse Jackson talks about the problem of "Black babies having babies."

DARRELL *(still visibly upset)*:   That's easy for a member of the Black middle class to say. These 14-year-olds you talk about were born into a poverty-stricken segment of society created by Whites!

Concerned that people's emotions had gotten out of hand, Harry called an end to the discussion. What was the problem?

From the African American viewpoint, no problem had occurred. The only problem was that the Anglo and African American discussion styles had clashed. As analyzed by Kochman (1981, 1990), African Americans value a very expressive style when they communicate. Perhaps due to years and years of being forced to hide their feelings and being forced to defer to Anglos (slavery, Jim Crow laws, and segregated schools, neighborhoods, and churches), African Americans developed this expressive communication style when in the company of other African Americans. The desire to express emotional intensity is part of humanity. People do not want to suppress it, so they use what opportunities they can to express themselves freely. For African Americans, these opportunities existed only when Anglos were not present: in churches, dance halls, street-corner rap sessions, and so forth. After the Civil Rights movement of the 1950s and 1960s and resulting legislation that allowed African Americans greater movement in society, African Americans did not have to limit their style according to the type of people they found in any given social setting. If they wanted to express themselves, they could do so, no matter who else was present!

Expressiveness includes the amount of emotion people put into their discussions about controversial matters. In the example, Darrell felt he should express his position vigorously and with clear emotional intensity. In fact, part of the norms surrounding the style is that by expressing his ideas in an intense manner, he was complimenting the others in the classroom. In effect, he was saying, "I respect you enough to express my position vigorously. I don't feel you want me to beat around the bush. If you disagree, that's fine, just pay me respect by expressing your position so that I can understand it clearly." Jennifer followed the expectations African Americans have by communicating her position in a manner just as intense as Darrell's. It is important to understand that Jennifer and Darrell did not necessarily view their contributions as attacks on each other. They showed each other respect by allowing each other to express their positions (note Jennifer's comment to Harry, "let him have his say!"). This example does not provide evidence that Jennifer and Darrell were upset with each other. They both had opinions; they disagreed; and they raised their voices. So what? They expressed themselves and showed respect for each other. This is what is important according to African American norms about communication. As Kochman (1990) points out:

> Blacks' capacity to deal with intense emotional outputs is relatively greater than that of Whites because Blacks have greater experience of being confronted with them. Reciprocally, this capacity also gives Blacks acting in response to their own feelings greater freedom to express them intensely, knowing that others have developed the capacity to receive them without becoming overwhelmed. (p. 204)

When interacting with African Americans who feel they should express themselves openly, Anglos often become upset. The norms for conversation, according to the Anglos' cultural background, is that people should not say things that might upset someone else. Because disagreements about important issues can upset people, it is better to find agreeable topics for conversation. Or if a controversial topic must be discussed, as they must in college classrooms, then people should do so in a calm, level tone of voice (recall Harry's request, "I think we should try to be less emotional . . ."). Thus Harry eventually became so uncomfortable that he tried to bring the conversation to a close.

As already noted, one problem people have in analyzing encounters such as this is that they are not prepared to talk about the fact that communication style, not just content, can cause difficulties. Given their inability to talk about style, they are likely to leave some intercultural encounters with the vague conclusion that the conversations did not go well and that they do not understand exactly why. Not knowing the reasons for difficulties causes stress, and the easiest way to avoid further stress is to avoid future intercultural encounters. If people understood that communication style can cause difficulties and if they had some concepts to use in their analysis of problematic intercultural encounters (e.g., differing views of silence, the importance of expressiveness), then they would not become as upset.

A Warm and Open Style

The two examples discussed previously dealt with American Indian and African American cultures. The approach taken was to analyze difficulties that an outsider might have when communicating with members of these two cultural groups. It must be kept in mind that all cultures have norms outsiders can misunderstand or can consider irritating (Moore & Levitan, 1993; Pittam et al., 1995). Consider the following example (drawn from the research of Klineberg & Hull, 1979; Triandis, Brislin, & Hui, 1988; and Yamaguchi, Kuhlman, & Sugimori, 1995) of behavior that draws on communication norms commonly held in middle-class Anglo culture in the United States. The discussion of individualism and collectivism in chapter 2 introduced concepts that are helpful for analyzing this example.

Simalee is an international student from Thailand studying at a large university in the midwestern United States. The university has an active program that encourages interaction among American and foreign students. In securing funding for this program, supporters argued (to the state legislature) that Americans must learn about interaction across national boundaries given developments in the world's economy and political systems. American students can prepare for international experiences in their later lives through cooperative activities with foreign students.

Shortly after her arrival on campus, Simalee was invited to a reception for new students at the university. The international programs office had organized this reception, and its staff also invited some American students. At the reception, Simalee met an American student named Lisa. Lisa was very warm and open, asked about Simalee's interests, and even suggested a few ways these interests could be pursued in the United States. Simalee and Lisa talked for about 15 minutes before Lisa left the conversation and began to talk with someone else at the reception. Just before leaving, Lisa said to Simalee, "I hope we get a chance to talk again soon."

About two weeks later, Simalee was walking across campus. She spotted Lisa about 100 feet away. As Lisa approached her, Simalee smiled and said "hello." Lisa looked at Simalee with a rather vague expression on her face, then suddenly remembered the interaction at the reception two weeks ago. Lisa also said "hello" but hurried on because she was late for her next class. Simalee walked back to her apartment, puzzled at the rather cool way Lisa treated her. In contrast, Lisa arrived at her class and did not give the interaction with Simalee much thought. What are possible reasons for these differing reactions?

Lisa was socialized to behave in a way that is quite puzzling and disconcerting to people from many other parts of the world. She learned a communication style that allows a person to meet others quickly, to put them at ease, to find conversation topics both can talk about, and then to leave the conversation in a way that is not considered abrupt (Hamid, 1994; Pittam et al., 1995). Part of the style involves a warm demeanor, much smiling, a relaxed body posture, and a sense of enthusiasm and excitement about the conversation. This style is useful for individualists like Lisa (chapter 2). Because she does not have a collective or a support group constantly with her, she has to solve her own problems. The category "problems" is meant to be broad and includes such items as the need to make friends, finding someone to fix a car, discovering how to drop a course, arranging for a ride home before holidays, and so forth. A communication style that allows an individual to meet others quickly and to discover whether or not others can help is very useful. People in Lisa's culture know about this style and can interpret her seeming warmth and enthusiasm as simply how people behave when they meet others for the first time.

Simalee, in contrast, is from a collective culture. Because she has a constant support group she can call on, she does not need to develop a communication style that allows her (as an individual) to meet others quickly. When she does have to go outside her collective, as she did to study overseas, she is much more likely than Lisa to be quiet, tentative, and careful during her conversations. So she is likely to be quite puzzled when she meets someone like Lisa at a party or at a reception. Her attribution (chapter 2) of Lisa's warm behavior was likely that "This woman is showing interest in me, personally." Because she had not met hundreds of people with a similar style, Simalee had not learned to view the style as typical among people in middle-class American culture. When she met Lisa two weeks later on campus, then, she was very puzzled that Lisa did not continue her warm style. At this point, she is likely to view Lisa's behavior as a personal rejection. Further, she is likely to make negative attributions about Lisa. Readers might want to guess these probable attributions. A hint is that the possible attributions consist of words familiar to native English speakers but words they do not necessarily use in the course of an entire month. Given this relative infrequency of use, native speakers are surprised to hear such words used by foreign students who are expressing themselves in a second or third language. The probable words are "superficial" and "insincere." Simalee is likely to conclude that because Lisa is so inconsistent in her behavior, warm one time and cold the next, that no further interaction is possible.

What are Lisa's likely attributions about the same behaviors? Lisa would argue she was simply using the social skills and the communication style her parents taught her. "Be polite, talk about things the other person is interested in, keep the conversation flowing," and so forth. She further would argue that she was simply being nice to the foreign students she met at the party. If asked to interpret the second interaction on campus, she would argue that she talked to many people at the reception and could not possibly remember the names of everyone. She also had talked to numerous people over the two-week period between the reception and meeting Simalee on campus, again interfering with her memory of any one encounter. She was also in a hurry to class—surely people understand that reason for being unable to stop and chat!

The contrast between the warm and open communication style familiar to many Americans and the more reserved style of people in other parts of the world can have more intense consequences than those in this example. D. P. S. Bhawuk, from Nepal, worked with me for two years and prepared a summary of his thinking about the movement of people across cultures (Bhawuk, 1997, 1998). One of his observations was that men and women from different cultures can make very different conclusions about romantic intentions. The danger is that if a young man from an Asian culture interacts with an American woman who employs the warm and exuberant style under discussion here, the man may attribute the style to a romantic interest in him, personally. For example, assume that an American woman helps an Asian man on a class assignment. The Asian man (following norms in his culture) offers a small gift to show his appreciation. The American woman responds, "I just love it! It's so great! How thoughtful of you!" The Asian man may conclude that the comment about "loving it" extends to him, personally. Training programs to prepare American women to live in Asia often include treatments of this issue. The advice is that when interacting with men, women should tone down any natural exuberance in their communication style. If this is not done, men will interpret the exuberance as a sign of romantic or sexual interest. This is difficult for many women to do because the style is so natural for them. Another reason for the difficulty of changing communication style, as previously mentioned, is that people are unaccustomed to talking about it. People have terms for disagreements about the content of their conversations but not as frequently terms for the conversation style. Once again, one of the ways to find out about subtle and underdiscussed issues of this kind is to seek training programs that prepare people for successful intercultural experiences.

A Direct Style

Two people who know each other quite well but who are not best friends meet on the street. One is dressed so that her choice of colors clashes in a hideous way. The other has changed his hair color from the gray of two months ago to a dark black that obviously has come out of a bottle that must have been on sale at the local drugstore. Do the people mention these facts in a straightforward manner, or do they use sentences such as, "That's an interesting outfit. Where did you buy it?" Or "You look different compared to the last time I saw you." If people say exactly what is on their minds, they are said to have a *direct style*. If they "circle around" what is on their minds and hide their exact thoughts behind neutral or even mildly positive phrases, they are said to have an *indirect style*.

Do some cultures commonly encourage a direct style, and does this style sometimes cause problems for people unfamiliar with it? The answers to both questions are yes. In Deaf culture, a direct style of communication is common (Moore & Levitan, 1993; Siple, 1994).

When Deaf culture members meet, directness is common. I studied American Sign Language (ASL) for three years and observed signed conversations that included sentences such as these: "I haven't seen you for six months—you've put on a lot of weight." "I've heard that your marriage is in bad shape and that you may get divorced—is this true?" At a social gathering where most of the participants were in their 30s and 40s, the one older woman left the room for a short period. One Deaf person signed to another, "Where's the old lady?" The hearing people at the gathering would have used a phrase such as "senior citizen" or "the woman who is a little older than most of us."

This direct style is used for at least two reasons, one based on the nature of the language and the other based on issues surrounding social interactions. Deaf people in the United States and Canada have their own language, American Sign Langue. Contrary to popular belief, this language is different from other sign languages (e.g., in England, France, or Japan), and fluent ASL signers cannot converse fluently with signers in England. ASL is a visual language, and it takes advantages of visual aspects in people's lives. A clear example of visual aspects is how people look and appear, so these aspects are paramount when Deaf people describe themselves and others. Another feature of the language's visual nature is that the information adjectives and adverbs convey is made visual. If "intense anger" is to be described, a sign for *anger* is given, and the adjective *intense* is shown in body movements such as an angry facial expression or a tightening of the body that occurs when someone gets angry. In oral languages, additional information about verbs is conveyed through adverbs. In American Sign Language, the distinction between the adverb-containing phrases "move slowly" and "move quickly" in one's car would be shown with the sign for *car* and then movement of that sign in a slow, perhaps plodding manner in contrast to a swift, steady movement across the viewer's visual field.

Once an American Sign Language user sets up objects in a signing space, she can refer to the objects simply by pointing to them.

In ASL, information is conveyed by movements through a visual space, also sometimes called the signing space. Picture Deaf person A interacting with Deaf person B. When A communicates in signing space, she communicates in an area B can readily see. Very roughly, the signing space resembles about the same area as a large television screen. It extends from the top of A's head to the waist and from arm movements that extend about 12 inches from each side of A's body. This is an area B can easily see. Interestingly, B may stand about 2½ to 3 feet from A. This allows B to see the entire signing space. Naive observers might conclude that A and B do not care for each other very much because they are maintaining a very "cool" distance from each other (Albert, 1996; Hall, 1966). In addition to covering the entire signing space, another benefit of this distance is that B is not poked in the face or chest when A uses signs that extend outward from the body (e.g., the sign for "far away").

Skillful signers set up a scene within the signing space and use movements as part of syntax. Assume the sentence "I took the book from my home to the library" is to be signed. It is possible to do this by following the English syntax: one sign for *I*, a second for *took*, a third for *book*, and so forth. A key point for Deaf culture, however, is that this is *not* American Sign Language. It is Signed English. The latter shares American Sign Language signs, but it attaches the signs to an English language word order. How would an ASL signer convey this sentence? Refer to the figure on page 257. Person A might sign *home* and then point in front of her with her finger. She next might indicate another point and sign *library*. Finally, she might sign *book* and then pick up the imaginary book from the first point and move it to the second. Note that all the original sentence's elements are in the visual picture established in signing space. Other aspects of such "setups" in signing space are interesting. The first point can be A's home for the rest of the conversation with B. Person A can describe a party she had in her home and she can describe a recent remodeling of her kitchen, and person B will know the place A described simply because the point for *home* has been indicated. Other information also can be conveyed visually. Person A's favorable opinion of the book can be conveyed through a positive rather than a scowling expression when she signs for *book*. She can also give her opinion of the library (dull place, interesting place) through choice of a facial expression.

The distinction between Signed English and American Sign Language is important in Deaf culture. ASL is a language with its own syntax, and it has unique features for native signers (people who learned ASL as their first language). Signed English is not a unique language: It uses signs, but not according to a syntax different from English. Many Deaf people are bilingual and can show this through use of both Signed English and American Sign Language. Many move smoothly between the two, a process known as code switching. Hearing people who learn ASL often put together their newly learned signs in an English language order, so they are really using Signed English. Deaf people show their relationship to Deaf culture by using their culture's language, much like membership in any culture is marked by skill in language use. Deaf people who are proud of their culture sometimes will criticize (in a direct manner!) friends who use Signed English. "You know ASL! Why do you use English language order of signs? Are you trying to send a message about your relationship to us?"

Now I will return to the discussion of directness and ASL's visual emphasis. Deaf people want to know if signers they are conversing with have reasons for using certain facial expressions and other aspects of body language. If a person is going through a divorce, this will have an effect on their facial expressions and thus the content of their communications. Some hearing people are surprised at references to seemingly personal matters, such as recent experiences with bodily functions. Again, issues such as the quality of recent bowel movements can impact facial expressions and thus communication. Within Deaf culture, it is considered polite to pass on information that is easily available to hearing people but not so easily to Deaf people. For example, people are at a lecture in an auditorium. An airplane flies overhead. It is polite for hearing people to mention this to Deaf people. The reason is that information from the sound of the airplane is available to hearing people but not the Deaf people. Unless Deaf people know an airplane is flying overhead, they would not know why some of the hearing people are glancing at the ceiling.

The Deaf culture norm for "passing on information" extends to information outsiders might consider personal: divorces, teenagers with drug or alcohol problems, who is dating whom, and so forth. Hearing people may be able to understand the importance of this norm if they consider how much they know and learn from overhearing conversations. Readers should examine what they have learned of relevance to them during the past week. Did they learn some of this through overheard conversations in the cafeteria, while standing in line to buy movie tickets, or while picking up their mail? Even though they may be quite socially skilled and may try to keep their mothers' socialization advice about "not eavesdropping," they still may hear and learn much. Deaf people do not have this advantage of learning from overheard conversations. Moreover, they also have the norm of "not eavesdropping." If two Deaf people are signing, it is considered impolite for a third person to watch the conversation closely. Thus if Deaf people are to learn about what is happening in their communities, someone must tell them directly. The norm about the importance of information sharing has interesting implications. One of my hearing friends is a fluent signer (much better than I!). She heard a rumor, involving a plan among Deaf community members, that would affect her career negatively. She asked a highly respected Deaf community leader, "Is the rumor true?" The leader said, "I haven't heard the rumor." My friend then knew the rumor was not true. If the leader hadn't heard it, it could neither be important nor true given the leader's respect in the Deaf community and the norm of information sharing. If the leader hadn't heard about it, it did not exist! My friend monitored developments in the community, and the leader was correct. Nothing happened that would have remotely affected my friend's career.

Another reason for the norm of direct communication stems from the fact Deaf people don't always have the opportunity to interact frequently. Especially during the workday, they must interact with hearing people. Even if certain hearing people know some sign language, few are fluent. Deaf people must interact with others using notes, pantomime, a few shared signs, some lip reading (which is far more imperfect than commonly believed, even among the best lip readers), and so forth. Given the daily struggle to communicate with hearing people on basic issues, Deaf people seldom have the opportunity to express themselves fluently in their own language. When they do get together with other Deaf people, then, they can communicate anything they wish in a smooth, fluent, unhesitant manner. Such interactions might occur during weekend social gatherings. Because they have limited time together, however, they spend the time communicating directly and sharing information. Why spend such limited time on indirectness and talking around topics? Another implication of limited time together can be seen in good-byes at the end of social gatherings. People sign good-bye, but then others ask them to stay. These attempted good-byes and "you must stay longer" exchanges can go on for a long time. Eventually, people will walk backward toward their cars while continuing to sign, and often they will continue to sign outside their car windows as they pull out of a driveway.

One more aspect of Deaf culture should be emphasized. The Deaf do not like the term "hearing impaired." They prefer "deaf" or "hard of hearing." Realizing the relation between the ear and the brain, they ask if people who use "hearing impaired" are questioning their mental abilities and are inferring their brains are damaged. Deaf people sometimes will add (in the direct manner under discussion), "Aren't you saying some people are better than others? Whose behavior is the standard? Why can't we refer to you as 'signing impaired'?" This challenge has a bit of tongue-in-cheek humor, but like much good humor, it captures some truth. If people are to use a term such as "impaired," then something else has to have "unimpaired" status. I once saw this exchange between a hearing African American and a Deaf woman, one of my ASL teachers. The African American man had used the term "hearing impaired," and my teacher issued this same retort. I remember telling my fluent signer friend about this exchange, and her reply was that "It not only reminds me of the value placed on direct communication but also on the fact that for Deaf people, their identity stemming from membership in Deaf culture is often more central than that of their race or ethnicity. For many, it is 'Deaf first.'"

TRAINING PROGRAMS FOR MORE EFFECTIVE INTERCULTURAL INTERACTION

When some people know they will be engaging in extensive intercultural interactions, they may have the self-insight to know they are not well prepared. Even when they know what culture is and know how cultural differences affect interpersonal encounters, they may say to themselves that they need more information. Many researchers and educators have been involved in the development of cross-cultural training programs, or formal efforts to prepare people to live and work in cultures other than their own (Bhawuk, 1990; Brislin, 1981, 1989; Brislin & Yoshida, 1994; Landis & Bhagat, 1996; Landis & Brislin, 1983; Martin, 1986; R. M. Paige, 1986). As mentioned before, the intercultural experiences people can be prepared for include assignments in another country (e.g., Americans about to work in Japan) and extensive interactions among members of culturally diverse groups within a large country (e.g., Hispanic Americans about to interact with Native Americans).

The goals of cross-cultural training are to prepare people for intercultural interactions so that they have a greater likelihood of meeting the four-part criteria of success discussed in the first part of this chapter. Once again, success involves (a) positive feelings about the development of intercultural relationships, (b) the reciprocation of these feelings from members of other cultural groups, (c) task accomplishment, and (d) minimal stress stemming from intercultural misunderstandings and difficulties. The content of training programs often includes attention to people's thinking and cognitions, to their attitudes and feelings, and to their actual behaviors. When encouraging people to consider their thoughts, feelings, and behaviors, the administrators of programs (most frequently called "trainers") often use critical incidents and case studies that capture commonly encountered intercultural difficulties (Cushner & Brislin, 1996). Ideally, the incidents and case studies include experiences all program participants (called "trainees") can identify with easily. Given that trainees identify with aspects of the incidents (e.g., disagreements, the breakup of romances, failure to perform well in a job interview, a poor grade on a test), trainers then can point out how culture and cultural differences affect the outcomes described in the incident, much like many of the examples in this book. Good critical incidents, then, have a two-part structure: elements everyone can identify with and additional information about cultural differences. Most often, the cultural information will be new and unfamiliar to trainees. But because they understand and can identify with some elements of the incident, they are likely to become interested in the cultural information so that they can diagnose the reasons for the familiar difficulties presented in the incident.

Another example here should make the use of critical incidents clear, and it also allows a later discussion of how the three-part analysis of thoughts, feelings, and actual behavior can be treated in training programs. Many training programs cover a critical incident similar to the following one (Cushner & Brislin, 1996; Foa & Chemers, 1967) because the difficulty treated is so commonly experienced.

Yoshiko is an international student from Japan studying for a graduate degree in the United States. At her university, she enrolled in several graduate seminars that had only 10 or 12 other students. The professors in these seminars expected the graduate students to contribute a great deal to discussions of current research issues and planned that long lectures would be an uncommon event. The professors assigned students to prepare short presentations on various topics. The students then had to present their ideas to class, and the other seminar participants would contribute to the discussion of the issues the presentation raised. Yoshiko was not familiar with this style of participation, given that she was far more accustomed to sitting quietly and taking careful notes after hearing lectures her professors prepared. She also was unaccustomed to asking questions of her professors, as this was not a common practice during her undergraduate education in Japan. Her American colleagues also were accustomed to taking notes, but they were more familiar with the professors' expectations that they contribute given their prior participation in small classes (e.g., senior seminars) during the last two years of their undergraduate studies.

Yoshiko was friendly with Barbara, one of the other students in her department, and the two were participants in the same graduate seminar that dealt with the most recent research in personality testing. The professor assigned Yoshiko to give a short presentation on projective tests. Yoshiko worked hard, prepared a clear handout for the rest of the class, and spoke for about 30 minutes. After her presentation, Barbara brought up several recent studies that Yoshiko had not discussed and mentioned that these were on the "cutting edge" of current thinking about personality and its measurement. Other students also made contributions based on their thinking about the present and future status of projective tests. Barbara thought the session went very well. After the session, however, Yoshiko told Barbara she could not go to lunch with her, as they had previously planned. Because Yoshiko seemed a little upset after the session, Barbara wondered if something was wrong. She couldn't think of anything. "Yoshiko presented some interesting material, and it stimulated a lot of discussion. I should think she would be pleased," Barbara thought.

Could a cultural difference be affecting the outcome (the broken luncheon engagement) of this incident? The answer is yes, and the reason involves a concept known as *differentiation* and, specifically, differences among the expectations about how friends behave. What behaviors are expected of friends? Most people will list answers such as spending free time together, sharing emotional experiences, helping one another out in times of need, and so forth. In the language of chapter 3, these are undoubtedly the etic or universal expectations of friendship. But other, emic elements, differ from culture to culture. In the United States, a friend can be a constructive critic who makes helpful suggestions in a public forum (I'll shorten this to "helpful public critic"). In the incident, Barbara feels she is being a good friend. She listened attentively to Yoshiko's presentation during the seminar and then made some helpful suggestions. The cultural difference here is that Yoshiko does not expect friends to make critical remarks in public, no matter how positive the motivations are behind the suggestions. Yoshiko's expectations are that friends engage in supportive behaviors, not public criticism. Regarding the concept introduced in the second sentence, Yoshiko applies more differentiated categories than Barbara to the behaviors experienced in this incident. Yoshiko has the same etic expectations for the behavior of friends (free time, sharing of emotions, etc.) but does not expect helpful public criticism. She may know helpful public critics in her life, but these are not her friends. Helpful public criticism is a behavior expected of people in another category. Consequently, Yoshiko feels betrayed. She had planned to engage in a friendly behavior, the lunch with Barbara, but felt that this was totally inconsistent with Barbara's public criticism.

Barbara, in contrast, does not differentiate the behaviors described in the incident. Her expectations of what friends do include the same etic elements as Yoshiko's, but they also include the behaviors associated with helpful public criticism. Consequently, Barbara does not see any difficulties with criticizing Yoshiko and then having lunch with her. The two behaviors are part of the same category, friendship.

The advice for people participating in cross-cultural training programs, then, is to examine incidents such as this one and to identify cultural differences that can be causing the difficulties. A good starting point is to assume people are trying to get along with others and trying to communicate effectively but that they have difficulties because they cannot recognize cultural differences. At times, insights into cultural differences can be gained by asking, "Are people from one culture making differentiations within a category that people in another culture are not making? If so, can this be causing difficulties?" Learning to understand difficulties based on differentiations can be useful for analyzing misunderstandings within one's own culture. Readers might try to identify a recent misunderstanding or irritations based on differentiation. For example, Protestants who call themselves "Baptists" recognize many distinctions within this category, and they are irritated when outsiders lump all Baptists together and make the same predictions about their religious beliefs. Faculty members have misunderstandings with secretaries when discussing instructions for document preparation. The faculty members may have one word processing program in mind that allows doing certain tasks easily, while the secretaries may have switched to another. Although not using the term, secretaries in effect may complain that the impatient professors are not making proper differentiations between what various word processing programs can do. Automobile mechanics find it difficult to help customers who complain of a rattle under the hood of their cars. The mechanics can differentiate the various car parts found under the hood. If all of these parts look and sound about the same to customers, communication is made difficult.

Looking for misunderstandings based on differentiations often can lead to very specific behaviors that allow effective communication. Yoshiko did not have "helpful public critic" as part of her expectations of what friends do. However, a friend can be a "helpful private critic." If Barbara decided to behave according to Yoshiko's expectations after the incident, she could schedule an informal private meeting before the next presentation. There, Barbara could calmly make suggestions that could lead to improvements in Yoshiko's work. Even within the activities of this meeting, Barbara would want to work within Yoshiko's expectations. Barbara should keep the tone of the meeting as pleasant as possible. She should tell some jokes and should make sure she says several good things about Yoshiko's presentations. Barbara should make suggestions for improvements only after these more positive preliminaries, and the advice probably should not take up more than 25% or 30% of the time Barbara and Yoshiko spend together.

Note how the elements of this critical incident meet the suggestions for good cross-cultural training materials. Virtually everyone has been in a social encounter where they received more criticism than they thought they would. Everyone also has been disappointed when friends behaved in a manner other than what was expected. Given these commonalities everyone can relate to, trainers then can add cultural differences to explain what can happen when the people involved are from different cultural backgrounds. In this case, people also can relate to one of the underlying bases for the difficulties, the differentiation of categories, given that this undoubtedly has caused some misunderstandings or irritations in their own lives.

Culture-General and Culture-Specific Training

The incident involving Barbara and Yoshiko brings up another important aspect of cross-cultural training: the difference between culture-specific and culture-general materials and concepts (Bhawuk & Triandis, 1996). *Culture-specific training* provides very precise information that will help people from one country who are about to live in another. For example, it is useful for Yoshiko to know the specific pieces of information that she will be expected to "speak up" in seminars and that others will criticize her presentations, ideally with the goal of improving Yoshiko's work. Yoshiko can learn that people she considers friends might offer this criticism. Earlier in the chapter, the example of silence in Native American culture was discussed. It is very useful for Anglo Americans to know the very specific piece of information that they probably will not be greeted with enthusiasm should they accept employment in a Native American community in Arizona or New Mexico. Rather, they should know that a value is placed on silence and that someone in the community may talk to them after a few months if the Anglos show they are honest people willing to contribute to the community.

Culture-general training deals with aspects of people's movement across cultures that are common to virtually all intercultural experiences. In the example about Yoshiko, the culture-general concept could be "differentiation": when and how people make distinctions, in this case "friend" versus "critic." In the American Indian example, the culture-general themes could include "anxiety" and "nonverbal behaviors." All sojourners, if they are at all concerned with making a good impression on others and with others' acceptance, will be anxious about these aspects of their life away from home. Many times, they will try to ascertain their acceptance through observations of people's nonverbal behaviors.

People who administer cross-cultural training programs often have to choose between a culture-general and a culture-specific approach. Or, they must know about the distinction if they are to work with a combination of the approaches. Many people about to live in another country prefer culture-specific training because it clearly has usefulness to their upcoming lives. A culture-specific program for Japan and for Native American communities might use materials based on the examples discussed. Decisions about training almost always have to take economic considerations into account. Culture-specific programs are feasible when enough people about to live in a certain country are enrolled, when training materials are available for that country, when trainers have expertise about that country, and so forth. A real difficulty, however, is that materials are not always available for country-specific programs. One reason is that the potential market of people interested in *any one country* may be small, and thus commercial publishers have little or no incentive to produce materials. Another reason for unavailable materials is that good materials are expensive to develop, so an organization that offers country-specific training may label their materials "proprietary" and not make them available to others. Possibly, in the future, country-specific materials might be available on Internet Web sites, but people have to have the motivation to post these materials. In addition, quality control always will be an issue, as it is with any information people might gather through the Internet.

Culture-general programs are most practical when individuals or group members are about to go to many different countries. For example, a large business might be sending people overseas, but those people may be headed for different countries. The two big advantages for general cross-cultural training is that materials are available from commercial publishers (e.g., Cushner & Brislin, 1996; Fowler & Mumford, 1995; Landis & Bhagat, 1996) and trainers can lead participants through the materials in a highly effective manner. Sessions, for instance, could focus on "the importance of understanding how cultures differentiate information," "dealing with anxiety," and "sensitivity to nonverbal behaviors." The big disadvantage is contained in the name of the approach to training. If an approach is "general," it cannot deal with the specific aspects of life in another culture, such as specific anxiety-causing episodes in Japan or the impact of months of silence in some Native American communities.

Many times, the approaches can be combined. A culture-general framework can be presented, and then critical incidents involving common intercultural problems can be introduced. Trainers with expertise in a certain culture then can use the general materials and incidents as guidance for suggesting specific applications to a specific country. Using the examples of nonverbal behavior (general) and silence (incident), I would say the following to people about to go to Japan:

> I hope you found this incident about silence in Native American culture interesting. People have had similar experiences in Japan. One of my colleagues, an American university professor and expert in Japanese Kabuki theater (James Brandon), told me about his first months in Japan. He went to work at the Kabuki theater to learn. Nobody spoke to him for months. He worked hard and tried to figure out how to be helpful. After several months and after he had demonstrated his commitment and interest, people began to talk with him and to invite him to after-work informal gatherings. He now tells others that they should expect similar behavior should they go to study any traditional art form in Japan.

My experience (Brislin & Yoshida, 1994) has been that trainers always will need to move between culture-specific and culture-general training. Many people feel that their life experiences in other cultures are so unique that they can't see the usefulness of culture-general materials. Even when culture-specific materials are suggested, they find fault that they are not "specific" enough. This leads to a piece of cross-cultural–trainer jargon used when talking with colleagues: "I was *specificed* by some of the people during my negotiations." I was involved in a conversation similar to the one that follows that would inspire use of this jargon. Community leaders in northern Alaska asked a trainer to offer a workshop for incoming drug, alcohol, and rehabilitation counselors. The leaders were Aleuts from Kotzebue, Alaska. The trainer had recently worked in Nome, Alaska. The conversation went like this:

COMMUNITY LEADER: What approach will you use?

TRAINER: I have some very good specific materials that colleagues and I used recently in Nome. The training group were counselors who were coming to Nome for the same reasons this new group will be coming to Kotzebue.

LEADER: Nome is a lot different from Kotzebue.

TRAINER: I think they have enough similarities to make the materials usable. The materials deal with adjustment to life in a small Alaskan town above the Arctic Circle and with interactions between newly arrived counselors and longtime residents of the town.

LEADER: When was the information gathered that formed the basis of the materials?

TRAINER: Six months ago.

LEADER: A lot of changes have occurred in the past six months. You know more flights have been added to our airline service, and the new high school has opened.

It is probably a human universal for people to view themselves (Baumeister, 1998) or their cultures as unique, and this can manifest itself in conversations about the usefulness of culture-general and culture-specific training materials. There is no attempt to create characters representing knowledgeable and less knowledgeable people. I have been in similar conversations where the "leader" might be, for example, an American college administrator planning a program for incoming international students. The "trainer" might be a person offering services to the University of Arizona based on material developed at Arizona State University. The comments, "These two universities are quite different, and Tempe and Tuscon are quite different," surely would be uttered.

Whether the training is general or specific, subsequent decisions have to be made about other aspects of program content. Yoshida and I (Brislin & Yoshida, 1994; see also Gudykunst, Guzley, & Hammer, 1996) argue that the best cross-cultural training programs guide people about their thinking, their feelings, and their actual behavior. In fact, recommendations about the content of training programs sometimes are organized according to these three aspects of people's reactions to intercultural encounters (Brislin & Yoshida, 1994). As mentioned earlier, it is useful to examine the critical incident involving Yoshiko and Barbara to make recommendations about the thinking, feelings, and behaviors of trainees who might find themselves in similar encounters.

Attention to People's Thinking

Good cross-cultural training makes people's thinking more sophisticated. For example, it can help people develop new categories so that they can understand specific examples of those categories during their cross-cultural encounters. Without categories that allow an understanding and interpreting of events, intercultural encounters become strange, puzzling, and upsetting. But with knowledge of appropriate categories, people can examine their encounters and put them in proper perspective (Frable, 1997; Gardner, 1985). This assists greatly in the development of tolerance for behaviors that previously would have been labeled as strange, backward, or inferior.

In the critical incident example, Barbara and Yoshiko had difficulties because their categories of "what friends do" have different elements. "Helpful public critic" is part of Barbara's category but not Yoshiko's. Further, Yoshiko differentiates behaviors into two categories: friend and public critic. People who, through training, understand how these two differentiate categories will be better prepared for such intercultural encounters. When faced with a difficulty similar to that the incident depicts, they can say, "I shouldn't become upset. The other person is simply using a category, 'friend,' that has different content than mine." With this understanding, people can continue in their intercultural relationships without the emotional reaction that they have been betrayed or that they have been treated in a manner totally inconsistent with previous behaviors.

Another way training can encourage more tolerance and sophistication is to help people understand the nature of thinking itself. For example, people are much more influenced when an event happens to them, personally, than when they read about an event (Baumeister, 1998; Brewer, 1979; Kahneman & Tversky, 1972). If people read about a 3-year-old child who needs a kidney transplant, for instance, they may sympathize with the child's parents but probably will forget about it quickly given the many events that compete for their attention during the typical day. If it is their 3-year-old child who needs the transplant, the parents obviously become intensely involved, and the search for a new kidney becomes the most important goal in their lives.

The difference in emotional intensity between reading about an incident and experiencing it personally will not always be as great as in this example of a child's health, but it always exists to some degree. When people personally target their behaviors at each other, those people will interpret them as more important, more impactful, and as demanding more attention. Exactly this aspect of people's thinking can be introduced in good cross-cultural training programs. In the example given, Barbara and Yoshiko certainly are involved in a personal way, and they are likely to interpret the behaviors as personally directed at them. This situation will cause more intense reactions than if they had read about the incident or if they had simply observed the same interaction between two other people in the seminar. If Barbara and Yoshiko react with intensity, however, it may be more difficult to "patch up" the misunderstandings at a later date. Instead, they may be able to maintain cordial communications if they understand the impact of events that seem personally directed. In effect, they can say to themselves, "I am tempted to interpret these behaviors as personally directed at me, and this can cause intense reactions. Because we are from different cultures, however, misunderstandings occur for many reasons. Probably nothing going on here is directed at me, personally. I'm going to wait until I find out more!"

Attention to People's Feelings

A strong relationship exists between people's thinking and their feelings or emotions (Markus & Zajonc, 1985; Zajonc, 1998). People observe or experience behaviors and then interpret them in various ways. If they are disagreeing with someone and interpret a certain statement as an insult, they will become upset. If they interpret that same statement as simply the other person's way of advancing the discussion, they will continue the discussion without negative feelings. In addition to helping people think about and interpret events so that their emotional reactions cause as few difficulties as possible, good cross-cultural training programs recognize that people cannot always simply "interpret away" all events that can cause intense reactions. Certain behaviors people experience are so contrary to their expectations, based on their socialization in their own culture, that they cause emotional reactions when encountered in other cultures. Good cross-cultural training can prepare people for these types of emotional challenges.

In the incident involving Barbara and Yoshiko, both individuals will have emotional reactions. Yoshiko will be upset because she thinks Barbara is withdrawing her friendship, and Barbara will be frustrated when she learns that the time and effort she put into being friendly was misunderstood. Even if the two individuals understand some of the underlying concepts, such as categorization, differentiation, and the expectations of what friends do in different cultures, they likely will still have emotional reactions. Sometimes, understanding the underlying concepts behind people's behaviors is enough to inhibit the emotions that stem from a reaction such as "strange" or "unfamiliar." If Americans doing business in Asia, for instance, realize that business cards are exchanged far more frequently than in the United States, they simply will pay $50 and have some cards made. As a result, they will be prepared to exchange cards and will experience no emotional problems when meeting Asian businesspeople. At other times, an understanding of underlying concepts is not sufficient to prevent emotional reactions. For example, people may know about the uses of silence, discussed earlier in this chapter. They may have participated in a good cross-cultural training program that shared information and a critical incident on "silence as communication." But when experiencing interactions that involve long periods of silence, they still become upset! I have been in such interactions and still find them bothersome. I am tempted to fill the empty time with small talk, and I have to constantly tell myself, "Filling time is not required in all cultures like it is where I was socialized!" But if measuring instruments were strapped onto my body, I am sure they would show increased blood pressure, increased heart rate, and increased respiratory rate during these silent periods.

One way to prepare people for emotional reactions is to encourage them to actually participate in impactful experiences during cross-cultural training programs. For example, Yoshiko would be confronted with criticism in a public setting, and Barbara would interact with a person who misunderstood her friendly manner. The specific technique is called *role-playing*, and it is quite an effective training approach (Elms, 1972; Gudykunst & Hammer, 1983; McCafferey, 1995). Trainers identify a set of potentially problematic intercultural experiences, and trainees then take various roles in the minidrama. For example, assume a training program prepares international students for their graduate-level degree programs in the United States. The trainers decide that "participating in a small seminar" covers a good set of experiences because Asian students are often unfamiliar with the expectations that they participate vigorously in interactions with professors and fellow graduate students. One Asian student would role-play Yoshiko, an American would play Barbara, and others would play the professor and graduate students who contribute to the discussion. The assumption behind role-playing is that by actually experiencing what frequently happens in real intercultural encounters, people become prepared for the emotional reactions that follow from such encounters. If the Asian playing Yoshiko faces disagreement from others, he or she will have an emotional reaction even in the somewhat artificial setting the trainers provide. The Asian will have other emotional reactions from the expectation to "speak up" in the seminar, because this unfamiliar behavior is what good graduate students are supposed to do. The student assigned to Barbara's role also will have an emotional reaction when she has to "play out" the experience of having her friendly behavior misunderstood. Other behaviors she might practice in the role are encouraging international students both to speak out and to accept criticism and constructive comments graciously.

Role-playing has several benefits. When actually playing out the behaviors, such as those involved in a seminar, people do not work from a completely prepared script. Rather, the trainer suggests general guidelines, and people then make up the script as they go along. When people play their roles in this manner, they frequently find themselves making statements they never had thought through completely prior to the training program. Later, they think through their statements and say to themselves, "Why did I say that? Did I really mean it?" These very private thoughts contribute to a unique and especially impactful learning experience, because the individuals involved created the script themselves as they role-played the scene and later analyzed it. For example, a student playing one of the graduate students in the seminar might find himself or herself saying, "Yoshiko, what do you think about this issue, based on your experience in Japan?" Later, that student might think, "I wonder if I said that because I was really interested in the viewpoint of people in other cultures." This is an important self-generated thought the person should carefully examine. The appreciation of other people's viewpoints, of course, is central to effective intercultural interactions.

Decisions about whether or not to use role-playing in intercultural programs should not proceed without considering its potential disadvantages. In a chapter with the especially intriguing title "The Role Play: A Powerful but Difficult Training Tool," McCafferey (1995) discusses a number of disadvantages. One is that the role-playing can become so emotionally arousing that the trainees become extremely upset, so much so that they cannot continue in the training program. Human behavior is very complex, and role-playing that seems totally innocent and unthreatening can trigger intense reactions in just one trainee. When one trainee is obviously debilitated, of course, the training must come to an end until that person's needs are thoroughly addressed. For example, a trainer might feel that some basic ideas about male-female dating relationships should be covered so that international students are introduced to some aspects of campus social life. The person role-playing a man who wants a date may just happen to have mannerisms similar to the person who tried to rape one of the trainees a few years ago. The trainee becomes very upset due to a specific set of circumstances that no trainer could possibly foresee. Reactions such as this happen frequently enough for McCafferey to have chosen the chapter title he did. The recommendation for role-playing as a training technique is that it should be used only by very experienced people who have guided its use many times. Inexperienced people should apprentice themselves to others who have used role-playing frequently, in many places, and with many different types of trainees.

In the training programs I have organized, I add several "rules" that all trainees agree to prior to their actual role-playing. These include (a) working together in small groups for about 30 minutes going over what actually will happen later in the role-playing; (b) working from one or more of a collection of 110 critical incidents (Cushner & Brislin, 1996) that everyone can read prior to role-playing; and (c) accepting the rule that once the basic events that will happen while role-playing have been formulated, no "surprises" can occur. No one can say anything (e.g., a criticism Barbara makes about Yoshiko) different from the sorts of statements people agreed to during the 30-minute planning session. The surprises cause the intense reactions because people are totally unprepared. This point is covered as part of the introduction to the role-playing exercises. In my experience, if people accept the rules, then the time devoted to role-playing is well spent. Even with careful avoidance of the possibility of intense emotional reactions, many behaviors still occur during role-playing that provoke discussion and that provide specific examples of newly introduced concepts.

Attention to People's Behavior

In addition to people's thinking and their emotional responses, cross-cultural training also can deal with their actual behavior. For this discussion, *behavior* refers to people's actions that they and others can observe. The "others" part of this informal definition is important, of course, because people's behaviors that others observe are often the only basis these others have to make decisions about matters such as the desire for future interactions. The "they" aspect is also important because people monitor their own behavior and make conclusions about it. For example, when deciding what courses to take next semester, a student might say to himself or herself: "Am I interested in this course in international diplomacy? I attend a lot of meetings organized by the international student group here on campus. I guess I can do OK in the course."

In good cross-cultural training programs, trainers can ask people to focus on the actual behaviors they perform in a wide variety of social settings (Brislin & Yoshida,

1994; Cushner, 1989; Singelis & Pedersen, 1997). Then, people can examine those behaviors and decide if some should be abandoned or modified so that the chances of success are increased when living in other cultures. For example, recall that one of the four criteria of success is that people from other cultures must develop positive relationships with hosts. So how, exactly, can this be done? Trainees might be asked to write down exactly how they would develop positive relations with others in their own culture. Then, trainers can guide their self-examinations of whether or not these same behaviors will help them develop relationships in the host culture. If the trainees are from collective cultures, for example, they might write down that they develop new relationships after relatives or long-term friends arrange introductions (Triandis, 1995). Help with meeting new people, then, is one of the expectations people have when they have given their loyalty to a collective. If they are living in an individualistic culture such as the United States, however, the trainees probably will not have a supportive collective that accompanies them. They will have to develop positive relationships through another set of behaviors. Trainers then can guide the people into listing a set of behaviors that are more appropriate in the host culture, and they can help trainees rule out behaviors that are possible but extremely difficult. For example, trainees might list that they can walk up to people—for instance, in the student union or library—and simply introduce themselves. Although this is a possibility, trainers would have to point out that this is difficult even for socially skilled people who have lived their entire lives in the United States. A better possibility is to attend gatherings where people are expected to introduce themselves, such as at receptions various groups on campus sponsor. Another possibility is to encourage trainees to list their interests and hobbies (e.g., dance, drama, politics, computers) and to guide them toward various clubs on campus where they can meet like-minded people.

If Barbara and Yoshiko attended a cross-cultural training program after the incident, they could list behaviors they could modify, abandon, or develop. Yoshiko could list that she needs to speak up and to accept criticism graciously, and she could practice these as part of role-playing exercises. She could also perform these as part of "homework" exercises outside the cross-cultural training session. Later, she could report back to the trainer and could discuss the results of her efforts. Especially when Barbara finds herself in social settings such as a seminar with Asian students who probably have not been exposed to a good cross-cultural training program, she could practice keeping her comments to herself during the seminar session when an Asian makes a presentation. She later could take her fellow student aside and give her feedback in the manner more acceptable to Asians. She also could practice explaining to an Asian student how constructive criticism is expected in American seminars and then practice giving the criticism, thus preparing the Asian student for future encounters in other seminars whose participants are not as knowledgeable as Barbara about cultural differences.

I have had arguments with many people about this segment of a cross-cultural training program. Others argue that people shouldn't be asked to modify their behavior because they then would be false to themselves. If they follow the advice to list and to modify behaviors, they will be inconsistent with their own natural preferences to behave as they always have. Further, they argue, people would be treating individuals from another culture in a dishonest and even disrespectful manner. In the case of public criticism, for example, some individuals argue that foreign students should learn to "take it" and that Americans are saying the students don't have the maturity to do so if Americans instead wait and give their comments in private. People in other cultures deserve our honest reactions to their behaviors, they argue. People will not understand one another if everyone modifies their preferred behaviors. I respond that people always modify their preferred behaviors to meet the demands of various social settings. If people have a proposal to make, they surely behave in a different manner when they share it with friends than when they discuss it with the power holders who have the authority to grant or withhold support. If people receive a perfectly dreadful gift from an 8-year-old child who made the present with his or her own hands, the people do not give the child their "honest" reactions. Rather, they modify their behavior and respond in a gracious manner, telling the child how wonderful the gift is. Modifying behavior to meet various demands in life is part of people's social skills (Baumeister, 1998; Brislin, 1991).

For interactions with people from different countries, the recommendation for this type of behavior modification is to take into account the other people's cultural background. Regarding the objection that people won't learn to understand one another if they are constantly modifying their behavior, my response is that good cross-cultural training programs recommend that trainees become involved in many activities within the host culture. In doing so, they will meet all kinds of people, many of whom will not know how to modify their behavior even if they wanted to do so. In the United States, for example, they will meet many Americans who engage in typically American behaviors! To maintain trainees' enthusiasm for continuing the recommended involvement, they must have some successes. These successes, especially during people's first few months in a new culture, are more likely to happen if hosts are sensitive enough to take people's cultural background into account when deciding about their (hosts') behavior.

Immersion Into Another Culture

In addition to increasing the chances of successful intercultural encounters, another reason to modify actual behaviors is that change is sometimes necessary for survival in another culture (Hammer, Nishida, & Wiseman, 1996). If such behaviors can be identified, they can be practiced during training programs. Trifonovitch (1977) has been involved in training Peace Corps volunteers and American schoolteachers who accept two-year assignments in rural villages on various small Pacific islands. Having lived on such an island, Trifonovitch knew the changes in everyday behaviors that would be necessary for survival and for a chance (after two years) that the volunteers and teachers would consider their sojourn successful. Consequently, he designed a training program that immersed people into another culture. All trainees flew into the airport in Honolulu, Hawaii. From there, they were taken to rural parts of Molokai or Oahu, two islands in the Hawaiian chain. There, they found the village they would live in during their two-week training program. The village was built to be as close as possible to the sorts of villages they would be living in for two years. There, trainees had to learn to meet their everyday needs in ways new to them. No grocery stores were near, so they had to gather their own food, such as coconuts and fish. They had no radio or television, so they had to entertain themselves. No plumbing was installed, so they had to find fresh water and provide for the disposal of human wastes. No public transportation existed, so they had to walk or learn to travel by boat, necessitating awareness of ocean currents and tides. They also had to learn to tell time by the position of the sun and stars in the eventuality that their clocks or watches might break—they had no access to repair shops. The staff for the training program included Pacific islanders who could teach the behaviors necessary for success and who also could teach language and make presentations about life in rural island villages.

This immersion program represents one of the most intense experiences ever developed for the preparation of people about to enter another culture. Some trainees learned what was necessary for success in a Pacific island community and left the training program well prepared for their two-year assignments. Others did not survive the training and went back to their homes, cancelling their agreements to serve in the Peace Corps or to become schoolteachers. Many reactions to the finding that some trainees dropped out are possible. One is concluding that the training program was too intense and "burned the trainees out." Consequently, the trainers should lessen the intensity of training to encourage more trainees to complete it. Another reaction is that the training program should retain its intensity and realism. After all, people will be living in remote island villages. They should be exposed to the demands of such intercultural assignments. Further, it is far less expensive and less stressful to leave a training program and return home than it is to leave the actual assignment sometime during the two-year period. Finally, a certain amount of dropping out occurs in all such programs.

Recognizing the complaints and the admitted stresses of organizing and administering immersion training programs, Trifonovitch (1977) argued along the lines of the second reaction. People should be exposed during training to the behaviors necessary for success and then should make their own decisions about the future. When people decided to leave the training program and cancel their two-year agreements, Trifonovitch responded in an interesting and intriguing manner. He threw a party for them! He announced that the party was to celebrate the people's self-discovery. Living on a Pacific island is not for everyone, he would say. Nothing is wrong with this fact—lots of very decent people simply would not be happy on such an assignment. They would be far happier spending the two years somewhere else. Other people learned a lot during training and were prepared to live in the Pacific. That's fine, too! But nothing is inherently better about one set of people compared to the other. By focusing on self-discovery, Trifonovitch encouraged the dropouts to view the training as a success rather than as a failure. Everybody involved learned much about themselves, and this is most important in their search for happiness in life.

Trifonovitch's decision about how to respond to trainee dropout is a good example of tolerant behavior and of positive managerial skills. Intolerance stems from insistence on one type of behavior and the demonstration of obvious disapproval when deviations from the preferred behaviors occur. In this intense training program example, an intolerant response would be insisting that everybody keep a stiff upper lip and "stick with" the training until its completion. Such intolerance, however, can lead to people adjusting poorly to their work. Extremely unhappy people will not be good schoolteachers or community volunteers, and young islander students and others will suffer.

Tolerating different behaviors and developing a sensitivity to the fact that not all people will find satisfaction in the same types of work are necessary if individuals are to become not only good cross-cultural trainers but also good leaders and managers in the workplace (Fried & Matsumoto, 1997; Stewart, 1995). The importance of understanding cultural differences as they apply to the work world is the topic of the next chapter.

CHAPTER SUMMARY

Even when people are unprejudiced and have no intention to discriminate against people from other ethnic groups, they still can have problems with their intercultural interactions. Some of the reasons, including the style people use when interacting with others, are very subtle and hard to understand. Further, no convenient and widely available language exists that allows people to discuss the intercultural difficulties that might be called "beyond prejudice and discrimination." Consequently, special training programs often have to be established for openly discussing the difficulties.

People who want to overcome cultural misunderstandings and to succeed more in their intercultural interactions must understand this type of success. A four-part definition of success has been suggested:

1. People enjoy interacting with individuals from various cultural backgrounds.

2. These feelings are reciprocated by those culturally diverse individuals.

3. The tasks people want to accomplish (e.g., obtaining a degree, negotiating a contract) are completed within a reasonable amount of time.

4. No additional stress arises because the people working together are from different cultural backgrounds.

Fulfilling all four parts are necessary for success: Three out of four is not sufficient! For example, interactions can be imagined where people (1) enjoy their interactions, (3) get their work done, and (4) feel little stress. However, individuals from other cultural groups (in reference to part 2 of the success definition) may dislike these people, may feel they are insensitive, and may argue that they are not bringing diverse viewpoints to the task at hand.

People with a certain set of traits and skills have a greater chance than others of achieving success in their intercultural interactions. If people are culturally *flexible*, they can make changes in their behavior that meet the demands of various social settings. Flexible American businesspeople in Japan, for example, are willing to engage in much more small talk than if they were doing business in their own country. The Japanese want to know their business counterparts as people. Chats about people's backgrounds and interests allow them to get to know one another. One reason is pragmatic. If problems arise in business dealings, the Japanese strongly prefer that the people involved work cooperatively, with mutual trust and goodwill, toward a solution. The Japanese do not want to bring in a team of lawyers. The long hours spent on small talk is a way to determine whether potential counterparts can be trusted and whether they bring goodwill to their negotiations.

Some people are actively *enthusiastic* about developing intercultural relationships. Rather than just tolerating such interactions as necessary for task completion, they actively look forward to the stimulation of intercultural relations (Brislin & Yoshida, 1994; Fontaine, 1990). Enthusiasm also encourages people to *use various ways of communicating* effectively with others. For example, they are willing to put in the hard work necessary to learn another language and to learn the nonverbal behaviors necessary for good communication. One of many reasons children seem to be better language learners than adults is that they are more willing to make mistakes in conversations. They are not as embarrassed as adults, learn from their mistakes, and continue conversing. Many adults, however, do not like making mistakes in public and consequently do not give sufficient time and attention to practicing their language skills. An enthusiasm about developing intercultural relations can help to overcome the discomfort from making mistakes.

Successful people also have *methods to resolve conflicts* effectively in intercultural interactions. Just as mistakes inevitably will be made when people struggle in another language, so will mistakes be made when they develop close intercultural relationships. No person can be prepared for every eventuality that will occur in their futures. Interestingly, the more people develop intercultural relations, the more difficulties they are likely to have. Culturally influenced norms will be violated, conversational topics will be raised at the wrong time, polite comments to pass time will be taken seriously, and so forth. It is relatively easy to avoid such intercultural mistakes—just avoid any interaction with people from other cultural backgrounds! The alternative to this decision is to learn skills that allow effective conflict resolution.

Black (1990) and Singelis and Pedersen (1997) identified such a style. If people could address difficulties in a collaborative manner, focus on issues instead of personalities, and work toward mutual understanding, conflicts did not necessarily interfere with the long-term development of intercultural relationships. Focusing on cultural differences frequently can be part of this conflict resolution approach. One person might say to another, "We disagreed the other day on an issue. I wonder if the fact we are from different cultures and have different ways of doing things could have been a part of the disagreement." Focusing on cultural differences takes away the more threatening focus on people's personalities. If people develop *cultural informants*, they can use this conflict resolution approach better. A cultural informant is a knowledgeable individual who can answer queries when difficulties arise. If a businessperson can't understand the reason for all the small talk in Japan, a Japanese cultural informant can point out, "It's a way of developing trust, and it is a lot cheaper than a team of lawyers!" Cultural informants are often individuals who have lived in another country. For instance, the Japanese cultural informant may have attended college in Europe. From these cultural experiences, the informant knows about adjustment to another culture, how people can misunderstand everyday encounters, how people's cultural background can affect their everyday behavior, and so forth.

Cultural informants also may be able to give advice about very subtle reasons for misunderstandings that well-meaning people who have not previously engaged in extensive intercultural interactions might miss. One set of subtle reasons can be summarized by the term *communication style*. People know vocabulary terms that allow them to talk about disagreements and misunderstandings that stem from the content of their communications with others. They are not as likely to know terms that allow them to discuss differences in the style people use when they communicate. Three examples of stylistic differences are the use of silence, expressiveness, and warmth and openness that seem to signal a desire for further communication. As with many examples of cultural differences, concepts become especially clear when the styles of people from different cultures are contrasted. In any discussion of style, it is important to remember the danger of stereotypes (chapter 6). Stylistic features can be discussed as commonly found among members from identifiable cultural groups. This does not mean all members of those cultures behave in the same manner. The possibility of individual differences must be constantly kept in mind.

Silence is commonly found as part of the communication style among American Indians. When Anglo Americans interact with Native Americans, they often want to fill silent periods, feeling that too much silence is a sign that interpersonal interactions are not proceeding well. As a consequence, Native Americans may conclude that these Anglos are frivolous people who talk even when they do not have anything to say. Native Americans use silence in social settings involving ambiguity. When they meet a stranger, for example, it is ambiguous whether or not the person brings goodwill or intends to take advantage of people. Native Americans prefer to wait until the stranger demonstrates his or her intentions before they engage in conversations with the person. When a young man or woman comes home from a year in an urban university, the family does not know whether or not the student has adopted "White man's ways." The family members feel it is best to remain silent until the student demonstrates whether or not Native American ways are still respected.

Many African Americans commonly employ a very expressive style of putting their emotions "up front" (Kochman, 1981, 1990). In contrast to the socialization of many Anglo Americans who are told to keep controversial opinions to themselves for fear of offending people, many African Americans feel they are showing respect to others when they communicate their feelings expressively. They then expect others to do the same. Disagreements are acceptable because the most important goal is to express oneself openly. Anglo Americans can leave such intercultural interactions with the feeling that African Americans were too intense and were not willing to listen to anyone else. African Americans may leave the same conversation feeling that the Anglos never have anything to say and are uncooperative when dealing with controversial issues because they keep their opinions to themselves.

Many Anglo Americans commonly employ a very warm and open style when meeting people for the first time. One reason is that they were socialized into an individualistic culture. Because they do not have a supportive collective to call on when they need assistance on everyday matters, such as obtaining help with job searches and repairing their cars, they develop a warm and open style that allows them to meet others quickly. Then, they can seek help from these newly met others. This style can be very confusing to people not familiar with it. People raised in a collective culture did not have to develop a style that allowed them to meet others quickly. Instead they could seek help from members of their supportive collective. When they do meet warm and open individuals, they feel those individuals are treating them in a manner that shows special interest. People from the two types of cultures make quite different attributions (chapter 2) when the Anglo American acts differently later. The individualists conclude they are simply using the various social skills their mother taught them. The collectivists conclude that the people they recently met are superficial and insincere.

Deaf people have a very direct communication style, which they often call "straight talk." If they observe something or know something, they are more likely to pass on this information in a straightforward manner rather than to communicate it indirectly. They do this for several reasons. One is that American Sign Language is visual, so visual aspects of people are likely to become part of how they are noticed and described. So if people have gained weight or lost hair, Deaf people are likely to note it. Another reason is that Deaf people struggle to communicate with hearing people during most of their waking hours. They often cannot express themselves fluently and without hesitation due to most hearing people's lack of ASL fluency. When Deaf people do get together, they have limited time to catch up on everyone's lives. They choose to spend their time communicating directly rather than finding indirect ways to soften potentially controversial observations.

Examples of such intercultural difficulties can be effectively addressed in cross-cultural training, or formal efforts to prepare people to live and work effectively in cultures other than their own. Good training programs address people's thinking, feelings, and actual behaviors. Assume, for example, that trainers want to cover the (commonly experienced) problem of how people can disagree with their friends. In some cultures, such as the middle-class United States, people can read a friend's proposals and then make public suggestions about how some points can be changed and the proposals thus improved. In other cultures this is not possible—friends do not disagree in public. When addressing people's thinking in this case, trainers would point out that people are differentiating roles. In some cultures, the category "friend" can include a person one spends much free time with and can disagree with in public. In other cultures, these roles are differentiated: The same people cannot engage in both behaviors. The people who are one's friends are different from people who can disagree with one in public. A person who differentiates the roles, then, would feel that an individual is withdrawing his or her friendship when engaging in the role of "disagreer."

Training can emphasize very specific aspects of the culture sojourners will be living in, or it can deal with general issues all sojourners face (e.g., anxiety, interpreting nonverbal behaviors). Many times, decisions about which of the two types to use will be guided by economic considerations. Specific training can be done economically only when numerous people are about to live in the same country and when training materials that can prepare people for a specific country are available. If such specific materials are proprietary to one organization, they will not be easily available to others. General materials are easily obtainable, different trainers know how to use them, and many of the materials have been evaluated to determine both their usefulness and how they can be improved.

When addressing people's feelings, trainers would encourage people to actually encounter challenges to their cultural background during the training program. The assumption is that people inevitably will encounter challenges after training, so it is best to prepare people during formal programs when helpful and knowledgeable individuals can assist in the process of adjusting to another culture. People become emotionally aroused when their expectations are disconfirmed. If, for instance, people expect friendship, they are upset to find a critic! During training, people can role-play such encounters. For the situation involving friendship, one trainee can act out a person who makes a short presentation, another can be the friend who disagrees, another can act as a cultural informant who has experienced such encounters in his or her own life, and so forth. If people learn about potential emotional challenges during training, they are better prepared to deal with them during their actual intercultural encounters (Cushner, 1989; Cushner, McClelland, & Safford, 1996).

When addressing people's behaviors, trainers would encourage people to think about changes in their daily actions that could increase the chances of success in intercultural interactions. Some examples already have been covered. Americans should be more willing to engage in extensive small talk in Japan; Anglo Americans should not rush to fill periods of silence when interacting with Native Americans; and African Americans might make sure they encourage Anglos to communicate their feelings openly and to hold nothing back. In the example involving friendship, people might practice responding to friends' disagreements in a gracious manner and practice using others' suggestions to improve their work. Or, people who might express their disagreement with a friend in a public meeting might wait and share their reactions in a private conversation with their friend.

When people are willing to modify their behaviors to meet the expectations of people in other cultures, they are demonstrating they are tolerant individuals. They are communicating the point that people can choose from many ways to behave and that the ones with which they are most familiar, from their own socialization, are not necessarily the best for all people in all parts of the world. People who happen to be socialized so that they are familiar with a different set of behaviors should be respected. Tolerance for the differences due to people's ethnic heritage, cultural background, religion, gender, sexual orientation, and medical history is becoming an increasingly important issue in various parts of the world. Just one reason is that tolerance, and ideally enthusiasm, about differences are necessary in the work world because leaders need to integrate the various contributions different people can offer. Leaders can encourage more contributions if they appreciate differences and avoid forcing everyone to behave in exactly the same manner. This is one of the topics addressed in the next chapter, which deals with cultural differences in the workplace.

C H A P T E R 8

CULTURE'S EFFECTS ON THE WORK WORLD

CHAPTER OVERVIEW

Over the course of their lives, people will spend more time working than doing virtually any other activity, with the possible exception of sleep. In the workplace, they will encounter cultural differences. To understand these differences, people need to distinguish two kinds of relationships among concepts. *Ecological correlations* refer to concepts that describe a culture or nation. Knowing ecological correlations gives insights into a culture's important norms and central values. *Individual correlations* refer to concepts that describe people. Many times, ecological correlations and individual correlations are in perfect harmony. For example, an ecological analysis can identify collective cultures (e.g., Japan, China, and Mexico), where the emphasis is on people's membership in groups rather than on their own beliefs and attitudes. In addition, an individual-level analysis can identify people who are comfortable behaving in ways called for in a collective culture. Other times, research will identify different types of relationships between the two types of analyses. There can be highly individualistic people in a collective culture, and they may take important roles such as entrepreneur and creative artist.

Extensive research has been done to identify concepts central to understanding behavior in the workplace. The results include detailed analyses of individualism and collectivism, the distribution of power, approaches to dealing with the inevitability of uncertainty, the role expectations of men and women, and the relative importance placed on long- and short-term planning. This latter concept is based on research into Confucian values and has been important for understanding economic growth in some Asian countries since World War II. Researchers also have made suggestions about the relation between cultural values and economic stagnation in Asia during the 1990s.

Culture gives guidance about what is expected of leaders and about how leaders actually should behave. A major difference among cultures is the degree supervisors become involved in the personal lives of their employees. In some cultures, supervisors introduce employees to potential marriage partners and take on the role of counselor when employees have personal problems. Other cultures make a sharp distinction between the workplace and employees' personal lives, and behaviors such as matchmaking are strongly discouraged. The term *paternal authoritative* is used to describe the leadership style that includes involvement in employees' personal lives. *Paternal* refers to activities similar to those of a father, and *authoritative* refers to the greater knowledge and worldly sophistication leaders are expected to possess.

There are so many cultural differences to understand, as well as other aspects of the global economy, that people become frustrated and are tempted to throw up their hands in disgust. Instead of this step, a wiser approach is to develop trusting relationships with people from other cultures. People who trust one another look after one another's interests. Research on trust is reviewed in this chapter, and its role in successful international cooperative alliances is discussed. People's sensitivity to culture and cultural differences is a major contributor to their development of trusting relationships.

CULTURE AND THE WORKPLACE

The prediction has been made several times in this book that in the future people will need to make more decisions about intercultural interactions. This fact about the future led to its treatment in two chapters, one on the difficulties to be overcome (such as prejudice, chapter 6) and the other on the more subtle issues involved once people have made the decision to seek intercultural interactions (e.g., communication style, chapter 7). One of the important aspects of people's decision making concerns the range of settings they encounter. In some settings, they have more freedom of choice about intercultural interactions than in others. Many people, for example, choose to live in neighborhoods where most other residents are from similar backgrounds as theirs. Or, they choose to spend most of their free time with people who are culturally similar. In other settings, they have fewer choices. In many countries, if parents want their children to attend public schools, the children inevitably will encounter classmates from a variety of cultural backgrounds. Laws in these countries dictate that schools are to be integrated and that discrimination cannot occur on the basis of skin color, ethnicity, and a number of other factors. If parents want to circumvent these laws, they have to find or establish private schools and must pay sizable tuitions. Even with private schools, governments can demand integration if the schools seek public funds (e.g., for school lunches, tax dollars that support military dependents, and so forth).

Another setting where people have less choice than in their free time is the workplace. Massive changes have occurred in the workforce composition in countries such as the United States over the past 50 years. Years ago, an American White man could accept a job in a large organization and find himself in the company of people who were much like himself. Today, a host of laws demand that organizations recruit and hire women, Blacks, Hispanics, people with disabilities (Gaylord-Ross, 1987), and so forth. In addition to increased intercultural interactions with coworkers, many American workers are taking jobs involving international contact. Either they accept overseas assignments (Adler, 1997) or they work in organizations located in the United States but owned by people from other cultures (Dorfman, 1996; Nath, 1988; Rigby, 1987). These same poeple may hire executives from their own and other countries, forcing Americans to work for a boss born and socialized in another country. The Americans, then, have a choice between (a) avoiding such jobs or quitting their jobs when such changes occur or (b) learning to work effectively with people from other cultures. This chapter is meant to provide helpful concepts for people who choose the second alternative.

Just as in the contrast between chapter 6, about prejudice, and chapter 7, about successful communication, people can bring a negative, neutral, or positive attitude toward intercultural relations in the workplace. With a negative attitude, people may act in a discriminatory way toward out-group members, denying them opportunities such as difficult assignments that allow them to prove their worth to the organization. With a neutral attitude, they may merely tolerate cultural differences and may try to minimize their influence in the workplace. With a positive attitude, however, people may actually look forward to the stimulation of cultural differences (Cushner & Brislin, 1996; Martin, 1989). They may benefit from the differences workers bring to their jobs. Employers, for instance, may value the diverse experiences some members of their workforce have had and may attempt to benefit from their varied backgrounds, language skills, types of education, travel experience, contacts with influential people in various communities, and so forth. With this positive attitude, cultural differences can be viewed as a potentially rich fruit orchard that should be treated with care and enthusiasm.

Five general topic areas involving the relation between culture and work will be covered in this chapter.

1. Because much relevant cross-cultural research on worker values is based on a method of statistical analysis involving ecological correlations, an understanding of the difference between this and the more familiar analysis based on individual-level correlations is necessary. Understanding the two types of correlations also allows further treatment of a theme introduced several times in previous chapters (e.g., chapters 1 and 5): the distinction between individual and cultural differences. When interpreting individual-level correlations, researchers can focus on aspects of people. When ecological correlations are based on data collected in various countries, researchers can suggest interpretations based on cultural differences.

2. When moving between cultures, people are likely to confront differences in work values that involve individualism and collectivism, power distance, uncertainty avoidance, masculinity and femininity, and (in Asia) Confucian dynamism.

3. Leadership has been a focus of active research, and investigations have moved beyond descriptions of the traits of leaders to a greater sensitivity to leadership's social context.

4. In many parts of Asia, employees prefer a leadership style known as "paternal authoritativeness." This is a very puzzling style for many Americans and is a source of difficulties for Americans who accept leadership positions in Asia.

5. To develop long-lasting and productive intercultural relations in the business world, people must cultivate trust. The meaning of trust and ways to develop it have been the topics of insightful research studies.

UNDERSTANDING ECOLOGICAL CORRELATIONS

When people work in a country other than their own or work in an organization owned and operated by foreign nationals, they inevitably will encounter numerous challenges to their expectations. These challenges will be especially impactful if they have held other jobs in their own country and have interacted with few coworkers from culturally different backgrounds. Many resulting frustrations will stem from the realization that the behaviors they thought appropriate in the workplace are considered unacceptable by the other culture's members.

A number of helpful guides have been developed to assist people's adjustment to the workplace in other cultures (Adler, 1997; Cushner & Brislin, 1996; Miller & Kilpatrick, 1987). An especially helpful set of five concepts has been developed by Geert Hofstede and his colleagues (e.g., Chinese Culture Connection, 1987; Hofstede, 1980, 1996; Hofstede & Bond, 1988), and they have generated much research by other scholars (e.g., Earley, 1989, 1997; Kim, Park, & Suzuki, 1990; P. Smith, Dugan, & Trompenaars, 1996). To use these concepts for analyzing intercultural behavior in the workplace, it is first necessary to understand the meaning of ecological correlations.

I'll begin the discussion with an explanation of "correlation," a topic students may have covered in other classes. A *correlation* is a mathematical statement that communicates the association between two variables. For example, most readers have taken tests during their high school years in anticipation of attending college. These test scores were part of the application materials people presented to various colleges. The test scores (the most common is the Scholastic Aptitude Test, or SAT) are considered valuable because performance on them is associated with success in college. The mathematical relationship, or correlation, between test scores and college grades is positive ($r = .30$ to $.45$, depending on the college). This is not a perfect relationship, but it does provide useful information to college administrators and counselors who work with students. The interpretation of correlations always must be made carefully. In this example, test scores do not cause good grades, of course. Rather, certain aspects of human behavior (such as verbal and mathematical skills) most likely are both tapped by the test and are useful in the college classroom.

The association between test scores and college grades is summarized by an individual-level correlation. The term *individual* indicates that each piece of information was gathered from distinct people: Person A provided both test scores and college grades, as did B, C, D, and so forth. A mathematical formula was applied to the two sets of information, and the results were summarized in the form of a *correlation coefficient* (indicated by the letter *r*, as mentioned earlier). Individual-level correlations allow researchers to suggest reasons for the association between test scores and college grades, and the reasons almost always focus on the traits, abilities, and other aspects of people. Researchers usually entertain a number of reasons for a correlation's existence. Some researchers suggest that these tests measure important abilities, such as reading comprehension, and that such abilities lead to good grades. More skeptical researchers say the tests simply measure test-taking skills, and these same skills are later used when students take midterms and finals in the college classroom. Note that both suggested explanations involve aspects of people.

Thus, for individual-level correlations, aspects of people are the units of analysis. Some important cross-cultural research has used ecological correlations (Chinese Culture Connection, 1987; Hofstede, 1980; Schwartz, 1992; Schwartz & Sagiv, 1995; P. Smith et al., 1996). For calculating ecological correlations, aspects of a society or countries as a whole are studied. The use of different countries probably provides the clearest example. The gross national product (GNP) of various countries might be listed in a study, along with the amount spent on public education for children ages 5 to 18 in the same countries. Thus two entries are listed for countries such as Japan, Canada, Great Britain, Australia, the United States, and so forth. A correlation coefficient can be computed, and an association established: The greater the GNP, the greater the amount spent on public education. Interpretations of ecological correlations must focus on aspects of the units of analysis, in this case the countries. One interpretation might be that countries with a high GNP have citizens who make good salaries, and these provide a tax base for funding public education. Just as with individual-level correlations, ecological correlations encourage more than one explanation. Another interpretation might be that countries with a high GNP can afford to support an efficient tax collection system, and this collection of taxes due is important for the funding of public education.

Ecological correlations also can involve analysis of society's norms. *Norms* refer to widely accepted guidelines about behavior. A norm in America is to teach children to read—large amounts of money are put into public schools to do so. This is a fact about society. Given this fact, individual differences (of course) exist; some children read better than others. As another example, a norm in many societies (that could be used to analyze an ecological correlation) is that people are expected to work well with others on group-defined tasks. As will be discussed later, this is a norm in collective societies (e.g., Japan), where people are more likely to pursue their goals in cooperation with others. Within such a society, individual differences exist. A given person may be able to work cooperatively with others better than another individual. That second person, however, may have to develop cooperative skills to accomplish goals, given the societal norm that people are expected to work well with others.

It is very important not to interpret ecological correlations as individual-level correlations (and vice versa) because mistakes easily can be made. In a classic treatment of ecological correlations, Robinson (1950; see also review by Nachmias & Nachmias, 1987; Triandis, 1995) analyzed the relation between birth outside the United States and literacy. When analyzed as an ecological correlation, the association was positive. Specifically, when major regions (e.g., the Northeast, Deep South, Midwest, Far West, etc.) were analyzed, the more people who were foreign born in a region, the higher the literacy rates were. When an individual-level correlation was computed, the association was in the opposite direction! That is, foreign-born individuals were less likely to be literate than native-born individuals. What could cause this striking difference? The key to analyzing the difference is to return to the basic advice presented previously. To interpret individual-level correlations, look at aspects of people. To interpret ecological correlations, look at aspects of the unit of analysis, in this case U.S. regions. One interpretation of the ecological correlation is that different U.S. regions have public education systems that differ greatly in quality. Ambitious, hard-working, or already-literate foreign-born immigrants tend to settle in regions with good educational systems. Thus certain regions attract many immigrants who already are or who quickly become literate. One interpretation of the individual-level correlation is that native-born people have had longer exposure to the language the literacy tests are given in (English), so they can be expected to perform better. Note that one explanation does not contradict the other. They both can be correct. One explanation deals with an association between information at the "ecological" level, and the other deals with information at the individual level. When people interpret ecological correlations as if they were individual-level correlations (a very easy temptation!), they are said to be guilty of the *ecological fallacy*.

In the subsequent treatment of ecological relationships in this chapter, the unit of analysis will be the country where people work. In an influential research project, Hofstede (1980, 1996; Hofstede & Bond, 1988; see also Dorfman, 1996; Earley, 1997) assessed workers' values in more than 40 countries. All of these people worked for branches of the same multinational organization, International Business Machine (IBM). The researchers analyzed the results from individual workers by examining the average score of people in various countries: Japan, the United States, Germany, the Philippines, and so forth. The statistical analysis then dealt with these average scores in relation to other aspects of different countries. For instance, the average score (on the values assessment instrument) of workers in Japan, the United States, Germany, and so forth could be compared to the gross national product of those same countries. The unit of analysis is at the country level. Consequently, to interpret the project's results, people must understand the nature of ecological correlations. People must focus on the unit of analysis, the countries in Hofstede's research, and examine aspects of those countries. Hofstede and his colleagues have identified five factors that they argue are helpful for understanding work differences in various countries.

VALUES THAT INFLUENCE BEHAVIOR
IN THE WORKPLACE

In this section, the five values that affect behavior in the workplace that Hofstede et al. (Hofstede, 1980, 1991, 1996; Hofstede & Bond, 1988) identified using ecological correlations will be discussed. Ecological correlations are sometimes more difficult to interpret than individual correlations. People know lots of others with different traits and abilities, so they can suggest reasons why two traits are correlated when information is gathered from these individuals (recall the example of test scores and college grades). However, it often is harder to identify aspects of societies or countries that assist in the interpretation of ecological correlations, because most people are not intimately familiar with very many societies other than the one where they were socialized. Yet knowing about aspects of various societies (or major segments within a society) is important for making decisions about people's behavior. Recall the ecological correlation between number of foreign-born people in a region and literacy rates. One suggested reason for this ecological correlation is that certain regions have good educational systems that attract immigrants eager to learn English. This fact could be very useful, for instance, to a teacher who has job offers from school systems in several American cities located in different regions. If the teacher feels he or she can make a contribution to the education of immigrants, the level of funding for educational programs in the different cities can be a factor in the decision about which job to accept.

One technique for interpreting ecological correlations, then, is to imagine living and working in different parts of the world. By imagining typical workplace behaviors in their own (familiar) country along with behaviors expected in other countries, people can clarify research based on ecological correlations. The following incident (adapted from a case study presented by Chernin, 1990) involving an American working in Japan should make the subsequent discussion of value differences clearer. In this incident, the American encounters differences in the five values Hofstede and his colleagues identified (Hofstede, 1980, 1991, 1996; Hofstede & Bond, 1988) and other researchers investigated (e.g., Janssens, Brett, & Smith, 1995).

Peter Reed is a computer software specialist who had developed a good reputation as a programmer in the United States. Seeking new challenges, he accepted an appointment as a software specialist in his company's branch office in Tokyo. In his own country, Peter had a reputation as a very creative programmer, and part of his preferred work style involved working on a number of different projects simultaneously. If one project had a stumbling block, Peter often found he could clear his mind by working on one or even two other projects. His mind refreshed, he then could return to the original project with a fresh outlook and a range of potential solutions to problems. Managers in the American branch encouraged this work style because they saw that Peter was very productive when allowed to work in his preferred manner. The managers also were tolerant when Peter (and other productive workers) deviated from written policy with such activities as lateness to work, lunch hours that extended beyond 60 minutes, number of work breaks during the day, and so forth. As long as the employees were productive, rules were loosely enforced.

Peter arrived in Tokyo and met his immediate supervisor, Hirumi Watanabe. The relationship between the two started out well because Watanabe recognized Peter's abilities and the quality of his work. After about three months, however, tensions began to arise. Peter enjoyed going off by himself when faced with a difficult problem, sometimes sequestering himself in the company library and forgoing lunch with his coworkers. When he did have lunch with coworkers, he was surprised that men usually ate with men and women ate with women. Accustomed to more integration of men and women in his own country, Peter sometimes would ask women to join his lunch group, but his invitations were received with obvious discomfort. When Peter was late coming back from lunch or late coming to work, Watanabe reacted negatively. At first, the negative reactions consisted of frowns. Finally, Watanabe had to ask Peter to be more careful about observing company policy. Watanabe also was frustrated at Peter's habit of working on different projects simultaneously and not giving enough attention to the one Watanabe considered the most important. Peter's supervisor did not seem to appreciate Peter's preferred style of working on a second and third project to eventually resolve difficulties he encountered in the first and highest priority project.

It was clear to everyone who knew of Peter's work that he was one of the company's most productive workers. He was clearly not abrasive, nor unpleasant, and he obviously enjoyed interacting with his Japanese coworkers. Yet he was unhappy in his assignment, and Watanabe was not pleased with Peter's contributions. Peter recognized that he was unhappy and that he was not getting along very well with Watanabe, but he was unable to "put his finger on" the reasons for the difficulties. Eventually, Peter was forced to consider changing companies.

What are the reasons, all involving cultural differences, for Peter's difficulties? Five reasons will be discussed here, all involving generalizations about culture and cultural differences. The generalizations follow:

1. Individualism contrasted with collectivism

2. Power distance between bosses and employees

3. Uncertainty avoidance

4. Masculine and feminine goals in the workplace

5. The influence of Confucian thought on people's values

As discussed at length in chapter 6, the possibility of exceptions always must be kept in mind whenever generalizations are applied to specific cases. I believe these generalizations provide a good starting point for the analysis of intercultural difficulties, but people always should be willing to move beyond the generalizations as they acquire increasing information from their own firsthand experiences.

Individualism and Collectivism

One of the strongest distinctions people adjusting to other societies must face is the relative emphasis on individualism and collectivism (Chen, Meindl, & Hunt, 1997; Freeman, 1997; Triandis, 1995). These concepts were introduced in chapter 2 as they apply to the behaviors of individuals in various cultures. Hofstede (1980, 1986) found that the concepts also were important at the ecological level. In collectivist societies, goals are much more likely to be attained through group effort, and the organization of various institutions within a society is more likely to be based on groups. Consequently, there is a great deal of value placed on people's participation in groups and on working toward their goals as group members. Individualist societies have more institutions that allow people to work toward their personal goals. If they choose, they can pursue some of these goals as part of groups. For instance, they can join a political action committee to work toward electing a certain candidate for governor. The formation of these groups in individualist versus collective societies involves at least two differences. In individualist societies, people have a choice. They can join a group to pursue a goal, or they can work toward the goal without much interaction with others. In collective societies, people are far less likely to consider working alone because the expectation is that they will integrate their wishes with those of others.

The second difference involves the time frame of group membership. In individualist societies, the group is likely to exist only as long as it serves the needs of the individual members. In the example of the political action committee, the group will exist until the election results for governor are counted. After the group's goal has been accomplished (or after failure is clear), the group's members are likely to go their separate ways. In collective societies, the groups people are involved with are likely to be a permanent part of their lives (Hui, 1990; Hui & Luk, 1997). People are far more likely in collectivist societies to have lengthy (if not lifelong) ties to their extended family, to their organization, to their school alumni group, and so forth.

Understanding individualist and collective societies has many important and interesting implications. When interacting in collective societies, people are not seen as just individuals with their own qualities. People also are seen as a member of some group. Before my first lecture tour in Japan, a knowledgeable colleague advised me,

> Be sure to have business cards made. On the business card, be sure to include your title within your organization. The higher sounding your title can be and still represent an honest indicator of your position, the better. You have to keep in mind that part of your identity as a person in Japan is your position in your organization. If people don't know where you stand in a group, you will not have an existence for them.

Socialization (chapter 4) in a collective society involves sensitivity to people's lifelong participation in groups. The work of Tobin, Wu, and Davidson (1989a, 1989b) in China, Japan, and the United States was discussed in chapter 5. As part of their work in Japan, they observed a very ill-mannered, unruly boy in one preschool classroom who was clearly interfering with the schoolwork of the other students. A few well-behaved students complained to the teacher. Although it might be expected that the teacher would intervene, she took a different approach. She told the well-behaved students that it was their job to deal with the unruly youngster. She told them that the ill-behaved student must learn to work cooperatively with others and that part of the class's responsibility is to try to integrate the isolated individual into the group. She also said cooperative students always will have to deal with a few unruly people later. It is best to learn during preschool how to get along with difficult people and how to avoid becoming upset at these individuals.

Returning to the case study of Peter Reed's adjustment to the Japanese branch of a multinational corporation, note that Watanabe felt that Peter was not cooperating enough. He worked too frequently by himself, and he did not participate in the smooth-functioning lunch groups his coworkers enjoyed and looked forward to as a major part of their workday. Many lunch-hour conversations in Japan are job oriented. Watanabe felt that if Peter had a problem with one of his projects, he could obtain assistance from others if he simply would share his difficulties and ask for suggestions. Recognizing Peter's talents, Watanabe also felt Peter could assist other coworkers when they needed suggestions. Peter, of course, was not as accustomed to making contributions through a group. As noted earlier, in the United States, his supervisors tolerated his preference to work alone, realizing this style allowed him to be highly productive.

The value collectivists place on working in groups has many implications for individualists. One has been documented by Gabrenya, Wang, and Latane (1985), who reasoned that less "social loafing" happens in collective societies. When social loafing occurs, people make fewer contributions while working with others than they would while working alone (Erez & Somech, 1996; Latane, Williams, & Harkins, 1979). If five individuals working alone each generate five solutions to a complex problem, then the individuals are responsible for 25 solutions. Assume all 25 of the solutions are quite different. If people are put into a five-person working group and if the group generates only 15 or 18 solutions, then people may be guilty of social loafing. Certain group members may have relaxed, letting others do most of the work. Another reason individuals may not work as hard in groups is that their personal efforts are less visible. If a group generates 28 or 30 solutions, the contributions of the individual members are hard to recognize. Realizing the relative invisibility of their efforts, individual group members may "slack off."

Gabreyna and his colleagues (1985) found that social loafing was more common in a individualist culture (United States) compared to a collective culture (Taiwan). The Americans in the study were more productive when working alone than when working with others. The Chinese not only avoided social loafing, but also they were more productive when working with others than when working alone. Gabrenya and his colleagues said this finding indicated the possibility of "social striving." The value placed on group membership is so strong in collective societies that people actually benefit from working with others. Working with others helps people raise their productivity beyond the level they would achieve when working alone. Watanabe's realization that groups can generate social striving is another reason for his disappointment with Peter's behavior. Watanabe, based on his own socialization and experiences in his culture, felt that Peter would be even more productive if he could integrate himself into the work group. Peter, in contrast, may have felt that the time and energy spent on working with others would interfere with his productivity and would reduce the originality and creativity of his unique contributions.

Power Distance

A second dimension that is important for understanding cultural differences in the workplace is called *power distance* (Peterson et al., 1995; Spencer-Oatey, 1997). This dimension refers to the amount of distinctiveness among various groups in their access to power and in their relative status levels. The word *amount* is important here. All societies have different status levels, and people with high status have more access to power and to various comforts society has to offer. People who are wealthy, who are well educated, who come from families that have wielded power for many generations, and who have many contacts in government and professional circles are likely to have more status than the less educated and the more impoverished individuals in a society. In the workplace everywhere, executives have more power than factory workers, and office managers have more power than secretaries.

The differences across various societies involve the amount of power high-status groups have relative to lower status groups, the degree the distinctions are built into societal institutions, and people's acceptance of power differences as normal. Cultures referred to as "low power distance" are guided by laws, norms, and everyday behaviors that make power distinctions as minimal as possible. The United States is considered a low-power-distance country. Yes, members of the U.S. Senate have a great deal of power, but the less powerful citizens can remove a senator up for reelection. Yes, American executives have more power than factory workers, but workers can join together in unions and challenge the policies the executives establish. Friendly contact also can occur between executives and workers when the individuals involved share similar interests, such as in golf, bridge, or other activities. Yes, American office managers have more power than secretaries. But office managers are very unwise if they do not treat secretaries well and if they fail to listen carefully to the secretaries' suggestions about workplace or task improvements. Further, the power managers possess has explicit limits, as can be seen in laws and company policies that attempt to prevent sexual harassment. In general, workers in low-power-distance countries feel more freedom to disagree with their bosses than workers in high-power-distance countries. Yes, it is never easy to meet with the boss to express disagreement. But again, the power distinction refers to the amount of comfort people feel when disagreeing. In low-power-distance countries, people feel more comfortable disagreeing. In high-power-distance countries, people feel very uncomfortable disagreeing, and often they feel so uncomfortable they don't do it.

In some high-power-distance countries, people accept status distinctions as normal and are not upset when high-status people exert their power (Earley, 1997). For example, Bond, Wan, Leong, and Giacalone (1985) compared people's reactions to insults in a high-power-distance country (Hong Kong) and in a low-power-distance country (United States). People in Hong Kong were less upset when they were insulted, as long as the insulter was of high status. When people accept status distinctions as normal, they accept that the powerful are different from the less powerful. The powerful can engage in behaviors the less powerful cannot, in this case insult people and have the insult accepted as part of their rights. My colleagues and I (Triandis, Brislin, & Hui, 1988) suggest that people from low-power-distance countries who were socialized not to accept such status distinctions will find this one of the most difficult cultural differences they will have to cope with in the workplace.

In a number of countries, people accept that sharp status distinctions exist but do not necessarily like this fact. Earley and Stubblebine (1989) studied the ways British workers used feedback their supervisors provided. Great Britain is not one of the countries highest in power distance, but it allows enough for people from a country very low on this dimension (e.g., Israel or New Zealand) to notice. Whereas studies in other high-power-distance countries (e.g., Japan: Reitsperger & Daniel, 1990) have shown that workers benefited from feedback, the British workers actually resented the information supervisors offered to them. Earley and Stubblebine (1989) offered this explanation:

> . . . English society is characterized by an entrenched class structure such that shop-floor workers perceive themselves as quite different from managers. . . . English workers have structured their unions so as to retain control over their environment. The trade union system can be interpreted as a formalized structure that reduces the capacity of managers to influence shop-floor workers. The high power distance found in England reflects a hands-off approach that workers expect from their superiors. (p. 177)

When managers in England give feedback, then, workers consider it inappropriate and are unlikely to use it.

Power distance is a factor in the case study involving Peter Reed and his Japanese boss. Japan is higher on the power distance dimension than is the United States. Watanabe believed the boss had a right to direct the behavior of his employees. He was accustomed to his workers saying the equivalent of "yes, sir!" when he made a suggestion. Peter certainly knew Watanabe was the boss, but he did not see the distinction between himself and his boss to the degree his Japanese coworkers did. For example, Peter undoubtedly felt freer to disagree with Watanabe than did his Japanese coworkers. In the case study, I mentioned that Watanabe frowned when Peter came back late from his lunches. Watanabe felt this was a message his employee should take seriously. Peter felt the frown carried a message but that he was free to place it into a category (see chapter 7) of "less important items." The more important category, from Peter's viewpoint, was the collection of behaviors that contributed to the conclusion "I am productive." Watanabe was likely to have a stronger category than Peter consisting of items related to his rights as a boss.

Another way to capture the distinction between low- and high-power-distance countries is to consider whether supervisors and employees can become friends. People in low-power-distance countries often will give a response such as "Sure, I'm on a first-name basis with my boss, and we spend free time together coaching a baseball team!" People in a high-power-distance country are far less likely to entertain the possibility of being on a first-name basis with their boss and of spending free time together.

Uncertainty Avoidance

The third factor Hofstede (1980) identified deals with a universal concern. People are concerned about uncertainty in the future (Greenberg, Solomon, & Pyszczynski, 1997). Regarding work, they might ask themselves the following: "Will we have enough money to live comfortably five years from now?" "Will the demand for the products our company sells continue into the future, or should we change our products?" "If we put pressure on the board of directors to fire the current company president, what are the chances a new president will be any more capable?" "If I propose a new policy, how much support am I likely to receive from my coworkers?" One way to reduce uncertainty is to adopt rules. If people know they and others will obey the rules, they will have more confidence about the future. Some uncertainty about the future can be reduced through the widespread use of such rules, which then become, over a number of years, part of the culture. For example, people are uncertain how much income they will have after they reach age 65 and no longer work for a salary. One way to reduce the uncertainty is to establish laws or rules that require people to make contributions to a retirement fund (e.g., Social Security, a company's pension plan).

Different societies have various numbers of rules, laws, and norms that deal with uncertainty (P. Smith et al., 1996) and that become an accepted part of their culture (like the air we breathe, as discussed in chapter 1). In the United States, for instance, all workers know they will have payroll deductions (which the self-employed pay as estimated taxes) that represent their contributions to the Social Security system. Most workers accept the need for such contributions, even though they often would prefer to spend the money on today's necessities. Abandonment of the Social Security system is almost unthinkable—it is part of American culture. Legislators who propose major changes in Social Security risk not being reelected! If they speak out about aspects of the system that might be improved, legislators run the risk of appearing not to care about America's elders. Social Security is now part of American culture, so people who attack it can be seen as attacking American culture.

All cultures have guidelines that help people avoid uncertainty, so differences among cultures refer to the number and extent of the rules, laws, norms, and informal guidelines people are expected to know (Smith et al., 1996). Countries considered high in *uncertainty avoidance* have large numbers of such rules. People in these countries are socialized to believe that uncertainty about the future is best dealt with if everyone behaves according to widely accepted guidelines. Consider the example of employment. People are uncertain about where they will be working 10 years from now. High-uncertainty-avoidance countries would have various rules and norms that reduce this uncertainty. For instance, people would expect long employment with the same company (Brislin & Hui, 1993). People working in one company today are likely to be working in that same company 10 years from now. Or consider the salaries people receive. People in high-uncertainty-avoidance countries would expect to find jobs where salaries go up slowly each year. People may not become wealthy working in jobs that yield slow and steady salary increases, but they will not go hungry and they can support a family. Important links exist between uncertainty and the stress people feel and that they know can affect their health. One reason for stress is that people are uncertain about what will happen to them. If they engage in a certain behavior, what exactly will be the result? If they do not know, they may experience stress. When many rules in a society guide people's behavior, stress can be reduced because uncertainty can be reduced. Consider the example of people accepting jobs in a company and showing up for work on their first day. This can be stressful. They ask themselves, "Will I fit in? Will coworkers accept me?" People will feel reduced first-day stress if they are members of a culture where the strong informal rule is that coworkers will approach the newcomers, talk to them, and express words of welcome.

People in low-uncertainty-avoidance countries are noticeably less concerned with unpredictability. They know they cannot predict exactly what they will be doing in 10 years, but they are less willing to deal with the unpredictability by establishing numerous rules and regulations. In fact, too many rules and regulations are considered undesirable because they limit freedom of movement in society. If people are expected to stay with the same company for 10 years, for instance, this norm limits the movement of people who want to try a new job, to move to a new community, to seek better promotion opportunities in another company, and so forth. More risk taking occurs in low-uncertainty-avoidance countries (Hofstede, 1986). It is easier to take risks such as seeking funds for a small business venture if few rules and regulations place limits on the search for funding. People in low-uncertainty-avoidance countries realize that the future is unpredictable, but they don't feel that extensive guidelines for behavior are the way to deal with an uncertain future.

The concept of uncertainty avoidance is at the center of many intercultural encounters. Consider interactions between American business people and their Chinese counterparts as they seek joint-venture opportunities in China (Fang, 1998). The United States is considered low and China is considered high on the uncertainty-avoidance dimension. One aspect of uncertainty is whether or not people's decisions today will bring praise or reprimands next year. In uncertainty-avoidance countries, workers are very hesitant to make decisions, because the decisions may be wrong. Consequently, workers try to avoid making decisions until they have the approval of people higher in the company hierarchy. Then, if the decision proves wrong, the workers will be spared blame because the higher level people approved the decision. This desire to avoid making decisions, however, makes it very difficult to find anyone willing to approve a new business venture (Holton, 1990). Hui (Brislin & Hui, 1993) uses the example of modifications in a product that has proved successful. In China, the general manufacturer of a factory that produced dinnerware refused to change the design of its upscale plates from a round shape to a slightly octagonal shape. He explained his decision: "If the original design was well-accepted by consumers in the past, why wouldn't it be in the future? Besides, who else but myself will take the blame if the change flops?"

Analyzing similar potential difficulties in American-Chinese business dealings, Baird, Lyles, and Wharton (1990) concluded that people

> need to have clear, specific and detailed rules and procedures governing all aspects of Sino-U.S. joint ventures set down beforehand. Also, the selection of American managers for the venture who can adapt to and understand the Chinese intolerance of uncertainty is important. (p. 64)

To add to the interpretation of the difficulties between Peter Reed and Hirumi Watanabe, people must understand that Japan is higher in uncertainty avoidance than the United States. To deal with uncertainty, such as the flow of future business into a company, the Japanese are more accepting of rules and regulations. These rules extend to such everyday behaviors as the proper time when work starts, the accepted amount of time for lunch hour, the desired way to deal with work difficulties that arise, and so forth. Coming from a country lower in uncertainty avoidance, Peter was not as likely to pay as much attention to these rules. When he came back late from lunch, to him it was not a terribly important violation of rules. In contrast, it was a significant violation to Watanabe and his coworkers. If asked, Watanabe could have defended his actions.

> If a potential customer wants to talk to Peter Reed, I want to know Peter will be available at certain times. If Peter respected company rules about such things as lunch hours, I would know exactly when Peter would be back from lunch and I could ask the customer to come by at a certain time.

Peter was more likely to feel that spending time and energy learning unimportant rules would interfere with his creativity and productivity.

Masculinity-Femininity

The fourth factor to be considered in this discussion of work values is known as *masculinity-femininity* (Hofstede, 1996). As will be discussed more fully in chapter 9, some gender differences are found in all societies (Buss & Kenrick, 1998). Two are that men are more aggressive and women are more concerned with relationships. When applied to work values, "masculinity" leads to assertiveness, competitiveness, and a tough approach to decision making that sometimes downplays the feelings of people affected by the decision. "Femininity" leads to a desire for cooperative and pleasant coworkers, good working conditions, and a "tender" approach to decision making that takes people's feelings into account. It is important to keep in mind that "masculinity-femininity" represents a continuum rather than a statement about exact opposites. The norm in some societies is that masculine approaches are considered more effective, and the norm in others is that feminine approaches are preferred. Many societies, however, recognize the value of both and consequently have work norms that represent combinations of masculine and feminine approaches.

As with the other factors under discussion, the distinction between masculinity and femininity refers to the amount of attention people give to different values when making decisions about important behaviors in the workplace (Earley, 1997; Hofstede, 1996). Child care provides a good example. Women and not men can bear children. This fact means that all societies have to consider policies such as women's leave from the workplace for a period before and after childbirth. Differences appear in the number of policies designed to help women. Differences among countries include the amount of guaranteed leave time, the relative assurance given to women that their jobs will be waiting for them when they return, the amount of government-sponsored child care, and whether or not husbands can have paid leave so that they can help with the newly arrived baby. Countries with many such policies that recognize the importance of women are considered feminine. Examples are the Scandinavian countries, where government policies ease women's burdens of leaving their job, bearing a child, and returning to work (Yuchtman-Yaar & Gottlieb, 1985).

In feminine countries, people consider important the many roles women can play. Consequently, they attend to women's special needs (such as the stresses and events surrounding childbirth). Another way to look at masculinity-femininity is to assess relative power. In feminine societies, men and women are more likely to share power. Therefore, women develop an effective political voice and can insist that political leaders hear their concerns. As a result, the likelihood is greater in feminine countries that people will establish policies to meet women's needs. Masculine countries are less likely to favor such policies given that women have not attained positions that allow government officials, executives, and other leaders in society to hear their requests.

In masculine societies, most workers with responsible positions are men, so their preferences about what happens in the workplace are given more weight than those of women. As a result, the goals men have in the workplace are likely to be the goals all workers pursue. Even if some workers would prefer other goals, they learn what goals power holders prefer, what rewards are available, how to attain those rewards, and so forth. If they are to retain their jobs and prosper, they have to adapt to the goals power holders prefer. In masculine societies such as Japan, Venezuela, and Italy, worker goals include job advancement, increased earnings, training, and opportunities to remain current in their specialities. I have called these the traditional goals in a masculine society (Brislin, 1984) because men long have preferred them given their breadwinner role. My use of the word *traditional* reminds people that as women in various countries increasingly assume responsible positions and assume or share the breadwinner role, these goals will change. Some changes will involve movement toward the feminine direction. Feminine societies have work goals that reflect their traditional preferences, given women's long-term influence and the value placed on their work. These goals include a friendly work atmosphere, position security, good physical conditions in the workplace, positive relations with supervisors, and cooperative relations with coworkers. Most of these goals are clearly related to the traditional female concern about positive relations with other people (Deaux & LaFrance, 1998).

Japan is a highly masculine country according to the criteria discussed here (Hofstede, 1980), and it is higher than the United States. This means predictions can be made about worker preferences in the two countries. Loscocco and Kalleberg (1988) analyzed work values and work commitment in the United States and Japan. One prediction from an understanding of cultural differences in worker values is that as workers become older, work will play a more central part in their lives if they live in masculine countries. Older workers, then, are more likely to achieve the masculine values of advancement, increased earnings, and modernity. These older workers (see chapter 4), researchers suggested, will be responsible for socializing younger colleagues into an acceptance of these values. As predicted, older workers in Japan were more committed to their work than were younger workers. The researchers suggested that seniority was a major reason. Promotions are based on seniority, and thus older workers most likely held the positions offering the masculine rewards.

One interesting finding may have implications for the future. Among the masculine values, younger Japanese workers expressed an interest in greater pay. This may reflect their desire to have more everyday comforts (good housing, entertainment, playgrounds for children) than their parents and grandparents expected after the World War II devastation. Loscocco and Kalleberg (1988) speculated on the implications of this concern for greater earnings among younger Japanese workers. "If this trend continues, the frugal and self-sacrificing Japanese employee may disappear entirely, with potentially severe consequences for the Japanese economy" (pp. 352–353). The researchers also found that young Japanese women are desirous of more pay, and this suggests that women will become increasingly demanding of equal treatment in the business world.

Although future changes in the treatment of women are likely in Japan, today it is a highly masculine society with men holding power. The lack of opportunities for women to achieve high-level leadership positions is a feature of Japanese society frequently underdiscussed in books about Japan as a world power and Japan as a major influence on American business (e.g., DeMente, 1989; Katz & Friedman-Lichtschein, 1985; Reed, 1993).

Returning to the case study, recall that in Japan Peter tried to arrange luncheon groups composed of both men and women. He was disappointed to find that this simply was not done in the company where he worked. Given the strong distinction between men as power holders and women as employees, the Japanese are far more accustomed to forming luncheon groups based on gender than are Americans. The men undoubtedly discuss business, and the women would be uncomfortable trying to participate because they do not have access to the same information about current business opportunities that would have been shared among the men. Peter did not come from a society where men and women share power equally, but he was from a country far less masculine than Japan. Peter was familiar with the fact opportunities for women have broadened in the United States over the past 50 years, and he was familiar with luncheon groups composed of both men and women. One of the reasons for his difficulties is that he had not recognized the greater masculinity of the Japanese workplace.

Confucian Dynamism

The fifth factor that influences workplace behavior is based on research carried out subsequent to the development of the first four factors (Cheung & Leung, 1998; Chinese Culture Connection, 1987; Hofstede & Bond, 1988). Called *Confucian dynamism*, this factor emerged from efforts to explain the startling economic growth of some of the Asian nations since about 1970. These countries include Japan, South Korea, Taiwan, Hong Kong, and Singapore (sometimes called the "five dragons"). If readers of this book examine their recent purchases, they almost surely have acquired products made in one or more of these countries. As guidelines, consider recent purchases of automobiles, clothing, toys, and electronic products. The changes in the quality of products from these countries has been enormous. During my elementary school years (the 1950s), students gave a product "made in Japan" only as a booby prize for the worst performance in a spelling bee, dance contest, or athletic event. The term "made in Japan" was a synonym for something cheap and shabby. Times do change. Now, people look to Japan for high-quality products such as videocassette recorders and cameras that they expect to stay out of the repair shop.

Several scholars have pointed to the influence of Confucian thought in Asia as one reason for increased economic development (Bond, 1986; Fang, 1998; Kahn, 1979). Kong Fu Ze was a high-ranking civil servant in China around the time of 500 B.C. Jesuit missionaries later changed his name to Confucius because the syllables in this name were easier for them to pronounce. He was a teacher rather than a religious figure, and he developed a set of practical ethical guidelines to guide everyday behavior. He attracted a large number of pupils, and these disciples recorded his teachings (much like the students of Socrates recorded his contributions). Some key principles of Confucian thought (Hofstede & Bond, 1988) follow:

1. *Unequal-status relationships lead to a stable society.* Confucius was not referring to master-slave or tyrant–submissive servant relations. Rather, he was

referring to such relations as the ruler-subject, father-son, or older brother–younger brother relations. Each of these relationships involves mutual obligations. For instance, the younger or less powerful person owes the senior person respect and obedience. The older or powerful person owes the junior person protection and consideration. A Chinese scholar (Wang Gung Wu) once told me that the senior-to-junior obligation can take interesting and important specific forms in some Chinese families. If a young 25-year-old wants to start a business, the youth can approach elders (father, uncles, older brothers) and ask for investments. If the business fails, the youth can expect the elders to bail him or her out and to find money to start a second business. The assumption is that the youth will have learned enough from mistakes to have a far greater chance of success with the second venture. If the second business fails, the elders will not be expected to find money for a third venture, but they will try to find a place for the youth somewhere in one of the businesses the family administers. The important point is that the youth can depend on certain obligations the seniors have. Especially during the development of the first business venture, it must be very comforting to know that elders will put up money for a second chance if the first venture fails.

2. *The family is typical of all social organizations.* A person is not socialized to view himself or herself as an individual. Rather, he or she must find identity as a group member, and the first group is the family (recall the discussion of collectivism in chapter 2). It is important to maintain harmony in the family so that it does not disintegrate into a bickering set of individuals. One way to do this is to maintain one's own and others' face, in other words, their dignity, self-respect, and prestige (Earley, 1997). Family members do not disagree with an elder in public; that would cause the elder to lose face. A young woman does not date a man who has not earned the family's approval. That would cause the family to lose face, and it also would cause the woman to lose face in the wider community where the family lives. People "give face" by showing their respect for others.

3. *Virtue in life consists of working hard, of acquiring useful skills and as much education as possible, of not being a spendthrift, and of persevering when faced with difficult tasks.* Acquiring an education, working hard, and developing a reputation for perseverance allow people to take responsible positions in society that can benefit their families. Further, if they are not excessive in their spending, they will have money to invest when they are older and are asked to assume the obligations of senior people in their families (see point number 1).

To test the possibility that acceptance of Confucian teachings affects economic growth in a country, a group of scholars led by Michael Bond formed a group called The Chinese Culture Connection and published some of the results under that title (Chinese Culture Connection, 1987; see also Cheung & Leung, 1998; Hofstede, 1991; Hofstede & Bond, 1988). The researchers began by asking numerous Chinese scholars to list values children are expected to learn during their socialization (chapter 4). This information was collected in the Chinese language and later translated into the English-language summaries paraphrased here. The research findings are complex, but one of the most important results was that the teachings of Confucius could be readily identified in the values the researchers identified. Research among respondents in 22 countries showed that people in some countries are more likely to be socialized with these values than are people in others. Further, respondents in four Asian countries where recent economic growth has increased scored at the top of the scale that measured value acceptance. These countries were Hong Kong, Taiwan, Japan, and South Korea, with the fifth of the five dragons (Singapore) 8th on the list of 22 countries.

The researchers labeled the set of values "Confucian dynamism." The "Confucian" aspect of the label is due to the fact that all of the values can be identified as the teachings of Confucius. The "dynamism" is due to the fact that greater emphasis is placed on some of the teachings compared to others. The following lists make this distinction. The first includes aspects of Confucianism that people in the economically successful countries emphasized relative to other aspects. The second list includes Confucian teachings that people in the economically successful countries downplayed relative to the teachings on the first list. Confucian dynamism, then, is said to place relative emphasis on these values:

Persistence and perseverance
Ordering relationships by status and observing this order
Thrift
Having a sense of shame

Confucian dynamism recognizes that the following four values exist but places relatively less emphasis on them:

Personal steadiness and stability
Protecting face
Respect for tradition
Reciprocation of greetings, favors, and gifts

This important pattern of what is emphasized and what is less emphasized needs further discussion. Keep in mind that the Chinese Culture Connection (1987) group chose to use the term *dynamic* when interpreting the pattern.

Although no interpretation is perfectly clear, most of the pattern can be understood by referring to the importance of "the future" and "hard work." The general interpretation, then, is that countries influenced by the teachings of Confucius emphasize different aspects of those teachings. Countries that emphasize the dynamic aspects involving the future and the importance of hard work have experienced economic growth in recent years. The first four emphasized aspects listed earlier reveal the concern with the future and with hard work. Persistence and perseverance are important when people face difficulties on the job. Rather than give up, people with these values will continue their efforts (Si, Rethorst, & Willimczik, 1995). At times, these efforts will involve bringing in the expertise of others (Rothbaum & Xu, 1995). If people respect the status and contributions of others (part of the "ordering relationships" concept in the list) and if the individuals consulted feel they have obligations to help as much as possible, then people's chances of solving problems increases. If people are thrifty, they will have money to invest in new businesses. Economists examining the amount of capital available for investment in various countries "have been struck by the high savings quotas in the Five Dragon countries" (Hofstede & Bond, 1988, p. 18). If people have a sense of shame, they will become upset with themselves if they do not work hard and if they do not contribute to group efforts. They also will be upset at themselves if they do not develop the expertise and savings that will allow them to fulfill their eventual obligations as elders in their groups.

As noted, countries that have experienced recent economic success place relatively less emphasis on the four other aspects of Confucian teachings listed earlier. The clearest is respect for tradition. An overemphasis on this aspect would prevent dynamic ventures aimed at future prosperity. Similarly, valuing personal steadiness and stability also can prevent actions that will be useful for the future. For example, people can be steady and stable with their excellent mathematical skills, and they may be able to demonstrate their competencies with paper and pencils, an abacus, or a small calculator. But this steadiness can prevent them from developing skills useful in a fast-moving economy, such as operating high-speed computers and telecommunications technology. People who are too stable also may be unwilling to take risks, and risks always will be part of any new business venture. If people are busy protecting their face, they will be spending time and energy on matters that may be relatively unimportant for future business success. Here it is useful to remember the interpretation involves a dynamic viewpoint. People may become upset if they feel they are losing face but, emphasizing the other values, may decide the best use of their time and energy may be to set their feelings aside and to contribute to efforts that will result in group prosperity. The final underemphasized aspect involves the reciprocation of greetings, favors, and gifts. The argument that these are not dynamic aspects of Confucian thinking is similar to that for saving face. If people put time and effort into reciprocating greetings and gifts, then they may be too concerned with the recent past (e.g., an uncle's gift two weeks ago) and with the present (e.g., the way people greet one another currently) to accomplish their work efficiently and to focus on the future. As Hofstede and Bond (1988) put it, the type of reciprocation under discussion here "is a social activity more concerned with good manners than with performance" (p. 18) that if underemphasized can lead to productivity in the workplace.

In everyday terms, Confucian dynamism involves choosing from an array of philosophical principles. This type of selectivity is not uncommon and is not limited to Confucianism. Christians are exposed to numerous principles: "love thy neighbor as thyself," "honor thy father and thy mother," "keep holy the Lord's day," "when insulted, turn the other cheek," "thou shalt not commit adultery," and so forth. Christians are familiar with all these principles, but many choose to emphasize some and to deemphasize others.

Further insights into the case study presented at the beginning of this chapter can be suggested. Japan is higher on the Confucian dynamism factor than is the United States. Peter Reed enjoyed working on a number of problems simultaneously. If he had difficulties with one, he would put it aside and work on another. This might have interfered with Watanabe's preference for persistence and perseverance, which Peter could have shown more easily if he had worked on one problem at a time. From Watanabe's perspective, Peter's work style could have come across as flippant. In addition, Peter was not "ordering relationships" according to the ideal of Confucian dynamism. From Watanabe's perspective, Peter should have found out the expertise and potential contributions of his coworkers. (He could have done this during lunch hours, but he frequently kept to himself!) Then, he should have shown respect to the coworkers and asked them to help him solve the problems he was encountering. Realizing they would be making contributions to a group effort, the coworkers would be likely to help as much as they could.

Confucian dynamism is probably the most difficult of the five work-value concepts for most readers to understand. This is not accidental: As discussed in chapter 2, the emic aspects of complex concepts are the hardest to understand. The other four concepts involve etic or culturally general concepts readers can relate to easily. Most readers have been torn between putting time and effort into their own goals and compromising so that a group effort could take place (individualism versus collectivism). Most readers have had a boss who did not participate much in informal activities with coworkers and who would be displeased if they attempted to establish a close relationship that involved use of first names (power distance). Many readers are familiar with institutions that have multiple rules and regulations and with others that have far fewer rules (uncertainty avoidance). Perhaps some readers have talked with friends who have gone to different schools. Some schools are noted for their many required courses students must take to graduate. Other schools are noted for their absence of required courses and their encouragement of students who want to develop their own undergraduate majors. Some readers will be familiar with enough different institutions and organizations to distinguish those where workers value good pay and advancement opportunities more than pleasant relations with coworkers (masculinity-femininity).

Confucian dynamism, in contrast, will be far more familiar to readers who are from or who have lived extensively in Asia. Among North Americans, for instance, not as many links occur between behaviors they are familiar with and the teachings of Confucius. This absence of links is often a sign that the concepts involved are emic (chapter 2) and that they will demand more study until they become familiar. One of the less familiar aspects of Confucian dynamism involves the obligations elders and leaders have to younger people who show respect. Understanding these obligations is important in the analysis of leadership in the intercultural workplace.

When I introduced this discussion on Confucian dynamism, I made a reference to economic growth in Asia. In the late 1990s, recessions in Asia began to occur (Ching, 1998; Krugman, 1997), with subsequent impacts such as bankruptcies, layoffs of workers, and difficult job markets for college graduates. Do problems arise, then, with the concept known as Confucian dynamism? Much can be said, and only a few points can be made here. One possibility is that in the late 1990s, Asian economies experienced downswings in the inevitability known as "the business cycle" (Thurow, 1996). In the 1980s and early 1990s, products were manufactured, consumers bought them, and economies prospered. But a time arrives when consumers have enough of a product. Airline companies have enough jet planes, companies have enough computers for their employees, and men and women have enough business suits. Consumers purchase less, leading to less manufacturing, and this in turn has a major impact on economies. After a period of time, consumer demand will increase again as the jets become old, the computers become outdated, and the suits become tattered and out of style. After the year 2000, then, newspaper headlines could be calling attention to "Economic Recovery in Asia."

Some researchers have analyzed how cultural values and economic problems interact. One analysis relates to a problem with collectivism. If people are collective members, it means they should look after one another. If they have investment possibilities, they might bring these to the attention of friends rather than to cautious investors who want evidence of careful money management and risk assessment. But favoring friends can lead to the careless "crony capitalism" that has been criticized as one reason for recent economic difficulties. Another reason relates to an aspect of Confucian dynamism discussed earlier. Thrift is a valuable Asian cultural trait. If people save money, then banks have money to lend. But when newspapers report economic troubles, many Asians start saving more! This means they are not purchasing various products and so are not helping stimulate their country's economy. If the business cycle swings up, leading to more positive media treatment of the economy, consumer spending should increase.

LEADERSHIP

Researchers attempt to identify the most important aspects of behavior in the workplace, and few topics have received more attention than leadership (Bass, 1997; Bass & Stogdill, 1990; Hollander, 1985; Muchinsky, 1996). Leadership has been studied both in highly industrialized nations and in countries undergoing recent economic development (Ayman & Chemers, 1983; Hughes, Ginnett, & Curphy, 1996; Ling, 1989; Sullivan, Suzuki, & Kondo, 1986). One way to approach the topic is to analyze some basic findings from work in North America and Europe, where a long tradition of research on leadership exists. Then, this discussion can move into the more recent cross-cultural literature and ask, "What more needs to be known to understand leadership as it is practiced outside North America and Europe?"

Good summaries exist of leadership research carried out in highly industrialized nations (Bass & Stogdill, 1990; Hollander, 1985; Hughes et al., 1996). Considering the many definitions of leadership suggested for 60 years, Hollander finds that "influence" is one of the most frequently mentioned leadership characteristics. Leadership involves people who influence others to act in certain ways so that goals are attained. Applying this insight to the workplace, Saal and Knight (1988) proposed this definition: "Leadership is social influence in an organizational setting, the effects of which are relevant to, or have an impact on, the achievement of organizational goals"(p. 336).

The emphases in this definition are influence, achievement, and goals. Even if they accept this general definition, researchers disagree about what leadership aspects are most important. Muchinsky (1996) lists six different leadership aspects, and one or more of them could be the focus of a research study. The six, all of which will be discussed, follow:

1. Power and influence
2. The traits of leaders

3. The study of followers of certain leaders

4. The mutual influences of leaders and followers

5. The influence of the social setting on leaders and followers

6. The emergence of leaders, especially when people are given overseas business as-signments in cultures other than their own

Leadership and Power

The first aspect of leadership Muchinsky (1996) identified involves power. If leaders can influence others, they must be sensitive to the nature of power. They must decide whether to emphasize the rewards and punishments they have control over or whether to appeal to their good relations with followers and put their efforts into persuasion rather than coercion. Leaders also must decide what sort of strategies and tactics to use (Brislin, 1991; Greenberg & Baron, 1997). In a study comparing Brazilian and American managers, for instance, Rossi & Todd-Mancillas (1987) found differences in how managers tried to settle disputes among company person-nel. Brazilian male managers were likely to use the strategy of exercising their power and authority and to give orders. American managers were more likely to use the strategy of communicating with and negotiating among the various parties who had an interest in the dispute. The researchers suggested that the cultural value of "ma-chismo" is more prevalent in Brazil than in the United States and that it could be in-fluencing the preferred management style among Brazilians. People socialized into the value of machismo learn to engage in traditionally masculine behaviors, such as showing strength, never showing weakness, and never showing doubt about their decisions.

The Traits of Leaders

Another approach to the study of leadership involves examining the traits leaders have (item 2 in list). This is one of the oldest ways to analyze leadership, and it is probably the first aspect that comes to mind when people are asked, "What makes a good leader?" They think of a leader's traits, such as confidence, dominance, ability to analyze problems, and so forth. Although it attracts extensive attention from re-searchers, the trait approach has not led to a full understanding of leadership (Bass, 1997; Bass & Stogdill, 1990). One reason is that it gives too little attention to the context where leaders behave. Still, the trait approach always will be part of leader-ship research, and it will be referred to again later in this chapter when the traits of preferred leaders in India are reviewed.

Context: Followers and Mutual Influence

Realizing that emphasizing traits ignores the context where leaders behave, re-searchers looked for other approaches that take context into account. One of the important lessons of cross-cultural research long has been, "Behavior must be under-stood in its context." This has been a major theme in this book. Chapter 5 (on for-mal educational programs), for instance, reviewed research showing that changing the context led to changes in student achievement. If the classroom context was changed to incorporate activities familiar to children (e.g., telling stories to one another), achievement in reading increased. Much of chapter 7 (on intercultural communication) dealt with how people might be encouraged to understand the contexts they encounter. If students from Japan take a small seminar in the United States, this may be an unfamiliar context for them if they are accustomed only to large classes where the professors lecture. Behaviors occur in this new context that the Japanese students would be wise to rehearse.

Applied to the study of leadership, four approaches (of the six Muchinsky, 1996, identified) deal explicitly with context. Current approaches to the study of leadership emphasize that the people who are led are as important as the leader (item 3). What do employees prefer from their supervisors? An example of this concern was reviewed earlier in this chapter. British workers, concerned with protecting themselves from the power of managers, were less accepting of direct feedback about their work (Earley & Stubblebine, 1989). Another part of the context in which leaders and followers communicate includes the nature of their interaction and mutual influence (item 4). Leaders do not simply communicate their preferences, and followers do not simply choose either to comply with the preferences or to ignore them (Bhawuk, 1997). Rather, leaders and followers interact, communicate, and negotiate over a long period (Hui & Luk, 1997; Tsang, 1998).

In some organizations, the interaction and communication lead to effectiveness and productivity. In Japan, workers and managers cooperate through participation in "quality circles." All people who have suggestions about the betterment of the workplace and the products the company manufactures are encouraged to share their ideas. Workers, over several years, learn how to give their suggestions without causing anyone to lose face. When they make suggestions in a respectful manner, the managers are not upset and threatened. The use of quality-control circles is frequently cited as one reason for the reliability of Japanese consumer products (Bocker & Overgaard, 1982; Ferris & Wagner, 1985; Hui & Luk, 1997). Who knows more about making good products than the people "on the line" doing the wiring, assembling, and inspecting? If their suggestions for improvement can be integrated, product quality should improve. Note that an analysis of quality circles is far different from an analysis of "leaders give orders, and others follow them." Rather, quality circles are an example of how communication and interaction among leaders and followers can lead to improvements in an organization.

Situational Descriptors

Some researchers have attempted to analyze directly the various situations in which leaders find themselves (item 5), testing the general hypothesis that people will be more effective leaders in some situations compared to others. Consider situations involving time pressures. Readers might think of people they know who fit each of two situations. If people have time pressures to complete a task (say, organizing the efforts of 15 diverse individuals into an effective fund-raising group within a week), do certain potential leaders come to mind? If the situation is changed so that the organizing can take place over a three-month period, do other potential leaders come to mind? If readers can imagine that some people will perform better under time pressures and that others will perform better when more time is available for planning and organizing, then they are sensitive to situational differences.

One approach to analyzing situations is to describe their characteristics, much like people describe the characteristics of others (Detweiler, Brislin, & McCormack, 1983). When the characteristics of people are described, terms such as *aggressive*, *dominant*, and *friendly* might be used. Although people probably do not think about situations quite as often, they could describe key characteristics of situations in similar ways. For example, some situations involve "time pressures" and some do not. Some situations (e.g., small seminars in college) call for "active participation" and others (large lectures) do not. Some situations have lots of rules and others do not. As previously discussed when research on uncertainty avoidance was reviewed, the workplace in Japan has more rules people are expected to follow. What might seem to a casual observer as similar situations, people designing computer software in an American and in a Japanese company, are quite different. The distinction between the two involves the number of rules (Henderson & Argyle, 1986), many of them not written down and consequently hard for outsiders to learn.

The best known theory of leadership that has explicitly examined situational variables was designed by Fred Fiedler (Fiedler, 1967; Fiedler & Garcia, 1987; reviews by Dorfman, 1996; Greenberg & Baron, 1997). Three situational variables are central to the theory: whether leader-follower relations are good or bad; the amount of structure in the group tasks; and the amount of power the leader has. The most favorable set of situations for the leader are when relations among people are good, when the task is structured, and when the power the leader possesses is high. In the computer software company example, leaders will be in favorable situations when workers like and can cooperate with one another. The situations leaders face will be even more favorable when high task structure exists and when they have high position power. For example, making corrections to remove the known "bugs" from a word processing program is a more structured task than designing a new program that will compete well in the marketplace. Leaders who have the power to hire and to fire, to give raises, and to assign desirable tasks to selected workers will be in more favorable situations from their viewpoint.

It is important to keep in mind that the three factors describe situational favorability for leaders. Followers may have other preferences, as cross-cultural research has shown. Workers in various countries have preferences that focus on different emphases in their work. Although good leader-worker relations are undoubtedly welcome in organizations in all countries, research has indicated that this situational factor is more important for Americans than for Germans (Friday, 1989). Americans desire work situations where they can develop good relationships with coworkers so that others like them. Germans are more tolerant of work groups whose members are efficient and hard working, but they do not expect friendliness to the degree Americans do. The desire for Americans to be liked by others has been frequently noted by researchers who study intercultural communication difficulties.

> The American's need to be liked is a primary aspect of his or her motivation to cooperate or not to cooperate with colleagues. . . . For Americans, the almost immediate and informal use of a colleague's first name is a recognition that each likes the other. While such informality is common among American business

personnel, this custom should probably be avoided with Germans." (Friday, 1989, p. 432)

Another situational factor about which workers have different preferences is the amount of power leaders have. Within their work groups, the Japanese prefer a high-status, powerful leader (Nakao, 1987). Americans prefer a leader who is closer in status to the other workers. Americans long have distrusted people who have too much power. The Constitution of the United States was written so that the president would not have excessive power (the possibility of a king was dismissed!) and so that any one part of government would have checks and balances on its use of power (Collier & Collier, 1986). When American workers are promoted to leadership positions, much of the advice they receive consists of how not to abuse the power they have been given (Brislin, 1991).

The Emergence of Leaders

The sixth approach to leadership Muchinsky (1996) identified deals with how people develop their leadership skills and how they become recognized as leaders by others. This dynamic aspect of leadership is especially important in international business ventures (Dorfman, 1996; Mendenhall & Oddou, 1985). Many people attempt to establish various cooperative business arrangements in other countries (Adler, 1997; Tung & Miller, 1990). One approach to developing these arrangements is for people from one country to accept long-term employment in another. For example, American managers might accept employment in Japan, Korea, or Sweden. A question centering on the dynamics of leadership is "Who becomes accepted as leaders by coworkers in the host country?" In the examples introduced here, the question becomes, "Which Americans will emerge as leaders in Japan, Korea, or Sweden from the viewpoint of coworkers in those countries?"

A general prediction is that when managers from one country can modify their behavior to meet the expectations of individuals in another country, they are more likely to be treated as leaders. In a study of American managers working in Korea, Lee and Larwood (1983) found that this general prediction was supported. In this study, the more the Americans adopted attitudes and behaviors that were sympathetic toward Korean culture, the more the Koreans accepted them. In addition, the Americans' job satisfaction increased as they adopted respectful attitudes toward Korea. Considering the case of individualists working in a collective country such as Korea, Triandis, Brislin, and Hui (1988) gave recommendations for such respectful attitudes and behaviors. In the workplace, they would include more incorporation of employees in the decision-making process, a greater sensitivity to the views of high-level executives, emphasizing cooperation and harmony, and cultivating long-term relations that will exist after the individualists return to their own country.

LEADERSHIP CONCERNS COMMON IN ASIA

The importance of encouraging long-term relations to exist after individuals cease employment with one company and join another is more familiar to people in collective cultures. Consequently, people from individualist cultures will have to spend extra time and energy understanding the importance of this concern if they are to succeed on a business assignment in a collective culture. Another important concern (Weiming Tu, 1989) more familiar to people in collective cultures is that the leader has obligations to his or her employees. That is, in exchange for their respect, employees have the right to expect a leader to look after their interests, to provide opportunities for them to advance, and to help them out in times of difficulty. Although people in individualist countries welcome such leaders, they don't necessarily expect to always find them. Take Americans. People in this highly individualist country do not view leaders as having obligations to behave in certain ways that benefit employees. In one study (summarized by Freiberg, 1991), Americans were satisfied if their leaders were merely competent. "It's no secret that bosses are unpopular with their employees. But what hasn't been realized, according to a recent two-year study, is that employees have good reason to dislike them: Most managers are incompetent and are the prime source of job stress" (p. 23).

The concept that supervisors have obligations to act as effective leaders is part of many research treatments of leadership in Asia (Bigones & Blakely, 1996; Casimir & Keats, 1996; Hui, 1990; Kumar & Saxena, 1983; Misumi, 1985). Kumar and Saxena explain what leaders are expected to do in different contexts, thus exemplifying several of the six approaches to leadership already reviewed (Muchinsky, 1996). Although Kumar and Saxena's explanations were developed to explain leadership behavior in India, the descriptions are useful for analyzing supervisor-employee relations throughout Asia. To understand leadership in India, people must understand people's sense of family identification and sense of obligation. Most leaders in India are men, so some of the language used to describe leaders (e.g., paternal, authoritative) is masculine rather than feminine or gender neutral. Cultural differences in Asian leadership can be introduced by considering a conversation between a boss and his female employee. The boss calls the employee into his office.

BOSS: I'd like to discuss an issue with you. How long have you been working in my section of the company?

FEMALE EMPLOYEE: About five years.

BOSS: And I've always been happy with your work. However, something is wrong. You're about 28 years old now and are not married, and I think that it's time you meet some eligible men. There's a young man in the accounting department who seems very hard working. I will arrange a lunch for four people: you, me, him, and his boss.

FEMALE EMPLOYEE: Thank you for your concern.

Could this conversation occur in the United States? Probably not very often. In fact, the boss might face charges based on the "hostile work environment" clause that is part of the sexual harassment codes many companies have adopted. But the conversation could take place in many Asian countries. To understand this conversation (which occurs frequently, because the workplace often provides the meeting place for eligible men and women), people need to understand the viewpoints of leaders and their employees. As mentioned, two concepts (Kumar & Saxena, 1983; see

Bosses in some cultures are asked to give advice about highly personal matters.

also Casimir & Keats, 1996) are especially important: a sense of family identification and a sense of obligation.

Sense of Family Identification

Some leaders in Asia view their employees as a group much like their family, and this is called the "own family" identification. With this view, leaders show concern for their employees much as a father shows concern for his children. Leaders nurture their followers, exercise their authority in a responsible manner, and behave in a warm, caring manner. So, just as a father is concerned about his daughter's marriage, a boss is concerned that his employees marry well. Some contexts in Asia, however, prevent this sense of family identification, especially very large organizations where executives cannot even know the names of all the people who work for them. Here, the view leaders take is called "other family." The workers are certainly part of the leader's thinking, but the sense of kinship or sense of belonging is not there as it is in the "own family" identification.

Sense of Obligation

As previously discussed, once leaders in Asia accept their high-status positions, they have obligations toward followers. The obligations include addressing employees' needs and taking an interest in their personal lives. Depending on the situation, the obligations can be either "personal" or "impersonal." When obligations are personal, the leader first develops expectations of what specific and known others can offer to the organization. For example, the leader learns that specific people, who become well known, can offer their enthusiasm, their skills, and their loyalty (Bhawuk, 1997; Lincoln, 1985). In return, the leader behaves according to the specific and personalized expectations those employees develop during their tenure with the organization. Leaders and followers, then, have debts to each other. "This indebtedness legitimizes a highly personalized [sense of] ethics in relationships" (Kumar & Saxena, 1983, p. 357).

This acceptance of personal relations with employees contrasts sharply with a more impersonal set of obligations some leaders are forced to accept in Asia. One reason, again, is the company's size, but another is the competitiveness of the industry. In highly competitive, fast-moving industries, such as the development of robots, employees have to be shifted quickly from task to task so that any one company maintains its competitive edge. Even though a given set of employees may enjoy interacting with their current work group, the leaders may have to break up this group and assign the workers to provide on-the-job training for newly hired personnel. The nature of the industry can encourage a more impersonal style if leaders have to keep "industrial competitiveness" foremost in their minds. Rather than internalizing and accepting a set of obligations, leaders in Asia who act according to the impersonal orientation behave out of a sense of duty. They learn what tradition dictates (e.g., salary increases, vacation time, job security) and then discharge their duty to lead their employees. They do so, however, without a sense of emotional interrelatedness with their workers.

Expectations About Leadership: Cultural Differences

Another short case study may make some of these concepts clearer. George Jackson is a midlevel manager in the petrochemical industry, and he has been assigned to a two-year sojourn at the company's branch plant in India. Within his home country, the United States, George has a good reputation as a manager and leader. His employees felt he was fair in his dealings, accepted suggestions well, encouraged a cooperative atmosphere in the workplace, and "knew his stuff" when it came to petrochemicals.

Sudesh Kumar was one of the Indian citizens on George Jackson's staff overseas. As assistant manager for fiscal affairs, she reported directly to George. For the first six months of George's sojourn in India, his relations with Sudesh were much like those between a leader and employee in the United States. George found that Sudesh was a competent worker, cooperated well with others, and contributed to a pleasant work environment. George accepted an invitation from Sudesh and her family to attend a birthday party for her 6-year-old son and had a good time at the party. Sudesh's son enjoyed the present George brought, a large plastic figure of a cartoon hero, because he had seen it on television but had never seen it in the stores.

One day, Sudesh asked George for an appointment to discuss some of her concerns. Because Sudesh obviously had been very busy recently with paperwork related to company finances, George thought the meeting was to deal with Sudesh's suggestions for handling the workload. But once the meeting started, George realized that all of Sudesh's concerns dealt with her personal life. She told of troubles with her marriage, her suspicions about the faithfulness of her husband, the stress her suspicions were causing her, her concern that she was not being a good mother to her son given the pressures of her job, and other problems involving her extended family. She asked for George's advice about exactly what she should do, especially about her husband. George was very uncomfortable with the discussion. He was familiar with giving advice to employees about work-related matters and considered himself quite good at this aspect of his job. He also was familiar with sharing certain types of information that touched on his employees' personal lives, such as the names of good schools in the community where parents might send their children, but he had never had discussions of the type Sudesh desired. In fact, he was hesitant to discuss issues such as the husband's possible unfaithfulness because company policies he was familiar with (in his own country) discouraged supervisors' involvement in the personal lives of employees.

After Sudesh finished the discussion of her problems, George tried to express his concern and his sympathy. Because he was not prepared for such a personal conversation, however, he could not make any specific suggestions. Recognizing George's discomfort, Sudesh mentioned that they perhaps could meet again at a later date, but she was puzzled at George's unwillingness to make specific recommendations about exactly what she should do. What cultural differences might explain the reasons for this unsuccessful meeting?

The Paternal-Authoritative Leader

Sudesh has expectations about what leaders should do that are distinctly different from the behaviors familiar to George. Following the concepts Kumar and Saxena (1983) suggest, Sudesh prefers a leader who has a sense that workers are part of his "own family" and a sense that his obligations are "personal." Sudesh expects a male leader to behave much like a father and to treat her in a way that takes her special, personal needs into account. A father should be concerned that his daughter suspects her husband is unfaithful. The father should take concrete action! And the concern should be personal and should be different from the concern that he would show to any employee in the workplace. Didn't George enjoy himself at the birthday party and go to the trouble of obtaining a gift that is generally unavailable in India? This showed his personal concern for Sudesh and her family, so she expected a continuation of this personal concern when she had difficulties to discuss with him. Similarly, the woman who learned that she will be attending a lunch to meet an eligible man appreciated her boss's efforts. By commenting on her lack of a husband at 28 years of age, the boss was showing his personal interest and concern.

The leadership style many Indians and other Asians prefer and expect (Kumar & Saxena, 1983; J. Sinha, 1980) can be called "paternal authoritativeness." The words are carefully chosen. "Paternal" captures the expectations of concern and nurturance and the belief that employees should be treated like the leader's own family members (Janssens, Brett, & Smith, 1995). "Authoritativeness" captures the expectations that leaders should know what to do in a wide variety of situations. Note that the word is not *authoritarian*: That word would have the additional implications that people must behave in the way leaders demand or else face negative consequences. Recognizing "authoritativeness" means employees are willing to defer to leaders because the leaders are experts and are obliged to give good advice. With the expectation that the leader treat workers like family members, people do not make the sharp distinction between their personal lives at home and the hours they spend at work. George is much more comfortable with a leadership style that involves expertise in the workplace but respect for the privacy of employees' lives once they go home.

The Impersonal–Other Family Orientation

When the two concepts discussed here are combined, the leadership style that contrasts most sharply with paternal authoritativeness might be called the "impersonal–other family orientation." The "impersonal" part of the style means that leaders act according to rules, to written and widely available guidelines, and to laws (e.g., that deal with collective bargaining, harassment in the workplace). As much as possible, the leaders should not behave according to any personal relationship they have with employees. Rather, they should treat employees equally.

Although this style may seem very cold and uncaring, it is meant to serve the needs of as many employees as possible. The style is more common in highly industrialized countries where companies are large and where leaders find it difficult to learn the personal needs of each employee (Hui & Luk, 1997). Readers may be able to appreciate the appropriateness of the impersonal style (in certain contexts) if they consider this example. Assume a professor sets an average score of 92 (out of 100) as the cutoff for a grade of A. Two students have average scores of 91.5. They visit the professor to see if they can persuade her to grant an A grade. If the professor had a personal approach to leadership as discussed here, she would consider her relationships with the two students. Perhaps one of them was a research assistant last semester who worked overtime but did not claim extra hours when submitting her pay sheet. Perhaps an A grade would be a recognition of this past work. But this can be seen as unfair to the second student who never had a chance to act as a research assistant. This second student would prefer a more impersonal style based on written guidelines and widely known precedents that ignore any special professor-student relationship. The second student would prefer considerations that focus on the class where the A or B grade will be given. Such considerations might be class participation, an extra-credit paper, or the regrading of an earlier paper so that a few extra points are granted. If the professor acts according to these more impersonal guidelines, neither student will be the beneficiary of favoritism based on a personal relationship.

When the "other family" aspect of this leadership style is added, it indicates that leaders will make sharp distinctions between their own family at home and their colleagues and employees in the workplace. Again, this movement away from feelings of closeness is more common in large companies. Even if they desire to develop a "family atmosphere" in the workplace, leaders with more than 100 employees will find it difficult to do so. If they attempt to create a family atmosphere in a large company, the danger is that some employees will be treated as in-group members and some will be treated as out-group members (Hui, 1990; terms also discussed in chapter 6). Tensions then would arise when some workers feel favored by the leaders compared to others who feel ignored. In the incident involving the two students who sought an A grade, the professor could treat them both warmly if they were attending a small college where small classes were the norm. "We encourage a family-like atmosphere" is a phrase administrators frequently use at small colleges. If the students were at a large state university, in contrast, the professor is more likely to behave in a cordial but proper manner with both. In large lecture classes, professors have to be careful about favoring some students because they might be accused of ignoring others. Given that the professors have so many students, they cannot become intimate friends with all of them, so they develop a more impersonal style and apply it to virtually all their students.

In the example involving George Jackson and Sudesh Kumar, a clash occurred between expectations about two quite different leadership styles. Sudesh expected to be treated much like a family member, and she expected George to take her personal needs into account. George preferred a more impersonal style of treating his many employees in as equal a manner as possible. Note that one person was not "right" and the other "wrong." Both leadership styles are appropriate in certain cultures and in certain contexts. I have been placed in situations similar to the one described in the example. I have worked at the East-West Center, an organization that sponsors hundreds of students and midcareer professionals each year as they pursue advanced degrees and research projects. When I have worked with graduate students from Nepal, India, Burma, or Thailand, I frequently have been asked about potential marriage partners, for directives (not advice!) about where to send children to school, for precise orders about topic choices for thesis research, and for specific recommendations for career development covering more than a 10-year period. I am uncomfortable giving such advice, but I realize that it is part of these students' expectations of what a leader does. Leaders who do not engage in such behaviors are considered unworthy of their position.

Compromises are sometimes possible. I personally have dealt with the request for paternal and authoritative advice by suggesting a range of possibilities. I suggest a range of good thesis topics; I introduce students to many members of the opposite sex; young professionals and I discuss various career goals and ways to attain them, and so forth. Because the graduate students and midcareer professionals who work with me are interested in culture and cultural differences, we can relate my recommendations to concepts such as individualism-collectivism and the preference for a paternal-authoritative leader. My work with these people, then, becomes specific examples of concepts they will need to know in their future work in intercultural and cross-cultural studies.

TRUST AND INTERCULTURAL INTERACTIONS

Willingness to make compromises, or movement toward behaviors all the people involved can accept as reasonable, is just one way to insure effective intercultural interactions. As I noted, some of my graduate students want very direct advice on thesis topics. Given that my position is at an American university and that they chose to study in America, I want them to choose their own topic. The compromise is that I suggest a range of important research areas and students can choose a specific topic from this range. I believe that one reason this approach has worked is that the students and I trust each other. They trust that I am looking out for their best interests. I trust that they want to engage in high-level research, rather than just do the minimal amount of work necessary to obtain a graduate degree.

One of the difficult realizations for all people who want to have effective and positive intercultural interactions is that people cannot know other cultures so well that they always will behave appropriately. Rather, people will make mistakes, will have misunderstandings, and will leave intercultural interactions with bad feelings about what occurred. Sometimes, they can understand the reasons if they examine cultural differences. Yet so many specific cultural differences exist that no one can be expected to know them all. One solution to this dilemma is for people to communicate that they can be trusted (Butler, 1991; Fukuyama, 1995; Johnson, Cullen, Sakano, & Takenouchi, 1996; Mayer, Davis, & Schoorman, 1995). In effect, they will be saying, "I realize that I cannot behave perfectly in all intercultural interactions. But I want to be respectful, I want to achieve mutual goals, and I want people to have positive feelings about my interactions with them. I want people to trust that our intercultural interactions will have these positive outcomes." In informal conversations with colleagues, I sometimes say that "trust can be a way of cutting through the fact that we can't know all cultural differences and that sometimes we will make mistakes."

People sometimes ask me this question: "You've written books on intercultural interactions. Do you sometimes get thrown by differences in your own interactions?" The answer is "Yes, I still miss some differences, and they can have an impact." Here's an example. Recently, I had a grant that allowed me to engage in a variety of activities outside my home university as long as the activities were related to cross-cultural research. A colleague from China was visiting Hawaii and asked me to travel to Shanghai to *teach* a course in cross-cultural studies and to consult with various professors about their *ongoing and proposed* research. I replied to my colleague: "I have to check with the funding agency to determine if the conditions of the grant allow me to teach and consult about research. The original conditions of the grant emphasized the actual carrying out of research." My reply was sincere. The guidelines for how grant money can be spent (from American agencies) are lengthy and complex, and I had to make sure whether or not this trip would be possible.

My colleague then left to return to Shanghai. We agreed he would write me a formal letter of invitation and that I would then send a copy of this letter to the funding agency officials. But I never received the letter, and I could not figure out why. Discussing this with other colleagues from Asia, one suggested that I had said no to the professor from Shanghai. She continued,

It was a polite "no," but a "no" nevertheless. One way to say no is to tell some-one how difficult it will be to accept an invitation. When you said that you had to check with the funding agency, the professor probably concluded that you didn't want to accept the invitation. But rather than [your] saying no directly, which would be rude, he interpreted your response as a polite "no."

I think I am open to the criticism that this is a cultural difference I should have understood at the time rather than missed. My story is doubly embarrassing, because the cultural differences involved are consistent with much of the material I reviewed in chapter 7 in the section titled "Difficulties in Face-to-Face Communication."

So I never went to Shanghai. The professor and I are still in contact, however, and we have worked successfully with some of the same graduate students. Certainly, a misunderstanding and possibly some temporary ill feelings had occurred. I believe we have continued to interact successfully because we have developed a trusting re-lationship. He trusts me to do the best I can given my position and limitations, and I trust him in a similar manner. Yes, I was disappointed that the trip to Shanghai did not occur. But the level of trust we had developed meant we could put this problem aside and work on present and future projects.

Trust: A Willingness to Deal With Vulnerability

Developing trust between two people means that each person becomes vulnerable to the other's actions. This emphasis on vulnerability is central to the definition of trust suggested by Mayer, Davis, et al., (1995):

> [T]rust . . . is the willingness of a party to be vulnerable to the actions of another party based on the expectation that the other will perform a particular action im-portant to the trustor, irrespective of the ability to monitor or control that other party. (p. 712)

To this definition I would add that the trusting parties are interested in helping each other meet their goals. The goals can be general, such as the development of good working relationships, or they can be specific, such as successful completion of a joint project in the workplace.

A clear example of the interrelationship of vulnerability, goals, and trust is when money is lent between acquaintances without guarantees of repayment written into a carefully formulated contract. One person trusts that the other will pay back the loan later and is vulnerable because the other may leave town and never be heard from again. Goals include the temporary use of money and its repayment, as well as the move from acquaintanceship to friendship, which is sometimes marked by the willingness to make and to accept such loans. In most extensive intercultural rela-tionships, people are vulnerable because they open themselves to misunderstandings, anxiety (chapter 2), and sometimes the displeasure of prejudiced individuals in their community. If two people from different cultural backgrounds have a trusting rela-tionship, they believe these potential problems can be overcome given that the two individuals are committed to looking after each other's best interests.

Various researchers have suggested the conditions for developing trust (Butler, 1991; Mayer, Davis, et al., 1995). For many of these conditions, people can exam-ine their own behavior and try to make sure they are sending out signals that these conditions exist. I have chosen seven for further discussion here because they are especially important in the workplace

Competence

In the workplace, people have goals they may need to obtain. These can include obtaining good job ratings, completing tasks supervisors assign, and advancement in the organization through the promotion process. If A feels that B is competent to help in the achievement of these goals, trust can develop. Trust is certainly not guaranteed, as will become clear as other necessary conditions are discussed.

Consistency and Fairness

To be trusted, people must be consistent in their daily behavior. If bosses signal that they approve of employees who seek advanced training programs, they must be consistent with this view over time. Otherwise, workers will complain that they can't figure out what their boss wants. Fairness should be added to consistency. If one worker with a certain set of qualifications is given advanced training opportunities, other people with similar qualifications also should have the same opportunities. This generalization involves additional issues. In some cultures, bosses are expected to look after members of their in-group and are considered poor bosses if they don't. In-groups can include members of one's family, long-term employees, and people who have long engaged in resource exchanges with the boss. In other cultures, social action programs can lead to benefits for designated people. Bosses might feel a need for affirmative action programs, and this may lead to training opportunities for members of culturally diverse groups in the workplace. In all such cases, a majority of people in the organization should view these actions by bosses as reasonable. If not, then bosses risk the possibility of not being trusted.

Loyalty

Once people establish a trusting relationship, they must demonstrate loyalty to each other, especially when challenges to the relationship arise. A person cannot seemingly have a good relationship with another on Monday but then put that same person at a disadvantage on Tuesday. In everyday language, a person cannot develop relationships and then backstab. If people are loyal to each other, they will come to each other's assistance in times of trouble and will not quickly cut each other off from future interactions.

Consider a case where X and Y have a trusting relationship. If Y is accused of a misdeed such as sexual harassment, embezzlement, or the betrayal of company secrets, then X should display loyalty. X might say, "These are accusations, not proven facts. We must wait for all the information to come in and not jump to conclusions. I personally can't believe that Y would do what Y is accused of." Clearly, X is vulnerable to the chastisement of others if the facts prove that Y is guilty. But as discussed earlier, the willingness to be vulnerable is part of trust.

Promise Fulfillment

If people make promises, they must "move heaven and earth" to follow through on their commitments. This aspect of trust is probably very clear and prominent in people's minds. If people don't keep their promises, they can't be trusted. Items to measure this aspect of trust are likewise clear and direct (from the scale discussed by Butler, 1991):

_____ follows through on promises made to me.

Keeping promises is a problem for _____. (This item would be reverse scored.)

Promise keeping and its lack are frequently the subject of stories employees tell to one another. In one organization, for example, a boss has an especially ornate mahogany door to his office. Employees report that he is very enthusiastic about and supportive of proposals suggested to him in his office. "He is with you all the way until you reach the door," employees comment.

In intercultural interactions, people have to be careful with this aspect of trust. In many cultures, once one of the people involved in a relationship thinks of it as collective, then casual discussions can be interpreted as commitments. For instance, one person says her company has a job opening. The other person, if he labels the relationship as collective, may interpret that casual comment as a commitment. He may think the individual will make special efforts to see that he gets the job. If he does not get an invitation for a serious job interview, he may feel betrayed. The person who mentioned the job surely will comment that she was only passing on a piece of information, but the trust relationship may dissolve due to this well-meaning clash.

Availability and Receptivity

By asserting that people must be available to others to form trusting relationships, I might be accused of communicating common sense. Unless people are available to others, it is difficult to develop any kind of relationship. The move away from calling this a commonsense notion occurs when the question is asked, "How and where are people available in other cultures?" Answers to this question take a great deal of study. As noted earlier, in Japan and Korea, for example, most power holders are men. One time and place for interactions, and for the possible development of trusting relationships, is at after-work gatherings at restaurants and bars. After dinner, people often move from one bar to another, causing outsiders to wonder how people possibly can drink so much and stay up so late. People from other countries who want to do business in Japan are told to expect such invitations, and they are told that business decisions can be affected by an unwillingness to participate.

In Australia, Bochner and Hesketh (1994) were interested in job attitudes among members of culturally diverse work teams. They also found that "drinking together" was a way people became available to one another. If people complained about poor working relationships, they also reported "feeling uncomfortable about having a drink after work with a colleague, which breaks one of the most sacrosanct norms in Australian society" (p. 253). Another problem was that workers from Asia were too modest about their abilities. While perhaps this was desirable in their home countries, it meant that Australian coworkers did not know what individuals could do. Consequently, the Australians did not make requests of the overly modest individuals and the people involved remained unavailable to one another. Interestingly, people did not want to attract too much attention to their abilities and credentials for another reason. They might encounter another Australian norm: "The tall poppy

In some cultures people develop good business relations through large entertainment budgets. This can be less expensive than hiring lawyers later.

gets cut down" (Triandis, 1995). The Asian coworkers must find a golden middle area. People must communicate what they can do well, but they must not be seen as braggarts.

People living in other cultures need to think about how to become available to others. If they do not drink alcohol, for example, it is acceptable to order a nonalcoholic drink in the three countries discussed here. Ideally, it will not look too different from what others order. The term *ginger ale* is used so frequently in discussions of acceptable drink orders that I have been tempted to invest in the stocks of soft drink companies. No special attention need be called to the drink ordered, and people should not comment on the drinking habits of others. For people who were socialized to be modest about their accomplishments, it can be admittedly very difficult for them to communicate what they have to offer others in the workplace. This is the sort of behavior that can be practiced in a cross-cultural training program (chapter 7) designed to assist people to make the move from one culture to another.

Once people are available, they also must be receptive. They should communicate to others that they want to be approached and that they will pay attention to the other's information, suggestions, and requests. Again, there are cultural specific indicators of receptivity behind this generalization. In some cultures, eye contact with others is a signal that people are receptive and are paying attention. In other cultures, a slightly bowed head leading to a lack of direct eye contact is the sign of respect. In some cultures, receptivity is marked by frequent touching during conversations. In other cultures, touching is frowned on, especially when the receiver could make connotations involving sexual interest. In some cultures, turn taking occurs during conversations. One person talks, others listen, and one of these others later takes a turn. In other cultures (e.g., local culture in Hawaii), constant overlap occurs. People interrupt one another with their contributions. This shows they are interested in what others are saying. If a person doesn't interrupt, others may make an assumption that the person is bored or (worse) not particularly interested in interacting with the culture's long-term residents.

Trust and International Alliances

The importance of trust has been investigated in a study of international cooperative alliances between American and Japanese companies (Johnson et al., 1996). These international alliances "involve agreements to cooperate in joint activities such as co-development of a new product or existing products to a new market. They span national boundaries and are most often based in one of the partner's home country" (p. 982). These alliances do not usually involve the creation of a new legal entity, so partners cannot depend on carefully crafted contracts to insure cooperation. Rather, the partners have to develop relationships based on trust.

Johnson and her colleagues investigated whether or not various international strategic alliances were integrated into the long-term strategies of organizations in both the United States and Japan. They measured the concepts listed here. A "focal firm" refers to a company that might engage in alliances, and a "partner firm" refers to an organization in another country subject to the possible alliance. When the researchers are investigating the plans of an American company, it would be the focal firm, and a company in Japan would be a potential partner firm.

1. *The complementarity of the partner's firm.* If one firm manufactures quality consumer products and the other firm has good marketing capabilities, the firms are said to be complementary.

2. *The focal firm's sensitivity to its partner and the partner's culture.* Of course, this is of special interest given the goals of this chapter and the entire book. The assumption is that the more people understand culture and cultural differences, the more they will succeed in building alliances.

3. *The partner's similarity.* If companies are similar on dimensions such as size, leadership style, salary structures, and promotion policies, they may look at alliances in similar ways. This similarity might lead to effective communication, problem solving, and transfer of knowledge between the companies.

4. *Trust between partners.* Johnson and her colleagues predict that complementarity, cultural sensitivity, and similarity will combine to effect the partner's trust in the focal firm. In turn, the partner's trust will lead to increases in the focal firm's trust. In other words, if A trusts B, that trust is likely to be reciprocated. The definition of *trust* here is similar to what has been discussed in this section and is measured by questions such as these (Johnson et al., 1996, p. 1001, italics added):

"We can always rely on our *(insert American or Japanese)* partner to do its part in our alliance."

"Our *(insert American or Japanese)* partner would go out of its way to make sure our firm is not damaged or harmed in this relationship."

"In this relationship, we feel like our . . . partner cares what happens to us."

The dependent variable in this study was the degree the companies integrated the international alliances into their long-term strategies and plans. For both Americans and Japanese, cultural sensitivity led to trust, and trust in turn led to the highest degree of strategic integration of international alliances. Given the importance of cultural sensitivity, some of the more specific results will be reviewed here. All of these results are consistent with the discussions of cultural differences presented earlier in this chapter, and many will remind readers of the story involving Peter Reed and Hirumi Watanabe. I will review the findings for American cultural sensitivity toward Japan (e.g., using more indirect communication). The findings for Japanese sensitivity toward Americans are parallel (e.g., using more direct communication).

To score high on intercultural sensitivity, American businesspeople had to agree with items such as the following (Johnson et al., 1996, p. 1001). I have included discussion of the items that gives more detail on the cultural differences involved.

- "Our managers are sensitive to the amount of time it takes Japanese managers to decide on an action." Given that collectivism gives guidance for behavior, all members of a collective must have an opportunity to give their suggestions. Consequently, it can take a long time for managers to make decisions because they have to consult with many other people.
- "Our managers and representatives know not to press individual Japanese managers for immediate decisions." In addition to the time needed for Japanese decision making, Americans must remember that another value is uncertainty avoidance. High uncertainty avoidance cultures have many norms and unwritten rules for proper action. Much time is needed to navigate these many rules and norms. In addition, no one person wants to be seen as responsible for a decision that may prove faulty, so this is another reason not to press any individual manager.
- "In our firm, we have worked very hard to familiarize ourselves with the Japanese legal and economic environment." One important realization for Americans is that Japan has fewer practicing lawyers. Rather than depend on contracts, the Japanese prefer to develop trusting relationships. If problems arise in a cooperative business alliance, the Japanese trust that their partners will address the problem for the benefit of all the parties involved.

In chapter 7 the importance of developing cultural informants was discussed. Questions about trust, such as the following, can be directed to these informants: "What sorts of social invitations must I accept?" "What signals can I send that hosts will interpret positively?" "How can I distinguish myself from others who use these trusting signals as a ploy to rip off hosts?" "How can I communicate that I want a long-term business relationship that will yield mutual benefits?" It is hard to overestimate the importance of trust. In a study of New Zealand businesspeople who had experience in Asia, the need to develop long-term trusting relationships was seen as the most important part of doing business in Japan (Hawkins, 1998).

THE FUTURE

It is always important to consider how people's preferences will change in future years. One of the most impactful influences on change will be the increasing presence of women in the workplace, a trend that may spread from highly industrialized to developing nations (Adler, 1997; Hofstede, 1996; Tung & Miller, 1990). As these women assume responsible positions, what will their preferences be? Given the reasonable generalization (Deaux & LaFrance, 1998) that women are more sensitive to relationships, will they be better able to develop trust with colleagues in the workplace? When leadership is considered, will women expect a paternal authoritative style, or will they reject it as contributing to the power base of men? Will they want personalized interventions into their lives, for example, when they receive unwelcome sexual attention at work? Or will they develop an appreciation of very impersonal, formalized rules that specify what is and what is not allowed when men and women interact in the workplace? Will men and women continue to have differing views about what is friendly banter and what is harassment (Deaux & LaFrance; Konrad & Guteck, 1986)? To understand the future, people must understand the importance of gender and gender differences and their relation to cultures. This is the focus of the next chapter.

CHAPTER SUMMARY

The workplace increasingly will become one of the most important social settings for intercultural interactions. People can either (a) tolerate the legal requirements that demand interaction across cultural barriers, or (b) they can look forward to the stimulation that such interactions can provide. When people examine cultural differences in the workplace, a good technique is to imagine working in a country other than their own. Will they face new challenges, or will expectations of workplace behavior be much the same as in their own country? Given that the answer to the first part of the question always will be yes and to the second part no, it is important to examine differences identified by cross-cultural researchers (Adler, 1997; Dorfman, 1996; Hofstede, 1980).

Some of the most helpful cross-cultural research is based on ecological correlations, and it is important to understand the difference between this type of correlation and the more common individual-level correlations. When interpreting individual-level correlations, researchers can examine (among other factors) traits and qualities of the individuals involved in the study. If a correlation exists between Americans' fluency in Chinese and their satisfaction with their overseas assignments in China, one set of interpretations can be based on traits of the individuals. Perhaps people who invest the time and effort in learning the Chinese language are also very committed to learning a great deal about the Chinese culture. This commitment may assist them in overcoming the inevitable difficulties they will face in China, so it also will have a long-term impact on their satisfaction. Note that this interpretation is based on people's qualities: their language skills, their commitment, their ability to overcome problems, and their eventual satisfaction with life in China.

Ecological correlations are based on units of analysis larger than individuals. Individuals may work hard and earn lots of money, and these sums might be included in an analysis of earnings in their city, region of the country, or nation. When a research study's results are based on the analysis of units such as salaries in a city, region, or country, the correlations are said to be "ecological." When interpreting such correlations, researchers must focus on aspects of those units. If ecological correlations are interpreted as if they are individual correlations (an all-too-common practice), then the interpreters are guilty of the "ecological fallacy."

Hofstede (1980, 1991, 1996) and Bond (Chinese Culture Connection, 1987; Hofstede & Bond, 1988) have identified five ecological concepts that assist in understanding intercultural interactions in the workplace. The five are masculinity-femininity; uncertainty avoidance; power distance; individualism and collectivism; and Confucian dynamism. The unit of analysis for these correlations is the country where people were socialized: Japan, the United States, Sweden, India, Great Britain, and so forth. The most recent treatments of these concepts are based on data from 50 countries (Hofstede, 1991). Given that they are ecological concepts based (in this case) on data from countries, interpretation must focus on aspects of the different countries.

Insights into the masculinity-femininity dimension can be obtained by looking at people's concerns and preferences in the workplace. In masculine countries, people emphasize salaries, job advancement, and opportunities to remain current. In feminine countries, people prefer a friendly work atmosphere and cooperative relations with supervisors and coworkers. In the most masculine countries, women will not be found in meetings where decisions are made because they are relatively powerless and are discouraged from making suggestions about important decisions.

Uncertainty avoidance refers to the number of rules and regulations commonly found within a country's businesses. One fact about the future for everyone is that we don't know exactly what will happen. Countries high in uncertainty avoidance have, over many years, dealt with this fact by imposing many rules and regulations that people hope will lessen the impact of negative events. Because the startup of new businesses involves risks, intercultural development of new ventures is often hard in uncertainty-avoidance countries. Would-be businesspeople find many rules and regulations (red tape), become frustrated, and take their business elsewhere.

Power distance refers to the distinctions between various groups that are part of a country's status hierarchy. All countries have hierarchies. The important factor here is the degree of difference that separates one hierarchical level from another. A boss has a higher level position than workers, but how distant do workers feel from their boss? In high-power-distance countries, people defer to bosses and only rarely disagree with them openly. In low-power-distance countries (e.g., the United States), people do not feel that their boss is much more able than they. Further, they enjoy developing cordial relations with their boss and feel it is possible to disagree with their boss.

Individualism and collectivism were discussed as individual-level variables in chapter 2. They also are ecological concepts, and this fact admittedly can make interpretations of cross-cultural research difficult. As ecological concepts, individualism and collectivism refer to the organization of society. To what degree does group membership determine whether or not goals are met? In collective societies, the answer is "very much." People have a difficult time achieving their goals unless they are long-term members of influential groups, such as a university alumni association or a well-known company. The phrase "long-term" is important: People must show loyalty to a group over a number of years to achieve their goals. In individualist societies people have an easier time achieving their goals independent of any long-term commitment to a group. For example, people can be members of a company but within that company can make their contributions working mostly by themselves. As long as the people are productive, company executives in individualist countries are far more tolerant of workers who choose to keep to themselves.

Confucian dynamism has been identified as an important factor in Asian countries that have seen economic growth over the past 20 years. This factor refers to the relative influence (high, moderate, low) of philosophical principles Confucius formulated. The principles related to the economic growth of countries involve the Confucian values of a concern with the future and with the good that hard work can bring, so this selected list of principles is called "Confucian dynamism." The principles include the importance of persistence and perseverance, the ordering of relationships and attention to the resulting mutual obligations, thrift, and having a sense of shame.

A case study was presented involving difficulties between an American employee and a Japanese boss. All five factors were involved. The American preferred to work alone; the boss preferred contributions through group effort (individualism and collectivism). The American wanted to include women in certain company gatherings; the male boss felt this was unnecessary (masculinity-femininity). The American was not attentive to company rules and did not respond to the boss's concern about rule breaking (uncertainty avoidance and power distance). The American felt he was most creative when he could work on several tasks simultaneously; the boss preferred persistence on one task (Confucian dynamism). As with many intercultural encounters, this one had no hero and no villain. When people's cultures come into contact well-meaning clashes (chapter 7) do occur. Concepts such as the five reviewed here assist in the understanding of such clashes.

Clashes will exist when people exercise the role of "leader" in cultures other than their own. Different researchers have adopted various approaches to the study of leadership (Dorfman, 1996; Hollander, 1985; Muchinsky, 1996). One centers on power and influence, and another focuses on the traits of successful leaders. A third approach recognizes that any analysis of leadership must focus both on followers and on leaders. A question researchers interested in this aspect of leadership ask is "What are followers' preferences and expectations about the behavior of their leaders?" A fourth and related approach involves the analysis of the mutual influence leaders and followers have on the effectiveness of leadership. The well-known Japanese practice of establishing "quality circles," where workers make suggestions about the improvement of a company's products, are an example. Leaders are expected to listen carefully to these suggestions, and they often integrate the workers' ideas into company policies. A fifth approach to leadership study focuses on various situations involving leaders, and one of its intriguing assumptions is that some people are better leaders in some settings compared to others. For example, some people are better leaders than others when the task is highly structured. Other people are better leaders when the task is unstructured and when effort has to be put into organizing exactly what different people will do given this relative lack of structure. The sixth approach studies the emergence of leaders. What sorts of people move from modest positions within their organizations to positions of power and influence? This is an especially important question for people organizing international business ventures, who may choose leaders for overseas assignments based on performance in their own country. In another country, however, host nationals may not recognize them as leaders unless they meet the expectations of people in that country (hence the third approach).

Americans working in Asia are frequently puzzled by the expectations employees have of their leaders. This discussion is based on research carried out in India (Kumar & Saxena, 1983; J. Sinha, 1980), and similar expectations about what leaders should do can be found in various Asian countries (Casimir & Keats, 1996; Hui, 1990; Misumi, 1985). Expectations can be summarized in the phrase "paternal authoritativeness." Many workers expect their leaders to behave much like concerned fathers. Because fathers know their own children well, the workers prefer to be treated in ways based on the leader's knowledge of their personal needs. Further, the leaders are expected to know a great deal about many aspects of life, so they are expected to be able to give authoritative advice on matters involving marriage, the socialization of children, and various community activities. These can be very difficult expectations for Americans working in Asia. Many Americans prefer the approach to leadership whereby they have responsibility toward their employees during the workday but their employees' personal lives are considered just that: personal. Of course, many American employees strongly prefer such leaders: They will accept a leader's directives at work but feel that leaders have no business intervening into their marriages, dating behavior, community activities, and so forth.

Many cultural differences have been discussed throughout this book, and a reasonable question is "Can I ever learn all the differences and act on them appropriately?" The answer is "probably not," but people still can have effective intercultural interactions. One way to "cut through" possible cultural misunderstandings is to develop relationships based on trust. People trust each other if they are confident that they will look after each other's best interests. Trust involves vulnerability. People who trust risk betrayal and the subsequent loss of money, reputation, or status. Qualities that lead to the development of trusting relationships include competence in areas that could have an impact on relationships, consistency in behavior over time, fairness in dealing with others, loyalty, careful attention to promise fulfillment, availability to others, and receptivity to the suggestions of others. Johnson and her colleagues (1996) found that cultural sensitivity led to trust in the development of international cooperative alliances between American and Japanese companies. In turn, trust led to the integration of the alliances into the long-term strategic plans of the companies.

When people consider the future of work-related behaviors in various parts of the world, one of the most important factors will be the presence of, and growing influence of, women. As discussed in chapter 4, women in many countries are dissatisfied if they are limited to the roles of wife, mother, and homemaker. Many women are seeking wage employment, both to expand their opportunities and to gain the benefits that can accrue to their families. The increased presence of women in the workplace will demand that leaders (many of whom will be women) understand culture's influence on gender and be willing to modify company policies to meet the needs of different workers. Insights gained from the study of culture and gender are covered in the next chapter.

C H A P T E R 9

CULTURE AND GENDER

CHAPTER OVERVIEW

Men often complain that they don't understand women. Women express the corresponding sentiment. When people's cultural background is considered, with its guidance for behaviors expected of men and women, even more complexity is added. A starting point to understanding the interrelationships among men, women, and culture is to make careful distinctions among terms such as sex, gender, sex role, and gender role. The distinctions discussed in this chapter include attention to people's capabilities in the reproduction and bearing of children and attention to the sets of behavioral expectations that people learn as part of the socialization in their cultures.

Different theoretical perspectives have been developed to provide frameworks for understanding sex and gender differences. "Parental investment" refers to the differing contributions and outcomes of male-female sexual contact. If women become pregnant, the contribution of men can be minimal and not time consuming. The investment of women is extensive: nine months of pregnancy and usually multiyear efforts in raising the child. This leads to differences in male-female interactions. For example, men tend to look for young and healthy women to bear children. Women are more careful about partner selection and tend to look for men with resources and a long-term commitment to looking after children.

Many of the intriguing differences that follow from an understanding of different parental investment strategies also can be explained by examining differences in the socialization of children. If a culture is to survive into the future, it is essential that men and women produce and rear children. Socialization pressures in a culture thus can lead to very different emphases: Men are socialized to be aggressive and status seeking so that they can obtain resources for their families. Women are socialized to be nurturing and relationship oriented because the major demands for raising children fall on them.

The differing expectations of men and women lead to gender stereotypes—more specifically, images and adjectives that come to mind the second the words *men* and *women* are heard. Adjectives for men are *domineering* and *aggressive*; for women, *passive* and *nurturing*. To deal with any one person fairly, people must be willing to move beyond these stereotypes and to take individual differences into account.

In some cases, research evidence can be put forward to document differences among men and women. Even here, however, exceptions should always be entertained along with general trends. Women are often very concerned with relationships and become upset when the relationships flounder. This can have both positive and negative impacts. Good leaders also are concerned with relationships. However, too many disappointments with relationships can lead to emotional burnout.

Exceptions to trends should be considered more frequently when cultures are clearly undergoing changes. In highly industrialized nations, many women are aggressive in their pursuit of successful careers. Many men are pleased to shed the shackles of societal expectations and take up careers in "nurturing" professions: elementary school teaching, nursing, and social work. A general guideline for executives who work with both men and women is to move beyond stereotypes and past cultural expectations. The case of women on international assignments is discussed in this chapter as an example. Executives often make decisions favoring men because they believe women do not want overseas assignments. When asked, however, many women express enthusiasm for such assignments and complete them successfully.

GENDER AND GENDER DIFFERENCES

As discussed in chapters 1 and 4, culture provides people with guidance about appropriate thoughts, feelings, and actions. Culture also gives guidance about differences in behavior expected of people who hold different roles. One of the most important distinctions occurs for behaviors considered appropriate for men compared to women. Gaining an understanding of cultural expectations for men and women is assisted by examining how humans process information and form categories.

The amount of information children must learn to become members of their culture, as well as the amount of information adults encounter every day of their lives, is so vast that various learning aids are necessary. An extremely important learning aid, with major implications for how people from different cultures interact with one another, is *categorizing*. People in different cultures put information into categories and then react to the categories when making decisions (Chaplin, John, & Goldberg, 1988; A. Fiske, Kitayama, Markus, & Nisbett, 1998; Gardner, 1985). Rather than spend time and energy on each piece of information they encounter, people can react based on the categories well-socialized members of their culture use. When encountering an unfamiliar plant, for instance, people will not be likely to spend time considering whether or not it is edible. Rather, they will immediately see that the plant is not part of the category their culture has labeled as common "edible foods." If they are searching for food, they will shift their attention immediately to other possibilities. This strategy has advantages and disadvantages. If people immediately shift their attention away from the unfamiliar plant, they are protecting themselves if it is poisonous. Yet the people may be ignoring a good source of nutrition simply because it is unfamiliar.

If people must draw specific information from their environment so that they can meet their basic physical needs (e.g., "What water is drinkable?" "What potential mates are available to me?" "Are these newcomers to my culture a threat?"), then it is certain the culture has categories that deal with this necessary information. If the information deals with aspects of life that all people must face no matter where they live, then certain categories will be culturally universal. Differences across cultures then are found in the exact content of the categories. The category "edible foods" is a universal. The content of this category varies from culture to culture. Young puppies are a delicacy in some cultures, as are baby birds still in their eggshells. Both of these items are not considered edible foods in other cultures. As might be expected, the difference in the content of categories may cause embarrassments during intercultural encounters. High-status visitors from a country such as the United States might be entertained in a rural village in the Philippines. They may be served a lavish meal with puppies and unhatched baby birds as entrees. Even the most well-traveled and interculturally sensitive Western visitors will have a difficult time at this meal.

It is extremely important to recognize that people categorize all kinds of information. This information does not consist solely of objects such as potential foods and drinkable water. The categorization extends to other people individuals encounter. Again, universal concerns about other people will be categorized in all cultures. One concern all people have is mating with someone and producing children. Another is caring for and providing for the children, who are completely helpless at birth (Best & Williams, 1997; Low, 1989). The procreation of children only can be carried out with a member of the opposite sex. Caring for young children demands dividing labor so that some members of a culture (often but not always men) venture out of the place of residence to find food and some members (almost always women) stay with and care for the child. Given that both men and women are needed to produce children, the existence of categories for both men and women are culturally universal. Just as with physical objects, differences exist in the content of the categories. What are men expected to do? What behaviors will opposite-sex members see as desirable? Are behaviors indicative of leadership encouraged in the young women of a certain culture, or are leadership behaviors expected only of men? Again, the cultural differences in the content of categories cause difficulties and misunderstandings. Recall the story about Peter Reed in chapter 8. He was an American working in Japan, and he tried to involve his female coworkers in the lunch gatherings he organized. He discovered, however, that women are not frequently included in gatherings where company managers meet and discuss business matters. The category "women" is less likely to include the possibility of "company leader" in Japan compared to the United States.

With the possible exception of the categories "race" and "ethnicity," probably more controversy arises in discussions of men and women than in any other topic that touches on human behavior. For every suggestion about possible differences and reasons for them, detractors point to other explanations (Fausto-Sterling, 1985; Fleming, 1985–1986; Hare-Mustin & Marecek, 1988; Hubbard, 1990; Jamieson,

1998). One of the most frequently cited possible differences (introduced in chapter 5 and discussed more fully later in this chapter) is the superior performance of men on tasks involving mathematical computations (e.g., Bellisari, 1989; Doyle & Paludi, 1995; Engelhard, 1990; Maccoby & Jacklin, 1974). Controversy focuses on both the existence of any difference in mathematical ability and (if a difference is acknowledged) on explanations of the research results. Analysts who focus on the importance of socialization ask if parents expect boys to perform as well as girls. Analysts who focus on the schools ask if counselors encourage adolescents to take advanced math courses (and if students say no the first time this possibility arises, do counselors argue more with boys than girls)? Analysts who focus on power differences within societies (e.g., Hubbard) argue that men are more likely to encourage other men in mathematics because it is so useful for retaining power in complex technological societies. These various arguments provide many perspectives on the admittedly complex study of gender differences, and readers desirous of participating in vigorous debate will have a difficult time finding a more attractive research area.

In my opinion, the study of gender and gender differences has enriched the study of culture and behavior by forcing researchers to consider a broader range of theoretical concepts and practical issues (e.g., issues related to female participation in the workforce). Indeed, I believe the emphasis on gender study is directly responsible for books such as this one. In the 1960s and 1970s, the percentage of female high school graduates who decided to attend college rose significantly. These women took courses in fields such as psychology, education, communication, and management and did not find information about themselves in their textbooks. Rather, they found that most of the research generalizations were drawn from was based on experiments, surveys, and behavioral observations of men. They began to demand that their professors include more research about women in their class presentations and to search out texts that integrated research studies that looked directly at the behavior of women. Given the success of these women in influencing their professors, other people began examining their texts and asking the question "Do I find myself in here?" For example, members of various ethnically diverse groups, international students, and "nontraditional" students returning to college after several years in the workforce or after years of raising children asked this question. These various students demanded that the diversity of the people they saw every day on campus be reflected in their coursework. Many professors responded positively, began to expand the scope of their research to examine gender and cultural differences, and provided the information that allow books like this one to be written.

The treatment of culture and gender in this chapter will be organized around six themes:

1. The clarification of concepts by attention to terms such as *sex, gender, sex role,* and *gender role*

2. Differences between men and women that stem from biological heritage, with special attention to behaviors that led to an evolutionary advantage for our ancestors. Although the study of evolution can lead to some important insights, it cannot explain all male-female differences. People are also strongly influenced

by the role models they observe during their childhood, and this leads to the necessity of studying the next four themes.

3. The socialization of children to behave according to a culture's norms about gender roles

4. The analysis of sex stereotypes. When many or most members of a sex behave in a certain way, a generalization or stereotype can develop. Some people, however, do not behave according to the traditional guidelines their cultures offer. Understanding both stereotypes and individual differences is necessary in the analysis of culture and gender.

5. The concept of relatedness to others. Many researchers have argued that women are more sensitive to, and concerned about, their relations with others in their culture. Many implications stem from this difference.

6. The importance of cultural change. Two reasons cultures change over time are contact with other cultures and the adoption of technological innovations. The changes often have an impact on the behaviors women consider acceptable. When cultures change, the activities of women often converge with behaviors that long have been observed among men (e.g., greater sexual expressiveness, more political participation).

RECOMMENDATIONS ABOUT TERMS

Confusion can result if research or discussion terms are inconsistently used. Prince (1985) offered recommendations for terms about men and women that make a great deal of sense. She makes a distinction between *sex* and *gender*, and other researchers (Best & Williams, 1997; Eagly, 1987; Jandt, 1998; Unger, 1979) have used the distinction. *Sex* refers to biological facts. Men and women have physiological differences, and the most obvious differences involve their reproductive systems. Men produce sperm, and women produce ova. Members of both sexes are necessary to produce offspring who will be socialized into their culture and who will be responsible for the culture's perpetuation. The need to produce children to assure a culture's survival is a universal demand people face. The term *sex roles* includes the activities of men and women necessary for one of the man's sperm to meet the woman's ovum when the woman is fertile. For women, the sex role also includes behaviors involved in the nursing of children because only women have breasts that provide milk. Male sexual identity includes men's awareness that they have the potential to impregnate women and their knowledge of the necessary behaviors. Female sexual identity includes women's awareness of their reproductive potential and their knowledge about behaviors that lead to pregnancy.

Gender, as distinct from *sex*, refers to a set of behaviors a culture defines as proper and acceptable for men and for women. As will be discussed further in the next section, the male *gender role* includes aggressiveness in behavior, and the female gender role includes the nurturance of others. Other gender roles many cultures have for men include leaving the home daily to find food or to earn wages, contributing to the security of the village or town through military means, and assuming leadership positions. The gender roles many cultures have for women include raising children, cooking, making clothes, keeping house, and tending small vegetable gardens near the home.

The importance of maintaining a distinction between the terms *sex* and *gender* can be seen most clearly in cases where members of the male sex and the female sex want to engage in behaviors a culture traditionally has deemed inappropriate. The desire to engage in "traditionally inappropriate" behavior frequently occurs during times of cultural change. For example, many men want to stay home and interact extensively with their children; many women want to earn wages and to assume leadership positions. People's desire to acquire gender roles considered inappropriate for their sex may lead to rejection and discrimination by a culture's members who are familiar and comfortable only with traditional roles.

In the American culture, the distinction between *sex* and *gender* can be seen clearly in the women's liberation movement. When Prince (1985) refers to "sociocultural conditions," she is referring to the limits a culture's norms places on the behaviors men and women can engage in without formal or informal sanctions from authority figures.

> The women seeking liberation may be female but they are not seeking liberation from their biological state (which would not be possible in any case) but from the sociocultural condition to which the word woman refers. In the interest of real equality let me also note that men too need liberation at least as much and probably more than women. (p. 96)

In this context, the liberation of men refers to behavioral expectations. If both men and women are free to pursue behaviors once considered proper for only one gender role, they will have greater chances of finding happiness because their goals are set by themselves, not by the traditional limits of society. Many readers undoubtedly have benefited from the relaxation of traditional limits. I play the harp, for example, and started doing so in the mid-1980s. I hesitate to think of my community's reactions if I started playing this traditionally female instrument in the 1950s when I first began my study of music.

To understand the reasons for traditional limits on gender roles, people need to understand the evolutionary history of our ancestors and the socialization practices of different cultures. These topics are covered in the next two sections.

THE EVOLUTIONARY ADVANTAGE OF SOME SPECIFIC GENDER ROLES

The purpose of this section is to introduce a controversial topic: that our genetic inheritance has an impact on some of our social behaviors and, more specifically, on some behaviors of men and women. The behaviors I will discuss deal with interactions among men and women, sexual attraction, mate selection, and child rearing. Even though this material represents a small fraction of the content covered in this book's first edition, professors told me that it led to the most vigorous discussions and disagreements among students. People have stopped me on the street to express their viewpoints concerning the material on genetic influences.

I believe the reason for the intense feelings centers on concepts such as personal control and free choice. Many people do not enjoy hearing arguments suggesting that genetics influences their relations with opposite-sex members or their selection of a mate for life. Such matters are so close to what they consider the essence of humanity that they hesitate to consider influences other than their own free and unconstrained choices (Wilson, 1998).

Various Biological Influences on Behavior

When I introduce this material to my students, I begin with the least controversial material on biological influences. I remind students that people can't do everything they want to do during a day. A biological fact called "fatigue" means people must rest. They also cannot eat and drink as much as they might like or else they will gain so much weight they will become physically unattractive and possibly illness prone. If people are stressed over some major life events, it is wise to avoid social situations that would lead to additional stress because the resulting physiological reactions (increased heart rate, blood pressure, and release of chemicals in the body) can have a negative impact on their health.

It may be easier for middle-aged or older people to accept biological and genetic influences. People who were athletes during high school and college years simply cannot match their peak performances in foot races, jumping events, and competitive team sports as they age. Award-winning high school basketball players, now 40 years old, find 16-year-olds dribbling past them. People who used to party until the wee hours prefer going to bed at 10:30 P.M. Professors (like me) who used to enjoy traveling abroad to conferences find themselves making decisions about travel based on how fatigued they will be from scheduled activities. Some of the smartest older people are frustrated in new learning situations. My colleague and friend Harry Triandis (who speaks several European languages fluently and whose work has been cited frequently in this book) told me how hard it was to study the Chinese language given that he began after age 60.

Genetic issues, then, perhaps become clearer with age and after certain visits to the doctor's office. My brother's physician informed him that his cholesterol was dangerously high. The physician recommended that my brother tell his siblings so that they could take possible actions. In the words of the physician, "You, and perhaps your siblings, were dealt a bad hand for cholesterol in terms of your genetic heritage. You can't do anything about what your parents gave you, but you can take actions to do the best you can given your circumstances." My brothers and sister are now changing their behavior due to genetics, such as increasing exercise, attending to diet, and (in one case) taking daily medication.

Intergroup Relations and Altruism

Before I cover relations between men and women, I will introduce two other research areas arguments about evolution have influenced. The basic argument in evolutionary thinking is that certain behaviors were important to the survival of our distant ancestors hundreds of thousands of years ago. Given that our ancestors engaged in these behaviors, they survived and passed on their genes to the next generation. The behaviors, then, had survival value.

Evolutionary thinking has been applied to *intergroup relations* (Brewer & Brown, 1998; chapters 6 and 7) in cases where clear physical differences exist between groups, such as skin color. The argument is that if our distant ancestors came across people from unknown out-groups and if it was clear these people were different, then it was adaptive for our ancestors to be wary, to be distrustful, and to be rejecting. The out-group members could have been dangerous, so wariness and rejection would be functional behaviors. People gain little by being accepting and gracious when they meet potentially dangerous other people. But they have much to lose from their acceptance and graciousness if the out-group members have evil intentions. This argument about a biologically based distrust of out-group members has entered the dialogue about race in America that President Clinton initiated. During a one-hour presentation (July 9, 1998), he very explicitly discussed the arguments about the biologically based distrust of physically different out-group members. Other panel members either agreed or chose not to disagree. President Clinton added that relations among different groups within the same country is at the heart of many violent conflicts around the world.

Whether or not people agree with these biologically based arguments, they should know about them given their importance in public policy discussions.

Evolutionary thinking also has been applied to *altruism* (Batson, 1998). The argument is that people are more likely to help relatives than unrelated people. This behavior has at least two possible reasons. One is that any person's collection of relatives is a potential support group. In times of danger and hardship, people can call on their kinship network. People skillful at participating in kin networks were more likely to survive the difficulties of the distant past and thus more likely to pass on their genes. A second argument is that if a person helps a brother or close cousin, his or her own genes have a greater chance of being passed on. If X has a brother (Y) and a first cousin (Z), then X has an interest in Y and Z's survival. Person X shares 50% of his or her genes with brother Y and 25% with first cousin Z. If Y and Z survive difficulties and have children, some of X's genes are passed on to the next generation.

Perhaps an example with questions will be helpful. Assume that you live in a medium-sized city with an airport about 20 miles from your home. Two other people are involved in this example. One is a first cousin whom you don't know well. He always has lived in another city and you simply never had a chance to get to know him well. The other person is an old friend who, because of his moves to different cities, has not been in touch with you for about 10 years. One of these people is traveling to your city by airplane, but one cue that you are close to neither person is that the other person did not tell you about his trip.

You receive a phone call at 3:30 A.M. The person says, "I'm sorry that I have to call, but I'm stuck at the airport. The plane was delayed and all the taxi drivers seem to have gone home. Can you help out?" However, your car is in a garage for servicing and you can do little but offer sympathy.

Assume the caller is your first cousin. How upset would you be that you can't help? Then, assume the caller is your old friend. How upset would you be that you can't help? And now the key question: What would upset you more, that you could not help your cousin or that you could not help your old friend?

The prediction from evolutionary thinking is that people in such situations will be more upset that they can't help a close relative rather than that they disappointed a friend. Our evolutionary heritage makes us sensitive to the needs of people who share a percentage of our genes.

It is important to point out here that an alternative set of explanatory principles for such behaviors is based on *social learning theory* (Best & Williams, 1997; Deaux & LaFrance, 1998). People learn these behaviors as part of their socialization. Regarding intergroup relations, children are taught to distrust outsiders, especially if they are physically different. Also, an extensive research literature emphasizes how negative stereotypes, prejudice, and discrimination are learned (S. Fiske, 1998). Regarding altruism, children often are taught to attend to the needs of relatives and that family obligations are important. Attention to social learning and to the roles people learn to play during their lifetimes will be given in a later discussion of male-female differences. With this assurance that these topics will be treated in this chapter, I would like to present the arguments about male-female differences derived from an evolutionary perspective.

Evolution and Gender Differences

The starting point for an analysis of gender differences based on arguments from evolutionary theory is a basic fact about people and societies mentioned earlier. For societies to maintain themselves, men and women must engage in the behaviors that produce children. Once men and women fulfill their sex roles (man impregnates woman, woman eventually gives birth to a baby), several possible gender roles could have become common in various cultures. For example, women could have left the home and could have assumed the responsibility for securing food and for settling arguments with neighbors. By undertaking these activities, women could have acquired communitywide power and status if they were especially skillful. Men could have stayed home and taken care of the children. For a number of reasons, this set of gender roles did not evolve from early humans. Rather, a different set of behaviors became common and achieved the status of conferring an evolutionary advantage on people who adopted them (Archer, 1996; Buss, 1991; Buss & Kenrick, 1998; Chodorow, 1974; Hadiyono & Kahn, 1985; Low, 1989). When thinking about human evolution and its implications for human behavior as experienced and observed today, people must think of the difficult, dangerous ecologies our ancestors lived in hundreds of thousands of years ago. An *evolutionary advantage* means that people who adopted certain behaviors were more likely to survive in their difficult environments, so they were more likely to pass their genes to future generations. Any genetic tendency that led people to favor engaging in those behaviors, then, would lead to a greater chance of people surviving, producing offspring, and thus passing their genes to others.

One of the clearest examples is the evolution of language in humans. Our *homo sapien* ancestors were not the strongest animals nor the swiftest nor the most prolific (having many children so that a few possibly would survive no matter how difficult the environment). However, they evolved into the primates scientists now call the most "intelligent," and the major factor in this evolution was their capacity for language. With language, our ancestors could share lessons about survival they learned in the recent past, could organize themselves for effective group activity in the present, and could plan for the future (e.g., storing food in anticipation of a possible famine). Our ancestors who did not develop a capacity for language were less likely to have these benefits that encompassed the past, present, and future and thus were less likely to survive and to pass their genes to later generations. Presently, humans have the capacity for language and use it for their benefit, and by doing so they are taking advantage of a capacity developed in their evolutionary past.

One of the most important gender distinctions found all over the world (Barry & Child, 1983; Doyle & Paludi, 1995; Low, 1989; Prince, 1985) is that women stay home and take care of children and men leave the home and acquire food or work to acquire it. The food or money is later brought home and shared with the women. These gender roles evolved for several reasons. One is that the behaviors involved in giving birth to children either (at best) take away from the strength and energy of women or (very frequently) actually debilitate women. Consequently, women were simply too weak after giving birth to forage for food. Further, women have an extremely beneficial food source for their babies: the milk from their breasts. Women who developed the gender role of staying home (to recover from childbirth and to regain their strength) and accepting food men supplied (needed to increase their own strength and to increase the breast milk supply for their babies) were more likely to survive.

Men also derived advantages. By supplying food for women, the men helped insure that their children would survive past infancy. The children later could help with work necessary for the culture's survival and (if the parents lived long enough) could provide a form of old-age insurance once the parents could no longer work productively. Another advantage to men was the opportunity for sexual expression. If they developed unions with women for whom they provided food and other life necessities, they could expect sexual intercourse in exchange. One implication (admittedly controversial, as will be discussed later) is that the two gender roles led to the development of certain traits that are differently distributed among men and women and that were passed genetically. If women stayed home and took care of their children, they developed the trait often called "nurturance," because they became the major caretakers of their offspring. Further, the women may have been so weak after childbirth that they needed help taking care of the children (given that the men were off finding food). Consequently, they may have developed positive relationships with other women, such as sisters, sisters-in-law, and cousins, who could help with the children. If the women were sensitive to the importance of developing such relations, they would become better able to care for children. This may have lead to the trait called "sensitivity to relationships," or, more concisely, "relatedness."

If men left the home to find food, they also may have developed certain traits. For example, the men who were most "aggressive" may have been the best food providers. They may have been willing to take more risks when hunting animals, or they may have been more willing to enter unfamiliar territories to search for edible plants. They also may have developed "leadership skills" if they organized the efforts of other men to hunt for large animals that one person would have found impossible to kill. Aggressiveness was also an important trait when hostile forces threatened a community. Again, because women may have been weak from childbirth and were responsible for looking after small children who did not have any knowledge about protecting themselves from enemies, men may have become responsible for a community's defense. Aggressive men may have become the most valued and may have achieved the highest status. With a combination of aggressiveness, responsibility for protecting women and children, and communitywide status, men became comfortable in relationships with women that involved dominance rather than equality.

Implications for Observable Behaviors Today

These evolved roles have implications for the behavior of men and women in today's world. These implications are, again, admittedly controversial, and they have received attention from theorists who feel they can be explained in terms of learning and socialization (Archer, 1996; Buss, 1991; Buss & Kenrick, 1998; Deaux & LaFrance, 1998; Stanislaw, 1991).

Readers may want to write down the answers to the following questions about heterosexual mate preferences and relatives and compare them with others. Given that the predicted results will be seen as male-female tendencies that exist only if many people are questioned (e.g., women more likely than men to answer in a certain way), readers ideally will compare their responses with about 20 others. This might be done as part of a class exercise.

1. How old are you? Assume you are unmarried and unattached to an opposite-sex member. However, you feel you might like to begin a relationship that could lead to a serious romance. What age range do you prefer for a person you would start dating? (This question is based on the research of Buss and his colleagues: Buss, 1989; Buss & Barnes, 1986; Buss et al., 1990; Buss & Kenrick, 1998.)

2. What is your height? Assume, as in question 1, you are currently unmarried and unattached. What height (or range of heights) do you prefer for a person you would start dating? (This question is suggested by the research of Walster, Aronson, Abrahams, & Rottmann, 1966; also Hatfield & Sprecher, 1986, 1995.)

3. Think back to your childhood and to your adolescence. Who did you interact more with, the relatives on your mother's side of your family or the relatives on your father's side of your family? (This question was suggested in a personal communication by Herbert Barry, and it is based on the findings of several research projects: Barry, Bacon, & Child, 1957; Barry & Child, 1983.)

Questions about mate preference have been asked in 33 countries (located on six continents) by Buss and his colleagues (1990; Buss, 1996). Several of their findings are consistent with predictions based on the evolutionary advantages of preferences in mate selection. One finding is that women are more likely to prefer becoming romantically involved with men who are older than they are, and men are more likely to prefer women younger than they are. The prediction of this result stemmed from the fact that older men are more likely to have stature in their communities and thus are more likely to have resources they can share with women. Women look to somewhat older men, then, to take care of them during the times they cannot provide for themselves (e.g., after childbirth, as discussed previously). Men, in contrast, look to younger women because age is related to the ability to have children. The younger a given woman is, the more likely she is to have childbearing years ahead of her. A biological fact about sex roles is that older men (in today's world, who are more than 50 years old) can impregnate young women, but older women cannot become pregnant.

Arguments about mate preference that involve women's ability to bear children extend beyond attention to age as a factor in men's choices. In the survey of respondents in 33 countries (Buss et al., 1990), men were more likely than women to place importance on physical attractiveness. Women were more likely to put emphasis on factors related to men's "earning potential," again consistent with their sensitivity to choices of men who could be good providers. Focusing on greater male preference for physical attractiveness in potential mates, Buss and Barnes (1986) commented:

> Specifically, women's reproductive value and fertility are closely tied to age and health (Symons, 1979). Aspects of physical appearance such as smooth and clear skin, good muscle tone, lively gait, white teeth, and lustrous hair are proximate cues to age and health. Therefore, past selection has favored men who enact a preference for those physical attributes (beauty) that are strong cues for age and health, and hence for reproductive capacity. (p. 569)

My prediction is that people's answer to question 2 about the height of preferred romantic partners will be consistent with suggestions from evolutionary thinking. When this is thought about carefully, women have no good reason in today's world (especially one influenced by feminist thinking) for preferring men who are taller than they are. Yet this preference clearly exists. In a study analyzing why people become attracted to opposite-sex members, Walster and her colleagues (1966) wanted to randomly pair men and women at an informal dance they organized as part of their research. They could not proceed in this manner. Women complained they simply would not become involved in the research project unless they were paired with a man taller than they. I doubt this preference among women has diminished since the mid-1960s. The explanation from evolutionary thinking is that women look to height as a sign that a given man is stronger than they are and that he can protect them from danger. Another biological fact is that (when the physical abilities of many people are studied) men are stronger than women (Khan & Cataio, 1984). For example, men can lift heavier weights and can lift heavy objects for longer periods than women. If women attach themselves to strong men, they will have an advantage if an enemy physically threatens them. My guess is that many female readers will admit that they feel more secure walking across a college campus at 10:30 P.M. in the company of a man taller, rather than shorter, than they are.

The answers to the third question, about memories of interactions with relatives, may reflect another aspect of evolutionary predictions. As mentioned previously, women stayed home with infants while men left the home in search of food they later brought back. Given that women were still weak from childbirth, it was to their advantage to involve others who could help with completing the necessary tasks in and around the home. Good candidates for this support group were the mother's relatives: her sisters, cousins, aunts, and perhaps her mother if she was still living. Consequently, women able to integrate others into support group activities had an advantage. As the children grew older, they were likely to interact frequently with members of this support group. Further, women were more responsible than men for introducing children to their culture's norms while the children were very young (Barry & Child, 1983; Doyle & Paludi, 1995; Low, 1989). During later childhood and adolescence, boys were likely to leave the home to interact with men and to learn gender appropriate skills such as hunting, but during early childhood members of both sexes were likely to remain home and to learn about their culture. A universal need of every culture is learning the norms about the appropriate ways of interacting with various other people: those older, those with more status, and so forth. The mother's relatives, because the mother was more likely to have them around for help, provided a readily accessible group of people who could assist in the task of introducing such aspects of their culture.

In today's world, women still are more likely to bear the responsibility of introducing children to others in their culture, so responses to question 3 tend to focus on people having more memories of interactions with the mother's side of the family. My guess is that if readers find this tendency for the responses they have access to (e.g., other class members), it will be the weakest tendency of the responses to the three questions. Given that increasingly women are entering the workforce and given that families often move from place to place and have little or no access to relatives on one or either side of the family, the involvement of extended family members as helpers during the child's socialization has diminished in highly industrialized nations.

The Advantages of Understanding Our Past

Discussions suggesting that people engage in behaviors today, and have certain traits today, because of our evolutionary past are very distasteful to many individuals. They feel such theories encourage a biological fatalism that dictates the opportunities people can pursue. One response to this reasonable complaint is that a knowledge of our past can suggest directions for our behavior in the present. Low (1989) explains:

> . . . the suggestion of differential paths to reproductive success for the two sexes in humans throughout evolutionary time may seem almost offensive to some. It is important, however, to understand past selective pressures if we wish to understand male-female differences or to be successful in modifying male-female patterns of behavior toward equality in our own society. (p. 316)

At times, people can take advantage of an evolutionary tendency and turn it to their advantage. As mentioned throughout this book, the future will see more frequent intercultural interactions, and success in arenas such as international business negotiations will depend on an understanding of cultural differences. Given women's traditional concern with relatedness and with preparing children for membership in their culture, it is quite possible women may be much more skillful than men in dealing with interactions across cultural boundaries and may be more sensitive to the stresses involved. Men, with their natural aggressiveness, may want to forge ahead too quickly during their intercultural interactions, failing to take the time to consider the viewpoints of people from other cultures.

The differences between men and women I have discussed so far are related to the universal demand that adults must produce children who survive so that their culture does not become extinct. Other differences arise from the socialization process, when adults expect different behaviors of boys and girls. As discussed in chapter 4, many socialization experiences involve interactions with various role models from whom children learn behaviors appropriate to their culture.

THE SOCIALIZATION OF BOYS AND GIRLS IN THEIR CULTURES

As discussed in chapter 4, socialization refers to the activities whereby children learn to be acceptable and contributing members of their cultures. Infants know absolutely nothing about their birth culture. Parents and other influential adults in a society have the responsibility to introduce their culture to children and to supervise various activities (consciously and unconsciously) that allow children to learn to behave in culturally appropriate ways (A. Fiske et al., 1998).

In the previous section, a case was made for the theory that the universal demand that adults produce children has implications for male and female roles. These roles (e.g., men as dominant, women as nurturant and relationship oriented) lead to the procreation, survival, and early caretaking of children. Given the evolutionary selection that favors various genes that may contribute to these role behaviors, it is possible that men are biologically more likely to engage in behaviors that express dominance and that women are more likely to engage in nurturant behaviors. These suggested likelihoods are reinforced during socialization. That is, adults and other elders encourage boys (with a possible biological predilection toward dominance) to behave in a dominant manner and encourage girls to engage in nurturant behaviors. Adults distribute various rewards (e.g., approval, attention, extra food) based on the behaviors of boys and girls that are gender appropriate. Studies examining these gender socialization practices are discussed in this section.

A basic fact about socialization (e.g. Barry & Child, 1983; Block, 1983; Valsiner & Lawrence, 1997) is that parents and other adults encourage children to engage in behaviors that are necessary for children to integrate themselves into the culture and to make contributions once they become adolescents and then adults. When all cultures have the same goal (e.g., the procreation of children), researchers can look for possible universal ways of meeting the goal. These can involve the encouragement of the same behaviors in children all over the world, and the example presented previously centered on male dominance compared to female nurturance. When cultures have somewhat different goals, or different ways of meeting universal goals such as procreation, then scholars can look for different behaviors and different emphases in children's socialization. Alternatively, they can examine differences in the relative emphases adults in various cultures place on certain behaviors in children. The universal fact of greater male aggressiveness, together with differences in the relative emphasis adults place on this aggressiveness in various cultures, provides a good example.

Male Aggressiveness

Perhaps the most widely accepted conclusion about gender differences is that men are more aggressive than women in all cultures documented (Best & Williams, 1997; Block, 1983; Goldstein & Segall, 1983; Harris, 1996; Khan & Cataio, 1984). Block summarizes numerous studies:

> Research findings surrounding aggression are perhaps the most consistent in the literature and indicate that males are more aggressive than females and from an early age. . . . Males engage in more rough-and-tumble play, attempt more often to dominate peers, engage in more physical aggression, exhibit more antisocial behavior, prefer television programs with more aggressive content [where TV exists, of course], and depending upon context, are more competitive than females. (p. 1337)

Given this universal observation, cultural differences exist: Boys in some cultures are socialized to be more aggressive than boys in other cultures. Low (1989) has examined male aggressiveness as it relates to competition for the attention of (and eventual possible mating with) women.

An interesting feature of most human societies is that they have polygynous marriage systems, and this implies that our ancestors were polygynous. Murdock (1981) reports that adequate information on marriage systems exists for 1,158 societies and, of these, 1,078 are polygynous. In 93% of these societies, then, men can mate with several women, while women can mate with only one man. This means that because some men have several mates, other men do not have any if the society's male-female population is roughly equal. Consequently, men have to compete for available mates if they are to produce children and if they are to have opportunities for heterosexual intercourse. Aggressiveness is valued in polygynous societies, and male children are socialized to become aggressive (Low, 1989; Munroe & Munroe, 1997). As noted earlier, if some men are more aggressive than others, they gain certain advantages. They can fight successfully for available mates. Further, they can compete successfully for a society's various resources (e.g., wealth, status, goods) that will allow them to attract one or more mates. Aggressiveness also allows men to compete successfully for resources related to survival (especially food, perhaps medicinal plants) once they produce children and are expected to provide for their families.

Female Nurturance and Obedience

Viewed in a specific way, the socialization of nurturance and obedience in women is the opposite side of the male-aggressiveness coin. If girls are socialized to be nurturant and obedient to others, they later may be favored by the community's most successful, high-status men. Men want women who will bear and nurture their children; women want the highest status men possible because they will be more likely to secure the resources necessary for survival. Obedience is important to men because women who possess this trait are more likely to (a) follow orders and thus reinforce the male's dominance and (b) regularly do the necessary tasks related to housekeeping and caretaking of children.

Other Influences on Aggressiveness and Obedience

Differences within various polygynous societies affect the relative emphases people place on aggressiveness and obedience (Low, 1989). Some societies have strong caste or class structures that limit people's strivings for a better life. In such societies, people are born into a certain class, and their opportunities in life are determined by this fact. During their socialization, children would not be rewarded for trying to better their lot in life and to move into a higher class. One of the opportunities predetermined for men is the type of mates available to them. If they can choose only from their social class (and thus do not have to compete with men from higher and lower classes), they have less need than men in other societies to be aggressive, assertive, and dominant.

Women face an interesting possibility in some societies with strong class or caste structures. Women can "marry up"; that is, it is permissible for them to marry a man from a higher class. According to Low (1989):

> A woman who marries up may not have more children than a woman who marries within her class, but her children are likely to be better-invested and survive better. The traits expressed as desirable in wives in [these] societies are chastity and obedience. (p. 315)

Possibly, men from higher classes who marry women from lower classes expect certain features, such as chastity and obedience. A chaste wife may be more likely to remain faithful to the high-status husband, so the husband can assure himself about the parenthood of his offspring (Buss & Kenrick, 1998). A status-generating feature for a man may be the fact he is the only person to have engaged in sexual intercourse with a certain woman. The advantages of female obedience already have been mentioned: Obedient women reinforce dominant men, and they will faithfully fulfill their household duties.

These findings may have implications for today's world. Women who marry up may be trading resources: chastity and obedience for the man's higher status and access to society's benefits. This is not unknown in monogamous cultures. My guess is that most readers know of women who were from the lower or working class, but they happened to have beauty-queen-level good looks. Some of these women may have traded this resource and married a high-status man with access to money, an exquisite home, and benefits for any eventual children. More speculatively, the fact that most of our ancestors lived in polygynous societies may have an impact. Readers might want to consider this question: "If you could act on your own preferences, how many sexual partners would you like to have in one month?" Men may answer with a higher number than women might. If our evolutionary background is polygynous, men had the opportunity to seek multiple mates and may have learned to prefer such an arrangement. Women were limited to one partner and may have learned to prefer this arrangement. Further, women may have learned to prefer close relationships with one person rather than several interactions limited to the sex act.

These preferences may have continued through time. A number of women have told me their feeling in words similar to the following: "I am more interested in a deep relationship with one person than in superficial relationships with many different people."

Activity Level

People can behave in quiet, restful ways that are passive and indicate no desire to have an impact on other individuals or on their living environment. Or, people can invest energy in activities involving much physical movement and leading to impacts on others and on their living environments (MacDonald, 1998). The term "high activity level" is used to describe the latter types of behaviors. When the behaviors of males and females are compared, males are more likely to engage in behaviors marked by a high activity level. Block (1983) summarizes much of the literature:

> Males have also been observed to be more curious and to engage in more exploration, behaviors that may reflect activity level (and also may reflect impulsivity and risk taking). . . . Boys engage in more manipulation of objects, react more strongly to barriers to attractive goal objects, and play more than girls in outdoor areas. Studies of older boys show that they perceive and describe themselves as more daring and adventurous than females. Consistent with males' greater adventurousness is the set of findings (Manheimer, Dewey, Mellinger, & Corsa, 1966) demonstrating, perhaps definitively, in an enormous and representative sample ($N = 8,874$) that boys have significantly more accidents requiring emergency medical treatment at every age level between 4 and 18 years. (p. 1338)

Several implications stem from the findings that males are more likely to have a higher activity level than females. Recall the discussion of socialization in chapter 4, especially the concept of guided participation suggested by Rogoff (1990; see also A. Fiske et al., 1998). Children have an important influence on many of their own socialization experiences. They often try out new behaviors, such as reading a book beyond their grade level. If they do not do as well as they hoped they would, they may communicate this feeling to adults either verbally or nonverbally. The adults then can intervene and offer assistance (the "guidance" in guided participation). In the reading example, perhaps an adult would explain a few of the longer words or break a complex sentence into several shorter phrases. The important point for the analysis of male-female differences is that the more activities children engage in, the more opportunities adults have to notice how they might help. If boys engage in more behaviors involving high activity levels, then adults will have more opportunities to engage the boys in guided participation. High activity level, then, leads to noticeability. Noticeability, in turn, leads to opportunities for guided participation during adult-child encounters.

One of the places where boys and girls might engage in high levels of noticeable activity is on the playing field or on the playground. Participation in games can bring many benefits (Anshel, Williams, & Hodge, 1997; Sutton-Smith & Roberts, 1981). If the games involve large teams, children may have to interact effectively with people from outside their immediate family. If the game is complex, they may have to practice a great deal, thus developing good work habits that may later bring respect in the community once children take on adult tasks. If the game allows participation by people with various skill levels, children can test their limits, gradually setting higher personal performance goals and increasing the risks they are willing to take. Note that these benefits could accrue to both male and female participants. Boys, however, are likely to benefit more. As discussed previously, boys are more aggressive. This can lead to higher performance levels in games that have aggressiveness as an element (e.g., American football, basketball, and baseball). If girls decide to play with boys, they may drop out because of possible harm to their bodies from aggressive competition.

One reason for the common observation of gender differentiation among children after age 6 (Maccoby, 1990; Munroe & Munroe, 1997) is that girls do not like the aggressive play boys favor. A second and more subtle reason is that when they make suggestions during playtime, boys do not pay much attention to girls. For example, all three of the American team sports mentioned above involve behaviors that lead to arguments: Was the pass dropped or caught? Was the person fouled while making the basket or not? Was the runner safe or out at second base? Perhaps because of their concern with dominance (discussed previously), boys are more likely to listen to others of the same sex when making decisions about applying the games's rules. Seeing that they have little influence, girls may drop out and play among members of their own sex. Examining possible distinctions between boys and girls in their attempts to influence others, Maccoby also suggests:

> . . . between the ages of 3 and a half and 5 and a half, children greatly increase the frequency of their attempts to influence their play partners. This indicates that children are learning to integrate their activities with those of others so as to be able to carry out coordinated activities. (p. 515)

However, the means of influence differed in the study. Girls were more likely to make polite suggestions. Boys were more likely to use direct commands. In addition, boys were not likely to be influenced (in decisions about their own behavior) by polite suggestions from anyone. Consequently, the style that girls used was ineffective during their interactions with boys. The girls were influential with each other, and they were effective in their interactions with teachers and other adults given that the latter prefer suggestions to demands! Still, the positive attention girls received for their politeness must have been irritating to boys, further reinforcing their preference for same-sex playgroups.

The female style just discussed will have more use in the long run given that intercultural and international interactions demand mutual respect and will proceed more smoothly if suggestions are offered rather than demands made (Adler, 1997). Admittedly, however, adults are asking young girls to wait a long time (during the seemingly endless period of late childhood and adolescence) before their influence style is useful. Young girls can become upset when they find they cannot engage in the high activity level thought appropriate for boys. In a study of satisfaction with gender roles carried out in Australia, Burns and Homel (1986) found that some young girls had a major complaint. While having generally positive self-concepts, 37% of the Australian girls from an Anglo background were dissatisfied with the restrictions placed on their participation in sports and games. For example, many wanted to play cricket, but boys had far more opportunities to participate in this sport. The other sports the girls mentioned (and all involved high activity levels) as restricted were soccer, skateboarding, and tree climbing. One reason for the girls' dissatisfaction was that their expectations were not met. They went to school and heard the claim that Australia offers equal opportunities to males and females. Yet when they tried to participate in some of these opportunities in the form of active sports, they met barriers.

Interestingly, other young girls Burns and Homel (1986) surveyed did not have this dissatisfaction. Young Australian girls from Mediterranean backgrounds (e.g., Greece, Turkey) did not express any gender role dissatisfaction. They did not participate in active sports, but they did not expect to and did not value such participation. Young girls from Mediterranean backgrounds had internalized other expectations during their earlier socialization. They had learned to value their contribution to family honor through their chastity and preparation for eventual motherhood. The young girls met these expectations through such activities as helping their mothers at home, so they were satisfied with their gender roles. The childhood outcomes that lead to satisfaction will change as women have more choices among roles. Research in India (Dorahy, Schumaker, Simpson, & Deshpande, 1996) indicates that as role expectations change, women want the benefits of the changes and will make conclusions about their life satisfaction based on acquiring these benefits. Changes and resulting benefits in India include access to advanced educational opportunities, salaried jobs and choices about how the money is spent, and shared decision making on issues such as the number of children a couple will have.

Deference During Interactions With Others

To prepare for this discussion of people's behaviors during interactions with others, I suggest that readers imagine they are participants in the two incidents described next. Because some readers are men and some are women and because the settings involve members of both sexes, people may want to predict typical reactions of same- and opposite-sex participants.

Incident 1: Imagine that a group of six women are discussing political developments in the Middle East. They argue back and forth, occasionally disagree, add ideas to one anothers arguments, point out flaws in one another's reasoning, and in general are having a vigorous discussion. An attractive man who is the same age as the women enters the room. What typical reactions are likely to occur?

Incident 2: Imagine that a group of six men are holding a similar discussion. The give and take between participants is as vigorous (but no more so) as in Incident 1. An attractive woman who is the same age as the men enters the room. Three of the men know the woman is particularly well read about the history and politics of the Middle East. What typical reactions are likely to occur?

A number of research findings suggest that in such situations many women are likely to defer to the man and to decrease the vigor of their discussions. Compared to the quality of the ideas they raise when interacting with members of their own sex, they may bring up less insightful ideas and present them in a quieter manner when a man enters the room (Maccoby, 1990; Weisfeld, Weisfeld, & Callaghan, 1982). In contrast, the men are not likely to decrease the vigor of their arguments and will show no decrease in the quality of the ideas they offer to the group. In fact, the men may not make any effort to integrate the woman who entered the room, even though three of them know she is well read in the area under discussion.

An important fact to keep in mind is that no differences exist in the ability of men and women to make vigorous contributions to discussions. This analysis is absolutely not a claim about a trait people possess, that is, an aspect of their personality or intellect. Rather, the suggestion is that men and women respond differently to the same type of social situation (Pratto, Stallworth, Sidanius, & Siers, 1997). When they find themselves in mixed-sex groups, women become less vigorous and may even show decreases in performance on the tasks called for in the situation (in the examples, the quality of ideas offered). Men do not show this decline in performance.

Maccoby (1990) suggests that differences in performance in same- and mixed-sex groups can be seen during childhood. In one of her studies, she observed the behavior of American children (average age of 33 months) playing with toys with either same-sex or opposite-sex partners. A score for each child was recorded based on his or her social behavior directed at another child. This "social behavior" score included both positive (e.g., offering a toy, hugging) and negative (e.g., grabbing a toy, pushing) behaviors. "Passive behavior," when the child simply was standing around doing little or nothing, was also recorded. Maccoby summarizes some of the findings:

> There was no overall sex difference in the frequency of [passive] behavior, but the behavior of girls was greatly affected by the sex of the partner. With other girls, passive behavior seldom occurred; indeed, in girl-girl pairs it occurred less often than it did in boy-boy pairs. However, when paired with boys, girls frequently stood on the sidelines and let the boys monopolize the toys. Clearly, the little girls in this study were not more passive than the little girls in any overall, trait-like sense. Passivity in these girls could be understood only in relation to the characteristics of their interactive partners. (p. 514)

Additional information on behavior in mixed-sex groups can be found in two interesting studies carried out among Hopi Indian children in Arizona and among Black American children in Chicago (Weisfeld et al., 1982). The researchers recorded the behavior of 12-year-old children during dodgeball games. In dodgeball, a person enters the center of a circle. A member of the circle throws a large inflated ball at the person in the center. If the individual throwing the ball scores a hit, he or she then enters the middle of the circle. If the person in the center is missed, others in the circle should compete for the ball so that they can make the next throw. The only way to get points is to be the person who scores a hit and subsequently enters the center of the circle. For every thrown ball avoided or dodged, the person in the center gets a point. The potential for competitive behavior in this game occurs when children try to get the ball to make the next throw. Children can run into each other when trying to get the ball, and tears can surface if someone falls to the ground.

Weisfeld and her colleagues (1982) chose this game because it was equally familiar to boys and girls. They found results that were similar to those Maccoby (1990) reported. When all the players were girls, the games proceeded vigorously. Some girls were very skillful players and consistently scored more points than their same-sex peers. However, when boys and the same girls played dodgeball together, the girls became passive. This reaction took place both among the Hopi in Arizona and among the Black Americans in Chicago. Further, female passivity occurred even when the girls had more ability than many of the boys they were playing with in mixed-sex dodgeball games. The researchers also recorded exactly how the female passivity occurred, and the findings are consistent with the discussions of individualism and collectivism presented in several places in this book (e.g., chapters 2 and 8). During mixed-sex competition, Hopi girls would not position their bodies so that they could move quickly if the dodgeball came near them. Rather, they would stand with their legs crossed and their arms folded, "hugging themselves" as if they were seeking protection. The Hopi girls also smiled, perhaps offering this as a sign of appeasement and as a request for harmony as called for in their collective. In contrast, the more individualistic Black American girls engaged in expressive behaviors even though they were clearly not competing. These girls "slipped away to form little cliques alongside the playing circle. In these small groups the girls engaged in extraneous behaviors, eating potato chips, talking, dancing, or teasing the active players" (Weisfeld et al., p. 39).

When attempting to explain these results, the researchers considered the implications of research on activity level as discussed in the previous section. Perhaps the girls felt that the boys were likely to be more physically aggressive in the dodgeball games and that they might be hurt when chasing the ball or, if they were to succeed, when they played the center role. If they avoided throwing the ball, they could avoid acting as targets. Or, the girls may have felt that their suggestions for improving the game or for settling disputes (was the person in the center hit or not on a close call?) would be ignored by the more assertive and dominant boys. Examining these possibilities, Weisfeld and her colleagues (1982) also studied behavior during spelling bees. As most readers will remember from their own schooling, a teacher or other adult reads words, and the participants try to spell the words. Usually, not as many disputes arise about applying the rules in spelling bees compared to athletic events. The researchers reported, "Girls usually spell better than boys, and these [American Indian and Black American participants] were no exceptions. They were matched on spelling ability in this study, and again female inhibition was observed" (p. 41).

STEREOTYPES AND INDIVIDUAL DIFFERENCES

A point about sex and gender differences that constantly should be kept in mind is that results such as those in both the Maccoby (1990) and Weisfeld (1982) studies represent trends among numerous boys and girls. In these studies, a majority of the boys and girls behaved in the manner reported: Girls became passive in mixed-sex competition, and boys did not. However, exceptions occur. In the study by Weisfeld and her colleagues, individual girls were just as active and just as assertive in mixed-sex as in same-sex competitions. Currently, researchers know too little about people who choose to interact in ways that differ from others of their sex. Yet this is a key to understanding the liberation of both men and women from traditional gender roles (Dorahy et al., 1996). My prediction is that the analysis of people who break with tradition and who interact in ways considered atypical in their cultures will be a more common research focus in the future (Adler, 1994).

Studies with this predicted emphasis on understanding people who break with traditional gender roles will need to explain two sets of research findings. One will involve the analysis of individuals who break patterns, and the other will focus on documenting the general trends if information is gathered from large numbers of people. Explanations for these latter findings are very useful in the analysis of sex stereotypes, gender stereotypes, and the self-images of men and women in various parts of the world (Best & Williams, 1997; Williams & Best, 1982, 1990a, 1990b). Images and stereotypes become part of people's thinking after they observe the behavior of many individuals. As discussed in chapter 6 (and reviewed briefly at the beginning of this chapter), stereotypes and images are types of generalizations useful for organizing the massive amounts of information people encounter. As with any generalization, the formation of stereotypes and images downplays the behavior of specific individuals in favor of trends across large numbers of people. After many observations of different individuals, people from all over the world are likely to see more aggressive behavior in men, more nurturant behavior in women, more assertion of leadership among men, and more passivity among women in mixed-sex groups. These observations become part of the universal stereotypes and images of men and women (Williams & Best, 1982, 1990b). Because observers do not focus on individual differences, they do not focus on the aggressive woman or the passive man.

One of the most important guidelines for professionals who deal with people from different cultures (e.g., counselors, clinicians, social workers) is that to be of assistance professionals must go beyond stereotypes and images and focus on the individual in question. Professionals should not begin a counseling session with a woman by imposing the stereotype "nurturant." They should move quickly into assessments of the woman's individual needs, desires, and reasons for seeking assistance. More information on the work of these professionals will be covered in the next chapter.

Even while constantly reminding themselves to move beyond generalizations about men and women and to focus on individuals, professionals and other people have good reasons to search for explanations for the generalizations. One is to understand why gender stereotypes and self-images are formed and why some are found all over the world. Another is to help individuals move away from the generalization if that is their goal. For example, a woman may want to seek a leadership position in her culture. She may be experiencing stress given that her extended family and friends prefer that she behave in the nurturant manner typical of gender role expectations. If she understands the reasons for the general expectation about female nurturance (and this can be dealt with in counseling sessions), she may experience a reduction in stress. One of the major reasons for extreme stress is that people feel that "I am the only one having a problem like this, and I also am weird for feeling the way I do about this." If the counselor can point out that virtually all women who seek leadership positions experience stress given that their cultures expect nurturance, the heavy psychological load stemming from the thought that "I am the only one!" can be lifted.

Consider the generalization (keeping in mind that exceptions occur) that women become more passive in mixed-sex groups compared to all-female groups. The reasons for this are puzzling, and the suggestions presented in this paragraph are the most speculative in the entire chapter. Weisfeld and her colleagues (1982) drew from

Callan's (1970) analyses and suggested that a possible explanation stems from the demands of child rearing. Recall some of the facts about procreation and child rearing reviewed earlier in the chapter. The act of childbirth is often debilitating to the mother, and this must have been more true in the past given the absence of modern medical practice. In addition, children are totally helpless for long periods. Children cannot obtain their own food, cannot look after themselves in times of trouble, and need to be instructed about proper behavior called for in their cultures. All this attention to children and child rearing takes a great deal of energy (Doyle & Paludi, 1995). If the mother and father constantly argue among themselves about who is to take on what tasks and who will make decisions in certain areas, the time and energy spent on such arguments cannot be invested in the children. In addition, given her weakness after childbirth, the mother does not have much energy to invest in arguments. To insure that time and energy go into the difficult work of raising children, the culturally universal roles of male dominance and female passivity (in the presence of men) may have arisen. Women who behaved in this passive manner were more likely to attract men, mate with them, successfully raise their children, and pass their genes to future generations.

Williams and Best (1982, 1990b; Best & Williams, 1997) found that passivity was part of people's stereotype of women in 25 cultures. Other parts of the stereotype were that women are deferent, nurturant, and affiliative. In addition to an explanation based on biological differences that lead to responsibilities for child care, Williams and Best (1990b) stated that other arguments need to be made about reasons for the stereotype. One argument is that people become comfortable believing that members of each sex either have or can develop the characteristics necessary to carry out tasks in a smooth-functioning society.

> If females are to have principal responsibility for the care of the young, it is reassuring to believe that they are—or can become—affectionate, gentle, patient, sympathetic, and so on. If males are to serve as hunters and warriors, it is comforting to believe that they can—or can become—adventurous, aggressive, courageous, energetic, independent, self-confident, and the like. . . . It may be in this context, the "justification of necessity" with regard to different social roles, that many of the sex-trait stereotypes originated. Once established, the beliefs concerning the psychological makeup serve as norms for the behavior of adult men and women and provide models for the socialization of girls and boys toward their assigned [gender] roles. (Williams & Best, 1990a, p. 237)

Another needed part of the explanation is consistent with some feminist approaches to the analysis of gender differences (e.g., Hare-Mustin & Maracek, 1988; Jamieson, 1998; Stockard & Johnson, 1979). Once men are socialized to act in a dominant manner (part of the male stereotype identified by Williams & Best, 1990a), they become comfortable with their power over women and develop norms that keep women in subservient positions. People who hold power learn to enjoy it (Brislin, 1991; Kipnis, 1976) and are unwilling to relinquish it. When men have power, they often develop beliefs that maintain it (e.g., "We are better able to make tough decisions"). Further, they develop other beliefs that make it difficult for women to gain access to power (e.g., "They are really happier in homemaker roles"). These arguments involving the importance of power are similar to those made in chapter 6

When men have power over women, they often develop a set of beliefs to justify and maintain their dominance.

about race relations. One reason for White prejudice toward Blacks in the United States and other parts of the world is that Whites enjoy the power they possess. By discriminating against Blacks and keeping them in subservient roles, Whites maintain their power.

Returning to the arguments about gender, note that the tendency for women to become passive in the company of men does not have to dictate behavior among adults in today's world. Knowledge of such research can lead to possible actions, a theme I dealt with in a book on the strategies and tactics for power use (Brislin, 1991; Brislin & Jane, 1997). With a knowledge of all the research reviewed in this chapter, for instance, one of the female graduate students who works with me has developed a plan. She realizes she tends to defer to men during the give-and-take of arguments about scholarly issues. She has observed, for instance, that when a speaker from another university gives a good presentation, almost all the questions come from the men in the audience. She makes a point, at every presentation she attends, of asking acute questions. She admits it was difficult to ask questions at first, but after a few times it became rather matter-of-fact to participate actively.

A label for behaviors such as women asking pointed questions in mixed-sex groups might be "moving beyond male-female tendencies." As mentioned several times in this chapter, the liberation that stems from moving beyond traditional gender roles can benefit members of both sexes. Men who tend to dominate meetings, for instance, may want to make a point of listening to and respecting others' contributions. They may find that the meetings will be much more productive. Time and energy will be spent on developing good ideas rather than on sorting out positions in the dominance hierarchy.

What other tendencies should men and women know about so that they can make appropriate decisions about their behavior? One of the most important tendencies, given its widespread implications, is that women are more concerned than men about their relationships with others.

WOMEN'S CONCERN WITH RELATEDNESS

Much research has examined the possibility that women are more concerned with their relationships with others than are men (Deaux & LaFrance, 1998; Low, 1989; Maccoby, 1990; Prince, 1985). As already reviewed, reasons include the universal fact that women bear children and must nurture them. Given their weakness after childbirth and the demands of raising children for many years, women who can develop and maintain good relationships can secure assistance with their difficult child-rearing demands. Women are responsible for introducing their young children to the norms of their culture, and good relationships with others in their community help them achieve this goal. Knowing the benefits of good relationships, adults in a culture encourage girls to develop relational skills during socialization. One reason for the frequent observation that girls are more often punished for aggressive behavior than are boys (Barry & Child, 1983; Hendrix & Johnson, 1985) is that aggressiveness in girls may interfere with their ability to develop relationships with others. The "concern with relatedness" has several important implications that have been the focus of different research studies.

Expectations People Have of Friendships

Morse (1983) has provided evidence that when men and women are asked the same questions about their expectations about friendships with members of the same sex, women expect more. Interviewing college students in Australia and Brazil about love relationships and friendships, he showed that emotional involvement and dependency distinguished love from friendship in both countries and that respect and reciprocal communication were important in both types of relationships. In both countries, women expected more of friendships. Men and women were presented with various characteristics of friendship, and they were asked to rate "what's important for you to become good friends with someone of the same sex" (Morse, p. 471).

Women gave 10 friendship features more importantance than men gave them, and these included the following:

- For this person to fulfill your emotional demands
- For you to feel committed to your relationship with this person
- To just like to be with this person
- To be able to confide in this person
- To feel self-confident when you're with this person
- To feel secure about your feelings toward this person

The first implication of the general tendency for women to be more concerned with relationships, then, is that they have more expectations of people they develop close friendships with. Further evidence comes from a study of Caucasian Americans and Black Americans attending college in the southern United States (Holland & Eisenhart, 1988). Women's happiness during their college years was strongly affected by the quality of their friendships with peers. Much of what they learned about themselves, and how they learned to evaluate their present behavior and their likely futures, came from age peers far more than from others, such as professors and employers. These findings suggest that if people want to encourage women to expand their thinking beyond the traditional gender roles society provides for them, people would be wise to work with individual women and their peer groups. If the peer group disapproves of any woman's plans, this can lead to a great deal of stress for her.

This discussion should not be interpreted as a claim that women are prisoners of their peer groups. Rather, the suggestion is that peer relationships are very important and that this fact must be kept in mind by people (e.g., teachers, employers) asked to help women achieve their goals.

The Importance of Good Relations With Authority Figures

Another implication of women's concern for relatedness is that they strongly prefer to have positive feelings about authority figures. Recall from chapter 8 that this was a feature of societies Hofstede (1991, 1996) labeled "feminine." In feminine societies, where the influence of women has been felt in the workplace, workers rank good relationships with coworkers and bosses as important when rating their job satisfaction. Wise bosses know this and make a point of maintaining good relationships because they realize people will work hard if they think positively about the bosses and their goals, policies, and treatment of workers.

In addition to its relevance to adults developing their careers, the importance of good relationships with authority figures also has been identified in research among schoolchildren. Buriel (1983) provided evidence that contradicts common sense. Assuming that everyday wisdom suggests that boys (because they are more active) seek more interactions with teachers and volunteer answers to questions more frequently, Buriel showed that this is not always the case. Working with fourth- and fifth-grade Mexican American and Anglo American children, Buriel found that girls initiated more work-related contacts with their teachers than did boys. Unfortunately, the teachers whose behavior was recorded did not always follow up on the work-related contacts their female students initiated. Although the general finding was that teachers who used the most praise (and low amounts of criticism) encouraged the greatest amount of student achievement, no reciprocal relationship was found between student-initiated contact and teacher response. In one of the three classrooms studied, Mexican American girls received the most praise; in another classroom, Mexican American boys received the most praise; and in the third, Anglo American girls received the most praise when they initiated contact with their teachers. Another important finding was that Mexican American students, possibly because of their more collective socialization with its emphasis on good relationships, responded more positively to teachers who praised good school-related efforts and who downplayed any temptations to criticize nonwork activities (e.g., excessive requests to use the bathroom). One practical application of these findings is that teachers should make sure they encourage and reinforce contacts all students initiate, and they should be especially careful that they are not treating boys and girls differently. Given that the girls initiated more contact in this study, it must have been frustrating when they experienced inconsistent responses to this type of behavior.

Sensitivity to Other's Problems

If women are more concerned with relationships, they also may be more sensitive to the problems others have that can interfere with smooth and stress-free interactions among people (Lai, Hamid, & Chow, 1996). Doherty and Obani (1986) provided evidence for this possibility in a study of sensitivity to people's disabilities. The researchers provided descriptions of people with various disabilities to adolescents in Great Britain and in Nigeria. In each country, boys and girls from various age groups were selected so that the influence of both maturity (development of sensitivity over several years) and sex could be investigated. The groups selected were ages 11, 13, 15, and 17.

Doherty and Obani (1986) asked a number of direct questions and also presented short case studies to respondents. For example, one of the direct questions was "Which handicap do you think is the worst to have? Why do you say so?" One of the case studies involved a young woman named Ida who was a popular teenager with an active social life. However, she developed an illness that caused paralysis in her left leg and arm and that also caused difficulties when she tried to speak. This led to much unhappiness for Ida. Respondents were asked, "Why do you think Ida was unhappy?"

The results of the study showed that as the age of respondents increased, they were more likely to provide insightful answers to the questions. At the more mature age levels, the answers were more comprehensive and showed more insight into and accurate analyses of the problems of people with disabilities than those of the younger respondents. In addition, the girls in both cultures showed more insight and understanding than the boys. Their answers were more complete and were more likely to reflect thinking that went beyond the concepts presented in the questions and the case studies. The results showed that girls were more able to recall their personal observations of people in their everyday lives and were more likely to apply their insights to the questions the researchers asked than the boys. For example, answering the question about the worst impairment, a British 17-year-old girl focused on mental disabilities. Part of her answer included the effects of a disability on others.

> . . . it is the worst one to handle from the family's point of view. To have a child that is unresponsive or at least less than a normal child must be very depressing and frustrating. There are a lot of problems involved and in many cases this is seen to have a destructive influence on the family unit. (Doherty & Obani, 1986, p. 298)

In response to the case study about Ida, a 15-year-old Nigerian girl also was aware of the effects of a disability on other people.

> . . . for one who has been the center of attraction for quite a long time, it is quite a hard blow to suddenly find out that you are partially paralyzed and you won't be able to enjoy as much. Also she would have to be dependent and she may think she is a burden on the household. (Doherty & Obani, 1986, p. 301)

If women are more sensitive than men to people's problems and to the impacts those problems have on others, this sensitivity is undoubtedly a reason why women traditionally have entered such fields as nursing, social work, day care, and special education.

The Possibility of Burnout

A sensitivity to others that attracts women to the helping professions may have certain negative implications (Schaufeli & Janczur, 1994). When people have the responsibility for offering assistance to others but find that their efforts are hindered, they can experience emotional burnout (Maslach & Leiter, 1997). The helpers find that they have put much effort (and a great deal of themselves) into their desire to offer assistance but find that their efforts do little or no good. For many reasons, good intentions do not lead to the delivery of actual assistance to those needing it: inadequate funds, an overly complex bureaucracy, a legal system that demands evidence "beyond a reasonable doubt" if someone is to be convicted of a crime such as spouse abuse, and caseloads that offer little time for any one client needing help. Potential helpers find that they cannot cope with "the system," become extremely angry and frustrated, experience dibilitating stress, and report that they are simply burned out in their attempts to help others.

If women are more concerned with relationships and with the effects of people's problems, they also may experience more burnout than men when frustrated in their attempts to help others. Etzion and Pines (1986) found that this was the case. They interviewed 503 human service professionals in the United States and Israel. In both countries, women reported more frustration and burnout than men. Other results presented information that might assist human service professionals who are experiencing stress. Among women in both countries, the coping strategy of "actively confronting the stress source" was effective in reducing burnout feelings. Even though women may prefer a less direct strategy (such as avoiding the source of stress) than men, Etzion and Pines demonstrated that when women were more confrontative than in the past, they experienced less burnout. When women experiencing burnout developed support groups, discussions and mutual advice giving about confronting stress directly was fruitful. For example, women could share information about how to confront uncaring supervisors, how to lobby more effectively for increased funding, or how to enlist the help of law enforcement officials in spouse- and child-abuse cases.

In addition to this direct method for coping with stress, some women in the study benefited from the more indirect approach of getting involved in other community activities. This was more effective among American than among Israeli women, and the reason for the difference between the two countries is not entirely clear. One possibility is that the United States has more community activities that allow people to "take their minds off" their troubles than Israel: bridge clubs, support groups for the opera and symphony, supervision of community activities for children. After the relaxation these activities provide, women might return to their stressful workplace with a fresher perspective. Given the long-standing conflicts between Arabs and Jews in Israel, the country may offer far fewer activities that allow Israelis to relax and temporarily forget the various stressors in their lives.

Interpreting Negative Emotions

One of the important implications of a greater concern with relationships is that women are sensitive to both the positive and negative aspects of their interactions with others. If relationships are not going well, people often want to intervene and to correct any difficulties. One way they learn about difficulties is through observations of others. If the others are sending out negative signals, people concerned with good relationships should be able to interpret these signals. Given that women are concerned with maintaining good relationships, they should be more responsive to the negative signals others are sending.

Several studies have investigated this possibility, and they have focused on the interpretation of nonverbal behaviors (N. Goldstein, 1996; McAndrew, 1986; Sogon & Izard, 1987). More specifically, researchers have been concerned with the nonverbal communication of emotions such as joy, surprise, fear, sadness, disgust, anger, and contempt. The nonverbal behaviors studied were body posture (Sogon & Izard) and facial expressions (McAndrew).

The method Sogon and Izard (1987) chose was to film Japanese actors who posed the emotions while facing away from the camera. Viewers, then, had to interpret the emotion the actors posed with only a view of the backs of their bodies. The films were shown to American men and women who were asked to guess the emotion the actors had in mind. The method McAndrew (1986) chose was to present photographs prepared and published by Ekman and Friesen (1975). McAndrew then showed the pictures for very short periods (less than 1 second, by means of a tachistoscope) to men and women in both the United States and Malaysia. Ekman and Friesen earlier had shown that certain emotions are easier to interpret than others: Happiness, for example, seems to be easy for people to display and easy for others to interpret. Other emotions are more difficult in the sense that they can be mistaken for others. For example, fear and surprise are frequently confused: People may think they are communicating surprise, but observers often interpret the emotional display as fear.

Whenever sex differences occurred in the two studies, women were more skillful at interpreting nonverbal presentations of emotions. Sogon and Izard (1987) showed that women were more skillful at identifying disgust, fear, and sadness. One interpretation the researchers suggested is consistent with the arguments presented earlier in this chapter. Because women are more sensitive to relationships, they are more sensitive to difficulties that may be occurring in their relationships. If they become skillful in interpreting such negative emotions as disgust, fear, and sadness, they will be better able to diagnose difficulties in their everyday relationships. This skill also helps women avoid unwanted confrontations. Another possibility is that given their lower social status in many societies, women learn to interpret negative emotions so as to avoid powerful people when they are in negative moods. If women learn to diagnose negative emotions and also learn to wait for powerful people to be in good moods, the women may have a higher probability of benefiting from their relationships with the powerful.

McAndrew (1986) found that women in both Malaysia and the United States were better than males at identifying and distinguishing between facial expressions of fear and surprise. The explanation that stems from the "female concern with relatedness" argument is that females spend more time examining the nonverbal behavior of others so that they can maintain good relationships and intervene in problematic relationships. McAndrew argued:

> Female superiority occurred primarily on the emotions of fear and surprise, which are traditionally the two most readily confused emotions. As one of the reasons for the confusion on fear and surprise is the great similarity in the facial configurations involved in these expressions, it may be that females do better simply because they spend more time looking at other people's faces and are therefore more aware of and sensitive to subtle differences between expressions than are males. (p. 221)

Just as in the arguments about sensitivity to people's problems (burnout arises if the sensitivity does not lead to positive actions), a dilemma stems from women's ability to interpret negative emotions. People who enforce a culture's norms can take advantage of this ability and place limits on the opportunities allowed women (Jamieson, 1998). Dorn (1986) argues that the behavior of women can be controlled by gossip, and gossip is not necessarily only verbal. A woman who is the subject of gossip, for instance, may not hear what people are saying about her. However, she might observe the facial expressions and body postures of people talking about her, for example, 20 or 30 meters from where she is standing. Given her ability to interpret these nonverbal behaviors, she is likely to receive the message that her behavior is under scrutiny and then might change her behavior to conform. Dorn studied the behavior of women in a Jewish community in Istanbul, Turkey. Many of the behaviors that would lead to gossip, as well as the nature of gossip itself, were summarized in proverbs. For example, women say to each other,

> No one knows what is happening in the pot except for the spoon that turns. Meaning: Everyone talks about what is happening in the house, but only insiders know what is really happening. Thus, gossip can only be speculative and not very dangerous about a woman who stays at home and who keeps to the traditional role. (p. 299)

Traditional roles, of course, are exactly what women complain about as they attempt to move more freely and to pursue the opportunities available in their culture. What happens when women move beyond traditional roles?

THE CONVERGENCE OF BEHAVIORS TYPICAL OF MEN AND WOMEN

As women decide to move into roles that were traditionally denied them, the number of sharp distinctions that once marked the behaviors of men and women decreases. School-related performance is an example. If a stereotype once existed that women perform less well than men in mathematics and better than men in language arts, the differences today are either nonexistent or too small to influence decision making about a school's curriculum (Deaux & LaFrance, 1998; Lummis & Stevenson, 1990; Maccoby, 1990; Maccoby & Jacklin, 1974). The reason involves access to instruction. Once women were allowed to take advanced mathematics courses and once men were encouraged to pursue interests in language and the arts, they could take advantage of a school's offerings without encountering the prejudice that "boys do better in math, and girls do better in areas involving verbal skills." They then disproved the prior prejudice with their performance. In an ideal world, once opportunities within a society are opened up to members of both sexes, individuals can pursue various goals based on their abilities and interests. Further, they can pursue their goals without the constant concern that eventually limits will be placed on them. This ideal world does not yet exist, but research in diverse cultures has given insights into how a society without unnecessary gender restrictions might appear. Research has focused on the pressures for movements away from traditional restrictions and on the results of the changes in how men and women behave. Many of these changes involve a convergence in, rather than a sharp differentiation between, the behaviors of men and women.

Pressures for Change

One of the most influential factors that had led to changes centers on the roles women play in their culture. Recall the proverb that Dorn (1986) discovered in her study of women carried out in Turkey. The lesson to be drawn from the proverb was that women should stay in the home because if they ventured out, they might break a norm and then become the subject of gossip. Yet many pressures encourage women to leave the home (Hanassab & Tidwell, 1996). One involves the need to bring in more money to the family, and this leads to the search for wage labor (Brown, Graves, & Williams, 1997). Another involves the influence of mass media: Women see the greater freedom of the people who are portrayed in television shows and want to experience some of the benefits freedom appears to bring. Another and related reason involves intercultural contact. With increasing amounts of air travel and with increasing competition for the tourist dollar, places in the world once considered inaccessible are now chosen as vacation spots. Residents of the area where tourists appear observe different behaviors and may decide to try some. Returning to the first pressure about jobs, consider how tourism often creates jobs that involve frequent face-to-face contacts between visitors and residents of an area. Yet another reason for change undoubtedly involves the basic human need for growth, development, and stimulation. Many women, seeing the behavior of others on the television or in face-to-face interactions, learn that they are subject to many limits placed on them. Many must want to move beyond these limits simply to exercise their initiative, intelligence, and creativity, features of human beings that differentiate us from other primates (Buss & Kenrick, 1998; Kenrick, 1987).

Once women make the move away from traditional roles in the home to the increased opportunities found in the community at large, they change their outlook on life. Paguio, Skeen, and Robinson (1987) investigated the ideals that employed and nonemployed mothers have for their children, and they interviewed mothers in both the Philippines and the United States. Compared to their nonemployed counterparts, women with jobs (in both countries) felt that an ideal female child should be confident, aggressive, and well adjusted. The employed mothers undoubtedly saw the advantages of these features given their experiences in the workplace, and they wished them for their daughters. An interesting study by Nevill and Perrotta (1985) showed that preparation to take jobs in the workplace did not necessarily interfere with a commitment to home and family. Adolescents in Australia, Portugal, and the United States were interviewed about various life roles. An unanticipated finding was that, in all three countries, young women expressed more commitment to both work and the family than did young men. The authors explained, "[This] is an unexpected finding given prevailing sex-role stereotypes and shows the effects of the increased role of women in the workplace. However, female high school students did not expect to realize more values through work than did male high school students" (p. 492). One interpretation of these results is that the female adolescents were "hedging their bets." By committing themselves to both work and the home, they may have increased the chances of experiencing a realization of some of their goals. If their efforts in the workplace were thwarted, they could attempt to realize their goals in the home. Given the high divorce rate in highly industrialized nations, the young women also may have been preparing themselves for possible disappointments in the home.

With respect to their knowledge of potential problems in the workplace, the female adolescents were, unfortunately, correct. When a society changes or when people have to adjust to the demands of an unfamiliar society, men seem to be able to adjust more quickly than women. "Adjustment" is indicated by such factors as language acquisition, employment in good-paying jobs, and subjective feelings of happiness. Several studies have been carried out among immigrants and minority groups within the United States and in other countries. Abramson and Imai-Marquez (1982) worked with Japanese Americans, Burnam et al. (1987) worked with Mexican Americans, and Liebkind (1996) worked with Vietnamese refugees in Finland. In all three studies, men adjusted more quickly to the demands of the dominant American or Finnish mainstream. One reason is that men were allowed more movement outside the home. They could take part-time jobs, join community activities, and travel to other parts of their cities to interact with different kinds of people. Given these experiences, they learned information and participated in experiences that were useful to their adjustment. Given the pressures to maintain at least some allegiance to their traditional roles, women were more likely to spend time in the home. This meant they could not meet large numbers of people, had fewer chances to practice the dominant culture's language (English and Finnish), and had fewer chances to learn about the possibilities that full participation in American and Finnish society allows.

Types of Changes: Male-Female Interactions and Autonomy

As mentioned earlier in this chapter, people always must keep in mind the difference between trends (e.g., men adjusting to another culture faster than women) and individual differences. Individual women do adjust quickly, do accept and benefit from changes, and do begin to behave in ways that move them beyond the guidelines and limits provided them during their socialization (see chapter 4). Both the trends and the behaviors of individuals will be discussed in this section. One of the most stressful sets of behaviors involves attempts to change traditional expectations about interactions between men and women.

In a study investigating the acculturation of immigrants from Hong Kong to either the United States or Australia, Feldman and Rosenthal (1990) found that adjustment to behavioral norms common in the two English-speaking countries was very gradual. Among the various norms, gender differences arose in the time teenagers originally from Hong Kong took to press their families for greater personal freedom. In general, boys adjusted more quickly than girls, probably because of traditional norms to keep girls attached to the home (Liebkind, 1996). The types of behaviors that changed quickly contrasted to those that changed relatively slowly are interesting to note. The types of behaviors that changed more quickly (among adolescents from Hong Kong adjusting to the norms of Australia or the United States) involved attending boy-girl parties, staying home alone at night when parents are out, choosing TV shows or movies to watch, choosing friends even in the face of parental disapproval, and staying home alone when ill. These behaviors indicated that the adolescents were pressuring their parents for more autonomy and individualism.

However, for other adolescent behaviors, very slow adjustment to the norms in the two English-speaking countries occurred. These behaviors involved preparing dinner when home alone, going out on dates, preferring to do things with friends rather than family, and smoking and drinking. A distinction must be made between the relatively quick adjustment involving male-female parties and the slower adjustment to dating norms. The parties did not necessarily involve one-on-one relationships, while dating did. Parents are much more interested in having an influence in the latter area. The adolescents' behaviors involving preparing their own meals and interacting with friends rather than family may seem uncontroversial, but meals and family activities are very important in collective cultures (chapter 2), and parents view these activities as important for maintaining strong family ties. As noted earlier, when gender differences were reported by Feldman and Rosenthal (1990), girls were slower to find success in their quest for autonomy. The adolescents' behaviors involving attending boy-girl parties at night, no longer telling parents where they are going when leaving the house, and overnight trips involving both sexes without adult supervision were all approved more slowly for girls than for boys. One reason is that these behaviors involve the possibility that the young women might engage in the sex act. I have worked with many students who originally came from cultures where the behaviors of young women were carefully monitored. When asked the question "Why are more limitations placed on the behaviors of girls compared to boys?" most of my students have answered, "Because my parents always told me that girls get pregnant and boys don't. And that statement was supposed to end the discussion!"

Several research studies have suggested that once women leave the home and spend large amounts of time in other activities within their communities, their heterosexual behavior becomes similar to that of men. Alzate (1989) interviewed unmarried university students in Colombia, and Clement (1989) interviewed men and women in Germany. In both cases, women reported engaging in as much premarital sexual behavior as men. Both authors indicated that their results suggest a move away from the traditional double standard of expecting men to have sexual experience prior to marriage and women to be chaste. Researchers must be careful, however, not to overinterpret these findings and to declare that the double standard is dead. For the Colombian study, especially, it must be kept in mind that Alzate worked with a very select sample of people. Far fewer women attend college in Colombia than in the United States, so the self-confidence and autonomy of those who do attend college in Colombia is undoubtedly very high. Further, Alzate found indications that men were still expected to have more sexual experience than women, and they achieved this by employing prostitutes.

Other research suggests that female college students may possess a positive self-concept that allows them to challenge traditional norms. Ezelio (1983) found no difference in the self-concepts of male and female college students in Nigeria. One interpretation is that the relatively rare woman who strives to pursue a college education in Nigeria must have a very positive view of herself. Another possibility is that the move away from the traditional confines of the home, and participation in the new opportunities provided in a college, increases women's self-concepts. Of course, both possibilities can occur for the same woman. A positive self-concept contributes to her decision to attend college, and her self-worth increases from successful experiences in this nontraditional environment.

The general point argued here is that once a society's norms "loosen up" so that unnecessary restrictions are not placed on women, then male-female distinctions often disappear (Watkins, Akande, Cheng, & Regmi, 1996). As another example, Clark and Clark (1987) carried out interviews in Yugoslavia and found no distinctions made between male and female participation in the political arena as long as both were part of society's "elite." Here, *elite* refers to the benefits membership in society's upper strata can bring. These include affording a certain amount of comforts, education, and time to think about political issues. Elite women in Yugoslavia had as many of these opportunities as elite men, so their political participation was similar. Among the fewer advantaged, men were more likely to participate in politics than were women. This distinction undoubtedly reflects that among the less advantaged, women had fewer benefits than men: less education, less encouragement to read newspapers, less free time away from the home for developing interests in political issues, and so forth.

DIFFERENCES TO BE OVERCOME

Arguments have been presented in this chapter about male-female differences. With a few exceptions, most of these differences are small and are only observable if large numbers of men and women are compared. Overlap always occurs in the distribution of scores that summarize an attitude or aptitude or skills, with the highest scoring women scoring better than the lowest performing men. Given that most relevant differences are small, they can be overcome if people are motivated to do so and if they have the opportunities to develop their skills.

This "differences to be overcome" position will have exceptions where it is less likely to apply. Several professions only attract the strongest men, so it is unlikely a large pool of women of equal strength will participate. One example is professional sports, especially sports with constant and intense physical contact, such as American football. Another example would be jobs where strength and speed are combined. Emergency assistance personnel (e.g., firefighters, medics) often must run a certain distance while carrying heavy items. Even here, however, individual women can pass these tests and should be given every chance of thriving in these careers.

Moving from discussions of physical differences to psychological differences, I am unaware of any research that has identified insurmountable sex barriers. Yes, sometimes differences occur, but these can be overcome with motivation, training, and a supportive organization. Men score higher than women on a few spatial abilities (and they are poorly understood: Buss & Kenrick, 1998), but these are not so large as to erect barriers for women desirous of overcoming the differences. As discussed in this chapter, women may have more skills than men at developing relationships with others (Deaux & LaFrance, 1998). If men want to improve their ability to interact and to work with others, however, they can do so given the motivation and opportunities. They may want to develop these skills if leadership positions in their organizations are being assigned to individuals who work well with others, who set a democratic tone for participation, and who integrate the contributions of diverse people.

Perhaps an anecdote about my musical studies will be helpful. I started my study of a completely different instrument and style, Hawaiian slack key guitar, in my late 40s. Opportunities to learn this music are offered to classes of 10 to 20 students through organizations such as the University of Hawaii or through city Parks and Recreation programs. Younger students in my classes, both men and women, made more progress in less time than I did. But I knew the research on the development of new musical skills, especially those that demand fast and precise physical movements such as guitar fingerpicking. It is easier for young people to develop such skills. Yet I was motivated to learn this musical style, realizing I would be slower, and kept at it. It took about six years, and I remember learning similar amounts in two years when I was younger, but I now can play this style during very pleasant weekend gatherings with others. An important point is that my knowledge about the research was an aide in keeping me going. If I had not known the research, I may have made attributions about myself based on memories of mastering instruments when younger. I might have become frustrated and quit. But knowing the research allowed me to say, "I know I will be slower than the young hotshots in the class, but that's the way it is, and I can't change that. What I can do is keep working at it over a longer period. It will come."

Often, stereotypes about gender differences have been challenged by cross-cultural research. Most readers probably have heard the cliché mentioned earlier, "Men do better at mathematics." Research in Asia (Stevenson, Chen, & Lee, 1993) has shown that this is not the case if teachers have high expectations of both men and women and if cultural norms support the importance of mathematics for all. Young women in Asia (specifically, Korea, Japan, and China) hear the cliché about men and mathematics less frequently. Consequently, it is less likely to become part of their self-images. If they get poor grades on an algebra test and later talk to their teachers, they will not receive sympathy based on the fact they are women. If they expect a tissue for their tears, they are more likely to receive an extra set of 100 mathematics problems to solve. As discussed in chapter 5, attributions about school performance in Asia are more likely to be based on effort rather than aptitude. Excuses about lacking "mathematical ability" are not acceptable. Given that success in mathematics is based on effort, then the solution to poor performance is more effort. Both men and women are expected to engage in this effort.

At times, conclusions about gender differences have no basis in fact and must be constantly challenged. Adler (1994) analyzed why relatively few women are offered assignments in their multinational organizations. She compared a set of myths with information based on interviews with more than 100 female managers. Three myths were especially prominent, and each will be discussed in detail.

Myth 1: *Women are reluctant to accept overseas positions*. The responses to this myth are, "Who says, who is doing the asking, and who is answering the question?" Ambitious women are sensitive to their company's criteria for promotion, and they are sensitive to changes in their industry. If company executives expect their best managers to undertake overseas assignments, then women will want such assignments. Rather than women having a reluctance to accept an overseas posting, Adler (1994) found that women had to put time and effort into persuading bosses to let them undertake such travel and relocation. At times, women had to take advantage of emergencies and last-minute changes in others' plans. One woman reported she wanted an assignment in Tokyo but had to wait for and react to a tragedy. The financial manager in Tokyo had a heart attack, and the company had to send someone in a hurry. The woman was available, moved to Tokyo and set herself up quickly, and did a good job. Seeing her success, the company let her stay.

Part of this myth undoubtedly is based on the stereotype of women as weaker than men and in need of protection. In athletics, major changes over the 20th century have occurred in views about women's capabilities. When my mother played basketball, no contact was allowed, players could dribble once, and then they had to shoot or pass. Now, a glance at the television shows full contact, especially "in the paint" (under the basket), at high school, college, and professional levels. When I participated in track and field, the farthest women were allowed to run was 800 meters. I specifically remember coaches saying they would worry about exhaustion and collapses if women were allowed in other events. Today, of course, women complete 26-mile marathons. As previously discussed, myths and stereotypes sometimes have the function of setting limits on people and discouraging people from setting their sights higher.

Myth 2: *Women in dual-career marriages face problems with overseas assignments.* No one questions that men and women who marry and then pursue dual careers must deal with important issues (Brown et al., 1997). These issues should not be underemphasized in the hard work of maintaining a successful marriage. When a married woman considers and pursues an overseas assignment, this question arises: "Will an overseas assignment bring on marital problems different from any challenging assignment that would be part of one's career development?" And further, "Who should make the decision, the wife and husband or the wife's supervisors?"

The married female managers in Adler's (1994) study accepted an overseas assignment as a challenge to be faced. Different couples opted for different solutions. Some maintained a long-distance marriage. Some husbands had "portable" careers that allowed them to work no matter where they lived. Examples were professional writers, laboratory scientists skillful at obtaining grants for their research, and physicians willing to work under the sometimes burdensome regulations of various host countries. In my experience, people skillful in statistics often can find good-paying work overseas given that many researchers need statistical consultants, also called "numbers crunchers" in the jargon of the field. Some couples decided that the woman should accept the overseas assignment and the man then would seek work, but with no guarantees of such work at the time the woman accepted the assignment.

At times, overseas assignments provide unexpected benefits for a marriage. In many countries (e.g., Philippines, Thailand), a couple can hire domestic workers who will take care of chores such as cooking and cleaning. Other people might be hired to take the roles of chauffeurs, butlers, and personal maids. This is a common practice among middle-class hosts, also, and involves lower costs than hiring such workers in the United States. Some couples reported that their marriages were enriched greatly because they did not have to worry about these chores and could spend more time with their spouses. I have to add, however, that interactions with people who take on the role of "domestic workers" or "servants" can bring on its own problems (Cushner & Brislin, 1996). Many Americans, for instance, are actively uncomfortable hiring servants and argue that it is not part of their culture to do so. The Americans may even appeal to the egalitarian nature of their culture and may even cite this book's discussion (chapter 8) of low power distance. Hosts, however, may point out that if the Americans do not hire domestic workers, then the high unemployment rate of the country remains the same. They might even argue, "You can behave according to your egalitarian principles if you like. But what other jobs are available for these people if you do not hire them?" Like many potential problems that people may encounter on an overseas assignment, it is best to prepare for these encounters rather than to be completely surprised by them.

Myth 3: *Female managers will face prejudice overseas.* Many companies feel that if they send women to countries where most executives and managers are men, then the women will not be taken seriously. Further, the presence of women will reflect badly on the sending organization. People are afraid executives in the other countries will say, "We won't do business with this organization because they show so little respect for us when they send a female."

The female managers in Adler's (1994) study reported that they had heard this myth but that they did not find that it hindered their work overseas. They had many different experiences, but all reflected a common theme: People certainly repeat this myth, but the myth does not have to translate into reality. One respondent reported that it was an advantage to be a woman because she was a novelty and was different from what people expected. This allowed her to be more memorable and for her products and business proposals also to be more memorable. This response reminded me of conversations I had with a colleague, Dr. Elaine Bailey, who has been very successful doing business in Asia. She asked me to consider this scenario. She visited companies in Asia to make proposals about joint ventures with her American organization. Certainly, other American companies also were represented. But keep in mind the Asian executives. They entertain 20 or so visits a day from representatives of American companies. Nineteen are men and one is a woman. Who is more likely to find a place in the long-term memories of the Asian executives?

Other women reported that some countries maintain a double standard, and it involves the belief that men are better executives and that women should stay home and raise children. But women from other countries are not held to this double standard and are considered exceptions. They are viewed as professionals first, then as women. If they demonstrate excellence in their roles as professionals, this is what remains in the memories of the host-country businesspeople. Still other women reported that they were the beneficiaries of some complex thinking. They felt that host-country executives viewed them favorably. Executives could think as follows: "The Americans must know that we don't have very many female executives and that we might think poorly of a company that sends women. But because they sent this specific woman, she must be first-rate or else they would have sent a man." With host-country executives holding this positive view, the women then presented their business proposals to a receptive audience.

SPECULATIONS ABOUT THE FUTURE

The example of women and overseas assignments is just one example of the greater mobility than in the past of women in their cultures. Given the numerous pressures people experience all over the world, I believe that many traditional practices that place severe limits on the movement of women will weaken over the next 30 or 40 years. These pressures include the worldwide movement toward democracy, increased air travel, the influence of the mass media, greater attention to universal literacy, advances in medical care, and so forth. One way to predict the future is to examine today's research literature and to list activities men engage in more frequently than women throughout the world. Most of these reflect differential emphases during socialization, not differences in innate abilities. The list includes more interest in computers (Sproull, Zubron, & Kiesler, 1986), the use of power (Brislin, 1991; Brislin & Jane, 1997; Davies, 1985), and the demonstration of creativity (Khaleefa, Erdos, & Ashira, 1996; Mar'i & Karayanni, 1983). The predictions are that with the removal of traditional barriers, women will not differ from men in the use of computers, in the responsible use of power, and in the expression of creativity.

Gender stereotypes may change as fathers spend more time taking care of their children.

The predictions also can be based on movements in the other direction: With the removal of barriers that limit their activities, men will be able to behave in ways traditionally considered unacceptable because of their "femininity." These include sensitivity to the needs of others (Deaux & LaFrance, 1998; Murphy-Berman, Singh, Pachauri, Berman, & Kumar, 1984), emotional self-disclosure (Snell, Miller, & Belk, 1988), and the distribution of resources within a marriage (Brown et al., 1997; Warner, Lee, & Lee, 1986).

These changes may come slowly. In a study of people's perceptions of an ideal opposite-sex person (Stiles, Gibbons, & de la Garza–Schnellmann, 1990), adolescents from the United States and Mexico drew pictures and also ranked numerous characteristics. Young men and women in both cultures valued someone who is fun to be with, kind, honest, and good-looking (with young men placing more emphasis on this factor, consistent with the earlier discussion in this chapter). In Mexico, other values were predictable from a knowledge of long-standing traditions. For example, Mexican adolescents placed a value on family ties, affiliation, and cooperation. However, their answers gave some hints that social changes are having an impact on the values adolescents express. Stiles and her colleagues noted, "[W]e saw some evidence of changing [gender] roles in the United States. A few adolescent girls showed the ideal man caring for children. A few adolescent boys drew the ideal woman working at a job" (p. 196).

These results are consistent with a finding Williams and Best (1990a; see also Best & Williams, 1997) reported based on a 10-year follow-up study of sex stereotypes in Norway. Comparing results gathered in 1977 and 1987, they found that the traditional male stereotype (e.g. active, dominant, less nurturant than women) was not as familiar among Norwegian 5-year-olds in 1987. One reason may be that "[I]n recent years, there has been an increase in participation in child care by Norwegian fathers, which might be expected to soften the more extreme versions of the male stereotype encountered by the children in the popular media and elsewhere" (p. 332).

Not all the changes that might occur in the future will necessarily be positive. If the behavior of men and women is to converge given the movement away from traditional roles, then women may begin to drink as much as men (Ames & Rebhun, 1996; Gilbert & Cervantes, 1986; Teahan, 1987) and may develop problems that lead to suicide attempts (Barraclough, 1987; Zhang, 1996), which are more common to men. Men may become more susceptible to depression (Dorahy et al., 1996; Golding & Karno, 1988) and may experience more conflict between their home and their work (Ottaway & Bhatnagar, 1988), issues women currently deal with more than men. These possibilities demand that people develop a greater knowledge about threats to their mental and physical health, and this is the subject of the next chapter.

CHAPTER SUMMARY

When people organize the massive amounts of information they encounter, two of the most frequently used categories are "what men do" and "what women do." The sharp distinctions people make about sex and gender stems from one of the most basic facts about life: Men impregnate women, and women bear children. These facts have very important implications, as demonstrated in various cross-cultural studies. Childbirth and child rearing involve a great investment of energy. Especially in the past, the act of giving birth weakened the mother, and the demands of children (who are virtually helpless for several years) encouraged the mother to stay near the home. The father, in contrast, was far more likely to engage in behaviors outside the home as he secured food and other resources for his family. This traditional division of labor led to traits that members of the two sexes used for selecting mates.

Especially in societies that have strong norms about gender roles, women are likely to seek competent men in their community who can care for them after childbirth and during the difficult child-rearing years. Men are likely to look for young and nurturant women who have the physical ability to bear children and the psychological readiness to look after them. In a study of mate preferences in 33 countries, Buss and his colleagues (1990) found that men and women still keep these traits in mind when thinking about the opposite sex. Women were more likely to value men who were well established in their community because such men could provide resources to a family. Men were more likely to value developing a romantic relationship with younger and attractive women because these two visible "signs" indicated to them that the women were capable (e.g., youth and good health) of bearing children.

The argument from evolutionary theory (Buss, 1991, 1996) is that men and women who had these preferences in the past mated, bore and raised children, and passed their genes on to future generations. These genetic tendencies remain with us today because they had survival value in our ancestral past. This type of analysis is thoroughly distasteful to many who encourage women and men to break free from the restrictions of traditional roles. A number of scholars (e.g., Buss & Kenrick, 1998; Low, 1989) argue that people must understand the origins of male-female differences if they hope to find ways to achieve equality between the sexes in today's society. It also must be kept in mind that the demands of today's world encourage the development of various skills and that men will be wise to become more attentive to behaviors that may be more natural for women. The future will involve more frequent intercultural interactions, and people from other cultures will demand respect when they put their suggestions forward. Women may be much more naturally skillful at listening carefully and integrating the contributions of others. If men tend to dominate their intercultural interactions, they may miss many opportunities that a softer style would have nurtured.

The analysis of evolutionary theory provides some interesting insights, but several other factors must be considered. Many differences between men and women arise from socialization experiences in their culture. One of the most frequently discussed differences, almost certainly a universal, is that boys are more aggressive than girls. Boys engage in more rough-and-tumble play, are punished less frequently for fighting than are girls, and experience more injuries. One explanation is that aggressive boys grow into men who can attract mates. Aggressive men engage in risk-taking activities that help them secure resources for their families. In the past, risky activities included hunting and exploring unknown areas for possible agricultural use. Another frequently discussed difference is that women are more nurturant and are more concerned about their relationships with others. One explanation is that nurturant women can attract the most successful men in a community because the men look for women who can provide a home and take care of the children they father. Given the difficulties of child rearing, women who are sensitive to their relationships can enlist the help of supportive people such as sisters, sisters-in-law, and other relatives. Because the woman has the responsibility of introducing very young children to the norms of society, her extended family provides a good core group of people the children can be integrated with. Various people in the extended family offer the children opportunities for learning a culture's norms: which people deserve respect, who has important information to share, why cooperation is more useful in the long run than constant conflict, and so forth.

One of the most intriguing findings from cross-cultural research is that women often defer to men if the possibility of conflict arises during an interaction. Research by Maccoby (1990) and by Weisfeld and her colleagues (1982) demonstrates that when women interact with members of their own sex, they are vigorous, forthright, and skillful in expressing their contributions. When men enter a social setting, however, women often become passive and defer to the contributions men offer. For example, Weisfeld and her colleagues organized dodgeball games and spelling bees for Hopi Indian children in Arizona and for Black American children in Chicago. When playing among members of their own sex, young girls were vigorous and were proud of performing well. When young boys entered the dodgeball games or the spelling bees, the young girls engaged in less vigorous activity and performed less skillfully. No overall difference exists between the skills of men and women. Rather, a differential performance of these skills occurs in mixed-sex groups. No one has proposed a thoroughly convincing explanation for these findings. One possibility returns to the families of our distant ancestors. The time and energy needed to raise children was so extensive that competition between mothers and fathers was unwise. Any time and energy spent on competition would have meant fewer resources were available for the task of child rearing. Consequently, the behavioral tendencies of male assertiveness and female deference (when the mother and father were in the same social setting) became valued and were encouraged during the socialization of children and adolescents.

Research has indicated several implications from women's concern with their relationships. These include more expectations of others once a friendship has been established (Morse, 1983); greater concern with developing and maintaining positive relationships with authority figures (Buriel, 1983); greater insights into the effects people's problems have on themselves and others (Doherty & Obani, 1986); and greater ability to interpret nonverbal expressions of emotions (Goldstein, 1996; McAndrew, 1986; Sogon & Izard, 1987). These expectations, insights, and skills can have both positive and negative results. One positive outcome is that women, more than men, can identify potential problems in relationships and can intervene quickly before the problems escalate. A negative outcome is that women may experience more burnout when they try to help others. If women are more insightful about people's problems and more concerned about offering assistance, they may seek careers using these skills. Then they may become frustrated if they experience bureaucratic obstacles and uncaring public officials. The frustration can lead to emotional burnout (Maslach & Leiter, 1996).

Some of the documented differences between men and women are striking. In the Sogon and Izard study (1987), American women were better able to distinguish disgust, fear, and sadness from observations of filmed Japanese actors who had their backs turned toward the camera. This ability to interpret nonverbal expressions of emotion has various possible explanations. One is that given their greater concern with relatedness, women pay more attention to other people and learn to decode subtle cues the others send out. Another is that given women's traditionally lower status in societies all over the world, women have had to diagnose the emotions of powerful people so as to increase their chances of receiving favorable attention. If women learn to approach powerful people when they are in good moods and learn to avoid the powerful when they are experiencing negative moods, then women increase the chances of a favorable hearing for their proposals.

A prediction about the future people can make with absolute certainty is that traditional sanctions limiting the movement of women will decrease in societies all over the world. One result is that, given that they can pursue goals long denied them, women will behave in ways similar to men and some stereotypes will cease to exist. For example, the stereotype once existed that women were not as good in mathematics as men. Once restrictions about the choice of mathematics courses disappeared and once women received as much encouragement as men, no sex distinction in mathematics occurred, as current research shows (Lummis & Stevenson, 1990; Maccoby, 1990; Stevenson et al., 1993).

Other types of changes also involve a convergence of the behaviors of men and women once traditional norms change. One of the major pressures for the weakening of behavioral restrictions results from the experiences of women who seek employment outside the home. Once they leave home and have a wider variety of successful experiences, women develop nontraditional views of themselves and less restrictive ideals for their children (Hanassab & Tidwell, 1996; Paguio et al., 1987). Other changes include premarital sexual experiences similar to those of men (Alzate, 1989); self-concepts as positive as those of men (Ezelio, 1983); and increased participation in the political process (Clark & Clark, 1987).

One example of changes in women's roles involves their willingness to accept overseas assignments within multinational organizations. Adler (1994) has argued that attention has to be given to the distinction between myths and realities. She identified three myths: women are reluctant to accept such assignments, women in dual-career marriages will experience problems with such assignments, and women will be the target of prejudice during their overseas assignments. Based on interviews with more than 100 successful female managers who had accepted international assignments, Adler concluded that these myths are based on discussions among the wrong people. Women should be asked about the issues identified in the myths! In her study, Adler found that women seek overseas assignments and approach them with enthusiasm. Yes, the issue of dual careers must be addressed, but many couples have to face potential problems stemming from dual careers. Such couples have to address issues such as the number of children to have, savings plans for the children's schooling, moves to other cities when a promotion is offered, and so forth. When the female managers were asked about prejudice, their responses varied greatly. Some women encountered prejudice early in their assignments but found they could overcome it with professionalism and hard work. Other women received benefits. If they were competing for the attention of executives in other countries, some women reported that their proposals were more memorable. Assume 19 men and 1 woman present investment opportunities to male executives in other countries. Who is likely to be remembered, even if for no other reason than novelty? I hope that women taking overseas assignments becomes part of people's thinking and that it guides them into (a) asking women what their goals are and then into (b) encouraging them to pursue their goals as part of their formal education, their seeking mentorship opportunities, and their professional skills development.

Just because men engage in certain behaviors, of course, is no reason for women to mimic them. A danger in the "convergence of behaviors" possibility is that women will engage in undesirable behaviors that threaten their mental and physical health (Ames & Rebhun, 1996). In many cultures, men drink more alcohol and engage in more suicide attempts than women. If men desire greater freedom from the traditional gender roles that have placed limits on the types of goals they set for themselves (Prince, 1985), they should be alert to the undesirable behaviors more common among women. These include depressive episodes and stresses emanating from conflicts between home and the workplace (Brown et al., 1997). People must give careful thought to the problem of minimizing the negative effects of the move beyond traditional gender roles while maximizing the benefits. This is a common theme in treatments of the relation between culture and health, and this is the subject of the next chapter.

C H A P T E R 10

CULTURE AND HEALTH

CHAPTER OVERVIEW

Cultural change has been discussed many times in previous chapters. An important example of change is that, in many countries, people now feel their behavior has impacts on their health. Fifty years ago, people who ate large amounts of vegetables, exercised regularly, and meditated for stress reduction were seen as quirky if not downright strange. Today, people routinely take these and other steps to maintain and to improve their health.

Because views about health are culturally influenced, an understanding of cultural differences can have impacts on the prevention and treatment of physical and mental illnesses. A troublesome difference is that in many cultures people see visits to physicians as a final step to take only after they consult family members and native healers. By the time people see a physician, the problem can be so severe that no intervention is possible. As with other important aspects of human behavior, understanding the difference between culture-common and culture-specific issues is central to health care delivery. In one study, a screening instrument for mental health difficulties identified some culture-common complaints, such as nervousness and trouble sleeping. Culture-specific symptoms also need to be understood. Among Vietnamese Chinese, "fullness in the head" is a complaint, and problems with memory is a complaint among Mexicans. Some cultures somaticize complaints. Rather than talk about stresses, depression, or anxiety, they complain about parts of their bodies. Schizophrenia and depression studies have benefited from analyses in terms of culture-common and culture-specific concepts. One finding is that the prognosis for schizophrenia can be more optimistic in collective cultures if family members form a support group for the distressed individual.

Cross-cultural research has been used in the development of lists of behaviors people should consider when they want to prevent health problems. Researchers compare cultures with certain common and uncommon behaviors and health practices and seek their relationships to the frequencies of various diseases. Advice about diet, body weight, avoiding the smoking habit, stress avoidance, safe sexual practices, and nurturance of support groups is now readily available. Intervention programs have taken cultural differences into account. Health care information must be presented in a manner, and in a place, comfortable for people. Examples include distributing information about safe sex in brothels and integrating information about nutrition into commonly known stories in a culture. Keeping in mind that culture-specific information always will need to be integrated, researchers study universals in health care delivery to provide important guidelines for intervention. These universals include applying a name to problems, putting problems in frameworks familiar to people, and delivering help at a special time and place. Qualities of the health care professional are also important, and training programs exist where positive qualities can be nurtured. Professionals need to come across to help seekers as competent, caring, approachable, and concerned. In some cultures, professionals should be careful to provide concrete help early or else clients will not make or keep follow-up appointments.

CONCERNS IN HEALTH SERVICES DELIVERY

People's satisfaction with their physical and mental health are two of the most important factors in their overall feelings about their happiness and their enjoyment of life (Beardsley & Pedersen, 1997; Draguns, 1990; Ilola, 1990). The unique challenge for health professionals sensitive to the concerns covered throughout this book is to deliver services and to encourage healthy lifestyles when they help people from different cultural backgrounds (England, 1986). In many ways, much of the material covered in earlier chapters has relevance to people's health and to intervention efforts when help is needed. The distinction between culture-general concepts and culture-specific concepts (chapter 3) must be understood when health professionals apply labels such as "schizophrenia" or "depression" to clients from a culture different from theirs. People can be socialized (chapter 4) into everyday practices that can have an impact on the prevention of health problems, such as choices about their diet, about alcohol and tobacco use, and about the nurturance of potential support groups. Training programs to prepare health professionals for intercultural encounters (e.g., Barrett, 1997; Fisher, Jome, & Atkinson, 1998; Wade & Bernstein, 1991; Westermeyer, 1987) use the same methods and concepts reviewed in chapters 5 and 6. The effective use of a country's health services is dependent on a well-educated citizenry (chapter 5), on a productive economy where job holders (chapter 8) are contributing tax dollars for the support of health services, and on the talents of all citizens (chapter 9) for both preventative and intervention activities (Beutler & Harwood, 1995; Hunter, 1990).

Even when health professionals are sensitive to the fact they may encounter cultural differences and even when clients are motivated to seek the help of professionals, the actual delivery of services can be fraught with difficulties. For example, Ahia (1984) pointed to the possibility of two biases. If people behave according to the "limitations bias," they fail to examine important concepts beyond those with which they are already familiar given their socialization in their own culture. Counselors and physicians socialized in an individualist society such as the United States, for instance, may diagnose accurately that a person is suffering from a depressive episode or has experienced a recent heart attack. If the client or patient is from a collective culture, however the health professional may fail to see that the problem also will be experienced by the person's extended family. The professional may be unable to move beyond the "limits" of his or her socialization. The limitations bias also can work among people seeking help. If people from a certain culture (e.g., the Japanese) know they have a healthy diet, they may not move beyond this knowledge and engage in other activities that assist in their maintenance of good health. For example, the Japanese may use tobacco products to excess (Beardsley & Pedersen, 1997; Ilola, 1990) and may consume excessive amounts of alcohol as part of expectations that they socialize with coworkers (Christopher, 1983).

Another potential problem Ahia (1984) identified is the "generalization bias." If a health professional discovers that a certain type of intervention or a certain approach to clients works well, then he or she may generalize this to the entire population of the clients' origin. The generalization bias, of course, is an example of the use of stereotypes reviewed in chapter 6. Health professionals (and all others who engage in extensive intercultural interactions) must realize that not all people behave according to the stereotypes and generalizations attached to their groups. Professionals must willingly move beyond generalizations and consider the unique circumstances of each client. For example, an American physician might discover that a Chinese American client frequently visits an herbalist for traditional Chinese medicines. The physician might explain the contents of a prescribed drug by linking it to the herbs familiar to the patient. This would be a culturally sensitive way to prepare the Chinese American patient to follow the physician's recommendation. It would be incorrect for the physician, however, to describe medicines in this way to all Chinese American patients. Many patients would be quite familiar with Western medical practices and would feel that an herbal discussion is patronizing.

As with the limitations bias, the generalization bias can occur with clients. Sue and Zane (1987; see also Fisher et al., 1998; Lefley, 1989) provided evidence that patients from a number of cultural backgrounds (e.g., Chinese Americans, Hispanics, and African Americans) expect health professionals to provide something of immediate benefit. That is, members of some minority groups expect to be helped within a very short time after they seek the help of professionals. If they do not experience such benefits, they may generalize from their interactions with one or a few professionals to all potential helpers. People who have good relations with clients might assist by pointing out that, often, improvements in physical and mental health do not always come quickly. Similarly, professionals who expect to have clients from a variety of cultural backgrounds can be told that if they do not provide some sort of benefit quickly (it does not have to be a total cure), then clients may terminate their visits.

Moving Beyond Potential Biases

One way to deal with these potential biases is to develop collaborative arrangements with people from the cultures professionals serve (Ahia, 1984; Barrett, 1997). The collaborators can check one another's work and insights to (a) point out potential biases, (b) contribute information on the cultural background of various clients, and (c) provide a range of professionals for client consultation. The health professionals also can improve their sensitivity to clients by constantly asking these questions (reviewed by Turner, 1990, p. 16):

1. How is this person (client or patient) like all human beings? For example (as will be reviewed), research has suggested that virtually all people with schizophrenia experience a universal core of symptoms.

2. How is this person like some human beings? For answering this question, information about the cultural background of the person can be useful.

3. How is this person like no other human being? If professionals constantly ask this question, they can move away from stereotypes and generalizations and move toward the person's unique problems, needs, and resources.

The Organization of the Chapter

No one chapter or even collection of books can cover all the important research on the interrelationships of culture and health. I have attempted to review some highlights that seem to be central to most discussions of health and health delivery, and the five themes I would like to develop follow:

1. Understanding reasons for differences in health care delivery among people in different cultural groups

2. Understanding culture-general and culture-specific concepts as they apply to the study of health

3. Analyzing the universal and culture-specific aspects of two important mental disorders: schizophrenia and depression

4. Examining behaviors meant to prevent problems with people's mental and physical health. At times, formal programs can be introduced that combine traditional treatments found within a culture with medical practices developed in highly industrialized nations

5. Developing an awareness of culturally sensitive treatments, with special attention to education and training programs for health professionals

DIFFERENCES IN HEALTH SERVICES DELIVERY

As discussed in chapter 4, children must learn a wide variety of behaviors so that they can become respected members of their culture. During their socialization, they learn about various behaviors that the elders of a culture believe will allow the children to make contributions to their communities. Some of these behaviors, learned during socialization, are supposed to increase the chances of good mental and physical health. Differences exist, however, between people's expectations about good health and about good health care and the actual status of people's health as documented in international research studies.

The health of infants is a good example. Many health professionals consider that the infant mortality rate of a country, or the rate among different ethnic groups within a large country, is one of the most sensitive indicators of the health care available to people (Garcia-Coll, 1990; Hunter, 1990). Looking at just the United States, differences in infant mortality rates occur within different ethnic groups. As Garcia-Coll points out:

> Traditionally, disadvantaged ethnic minority populations in the United States have had higher death rates. Despite improvements, infant mortality rates for African-Americans remains high. Moreover, African-American neonatal and infant mortality is elevated at all income levels. . . . Higher rates of prematurity and low birth weight are contributing factors to infant mortality and represent "at risk" factors for poorer developmental outcomes for survivors. Again, differential rates are seen among different minority groups. (p. 275)

The health of infants involves a very complex combination of genetic, economic, cultural, and linguistic factors. Certain diseases are more prevalent in certain minority groups, and these involve a genetic component. Examples are sickle cell anemia among African Americans, cystic fibrosis among Pueblo Indians, and lactose intolerance among Asians and Asian Americans (Diamond, 1997; Garcia-Coll, 1990; Overfield, 1985). Lactose intolerance can lead to diarrhea and dehydration if infants receive too much food containing milk products. Regarding the care given to infants with these and the many other illnesses children can have, socioeconomic and cultural factors play a major role. In countries without a policy of health insurance for all citizens (such as the United States), lack of personal insurance or money forces people to stay away from health professionals. When the members of various ethnic minority groups are overrepresented among a nation's poor, then the delivery of health services becomes associated with ethnic status. Given their lack of money or personal insurance, many people seek professionals only after illnesses have advanced to stages where they may be untreatable. Rather than approaching health professionals at the first signs of a problem, impoverished people may use traditional remedies long used in their cultures. These may prove beneficial. If they do not, however, problems may reach a point where no intervention, traditional or modern, can be effective. Hence, infants in these cultures die more frequently than in other cultures.

Understanding various cultural barriers to health treatment are difficult because of the following:

1. They differ among cultures (Braun, Takamura, & Mougeot, 1996; Qureshi, 1989).

2. They are less visible than factors such as the lack of an insurance policy or lack of money.

3. Health professionals have few opportunities to learn about them.

4. Even the most culturally sensitive health professionals are sometimes viewed as outsiders who are to be trusted less than fellow members of a culture.

In a study of the expectations mothers have about their children's development, Hopkins and Westra (1989; see also Chao, 1996) were interested in the health-care-seeking activities of mothers. They attempted to discover the expectations mothers had for their children's normal developmental behaviors and to discover when mothers would seek professional help if children were slow to achieve these behaviors. Examples of the behaviors include the ages children would sit by themselves, crawl, walk, and so forth. Working with Jamaican, Indian, and English women in Great Britain, Hopkins and Westra were surprised to find that mothers did not contact physicians to obtain information about the normal progress of children. Rather, the mothers obtained this information from other women in their communities. This dependence on others from the same cultural background, incidentally, is a common finding across quite different types of behaviors. For example, Pedersen (1991a) found that foreign students at a large American university were likely to approach same-culture peers when they had a problem, whether it was academic, social, or medical. They preferred contacting peers to consulting professionals such as highly experienced international-student advisers the university employed.

Hopkins and Westra (1989), in their work among mothers of young children, found that the women's cultural background had an impact on their expectations. Jamaican mothers, for instance, were sensitive to the age at which their children could sit up by themselves. They were not very concerned with the age the children learned to crawl, as they considered this "hazardous and non-human" (p. 388). The Jamaican mothers felt sitting alone quietly was important because they used this milestone as a sign that they were successfully training children to become polite adults later. If the children could not sit alone by age 6 or 7 months, the mothers became upset. Knowing these facts, health professionals can increase the chances of their recommendations being accepted by linking them to the mothers' concerns.

Health professionals admittedly have a difficult task. They have the responsibility to deliver the best possible services they can, but they must do so in (a) a culturally sensitive manner to (b) people who do not always recognize the value of their services (Fisher et al., 1998). At times, professionals must press forward with their recommendations even at the risk of violating traditions. Breast-feeding is a good example. Mother's milk has numerous advantages over bottled milk. Babies more easily digest it, and, among other biological advantages, it can transfer to the baby the mother's immunities to locally common diseases. However, women in some cultures do not want to breast-feed because they feel their husbands will disapprove (Winikoff & Laukaran, 1989). Professionals often have to assume the role of educators, explaining the benefits of uncommon or frowned on health practices in a culture.

A number of professionals have made recommendations about universal goals in health care, realizing that cultural factors influence the actual delivery of such care. Broad goals for any nation's health policy (Beardsley & Pedersen, 1997; Ilola, 1990; World Health Organization, 1987) include the following recommendations:

- Spending 5% or more of a country's gross national product on health
- Equitably distributing resources across social classes
- Keeping infant mortality at less than 50 per 1,000 live births

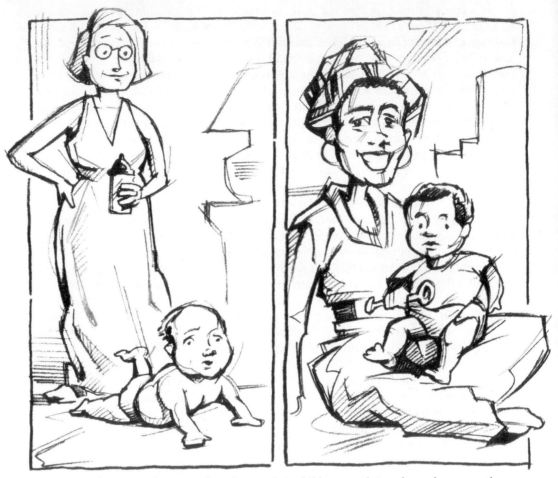

In some cultures, mothers attend to the age their children crawl. In other cultures, mothers attend to the age their children sit up by themselves.

- Ensuring that life expectancy at birth is greater than 60 years
- Seeking greater than 70% adult literacy for both sexes

More specifically, the World Health Organization recommends that (a) safe water be available within a 15-minute walking distance, (b) children and adults receive the basic immunizations, (c) approximately 20 essential drugs be available in local health care facilities, and (d) 90% of newborns weigh 2,500 grams or more at birth.

These recommendations from the World Health Organization are meant to be examples of universal goals and requirements for minimal health care. Understanding the nature of such universals (also called culture-general concepts) together with culture-specific concepts is one of the central challenges of cross-cultural research and its applications.

CULTURE-COMMON AND CULTURE-SPECIFIC CONCEPTS

One of the most important guidelines for cross-cultural research (reviewed in chapter 3) is that investigators should be prepared for the fact their measuring instruments may be less successful when they gather data in other cultures than when they do so in the original culture (Butcher, Lim, & Nezami, 1998). Among the many reasons (e.g., translation errors, respondents' lack of familiarity with the responses the instruments require), one of the most important is that complex concepts do not have exactly the same meaning in all cultures. Consider the concept "good health." In the United States, the concept includes the absence of harmful bacteria and of chemical imbalances. In China, the concept involves Yin and Yang, which "are the primogenial elements from which the universe was evolved. Health is achieved when Yin and Yang are in harmony. Disharmony or undue prevalence by either would result in ill-health and death" (Cheng & Lee, 1988, p. 208). In addition to these culture-specific components of good health, culture-common components also are important for analyzing good health in all cultures. These include subjective feelings of well-being, adequate energy to do daily tasks, sexual activity appropriate to age and position in society (e.g., husband, monk), adequate support from important others, and feeling able to develop positive emotional ties with others (Draguns, 1990; Nishimoto, 1988; Qureshi, 1989; Salovey, Rothman, & Rodin, 1998).

The recommendation for people involved in health services delivery across cultural boundaries, then, is to be prepared to deal with both culture-common and culture-specific components of complex concepts (Siegert & Chung, 1995). A research study by Nishimoto (1988) provides a good example. He was interested in the concept of people's ability to meet the everyday challenges of life in an effective way, free of debilitating mental health problems. Realizing that this complex concept undoubtedly would have both culture-common and culture-specific components, he designed his research so that he could identify both types of components. As his measuring instrument, he chose the Langer (1962) index of psychiatric symptoms, one of the most frequently used screening instruments health professionals use to identify people who are not institutionalized but who have psychological disorders that disrupt their everyday functioning. Nishimoto analyzed data gathered from three groups: Anglo Americans from Nebraska, Vietnamese Chinese living in Hong Kong, and Mexicans living either in El Paso, Texas, or Ciudad Juarez, Mexico.

Nishimoto (1988, p. 57) found that 12 of people's reported symptoms were useful for diagnosing mental health difficulties. Health professionals, then, could use these 12 complaint indicators in all three cultures to identify people who need health services based on whether they reported these symptoms when thinking about their lives:

weak all over	restlessness
personal worries	can't get going
(I'm the) worrying type	feel apart, alone
low spirits	nervousness

nothing turns out well   hot all over
(I can't do) anything worthwhile   trouble sleeping

In addition to these cultural general symptoms, Nishimoto (1988) also identified symptoms that were useful for diagnostic purposes within each culture. Each set of symptoms would be useful for diagnosis within a specific culture, but not in another. For the Anglo American respondents, five additional symptoms were reported by people with mental health difficulties:

heart beating hard   hands tremble
acid stomach   headaches
shortness of breath

The Vietnamese Chinese respondents gave three additional symptoms:

heart beating hard
acid stomach
fullness in head

And the Mexican respondents named two additional symptoms:

(problems with) memory
headaches

It is probably no accident that the researchers documented that the Anglo American respondents reported the largest number of symptoms. The original measuring instrument was developed by an American who had access to numerous respondents from his own country. It is only natural that with these two facts, the symptoms identified were meaningful to Americans. Whenever instruments developed in one country are used, an important research step is to seek actively other items that may be diagnostic in the various cultures where the instrument is to be administered (as discussed in the addendum to chapter 3 on p. 108). Nishimoto's findings can be interpreted as supporting the general usefulness of the 22-item index Langer (1962) developed, but they also are a reminder that undoubtedly other symptoms could be added to the instrument. Americans may report these other symptoms infrequently, but respondents in other cultures may report them far more often.

As will be discussed more fully later in this chapter, health professionals must be prepared for cultural differences in people's reports about their physical and mental health. A good exercise is to study carefully the reports by researchers such as Nishimoto and to ask, "Which of these symptoms are familiar to me, given my own cultural background, and which seem strange?" One reason for people finding that a symptom is strange, of course, is that they have not encountered it during their socialization. If Americans study the lists presented, I believe most will find that the core set of 12 symptoms and the additional culture-specific 5 symptoms for Americans will be familiar. Either they have experienced them from time to time during periods of personal psychological distress or they have talked with others who have experienced them. Several of the culture-specific symptoms for the Vietnamese Chinese and the Mexicans, however, may seem unfamiliar to Americans as indicators of distress. Many Americans will not be familiar with the "fullness in the head" symptom the Vietnamese Chinese reported, nor will most be familiar with the memory problems the Mexicans reported. This does not mean Americans do not occasionally experience fullness in the head or memory problems. It means these two symptoms are not as frequently experienced as part of a more general psychological distress that interferes with everyday functioning.

To emphasize, looking for symptoms that seem strange is a good exercise for two reasons. It can sensitize people to the presence of cultural differences. Further, it can encourage a constant awareness that strangeness is simply a sign that people have not encountered a concept during their own socialization. I told a colleague from India, Meheroo Jussawala, about Nishimoto's finding that Vietnamese Chinese did not report headaches as a symptom of distress. She told me that while she was growing up in India, she never had headaches. When she or her Indian friends were upset, they experienced an upset stomach. After moving to the United States, she was surprised to see so many commercials on television that advertise remedies for headaches: aspirin, Tylenol, Ibuprofin, and so forth. Given that she never had headaches (and still does not), she is fascinated by all the fuss made about pain killers. But when her students or colleagues complain about headaches, she can interpret their complaints as a sign they are experiencing stress, even though she does not react to stress in the same way.

Reasons for Culture-Specific Reports of Symptoms

One of the most interesting concepts in the analysis of culture and health is that people learn to express symptoms of distress in ways acceptable to others in their culture (Cook, 1994; Edman, 1997). As part of their socialization, they learn that certain complaints about distress are acceptable and elicit understanding and that other complaints are unacceptable. Several examples already were presented in the previous section. Americans learn that when encountering significant distress, they will earn more sympathy when they complain about headaches rather than about memory problems. Mexicans learn that complaints about memory are acceptable, and the Vietnamese learn that others in the culture will understand complaints about fullness in the head. If my colleague is correct, Indians learn that appeals to their stomach aches elicit more sympathy than claims about their headaches.

Readers may want to examine their own lives to determine if at times they appealed to certain symptoms because of their acceptability to others. When I was about 12 years old and playing my first year of Little League baseball, my talents kept me sitting on the bench during games. I played before the era of mandatory "two innings of play per player," a policy now common in many if not most American communities. In fairness to my coaches, their choice of where to place me during games was in line with my abilities. Still, I became bored and frustrated with baseball. Before one of the more important games, I reported to my mother that I had a headache and could not go to the game. In reality, I had an upset stomach because I knew that a certain female classmate would be coming to see her brother play for the opposing team. I did want her to see me sitting on the bench for the entire game. Although I did not know about the phrase "acceptable symptoms within a culture," I felt that my mother would show more sympathy if I told her about my headache rather than my upset stomach and embarrassment stemming from my classmate's planned presence at the game.

Somatization

If I actually had felt the headache, it would have been an example of *somatization*. More frequently reported among Asians, Africans, and Latin Americans than among North Americans (E. H. B. Lin, Carter, & Kleinman, 1985; Tseng & Hsu, 1980), somatization refers to people reporting physical symptoms when they are experiencing psychological distress (Salovey et al., 1998). For example, Carden and Feicht (1991) studied homesickness among female college students from the United States and Turkey. They found that homesick students reported somatic symptoms such as gastrointestinal problems, nausea, tightness in the head/chest, and menstrual irregularities. Further, somatization infers that no identifiable organic causes of the physical symptoms exist, but people report them as real and troublesome. One of the major reasons for somatization is that it is socially acceptable in many cultures. People in such cultures are socialized to believe that complaints about anxieties, worries, and depression are signs of weakness. These complaints signal to others that people are somehow sick in the head, and many cultures have far less tolerance for mental illness than for physical illness. Consequently, when people experience psychological stress due to their inability to meet everyday goals (e.g., good relations with in-laws), they find more acceptance by reporting physical symptoms.

Somatization is so prevalent that it is a frequently used term in programs to prepare professionals who administer various intercultural programs. In a set of materials for these professionals, colleagues and I (Cushner & Brislin, 1996) described an overseas student from Asia studying at a large American university. He was having problems with both his relations and his studies, went to the student health center complaining about pains in various parts of his body, and received a powerful drug from a physician. The underlying reason for his difficulties went unaddressed, and he ran the risk of becoming addicted to the painkiller. Many health care professionals who work with various types of sojourners (foreign students, immigrants, overseas businesspeople and their families) know about the possibility of somatization and examine stress-reducing possibilities other than drugs.

In some cultures, somatic complaints are very well established for certain types of health problems. Guarnaccia, Good, and Kleinman (1990) argue that health professionals who work with Puerto Ricans and other Latinos must understand the concepts underlying the complaints of *nervios* (nerves) and *ataques de nervios* (attacks of nerves). "Nervios" refers to chronic feelings of stress that result from various difficulties in facing life's challenges: a bad marriage, looking for employment during a long recession, and so forth. The symptoms include various "psychosomatic experiences, most prominently headaches, heart palpitations, a sense of heat in the chest, generalized body pains, trouble sleeping, and persistent worrying" (Guarnaccia et al., p. 1449). An "ataque de nervios" is a well-known response (within the culture) to acute stressful experiences, such as the death of a loved one or a specific and unexpected conflict within a family. The symptoms include "trembling, heart palpitations, a sense of heat in the chest rising into the head, faintness, and seizure-like episodes. A typical attack occurs at a culturally appropriate time, such as during a funeral, at the scene of an accident, or during a family argument or fight" (p. 1450).

When people have such an attack, others will understand it well , and they will offer what assistance they can (Tanaka-Matsumi & Draguns, 1997).

Various benefits stem from knowledge of culture-specific reactions such as nervios. In comparative studies of symptomatology, researchers will be able to interpret the (culture-common) finding that people from different cultures report differential rates of various symptoms. As Tseng and Hsu (1980) reported, for instance, "Latin groups in Europe and America generally tended toward somatization, as did North Africans, while English-speaking populations expressed their distress to a greater extent through anxiety and depression" (p. 81). Health delivery professionals then can offer more effective services. Assume, for example, that English-speaking Americans are working among Latino immigrants in New York City. The least familiar distress symptom clients would report (from the list presented earlier) probably would be "a sense of heat in the chest rising into the head." But with knowledge about the culturally appropriate responses to stress known as "nervios" and "ataques de nervios," the professionals could formulate various questions about other symptoms. Realizing that the professionals understand what they are experiencing, clients would be likely to feel they could be helped. Such beliefs in the possibility of positive outcomes are central to the delivery and acceptance of health services (Draguns, 1990; Fisher et al., 1998; Sue & Zane, 1987).

A Further Example: Behavioral Problems

Another example of the importance of understanding culture-common and culture-specific components involves a critical incident. George Andrews and Anna Tanaka were teachers at a preschool in New Mexico. Along with other teachers, they organized a orientation at their school, inviting parents and students new to the community, and held it a few days before classes were to start. The purpose was to familiarize the students with the school and to give them an opportunity to meet teachers and some fellow students prior to the intense activities surrounding the first few weeks of the actual school year.

George was originally from New England and, like the students participating in the orientation, was new to the community. Anna had worked at the school for eight years and also enjoyed traveling south to Mexico, where she previously had participated in two summer-long study tours. Both George and Anna interacted with many of the same students during the orientation. One, Robert, was an Anglo originally from the state of Washington. He found it difficult to concentrate during the activities held at the orientation (e.g., games, practice in following school rules, etc.). He occasionally became restless, was boisterous, and was generally uncooperative in contributing to the orientation program's success. Another student, Manuel, was originally from Mexico, his parents having moved north to seek better-paying jobs. Manuel also found it difficult to concentrate and often was sluggish and inactive during the orientation.

After the orientation, the teachers met to discuss the strong points and the shortcomings of the program, with the goal of improving it in future years. George and Anna happened to converse about the students they both had met, and their discussion turned to the question "Which students might need special attention and help this year?" George felt that Robert would be a disruptive student whose behavioral problems might lead to the need for interventions, such as extra sessions with his parents. Although not disagreeing about Robert, Anna also felt that Manuel showed signs he would have difficulties in school. George disagreed, feeling that Manuel was simply a quiet student who might become more active after he became more familiar with the new school. Why did George and Anna have different reactions to the students?

Given her eight years of experience at the school in New Mexico and her experiences in Mexico, Anna had learned that the sluggishness and inactivity Manuel showed could be a culture-specific manifestation of problematic reactions to the challenges of preschool. In a study of behavioral problems among Anglo American and Mexican American preschool children, O'Donnell, Stein, Machabanski, and Cress (1982) found one culture-common factor. They labeled this component "anxiety-withdrawal," and they associated it with specific behavioral manifestations such as the following:

(the child is) self-conscious	is shy, bashful
is sad, unhappy, depressed	doesn't show feelings
is aloof, socially reserved	doesn't have fun

The researchers also identified culture-specific factors, and one of the most important findings involved the behavior "easily distracted." Among the Anglo Americans, this item was associated with others in a factor called "distractible-hyperactive." These other behaviors included the following:

is restless, fidgety	is boisterous
is easily excited	is uncooperative
is disruptive	is impulsive

An Anglo teacher such as George is likely to have these behaviors in mind when predicting that a certain student might have problems in school.

In sharp contrast, the item "easily distracted" was associated with very different behaviors among the Mexican Americans. O'Donnell and his colleagues (1982) labeled the factor "distractible-hypoactive," with the prefix "hypo" referring to "less than normal level of activity." These other behaviors included the following:

lazy in school	daydreams
short attention span	sluggish, inactive
irresponsible	passive, suggestible

Given her far greater familiarity with Mexican American students than George, Anna had these behaviors in mind when commenting on preschoolers who might face more difficulties than their peers.

O'Donnell and his colleagues (1982) summarized their results: ". . . temperamentally distractible Anglo children confronted with the stress of accommodating to

In some cultures, the unruly student causes the teacher to be concerned. In other cultures, the quiet and passive student causes concern.

the school's demands for concentration react with restless, boisterous behaviors, whereas distractible [Mexican American] children react to a similar situation with inactive, passive behaviors that suggest daydreaming to their teachers" (p. 649). The researchers caution against overinterpreting this summary statement, pointing out that many individual differences exist among both Anglo and Mexican American students and that differences also are associated with students' socioeconomic background, age, and residential location in the United States. Still, if teachers and counselors become aware of the possibility of cultural differences among students and in their behaviors, they will be better able to intervene in the early stages of children's difficulties with their schooling. If such difficulties are identified early, then problems can be addressed before they become so complex as to defy professional interventions.

CULTURE-COMMON AND CULTURE-SPECIFIC ASPECTS OF TWO MAJOR PSYCHOLOGICAL DISORDERS

Two of the major psychological disorders that greatly interfere with people's everyday functioning are schizophrenia and depression. Both are found in all parts of the world, and both have been analyzed in terms of culture-common and culture-specific concepts.

Schizophrenia

The clinical diagnosis most misused by nonspecialists is undoubtedly *schizophrenia*. Many people use it to refer to a split personality and may even use it to describe themselves. For example, if people find themselves behaving quite differently with their parents compared to their age peers, they may call themselves "schizophrenic." This usage is quite different from its use by clinical psychologists and psychiatrists. They might use the word *split*, but the more accurate description is that people with schizophrenia have a split from reality. They cannot relate their thoughts, attitudes, and actions to their everyday reality. For example, they engage in bizarre thinking with frequent delusions about who they are or about the other people in their lives. It is difficult to converse with people who are schizophrenic because no relation exists between one of their statements and another. Hallucinations are common, and people with schizophrenia report that various unseen beings are speaking to them. Emotional relations with others are inconsistent: When schizophrenic, people show anger, happiness, and sorrow for unclear (to the targets of these emotions) reasons. Their behaviors also do not match the culture's guidelines for social situations. People with schizophrenia may laugh at funerals or remain motionless for hours during family gatherings, sometimes involved only in their own idiosyncratic thoughts.

Of the major psychological disorders, the largest number of culture-common symptoms has been reported for schizophrenia (Draguns, 1990; K. Lin & Kleinman, 1988; Tanaka-Matsumi & Draguns, 1997; World Health Organization, 1979). The cross-cultural commonality of schizophrenia, together with the sizable number of culture-common symptoms, is one of the major arguments for suggesting that this major illness has a biological basis. These core symptoms, identified through research in nine locations in Asia, Africa, Europe, South America, and North America, are:

- Restricted affect, or the inability to form emotional ties with others
- Poor insight into the reason's for one's problems or one's current thinking
- Thinking aloud
- Poor rapport with others, including professionals who might offer help
- Incoherent speech, with phrases or sentences seeming to bear no relation to one another

■ Unrealistic information that objective facts would contradict if the person could consider these facts (in the United States, for example, a person cannot buy a new car for $1,000)

■ Widespread, bizarre, and often *nihilistic* delusions. Nihilism is marked by feelings that existence is useless and that nothing is worth living for.

Three other indicators demonstrated the possibility of a culture-common core of symptoms that *do not* indicate schizophrenia. That is, if patients demonstrated these symptoms, clinicians would entertain diagnoses other than schizophrenia. Called *counterindicators*, these three symptoms (Draguns, 1990) are depressed facial features, waking up early after sleeping, and expressions of elation.

Even with this large core of culture-common symptoms, many possibilities exist for the impact of culture-specific factors on schizophrenia. For example, culture-specific factors can influence the forms of schizophrenic symptoms, the specific reasons for the onset of the illness, and the prognosis about outcomes for people afflicted with the disease.

The Forms of Schizophrenic Symptoms

The clearest examples of culture's effects on schizophrenia can be seen in the forms symptoms take. For example, the symptoms of unrealistic information and widespread delusions can be seen in claims that people are hearing voices or that unseen forces are invading their minds. In North America and Europe, these forces keep current with technology. In the 1920s, they were voices from the radio; in the 1950s, they were voices from the television; in the 1960s they could be voices from satellites in outer space; and in the 1970s and 1980s they could be spirits transmitted through people's microwave ovens. In cultures where witchcraft is considered common, the voices or spirits are unseen forces that demons control.

Katz and his colleagues (1988) argue that the exact forms of schizophrenic symptoms can be understood by looking at predominant cultural values. In Agra, India, people with schizophrenia separated themselves from others and emphasized the self-centered behavior indicated in the core symptoms listed previously. This emphasis interfered with the value placed on the collective in India. As Katz et al. argue: "In India, in light of the strong emphasis on family and on mystical life, expressions of self-centeredness would clash with societal values. Release of such emotions and egocentric behaviors reflects the breakdown of [reality and control in one's thinking]" (p. 351). In Ibadan, Nigeria, people with schizophrenia had symptoms that emphasized a highly suspicious orientation toward others, with many bizarre fears and thoughts. This set of symptoms reflects how many Nigerians view illnesses. It is normal in Nigeria to view illness as caused by unseen evil forces, and sometimes enemies and witches direct these forces at a person. The reactions of people with schizophrenia are an exaggeration of this normal view, with attributions to enemies, witches, and unseen forces considered bizarre by other Nigerians with a basic belief in the existence of spirits.

To deviate only slightly, this set of findings suggests that some mental illnesses can be seen as exaggerated versions of the values considered normal in a culture (Draguns, 1973). When discussing the Nigerian findings, for instance, Katz and his colleagues (1988) argue that "the paranoid aspects of the disorder appear to represent an exaggeration and distortion of the 'normal' state" (p. 352). Draguns once asked people to consider this argument about "exaggeration of the normal" by imagining a visit to a carnival with a funhouse full of twisted mirrors. People recognize themselves in funhouse mirrors, but their head, neck, abdomen, or legs are exaggerated. These distortions are not only funny but also slightly disturbing. The metaphor is similar for some mental illnesses. In the United States, for example, hard work is valued. An overemphasis or exaggeration can lead a person to become a workaholic. Likewise, it is smart to suspect salespeople with offers that sound too good to be true. If this suspicion of strangers is exaggerated and expanded, it can lead to paranoia.

The Onset of Schizophrenia

One theory about schizophrenia is that it has a biological basis, placing certain people at risk. If these "at risk" people lead relatively stress-free lives, visible schizophrenic symptoms do not appear. If they are exposed to unanticipated stressful events, however, they may experience the acute onset of schizophrenia (Draguns, 1990; Sanua, 1980; Tanaka-Matsumi & Draguns, 1997). The distinction between being "at risk" and demonstrating obvious symptoms parallels other types of health problems. A 12-year-old boy may have weak tendons in his right arm, but this might never pose a problem during his everyday physical activities. The weak tendons may lead to obvious problems only with intense activity. For example, if he becomes a baseball pitcher and tries to master both a fastball and a curveball, he might damage his arm severely.

Working in nine research sites in the United States (including Hawaii), Asia, Europe, and South America, Day and his colleagues (1987) presented evidence that acute schizophrenic attacks were associated with stressful events, often more than one. Further, they argued that these stressful events could be described as external to individuals (not initiated by them), and the events tended to cluster in a period two to three weeks before the onset of obvious symptoms. Examples of stressful events include a spouse's unexpected death , the loss of a job, or the divorce of parents. Some stressful events were interpretable only if the researchers had considerable information about the cultural background of the people in the various samples. For example, using witchcraft as one explanation of disease in Nigeria already has been mentioned. One case study involved a Nigerian man (referred to as T. O.) who was employed as both an electrician and a taxi driver. One day his mother, complaining of an eye condition, went to a religious healer. While receiving treatment, T. O.'s mother announced to the entire congregation that she practiced witchcraft. About six weeks after this episode (somewhat longer than the typical two to three weeks mentioned), T. O. began to show symptoms of an acute schizophrenic attack. He went into a trance at a religious ceremony, heard voices, saw visions, and continued to behave in an abnormal way after the ceremony. Later, he received "an unexpected bill for his children's education. He threatened to kill his wife and children, became restless, and went without sleep. He developed auditory and visual hallucinations . . ." (Day et al., p. 186).

The purpose of the study Day and his colleagues (1987) designed was to document the relation between external events and the acute onset of schizophrenia. In doing so, they were careful to label an event as "external" only if it occurred in people's environment and was not initiated by them. Note that in T. O.'s case the facts of his mother's confession of witchcraft and the unexpected bill occurred as "external" to him. They had a strong impact on him but occurred independent of his behavior. By deciding to examine life events in this manner, Day and his colleagues admitted they may have underestimated the relation between life stress and schizophrenia. For example, they presented the case of a young woman in Colombia who experienced the symptoms of anxiety, insomnia, and a loss of appetite. She feared she had been bewitched and went to a fortune teller. The fortune teller confirmed the young woman's suspicions and recommended a perfume for protection. The prescription for the perfume included some of the secretions from the young woman's body. She became guilty about using this perfume, and her condition worsened. She deteriorated rapidly and had to seek treatment at a nearby university health clinic.

Day and his colleagues (1987) did not categorize this story as contributing to the proposed link between stressful events and the onset of acute schizophrenia. Even though many people would argue that at least two external stressful events (the fortune teller's confirmation and the perfume use) occurred, the researchers categorized these as involving activity the young woman initiated. The woman was experiencing some symptoms and thus sought the fortune teller. This contrasts with the experiences of T. O., who did not initiate the external events that contributed to his difficulties. Future research activities undoubtedly will examine the relative contributions of (a) unexpected external stresses that clearly do not involve the individual's contributions and (b) external stresses the individual plays a part in. For example, the loss of a job during a severe recession often can be considered an example of an external stress as described in category (a) (McCormick & Cooper, 1988). The loss of a job in a recession when a person had received only mediocre performance ratings during the past three years would be an example of category (b). These two categories are admittedly difficult to separate in actual research, but it is important to do so because people frequently contribute to the external events that affect them.

The Prognosis for Patients With Schizophrenia

Prognosis refers to the anticipation of recovery from illness given the treatments available to patients. K. Lin and Kleinman (1988) have argued that the prognosis for the successful treatment of people with schizophrenia is better in nonindustrialized societies. At first glance, this is a surprising claim given the availability of drugs, trained psychiatrists, and advanced treatment facilities in highly industrialized nations. The explanation is that functioning members of a "highly industrialized" nation need skills that are very difficult for people with schizophrenia to demonstrate. Recall the core schizophrenic symptoms. Many of them involve relating to others: difficulty forming emotional ties, poor rapport with others, speech that listeners consider incoherent, and ignoring facts accepted in one's community. As discussed previously (chapters 2 and 8), individualism is valued in most highly industrialized nations. Individuals must develop rapport and emotional ties with others without an automatic support group to help with these tasks. In years past the nuclear family might have helped, but its members are often so affected by divorce and intrafamilial strife (Sanua, 1980) that they can be stressors rather than supportive. As K. Lin and Kleinman explain:

> Along with their heavy emphasis of independence, self-reliance, and personal free-dom, individualist value orientations also tend to foster fierce competition, fre-quent life changes, and alienation, and they do not usually provide the kind of structured, stable, and predictable environments that allow schizophrenic pa-tients to recuperate at their own pace and to be reintegrated into the society. (p. 561)

In contrast, the slower lifestyle and more integrated collectives commonly found in less industrialized nations may provide a more supportive environment for pa-tients with schizophrenia. The likelihood of finding productive work for the individ-ual who has the illness, perhaps as part of family agricultural or business activities, may be greater, leading to the person's sense of self-worth. After accepting work, the individual is likely to be in the company of supportive people who are more tolerant of mistakes than are employers and coworkers in large, impersonal companies. In collective societies, more people feel obligated to offer help in times of troubles than in individualist societies (P. Cook, 1994; E. Imamoglu, R. Kuller, V. Imamoglu, & M. Kuller, 1993). These people are not just mothers, fathers, sisters, and brothers; they also include cousins, uncles, and longtime family friends who have various hon-orary types of collective membership (e.g., godparents). If one collective member can-not communicate with a person who is schizophrenic, the chance is that someone else in the collective can. The extended family, in contrast to the smaller and often troubled nuclear family found in individualist societies, may have more resources to offer help to their member with schizophrenia. The results of K. Lin and Kleinman's (1988) analysis are a reminder of the importance of social support in one's life, and I will return to this concept several times in this chapter.

Depression

An understanding of depression is as necessary in today's world as an understanding of inoculations against diseases, of dietary habits that increase the chances of good health, and of the dangers of alcohol abuse. In a study designed to predict the chances in England of a severe depressive episode during a person's life, Sturt, Kumakura, and Der (1984) estimated that the chances are 11.9% for men and 20.2% for women. These estimates are similar to those calculated independently for residents of Den-mark, Iceland, and the United States (Wing & Bebbington, 1985). This means that the majority of this book's readers will either experience a depressive episode in their lives or have relatives or friends, with whom they have strong relationships, who will have a depressive episode.

The evidence for a culture-common core of depressive symptoms is not as strong as for the core schizophrenic symptoms already reviewed. Depression is expressed in more ways than schizophrenia. Based on research in four countries (Iran, Japan, Canada, and Switzerland: World Health Organization, 1983) and on a study in Colombia and the United States (Escobar, Gomez, & Tuason, 1983), the best evi-dence to date suggests this culture-common core of depressive symptoms:

- *Sad affect.* Everyone occasionally feels the emotion of sadness. When the emo-tion is frequent, intense, and occurs for long periods, it becomes a symptom of depression (Dorahy, Schumaker, Simpson, & Deshpande, 1996). In the study by Escobar and his colleagues, patients in the United States and Colombia could point to the fact they were depressed.

- *Loss of enjoyment.* People seem to take no pleasure in life and fail to find enjoyment in activities they once participated in with enthusiasm.
- *Anxiety.* People experience anxiety about their lives and apprehension about forthcoming events in their lives.
- *Concentration.* People experience difficulties concentrating on tasks necessary for everyday functioning.
- *Energy level.* The energy necessary for setting simple goals and for working toward their accomplishment is lacking.

In addition to this culture-common core is a set of less frequent but commonly found symptoms. These symptoms often are included in diagnostic instruments meant to identify people with depressive disorders (Draguns, 1990; Escobar et al., 1983; Tanaka-Matsumi & Draguns, 1997):

- Loss of sexual interest
- Loss of appetite
- Weight reduction
- Feelings of hopelessness about doing anything positive to improve one's mental health
- Self-accusations about the cause of the difficulties that have led to one's depressive state

Important research also has addressed culture-specific symptoms, the greater frequency of depression among women, and how people with depression think.

Culture-Specific Symptoms

Depression manifests itself in various ways in different parts of the world. In North America and Europe, feelings of guilt are more common than in other parts of the world. Research in Nigeria, for instance, identified many people with depression who did not show evidence of guilt (Marsella, 1980). In fact, cross-cultural research has provided a corrective to the analysis of depression (Draguns, 1990), since guilt was once thought to be central to its existence as a psychological disorder. Kleinman (1982) argued that somatization was more frequent in China than in other parts of the world. As Draguns summarized, "In China, as well as in many other cultures, somatization serves as the channel of communication for the experience of helplessness and even despair, as a culturally sanctioned and generally understood cry for help" (p. 311).

Depression often is associated with suicidal behavior (Diekstra, 1989), but suicidal intentions are not part of the core because exceptions occur. Chiles and his colleagues (1989) compared support group reactions to suicidal threats by people with depression in the United States and China. In the United States, if a person threatens suicide, members of the support group are likely to bring the person to a hospital. There, the patient is treated well and, perhaps, is taken out of a stressful environment at home and the workplace. The suicidal threats, then, are reinforced. They lead to positive outcomes, and one of the most basic concepts in psychology is that reinforced behaviors are likely to be repeated. In China, however, suicidal intentions do not elicit sympathy from a person's support group.

> [In China], suicidal behavior tends to be seen less as a symptom of illness or psychological distress and more as a condition that brings embarrassment and shame to one's family and, to a lesser extent, to one's work group. . . . The immediate consequence of a suicide attempt is likely to be stern discussions with the support group, with the emphasis on, "You must stop this," rather than, "Now that we recognize your pain, how can we help you?" (Chiles et al., p. 344)

Finding that suicidal behaviors do not bring reinforcement, the person with depression is less likely to repeat them.

Depression Among Women

The finding that women are more likely to express depressive symptoms than men has been documented so frequently, in different parts of the world, that it is one of the most widely accepted conclusions in the analysis of mental illnesses (Castillo, 1997; Fugita & Crittenden, 1990). This finding calls for the analysis of possible reasons. No single reason for the difference (which can be on the order of two women for every man with depression: Boyd & Weissman, 1981) has been widely accepted, and the eventual conclusion undoubtedly will be that several factors work in combination. Research to date has dealt both with biological and with social factors. For example, hypothyroidism is higher in women than men, leading to behavior marked by low energy, which is one symptom of depression. Hormonal changes associated with different stages of women's menstrual cycle, which often lead to observable changes in mood, also have been investigated (Thase, Frank, & Kupfer, 1985).

Social factors include the relative powerlessness of women in almost all societies and the subsequent frustrations stemming from their inability to achieve their goals (Castillo, 1997). Recall the discussion in chapter 9: Boys are frequently allowed more freedom of movement outside the home than girls. Analyzing data from a longitudinal study in the United States, Block, Gjerde, and Block (1991), pointed to the difficulties bright young girls can face:

> Over time, bright girls, with their greater emergent awareness of their self and of the world in which they are allowed to function, may build up a sense of stultification and depression about the way their life is being shaped and the criteria on which they are evaluated. (p. 735)

Depression, then, can be a response to societal norms that place limits on the movement of women.

Another discussion in chapter 9 centered on the greater amount of aggressive behavior found in boys than in girls, and this was suggested as a cultural universal. One explanation for the lower amount of depression among men is that they act out their problems in more active, vigorous behaviors than women (Castillo, 1997). Thase and his colleagues (1985) argue: ". . . it is assumed that the lower rate of depression in males results, in part, from expression of the depressive disorder in the form of alcoholism or antisocial behavior" (p. 871). In support of this possibility, Egeland and Hostetter (1983) worked among the Amish, a culture with very strong norms against alcohol abuse and antisocial behavior. Among the Amish, men and women have

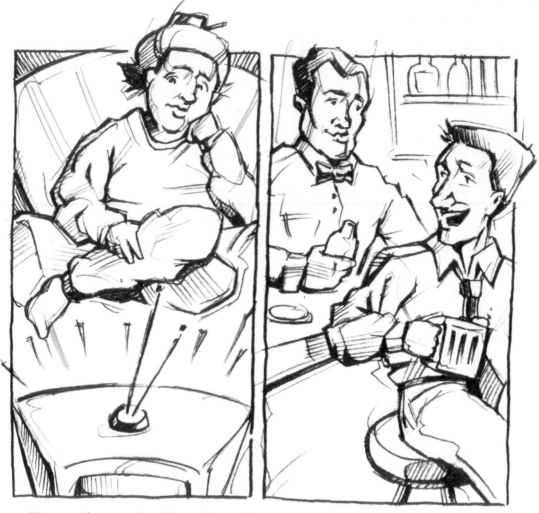

Women with personal problems often turn inward and become depressed. Men with similar problems often "act out" by abusing alcohol and behaving antisocially.

equal rates of depression as expressed in the types of symptoms previously reviewed (low energy, loss of enjoyment, and so forth).

How People With Depression Think

The thought processes of people with depression are marked by large numbers of negative thoughts involving the acceptance of self-blame for any difficulties they encounter (Seligman, 1989, 1998). Assume a person does not receive a job offer after an interview. A healthy response would be, "Well, I just have to keep trying. Perhaps I should look over my résumé and make sure it describes my qualifications clearly." A response indicative of depression would be, "This shows I am not qualified and that the employer was wise to reject me." In particular, people with depression have three features in their thinking.

1. Their thinking is *internal*, meaning they take the blame for problems, even when their thinking could focus on external factors (e.g., a very competitive job market).

2. Their thinking focuses on *stable factors*, such as a permanent unsuitability for the work world, which is self-defeating because it allows little opportunity for positive change. Focusing thinking on unstable factors is more healthy, because it allows for positive change. If a factor is unstable, it may change so that it favors a person.

3. Their thinking is also *universal*. Not only do they feel unsuitable for the job market, they also feel unsuitable for any role in life. Therapists who work with people who are depressed frequently focus on their patients' thinking, encouraging them to avoid excessive amounts of self-blame, to examine aspects of their lives that can be changed in positive directions, and to avoid generalizing from a specific (and potentially modifiable) difficulty to conclusions about their entire life (Seligman, 1989, 1998).

This analysis of how people with depression think was developed in the United States, and it has been tested in other cultures. Crittenden and Lamug (1988) tested the model in the Philippines and found that Filipino people with depression thought in similar ways. Other important findings in the Philippines can be interpreted as culture-specific additions to the culture-common core of internal, stable, and universal thinking among people with depression. For example, the depressive thinking pattern predicted somatic symptoms among respondents in the Philippines but not among the Americans interviewed in the study. This may reflect that Filipinos, as part of their socialization, learn that somatic symptoms such as sleep disturbance, decreased libido, decreased weight, and constipation are part of the depressive state. Americans learn to focus more on psychological symptoms, such as indecisiveness, emptiness, and hopelessness. Filipinos are also more likely to express depression through psychomotor agitation (Fugita & Crittenden, 1990), in contrast to the more listless behavior of Americans. These findings provide other examples of a point argued in several places throughout this chapter: As part of their socialization, people learn to express psychological disturbances in ways that are acceptable within their culture, in ways that will be understood, and in ways that will generate sympathy from others.

THE PREVENTION OF HEALTH PROBLEMS

In the discussion of schizophrenia and depression, several factors were mentioned as lessening the chances people would be debilitated by these illnesses. These factors included the avoidance of stress, the nurturance of a group of supportive individuals, creating opportunities to engage in positive thoughts about one's life, and others.

Much research in recent years has focused on various behaviors in which people can engage that will increase their chances of good health and decrease their chances of illness. The shorthand term *preventive health* often has been used to identify these types of behaviors. Given that people are concerned about their health, summaries of this research have been given extensive coverage in the mass media (e.g., Cowley, 1998; "Feeding Frenzy," 1991; "Health Guide," 1991). In addition, summaries of the research are often provided to members of Health Maintenance Organizations (e.g., Healthwise staff, 1997).

Cross-cultural research has played a solid role in developing various recommendations people can consider when making decisions about their behavior. For example, recommendations have been made about diet (Zaldivar, 1998a), about alcohol use, and about sex education for teenagers. One way to determine the probable effects if such recommendations are followed is to examine the health of people in various countries who behave differently in relation to these factors. For their diet, for example, people in other countries typically obtain fewer of their calories from fat than do people in the United States (Ilola, 1990; Zaldivar, 1998a). Regarding alcohol consumption, people in some countries (e.g., France, Portugal) typically consume more than do citizens in others (e.g., Norway, South Africa: Smart, 1989). By examining data such as mortality figures due to heart disease in these countries, researchers can estimate the effects of behaviors such as adopting a low-fat diet or moderating alcohol intake.

Space limitations prevent extensive discussions of all the relevant literature. I will summarize key research findings by listing the recommended behaviors, briefly discussing some cross-cultural research that contributed to the recommendations, and indicating where sensitivity to culture and cultural differences can play a part in the development of preventive health programs.

Diet, Especially Calories From Animal Fats

In Hawaii, native Hawaiians have the shortest life expectancy of any ethnic group. Threats to the health of native Hawaiians include high cholesterol, obesity, high blood pressure, and diabetes. One possible reason is that when adjusting to the modernity pressures Americans of European ancestry introduced, early Hawaiians adopted the high-fat diet typical of Caucasian Americans. In contrast, the native diet was much healthier, with its emphasis (in today's terms) on low fat, on an abundance of complex carbohydrates, and on a great deal of bulk. A recently established intervention project encouraged Hawaiians to move back to their more traditional diet (Shintani & Devenot, 1998; Shintani, Hughes, Beckham, & O'Connor, 1991). The diet's contents included large amounts of sweet potatoes and poi, the latter a vegetable product produced from the taro plant. Other acceptable items were breadfruit, a variety of vegetables, seaweed, fruit, fish, and chicken. Note the absence of animal fats in products such as red meat, eggs, milk, and cheese. Results of a 21-day program indicated that participants lost an average of 17.1 pounds, lowered their serum cholesterol by an average of 14%, and also significantly lowered both their systolic (7.8%) and diastolic (11.5%) blood pressure.

Weight

Recommendations about diet, of course, will impact people's weight. With the possible exception of avoiding the smoking habit (Zaldivar, 1998b), few preventive health recommendations are suggested more frequently than keeping weight at levels appropriate to sex, age, and height. When examining the health of the Amish culture within the United States, Fuchs, Levinson, Stoddard, Mullet, and Jones (1990) concluded that the relative infrequency of obesity is a positive feature of the Amish lifestyle and an important contributor to their good health.

Exercise

In addition to its role in assisting people to maintain their weight at desired levels, regular exercise has a positive impact on people's cardiovascular fitness, their muscle tone, and their stamina (Avlund, Luck, & Tinsley, 1996). In contrast to diet, where the influence of Westernization often has led to increases in the intake of animal fats (discussed earlier) in some cultures, people with modern outlooks on life appear to make a point of adding regular exercise to their lives. Among Chinese living in Malaysia, Quah (1985) found that "young, educated, and well-informed [from the mass media and public health campaigns] Chinese are more likely to exercise regularly than their older, less educated, and less informed counterparts" (p. 355). In contrast to the convergence of male and female behaviors once traditional restrictions are lifted (chapter 9), differences in exercise behavior among men and women were small when comparisons were made among the young and well educated. Among the less well educated, men were more likely to exercise than women were, perhaps because they had more opportunities for activities outside the home.

Exercise is one of the few treatments proven successful in the prevention and treatment of low back pain (Deyo, 1998). This conclusion holds for sufferers of both acute and chronic back pain. It has been very difficult to document the benefits of back surgery. This lack of proven efficacy is probably one reason surgery quantity rates for back pain vary greatly across industrialized nations. In some countries, people carefully study research on the efficacy of various treatments prior to choosing surgery because insurance programs mandate this step. The United States has the highest back surgery rate, five times that of Scotland. When exercise instead becomes the chosen treatment or method of prevention, recommendations call for a combination of general fitness training through aerobics and "specific training to improve the strength and endurance of the back muscles" (Deyo, p. 51).

Drugs and Alcohol

Discussions of problems from drug and alcohol use often are covered under discussions of "substance abuse" (Ames & Rebhun, 1996; Foxcroft, 1996; O'Nell & Mitchell, 1996; Reeves, 1998). Among Native Americans, numerous alcohol-related health problems are more prevalent than in any other ethnic group in the United States. They include cirrhoses, diabetes, fetal abnormalities, accident fatalities, and homicides. The American Indian use of substances such as marijuana, inhalants (e.g., glue), and other illicit drugs contribute to educational difficulties when children attend school, criminal acts among adults, and severe pressures on family economic resources. After reviewing these and other difficulties, Moncher, Holden, and Trimble (1990) attempted to identify Native American youth who were at risk for substance abuse. More specifically, they attempted to predict the abuse of tobacco, smokeless tobacco, alcohol, inhalants, cannabis, and cocaine/crack. They identified a number of predictors that could identify Native American youth who (a) were at risk and who (b) might become participants in educational and health delivery programs aimed at preventing problems before they occurred.

The various risk factors included the fact an individual's family members smoked or used smokeless tobacco; the presence of peers who smoked; the presence of peers who used alcohol; the quality of family life; school adjustment; deviant behaviors not directly related to substance abuse; religiosity; and cultural identification. This last factor, cultural identification, refers to an individual's feelings about his or her status as a Native American, and it also refers to the individual's ability to function effectively in the dominant Anglo American culture. Skills for functioning in the dominant culture are important because they are often the source of advanced educational opportunities, employment, and receiving health delivery services. The goals of many intervention programs include *biculturalism*, or the ability to be comfortable in interactions whether they take place among Native Americans or among any other ethnic group members. As LaFromboise (1982) noted, bicultural skills allow young people to "blend the adaptive values and roles of both the culture in which they were raised and the culture by which they are surrounded" (p. 12). People's frustrations in their ability to maneuver effectively can be one reason for escape by using various health-threatening substances (LaFromboise, Coleman, & Gerton, 1993).

Acting to Prevent Health Difficulties

Whenever a discussion of activities such as avoiding harmful substances or developing skills useful in a society occurs, attention must be given to individual initiative (Braun, Takamura, & Mougeot, 1996). At some point, individuals have to monitor their diet, watch their weight, set time aside for exercise, make decisions about their sexual activity, avoid drug use, develop certain skills, and so forth. If programs are established for recommending these activities, people have to attend the programs and do the recommended activities after the program ends (Avlund et al., 1996).

Various health delivery programs are more common in some countries than in others. Many countries (not the United States) have national health insurance programs so that people can consult physicians without the worry of a drain on their finances. The number of visits to physicians varies across countries. In Germany, for example, people see a physician an average of 12 times a year, compared to an average of 4.7 visits for Americans and 5.2 for the French (Payer, 1988). Germans (specifically, West Germany before reunification) also receive large numbers of prescription items: 11.2 prescriptions per year compared to the 6.5 prescriptions the average patient in Great Britain receives. The interesting question arises, "Does all this attention from physicians, and easy access to health professionals, interfere with people's initiative in maintaining their health?" After investigating health care in the United States and West Germany, Cockerham, Kunz, and Lueschen (1988) would answer no. This answer has important implications for social policy because proponents of a national health insurance program can argue that people still take the initiative to maintain their health even if far more government services become available to them. Cockerham and his colleagues describe the German system:

> . . . the state provides comprehensive health insurance, featuring free medical and dental treatment, drugs, and hospitalization for an indefinite period of time. Sick or injured workers also receive full wages from their employers for six weeks; they receive their approximate take-home pay from public health benefits for 78 weeks thereafter. . . . Extensive maternity and death benefits also are paid through public health insurance. (p. 117)

In addition to actually receiving these benefits, the Germans in the study had adopted the philosophy that they were entitled to these types of services from their government. Many Americans were more distrustful than Germans were of having too many government programs that might affect their lives.

With the possible exception that they consumed greater quantities of alcohol (beer was the most common drink), Germans were as concerned as Americans were with preventive health behaviors. Germans were more likely to be careful about the food they ate and to seek relaxation time; Americans were more likely to be careful about their alcohol consumption and to be concerned about their appearance (e.g., good complexion, good posture). Both Americans and Germans gave attention to exercise and if they had the smoking habit were making attempts to quit. Overall, the respondents were equally attentive to maintaining a healthy lifestyle, even though they gave more emphasis to some factors relative to others. Cockerham and his colleagues (1988) conclude: "West Germans, with their more extensive state-sponsored health benefits, appear to work just as hard to stay fit as do Americans, who have more individual responsibility for obtaining and maintaining coverage for health services" (p. 125). Thus government programs do not necessarily interfere with personal incentives to engage in a healthy lifestyle.

Avoiding Stress

One of the factors in a healthy lifestyle Germans emphasized more than Americans was time for relaxation. This emphasis is part of the more general advice to avoid stress whenever possible and to seek relaxing activities in the form of hobbies, time with family and friends, vacations, and so forth. People in individualist countries such as the United States and Canada seem to have more stress-related illnesses than people in collective countries such as China, Thailand, and India (Bond, 1991). One reason is that individualists have to do so much on their own: find a job, work effectively at the job, find a spouse, raise children, provide for the financial security of the nuclear families, and so forth. In collective cultures, others help in major ways with these tasks (as discussed in chapter 2), so any one person has less stress than individualists have. The stress-related illnesses individualists are more prone to include ulcers, heart diseases, strokes, and cancers of the stomach, colon, and rectum (Bond).

Stress has impacts on other health problems (Bagley & Mallick, 1995). As previously discussed, people in various parts of the world who are at risk for schizophrenia are more likely to have acute attacks after stressful episodes in their lives (Day et al., 1987). Summarizing research in seven countries, McCormick and Cooper (1988) argue that job loss and family conflicts are two of the most stressful life events. The stress resulting from job loss may be less (a) in countries where companies have a tradition of never laying off employees or doing so only under the most extreme circumstances or (b) in countries where unemployment is so low that people can find jobs easily. Stress from conflicts within the nuclear family can be lessened in collective cultures if the extended family or organization has supportive members who can offer various forms of assistance (Golding & Baezconde-Garbanati, 1990).

Nurturing a Support Group

This discussion of the relationship between collectivism and the lower frequency of stress-related diseases compared to individualists leads to another piece of advice for a healthy lifestyle. If people do not naturally have a supportive group in the form of an extended family or of employment in a paternal organization (as discussed in chapter 8), they should strongly consider developing a network of people who can offer assistance in difficult times. In many types of jobs, stress cannot be eliminated. However, stress can be managed in ways that decrease the chances of negative impacts on people's health. One way people can decrease stress is to have supportive others in their life who can act as buffers between stressful events and harmful effects on their health (P. Cook, 1994; Harari, Jones, & Sek, 1988; Kelley & Kelley, 1985).

Stress cannot be totally eliminated in job situations such as air traffic controllers working when the weather is bad at busy airports, retail sales workers just before the major holidays when gifts are exchanged, and social workers dealing with clients unwilling to accept bureaucratic procedures for receiving public assistance. The presence of people who care about the difficulties in one's life can have major impacts on reducing stress. In a discussion of suicide attempts in 19 European countries, with special emphasis on information from the Netherlands, Diekstra (1989) presented an argument consistent with the gender discussion in chapter 9. As noted, women, compared to men, expect more from their friends (Morse, 1983). These expectations can include listening to discussions about the stresses in their life. Men are either less likely to expect that friends will want to hear about their stresses or are less comfortable discussing their emotions. When women experience depression or suicidal thoughts, the fact that they discuss their emotions with others has several benefits. The others may offer various types of support, or at least they may not allow the troubled individual to find herself alone. It is very difficult to commit suicide when others are present. Diekstra summarizes:

> . . . although women may indeed more often experience [depressive] feelings, they also seem more inclined to admit and communicate such feelings to others (even in the form of nonfatal suicide attempts), while men are less inclined to do so and more often cope with them by substance abuse. . . . [This increases] the probability of not only worsening such feelings but also of more severe social, interpersonal and physical disruption, that in turn increases their risk for . . . suicide attempts and completed suicides. (p. 205)

Intervention programs aimed at men often include the recommendation that they learn to discuss their emotions more openly with support group members (Kelley & Kelley, 1985).

Varying and Increasing Activities

Support groups often develop out of people's activities. Positive interactions take place with colleagues in the workplace, with other community-minded people during volunteer activities, and with friends who share activities associated with a variety of hobbies. Varying and increasing activities is associated with good health (Avlund et al., 1996). In an eight-year longitudinal study of Mexican Americans and Anglo Americans age 60 and older, Markides and Lee (1990) investigated the relation between health and activities such as going to movies, dances, picnics, museums, zoos, or sporting events; hunting or fishing; attending parades or fiestas; meeting with friends or neighbors; and sightseeing. Activity level decreased with age, suggesting "the importance of targeting activity programs at the very old" (Markides & Lee, p. S72). The model the researchers presented suggests a relationship between health and activity level. The exact nature of the relationship is admittedly ambiguous: Good health allows people to increase their activities, and poor health (for reasons unassociated with an active lifestyle) can force people to decrease their activities. As with many complex behavioral analyses, the relationship between health and activity can exist for several reasons. In addition to activity affecting health and vice versa, a third variable can affect both. People's socioeconomic status can affect their access to a healthy diet; a good diet can affect their energy level (Palmore, Nowling, & Wang, 1985; S. Taylor, Repette, & Seemen, 1997); energy level can affect their number of activities; and the number of activities can affect their health.

People often obtain approval from others if they engage in work-related activities considered important in a culture. K. Lin and Kleinman (1988) suggest that people at risk for schizophrenia are less likely to have acute attacks if they participate in a culture's workforce. If they can carry out tasks successfully that benefit a society (e.g., agricultural work, construction work), they receive approval, social support, and a sense of meaning in their lives. People with schizophrenia who are members of collective cultures sometimes fit well into the workforce because supportive group members (a) see that they obtain jobs not beyond their abilities and (b) keep an eye on them so that as many problems as possible can be avoided.

Participating in Intervention Programs

At times, the activities people should engage in are either formal programs designed to prevent health problems or programs to deal with problems should they arise (Coates & Collins, 1998). Preventive programs are often the most cost effective to operate. The treatment of certain diseases, such as alcoholism, can be very expensive, and the expenses multiply if a disease is especially prevalent in a culture. Programs to prevent problems before they occur are not only often far less expensive but also, of course, can have additional positive impacts on family members who do not participate directly (see chapter 5). Relatives can reap benefits if illness does not strike the spouse, son, or daughter who is an active program participant.

Adolescents all over the world are exposed to temptations to abuse alcohol (Foxcroft, 1996; O'Nell & Mitchell, 1996). Whenever adolescents congregate for social purposes, alcohol use often becomes one of the expected activities. Perry and her colleagues (1989) introduced school-based alcohol education programs in four countries: Australia, Chile, Norway, and Swaziland. The target population was 13- and 14-year-olds in these countries, and the goal was to encourage the adolescents to minimize their alcohol use. A group of age peers were carefully trained to be comfortable with leading the educational program, which included presenting information about alcohol's effects, organizing small group discussions, role-playing, and synthesizing information material with participant suggestions. The leaders gave special attention to developing skills such as examining the promises made in advertisements for alcohol, analyzing peer influences to use alcohol at parties, and refusing invitations to use alcohol in a way that does not alienate friends.

The researchers compared the effectiveness of peer-led programs with teacher-led programs, and (perhaps surprisingly) the peer-led programs were more effective in all four countries. Reasons for this finding include the possibility that participants viewed peers as more knowledgeable about the pressures adolescents face when confronted with invitations to use alcohol. Perry and her colleagues (1989) further suggest:

> . . . teachers are often viewed as authority figures and [are] not seen as "experts" on adolescent social decisions. . . . Peer leaders may be more credible role models since they employ the social language of their classmates. They also carry the message with them into the social environment outside the school of classroom. (p. 1167)

Of course, some major tasks remain for adults who decide to use peer-led education programs. Adults can select the most influential adolescents, can prepare materials for training, can organize the training programs for peer leaders, and can evaluate the entire set of intervention efforts so that improvements can be made.

Yao (1990) made similar recommendations for AIDS awareness workshops among youth in Africa, where AIDS has been transmitted through heterosexual contact more frequently than in other parts of the world (Krieger & Margo, 1991). Youths may be more willing to listen to one another make recommendations about sexual activity, rather than listening to adults. Adults still would have much to do: workshop preparation, youth leader selection, and follow-up activities such as evaluations months and years after young people participate in the workshops. It is important to note that the statement about more transmission through heterosexual contact in Africa is based on data gathered through 1990. Many analysts (e.g. Erlanger, 1991) fear that AIDS will spread in countries such as Thailand, where prostitution is common, where extramarital sex is tolerated, and where public health education programs are underfinanced (Martinez & Fisher, 1997; see later discussion).

At times, intervention programs require detailed knowledge of a culture. Bastien (1987) described a program he developed for physicians working in Andean communities (with speakers of the Aymara and Quechua languages) in Bolivia. Recommended medical practices sometimes could be communicated to Andeans through familiar myths and stories. Physicians often tried to communicate the seriousness of diarrhea. People (especially young children) with diarrhea can become dehydrated, and death from dehydration was common. The physicians' recommendation that people with diarrhea drink fluids was communicated by appealing to the story about Sajima, which is well known to Andeans. Sajima was a mountain that lost all its water because gophers drilled so many holes in it. Sajima was dying because of water loss, and a condor had to fly to neighboring mountains to bring back a special type of water. Because of the water, Sajima was saved. When presenting this story to Andeans, physicians added details about the special water. They said that to make a liter of water special so that it could be used similarly to saving Sajima, people should add two soupspoons of sugar and small amounts of salt and bicarbonate of soda. A child who has lost water, like Sajima, should receive small amounts of this special liquid every 5 minutes. Given that the physicians' recommendations were linked to a story the Andeans already knew, they were more likely to consider diarrhea and dehydration as serious problems and to take appropriate action.

Researchers and practitioners have been sensitive to the need for cultural knowledge when developing programs for AIDS prevention (Barrett, 1997; Coates & Collins, 1998; Martinez & Fisher, 1997). Efforts to develop intervention programs, with careful analyses of successes and failures, have led to checklists of concepts people should keep in mind. The following list of five points uses the analysis of Coates and Collins as its starting point and includes detailed discussions of each point.

1. *Educational programs should be targeted.* Especially because funding for AIDS prevention is limited, programs should be targeted where they will do the most good. Unfortunately, targeting can reinforce negative images of people and of places as "hotbeds of disease" that, as such, do not deserve the attention of politicians who hold the purse strings of needed funds. This is undoubtedly a problem that must be accepted as part of realistic efforts to combat AIDS. In San Francisco, information was prepared especially for gay community members and presented to them through media they consult regularly and in places where they meet. These included gay publications, meeting places of gay societies, and churches.

Thailand has a long tradition of a commercial sex industry including brothels (Barrett, 1997). This fact leads to tolerated outcomes when they are not encouraged. Young men often have their first sexual experience in these brothels. Impoverished but pretty young women are recruited from rural villages and are brought to big cities to become commercial sex workers (CSWs). The tacit knowledge is that husbands will pay for the services of CSWs and their wives may disapprove but have little power to change the norm that "men will be men." Organized tours are established for people who want to travel to Thailand to avail themselves of frequent, relatively low-cost sex acts. The amount of money generated from the commercial sex industry and the number of jobs created provide incentives for politicians to avoid major changes in the status quo.

AIDS intervention efforts in Thailand have involved a variety of activities introduced in the brothels. Condoms have been provided to CSWs. Instructions have been offered about how to encourage customers to use them. Given that too few well-trained professionals are available to present programs in all needed places, computer programs on disks and videotapes have been produced. The disks are presented with a laptop computer, and their use stimulates interest because CSWs are not familiar with a laptop but find it fascinating to press keys and to click the mouse. A practical piece of advice is to always have backup materials. Videotapes could not be used in some Thai brothels because of broken equipment, so simple and self-paced presentations based on inexpensive flip charts should be available (Martinez & Fisher, 1997).

2. *People who deliver the interventions should be carefully selected.* No generalizations exist about who should be chosen to deliver AIDS interventions. Each social situation must be carefully studied, and the recommendations of many knowledgeable people should be sought. In some situations, the choice will be the peers of the targeted individuals. In small cities in the United States, opinion leaders within the gay community were identified. These individuals were respected by many gays, knew where gays meet, could talk comfortably with them, and so forth. These opinion leaders were trained about methods to promote safe sex practices, and they then communicated this information within their communities. Follow-up research showed significantly more safe sex practices: more condom use, less anal intercourse, and fewer cases of multiple sex partners (Coates & Collins, 1998).

In Thailand, the recruitment of CSW peers was not as successful (Barrett, 1997). Some CSWs meet in or work out of bars. Although it might seem reasonable to recruit some of the bar patrons and to train them in interventions for AIDS prevention, this may not be wise in this context. Barrett (1997) argues that bars in Thailand should be analyzed as a microsociety where people have clear roles and behave according to well-accepted norms. If professionals choose a bar patron and offer training, they are removing the patron from his or her microsociety and are upsetting the established social order. A better procedure is to introduce a new person to the microsociety who takes on the roles of counselor and AIDS-prevention information provider. Other people in the bar (owner, bartenders, waiters) then can refer one another and bar patrons to this "outsider" who has a clear role that does not interfere with previous hierarchies and well-established social relationships.

After assuming a role, the intervention worker must be prepared for a wide variety of conversations with CSWs. For example, some CSWs in Thailand are paid based on the number of clients served during a day. They are reluctant to ask customers to use condoms not out of shyness but out of a concern that condom use will prolong interactions with customers and thus cut into profits (Martinez & Fisher, 1997). This concern stems from the belief that condom use decreases sensitivity and consequently increases the amount of time customers need to achieve sexual release. The intervention worker must be prepared to discuss the health benefits of condom use and to discuss other ways of increasing sensitivity. Professionals uncomfortable with such discussions will not be good health intervention workers in these specific circumstances.

3. *As many people as possible should be involved in programs.* The developers of many successful AIDS prevention programs are not satisfied to work only with women or with male CSWs. Whenever possible, partners and customers should be included. In Rwanda, counselors refer to heterosexual couples as "discordant" if one partner is HIV positive and one is not. After people receive the medical report that they are HIV positive, counseling is offered to them and to their uninfected partners. Condom use rose from 3% to 57% after counseling (Coates & Collins, 1998).

Given that AIDS intervention programs are expensive and budgets for them are sparse, people at risk who find themselves in the same place often are targeted (Martinez & Fisher, 1997). For users of CSWs, this often demands knowledge of (a) what groups of people are likely to pay for sex and (b) who can be targeted for group programs. In Thailand, this can include college students (at their schools or in their dormitories) and military personnel (at their barracks). In India, this can include truck drivers who congregate at known eating establishments. In Japan, this can include businesspeople out for a night of entertainment in a city's red-light district. In some cities, these red-light districts are so well known that intervention workers can pass out leaflets as the businesspeople enter the district.

4. *Information should be presented in culturally acceptable ways.* People learn information through different means, through different examples of concepts, and through different media. Intervention workers can ask themselves, "How do people in this culture learn new information? Can we present our intervention messages in ways familiar to people?" As in the discussion of groups of people likely to pay for sex, answers to these questions demand very specific cultural knowledge.

A knowledge of collectivism has helped interventions in Thailand (Barrett, 1997). People are asked to imagine one person who has AIDS. Then, they are asked to consider the impact of this person on a community as a whole. If they are uncomfortable talking about themselves as the one person, they can draw a picture of a person on the floor or elsewhere and then speculate about this person. Of course, the speakers often project their own goals, desires, and fears in their presentations about this other person. Another exercise uses the knowledge that Thais often diagnose their own symptoms and then buy their own pharmaceuticals (available without prescription far more readily than in North America). With this approach to self-help, they do not seek professional medical diagnoses and intervention. In the exercise, different symptoms are presented, and participants decide on a diagnosis. The goal is to persuade participants that no one-to-one relationship exists between symptoms and diagnosis and that many diseases have similar symptoms. Especially with sexually transmitted diseases, self-diagnoses are dangerous, and professional help should be sought as soon as symptoms are noticed.

In Thailand, street theater is a form of entertainment, so intervention workers have staged short plays in parts of cities where pedestrians commonly encounter public dramatic presentations. In cultures where church attendance is highly valued, leaders can incorporate preventive health practices in presentations to their congregations. In the United States, actors on television soap operas and nighttime dramatic shows have stopped in the middle of seduction scenes and have gone to their bedroom dressers to retrieve condoms.

5. *Avoiding what does not work.* In their review of how to best introduce preventive measures for HIV transmission, Coates and Collins (1998) covered methods that have proven successful as well as methods that have failed. A knowledge of the latter helps in the development of programs likely to succeed. For example, a one-time exposure to information is less successful than programs that teach skills. A piece of insufficient information is "condoms reduce but do not eliminate risk." Communicating this is less successful than programs that teach assertiveness skills for social situations where condom use must be negotiated. In addition, program

directors must teach the exact use of condoms and should *not* take for granted that instructions on use are the same as realistic demonstrations and actual practice. *Single messages* are ineffective. The repetition of information combined with practice opportunities is highly recommended. This advice is reminiscent of what long has been standard practice in education and training programs. Years ago my mentors pointed out that if you tell people information only once they may not hear it, they may misunderstand it, or they may forget it.

For preventing sexually transmitted diseases, *abstinence-only programs* are not the best choice. It may be politically efficacious for government officials to recommend them and to vote for their funding, but independent evaluations have shown they are unrealistic. Programs can recommend abstinence and perhaps reach some participants with this message, but the programs also should provide information and behaviors "to protect the young from HIV" (Coates & Collins, 1998, p. 97). *Coercive programs* are likely to backfire. For example, forcing HIV-infected people to provide the names and addresses of sexual partners can cause the people to distrust and to be uncomfortable with the health care system. Such programs also can yield much useless information in the form of false names and incomplete lists. The time and effort to develop coercive programs is better spent on programs that guarantee anonymity and that offer confidential testing.

DEVELOPING CULTURAL SENSITIVITY IN HEALTH CARE DELIVERY

When health specialists modify their behaviors so that their recommendations are placed into frameworks familiar to patients (as in the example of AIDS prevention programs in Thailand), they are demonstrating a sensitivity to culture and to cultural differences. Many researchers and practitioners have made recommendations or have developed programs to encourage the development of cultural sensitivity among health workers (e.g., Ahia, 1984; Castillo, 1997; Draguns, 1975, 1990; Fisher et al., 1998; Lefley, 1990; Pedersen, 1991b; Ponterotto & Benesch, 1988; Weiss & Parish, 1989). Several people concerned with the development of cultural sensitivity feel that a good starting point is to analyze universal aspects of health care delivery. If universal aspects can be identified, people have a convenient framework to think about and plan health care delivery in their own culture. In addition, they have a framework for examining other cultures so that they can identify how the universal aspects operate.

Universals in Health Care Delivery

Several scholars have examined interactions between health professionals and people seeking help in various parts of the world. Although the emphasis has been services for people with psychological complaints, I believe the universal aspects these scholars (Barsh, 1997; Draguns, 1975, 1990; Ponterotto & Benesch, 1988; Torrey, 1986) identified are applicable to interactions between professionals and clients about any type of health problem. It is important to note that the term "professionals" is meant to be very broad here. It includes people with advanced degrees in highly industrialized nations who citizens label as "physician," "psychiatrist," "public health worker," and so forth. It also includes people in less industrialized nations such as native healers, shamans, and herbalists. Six universal aspects will be reviewed here.

1. Health care specialists *apply a name to a problem*. When clients learn that their problem has a name, it seems to be a positive step toward identifying solutions for the problem. I remember when one of my children, then about 18 months, was constantly fussy. My wife and I went to the doctor and learned that an appropriate label (in the United States) was that the baby suffered from "colic." Even though I knew that the label "colic" said little more about our baby than the symptom of fussiness we already knew, realizing the problem had a label was comforting. Perhaps one reason for the comfort is learning we were not unique (and perhaps not inadequate) as parents. Other parents have colicky babies. In the example of Sajima presented previously, the name given to babies with diarrhea is "water loss," and this label is familiar to Andean parents.

2. *Qualities of the health professional are important* (Sue & Zane, 1987). Clients must see them as caring, competent, approachable, and concerned with identifying and finding solutions to problems. These qualities contribute to the client's belief that a solution can be found and that the physical or psychological pain that led to the search for help will be relieved. When discussing interventions for minority groups in the United States, Sue and Zane (1987) emphasized that professionals must communicate a sense of credibility that they can help. Further, they should offer benefits of some kind as soon as they can. If professionals do not offer benefits, they risk clients terminating contact, for instance, by not keeping appointments. "Offer benefits" does not mean providing a total cure. It can entail smaller contributions such as helpful advice for the problem; a concrete suggestion about some aspect of the patient's life, such as developing a good résumé for a job search, or introductions to people from the same cultural background who might become part of a support group (e.g., Alcoholics Anonymous for a person with a drinking problem).

3. The *establishment of credibility* can be assisted through symbols and status trappings familiar in a culture. In highly industrialized nations, people are put at ease if they seek help from a professional who works out of an attractive office, has diplomas on the wall, and dresses in a certain way. Among professionals known as native healers, credibility would be established if clients know the healer has served many years as an apprentice to a person enshrined in the culture's oral legends. In all cultures, professionals can increase their credibility by positive word of mouth, that is, by testimonials from former patients who speak highly of the professionals' abilities.

4. Credibility is also related to *placing the client's problem in a familiar framework*. If long-held beliefs in a culture center on witchcraft as the cause of certain problems, healers are likely to present their exact diagnoses and recommended treatments in terms of evil spirits rather than bacteria. In contrast, physicians in industrialized nations are far more likely to appeal to bacteria, diet, unsafe sex,

or the smoking habit as causes of medical problems because these are familiar to patients. One reason people choose one psychotherapist over another involves the frameworks different mental health specialists offer (Edman, 1997). If a person seeking help had a difficult childhood and accepts the possibility that parent-child relations have major impacts 20 years later, he or she may find it attractive to work with a therapist trained in Freudian analysis. People who do not find explanations based on childhood appealing and who want to focus on very specific problems, such as hostility or depression in their current lives, may expect more success working with a clinician trained in behavioral or cognitive therapies.

5. After the problem is identified, a professional then *applies a set of techniques meant to bring relief*. These techniques also should fit into the patients' worldview about the problems that brought them to seek professional help. If patients are familiar with the work of psychiatrists, for example, they will not be surprised when asked to talk profusely about themselves. If they are familiar with the germ theory of disease, they will accept injections meant to either kill bacteria or to stimulate the body's own immune system. If they are familiar with the presence of spirits, they will look forward to rituals that rid the body of demons. Within industrialized nations, differences within psychotherapies are based on the source of advice that will lead to relief. In some therapies, patients are expected to become gradually aware of possible solutions, and the clinician is expected to encourage this process. In other therapies, the clinician is expected to give direct advice the client is expected to follow. Minority group members in the United States often expect direct advice (Castillo, 1997; Sue, 1988; Sue & Zane, 1987), and clinicians unwilling to offer it often find that patients fail to keep appointments.

6. Interactions between professionals and clients occur at *a special time and place* (Draguns, 1975, 1990). The special places vary across cultures, of course, and take the form of doctor's offices, hospitals, ceremonial huts, and areas taboo to anyone but healers and people they designate as acceptable visitors. Professional-client interactions often take the form of an acceptable period of "time out" from the problems that caused the clients to seek help. But within this limited period, professionals and their clients engage in intense, concentrated, and emotionally charged activities that have the goals of diagnosis and recommended solutions to problems. Given that clients are interacting with a credible professional who they believe will offer help and that they are focusing solely on their problem and are setting aside their other life concerns, they experience intense emotions. "The opportunity to behave, think, and feel differently from one's day-to-day experience is another common denominator of many very different therapeutic procedures" (Draguns, 1975, p. 286).

More on the Characteristics of Helpers: Cultural Sensitivity

Other issues in the delivery of health services can be introduced in a short critical incident. Jane McKenna is an Anglo American from a small city in the American

Midwest. She was active in community organizations during her high school years. She became interested in the helping professions during the two years she spent as a volunteer at a social services agency. After entering college, she took several psychology courses and eventually attended graduate school with the aim of becoming a counseling psychologist. She did well in her coursework and accepted an internship at a mental health clinic in Chicago. On her first day there, she learned that she would be working with a number of African American clients from the inner city. Jane wondered if she really could be of assistance. She feared that because she was Anglo and some of her clients were African American, a lack of effective communication and of client acceptance of her as their counselor might occur. Can Jane be an effective counselor at this mental health clinic?

The answer is yes, and the key issue is Jane's sensitivity to culture and to cultural differences. When researchers make recommendations about the selection and training of professionals who could offer help to clients from other cultural backgrounds, the term "cultural sensitivity" is used repeatedly (Fisher et al., 1998; Gim, Atkinson, & Kim, 1991; Lefley, 1990; Newhill, 1990; Ponterotto & Benesch, 1988). It is important to understand this concept in this context, because several research studies (Campion, 1982; Hess & Street, 1991; Sue, 1988; Wade & Bernstein, 1991) indicate that professionals can interact effectively with clients from other cultural groups and can offer help as long as they possess "cultural sensitivity." This familiar term refers to, in this case, a health professional's knowledge of culture and cultural differences, and examples of this sensitivity can be found throughout this book. But knowledge is not enough. Sensitivity also includes professionals' willingness to bring their knowledge to interactions with different clients and their ability to take culture into account during discussions of important topics such as recommendations about the alleviation of pain and stress.

Training programs have been established to encourage intercultural sensitivity among health care professionals. Often, programs use a variety of approaches so that the various aspects of sensitivity are addressed: knowledge about culture, willingness to incorporate this knowledge into health care delivery, and actual practice in doing so. One training method can be borrowed from the efforts of Gim and her colleagues (1991), who developed audiotapes that present examples of culturally sensitive counseling. Trainees can listen to these tapes and identify examples of good counselor-client interactions. In this exercise, an important distinction is between empathy and cultural sensitivity. All of the counselor's comments in the examples presented here show empathy, or clear attempts to understand and share the clients' feelings, and this characteristic of counselors is considered essential in all types of interventions. But not all examples show cultural sensitivity, the characteristic considered necessary when counselors and clients are from different cultural backgrounds. In this conversation taken from the audiotapes Gim and her colleagues prepared, the material in brackets provides examples of cultural sensitivity that go beyond empathy. The client is an Asian American female.

CLIENT: But, you know, more than anything else, I feel really different from everybody. I grew up in a big city with a lot of Asians and other minority groups. My high school was pretty mixed; but here, I feel out of place, I miss my friends a lot.

COUNSELOR: Yes, it's hard to leave behind a familiar place and start all over in a new place. [But it also sounds like you're feeling alienated because not many people here share your cultural background.]

CLIENT: Yeah, it's really hard on me sometimes. I wish there were more Asians here.

COUNSELOR: I can see that this situation is affecting you a great deal. [In addition to the usual difficulties of adjusting to a new place, you also feel culturally isolated.] (p. 58)

Other culturally sensitive remarks could focus on the client's relation with her family (chapter 4), communication difficulties when making friends that might be based on communication styles familiar in different cultures (chapter 7), and expectations that different cultures place on women (chapter 9).

Another method for developing sensitivity is for trainees to engage in role-playing, as introduced in chapter 7. Paul Pedersen (1988) has developed a unique version of role-playing called the *triad model*, with three people simulating counseling sessions. Two of the people play the well-known roles of client and counselor, and a third person acts in a variety of ways meant to assist or to challenge the counselor and client. For example, the third person can act as someone very knowledgeable about the client's culture. Or, the third person can act as the problem and can try to maintain its existence. If the client brings the problem of alcohol use to the counseling session, the third person would make comments such as the following: "But you're so much fun when you've had a couple of drinks. It's nice to look forward to a couple of relaxing drinks when you are having a stressful day at work. Keep in mind how frequently alcohol is served at social gatherings in your culture." The person role-playing the counselor has to deal with these comments in various ways and keep the client focused on why help was sought.

The purposes of the triad model are to encourage trainees (a) to describe and explain the client's problem so that cultural factors are clearly identified, (b) to deal with client resistance (for instance, resistances stemming from the fact client and counselor are from different cultural backgrounds), (c) to recognize and deal with any defensiveness people may be expressing as counselors, and (d) to recover from any mistakes made during counseling sessions. Wade and Bernstein (1991) evaluated the effects of a cultural sensitivity training program that included the triad model. The clients in the evaluation study were African American women. Some clients were assigned to experienced counselors who had not participated in the training program, and other clients were assigned to program graduates. Clients rated trained counselors higher than the graduates on a number of important dimensions: expertness, trustworthiness, ability to show positive regard, and empathy. However, clients assigned to the program graduates expressed greater satisfaction with their experience in counseling and returned for more follow-up sessions. One conclusion of this evaluation study is that cultural sensitivity is a characteristic of good counseling that can be developed in well-thought-out programs.

Another conclusion is that well-prepared counselors can work across cultural barriers. Both African American and Anglo counselors participated in the study, but the African American clients did not prefer specific counselors just because they were from the same ethnic group. As Wade and Bernstein (1991) concluded, ". . . Black female clients' perceptions of counselors and the counseling process were affected more by cultural sensitivity training of the counselors than by counselor race" (p. 13). I believe that this finding, consistent with other evidence Sue (1988) reviewed, shows that health delivery professionals can increase their knowledge of culture and cultural differences and become more effective as a result. It also supports one of the themes presented throughout this book. Whether people are teachers, businesspeople, health care deliverers, government officials, or members of other professions, they can work effectively with individuals who happen to come from different cultural backgrounds. The culture people were socialized in does not necessarily place an insurmountable barrier on their ability to carry out their professional goals. Instead, a knowledge of culture may provide guidelines for achieving the goals (the best education possible, excellent health care, respect for contributions in the workplace) more effectively. If people put time and effort into understanding culture's influence on their own behavior and on others' behavior, they even may look forward to the challenges and stimulation of intercultural interactions.

CHAPTER SUMMARY

As people increasingly move across cultural boundaries, the people they seek health care from will be from different backgrounds. Learning the importance of culture and cultural differences for effective health services delivery will become an essential part of training programs in the health professions. Various biases will have to be overcome, such as the difficulty of moving beyond the guidelines for behavior people learn in their own culture (the *limitations bias*) or the tendency to repeat new behaviors if they have been successful with one person from another culture (the *generalization bias*). A good basic guideline for dealing with cultural differences is to nurture professional relationships with colleagues from different backgrounds. Collaborators in health services delivery then can identify potential biases their colleagues may be carrying, can contribute information about the different cultures involved, and can provide several helpers clients can choose among for consultation.

The task of integrating cultural knowledge into health care delivery is not easy. Cultural influences vary greatly among cultures, demanding very specific knowledge. For instance, Jamaican mothers living in Great Britain were sensitive to the age their children learned to sit up by themselves but were not concerned with the age crawling started (Hopkins & Westra, 1989). Pediatricians have to know this fact if they encourage mothers to secure professional assistance when their babies develop slowly. Another difficulty is that people frequently seek medical advice from friends and family members rather than from professionals. By the time they finally see professionals, the problems may have become so severe that any form of intervention will be unsuccessful (Coates & Collins, 1998; Pedersen, 1991a). At times, professionals will have to make recommendations that go against cultural norms. Mothers in some cultures are hesitant to breast-feed their infants because their husbands disapprove. Given the benefits of breast milk, such as the transfer of immunities from mothers to babies, professionals may have to risk the charge of "cultural insensitivity" to deliver the best health care possible.

Identifying the Impact of Culture

Many health problems have both culture-common and culture-specific components. Analyzing an instrument meant to identify people who are at risk for mental health difficulties, Nishimoto (1988; see also Siegert & Chung, 1995) worked with Anglo Americans, Vietnamese Chinese, and Mexicans. A number of indicators of mental health difficulties were common to all three cultures, and these included nervousness, trouble sleeping, and feeling weak all over. Additional symptoms were useful in one of the cultures but not the others. For instance, shortness of breath was an identifying symptom among Anglo Americans; fullness in the head was a symptom among Vietnamese Chinese, and problems with memory was a symptom among Mexicans. People from one cultural background naturally will feel a sense of strangeness when considering the symptoms specific to other cultures. This sense of strangeness should be taken as a reminder that culture plays a role in the diagnosis and treatment of health problems and that professionals should be constantly alert to discover culturally influenced factors that can improve health services. One factor occurs so often that professionals surely will encounter it. People from many cultures *somatize* their psychological problems. Rather then describe symptoms such as an inability to carry out their daily routines, people describe their problems in physical terms, such as claiming headaches and back pains. If physicians are unaware of the frequency some people somatize, they are likely to prescribe drugs that address the reported symptoms but not the underlying problems.

The distinction between culture-common and culture-specific symptoms has been very helpful in the study of schizophrenia and depression. People with schizophrenia cannot relate their thoughts, attitudes, and actions to daily reality. "Reality" includes the expectations people have of appropriate behavior in a culture: A funeral is not a wedding, and an informal chat with a close friend is not a confrontation with a total stranger. People with schizophrenia make so many responses inconsistent with others' expectations of appropriate behavior (getting angry at a friend for no apparent reason) that they have severe difficulties meeting the society's demands on people. Culture-common symptoms of schizophrenia include difficulties forming emotional ties with others, poor self-insight, thinking aloud, poor rapport with others, incoherent speech, and widespread delusions. Culture-specific factors deal with the form these general symptoms take, with the reasons for the onset of illness, and the prognosis for people afflicted with the disease. In Ibadan, Nigeria, the symptoms of schizophrenia emphasize an intense suspicion of others, with many bizarre fears and thoughts (Katz et al., 1988). Many Nigerians believe illness is caused by evil forces, but people with schizophrenia move beyond this belief into bizarre suspicions about unseen forces. These suspicions become so intense that they interfere with people's everyday functioning as judged by other Nigerians.

Acute schizophrenic attacks tend to be associated with stressful events in people's lives that occur approximately two to three weeks before the disease's onset. Some of these events are interpretable only with cultural knowledge. The common belief in evil forces among Nigerians has been mentioned already. One Nigerian man experienced an acute attack of schizophrenia after his mother confessed to the practice of witchcraft in an open forum within their community. Evil forces may have existed for the Nigerian male, but the sudden realization that his mother practiced witchcraft, along with another stressful event, became too overwhelming for his coping resources. Interestingly, it is possible this individual, like other people in less industrialized nations, may have a better prognosis for improvement than people with schizophrenia in highly industrialized nations (K. Lin & Kleinman, 1988). People with schizophrenia in less industrialized nations may have a more active support group and may be able to find work (e.g., a simple but important agricultural job) valued in the culture. Recall from chapters 2 and 8 that industrialization is associated with individualism. In individualist societies, people have greater responsibilities for taking care of themselves than in collective societies. People with schizophrenia, with their delusional thoughts and problems establishing rapport with others, have difficulties in such necessary efforts as finding and retaining a job, developing and maintaining a support group, keeping appointments with health professionals, and so forth.

For depression, research evidence suggests this culture-common core: frequent and intense sad affect, loss of enjoyment, anxiety, difficulties when concentrating, and lack of energy. Culture-specific components of depression also exist. Feelings of guilt are found more often in North America and Europe than in other parts of the world. Somatic complaints are often heard from people with depression in China. Women may be twice as likely to have a depressive episode in their lives compared to men. Many reasons have been suggested, including the relative powerlessness of women. Another is that men have as many problems but (given that they are more aggressive: chapter 9) are more likely to act out their negative feelings in antisocial behaviors and by alcohol abuse. Women are more likely to turn their negative feelings inward. Intervention efforts aimed at helping people with depression often focus on their thinking. They can be encouraged to intercept their negative thoughts and to avoid overgeneralizing from the discouragements everyone experiences in their daily lives. For example, people who feel depressed may interpret an unsuccessful job interview as a total rejection of their suitability for employment. People not experiencing depression are more likely to view an unsuccessful interview as a learning experience and to identify ways to improve their chances with the next potential employer.

Preventive Health Measures

Cross-cultural research has been a major contributor to lists of recommended actions people can take to prevent threats to their health. For example, people in some cultures consume diets far lower in fat than people in other cultures. If one type of diet leads to fewer health problems than another, this can lead to recommendations for intervention programs. For example, Shintani and his colleagues (1991; Shintani & Devenot, 1998) documented that if native Hawaiians returned to their traditional diet, as compared to the diet many have adopted since European contact, then their health improved.

Many of the preventive health recommendations seem familiar because they have been covered in the mass media. The recommendations include the following:

1. Adopting a low-fat diet high in bulk and complex carbohydrates

2. Keeping weight at levels appropriate to age and body size

3. Maintaining a regular program of exercise

4. Avoiding drugs (including tobacco) and using alcohol in moderation

5. Adopting the general outlook that people can positively impact their health if they take the initiative and adopt a healthy lifestyle

6. Avoiding stress as much as possible

7. Contributing to and drawing from the resources of a support group

8. Increasing activities and nurturing a variety of interests

People also can be encouraged to participate in various intervention programs designed either to promote a healthy lifestyle or to help people cope with problems currently threatening their health (Coates & Collins, 1998). In a program designed to prevent alcohol abuse among teenagers, Perry and her colleagues (1989) worked in Australia, Chile, Norway, and Swaziland. They found that programs trained adolescents led were more effective than programs teachers led. One possible reason is that program participants viewed peers as more knowledgeable about the pressures teenagers face when they are handed a drink at a social gathering. Even though adults may not be the most effective leaders once a program starts, they have many roles in these programs. They can select the most influential adolescents, train them in the skills necessary for effective program leadership, prepare impactful materials for the program, and evaluate the program to identify points where improvements are possible.

Intervention programs often demand a detailed knowledge of the culture where health professionals are working. Bastien (1987) found, for example, that recommendations to take diarrhea seriously could be communicated to Andeans in Bolivia if links were made to stories and legends familiar to the Andeans. The administrators of programs to prevent HIV transmission have developed a number of general principles. These include working with at-risk people where they congregate, whether these places are brothels, bars, or social clubs. The people who deliver information about HIV prevention must be carefully selected. They must be willing to take on roles they previously have had little experience with, such as an informal counselor who frequents the same bars as commercial sex workers. They also must be willing and able to engage in very candid discussions about issues such as condom use, sensitivity when condoms are used, and the number of clients CSWs serve during a given period. Within intervention programs, experience has shown (Coates & Collins, 1998) that (a) skill training is essential, (b) messages must be repeated, (c) recommendations for abstinence only are unrealistic, and (d) coercive programs can drive people away from clinics where they would receive medical attention.

Delivering Health Care

Whenever health professionals interact with clients to offer assistance, it involves several universal elements (Castillo, 1997; Fisher et al., 1998). Professionals (a) give the client's problem a name. They present themselves as (b) caring, competent, and concerned, and they (c) establish credibility by using symbols respected in their culture. They (d) place the client's problem in a familiar framework and (e) apply techniques meant to bring relief. Especially in contrast to times when people seek help from friends and family members, professionals (f) provide help at a special time and place. Further, the help is a sort of "time out" from the daily hassles that contributed to the client's problems.

Culturally sensitive professionals have a characteristic that goes beyond the (very necessary) qualities of concern, empathy, and credibility. Sensitive professionals have the knowledge, willingness, and ability to take clients' cultural background into account during help-giving interactions. If they wish to do so, health professionals can develop this quality. Wade and Bernstein (1991) evaluated a program for training counselors who had clients seeking help with their personal problems. They found that African American female clients preferred training program graduates more than other experienced counselors. Further, they were more satisfied with the counseling process and were more likely to keep later appointments than were age peers who interacted with untrained counselors. An important additional finding was that the African American female clients did not have an automatic preference for counselors of their own race. Rather, they preferred trained counselors, whether the helpers were African or Anglo American.

This finding is consistent with other research evidence (Sue, 1988) that people from one cultural background can offer assistance to people from another as long as they are well prepared. Cultural barriers can be overcome in the delivery of health care. As people increasingly engage in extensive intercultural interactions, it is hoped that "culture" will be seen as more than a hurdle to overcome. Culture and cultural differences ideally will be viewed as important and stimulating challenges that, at times, will provide insights about health that people can apply to their own lives.

CHAPTER 11

SOME PREDICTIONS
FOR THE FUTURE

CHAPTER OVERVIEW

Although predicting the future can bring embarrassment when a person's words are reviewed 10 years hence, I believe certain broad trends are more likely to occur than not. As noted several times, people will continue to increase their intercultural contacts, and this will challenge the ethnocentric assumptions people bring to such interactions. These contacts can have benefits, such as stimulating people to consider alternatives in their life. Women will not be blind to such stimulation and will continue to challenge limitations placed on what their cultures view as acceptable roles. People will become more familiar with terms today's research specialists use and will be more comfortable examining culture's influences on their behavior and the behavior of others. Given their increased familiarity with cross-cultural concepts, these same people will want to see their tax dollars spent on cross-cultural research that has clear, practical implications.

This increased sophistication will be turned inward. People will be more willing to talk about both the positive and negative aspects of intercultural contact, and this in turn will lead to an impatience with glib stereotypes and simplistic explanations for difficult problems. Given their realization that culture is complex, dynamic, and multifaceted, people will become more willing to match their thinking with this reality.

INTERCULTURAL INTERACTIONS AND THE FUTURE

A prediction about the future that can be made with certainty is that people will engage in extensive intercultural contacts. College students, instructors, and other employees will interact with students from other countries; managers in businesses and industries will interview immigrants or their sons and daughters; people will find employment in companies foreign nationals own; tourism will be adopted as an industry in more countries; schoolchildren will interact with peers from different ethnic and cultural backgrounds; and legal decisions will assist people so they can move to certain neighborhoods once denied them given their skin color. Even if people would prefer to interact with others who have the same cultural background, same skin color, same accent, and same general interests, they will find themselves in the company of numerous diverse individuals. This contact will not automatically lead to positive relationships (Allport, 1954; Brewer & Brown, 1998; Stephan, 1985). Many people will continue to hold their prejudicial attitudes (chapter 6), but others will accept the challenge of developing positive intercultural relationships (chapter 7).

THE EFFECTS OF EXTENSIVE INTERCULTURAL CONTACTS

The increasing frequency of intercultural interactions will have several specific effects I would like to discuss in this final chapter:

1. The interactions will challenge people's ethnocentric viewpoints, and this will force people to expand their thinking.

2. Women will be more concerned than ever about their abilities to make choices about their lives.

3. People will be able to analyze the roles culture and cultural differences play as they think about their lives and about policies in their own societies.

4. As people become involved in new research ventures in other cultures, either as investigators, participants, funders, or gatekeepers who can approve or disapprove proposals, the importance of practical applications will become paramount.

5. Basic information about the benefits and potential pitfalls of intercultural interactions will be widely discussed among people, and such thinking will make acceptance of simplistic stereotypes far less likely.

6. The benefits of complex thinking about intercultural interactions will achieve greater recognition.

Challenges to Ethnocentrism

Part of everyone's socialization is the right and wrong ways to do everyday tasks such as eating, sleeping, working, and interacting with others. As noted earlier, *ethnocentrism* refers to the universal feeling that not only have members of a specific culture found the right and wrong ways but also that other cultures have not. Further, people who engage in ethnocentric thinking judge the behavior of others with their own standards of right and wrong in mind. One guaranteed outcome of extensive intercultural interactions is that the ethnocentric tendencies of people will be challenged. They will observe behaviors they find irritating, incorrect, or boorish based on their own standards. But instead of immediately thinking of a negative label for the behaviors and applying it, people might look at the challenge as an opportunity to learn more about culture and cultural differences.

Consider this incident that North Americans and Europeans working in Japan frequently report (Sakamoto & Naotsuka, 1982).

JAPANESE MALE: I just got married and I would like you to come to our house for dinner next Saturday.

AMERICAN FEMALE: That's wonderful! Congratulations! Thank you, I'd love to. I'm looking forward to meeting your wife.

JAPANESE MALE: She's not beautiful, and she can't cook very well. But I hope you'll come. (p. 1)

The American woman clearly will be tempted to dismiss the Japanese man's behavior as rude and unkind. But she also might consider the possibility that such a conclusion would be ethnocentric, and instead she might explore the incident to determine if cultural factors are involved.

Several exist. One is that the Japanese man considers his wife part of his collective identity (chapter 2). He should be modest about himself, and because his wife is part of his identity, he also should be modest about her. The wife, incidentally, might use similar negative terms when discussing him among her friends: "He is not very good looking and rather lazy." Another cultural difference is that in Japan people are more likely to be considered a permanent part of their collective. Americans have an easier time than Japanese when asked the question "Could you please give me the names of people with whom you were once very close but with whom you currently do not interact?" One implication is that the Japanese do not give much attention to special personalized acts that help to maintain and to develop a marriage. The marriage *is*: there is not an emphasis on consciously thinking about behaviors that might be pleasing to a spouse so that the marriage bond is strengthened. In the United States, however, many people make a point of engaging in behaviors that will keep the marriage fresh. Husbands buy flowers for their wives; wives discover their husband's favorite aftershave lotion and purchase it. Either spouse surprises the other with breakfast in bed. Because the marital bond is not treated as something permanent and indissoluble (50% of marriages in the United States end in divorce), people have to take steps to keep a marriage successful.

Examining intercultural incidents in this manner (a) allows people to explore the influence of culture in people's lives and (b) allows them to develop fresh insights into their own behavior. It also allows (c) interventions into difficulties. I have counseled many American women married to Japanese men who complain of their husband's cavalier treatment of them in public. An American women does not like working in the kitchen for 6 hours only to hear her husband make apologies to his friends once the first course is served. Seeing his American wife's reaction, the Japanese husband becomes upset about her inappropriate behavior in front of his friends. When the cultural background for the husband's behavior and the wife's irritation are discussed openly, the two are less likely to interpret the behaviors as personal attacks on them as individuals. If they can learn to identify some of their own and their spouse's behaviors as due to their cultural backgrounds, they will be more able to develop compromises that will increase the chances of marital harmony.

Once people understand some basic examples of how to move beyond ethnocentric thinking, they might examine intercultural interactions in their own lives. As discussed often throughout this book, a frequent reaction to intercultural encounters is that they are puzzling. "Why did that person react as she did? Why did that person behave as he did? I would not have behaved that way. I would not have reacted to that social situation in the same way!" People are tempted to make negative attributions: The other person was socially unskilled, rude, or consciously behaving to create social distance. Given knowledge of culture and cultural differences, people might postpone and possibly avoid these negative attributions. They can do this by purposefully asking questions of themselves during the period between observed behaviors and their temptation to make attributions (G. Gilbert, 1998). These questions can include, "Is this person from a cultural background different from mine? Is this person behaving in a way that is socially appropriate for her cultural background? Is it possible for me to suggest a precise reason for the cultural difference?"

Carefully thinking about these questions often will yield answers that indicate people are not being rude and prejudicial. Rather, they are behaving according to the guidelines for behavior they learned during childhood and adolescence in their own cultures. It is useful to review here examples discussed in earlier chapters. Native Americans are not being rude when they avoid talking with newcomers who take jobs in their communities. Rather, they are engaging in a "wait and see" approach to interpersonal interactions. If the newcomers seem to be trustworthy, someone might talk to them in 6 months. If Deaf people describe a person's physical features with uncanny, if uncomfortable, accuracy, they are not making fun of that person. Rather, they are differentiating one person from another by pointing to their visual features, and this matches the visual nature of American Sign Language. If Americans are enthusiastic when meeting international students from Asia but seem to forget meeting these same students a month later, it does not mean they are superficial and uncaring. Enthusiasm when meeting people for the first time is a social skill Americans learn, and only a few are aware that people from other cultures might take it as a sign of "special attention." An awareness of such cultural differences takes the sting away from feelings of personal rejection during and after interpersonal interactions. People can leave a problematic intercultural encounter with the conclusion that, maybe, a cultural difference exists that they don't yet understand.

Another advantage of moving beyond ethnocentrism, and of knowing about cultural differences, is that it helps people face the challenges of movement between two (and sometimes more) cultures. Some people have *bicultural* membership and thus face unique challenges (LaFromboise, Coleman, & Gerton, 1993). They are expected to behave as good and productive members of two cultures, but sometimes the behaviors called for are quite different. Take the example of international students from Korea or China. If they are studying in North America or Europe, they are expected to speak up in class and to disagree with others when appropriate. At times, they may even take positions opposite to those of their professors. The students are encouraged to develop their intellectual and self-presentational skills through such behaviors.

Back in Korea or China, however, no value is placed on speaking up, and certainly no rewards are given for disagreeing publicly with bosses or professors.

A knowledge of cultural differences and cultural adjustment can help such people. For a person challenged by biculturalism, it is extremely comforting to know that she or he is not the only individual going though the discomfort of adjusting to different cultures. If knowledgeable people such as professors and counselors can point out to bicultural people that virtually all such people face these challenges, that single point can relieve stress significantly. In the case just presented, a knowledge of cultural differences provides further help. The United States and Canada are high in individualism and low in power distance (chapter 8). It follows, then, that students can disagree with others and with professors. Korea and China are high in both collectivism and power distance. It follows that disagreeing with others can interfere with the harmony collectivism requires, and disagreeing with professors can interfere with well-established status hierarchies. Behaviors of people from all these cultures can begin to make sense if culture and cultural differences are understood.

I have had conversations similar to the following with international students. They come to me having read the first edition (1993) of this book and knowing of my interest in people's movements across cultural boundaries (Cushner & Brislin, 1996). Their visits have been stimulated by the thought that they will be returning to their home country after studying in the United States for two or more years.

VISITOR: I'll be returning to my home country soon. I know a few of the intercultural concepts. One, for instance, is power distance. Here in the United States, I took courses in public speaking and know how to communicate my views clearly. But if I speak up with my views in front of my father at the dinner table, I'm afraid that I will be a total jerk.

RWB: I'd like to start by saying that the sort of potential problem you have identified has been faced by many people returning to their own country after study in another. And, it happens with people in their own culture. My grandfather was a railroad conductor, and part of his training was supervision of work crews who could put railroad cars back on tracks after a bad accident. I would come home from college with my texts dealing with the transportation industry. My grandfather would look at them and ask, "Has the author of this book ever cleaned up after a train wreck?"

VISITOR: Right! I'll share an idea with my father on modern business practices, and he will ask if my professors ever had a job where they had to meet a payroll.

During such a conversation I introduce the biculturalism concept. Different cultures offer different guidances for behaviors. Many times, these behaviors are different given similar social situations, such as dinner-table conversations and interactions with parents, grandparents, and coworkers. Some of my advice deals with people's goals. I point out that they clearly have goals for their return home or they would not have visited me. One goal in this example is that the person did not want to irritate her father. I ask these visitors to think carefully about various outcomes they desire given their interactions with others at home. With this list of outcomes or goals, I then recommend that they think about behaviors necessary to achieve these goals. In the example, what might the person's goals be? In actually answering this question, she listed four: respecting her father, being able to present her opinions, maintaining skills learned in America, and making career progress after returning to her job. We then discussed behaviors that would help her reach these goals. These included asking her father about recent locally important events that might not have received international news coverage. They also included behaviors such as presenting her opinions during informal one-on-one chats with her father away from the confrontational possibilities of the family dining table. The father also could be invited to present his disagreements. For maintaining skills, taking evening courses at a nearby college is a possibility, as is membership in clubs. In many mid- to large-sized cities, there are organizations whose commonality among members is that they have lived overseas. A foreign nation's embassy sometimes sponsors these. To make career progress, she could schedule meetings with her bosses to review recent developments (similar to conversations with her father). During these meetings, she could communicate information about her newly developed skills and could make suggestions that she could help customers from North America making business visits.

The key to understanding biculturalism, then, is to realize that people behave to achieve goals but the exact behaviors vary according to the guidance of different cultures.

When people live for a long period in another culture, they often learn new behaviors. If they can successfully match these behaviors with goals in different cultures, they are said to be bicultural. As more and more people move across cultural boundaries, I believe the term *biculturalism* will become part of people's everyday language.

Women and Choices

Examining cultural influences on one's life and making modifications in one's behaviors are not easy. Consider, again, the incident from the previous section that described an interaction between a Japanese man and an American woman. When readers first considered this incident and my recommendation to look for cultural influences, many may have experienced the same reaction as some women I have counseled. "I can understand why criticizing me in public can be seen as part of his cultural background and why I should not take it personally. But I am still extremely irritated!" This is a common reaction, and it will continue to occur in the future. People enjoy being treated well, having nice things said about them, being verbally reinforced at work when they put in extra effort, and being consulted about decisions that will affect them. If a culture's norms do not include the recommendation that people praise, recognize, and consult others, then the pressures of cultural contact, industrialization, and modernization will encourage people's adoption of these behaviors (Hofstede, 1998). One of my colleagues is a Japanese woman who received one of her college degrees in Japan and a second degree in the United States. She reports, "It's a lot more enjoyable to receive flowers and compliments from my American boyfriend than to be told how fat I am by my [former] Japanese boyfriend."

Given various technological advances, women worldwide will be exposed to differences, and many will be attracted to them. The innovations include air travel and development in the tourist industry, leading to face-to-face interactions among women raised in traditional and highly industrialized societies. The entertainment industry also has its impact: People worldwide see movies and television shows that

Bicultural people can move between two cultures. A Chinese American might enjoy football and traditional martial arts.

depict alternative ways of behaving in a variety of social situations. Many women raised according to traditional norms will become attracted to these alternatives, whether they include better treatment by men, greater opportunities in the job market, and decisions about the number of children to bear (Hofstede, 1998). Other women will not be attracted to such changes and will have a greater chance of finding happiness by behaving according to traditional norms. The key point is that many women will want to make their own choices and will resist having traditional authority figures control their actions. This will lead to changes in their cultures and to stresses in the lives of all involved. Both of these topics will be important areas of research well into the 21st century.

The increasing ability of women to make choices will have important impacts on many social issues. Basset and Mhloyi (1991; see also Coates & Collins, 1998) predicted possible implications of women's expanded choices concerning sex and AIDS transmission in Zimbabwe, Africa. As discussed in chapter 10, AIDS has been spread through heterosexual contact in Africa. One reason is that traditions of male dominance and of limited job opportunities for women in Zimbabwe have forced many women into subservient positions within their society. Further, husbands traditionally have left their wives home and have accepted work as migrant laborers, leading to transmission of the HIV virus through extramarital sex. Because women have less power, they are inexperienced at asserting themselves and at requesting that their partners use condoms. Given the limited opportunities women have for wage employment, some must enter the sex industry to survive. If women in Zimbabwe acquire the freedom to make more of their own choices, then the number of AIDS cases may diminish given women's demands for protection during sexual intercourse and their ability to find employment outside the sex industry.

The movement from traditional roles to roles based on choices is not a simple one. Moghaddam, Ditto, and Taylor (1990) interviewed immigrant women from India living in Montreal, Canada. The more changes from traditional expectations the women desired, the more distress they experienced. The changes the most distressed women desired included movement away from the traditional role of homemaker, greater opportunities in the job market, unwillingness to pass on traditional gender roles to their children, and the desire for an egalitarian relationship with their husbands. The desire (and movement toward) these changes led to stress, however, and resulted in the same sorts of symptoms discussed in chapter 10: psychosomatic complaints, trouble sleeping, feelings of depression, anxiety, and so forth. Reasons for the distress included a lack of familiarity with the behaviors necessary to achieve the newly formulated goals, lack of support from husbands and extended family members, and prejudicial reactions from members of the dominant society. Research on the most effective content and structure of various intervention programs to assist people to deal with these stresses will continue as a high-priority need (Brislin & Horvath, 1997).

One of the driving forces behind societal changes is people's desire for freedom to make choices about their life. In recent years, this desire has been part of worldwide political movements as people have expressed their demands for elected governments to replace traditional and authoritarian ruling bodies. These demands have been seen in the former U.S.S.R, South Africa, East Germany before reunification with West Germany, Nepal, Romania, China, the Philippines, Cuba, and other countries. One of the graduate students I worked closely with recently returned to one of these countries after two years in the United States. I asked him what he would miss most about his two-year sojourn, and he said simply "freedom." I believe he meant the ability to make his own choices about where he would work, about how he could criticize authority figures, about where he could travel, about the right to vote in honest and open elections, and so forth. He went home and almost immediately joined the democracy movement in his country. Bullets flew over his head during a demonstration, and he spent time in jail. The movement was successful, his country has an elected legislative body, and he and others are struggling to make democracy work. The universal desire for freedom is extremely strong, and I believe people will continue to see its impact worldwide.

Cultural Factors in Major Policy Changes

As people move toward more democratic forms of government, cultural factors will impact how quickly the move will occur, as well as the stresses people will experience. Democracy, with its emphasis on citizen participation in decision making, sounds fine as an ideal. It is very hard to put into practice. One reason is that people in some cultures are socialized to be much more respectful of, and deferent to, authority than are people in other cultures (chapter 8). Such people will be uncomfortable when they actually have to make decisions themselves in contrast to talking about their desire to make decisions. Further, people socialized to respect authority will be uncomfortable when asked to vote someone out of office who is from a respected family but who has been engaging in graft or other forms of power corruption.

Further, people in newly developing democracies will have to develop ways of choosing among various proposals for scarce resources. Again, the distinction between the ideal and the real is involved. Ideally, people in democracies can speak freely and make demands on their governments. In reality, government representatives have to choose among these demands because no country has enough resources (especially money) to satisfy everyone. In a book that analyzed people's acquisition of and use of power, I discussed the worldwide movement toward democracy (Brislin, 1991):

> In a democracy, people can speak their minds, can disagree with authority figures, and can assume leadership roles as long as they can persuade others to follow them. . . . Given the movement toward democratic governments today in various parts of the world, more and more people will be able to put their ideas forward and to pursue their goals without concern of reprisals from traditional authority figures. These ideas will not be put forward only by people concerned with their countries' formal political systems. New ideas will also be introduced by people concerned with education, social welfare, religion, the status of women and minority groups, expansion of businesses, international relations, and so forth. But who will be successful in putting their ideas forward and who will be ignored? (p. xiv)

Important research will investigate leadership development, the creation of various mechanisms that allow choices among competing proposals, and the treatment of proposals by various ethnic groups competing for their government's resources.

Understanding cultural differences sometimes can bring insights into arguments about government in one's own country. The United States, in sharp contrast to European countries, does not have a policy of universal health insurance funded by the government. It is possible the cultural norm of individualism in the United States is having an impact on this issue. It is possible that when American leaders consider competing proposals for government funding (education, transportation, Social Security), many decide from the belief people should take care of their own health insurance. Further, the American desire for individualism leads people to distrust programs that allow government agencies to tell them what they can and cannot do. With national health insurance, a government agency would become involved in decisions about health care, especially elective surgery. Government officials would have to interpret policies and tell people what medical care they can and cannot receive. Many individualists are very unhappy when they have to deal with government agencies that can limit their behavior.

Cultural differences also impact people's acceptance of intervention programs meant to address major social problems. Ilola (1990) analyzed the Finnish government's efforts to encourage its citizens to adopt healthier lifestyles. In 1972, after seeing figures that Finland had one of the highest mortality rates due to cardio-vascular diseases, government leaders instituted several programs. Programs were established to treat hypertension, to discourage the consumption of foods high in fat such as butter and cream, to reduce the smoking habit, and to reduce alcohol consumption. For example, the government prevented the tobacco industry from advertising in the mass media or on billboards, and it established luxury taxes on cigarettes that made their use prohibitively expensive for many. Alcohol consumption was discouraged through strict controls on sales and severe penalties for driving under the influence, including jail time and automatic loss of drivers' licenses. A key factor is that in Finland, compared to the United States, people are more likely to respect and to defer to the decisions of government leaders. In the United States, decisions about tobacco advertising can (and have) brought lawsuits about restrictions on the freedom of speech. Decisions about withdrawing drivers' licenses surely would bring lawsuits concerned with the violation of people's constitutional rights. As Ilola summarizes: "It is clear that health education efforts will be more successful in a culture such as Finland, where institutional intervention and support is viewed as positive and not a violation of individual rights or responsibilities" (p. 291). Research on how best to develop culturally appropriate intervention programs for problem areas such as health, education, and worker productivity will become a necessity rather than an academic luxury.

The Potential for Applying Research Findings

This discussion of scarce resources and academic luxuries is closely related to an issue researchers from less industrialized nations frequently discuss (e.g., Kagitcibasi, 1997; Sinha, 1983; Zaidi, 1979). To be acceptable, cross-cultural research projects will have to address topics with clear potential applications for the alleviation of social problems (Hui & Luk, 1997). Many cultures simply do not have enough resources, such as money and the time of research collaborators from various cultures, to allow the pursuit of inquiry into theoretically interesting but practically unimportant topics. Given these statements, my purpose is not to draw a sharp distinction between theoretical and applied topics. Many times, researchers can investigate theoretically important topics as long as they link them to potential applications of interest to practitioners. In chapter 4, for instance, the theoretically important work of Rogoff (1990) on guided participation was reviewed. This is an important concept for teachers as they develop tasks that build on students' existing abilities. Further, knowledge of guided participation allows teachers to encourage students to improve their skills so that they can take on more difficult tasks as they move toward mastery of topics areas of special interest to them.

The need for attention to applied topics also has been recommended for researchers who are themselves citizens of less industrialized nations. D. Sinha (1983) argues that there is a

> need for certain attitudes and sensitivity, if he [or she] is to be engaged in cross-cultural research. Apart from [his or her] general competence in the subject, [the

investigator] has to be highly sensitive to the country's problems so that the research effort has some relevance to the national needs. (p. 13)

The research results I reviewed in this book lean in the direction of studies with potential applications in education, employment, health, cultural change, and programs encouraging positive intercultural contact. I believe such studies have many benefits. A knowledge of theory can guide the selection of concepts that serve as the basis of intervention programs. In turn, theoretical advances are made if a concept can survive the test of application in the "real world" of scarce resources, of competition for people's attention, and of other concepts that can work against an intervention into social problems. Further, theoretical concepts can be sharpened when researchers carefully examine the results of their application. For example, Kagitcibasi's work on home-based schooling was reviewed in chapter 5. Some of the concepts that guided the interventions were based on a knowledge of collectivism, which included mothers' concerns that success in Turkey's schools could lead to a distancing between children and parents. Despite scarce resources for putting family programs into practice and the busy schedules of mothers and schoolchildren, the researchers found that programs to involve mothers had several benefits, including the mothers' realization that autonomy and family loyalty are not incompatible. The theoretical understanding of collectivism also was increased as researchers noted unexpected results, such as the learning of new knowledge by the target children's younger siblings. The younger children learned this knowledge as they listened while on the fringes of sessions between researchers, mothers, and older children and as part of postsession activities when older children took the teacher's role and passed on what they had learned to their younger siblings.

Widespread Discussions of Intercultural Interactions

If contact across cultural boundaries is to become commonplace, as predicted throughout this book, then people will discuss the benefits and difficulties of intercultural interactions among themselves. I hope they will use sophisticated concepts when doing so. I once asked a well-known physician, "What do you think is the major advance in medicine that has helped people over the past 30 years?" His response was "the concept of 'blood pressure.'" When discussing his answer, he referred to people's knowledge about and use of this concept. "Blood pressure" is a concept people can understand and discuss, and it is a measurement they can monitor themselves. If their blood pressure is too high, they can take steps to reduce it (e.g., reducing stress in their lives, modifying their diet). Developing a goal for blood pressure reduction also gives people a target to work toward. Further, once people develop an interest in their blood pressure, they might add other targets for preventative health care, such as exercising, smoking cessation, and a low-fat diet, to their changing lifestyles.

Cross-cultural research has led to insights that can assist people's discussions as they analyze the intercultural interactions in their lives. Covered throughout this book, especially in chapters 6 and 7, these concepts can help people clarify puzzling and difficult interactions. For example, people always will have a very difficult time avoiding the temptation to stereotype (chapter 6). People meet and observe so many individuals that it is necessary to form categories that capture a few key features of these individuals: all the conservatives, all the young women, all the Blacks, all the immigrants, and so forth. However, it is *not* necessary for people to make decisions about these individuals based on their stereotyped groupings (S. Fiske, 1998). People can quite consciously stop themselves when they are tempted to make decisions based on stereotypes and can remind themselves that they should keep individuals in mind. For example, high school counselors can say, "I should not withhold my recommendations about advanced math classes just because I am dealing with a young woman. I should examine her individual record, preparation, and goals to determine if advanced math is an option she should consider." Similarly, students can learn to avoid making decisions based on stereotypes and look to individual interests and abilities as they invite classmates to join various academic, athletic, and social activities.

These goals for discussion and implementation are based on the assumption people can learn about concepts such as "stereotypes" and "individual differences." I believe this is a realistic possibility. Concepts such as "stereotypes," "prejudice," and "interaction style" (chapter 7) are no more difficult and complex than concepts such as "blood pressure," "cholesterol," and the "fat content" of diets. Concepts to help people analyze their intercultural interactions can be presented in the same places as concepts related to their health: in the mass media (e.g., Goleman, 1991; Hirsh, 1997), in high school and university coursework (Rogers & Steinfatt, 1999), and in public outreach programs sponsored by colleges, governmental agencies, and community volunteer groups. As concepts dealing with intercultural interactions are discussed widely, a general tone of tolerance, understanding, and mutual enrichment hopefully will become the norm people will accept and disseminate for the discussions and especially the interactions. Again, setting norms in this way has parallels with health. In many parts of the United States today, smoking in public areas is no longer acceptable. Nonsmokers, concerned about their health, have successfully set the norm that smokers have to modify their behavior. Similarly, people concerned with positive intercultural interactions can set the norm that understanding and enrichment are reasonable goals and that intolerance will not be socially acceptable.

The Advantages of Complex Thinking

One of my goals in writing this book was to introduce concepts that allow people to talk comfortably about culture and cultural differences and that allow them to do so in a complex manner. Certainly, some concepts deal with negative aspects of people's behavior, for instance, prejudice and discrimination as discussed in chapters 6 and 7. For many other concepts, I emphasized not labeling them as good or bad. For example, after I present material on individualism and collectivism (chapter 8 and elsewhere) to my students, some ask, "Which is better?" I respond,

> Like many concepts in the study of culture and behavior, the issue is not what is better. These are concepts that need to be understood, and it is understanding, rather then conclusion drawing, that will serve us well as we interact with people

from different cultural backgrounds. To move immediately to "better and worse" runs the risk of ethnocentric thinking.

Negative comments are not disallowed given this emphasis on understanding. Humans are imperfect and cannot improve (e.g., in their health care practices: chapter 10) until problems are identified. Many times, a collection of concepts can be examined for a *pattern* of implications for human behavior. Some specific behaviors within the pattern may have a good or a bad connotation, at least from the viewpoint of people from one culture examining another. The overall pattern, however, may indicate a balance among the concerns people must deal with in any culture. Reviewing the concepts Hofstede (1980, 1998) developed is useful given that they form patterns representing various choices and dilemmas people long have faced. Individualism is desirable for well-educated and articulate people with resources to offer their culture, but it is less desirable for people in need of the social support available from a collective (chapter 9). Collectivism leads to support from members of a person's in-group, but it can lead to sharp exclusion of people not in the collective. This has very practical implications. Before students return to their home countries, I often can give them the names of people they might contact for job leads, for follow-up of research projects we have discussed, and for other useful information. But I always have to say,

> In individualistic cultures, strangers can call each other on the phone without needing a go-between. It is helpful if the caller can say, "so-and-so suggested I call." But in collective cultures, this may not be as easy for the very reason the caller is most often a stranger to the person being called. Are you comfortable placing a call to a person I know but whom you have not met yet?

Other concepts Hofstede (1980, 1998) developed that reveal patterns of choices and dilemmas involve power distance and masculine/feminine cultures. Low power distance encourages workers to communicate their ideas to supervisors, but it can lead to slow decision making if many people want their views heard. High-power-distance cultures have leaders who command respect and who provide clear role models for young people. However, this same concept can lead to corruption if the leaders conspire among themselves and ignore their followers' needs. The problems associated with a masculine culture are especially clear. Women can be denied access to leadership opportunities and to career growth and instead can be relegated to a small number of roles. But feminine cultures also have their frailties. If people in such cultures strive according to the more masculine values of achievement, advancing on the job, and earning large amounts of money, they may face much envy from others.

Learning about Confucian dynamism encourages another type of move away from ethnocentric thinking. This move involves consideration of whether or not people move along *different* paths in their pursuit of *similar* goals. Research on Confucian dynamism (chapter 8) suggests that if adults in a culture emphasize certain concepts in the socialization of children, this emphasis contributes to economic growth. The argument continues that if children learn to be persistent and thrifty, if they learn to order the relationships in their lives, and if they develop a sense of shame, they will be successful workers in healthy economies. As was discussed in chapter 8, Confucian dynamism (Chinese Culture Connection, 1987) is the hardest of the five concepts to understand for people socialized in North America and western Europe. It is certainly the concept I spend the most time on in my own college classes.

Some students look at Confucian dynamism and conclude that people in other parts of the world are "worse off" for not giving it sufficient attention. My argument is that another way to move from such conclusions is to ask about different roads people take in their move toward the same goals as the Chinese. The Confucian goal is a healthy economy and active participation in such an economy. People in various cultures take other paths toward this goal. In many parts of the world where successful economies exist, people are socialized into a Judeo-Christian work ethic. This socialization includes the concepts that hard work is good and can be part of people's self-identity, that people develop positive reputations in their communities because of their work and voluntary public service, and that a good education prepares people for success in their work. If people socialized this way feel that work is not an important part of their status and public image, they might consider this scenario. A 25-year-old calls his or her parents and says, "I have been dating a person for quite a while, and we are beginning to talk about marriage." What will be one of the first three questions the parents ask? Most people from cultures influenced by Judeo-Christian thinking agree that early questions will be "What does this person do?" or "What is the person's major?" These questions are designed to establish the part of the person's identity that deals with his or her relationship to the work world.

The concepts emphasized in Confucian dynamism and the Judeo-Christian work ethic are different, but the outcome of participation in a healthy economy is quite similar. Incidentally, I recently asked this question of students in my upper-division class. One American woman recently had become engaged, and she told me the first question her parents asked was "Where does he work?" A Japanese woman reported that she had recently called home to inform her parents about her engagement. Her parents' first question was "Is he an oldest son within his family?" The parents were interested in the fiance's experience with the importance of ordering relationships and of placing proper emphasis on these relationships. The parents assumed that an oldest son would have this experience. This is part of Confucian dynamism (the arguments for how this relates to healthy economies were presented in chapter 8).

Understanding culture and cultural differences involves complex analyses of multiple concepts. I hope that in the future people's simplistic analyses based on one concept will be met with comments that people thinking about important social issues must consider multiple concepts. Further, they should add to their analysis the reasons one culture emphasizes some concepts over others and explain how trade-offs often exist when multiple concepts are considered. To add even more to the admitted complexity, individual differences occur within cultures (chapters 1 and 5). For example, some people very interested in pursuing their own goals are members of collective cultures, and some people very sensitive to their group's goals were socialized in individualist cultures. All these considerations admittedly add to the complexity needed for people's thinking about culture (Pedersen, 1997), but this is desirable rather than annoying. People cannot use oversimplified stereotypes (chapter 6) while engaging in complex thinking that integrates analyses of multiple concepts.

THE IMPORTANCE OF CULTURE IN THE STUDY OF HUMAN BEHAVIOR

As I mentioned in chapter 9, I am delighted that various groups have insisted that researchers give more attention to issues such as gender, ethnicity, and culture. In the past, people have examined textbooks and have found that their authors describe the behavior of Caucasian men in an adequate manner but that women, members of other ethnic groups, and people from different cultural backgrounds seem absent. A final prediction is that when authors contemplate writing a text, they automatically will be inclined to address human diversity defined by cultural, ethnic, and gender differences. The importance of these concepts will become so widely accepted that authors will not have to stop and make a point to integrate them into their writings. Terms such as "cross-cultural psychology" and "intercultural interactions" will become less commonly used because analyses of human behavior will, of necessity, consider cultural influences.

REFERENCES

Aberle, D., Cohen, A., Davis, A., Levy, M., & Sutton, F. (1950). The functional prerequisites of a society. *Ethics, 60,* 100–111.

Abramson, P., & Imai-Marquez, J. (1982). The Japanese-American: A cross-cultural, cross-sectional study of sex guilt. *Journal of Research in Personality, 16,* 227–237.

Adler, N. (1994, April). Women managers in a global economy. *Training and Development,* 31–36.

Adler, N. A. (1997). *International dimensions of organizational behavior* (3rd ed.). Boston: PWS-Kent.

Ahia, C. (1984). Cross-cultural counseling concerns. *Personnel and Guidance Journal, 62,* 339–341.

Albert, R. (1996). A framework and model for understanding Latin American and Latino/Hispanic cultural patterns. In D. Landis & R. Bhagat (Eds.), *Handbook of intercultural training* (2nd ed., pp. 327–348). Thousand Oaks, CA: Sage.

Allport, G. (1954). *The nature of prejudice.* Reading, MA: Addison-Wesley.

Althen, G. (1995). *The handbook of foreign student advising* (Rev. ed.). Yarmouth, ME: Intercultural Press.

Altman, I., & Chemers, M. M. (1980). Cultural aspects of environment-behavior relationships. In H. C. Triandis & R. W. Brislin (Eds.), *Handbook of cross-cultural psychology* (Vol. 5, pp. 355–393). Boston: Allyn & Bacon.

Alzate, H. (1989). Sexual behavior of unmarried Colombian university students: A follow-up. *Archives of Sexual Behavior, 18,* 239–250.

Ames, G., & Rebhun, L. (1996). Women, alcohol, and work: Interactions of gender, ethnicity, and occupational culture. *Social Science and Medicine, 43,* 1649–1663.

Amir, Y. (1969). Contact hypothesis in ethnic relations. *Psychological Bulletin, 71,* 319–343.

Anastasi, A. (1988). *Psychological testing* (6th ed.). New York: Macmillan.

Anderson, C., & Bowman, M. (1965). *Education and economic development.* London: Frank Cass.

Anshel, M., Williams, L., & Hodge, K. (1997). Cross-cultural and gender differences on coping style in sport. *International Journal of Sport Psychology, 28,* 141–156.

Arbeiter, S. (1984). *Profiles, college-bound seniors, 1984.* New York: College Entrance Examination Board.

Archer, J. (1996). Sex differences in social behavior: Are the social role and evolutionary explanations compatible? *American Psychologist, 51,* 909–917.

Argyle, M., Furnham, A., & Graham, J. (1981). *Social situations.* Cambridge, England: Cambridge University Press.

Aronson, E., & Osherow, N. (1980). Cooperation, prosocial behavior, and academic performance: Experiments in the desegregated classroom. In L. Bickman (Ed.), *Applied social psychology annual.* Beverly Hills, CA: Sage.

Aronson, E., Wilson, T., & Akert, R. (1999). *Social psychology: The heart and the mind* (3rd ed). New York: Addison-Wesley.

Arsenault, R. (1989). Air-conditioning. In C. R. Wilson & W. Ferris (Eds.), *Encyclopedia of southern culture* (pp. 321–323). Chapel Hill, NC: University of North Carolina Press.

Ashmore, R. (1970). The problem of intergroup prejudice. In B. Collins, *Social Psychology* (pp. 245–296). Reading, MA: Addison-Wesley.

Atkinson, D., Morten, G., & Sue, D. (1989). Minority group counseling: An overview. In D. Atkinson, G. Morten, & D. Sue (Eds.), *Counseling American minorities: A cross-cultural perspective* (pp. 11–34). Dubuque, IA: William C. Brown.

Avlund, K., Luck, M., & Tinsley, R. (1996). Cultural differences in functional ability among elderly people in Birmingham, England, and Glostrup, Denmark. *Journal of Cross-Cultural Gerontology, 11,* 1–16.

Ayman, R., & Chemers, M. (1983). Relationship of supervisory behavior ratings to work group effectiveness and subordinate satisfaction among Iranian managers. *Journal of Applied Psychology, 68,* 388–341.

Bagley, C., & Mallick, K. (1995). Negative self-perception and components of stress in Canadian, British, and Hong Kong adolescents. *Perceptual and Motor Skills, 81,* 123–127.

Baird, I., Lyles, M., & Wharton, R. (1990). Attitudinal differences between American and Chinese managers regarding joint ventures management [Special issue]. *Management International Review, 30,* 53–68.

Bandura, A. (1986). *Social foundations of thought and action: A social-cognitive view.* Englewood Cliffs, NJ: Prentice Hall.

Bandura, A. (1989). Human agency in social cognitive theory. *American Psychologist, 44,* 1175–1184.

Barayuga, D. (1998, March 3). Kamehameha Schools: "Shibai" came, outreach went. *Honolulu Star Bulletin,* pp. A1, A8.

Barna, L. (1983). The stress factor in intercultural relations. In D. Landis & R. Brislin (Eds.), *Issues in training methodology: Handbook of intercultural training Vol. 2.* (pp. 19–49). Elmsford, NY: Pergamon.

Barraclough, B. (1987). Sex ratio of juvenile suicide. *Journal of the American Academy of Child and Adolescent Psychology, 26,* 434–435.

Barrett, M. (1997). HIV prevention approaches in Thailand: Lessons learned from the field. *Asian Psychologist, 1,* 40–46.

Barry, H., Bacon, M., & Child, I. (1957). A cross-cultural survey of some sex differences in socialization. *Journal of Abnormal and Social Psychology, 55,* 327–332.

Barry, H., & Child, I. (1983). Cultural variations in motivational satisfactions for men and women. *Behavior Science Research, 18*, 306–322.

Barry, H., & Schlegel, A. (1991). *Adolescence: An anthropological inquiry.* New York: Free Press.

Barsh, R. (1997). The epistemology of traditional healing systems. *Human Organization, 56*, 28–37.

Bar-Tel, D. (1997). Formation and change of ethnic and national stereotypes: An integrative model. *International Journal of Intercultural Relations, 21*, 491–523.

Bass, B. (1997). Does the transactional-transformational leadership paradigm transcend organizational and national boundaries? *American Psychologist, 52*, 130–139.

Bass, B., & Stogdill, R. (1990). *Bass and Stogdill's handbook of leadership* (3rd ed). New York: Free Press.

Bassett, M., & Mhloyi, M. (1991). Women & AIDS in Zimbabwe: The making of an epidemic. *International Journal of Health Services, 21*, 143–156.

Basso, K. (1970). "To give up on words": Silence in Western Apache culture. *Southwestern Journal of Anthropology, 26*, 213–230.

Bastien, J. (1987). Cross-cultural communication between doctors and peasants in Bolivia. *Social Science and Medicine, 24*, 1109–1118.

Batson, C. (1998). Altruism and prosocial behavior. In D. Gilbert, S. Fiske, & G. Lindzey (Eds.), *The Handbook of Social Psychology* (4th ed., vol. 2, pp. 282–316). New York: McGraw-Hill.

Baumeister, R. (1998). The self. In D. Gilbert, S. Fiske, & G. Lindzey (Eds.), *The handbook of social psychology* (4th ed., Vol. 1, pp. 680–740). New York: McGraw-Hill.

Beardsley, L., & Pedersen, P. (1997). Health and client-centered intervention. In J. Berry, M. Segall, & C. Kagitcibasi (Eds.), *Behavior and Applications: Vol. 3. Handbook of cross-cultural psychology* (2nd. ed.), pp. 413–448). Boston: Allyn & Bacon.

Befus, C. (1988). A multilevel treatment approach for culture shock experienced by sojourners. *International Journal of Intercultural Relations, 12*, 381–400.

Belle, D. (1990). Poverty and women's health. *American Psychologist, 45*, 385–39.

Bellisari, A. (1989). Male superiority in mathematical aptitude: An artifact. *Human Organization, 48*, 273–279.

Ben-Ari, R., Schwarzwald, J., & Horiner-Levi, E. (1994). The effects of prevalent social stereotypes on intergroup attribution. *Journal of Cross-Cultural Psychology, 25*, 489–500.

Berry, J. (1969). On cross-cultural comparability. *International Journal of Psychology, 4*, 119–128.

Berry, J. (1979). A cultural ecology of social behavior. In L. Berkowitz (Ed.), *Advances in experimental social psychology* (Vol. 12). New York: Academic Press.

Berry, J. (1984). Towards a universal psychology of cognitive competence. *International Journal of Psychology, 19*, 335–361.

Berry, J. (1990). Psychology of acculturation: Understanding individuals moving between cultures. In R. Brislin (Ed.), *Applied cross-cultural psychology* (pp. 232–253). Newbury Park, CA: Sage.

Berry, J. (1997). Preface. In J. Berry, Y. Poortinga, & J. Pandey (Eds.), *Theory and method: Vol. 1. Handbook of cross-cultural psychology* (2nd. ed., pp. x–xv). Boston: Allyn & Bacon.

Berry, J., Poortinga, Y., & Pandey, J. (Eds.). (1997). *Theory and method: Vol. 1. Handbook of cross-cultural psychology* (2nd. ed.). Boston: Allyn & Bacon.

Berry, J., & Sam, D. (1997). Acculturation and adaptation. In J. Berry, M. Segall, & C. Kagitcibasi (Eds.), *Behavior and applications: Vol. 3. Handbook of cross-cultural psychology* (2nd. ed., pp. 291–326). Boston: Allyn & Bacon.

Best, D., & Ruther, N. (1994). Cross-cultural themes in developmental psychology: An examination of texts, handbooks, and reviews. *Journal of Cross-Cultural Psychology, 25*, 54–77.

Best, D., & Williams, J. (1997). Sex, gender, and culture. In J. Berry, M. Segall, & C. Kagitcibasi (Eds.), *Behavior and applications: Vol. 3. Handbook of cross-cultural psychology* (2nd. ed., pp. 163–212). Boston: Allyn & Bacon.

Beutler, L., & Harwood, M. (1995). Prescriptive psychotherapies. *Applied & Preventive Psychology, 4*, 89–100.

Bhawuk, D. P. S. (1989). *Cross-cultural sensitivity and its relation to individualism and collectivism.* Unpublished master's thesis, College of Business Administration, University of Hawaii, Honolulu, HI.

Bhawuk, D. P. S. (1990). Cross-cultural orientation programs. In R. Brislin (Ed.), *Applied cross-cultural psychology* (pp. 325–346). Newbury Park, CA: Sage.

Bhawuk, D. (1997). Leadership through relationship management: Using the theory of individualism and collectivism. In K. Cushner & R. Brislin (Eds.), *Improving intercultural interactions: Modules for cross-cultural training programs* (Vol. 2, pp. 40–56). Thousand Oaks, CA: Sage.

Bhawuk, D. (1998). The role of culture theory in cross-cultural training: A multidimensional study of culture-specific, culture-general, and culture theory–based assimilators. *Journal of Cross-Cultural Psychology, 29*, 630–655.

Bhawuk, D., & Triandis, H. (1996). The role of culture theory in the study of culture and intercultural training. In D. Landis & R. Bhagat (Eds.), *Handbook of intercultural training* (2nd ed., pp. 17–34). Thousand Oaks, CA: Sage.

Biernat, M. (1991). Gender stereotypes and the relationship between masculinity and femininity: A developmental analysis. *Journal of Personality and Social Psychology, 61*, 351–365.

Biernat, M., & Wortman, C. (1991). Sharing of home responsibilities between professionally employed women and their husbands. *Journal of Personality and Social Psychology, 60*, 844–860.

Bigones, W., & Blakely, G. (1996). A cross-national study of managerial values. *Academy of International Business, 27*, 739–752.

Biswas, U., & Pandey, J. (1996). Mobility and perception of socioeconomic status among tribal and caste group. *Journal of Cross-Cultural Psychology, 27*, 200–215.

Black, J. (1990). The relationship of personal characteristics with the adjustment of Japanese expatriate managers. *Management International Review, 30*, 119–134.

Blake, B., Heslin, R., & Curtis, S. (1996). Measuring impacts of cross-cultural training. In D. Landis & R. Bhagat (Eds.), *Handbook of intercultural training* (2nd ed., pp. 165–182). Thousand Oaks, CA: Sage.

Block, J. (1983). Differential premises arising from differential socialization of the sexes: Some conjectures. *Child Development, 54*, 1335–1354.

Block, J., Gjerde, P., & Block, J. (1991). Personality antecedents of depressive tendencies in 18 year-olds: A prospective study. *Journal of Personality and Social Psychology, 60*, 726–738.

Bobo, L. (1983). Whites' opposition to busing: Symbolic racism or realistic group conflict. *Journal of Personality and Social Psychology, 45*, 1196–1210.

Bochner, S. (1994). Culture shock. In W. Lonner & R. Malpass (Eds.), *Psychology and culture* (pp. 245–251). Needham Heights, MA: Allyn & Bacon.

Bochner, S., & Hesketh, B. (1994). Power distance, individualism/collectivism, and job-related attitudes in a culturally diverse work group. *Journal of Cross-Cultural Psychology, 25*, 233–257.

Bock, P. (Ed.). (1970). *Culture shock: A reader in modern cultural anthropology.* New York: Knopf.

Bocker, H., & Overgaard, H. (1982). Structuring quality circles: A management challenge to combat ailing productivity. *Leadership and Organization Development Journal, 3*(5), 17–29.

Bond, M. (Ed.). (1986). *The psychology of the Chinese people.* New York: Oxford.

Bond, M. (1991). Chinese values and health: A cultural level examination. *Psychology and Health, 5*, 137–152.

Bond, M. (1995). Doing social psychology cross-culturally: Into another heart of darkness. In G. Brannigan & M. Merrens (Eds.), *The social psychologists: Research adventures* (pp. 187–205). New York: McGraw-Hill.

Bond, M., Wan, K., Leong, K., & Giacalone, R. (1985). How are responses to verbal insult related to cultural collectivism and power distance? *Journal of Cross-Cultural Psychology, 16*, 111–127.

Boyd, J. H., & Weissman, M. M. (1981). Epidemiology of affective disorders. A reexamination and future directions. *Archives of General Psychiatry, 38*, 1039–1046.

Braithwaite, C. (1990). Communicative silence: A cross-cultural study of Basso's hypothesis. In D. Carbaugh (Ed.), *Cultural communication and intercultural contact* (pp. 321–327). Hillsdale, NJ: Lawrence Erlbaum.

Braun, K., Takamura, J., & Mougeot, T. (1996). Perceptions of dementia, caregiving, and help-seeking among recent Vietnamese immigrants. *Journal of Cross-Cultural Gerontology, 11*, 213–228.

Braunwald, S., & Brislin, R. (1979a). The diary method updated. In E. Ochs & B. Schieffelin (Eds.), *Developmental pragmatics* (pp. 21–42). New York: Academic Press.

Braunwald, S., & Brislin, R. (1979b). On being understood: The listener's contribution to the toddler's ability to communicate. In P. French (Ed.), *The development of meaning* (pp. 71–113). Hiroshima, Japan: Bunka Hyoran.

Brewer, M. (1979). Ingroup bias in the minimal intergroup situation: A cognitive-motivational analysis. *Psychological Bulletin, 86*, 307–324.

Brewer, M., & Brown, R. (1998). Intergroup relations. In D. Gilbert, S. Fiske, & G. Lindzey (Eds.), *The handbook of social psychology* (Vol. 2, 4th ed., pp. 554–594). New York: McGraw-Hill.

Brewer, M., & Miller, N. (1984). Beyond the contact hypothesis: Theoretical perspective on desegregation. In N. Miller & M. Brewer (Eds.), *Groups in contact: The psychology of desegregation* (pp. 281–302). Orlando, FL: Academic Press.

Brewin, C. (1996). Theoretical foundations of cognitive-behavioral therapy for anxiety and depression. *Annual Review of Psychology, 47*, 33–57.

Brislin, R. (1970). Back-translation for cross-cultural research. *Journal of Cross-Cultural Psychology, 1*, 185–216.

Brislin, R. (1980). Translation and content analysis of oral and written materials. In H. Triandis & J. Berry (Eds.), *Methodology: Vol. 2. Handbook of cross-cultural psychology* (pp. 389–444). Boston: Allyn & Bacon.

Brislin, R. (1981). *Cross-cultural encounters: Face-to-face interaction.* Elmsford, NY: Pergamon.

Brislin, R. (1984). Cross-cultural psychology. In R. Corsini (Ed.), *Encyclopedia of psychology* (Vol. 1, pp. 319–327). New York: John Wiley.

Brislin, R. (1986a). Prejudice and intergroup communication. In W. Gudykunst (Ed.), *Intergroup communication* (pp. 74–85). London & Baltimore: Edward Arnold.

Brislin, R. (1986b). The wording and translation of research instruments. In W. Lonner & J. Berry (Eds.), *Field methods in cross-cultural research* (pp. 137–164). Newbury Park, CA: Sage.

Brislin, R. (1988). Increasing awareness of class, ethnicity, culture, and race by expanding on students' own experiences. In I. Cohen (Ed.), *The G. Stanley Hall lecture series* (Vol. 8, pp. 137–180). Washington, DC: American Psychological Association.

Brislin, R. (1989). Intercultural communication training. In M. Asante & W. Gudykunst (Eds.), *Handbook of international and intercultural communication* (pp. 441–457). Newbury Park, CA: Sage.

Brislin, R. (1991). *The art of getting things done: A practical guide to the use of power.* New York: Praeger.

Brislin, R. (1997). Introducing active exercises in the college classroom for intercultural and cross-cultural courses. In K. Cushner & R. Brislin (Eds.), *Improving intercultural interactions: Modules for cross-cultural training programs* (Vol. 2, pp. 91–108). Thousand Oaks, CA: Sage.

Brislin, R., Cushner, K., Cherrie, C., & Yong, M. (1986). *Intercultural interactions: A practical guide.* Newbury Park, CA: Sage.

Brislin, R., & Horvath, A. M. (1997). Cross-cultural training and multicultural education. In J. Berry, M. Segall, & C. Kagitcibasi (Eds.), *Behavior and applications: Vol. 3. Handbook of cross-cultural psychology* (2nd. ed., pp. 327–369). Boston: Allyn & Bacon.

Brislin, R., & Hui, C. H. (1993). The preparation of managers for overseas assignments: The case of China. In O. Shenkar & N. L. Kelley (Eds.), *International business in China* (pp. 233–258). London: Routledge.

Brislin, R., & Jane, S. (1997). Power in the service of leadership. In K. Cushner & R. Brislin (Eds.), *Improving intercultural interactions: Modules for cross-cultural training programs* (Vol. 2, pp. 21–39). Thousand Oaks, CA: Sage.

Brislin, R., & Keating, C. (1976). Cultural differences in the perception of a three-dimensional Ponzo illusion. *Journal of Cross-Cultural Psychology, 7,* 397–411.

Brislin, R., Landis, D., & Brandt, E. (1983). Conceptualizations of intercultural behavior and training. In D. Landis & R. Brislin (Eds.), *Issues in theory and design: Vol. 1. Handbook of intercultural training* (pp. 1–35). Elmsford, NY: Pergamon.

Brislin, R., Lonner, W., & Thorndike, R. (1973). *Cross-cultural research methods.* New York: Wiley.

Brislin, R., & Pedersen, P. (1976). *Cross-cultural orientation programs.* New York: Wiley/Halsted.

Brislin, R., & Yoshida, T. (1994). *Intercultural communication training: An introduction.* Thousand Oaks, CA: Sage.

Broaddus, D. (1986). *Use of a culture-general assimilator in intercultural training.* Unpublished doctoral dissertation, Indiana State University, Terre Haute, Indiana.

Brophy, W. (1989). Defense of segregation. In C. R. Wilson & W. Ferris (Eds.), *Encyclopedia of southern culture* (pp. 1176–1178). Chapel Hill, NC: University of North Carolina Press.

Brown, N. (1997). Child's talk. *Research / Penn State, 18*(3), 33–38.

Brown, T., Graves, T., & Williams, S. (1997). Dual-earner families: The impact of gender and culture on this normative family structure and the implications for therapy. *Family Therapy, 24,* 177–189.

Burg, B., & Belmont, I. (1990). Mental abilities of children from different cultural backgrounds in Israel. *Journal of Cross-Cultural Psychology, 21,* 90–108.

Buriel, R. (1983). Teacher-student interactions and their relationship to student achievement: A comparison of Mexi-can-American and Anglo-American children. *Journal of Educational Psychology, 75,* 889–897.

Burnam, M. A., Telles, C. A., Karno, M., Hough, R., & Escobar, J. (1987). Measurement of acculturation in a community population of Mexican Americans. *Hispanic Journal of Behavioral Sciences, 9,* 105–139.

Burns, A., & Homel, R. (1986). Sex role satisfaction among Australian children: Some sex, age, and cultural group comparisons. *Psychology of Women Quarterly, 10,* 285–296.

Buss, D. (1989). Sex differences in human mate preference: Evolutionary hypotheses tested in 37 cultures. *Behavior and Brain Sciences, 12,* 1–49.

Buss, D. (1991). Evolutionary personality psychology. *Annual Review of Psychology, 42,* 459–491.

Buss, D. (1996). The evolutionary psychology of human social strategies. In E. T. Higgins & A. Kruglanski (Eds.), *Social psychology: Handbook of basic principles* (pp. 3–38). New York: Guilford.

Buss D., Abbot, M., Angeleitner, A., Asherian, A., et al. (1990). International preferences in selecting mates: A study of 37 cultures. *Journal of Cross-Cultural Psychology, 21,* 5–47.

Buss, D. M., & Barnes, M. F. (1986). Preferences in human mate selection. *Journal of Personality and Social Psychology, 50,* 559–570.

Buss, D., & Kenrick, D. (1998). Evolutionary social psychology. In D. Gilbert, S. Fiske, & G. Lindzey (Eds.), *The Handbook of Social Psychology* (Vol. 2, 4th ed., pp. 554–594). New York: McGraw-Hill.

Butcher, J., Lim, J., & Nezami, E. (1998). Objective study of abnormal personality in cross-cultural settings: The Minnesota Multiphasic Personality Inventory (MMPI-2). *Journal of Cross-Cultural Psychology, 29,* 189–211.

Butler, J. (1991). Toward understanding and measuring conditions of trust: Evolution of a conditions of trust inventory. *Journal of Management, 17,* 643–663.

Button, K., & Bart, C. (1998). Conscience or competitive edge? In A. Francesco & B. Gold (Eds.), *International organizational behavior* (pp. 445–448). Upper Saddle River, NJ: Prentice Hall.

Callan, H. (1970). *Ethology and society: Toward an anthropological view.* Oxford, England: Clarendon Press.

Camilleri, C., & Malewska-Peyre, H. (1997). Socialization and identity strategies. In J. Berry, P. Dasen, & T. Saraswathi (Eds.), *Basic processes and human development: Vol. 2. Handbook of cross-cultural psychology* (2nd ed., pp. 41–67). Boston: Allyn & Bacon.

Campbell, D. (1964). Distinguishing differences in perception failures of communication in cross-cultural studies. In F. Northrop & H. Livingston (Eds.), *Cross-cultural understanding: Epistemology in anthropology.* New York: Harper & Row.

Campion, J. (1982). Young Asian children with learning and behaviour problems: A family therapy approach. *Journal of Family Therapy, 4,* 153–163.

Caporael, L. (1997). The evolution of truly social cognition: The core configurations model. *Personality and Social Psychology Review, 1*(4), 276–298.

Carbaugh, D. (Ed.). (1990a). *Cultural communication and intercultural contact.* Hillsdale, NJ: Lawrence Erlbaum.

Carbaugh, D. (1990b). Toward a perspective on cultural communication and intercultural contact. *Semiotica, 80,* 15–35.

Carden, A., & Feicht, R. (1991). Homesickness among American and Turkish college students. *Journal of Cross-Cultural Psychology, 22,* 418–428.

Carson, R. (1989). Personality. *Annual Review of Psychology, 40,* 227–248.

Cashmore, J. A., & Goodnow, J. L. (1986). Influence of Australian parents' values: Ethnicity versus socioeconomic status. *Journal of Cross-Cultural Psychology, 17,* 441–454.

Casimir, G., & Keats, D. (1996). The effects of work environment and in-group membership on the leadership preferences of Anglo-Australians and Chinese Australians. *Journal of Cross-Cultural Psychology, 27,* 436–457.

Castillo, R. (1997). *Culture and mental illness: A client centered approach.* Pacific Grove, CA: Brooks/Cole.

Chaika, E. (1989). *Language: The social mirror.* New York: Newbury House.

Chang, D. (1989). "Heaven is high, and the emperor is far away." *Harvard Business Review, 67*(6), 33–36.

Chao, R. (1996). Chinese and European mothers' beliefs about the role of parenting in children's school success. *Journal of Cross-Cultural Psychology, 27,* 403–424.

Chaplin, W., John, O., & Goldberg, L. (1988). Conceptions of states and traits: Dimmensional attributes with ideals as prototypes. *Journal of Personality and Social Psychology, 54,* 541–547.

Chen, C., Meindl, J., & Hunt, R. (1997). Testing the effects of vertical and horizontal collectivism: A study of reward allocation preferences in China. *Journal of Cross-Cultural Psychology, 28,* 44–70.

Chen, G.-M. (1995). Differences in self-disclosure patterns among Americans versus Chinese: A comparative study. *Journal of Cross-Cultural Psychology, 26,* 84–91.

Cheng, Y., & Lee, P. (1988). Illness behaviour in Chinese medical students. *Psychologia: An International Journal of Psychology in the Orient, 31,* 207–216.

Chernin, D. (1990). An American learns to work in Japan. *World Monitor, 3*(7), 50–56.

Chesanow, N. (1985). *The world-class executive.* New York: Rawson.

Cheung, C.-K., & Chan, C.-F. (1996). Television viewing and mean world value in Hong Kong's adolescents. *Social Behavior and Personality, 24,* 351–364.

Cheung, F., & Leung, K. (1998). Indigenous personality measures: Chinese examples. *Journal of Cross-Cultural Psychology, 29,* 233–248.

Cheung, F., Leung, K., Fan, R., Song, W.-Z., Zhang, J.-X., & Zhang, J.-P. (1996). Development of the Chinese Personality Assessment Inventory. *Journal of Cross-Cultural Psychology, 27,* 181–199.

Chick, J. (1990). The interactional accomplishments of discrimination in South Africa. In D. Carbaugh (Ed.), *Cultural communication and intercultural contact* (pp. 225–252). Hillsdale, NJ: Lawrence Erlbaum.

Child, I. L. (1954). Socialization. In G. Lindzey (Ed.), *Handbook of social psychology* (Vol. 2, pp. 655–692). Cambridge, MA: Addison-Wesley.

Chiles, J., Strosahl, K., & Ping, Z., Michael, M., et al. (1989). Depression, hopelessness, and suicidal behavior in Chinese and American psychiatric patients. *The American Journal of Psychiatry, 146,* 339–344.

Chinese Culture Connection. (1987). Chinese values and the search for culture-free dimensions of culture. *Journal of Cross-Cultural Psychology, 18,* 143–164.

Ching, F. (1998, January 22). Are Asian values finished? *Far Eastern Economic Review,* p. 32.

Chodorow, N. (1974). Family structure and feminine personality. In M. Z. Rasaldo & L. Lamphere (Eds.), *Women, culture and society.* Stanford, CA: Stanford University Press.

Christopher, R. (1983). *The Japanese mind.* New York: Fawcett Columbine.

Church, A., & Lonner, W. (Eds.). (1998). Personality and its measurement in cross-cultural perspective. *Journal of Cross-Cultural Psychology, 29,* 5–270.

Cialdini, R. (1990). Personal communication. Arizona State University, Tempe, AZ.

Clark, C., & Clark, J. (1987). The gender gap in Yugoslavia: Elite versus mass levels. *Political Psychology, 8,* 411–426.

A clash of cultures (1986). Part 8 in *The Africans* [Film, WETA's Annenberg/CPB collection]. (Available from Intellimation, Santa Barbara, CA.)

Clement, U. (1989). Profile analysis as a method of comparing intergenerational differences in sexual behavior. *Archives of Sexual Behavior, 18,* 229–237.

Coates, T., & Collins, C. (1998). Preventing HIV infection. *Scientific American, 279*(1), 96–97.

Cockerham, W., Kunz, G., & Lueschen, G. (1988). Social stratification and health lifestyle in two systems of health care delivery: A comparison of the United States and West Germany. *Journal of Health and Social Behavior, 29,* 113–126.

Cole, M., Gay, J., Glick, J. A., & Sharp, D. W. (1971). *The cultural context of learning and thinking.* New York: Basic Books.

Cole, M., & Scribner, S. (1974). *Culture and thought: A psychological introduction.* New York: John Wiley.

Collier, C., & Collier, J. (1986). *Decision in Philadelphia: The Constitutional Convention of 1787.* New York: Random House.

Compton, J. N. (1998). Critical incidents in interactions with Russians. In R. Moody (Ed.), *Proceedings of the Conference on Culture and Type, Honolulu, Hawaii.*

Gainesville, FL: Center for Applications of Psychological Type.

Condon, R. (1995). The rise of the leisure class: Adolescence and recreational acculturation in the Canadian arctic. *Ethos, 23*(1), 47–78.

Cook, P. (1994). Chronic illness beliefs and the role of social networks among Chinese, Indian, and Anglocentric Canadians. *Journal of Cross-Cultural Psychology, 25,* 452–465.

Cook, S. W. (1969). Motives in a conceptual analysis of attitude-related behavior. In W. J. Arnold & D. Levine (Eds.), *Nebraska symposium on motivation.* Lincoln, NE: University of Nebraska Press.

Cowley, G. (1998, July 27). Vaccine revolution. *Newsweek, 132*(4), 48–49.

Crick, B. (1982). *In defense of politics* (2nd ed.). New York: Penguin.

Crittenden, K., & Lamug, C. (1988). Causal attribution and depression: A friendly refinement based on Philippine data. *Journal of Cross-Cultural Psychology, 19,* 216–231.

Crocker, J., Major, B., & Steele, C. (1998). Social stigma. In D. Gilbert, S. Fiske, & G. Lindzey (Eds.), *The handbook of social psychology* (Vol. 2, 4th ed., pp. 504–553). New York: McGraw-Hill.

Crosby, F., Bromley, S., & Saxe, L. (1980). Recent unobtrusive studies of Black and White discrimination and prejudice: A literature review. *Psychological Bulletin, 87,* 546–563.

Cross, S. (1995). Self-construals, coping, and stress in cross-cultural adaptation. *Journal of Cross-Cultural Psychology, 26,* 673–697.

Crowne, D., & Marlowe, D. (1964). *The approval motive.* New York: Wiley.

Crozier, G. (1996). Black parents and school relationships: A case study. *Educational Review, 48,* 253–267.

Cui, G., & Van Den Berg, S. (1991). Testing the construct validity of intercultural effectiveness. *International Journal of Intercultural Relations, 15,* 227–241.

Cummins, J. (1976). The influence of bilingualism on cognitive growth: A synthesis of research findings and explanatory hypothesis. *Working Papers on Bilingualism, 9,* 1–43.

Curtain, P. (1992). The slavery hypothesis for hypertension among African Americans: The historical evidence. *American Journal of Public Health, 82,* 1681–1686.

Cushner, K. (1989). Assessing the impact of a culture-general assimilator. *International Journal of Intercultural Relations, 13,* 125–146.

Cushner, K. (1990). Cross-cultural psychology and the formal classroom. In R. Brislin (Ed.), *Applied cross-cultural psychology* (pp. 98–120). Newbury Park, CA: Sage.

Cushner, K. (1994). Preparing teachers for an intercultural context. In R. Brislin & T. Yoshida (Eds.), *Intercultural interactions: A practical guide* (pp. 91–128). Thousand Oaks, CA: Sage.

Cushner, K., & Brislin, R. (1996). *Intercultural interactions: A practical guide* (2nd ed). Thousand Oaks, CA: Sage.

Cushner, K., McClelland, A., & Safford, P. (1996). *Human diversity in education: An integrated approach* (2nd ed.). New York: McGraw-Hill.

Damen, L. (1987). *Culture learning: The fifth dimension in the language classroom.* Reading, MA: Addison-Wesley.

Dane, F. (1990). *Research methods.* Pacific Grove, CA: Brooks/Cole.

Dasen, P. (1984). The cross-cultural study of intelligence: Piaget and the Baoule. *International Journal of Psychology, 19,* 407–434.

Dasen, P. R., & Heron, A. (1981). Cross-cultural tests of Piaget's theory. In H. C. Triandis & A. Heron (Eds.), *Psychology: Vol. 4. Handbook of cross-cultural psychology* (pp. 295–342). Boston: Allyn & Bacon.

Davies, J. (1985). Why are women not where the power is? An examination of the maintenance of power elites. *Management Education and Development, 16,* 278–288.

Daws, G. (1977). Looking at islanders: European ways of thinking about Polynesians in the eighteenth and nineteenth centuries. In R. Brislin (Ed.), *Culture learning: Concepts, applications, and research* (pp. 176–181). Honolulu, HI: University Press of Hawaii.

Day, R., Nielsen, J., Korten, A., Ernberg, G., et al. (1987). Stressful life events preceding the onset of schizophrenia: A cross-national study from the World Health Organization. *Culture, Medicine, and Psychiatry, 11,* 123–205.

Deaux, K., & LaFrance, M. (1998). Gender. In D. Gilbert, S. Fiske, & G. Lindzey (Eds.), *The Handbook of Social Psychology* (Vol. 1, 4th ed., pp. 788–827). New York: McGraw-Hill.

DeMente, B. (1989). *The Japanese influence on America.* Lincolnwood, IL: Passport Books.

Deregowski, J. B. (1980). Perception. In H. C. Triandis & W. J. Lonner (Eds.), *Basic processes: Vol. 3. Handbook of cross-cultural psychology* (pp. 21–115). Boston: Allyn & Bacon.

Detweiler, R., Brislin, R., & McCormack, W. (1983). Situational analysis. In D. Landis & R. Brislin (Eds.), *Issues in training methodology: Vol. 2. Handbook of intercultural training* (pp. 100–123). Elmsford, NY: Pergamon.

Deutsch, M., & Collins, M. (1951). *Interracial housing: A psychological evaluation of a social experiment.* Minneapolis, MN: University of Minnesota Press.

Devine, P. (1995). Getting hooked on research in social psychology: Examples from eyewitness identification and prejudice. In G. Brannigan & M. Merrens (Eds.), *The social psychologists: Research adventures* (pp. 161–184). New York: McGraw-Hill.

Devine, P. G. (1996). Breaking the prejudice habit. *Psychological Science Agenda, 9,* 10–11.

Devine, P., & Elliot, A. (1995). Are racial stereotypes *really* fading: The Princeton triology revisited. *Personality and Social Psychology Bulletin, 21,* 1139–1150.

Devine, P., Monteith, M., Zuwerink, J., & Elliot, A. (1991). Prejudice with and without compunction. *Journal of Personality and Social Psychology, 60,* 817–830.

Deyo, R. (1998). Low-back pain. *Scientific American, 279* (2), 49–53.

Diamond, J. (1997). *Guns, germs, and steel: The fates of human societies.* New York: Norton.

Dichtl, E., Koeglmayr, H. G., & Mueller, S. (1990). International orientation as a precondition for export success. *Journal of International Business Studies, 21,* 23–40.

Diekstra, R. (1989). Suicidal behavior and depressive disorders in adolescents and young adults. *Neuropsychobiology, 22,* 194–207.

Dinges, N., & Baldwin, K. (1996). Intercultural competence: A research perspective. In D. Landis & R. Bhagat (Eds.), *Handbook of intercultural training* (2nd ed., pp. 81–105). Thousand Oaks, CA: Sage.

Doherty, J., & Obani, T. (1986). The development of concepts of handicap in adolescence: A cross-cultural study: III. *Educational Studies, 12,* 291–311.

Dong, Q., Weisfeld, G., Boardway, R., & Shen, J. (1996). Correlates of social status among Chinese adolescents. *Journal of Cross-Cultural Psychology, 27,* 476–493.

Dorahy, M., Schumaker, J., Simpson, P., & Deshpande, C. (1996). Depression and life satisfaction in India and Australia. *Journal of Personality and Clinical Studies, 12,* 1–7.

Dorfman, P. (1996). International and cross-cultural leadership. In B. Punnett & O. Shenkar (Eds.), *Handbook for international management research* (pp. 267–349). Cambridge, MA: Blackwell.

Dorn, P. (1986). Gender and person level: Turkish Jewish proverbs and the politics of reputation. *Women's Studies International Forum, 9,* 295–301.

Doyle, J., and Paludi, M. (1995). *Sex and gender: The human experience* (3rd ed.). Madison, WI: Brown and Benchmark.

Draguns, J. G. (1973). Comparison of psychopathology across cultures: Issues, findings, directions. *Journal of Cross-Cultural Psychology, 4,* 9–47.

Draguns, J. (1975). Resocialization into culture: The complexities of taking a worldwide view of psychotherapy. In R. Brislin, S. Bochner, & W. Lonner (Eds.), *Cross-cultural perspectives on learning* (pp. 273–289). Beverly Hills, CA: Sage.

Draguns, J. (1990). Applications of cross-cultural psychology in the field of mental health. In R. Brislin (Ed.), *Applied cross-cultural psychology* (pp. 302–324). Newbury Park, CA: Sage.

Durodoye, B. (1997). Factors of marital satisfaction among African American couples and Nigerian Male/African American female couples. *Journal of Cross-Cultural Psychology, 28,* 71–80.

Dutton, D. (1976). Tokenism, reverse discrimination, and egalitarianism in interracial behavior. *Journal of Social Issues, 32*(2), 93–107.

Eagly, A. (1987). *Sex differences in social behavior: A social role interpretation.* Hillsdale, NJ: Erlbaum.

Eagly, A., & Chaiken, S. (1998). Attitude structure and function. In D. Gilbert, S. Fiske, & G. Lindzey (Eds.)., *The handbook of social psychology* (Vol. 1, 4th ed., pp. 269–322). New York: McGraw-Hill.

Earley, P. (1989). Social loafing and collectivism: A comparison of the United States and the People's Republic of China. *Administrative Science Quarterly, 34,* 565–581.

Earley, P. C. (1997). *Face, harmony, and social structure: An analysis of organizational behavior across cultures.* New York: Oxford University Press.

Earley, P., & Stubblebine, P. (1989). Intercultural assessment of performance feedback. *Group and Organizational Studies, 14,* 161–181.

Eckensberger, L., & Zimba, R. (1997). The development of moral judgment. In J. Berry, P. Dasen, & T. Saraswathi (Eds.), *Basic processes and human development: Vol. 2. Handbook of cross-cultural psychology* (2nd ed., pp. 299–338). Boston: Allyn & Bacon.

Edman, J. (1997). Cultural differences in illness schemas: An analysis of Filipino and American illness attributions. *Journal of Cross-Cultural Psychology, 28,* 252–265.

Egeland, J. A., & Hostetter, A. M. (1983). Amish study: I. Affective disorders among the Amish. *American Journal of Psychiatry, 140,* 56–61.

Ehrenhaus, P. (1983). Culture and the attribution process. In W. Gudykunst (Ed.), *Intercultural communication theory.* Newbury Park, CA: Sage.

Ekman, P., & Friesen, W. V. (1975). *Unmasking the face: A guide to recognizing emotions from facial clues.* Englewood Cliffs, NJ: Prentice Hall.

Elms, A. (1972). *Social psychology and social relevance.* Boston: Little, Brown.

Embretson, S. (1997). The new rules of measurement. *Psychological Assessment, 8,* 341–349.

Engelhard, G. (1990). Gender differences in performance on mathematics items: Evidence from the United States and Thailand. *Contemporary Educational Psychology, 15,* 13–26.

England, J. (1986). Cross-cultural health care. *Canada's Mental Health, 34*(4), 13–15.

Erez, M., & Somech, A. (1996). Is group productivity loss the rule of the exception? Effects of culture and group-based motivation. *Academy of Management Journal, 39,* 1513–1537.

Erlanger, S. (1991, July 14). A plague awaits. *New York Times Magazine,* pp. 24–26, 49–53.

Escobar, J., Gomez, J., & Tuason, V. (1983). Depressive phenomenology in North and South American patients. *American Journal of Psychiatry, 140,* 47–51.

Etzion, D., & Pines, A. (1986). Sex and culture in burnout and coping among human service professionals: A social psychological perspective. *Journal of Cross-Cultural Psychology, 17,* 191–209.

Ezelio, B. (1983). Age, sex, and self concepts in a Nigerian population. *International Journal of Behavioral Development, 6*, 497–502.

Fang, T. (1998). *Chinese business negotiating style: A middle kingdom perspective*. Thousand Oaks, CA: Sage.

Farver, J., Kim, Y., & Lee, Y. (1995). Cultural differences in Korean- and Anglo-American preschoolers' social interaction and play behaviors. *Child Development, 66*, 1088–1099.

Fausto-Sterling, A. (1985). *Myths of gender: Biological theories about men and women*. New York: Basic Books.

Feeding frenzy. (1991, May 27). *Newsweek, 117*(21), 46–53.

Feldman, S., & Rosenthal, D. (1990). The acculturation of autonomy expectations in Chinese high schools residing in two Western nations. *International Journal of Psychology, 25*, 259–281.

Ferdman, B., & Brody, S. (1996). Models of diversity training. In D. Landis & R. Bhagat (Eds.), *Handbook of intercultural training* (2nd ed., pp. 282–303). Thousand Oaks, CA: Sage.

Ferris, G., & Wagner, J. (1985). Quality circles in the United States: A conceptual re-evaluation. *Journal of Applied Behavioral Science, 21*, 155–167.

Fiedler, F. E. (1967). *A theory of leadership effectiveness*. New York: McGraw-Hill.

Fiedler, F. E., & Garcia, J. E. (1987). *New approaches to leadership: Cognitive resources and organizational performance*. New York: Wiley.

Finn, J., & Rock, D. (1997). Academic success among students at risk for school failure. *Journal of Applied Psychology, 82*, 221–234.

Fisher, A., Jome, J., & Atkinson, D. (1998). Reconceptualizing multicultural counseling: Universal healing conditions in a culturally specific context. *The Counseling Psychologist, 26*, 525–588.

Fiske, A. (1991). *Structures of social life*. New York: Free Press.

Fiske, A., Kitayama, S., Markus, H., & Nisbett, R. (1998). The cultural matrix of social psychology. In D. Gilbert, S. Fiske, & G. Lindzey (Eds.), *The handbook of social psychology* (Vol. 2, 4th ed., pp. 357–411). New York: McGraw-Hill.

Fiske, S. (1998). Stereotyping, prejudice, and discrimination. In D. Gilbert, S. Fiske, & G. Lindzey (Eds.), *The handbook of social psychology* (Vol. 2, 4th ed., pp. 357–411). New York: McGraw-Hill.

Fiske, S., Bersoff, D., Borgida, E., Deaux, K., & Heilman, M. (1991). Social science research on trial: Use of sex stereotyping research in Price Waterhouse v. Hopkins. *American Psychologist, 46*, 1049–1060.

Flavell, J. H. (1963). *The developmental psychology of Jean Piaget*. Princeton, NJ: Van Nostrand.

Fleming, A. (1985–1986). Sex differences and cross-cultural studies. *Women and Therapy, 4*, 23–32.

Foa, U., & Chemers, M. (1967). The significance of role behavior for cross-cultural interaction training. *International Journal of Psychology, 2*, 45–57.

Fontaine, G. (1990). Cultural diversity in intimate intercultural relationships. In D. Cahn (Ed.), *Intimates in conflict: A communication perspective* (pp. 209–224). Hillsdale, NJ: Lawrence Erlbaum.

Fowler, S., & Mumford, M. (1995). *Intercultural sourcebook: Cross-cultural training methods* (Vol. 1). Yarmouth, ME: Intercultural Press.

Foxcroft, D. (1996). Adolescent alcohol use and misuse in the UK. *Educational and Child Psychology, 13*, 60–68.

Frable, D. (1997). Gender, racial, ethnic, sexual, and class identities. *Annual Review of Psychology, 48*, 139–162.

Francesco, A., & Gold, B. (1998). *International organizational behavior*. Upper Saddle River, NJ: Prentice Hall.

Freed, R., & Freed, S. (1981). Enculturation and education in Shanti Nagar. *Anthropological Papers of the American Museum of Natural History* (Vol. 57, Part 2). New York: American Museum of Natural History.

Freeman, M. (1997). Demographic correlates of individualism and collectivism: A study of social values in Sri Lanka. *Journal of Cross-Cultural Psychology, 28*, 321–341.

Freiberg, P. (1991, January). Surprise: Most bosses are incompetent. *The American Psychological Association Monitor, 22*(1), 23.

Freimanis, C. (1994). Training bilinguals to interpret in the community. In R. Brislin & T. Yoshida (Eds.), *Intercultural interactions: A practical guide* (pp. 313–341). Thousand Oaks, CA: Sage.

Friday, R. (1989). Contrasts in discussion behaviors of German & American managers. *International Journal of Intercultural Relations, 13*, 429–446.

Fried, J., & Matsumoto, I. (1997). Everyday work experiences of people designated as diverse: A focus on strategies. In K. Cushner & R. Brislin (Eds.), *Improving intercultural interactions: Modules for cross-cultural training programs* (Vol. 2, pp. 57–73). Thousand Oaks, CA: Sage.

Fuchs, J., Levinson, R., Stoddard, R., Mullet, M., & Jones, D. (1990). Health risk factors among the Amish: Results of a survey. *Health Education Quarterly, 17*, 197–211.

Fugita, S., & Crittenden, K. (1990). Towards culture—and population-specific norms for self-reported depressive symptomatology (Korea, the Philippines, Taiwan, and the United States). *The International Journal of Social Psychiatry, 36*, 83–92.

Fukuyama, F. (1995). *Trust: The social virtues and the creation of prosperity*. New York: Free Press.

Funder, D., & Colvin, C. R. (1991). Explorations in behavioral consistency properties of persons, situations, and behaviors. *Journal of Personality and Social Psychology, 60*, 773–794.

Furnham, A., & Bochner, S. (1986). *Culture shock: Psychological reaction to unfamiliar environments*. London & New York: Methuen.

Gabrenya, W., Wang, Y. & Latane, B. (1985). Social loafing on an optimizing task: Cross-cultural differences among Chinese and Americans. *Journal of Cross-Cultural Psychology, 16*, 223–242.

Gaertner, S. & Dovidio, J. (1986). The aversive form of racism. In J. Dovidio & S. Gaertner (Eds.), *Prejudice, discrimination, and racism* (pp. 61–89). San Diego: Academic Press.

Garber, H. L. (1988). *The Milwaukee Project: Preventing mental retardation in children at risk*. Washington, DC: American Association on Mental Retardation.

Garcia-Coll, C. (1990). Developmental outcome of minority infants: A process-oriented look into our beginnings. *Child Development, 61*, 270–289.

Gardner, H. (1985). *The mind's new science: The history of the cognitive revolution*. New York: Basic Books.

Gaskins, S., & Lucy, J. (1987). *The role of children in the production of adult culture: A Yucatec case*. Paper presented at the meeting of the American Ethnological Society, San Antonio, TX.

Gauvin, M. (1998). Culture, development, and theory of mind: Comment of Lillard (1998). *Psychological Bulletin, 123*, 37–42.

Gaylord-Ross, R. (1987). Vocational integration for persons with mental handicaps: A cross-cultural perspective. *Research in Development Disabilities, 8*, 531–548.

Georgas, J., Christakopoulous, S., Poortinga, Y., Angleitner, A., Goodwin, R., Charalambous, N. (1997). The relationship of family bonds to family structures and function across cultures. *Journal of Cross-Cultural Psychology, 28*, 303–320.

Georgie-Hyde, D. M. (1970). *Piaget and conceptual development*. London: Holt, Rinehart and Winston.

Gersten, R., & Woodward, J. (1995). A longitudinal study of transitional and immersion bilingual education programs in one district. *Elementary School Journal, 95*, 223–239.

Gerver, D., & Sinaiko, H. W. (Eds.). (1978). *Language interpretation and communication*. New York: Plenum.

Gilbert, D., & Kahl, J. A. (1982). *The American class structure: A new synthesis*. Homewood, IL: Dorsey.

Gilbert, G. (1998). Ordinary personology. In D. Gilbert, S. Fiske, & G. Lindzey (Eds.), *The handbook of social psychology*, (Vol. 2, 4th ed., pp. 89–150). New York: McGraw-Hill.

Gilbert, M. J., & Cervantes, R. (1986). Patterns and practices of alcohol use among Mexican Americans: A comprehensive review. *Hispanic Journal of Behavioral Sciences, 8*, 1–60.

Gim, R, Atkinson, D., and Kim, S. (1991). Asian-American acculturation, counselor ethnicity and cultural sensitivity, and ratings of counselors. *Journal of Counseling Psychology, 38*, 57–62.

Ginsburg, H. P., & Opper, S. (1969). *Piaget's theory of intellectual development: An introduction*. Englewood Cliffs, NJ: Prentice Hall.

Glaser, W. (1978). *The brain drain*. Elmsford, NY: Pergamon.

Glickman, H. (1983). *Basic psychology*. New York: Norton.

Golding, J., Baezconde-Garbanati, L. (1990). Ethnicity, culture, and social resources. *American Journal of Community Psychology, 18*, 465–486.

Golding, J., & Karno, M. (1988). Gender differences in depressive symptoms among Mexican Americans and non-Hispanic Whites. *Hispanic Journal of Behavioral Sciences, 10*, 1–19.

Golding, J., Karno, M., & Rutter, C. (1990). Symptoms of major depression among Mexican-American and non-Hispanic Whites. *American Journal of Psychiatry, 147*, 861–866.

Goldstein, A., & Segall, M. (1983). *Aggression in global perspective*. Elmsford, NY: Pergamon.

Goldstein, N. (1996). Knowledge of American Sign Language and the ability of hearing individuals to decode facial expressions of emotion. *Journal of Nonverbal Behavior, 20*, 111–122.

Goldstein, S. (1995). Cross-cultural psychology as a curriculum transformation resource. *Teaching of Psychology, 22*, 228–232.

Goleman, D. (1991, July 16). New way to battle bias: Fight acts, not feeling. *New York Times*, pp. B1, B9.

Goto, S., & Abe-Kim, J. (1998). Asian Americans and the model minority myth. In T. Singelis (Ed.), *Teaching about culture, ethnicity, and diversity* (pp. 151–157). Thousand Oaks, CA: Sage.

Gough, H. G. (1969). *California psychological inventory*. Palo Alto, CA: Consulting Psychologists Press.

Greenberg, Jeff, Solomon, S., & Pyszczynski, T. (1997). Terror management theory of self-esteem and cultural worldviews: Empirical assessments and conceptual refinements. In M. Zanna (Ed.), *Advances in experimental social psychology* (Vol. 30). San Diego, CA: Academic Press.

Greenberg, Jerald, & Baron, R. (1997). *Behavior in organizations* (6th ed.). Upper Saddle River, NJ: Prentice Hall.

Greenfield, P. M. (1984). A theory of the teacher in the learning activities of everyday life. In B. Rogoff & J. Lave (Eds.), *Everyday cognition* (pp. 117–138). Cambridge, MA: Harvard University Press.

Greenfield, P. (1997a). Culture as process: Empirical methods for cultural psychology. In J. Berry, Y. Poortinga, & J. Pandey (Eds.), *Theory and method: Vol. 1. Handbook of cross-cultural psychology* (2nd. ed., pp. 301–346). Boston: Allyn & Bacon.

Greenfield, P. (1997b). You can't take it with you: Why ability assessments don't cross cultures. *American Psychologist, 52*, 1115–1124.

Greenfield, P. M., & Lave, J. (1982). Cognitive aspects of informal education. In D. A. Wagner & H. W. Stevenson (Eds.), *Cultural perspectives on child development* (pp. 181–207). San Francisco: W. H. Freeman.

Grimm, L., & Yarnold, P. (Eds.). (1995). *Reading and understanding multivariate statistics*. Washington, DC: American Psychological Association.

Guarnaccia, P., Good, B., & Kleinman, A. (1990). A critical review of epidemiological studies of Puerto Rican mental health. *American Journal of Psychiatry, 147,* 1449–1456.

Gudykunst, W., & Bond, M. (1997). Intergroup relations across cultures. In J. Berry, M. Segall, & C. Kagitcibasi (Eds.), *Social behavior and applications: Vol. 3. Handbook of cross-cultural psychology* (2nd ed., pp. 119–161). Boston: Allyn & Bacon.

Gudykunst, W., Guzley, R., & Hammer, M. (1996). Designing intercultural training. In D. Landis & R. Bhagat (Eds.), *Handbook of intercultural training* (2nd ed., pp. 61–80). Thousand Oaks, CA: Sage.

Gudykunst, W., & Hammer, M. (1983). Basic training design: Approach to intercultural training. In D. Landis & R. Brislin (Eds.), *Issues in theory and design: Vol. 1. Handbook of intercultural training* (pp. 118–154). Elmsford, NY: Pergamon.

Gudykunst, W., & Hammer, M. (1988). Strangers and hosts. In Y. Y. Kim & W. Gudykunst (Eds.), *Cross-cultural adaptation* (pp. 106–139). Newbury Park, CA: Sage.

Gudykunst, W., & Kim, Y. (1984). *Communicating with strangers: An approach to intercultural communication.* Reading, MA: Addison-Wesley.

Gudykunst, W., & Nishida, T. (1989). Theoretical perspectives for studying intercultural communication. In M. Asante & W. Gudykunst (Eds.), *Handbook of international and intercultural communication* (pp. 17–46). Newbury Park, CA: Sage.

Guthrie, G., & Lonner, W. (1986). Assessment of personality and psychopathology. In W. Lonner & J. Berry (Eds.), *Field methods in cross-cultural research* (pp. 231–264). Newbury Park, CA: Sage.

Hadiyono, J., & Kahn, M. (1985). Personality differences and sex similarities in American and Indonesian college students. *Journal of Social Psychology, 125,* 703–708.

Hakuta, K. (1986). *Mirror of language: The debate on bilingualism.* New York: Basic Books.

Hall, E. (1959). *The silent language.* Garden City, NY: Doubleday.

Hall, E. (1966). *The hidden dimension.* Garden City, NY: Doubleday.

Hall, E. (1976). *Beyond culture.* Garden City, NY: Anchor.

Hamid, P. (1994). Self-monitoring, locus of control, and social encounters of Chinese and New Zealand students. *Journal of Cross-Cultural Psychology, 25,* 353–368.

Hamilton, V. L., Blumenfeld, P., Akoh, H., & Miura, K. (1991). Group and gender in Japanese and American elementary classrooms. *Journal of Cross-Cultural Psychology, 22,* 317–346.

Hammer, M. (1989). Intercultural communication competence. In M. Asante & W. Gudykunst (Eds.), *Handbook of international & intercultural communication* (pp. 247–260). Newbury Park, CA: Sage.

Hammer, M. R., Gudykunst, W. B., & Wiseman, R. L.

(1978). Dimensions of intercultural effectiveness: An exploratory study. *International Journal of Intercultural Relations, 2,* 382–392.

Hammer, M., Nishida, H., & Wiseman, R. (1996). The influence of situational prototypes on dimensions of intercultural communication competence. *Journal of Cross-Cultural Psychology, 27,* 267–282.

Hanassab, S., & Tidwell, R. (1996). Sex roles and sexual attitudes of young Iranian women: Implications for cross-cultural counseling. *Social Behavior and Personality, 24,* 185–194.

Harari, H., Jones, C., & Sek, H. (1988). Stress syndromes and stress predictors in American and Polish college students. *Journal of Cross-Cultural Psychology, 19,* 243–255.

Hare-Mustin, R., & Marecek, J. (1988). The meaning of differences: Gender theory, postmodernism, and psychology. *American Psychologist, 43,* 455–464.

Harper, D. (1997). Children's attitudes toward physical disability in Nepal: A field study. *Journal of Cross-Cultural Psychology, 28,* 710–729.

Harris, J. G. (1973). A science of the South Pacific: An analysis of the character structure of the Peace Corps volunteer. *American Psychologist, 28,* 232–247.

Harris, M. (1996). Aggressive experiences and aggressiveness: Relationship to ethnicity, gender, and age. *Journal of Applied Social Psychology, 26,* 843–870.

Hatfield, E., & Sprecher, S. (1986). *Mirror, mirror: The importance of looks in everyday life.* Albany: State University of New York Press.

Hatfield, E., & Sprecher, S. (1995). Men's and women's preferences in marital partners in the United States, Russia, and Japan. *Journal of Cross-Cultural Psychology, 26,* 728–750.

Hawes, F., & Kealey, D. J. (1981). An empirical study of Canadian technical assistance. *International Journal of Intercultural Relations, 5,* 239–258.

Hawkins, M. (1998). Understanding Japanese business practice: Implications for New Zealand firms. Unpublished master's thesis, University of Aukland, New Zealand.

Headland, T., Pike, K., & Harris, M. (Eds.). (1990). *Emics and etics: The insider/outsider debate.* Newbury Park, CA: Sage.

Health guide. (1991, May 20). *U. S. News and World Report, 110*(19), 68–99.

Healthwise staff. (1997). *Healthwise handbook.* Boise, ID: Healthwise.

Heath, S. (1983). *Ways with words: Language, life, and work in communities and classroom.* Cambridge, England: Cambridge University Press.

Heber, R., & Garber, H. (1975). The Milwaukee Project: A study of the use of family intervention to prevent cultural-familial mental retardation. In B. Z. Friedlander, G. M. Sterrit, & G. E. Kirk (Eds.), *Assessment and intervention: Vol. 3. Exceptional infant.* New York: Brunner/Mazel.

Henderson, M., & Argyle, M. (1986). The informal rules of working relationships. *Journal of Occupational Behaviour, 7,* 259–275.

Hendrix, L., & Johnson, G. D. (1985). Instrumental and expressive socialization: A false dichotomy. *Sex Roles, 13,* 581–595.

Herskovits, M. (1948). *Man and his works.* New York: Knopf.

Hess, R., Azuma, H., Kashiwaga, K., Dickson, W., Nagano, S., Holloway, S., Miyake, K., Price, G., Hatano, G., & McDevitt, T. (1986). Family influence on school readiness and achievement in Japan and the United States: An overview of a longitudinal study. In H. Stevenson, H. Azuma, & K. Hakuta (Eds.), *Child development and education in Japan.* New York: Freeman.

Hess, R. D., Chang, C. M., & McDevitt, T. M. (1987). Cultural variations in family beliefs about children's performance in mathematics: Comparisons among People's Republic of China, Chinese-American, and Caucasian-American families. *Journal of Educational Psychology, 79,* 179–188.

Hess, R., & Street, E. (1991). The effect of acculturation on the relationship of counselor ethnicity and client ratings. *Journal of Counseling Psychology, 38,* 71–75.

Higgins, E. T., & Bargh, J. (1987). Social cognition and social perception. *Annual Review of Psychology, 38,* 369–425.

Hilton, J., & von Hippel, W. (1990). The role of consistency in the judgment of stereotype-relevant behaviors. *Personality and Social Psychology Bulletin, 16,* 430–448.

Hijirida, K., & Yoshikawa, M. (1987). *Japanese language and culture for business and travel.* Honolulu, HI: University of Hawaii Press.

Hirsh, M. (1997, June 29). Tricks of trade. *Newsweek, 131* (26), 40–42.

Ho, D. (1998). Indigenous psychologies: Asian perspectives. *Journal of Cross-Cultural Psychology, 29,* 88–103.

Hofstede, G. (1980). *Culture's consequences: International differences in work-related values.* Newbury Park, CA: Sage.

Hofstede, G. (1986). Cultural differences in teaching and learning. *International Journal of Intercultural Relations, 10,* 301–320.

Hofstede, G. (1991). *Cultures and organizations: Software of the mind.* New York & London: McGraw-Hill.

Hofstede, G. (1996). Gender stereotypes and partner preferences of Asian women in masculine and feminine cultures. *Journal of Cross-Cultural Psychology, 27,* 533–546.

Hofstede, G. (1998). *Masculinity and femininity: The taboo dimension of national cultures.* Thousand Oaks, CA: Sage.

Hofstede, G., & Bond, M. H. (1988). Confucius & economic growth: New trends in culture's consequences. *Organizational Dynamics, 16*(4), 4–21.

Holland, D., & Eisenhart, M. (1988). Moments of discontent: University women and the gender status quo. *Anthropology and Education Quarterly, 19,* 115–138.

Hollander, E. (1985). Leadership and power. In G. Lindzey & E. Aronson (Eds.), *The Handbook of Social Psychology* (Vol. 2, 3rd ed., pp. 485–537). New York: Random House.

Holton, R. (1990). Human resource management in the People's Republic of China [Special issue]. *Management International Review, 30,* 121–136.

Holtzman, W. (1997). Community psychology and full-service schools in different cultures. *American Psychologist, 52,* 381–389.

Hopkins, B., & Westra, T. (1989). Material expectations of their infants' development: Some cultural differences. *Developmental Medicine and Child Neurology, 31,* 384–390.

Horenczyk, G., & Bekerman, Z. (1997). The effects of intercultural acquaintance and structured intergroup interaction on ingroup, outgroup, and reflected ingroup stereotypes. *International Journal of Intercultural Relations, 21,* 71–83.

Howard, G. (1991). Culture tales: A narrative approach to thinking, cross-cultural psychology, and psychotherapy. *American Psychologist, 46,* 187–197.

Hsia, J. (1988). Limits on affirmative action: Asian American access to higher education. *Educational Policy, 2,* 117–136.

Hsiao-Ying, T. (1995). Sojourner adjustment: The case of foreigners in Japan. *Journal of Cross-Cultural Psychology, 26,* 523–536.

Hsu, F. L. K. (1981). *American and Chinese: Passage to differences* (3rd ed.). Honolulu, HI: University Press of Hawaii.

Hubbard, R. (1990). *The politics of women's biology.* New Brunswick, Canada: Rutgers University Press.

Hudson, R. (1981). Some issues on which linguists can agree. *Journal of Linguistics, 17,* 333–343.

Hughes, R., Ginnett, R., & Curphy, G. (1996). *Leadership: Enhancing the lessons of experience* (2nd ed.). Chicago: Irwin.

Hui, C. H. (1990). Work attitudes, leadership styles, and managerial behaviors in different cultures. In R. Brislin (Ed.), *Applied cross-cultural psychology* (pp. 186–208). Newbury Park, CA: Sage.

Hui, C. H., & Luk, C. (1997). Industrial/Organizational psychology. In J. Berry, M. Segall, & C. Kagitcibasi (Eds.), *Behavior and applications: Vol. 3. Handbook of cross-cultural psychology* (2nd. ed., pp. 371–411). Boston: Allyn & Bacon.

Hui, C. H., & Triandis, H. (1985). Measurement in cross-cultural psychology: A review and comparison of strategies. *Journal of Cross-Cultural Psychology, 16*(2), 131–152.

Hunter, S. (1990). Levels of health development: A new tool

for comparative research and policy formulation. *Social Science and Medicine, 31,* 433–444.

Hyde, J., Fennema, E., & Lamon, S. (1990). Gender differences in mathematics performance: A meta-analysis. *Psychological Bulletin, 107,* 139–155.

Ilola, L. (1990). Culture and health. In R. Brislin (Ed.), *Applied cross-cultural psychology* (pp. 278–301). Newbury Park, CA: Sage.

Imamoglu, E., Kuller, R., Imamoglu, V., & Kuller, M. (1993). The social psychological worlds of Swedes and Turks in and around retirement. *Journal of Cross-Cultural Psychology, 24,* 26–41.

Irvine, S., & Berry, J. (Eds.). (1988). *Human abilities in cultural context.* Cambridge, England: Cambridge University Press.

James, W. (1890). *Principles of psychology.* New York: Henry Holt.

Jamieson, L. (1998). *Intimacy.* Cambridge, England, & Malden, MA: Polity Press and Blackwell Publishers.

Jandt, F. (1998). *Intercultural communication: An introduction* (2nd ed.). Thousand Oaks, CA: Sage.

Janssens, M., Brett, J., Smith, F. (1995). Confirmatory cross-cultural research: Testing the viability of a corporation-wide safety policy. *Academy of Management Journal, 38,* 364–382.

Johnson, D., & Johnson, R. (1987). *Learning together and alone: Cooperative, competitive, and individualistic learning* (2nd ed.). Englewood Cliffs, NJ: Prentice Hall.

Johnson, J., Cullen, J., Sakano, T., & Takenouchi, H. (1996). Setting the stage for trust and strategic integration in Japanese-U.S. cooperative alliances. *Journal of International Business Studies, 27,* 981–1004.

Johnson, J. D., & Tuttle, F. (1989). Problems in intercultural research. In M. Asante & W. Gudykunst (Eds.), *Handbook of international and intercultural communication* (pp. 461–483). Newbury Park, CA: Sage.

Jones, E. (1979). The rocky road from acts to dispositions. *American Psychologist, 34,* 107–117.

Jordan, C., & Tharp, R. (1979). Culture and education. In A. Marsella, R. Tharp, & T. Ciborowski (Eds.), *Perspectives on cross-cultural psychology* (pp. 265–285). New York: Academic Press.

Jordan, W. (1989). Racial attitudes. In C. Wilson & W. Ferris (Eds.), *Encyclopedia of Southern Culture* (pp. 1118–1120). Chapel Hill, NC: University of North Carolina Press.

Joshi, M., & MacLean, M. (1997). Maternal expectations of child development in India, Japan, and England. *Journal of Cross-Cultural Psychology, 28,* 219–234.

Kagan, S. (1990). The structural approach to cooperative learning. *Educational Leadership, 47*(4), 12–15.

Kagitcibasi, C. (1988). Diversity of socialization and social change. In P. Dasen, J. Berry, & N. Sartorius (Eds.), *Health and cross-cultural psychology: Toward applications* (pp. 25–47). Newbury Park, CA: Sage.

Kagitcibasi, C. (1990). Family and home based intervention.

In R. Brislin (Ed.), *Applied cross-cultural psychology* (pp. 121–141). Newbury Park, CA: Sage.

Kagitcibasi, C. (1997). Individualism and collectivism. In J. Berry, M. Segall, & C. Kagitcibasi (Eds.), *Behavior and applications: Vol. 3. Handbook of cross-cultural psychology* (2nd. ed., pp. 1–49). Boston: Allyn & Bacon.

Kagitcibasi, C., & Berry, J. (1989). Cross-cultural psychology: Current research and trends. *Annual Review of Psychology, 40,* 493–531.

Kagitcibasi, C., Sunar, D., & Bekman, S. (1989). *Preschool education project.* Ottawa, Canada: International Research Development Council Final Report.

Kahn, H. (1979). *World economic development: 1979 and beyond.* Boulder, CO: Westview.

Kahneman, D., & Tversky, A. (1972). On the psychology of prediction. *Psychological Review, 80,* 237–251.

Kahneman, D., & Tversky, A. (1984). Choices, values, and frames. *American Psychologist, 39,* 341–350.

Kaiser, R. (1984). *Russia: The people and the power.* New York: Washington Square Press.

Kakkar, S. (1970). Family conflict and scholastic achievement. *Indian Journal of Psychology, 45,* 159–164.

Kaniel, S. (1990). The influence of mediation on working memory: Differences between Ethopian immigrants and Israelis. *Psychologia: Israel Journal of Psychology, 2*(1), 57–67.

Kapur, P. (1970). *Marriage and the working women in India.* New Delhi, India: Vikas.

Karpov, Y., & Haywood, H. (1998). Two ways to elaborate Vygotsky's concept of mediation: Implications for instruction. *American Psychologist, 53,* 27–36.

Katriel, T. (1990). "Griping" as a verbal ritual in some Israeli discourse. In D. Carbaugh (Ed.), *Cultural communication and intercultural contact* (pp. 99–113). Hillsdale, NJ: Lawrence Erlbaum.

Katriel, T., & Philipsen, G. (1981). "What we need is communication": "Communication" as a cultural category in some American talk. *Communication monographs, 48,* 301–317.

Katz, D. (1960). The functional approach to the study of attitudes. *Public Opinion Quarterly, 24,* 164–204.

Katz, J. (1977). The effects of a systematic training program on the attitudes and behaviors of White people. *International Journal of Intercultural Relations, 1,* 77–89.

Katz, J., & Friedman-Lichtschein, T. (Eds.). (1985). *Japan's new world role.* Boulder, CO: Westview.

Katz, M., Marsella, A., Dube, K., Olatawura, M., et al. (1988). On the expression of psychosis in different cultures: Schizophrenia in an Indian and in a Nigerian community: A report from the World Health Organization Project on Determinants of Outcome of Severe Mental Health Disorders. *Culture, Medicine, and Psychiatry, 12,* 331–355.

Kawakami, K., Dion, K., & Dovidio, J. (1998). Racial prejudice and stereotype activation. *Personality and Social Psychology Bulletin, 24,* 407–416.

Kealey, D. (1988). *Explaining and predicting cross-cultural adjustment and effectiveness: A study of Canadian technical advisors overseas*. Hull, Quebec, Canada: Canadian International Development Agency.

Kealey, D. (1989). A study of cross-cultural effectiveness: Theoretical issues, practical applications. *International Journal of Intercultural Relations, 13*, 387–428.

Kealey, D. (1996). The challenge of international personnel selection. In D. Landis & R. Bhagat (Eds.), *Handbook of intercultural training* (2nd ed., pp. 106–123). Thousand Oaks, CA: Sage.

Kealey, D. J., & Ruben, B. D. (1983). Cross-cultural personnel selection: Criteria, issues and methods. In D. Landis & R. Brislin (Eds.), *Issues in theory and design: Vol. 1. Handbook of intercultural training* (pp. 155–175). Elmsford, NY: Pergamon.

Keller, H. (1997). Evolutionary approaches. In J. Berry, Y. Poortinga, & J. Pandey (Eds.), *Theory and method: Vol. 1. Handbook of cross-cultural psychology* (2nd. ed., pp. 171–213). Boston: Allyn & Bacon.

Kelley, P., & Kelley, V. (1985). Supporting natural helpers: A cross-cultural study. *Social Casework, 66*, 358–366.

Kenrick, D. (1987). Gender, genes, and the social environment: A biosocial interactionist perspective. In P. Shaver & C. Hendrick (Eds.), *Sex and gender (Review of Personality & Social Psychology*, Vol. 7, pp. 14–43). Newbury Park, CA: Sage.

Khaleefa, O., Erdos, G., & Ashira, I. (1996). Gender and creativity in an Afro-Arab Islamic culture: The case of Sudan. *Journal of Creative Behavior, 30*, 52–60.

Khan, A., & Cataio, J. (1984). *Men and women in biological perspective*. New York: Praeger.

Kim, K., Park, H. J., & Suzuki, N. (1990). Reward allocations in the United States, Japan, and Korea: A comparison of individualistic and collectivistic cultures. *Academy of Management Journal, 33*, 188–198.

Kim, M.-S. (1998). Conversational constraints as a tool for understanding communication styles. In T. Singelis (Ed.), *Teaching about culture, ethnicity, and diversity* (pp. 101–109). Thousand Oaks, CA: Sage.

Kim, U. (1990). Indigenous psychology: Science and applications. In R. Brislin (Ed.), *Applied cross-cultural psychology* (pp. 142–160). Newbury Park, CA: Sage.

Kim, U., & Berry, J. (Eds.).(1993). *Indigenous psychologies*. Newbury Park, CA: Sage.

Kinder, D. (1986). The continuing American dilemma: White resistance to racial change 40 years after Myrdal. *Journal of Social Issues, 42*, 151–171.

Kipnis, D. (1976). *The powerholders*. Chicago: University of Chicago Press.

Kipnis, D. (1984). The use of power in organizations and in interpersonal settings. In S. Oskamp (Ed.), *Applied social psychology annual*, (Vol. 5, pp. 179–210). Newbury Park, CA: Sage.

Kleinhesselink, R., & Rosa, E. (1991). Cognitive representation of risk perceptions: A comparison of Japan and the United States. *Journal of Cross-Cultural Psychology, 22*, 11–28.

Kleinman, A. (1982). Neurasthenia and depression: A study of somatization and culture in China. *Culture, Medicine, and Psychiatry, 6*, 117–190.

Klineberg, O., & Hull, F. (1979). *At a foreign university*. New York: Praeger.

Knappman, E. (Ed.). (1995). *American trials of the 20th century*. Detroit, MI: Visible Ink Press.

Kochman, T. (1981). *Black and White style in conflict in communication*. Chicago: University of Chicago Press.

Kochman, T. (1990). Force field in Black and White communication. In D. Carbaugh (Ed.), *Cultural communication and intercultural contact* (pp. 193–217). Hillsdale, NJ: Lawrence Erlbaum.

Kohn, M. L. (1977). *Class and conformity* (2nd ed.). Chicago: University of Chicago Press.

Konrad, A. M., & Gutek, B. A. (1986). Impact of work experiences on attitudes toward sexual harassment. *Administrative Science Quarterly, 31*, 422–438.

Krauss, R., Chen, Y., & Chawla, P. (1996). Nonverbal behavior and nonverbal communication: What do conversational hand gestures tell us? In M. Zanna (Ed)., *Advances in experimental social psychology* (Vol 29, pp. 389–450). San Diego, CA: Academic Press.

Krieger, N., & Margo, G. (1991). Women and AIDS: Introduction. *International Journal of Health Services, 21*, 127–130.

Kroeber, A. L., & Kluckhohn, C. (1952). *Culture: A critical review of concepts and definitions* (Peabody Museum Papers, Vol. 47, No. 1). Cambridge, MA: Harvard University.

Krugman, P. (1997, August 18). First: Whatever happened to the Asian miracle? *Fortune*, 26–28.

Kumar, U., & Saxena, S. (1983). Interpersonal construct system and work styles of Indian managers. In J. Deregowski, S. Dziurawiec, & R. Annis (Eds.), *Expiscations in cross-cultural psychology*. Lisse, The Netherlands: Swets & Zeitlinger.

Laboratory of Comparative Human Cognition. (1986). Contribution of cross-cultural research to educational practice. *American Psychologist, 41*(10), 1049–1058.

LaFromboise, T. (1982). *Assertion training with American Indians: Cultural/behavioral issue for trainers*. Las Cruces: New Mexico State University.

LaFromboise, T., Coleman, H., & Gerton, J. (1993). Psychological impact of biculturalism: Evidence and theory. *Psychological Bulletin, 114*, 395–412.

Lai, J., Hamid, N., & Chow, P. (1996). Gender difference in hassles and symptom reporting among Hong Kong adolescents. *Journal of Social Behavior and Personality, 11*, 149–164.

Lambert, M., Knight, F., Taylor, R., & Achenbach, R. (1996). Comparisons of behavioral and emotional problems among children of Jamaica and the United States. *Journal of Cross-Cultural Psychology, 27*, 82–97.

Lambert, W., Genesee, F., & Holobow, N. (1993). Bilingual education for majority English-speaking children. *European Journal of Psychology of Education, 8,* 3–22.

Lambert, W. E., Hamers, J. F., & Frasure-Smith, N. (1979). *Child-rearing values: A cross-national study.* New York: Praeger.

Lambert, W. E., & Tucker, G. R. (1972). *Bilingual education of children: The St. Lambert experiment.* Rowley, MA: Newbury House.

Landis, D., & Bhagat, R. (Eds.). (1996). *Handbook of intercultural training* (2nd ed.). Thousand Oaks, CA: Sage.

Landis, D., & Brislin, R. (Eds.). (1983). *Handbook of intercultural training* (3 vols.). Elmsford, NY: Pergamon.

Landis, D., Brislin, R., & Hulgus, J. (1985). Attributional training versus contact in acculturative learning: A laboratory study. *Journal of Applied Social Psychology, 15,* 466–482.

Landy, F. (1986). Stamp collecting versus science: Validation as hypothesis testing. *American Psychologist, 41,* 1183–1192.

Landy, F. (1989). *Psychology of work behavior* (4th ed.). Belmont, CA: Brooks/Cole.

Langer, T. (1962). A twenty-two item screening score of psychiatric symptoms indicating impairment. *Journal of Health and Human Behavior, 3,* 269–276.

Latane, B., Williams, K., & Harkins, S. (1979). Many hands make light the work: Causes and consequences of social loafing. *Journal of Personality and Social Psychology, 37,* 822–832.

Lebra, T. (1976). *Japanese patterns of behavior.* Honolulu, HI: University of Hawaii Press.

Lebra, T. (1995). Skipped and postponed adolescence of aristocratic women in Japan: Resurrecting the culture/nature issue. *Ethos, 23*(1), 79–102.

Lee, Y., & Larwood, L. (1983). The socialization of expatriate managers in multinational firms. *Academy of Management Journal, 26,* 657–665.

Lefley, H. (1989). Empirical support for credibility and giving in cross-cultural psychotherapy. *American Psychologist, 44,* 1163.

Lefley, H. (1990). Culture and chronic mental illness. *Hospital and Community Psychiatry, 41,* 277–286.

Leibowitz, H. W., Brislin, R., Perlmutter, L., & Hennessey, R. (1969). Ponzo perspective illusion as a manifestation of space perception. *Science, 166,* 1174–1176.

Leong, F., & Kim, H. (1991). Going beyond cultural sensitivity on the road to multiculturism: Using the Intercultural Sensitizer as a counselor training tool. *Journal of Counseling and Development, 70,* 112–118.

Leung, K., & Iwawaki, S. (1988). Cultural collectivism and distributive behavior. *Journal of Cross-Cultural Psychology, 19,* 35–49.

Leung, K., & Wu, P. G. (1990). Dispute processing: A cross-cultural analysis. In R. Brislin (Ed.), *Applied cross-cultural psychology* (pp. 209–231). Newbury Park, CA: Sage.

Levine, R. (1997). *A geography of time.* New York: Basic Books.

LeVine, R., & Campbell, D. (1972). *Ethnocentrism.* New York: Wiley.

Liebkind, K. (1996). Acculturation and stress: Vietnamese refugees in Finland. *Journal of Cross-Cultural Psychology, 27,* 161–180.

Lin, E. H. B., Carter, W., & Kleinman, A. M. (1985). An exploration of somatization among Asian refugees and immigrants in primary care. *American Journal of Public Health, 75,* 1080–1084.

Lin, K., & Kleinman, A. (1988). Psychopathology and clinical course of schizophrenia: A cross-cultural perspective. *Schizophrenia Bulletin, 14,* 555–567.

Lincoln, J. (1985). Work organization and workforce commitment: A study of plants and employees in the U.S. and Japan. *American Sociological Review, 50,* 738–760.

Lindgren, H. C., & Suter, W. N. (1985). *Educational psychology in the classroom* (7th ed.). Monterey, CA: Brooks/Cole.

Lindholm, K. (1991). Theoretical assumptions and empirical evidence for academic achievement in two languages. *Hispanic Journal of Behavioral Sciences, 13,* 3–17.

Ling, W. (1989). Pattern of leadership behavior assessment in China. *Psychologia: An International Journal of Psychology in the Orient, 32,* 129–134.

Lonner, W. (1980). The search for psychological universals. In H. Triandis & W. Lonner (Eds.), *Perspectives: Vol 1. Handbook of cross-cultural psychology* (pp. 143–204). Boston: Allyn & Bacon.

Lonner, W. (1985). Television in the developing world [Special issue]. *Journal of Cross-Cultural Psychology, 16*(3), 259–397.

Lonner, W. (1990). An overview of cross-cultural testing and assessment. In R. Brislin (Ed.), *Applied cross-cultural psychology* (pp. 56–76). Newbury Park, CA: Sage.

Lonner, W., & Berry, J. (Eds.). (1986). *Field methods in cross-cultural research.* Newbury Park: Sage.

Loscocco, K., & Kalleberg, A. (1988). Age and the meaning of work in the United States and Japan. *Social Forces, 67,* 337–356.

Low, B. (1989). Cross-cultural patterns in the training of children: An evolutionary perspective. *Journal of Comparative Psychology, 103,* 311–319.

Lummis, M., & Stevenson, H. (1990). Gender differences in beliefs and achievement: A cross-cultural study. *Developmental Psychology, 26,* 254–263.

Luo, Y., & Chen, M. (1996). Managerial implications of guanxi-based business strategies. *Journal of International Management, 2,* 293–316.

Maccoby, E. (1990). Gender and relationships: A developmental account. *American Psychologist, 45,* 513–520.

Maccoby, E. E., & Jacklin, C. N. (1974). *The psychology of sex differences.* Stanford, CA: Stanford University Press.

MacDonald, K. (1998). Evolution, culture, and the five-factor model. *Journal of Cross-Cultural Psychology, 29*, 119–149.

Mackey, W. F., & Beebe, V. N. (1977). *Bilingual schools for a bicultural community: Miami's adaption to the Cuban refugees.* Rowley, MA: Newbury House.

Magnusson, D., & Endler, N. (Eds.). (1977). *Personality at the crossroads.* New York: Wiley.

Malinowski, B. (1927). *Sex and repression in savage society.* London: Kegan Paul.

Malpass, R., & Poortinga, Y. (1986). Strategies for design and analysis. In W. Lonner & J. Berry (Eds.), *Field methods in cross-cultural research* (pp. 47–83). Newbury Park, CA: Sage.

Manheimer, D. L., Dewey, J., Mellinger, G. D., & Corsa, L. (1966). 50,000 child-years of accident injuries. *Pacific Health Reports, 81*, 519–533.

Mar'i, S., & Karayanni, M. (1983). Creativity in Arab culture: Two decades of research. *Journal of Creative Behavior, 16*, 227–238.

Marin, G., & Marin, B. V. (1991). *Research with Hispanic populations.* Beverly Hills, CA: Sage.

Markides, K., & Lee, D. (1990). Predictors of well-being and functioning in older Mexican Americans and Anglos: An eight-year follow-up. *Journal of Gerontology, 45*, S69–S73.

Markus, H., & Kitayama, S. (1991). Culture and the self: Implications for cognition, emotion, and motivation. *Psychological Review, 98*, 224–253.

Markus, H., & Kitayama, S. (1998). The cultural psychology of personality. *Journal of Cross-Cultural Psychology, 29*, 63–87.

Markus, H., & Zajonc, R. (1985). The cognitive perspective in social psychology. In G. Lindzey & E. Aronson (Eds.), *Theory and method: Vol. 1. Handbook of social psychology* (3rd ed., pp. 137–230). New York: Random House.

Marsella, A. (1980). Depressive experiences and disorder across cultures. In H. Triandis & J. Draguns (Eds.), *Psychopathology: Vol. 6. Handbook of cross-cultural psychology* (pp. 237–289). Boston: Allyn & Bacon.

Martin, J. (Ed.). (1986). Theories and methods in cross-cultural orientation [Special issue]. *International Journal of Intercultural Relations, 10*(2), 103–254.

Martin, J. (Ed.). (1989). Intercultural communication competence [Special issue]. *International Journal of Intercultural Relations, 13*(3), pp. 227–428.

Martin, J., & Harrell, T. (1996). Reentry training for intercultural sojourners. In D. Landis & R. Bhagat (Eds.), *Handbook of intercultural training* (2nd ed., pp. 307–326). Thousand Oaks, CA: Sage.

Martinez, T., & Fisher, J. (1997). Applications of an information-motivation-behavioral skills model to reducing AIDS risk behavior in Asia's developing countries. *Asian Psychologist, 1*, 24–39.

Maslach, C., & Leiter, M. (1997). *The truth about burnout.* San Francisco: Jossey-Bass.

Mayer, R., Davis, J., & Schoorman, F. (1995). An integrative model of organizational trust. *Academy of Management Review, 20*, 709–734.

Mayer, R., Sims, V., & Tajika, H. (1995). A comparison of how textbooks teach mathematical problem solving in Japan and the United States. *American Educational Research Journal, 32*, 443–460.

McAndrew, F. (1986). A cross-cultural study of recognition thresholds for facial expressions of emotion. *Journal of Cross-Cultural Psychology, 17*, 211–224.

McCafferey, J. (1995). Role plays: A powerful but difficult training tool. In S. Fowler & M. Mumford (Eds.), *Intercultural sourcebook: Cross-cultural training methodologies* (pp. 17–25). Yarmouth, ME: Intercultural Press.

McConahay, J., & Hough, J. (1976). Symbolic racism. *Journal of Social Issues, 32*(2), 23–45.

McCormick, I., & Cooper, C. (1988). Executive stress: Extending the international comparison. *Human Relations, 41*, 65–72.

McCrae, R., & Costa, P. (1997). Personality trait structure as a human universal. *American Psychologist, 52*, 509–516.

McInerney, D., Roche, L., McInerney, V., & Marsh, H. (1997). Cultural perspectives on school motivation: The relevance and application of goal theory. *American Educational Research Journal, 34*, 207–236.

Mead, M. (1928). *Coming of age in Samoa.* New York: William Morrow.

Meichenbaum, D. (1977). *Cognitive-behavior modification: An integrative approach.* New York: Plenum.

Mendenhall, M., & Oddou, G. (1985). The dimensions of expatriate acculturation. *Academy of Management Review, 10*, 39–47.

Messick, D., & Mackie, D. (1989). Intergroup relations. *Annual Review of Psychology, 40*, 45–81.

Miller, D. (Ed.). (1991). *Handbook of research design and social measurement.* Newbury Park, CA: Sage.

Miller, J. (1984). Culture and the development of everyday social explanation. *Journal of Personality and Social Psychology, 46*, 961–978.

Miller, J. (1997). Theoretical issues in cultural psychology. In J. Berry, Y. Poortinga, & J. Pandey (Eds.), *Theory and method: Vol. 1. Handbook of cross-cultural psychology* (2nd. ed., pp.85–128). Boston: Allyn & Bacon.

Miller, J., & Bersoff, D. (1995). Development in the context of everyday family relationships: Culture, interpersonal morality, and adaptation. In M. Killen & D. Hart (Eds.), *Morality in everyday life: Developmental perspectives* (pp. 259–282). New York: Cambridge University Press.

Miller, J., & Kilpatrick, J. (1987). *Issue for managers: An international perspective.* Homewood, IL: Irwin.

Miller, N., & Brewer, M. (Eds.). (1984). *Groups in contact: The psychology of desegregation.* Orlando, FL: Academic Press.

Mishra, R. (1997). Cognition and cognitive development. In

J. Berry, P. Dasen, & T. Saraswathi (Eds.), *Basic processes and human development: Vol. 2. Handbook of cross-cultural psychology* (2nd ed., pp. 143–175). Boston: Allyn & Bacon.

Misumi, J. (1985). *The behavioral science of leadership: An interdisciplinary Japanese research program*. Ann Arbor, MI: University of Michigan.

Mizokawa, D., & Rychman, D. (1990). Attributions of academic success and failure: A comparison of six Asian-American ethnic groups. *Journal of Cross-Cultural Psychology, 21,* 434–451.

Moghaddam, F., Ditto, B., & Taylor, D. (1990). Attitudes and attributions related to psychological symptomatology in Indian immigrant women. *Journal of Cross-Cultural Psychology, 21,* 335–350.

Moghaddam, F., Taylor, D., Lambert, W., & Schmidt, A. (1995). Attribution and discrimination: A study of attributions to the self, the group, and external factors among Whites, Blacks, and Cubans in Miami. *Journal of Cross-Cultural Psychology, 26,* 209–220.

Mohanty, A., & Perregaux, C. (1997). Language acquisition and bilingualism. In J. Berry, P. Dasen, & T. Saraswathi (Eds.), *Basic processes and human development: Vol. 2. Handbook of cross-cultural psychology* (2nd ed., pp. 217–253). Boston: Allyn & Bacon.

Moncher, M., Holden, G., & Trimble, J. (1990). Substance abuse among Native-American youth. *Journal of Consulting and Clinical Psychology, 58,* 408–415.

Moore, M., & Levitan, L. (1993). *For hearing people only*. Rochester, NY: Deaf Life.

Morrison, A., & Von Glinow, M. (1990). Women and minorities in management. *American Psychologist, 45,* 200–208.

Morse, S. (1983). Requirements for love and friendship in Australia and Brazil. *Australian Journal of Psychology, 35,* 469–476.

Muchinsky, P. (1996). *Psychology applied to work* (5th ed.). Pacific Grove, CA: Brooks/Cole.

Mukai, T., & McCloskey, L. (1996). Eating attitudes among Japanese and American elementary schoolgirls. *Journal of Cross-Cultural Psychology, 27,* 424–435.

Munroe, R., & Munroe, R. (1997). A comparative anthropological perspective. In J. Berry, Y. Poortinga, & J. Pandey (Eds.), *Theory and Method: Vol. 1. Handbook of cross-cultural psychology* (2nd. ed., pp. 171–213). Boston: Allyn & Bacon.

Murdock, G. P. (1981). *Atlas of world cultures*. Pittsburgh, PA: University of Pittsburgh Press.

Murphy-Berman, V., Singh, P., Pachauri, A., Berman, J., & Kumar, P. (1984). Factors affecting allocation to needy and meritorious recipients: A cross-cultural comparison. *Journal of Personality and Social Psychology, 46,* 1267–1272.

Nachmias, D., & Nachmias, C. (1987). *Research methods in the social sciences*. New York: St. Martin's Press.

Nagar, D., & Paulus, P. (1988). *Residential crowding experience scale: Assessment and validation*. Arlington, TX: University of Texas at Arlington.

Nakao, K. (1987). Analyzing sociometric preferences: An example of Japanese and U.S. business groups. *Journal of Social Behavior and Personality, 2,* 523–534.

Naroll, R. (1983). *The moral order*. Beverly Hills, CA: Sage.

Nath, R. (Ed.). (1988). *Comparative management*. Cambridge, MA: Ballinger.

Neal, A., & Turner, S. (1991). Anxiety disorders research with African Americans: Current status. *Psychological Bulletin, 109,* 400–410.

Nevill, D., & Perrotta, J. (1985). Adolescent perceptions of work and home: Australia, Portugal, and the United States. *Journal of Cross-Cultural Psychology, 16,* 483–495.

The new whiz kids. (1987, August 31). *Time Magazine, 130*(9), 42–51.

Newhill, C. (1990). The role of culture in the development of paranoid symptomatology. *American Journal of Orthopsychiatry, 60,* 176–185.

Nishimoto, R. (1988). A cross-cultural analysis of psychiatric symptom expression using Langer's twenty-two item index. *Journal of Sociology and Social Welfare, 15*(4), 45–62.

Oberg, K. (1958). *Culture shock and the problem of adjustment to new cultural environments*. Washington, DC: Department of State, Foreign Service Institute.

O'Brien, G., Fiedler, F., & Hewlett, T. (1971). The effects of programmed culture training upon the performance of volunteer medical teams in Central America. *Human Relations, 24,* 209–231.

O'Brien, G., & Plooj, D. (1977). Development of culture training manuals for medical workers with Pitjantiatjara aboriginals: The relative effects of critical incident and prose training upon knowledge, attitudes, and motivation. In G. Kearney & D. McElwain (Eds.), *Aboriginal cognition: Retrospect and prospect* (pp. 383–396). Canberra, Australia: Australian Institute of Aboriginal Studies.

O'Donnell, J., Stein, M., Machabanski, H., & Cress, J. (1982). Dimensions of behavior problems in Anglo-American and Mexican-American preschool children: A comparative study. *Journal of Consulting and Clinical Psychology, 50,* 643–651.

Offermann, L., & Gowing, M. (1990). Organizations of the future: Changes and challenges. *American Psychologist, 45,* 95–108.

O'Nell, T., & Mitchell, C. (1996). Alcohol use among American Indian adolescents: The role of culture in pathological drinking. *Social Science and Medicine, 42,* 565–578.

Ottaway, R., & Bhatnagar, D. (1988). Personality and biographical differences between male and female managers in the United States and India. *Applied Psychology: An International Review, 37,* 201–212.

Overfield, T. (1985). *Biological variation in health and illness*. Reading, MA: Addison-Wesley.

Padila, A., Lindholm, K., Chen, A., Durán, R., Hakuta, K., Cambert, W., & Tucker, G. (1991). The English-only movement: Myths, reality, and implications for psychology. *American Psychologist, 46*, 120–130.

Paguio, L. P., Skeen, P., & Robinson, B. (1987). Perceptions of the ideal child among employed and nonemployed American and Filipino mothers. *Perceptual and Motor Skills, 65*, 707–711.

Paige, M. (1990). International students: Cross-cultural psychological perspectives. In R. Brislin (Ed.), *Applied cross-cultural psychology* (pp. 161–185). Beverly Hills, CA: Sage.

Paige, R. M. (1986). *Cross-cultural orientation: New conceptualizations and applications*. Lanham, MD: University Press of America.

Palmore, E., Nowlin, J., & Wang, H. (1985). Prediction of function among the old-old: A ten-year following. *Journal of Gerontology, 40*, 244–250.

Pandey, J. (1990). The environment, culture, and behavior. In R. Brislin (Ed.), *Applied cross-cultural psychology* (pp. 254–277). Newbury Park, CA: Sage.

Paniagua, F. (1994). *Assessing and treating culturally diverse clients: A practical guide*. Thousand Oaks, CA: Sage.

Pascale, R., & Athos, A. (1981). *The art of Japanese management: Applications for American executives*. New York: Simon & Schuster.

Paulston, C. B. (1980). *Bilingual education: Theories and issues*. Rowley, MA: Newbury House.

Paunonen, S., Jackson, D., Trzebinski, J., & Forsterling, F. (1992). Personality structure across cultures: A multimethod evaluation. *Journal of Personality and Social Psychology, 62*, 447–456.

Payer, L. (1988). *Medicine and culture*. New York: Holt.

Pedersen, P. (1988). *A handbook for developing multicultural awareness*. Alexandria, VA: American Association for Counseling and Development.

Pedersen, P. (1991a). Counseling international students. *The Counseling Psychologist, 19*(1), 10–58.

Pedersen, P. (Ed.). (1991b). Multiculturalism as a fourth force in counseling [Special issue]. *Journal of Counseling and Development, 70*(1).

Pedersen, P. (1997). *Culture-centered counseling interventions: Striving for accuracy*. Thousand Oaks, CA: Sage Publications.

Peeters, R. (1986). Health and illness of Moroccan immigrants in the city of Antwerp, Belgium. *Social Science and Medicine, 22*, 679–685.

Pepitone, A. (1987). The role of culture in theories of social psychology. In C. Kagitcibasi (Ed.), *Growth and progress in cross-cultural psychology* (pp. 12–21). Lisse, The Netherlands: Swets & Zeitlinger.

Perry, C., Grant, M., Ernberg, G., Florenzano, R., et al. (1989). WHO collaborative study on alcohol education and young people: Outcome of a four-country pilot study. *International Journal of the Addictions, 24*, 1145–1171.

Peterson, M., Smith, P., Akande, A., Ayestaran, S., Bochner, S., Callan, V., Cho, N. G., Jesuino, J. C., D'Amorim, M., Francois, P. H., Hofmann, K., Koopman, P. L., Leung, K., Lim, T. K., Mortazavi, S., Munene, J., Radford, M., Ropo, A., Savage, G., Setiadi, B., Sinha, T. N., Sorenson, R., & Viedge, C. (1995). Role conflict, ambiguity, and overload: A 21-nation study. *Academy of Management Journal, 38*, 429–452.

Pettengill, S., & Rohner, R. (1985). Korean-American adolescents' perceptions of parental control, parental acceptance-rejection, and parent-adolescent conflict. In I. Reyes Lagunes & Y. Poortinga (Eds.), *From a different perspective: Studies of behavior across cultures* (pp. 241–249). Lisse, The Netherlands: Swets & Zeitlinger.

Pettigrew, T. (1997). Generalized intergroup contact effects on prejudice. *Personality and Social Psychology Bulletin, 23*, 173–185.

Pettigrew, T. (1998). Intergroup contact theory. *Annual Review of Psychology, 49*, 65–85.

Pettigrew, T., & Meertens, R. (1995). Subtle and blatant prejudice in western Europe. *European Journal of Social Psychology, 25*, 57–75.

Petty, R., & Wegener, D. (1998). Attitude change: Multiple roles for persuasion variables. In D. Gilbert, S. Fiske, & G. Lindzey (Eds.), *The handbook of social psychology* (Vol. 1, 4th ed., pp. 323–390). New York: McGraw-Hill.

Philipsen, G. (1975). Speaking "like a man" in Teamsterville: Cultural patterns of role enactment in an urban neighborhood. *Quarterly Journal of Speech, 62*, 15–25.

Philipsen, G. (1990a). Reflections on "communication" as a cultural category of some American speech. In D. Carbaugh (Ed.), *Cultural communication and intercultural contact* (pp. 95–97). Hillsdale, NJ: Lawrence Erlbaum.

Philipsen, G. (1990b). Reflections on speaking "like a man" in Teamsterville. In D. Carbaugh (Ed.), *Cultural communication and intercultural contact* (pp. 21–26). Hillsdale, NJ: Lawrence Erlbaum.

Phillips, H. (1960). Problems of meaning and translation in field work. *Human Organization, 18*, 184–192.

Piaget, J. (1966). Necessite et signification des recherches comparatives en psychologie genetique. *Journal International de Psychologie, 1*, 3–13. Need and significance of cross-cultural studies in genetic psychology (C. Dasen, Trans.). In J. W. Berry & P. R. Dasen (Eds.), 1974, *Culture and cognition* (pp. 299–309). London: Methuen.

Piaget, J. (1970). Piaget's theory. In P. H. Mussen (Ed.), *Carmichael's manual of child psychology* (Vol. 1, 3rd ed., pp. 703–732). New York: John Wiley.

Piedmont, R., & Chae, J. H. (1997). Cross-cultural generalizability of the five-factor model of personality: Development and validation of the NEO-PI-R for Koreans. *Journal of Cross-Cultural Psychology, 28*, 131–155.

Pines, A. (1994). The Palestinian Intifada and Israelis'

burnout. *Journal of Cross-Cultural Psychology, 25,* 438–451.

Pittam, J., Gallois, C., Iwawaki, S., & Krooneberg, P. (1995). Australian and Japanese concepts of expressive behavior. *Journal of Cross-Cultural Psychology, 26,* 451–473.

Ponterotto, J., & Benesch, K. (1988). An organizational framework for understanding the role of culture in counseling. *Journal of Counseling & Development, 66,* 237–241.

Ponterotto, J., Casas, J., Suzuki, L., Alexander, C. (Eds.). (1995). *Handbook of multicultural counseling.* Thousand Oaks, CA: Sage.

Poortinga, Y. (1997). Towards convergence? In J. Berry, Y. Poortinga, & J. Pandey (Eds.), *Theory and method: Vol. 1. Handbook of cross-cultural psychology* (2nd ed., pp. 347–387). Boston: Allyn & Bacon.

Poortinga, Y., & Malpass, R. (1986). Making inferences from cross-cultural data. In W. Lonner & J. Berry (Eds.), *Field methods in cross-cultural research* (pp. 17–46). Newbury Park, CA: Sage.

Prasse, D., & McBride, J. (1991, August). *The Milwaukee Project: Follow-up through high school.* Paper presented at the Annual Meeting of the American Psychological Association, San Francisco, CA.

Pratto, F., Stallworth, L., Sidanius, J., & Siers, B. (1997). The gender gap in occupational role attainment: A social dominance approach. *Journal of Personality and Social Psychology, 72,* 37–53.

Price-Williams, D. R., Gordon, W., & Ramirez, M. (1969). Skill and conservation. *Developmental Psychology, 1,* 769.

Prince, V. (1985). Sex, gender, and semantics. *Journal of Sex Research, 21,* 92–96.

Quah, S. (1985). The health, belief model and preventive health behavior in Singapore. *Social Science and Medicine, 21,* 351–363.

Qureshi, B. (1989). *Transcultural medicine: Dealing with patients from different cultures.* Dordrecht, The Netherlands: Kluwer Academic Publishers.

Ramsey, S., & Birk, J. (1983). Preparation of North Americans for interaction with Japanese: Considerations of language and communication style. In D. Landis & R. Brislin (Eds.), *Area studies in intercultural training: Vol. 3. Handbook of intercultural training* (pp. 227–259). Elmsford, NY: Pergamon.

Randolph, G., Landis, D., & Tseng, O. (1977). The effects of time and practice upon culture assimilator training. *International Journal of Intercultural Relations, 1*(4), 105–119.

Reed, D., McGee, D., Cohen, J., Yano, K., Syme, S., & Feinlab, M. (1982). Acculturation and coronary heart disease among Japanese men in Hawaii. *American Journal of Epidemiology, 115*(6), 894–905.

Reed, S. (1993). *Making sense of Japan.* Pittsburgh, PA: University of Pittsburgh Press.

Reeves, T. (1998, August 3). Harsh lives take heavy toll on Native Americans' health. *The Seattle Times,* p. A2.

Reitsperger, W., & Daniel, S. (1990). Japan vs. Silicon Valley: Quality-cost trade-off philosophies. *Journal of International Business Studies, 21,* 289–300.

Return to paradise. (1987). In BBC (producers) *New Pacific Series.* (Available from Films Incorporated, Chicago, IL.)

Rigby, J. M. (1987). The challenge of multinational team development [Special issue: Multicultural management development]. *Journal of Management Development, 6,* 65–72.

Riordan, C. (1978). Equal-status interracial contact: A review and revision of the concept. *International Journal of Intercultural Relations, 2,* 161–185.

Ritter, P. L., & Dornbusch, S. M. (1989, March). *Ethnic variation in family influences on academic achievement.* Paper presented at the American Educational Research Association Meetings, San Francisco.

Robbins, S. (1998). *Organizational behavior* (8th ed.). Upper Saddle River, NJ: Prentice Hall.

Roberts, K. (1970). On looking at an elephant: An evaluation of cross-cultural research related to organizations. *Psychological Bulletin, 74,* 327–350.

Robinson, W. (1950). Ecological correlations and the behavior of individuals. *American Sociological Review, 15,* 351–357.

Rogers, E. (1989). Inquiry in development communication. In M. Asante & W. Gudykunst (Eds.), *Handbook of international and intercultural communication* (pp. 67–86). Newbury Park, CA: Sage.

Rogers, E., & Steinfatt, T. (1999). *Intercultural communication.* Prospect Heights, IL: Waveland Press.

Rogoff, B. (1981). Schooling and the development of cognitive skills. In H. C. Triandis & A. Heron (Eds.), *Developmental psychology: Vol. 4. Handbook of cross-cultural psychology* (pp. 233–294). Boston: Allyn & Bacon.

Rogoff, B. (1990). *Apprenticeship in thinking: Cognitive development in social context.* New York: Oxford University Press.

Rogoff, B., & Chavajay, P. (1995). What's become of research on the cultural basis of cognitive development? *American Psychologist, 50,* 859–877.

Rohner, R. (1986). *The warmth dimension.* Newbury Park, CA: Sage.

Rohner, R., & Pettengill, S. (1985). Perceived parental acceptance-rejection and parental control among Korean adolescents. *Child Development, 56,* 524–528.

Romano, D. (1997). *Intercultural marriage* (2nd ed.). Yarmouth, ME: Intercultural Press.

Rossi, A., & Todd-Mancillas, W. (1987). Machismo as a factor affecting the use of power and communication in the managing of personnel disputes: Brazilian versus American male managers. *Journal of Social Behavior and Personality, 2*(1), 93–104.

Rothbaum, F., & Xu, X. (1995). The theme of giving back

to parents in Chinese and American songs. *Journal of Cross-Cultural Psychology, 26*, 698–713.

Russell, P., Deregowski, J., & Kinnear, P. (1997). Perception and aesthetics. In J. Berry, P. Dasen, & T. Saraswathi (Eds.), *Basic processes and human development: Vol. 2. Handbook of cross-cultural psychology* (2nd ed., pp. 107–142). Boston: Allyn & Bacon.

Saal, F., & Knight, P. (1988). *Industrial/Organizational Psychology: Science and Practice*. Pacific Grove, CA: Brooks/Cole.

Sakamoto, N., & Naotsuka, R. (1982). *Polite fictions: Why Japanese and Americans seem rude to each other*. Tokyo: Kinseido.

Salgado, J. (1997). The five factor model of personality and job performance in the European community. *Journal of Applied Psychology, 82*, 30–43.

Salovey, P., Rothman, A., & Rodin, J. (1998). Health behavior. In D. Gilbert, S. Fiske, & G. Lindzey (Eds.), *The handbook of social psychology* (Vol. 2, 4th ed., pp. 633–683). New York: McGraw-Hill.

Sanua, V. (1980). Familial and sociocultural antecedents of psychopathology. In H. Triandis & J. Draguns (Eds.), *Psychopathology: Vol. 6. Handbook of cross-cultural psychology* (pp. 175–236). Boston: Allyn & Bacon.

Saraswathi, T., & Dutta, R. (1988). Current trends in developmental psychology: A life-span perspective. In J. Pandey (Ed.), *Personality & mental processes: Vol. 1. Psychology in India: The-state-of-the-art* (pp. 93–152). New Delhi, India: Sage.

Scarberry, N., Ratcliff, C., Lord, C., Lanicek, D., & Desforges, D. (1997). Effects of individuating information on the generalization part of Allport's contact hypothesis. *Personality and Social Psychology Bulletin, 23*, 1291–1299.

Schaufeli, W., & Janczur, B. (1994). Burnout among nurses: A Polish-Dutch comparison. *Journal of Cross-Cultural Psychology, 25*, 95–113.

Schlegel, A. (1995a). A cross-cultural approach to adolescence. *Ethos, 23*(1), 15–32.

Schlegel, A. (1995b). Introduction: Special issue on adolescence. *Ethos, 23*(1), 3–14.

Schneider, D. (1991). Social cognition. *Annual Review of Psychology, 42*, 527–561.

Schoonhals, M. (1994). Encouraging talk in Chinese classrooms. *Anthropology and Education Quarterly, 25*, 399–412.

Schutte, J., Valerio, J., & Carrillo, V. (1996) Optimism and socioeconomic status: A cross-cultural study. *Social Behavior and Personality, 24*, 9–18.

Schwartz, S. (1992). Universals in the content and structure of values: Theoretical advances and empirical tests in 20 countries. In M. Zanna (Ed.), *Advances in experimental social psychology* (Vol. 25, pp. 1–65). San Diego: Academic Press.

Schwartz, S., & Sagiv, L. (1995). Identifying culture-specifics in the content and structure of values. *Journal of Cross-Cultural Psychology, 26*, 92–116.

Scribner, S., & Cole, M. (1981). *The psychology of literacy*. Cambridge, MA: Harvard University Press.

Sears, D., & Funk, C. (1991). The role of self-interest in social and political attitudes. In M. Zanna (Ed.), *Advances in experimental social psychology* (Vol. 24, pp. 1–91). San Diego: Academic Press.

Segall, M., Campbell, D., & Herskovits, M. (1966). *The influence of culture on visual perception*. Indianapolis, IN: Bobbs-Merrill.

Segall, M., Dasen, P., Berry, J., & Poortinga, Y. (1990). *Human behavior in global perspective*. Elmsford, NY: Pergamon.

Segall, M., Lonner, W., & Berry, J. (1998). Cross-cultural psychology as a scholarly discipline: On the flowering of culture in behavioral research. *American Psychologist, 53*, 1101–1110.

Seligman, M. (1989). Research in clinical psychology: Why is there so much depression today? In I. Cohen (Ed.), *The G. Stanley Hall Lecture Series* (Vol. 9). Washington, DC: American Psychological Association.

Seligman, M. (1998). *Learned optimism*. New York: Pocket Books.

Serpell, R. (1982). Measures of perception, skills, and intelligence: The growth of a new perspective on children in a Third World country. In W. Hartrup (Ed.), *Review of child development research* (Vol. 6). Chicago: University of Chicago Press.

Serpell, R., & Hatano, G. (1997). Education, schooling, and literacy. In J. Berry, P. Dasen, & T. Saraswathi (Eds.), *Basic processes and human development: Vol. 2. Handbook of cross-cultural psychology* (2nd ed., pp. 339–376). Boston: Allyn & Bacon.

Sherif, M. (1966). *In common predicament: Social psychology of intergroup conflict and cooperation*. New York: Houghton Mifflin.

Sherman, S., Judd, C., & Park, B. (1989). Social cognition. *Annual Review of Psychology, 40*, 281–326.

Shintani, T., & Devenot, C. (1998). *Hawaii diet cookbook*. Honolulu, HI: Halpax.

Shintani, T., Hughes, C., Beckham, S., & O'Connor, H. (1991). Obesity and cardiovascular risk intervention through the ad libitum feeding of traditional Hawaiian diet. *American Journal of Clinical Nutrition, 53*, 1647S–1651S.

Shweder, R. (1991). *Thinking through cultures: Expeditions in cultural psychology*. Cambridge, MA: Harvard University Press.

Shweder, R., & Bourn, E. (1984). Does the concept of the person vary cross-culturally? In R. Schweder & R. Levine (Eds.), *Culture theory* (pp. 158–199). New York: Cambridge University Press.

Si, G., Rethorst, S., & Willimczik, K. (1995). Causal attribution perception in sports achievement: A cross-cultural study on attributional concepts in Germany and China. *Journal of Cross-Cultural Psychology, 26,* 537–553.

Sidanius, J., Pratto, F., & Bobo, L. (1996). Racism, conservatism, affirmative action, and intellectual sophistication: A matter of principled conservatism or group dominance? *Journal of Personality and Social Psychology, 70,* 476–490.

Siegert, R., & Chung, R. (1995). Dimensions of distress: A cross-cultural factor replication. *Journal of Cross-Cultural Psychology, 26,* 169–175.

Singelis, T. (Ed.). (1998). *Teaching about culture, ethnicity, and diversity: Exercises and planned activities.* Thousand Oaks, CA: Sage.

Singelis, T., & Pedersen, P. (1997). Conflict and mediation across cultures. In K. Cushner & R. Brislin (Eds.), *Improving intercultural interactions: Modules for cross-cultural training programs* (Vol. 2, pp. 205–220). Thousand Oaks, CA: Sage.

Singleton, W., Spurgeon, P., & Stammers, R. (Eds.). (1980). *The analysis of social skills.* New York: Plenum.

Sinha, D. (1983). Cross-cultural psychology: A view from the Third World. In J. B. Deregowski, S. Dziurawiec, & R. C. Annis (Eds.), *Expisications in cross-cultural psychology* (pp. 3–17). Lisse, The Netherlands: Swets and Zeitlinger.

Sinha, D. (1988). The family scenario in a developing country and its implications for mental health: The case of India. In P. Dasen, J. Berry, & N. Sartorius (Eds.), *Health and cross-cultural psychology: Toward applications* (pp. 48–70). Newbury Park, CA: Sage.

Sinha, D. (1989). Personal communication, Honolulu, Hawaii.

Sinha, D. (1990). Interventions for development out of poverty. In R. Brislin (Ed.), *Applied cross-cultural psychology* (pp. 77–97). Newbury Park, CA: Sage.

Sinha, D. (1997). Indigenizing psychology. Theoretical issues in cultural psychology. In J. Berry, Y. Poortinga, & J. Pandey (Eds.), *Theory and method: Vol. 1. Handbook of cross-cultural psychology* (2nd ed., pp.129–169). Boston: Allyn & Bacon.

Sinha, J. (1980). *The nurturant task leader.* New Delhi: Sage.

Siple, L. (1994). Cultural patterns of Deaf people. *International Journal of Intercultural Relations, 18,* 345–367.

Slovic, P., Fischhoff, B., & Lichtenstein, S. (1985). Characterizing perceived risk. In R. Kates, C. Hohenemser, & R. Kasperson (Eds.), *Perilous progress: Managing the hazards of technology* (pp. 91–125). Boulder, CO: Westview.

Smart, R. (1989). Is the postwar drinking binge ending? Cross-national trends in per capita alcohol consumption. *British Journal of Addiction, 84,* 743–748.

Smith, E. (1998). Mental representation and memory. In D. Gilbert, S. Fiske, & G. Lindzey (Eds.), *The handbook of social psychology* (Vol. 1, 4th ed., pp. 391–445). New York: McGraw-Hill.

Smith, H. (1988). *The power game: How Washington works.* New York: Random House.

Smith, K. (1998). Applying Berry and Kim's acculturative framework to documentaries on culture contact. In T. Singelis (Ed.), *Teaching about culture, ethnicity, and diversity* (pp. 81–91). Thousand Oaks, CA: Sage.

Smith, P., Dugan, S., & Trompenaars, F. (1996). National culture and the values of organizational employees: A dimensional analysis across 43 nations. *Journal of Cross-Cultural Psychology, 27,* 231–264.

Snell, W., Miller, R., & Belk, S. (1988). Development of the emotional self-disclosure scale. *Sex Roles, 18,* 59–73.

Snell, W., Miller, R., Belk, S., & Garcia-Falconi, R., et al. (1989). Men's and women's emotional disclosures: The impact of disclosure recipient, culture, and the masculine role. *Sex Roles, 21,* 467–486.

Sogon, S., & Izard, C. (1987). Sex differences in emotion recognition by observing body movements: A case of American students. *Japanese Psychological Research, 29,* 89–93.

Solomon, S., Greenberg, J., & Pyszczynski, T. (1991). A terror management theory of social behavior: The psychological functions of self-esteem and cultural worldviews. In M. Zanna (Ed.), *Advances in experimental social psychology* (pp. 93–159). San Diego: Academic Press.

Spencer-Oatey, H. (1997). Unequal relationships in high and low power distance societies: A comparative study of tutor-student role relations in Britain and China. *Journal of Cross-Cultural Psychology, 28,* 284–302.

Spiro, M., & Swartz, L. (1994). Mothers' reports of behaviour problems in three groups of South African preschool children: Prevalence, perceptions, and management strategies. *Journal of Cross-Cultural Psychology, 25,* 339–352.

Spitzberg, B. (1989). Issues in the development of a theory of interpersonal competence in the intercultural context. *International Journal of Intercultural Relations, 13,* 241–268.

Spodek, B., & Saracho, O. (1996). Culture and the early childhood curriculum. *Early Childhood Development and Care. 123,* 1–14.

Sproull, L., Zubrow, D., & Kiesler, S. (1986). Cultural socialization to computing in college. *Computers in Human Behavior, 2,* 257–275.

Stanislaw, H. (1991). Why aren't we all Darwinians? *American Psychologist, 46,* 248.

Steel, R., & Rentsch, J. (1997). The dispositional model of job attitudes revisited: Findings of a 10-year study. *Journal of Applied Psychology, 82,* 873–879.

Stenlund, K. (1995). Teacher perceptions across cultures: The impact of students on teacher enthusiasm and discouragement in a cross-cultural context. *American Journal of Educational Research, 41,* 145–161.

Stephan, W. (1985). Intergroup relations. In G. Lindzey & E. Aronson (Eds.), *The handbook of social psychology* (Vol. 2, pp. 599–658). New York: Random House.

Stephan, W., & Stephan, C. W. (1984). The role of ignorance in intergroup relations. In N. Miller & M. B. Brewer (Eds.), *Groups in contact: The psychology of desegregation* (pp. 229–255). Orlando, FL: Academic Press.

Stephan, W., Ybarra, O., Martinez, C., Schwartzwald, J., & Tur-Kaspa, M. (1998). Prejudice toward immigrants to Spain and Israel: An integrated threat theory analysis. *Journal of Cross-Cultural Psychology, 29,* 559–576.

Stevenson, H., Azuma, H., & Hakuta, K. (Eds.). (1986). *Child development and education in Japan.* New York: Freedman.

Stevenson, H., Chen, C., & Lee, S.-Y. (1993). Mathematics achievement of Chinese, Japanese, and American children: Ten years later. *Science, 259,* 53–58.

Stewart, E. (1995). Contrast-culture training. In Fowler, S., & Mumford, M. (Eds.), *Intercultural sourcebook: Cross-cultural training methods* (Vol. 1, pp. 47–57). Yarmouth, ME: Intercultural Press.

Stiles, D., Gibbons, J., & de la Garza-Schnellmann, J. (1990). Opposite sex ideal in the U.S.A. and Mexico as perceived by young adolescents. *Journal of Cross-Cultural Psychology, 21,* 180–199.

Stockard, J., & Johnson, M. (1979). The social origins of male dominance. *Sex Roles, 5,* 199–218.

Sturt, E. S., Kumakura, N., & Der, G. (1984). How depressing life is: Lifelong risk of depression in the general population. *Journal of Affective Disorders, 7,* 109–22.

Sue, S. (1988). Psychotherapeutic services for ethnic minorities: Two decades of research findings. *American Psychologist, 43,* 301–308.

Sue, S., & Okazaki, S. (1990). Asian-American educational achievements: A phenomenon in search of an explanation. *American Psychologist, 45,* 913–920.

Sue, S., & Zane, N. (1987). The role of culture and cultural techniques in psychotherapy: A critique and reformulation. *American Psychologist, 42,* 37–45.

Sue, S., Zane, N., & Ito, J. (1979). Alcohol drinking patterns among Asian and Caucasian Americans. *Journal of Cross-Cultural Psychology, 10,* 41–56.

Sullivan, J., Suzuki, T., & Kondo, Y. (1986). Managerial perceptions of performance: A comparison of Japanese American work groups. *Journal of Cross-Cultural Psychology, 17,* 379–398.

Super, C., & Harkness, S. (1986). The developmental niche: A conceptualization at the interface of society and the individual. *International Journal of Behavioral Development, 9*(4), 545–570.

Super, C., & Harkness, S. (1997). The cultural structuring of child development. In J. Berry, P. Dasen, & T. Saraswathi (Eds.), *Basic processes and human development: Vol. 2. Handbook of cross-cultural psychology* (2nd ed., pp. 1–39). Boston: Allyn & Bacon.

Sutton-Smith, B., & Roberts, J. (1981). Play, toys, games, and sports. In H. Triandis & A. Heron (Eds.), *Handbook of cross-cultural psychology, Vol. 4: Developmental psychology* (pp. 425–471). Boston: Allyn & Bacon.

Symons, D. (1979). *The evolution of human sexuality.* New York: Oxford University Press.

Talbot, L. (1972). Ecological consequences of rangeland development in Masailand, East Africa. In M. Farvar & J. Milton (Eds.), *The careless technology: Ecology and international development* (pp. 694–711). Garden City, NY: Natural History Press.

Tanaka-Matsumi, J., & Draguns, J. (1997). Culture and psychopathology. In J. Berry, M. Segall, & C. Kagitcibasi (Eds.), *Behavior and applications: Vol. 3. Handbook of cross-cultural psychology* (2nd. ed., pp. 449–491). Boston: Allyn & Bacon.

Taylor, D., Dube, L., & Bellerose, J. (1986). Intergroup contact in Quebec. In M. Hewstone & R. Brown (Eds.), *Contact and conflict in intergroup encounters* (pp. 107–118). Oxford, England, & New York: Basil Blackwell.

Taylor, S. (1991). *Health psychology* (2nd ed.). New York: McGraw-Hill.

Taylor, S., Repette, R., & Seeman, T. (1997). Health psychology: What is an unhealthy environment and how does it get under the skin? *Annual Review of Psychology, 48,* 411–447.

Teahan, J. (1987). Alcohol expectancies, values, and drinking of Irish and U.S. collegians. *International Journal of the Addictions, 22,* 621–638.

Thacore, V. (1973). *Mental illness in an urban community.* Allahabad, India: United Publishers.

Thase, M., Frank, E., & Kupfer, D. (1985). Biological processes in major depression. In E. Beckman & W. Leber (Eds.), *Handbook of depression: Treatment, assessment, and research* (pp. 816–913). Homewood, IL: Dorsey Press.

Thurow, L. M. (1987). A surge in inequality. *Scientific American, 256*(3), 30–37.

Thurow, L. (1996). *The future of capitalism.* New York: William Morrow.

Tobin, J., Wu, D., & Davidson, D. (1989a, April). How three key countries shape their children. *World Monitor,* pp. 36–45.

Tobin, J., Wu, D., & Davidson, D. (1989b). *Preschool in three cultures: Japan, China, & the United States.* New Haven: Yale University Press.

Torbiorn, I. (1988). Culture barriers as a social psychological construct: An empirical validation. In Y. Kim & W. Gudykunst (Eds.), *Cross-cultural adaption: Current approaches* (pp. 168–190). Newbury Park, CA: Sage.

Torrey, E. (1986). *Witchdoctors and psychiatrists: The common roots of psychotherapy and its future.* New York: Harper & Row.

Toupin, E., & Son, L. (1991). Preliminary findings on Asian Americans: The "model minority" in a small private East Coast college. *Journal of Cross-Cultural Psychology, 22,* 403–417.

Tran, T. (1990). Language acculturation among older Vietnamese refugee adults. *Gerontologist, 30*, 94–99.

Triandis, H. (1972). *The analysis of subjective culture.* New York: Wiley.

Triandis, H. (1977). *Interpersonal behavior.* Monterey, CA: Brooks/Cole.

Triandis, H. (1989). The self and social behavior in differing cultural contexts. *Psychological Review, 96*, 506–520.

Triandis, H. (1990). Theoretical concepts that are applicable to the analysis of ethnocentrism. In R. Brislin (Ed.), *Applied cross-cultural psychology* (pp. 34–55). Newbury Park, CA: Sage.

Triandis, H. (1995). *Individualism & collectivism.* Boulder, CO: Westview.

Triandis, H., & Berry, J. (Eds.). (1980). *Methodology: Vol. 2. Handbook of cross-cultural psychology.* Boston: Allyn & Bacon.

Triandis, H., Brislin, R., & Hui, C. H. (1988). Cross-cultural training across the individualism-collectivism divide. *International Journal of Intercultural Relations, 12*, 269–289.

Triandis, H., & Davis, E. (1965). Race and belief as determinants of behavioral intentions. *Journal of Personality and Social Psychology, 2*, 715–725.

Triandis, H., Kurowski, L., & Gelfand, M. (1994). Workplace diversity. In H. Triandis, M. Dunnette, & L. Hough (Eds.), *Handbook of industrial and organizational psychology* (Vol. 4, 2nd ed., pp. 769–827). Palo Alto, CA: Consulting Psychologists Press.

Triandis, H., Kurowski, L., Tecktiel, A., & Chan, D. (1993). Extracting the emics of cultural diversity. *International Journal of Intercultural Relations, 17*, 217–234.

Triandis, H., Lambert, W., Berry, J., Lonner, W., Heron, A., Brislin, R., & Draguns, J. (Eds.). (1980). *Handbook of cross-cultural psychology* (6 vol.). Boston: Allyn & Bacon.

Trifonovitch, G. (1977). On cross-cultural orientation techniques. In R. Brislin (Ed.), *Culture learning: Concepts, applications, and research* (pp. 213–222). Honolulu, HI: University Press of Hawaii.

Tsai, H.-Y. (1995). Sojourner adjustment: The case of foreigners in Japan. *Journal of Cross-Cultural Psychology, 26*, 523–526.

Tsang, E. (1998). Can Guanxi be a source of sustained competitive advantage for doing business in China? *Academy of Management Executive, 12*(2), 64–73.

Tseng, W., & Hsu, J. (1980). Minor psychological disturbances of everyday life. In H. C. Triandis & J. Draguns (Eds.), *Psychopathology: Vol 6. Handbook of cross-cultural psychology* (pp. 61–97). Boston: Allyn & Bacon.

Tu, Weiming. (1989). *The way, learning, and politics: Essays on the Confucian intellectual.* Singapore: Institute of East Asian Philosophies.

Tulananda, O., & Young, D. (1994). Thai and American fathers' involvement with preschool-age children. *Early Child Development and Care, 97*, 123–133.

Tung, R. (1984). *Business negotiations with the Japanese.* Lexington, MA: Lexington Books.

Tung, R., & Miller, E. (1990). Managing in the twenty-first century: The need for global orientation. *Management International Review, 30*, 5–18.

Turner, F. (1990). Social work practice theory: A transcultural resource for health care. *Social Science and Medicine, 31*, 13–17.

Unger, R. (1979). *Female and male: Psychological perspectives.* New York: Harper & Row.

Valsiner, J., & Lawrence, J. (1997). Human development in culture across the life span. In J. Berry, P. Dasen, & T. Saraswathi (Eds.), *Basic processes and human development: Vol. 2. Handbook of cross-cultural psychology* (2nd ed., pp. 69–106). Boston: Allyn & Bacon.

van de Vijver, F., & Leung, K. (1997). Methods and data analysis of comparative research. In J. Berry, Y. Poortinga, & J. Pandey (Eds.), *Theory and method: Vol. 1. Handbook of cross-cultural psychology* (2nd. ed., pp. 257–300). Boston: Allyn & Bacon.

Veilleux, F., & Tougas, F. (1989). Male acceptance of affirmative action programs for women: The results of altruistic or egotistical motives. *International Journal of Psychology, 24*, 485–496.

Vernon-Feagans, L. (1996). *Children's talk in communities and classrooms.* Cambridge, MA: Blackwell.

Vitz, P. (1990). The use of stories in moral development: New psychological reasons for an old education method. *American Psychologist, 45*, 709–720.

Vogt, L., Jordan, C., & Tharp, R. (1987). Explaining school failure, producing school success: Two cases. *Anthropology and Education Quarterly, 18*, 276–286.

Vrij, A., & Winkel, F. (1994). Perceptual distortions in cross-cultural interrogations: The impact of skin color, accent, speech style, and spoken fluency on impression formation. *Journal of Cross-Cultural Psychology, 25*, 284–295.

Vygotsky, L. (1987). Thinking and speech. In R. Bieber & A. Carton (Eds.), *The Collected Works of L. S. Vygotsky.* (N. Minick, Trans.). New York: Plenum.

Wade, P., & Bernstein, B. (1991). Culture sensitivity training and counselor's race: Effects on Black female clients. *Journal of Counseling Psychology, 38*, 9–15.

Wagner, D. (1977). Ontogeny of the Ponzo illusion: Effects of age, schooling, and environment. *International Journal of Psychology, 12*, 161–176.

Wagner, D. (1988). "Appropriate education" and literacy in the Third World. In P. Dasen, J. Berry, & N. Santorious (Eds.), *Health and cross-cultural psychology: Towards applications* (pp. 93–111). Newbury Park, CA: Sage.

Walster, E., Aronson, V., Abrahams, D., & Rottmann, L. (1966). Importance of physical attractiveness in dating behavior. *Journal of Personality and Social Psychology, 4*, 508–516.

Ward, C. (1996). Acculturation. In D. Landis & R. Bhagat (Eds.), *Handbook of intercultural training* (2nd ed., pp. 124–147). Thousand Oaks, CA: Sage.

Ward, C., & Kennedy, A. (1993). Where's the "culture" in cross-cultural transition? Comparative studies of sojourner adjustment. *Journal of Cross-Cultural Psychology, 24,* 221–249.

Ward, M. C. (1971). *Them children: A study in language learning.* New York: Holt, Rinehart and Winston.

Warner, M. G. (1990, January 29). Hired guns for Hungary. *Newsweek, 115,* 48.

Warner, R., Lee, G., & Lee, J. (1986). Social organization, spousal resources, and marital power: A cross-cultural study. *Journal of Marriage and the Family, 48,* 121–128.

Watkins, D., Akande, A., Cheng, C., & Regmi, M. (1996). Culture and gender differences in the self-esteem of college students: A four-country comparison. *Social Behavior and Personality, 24,* 321–328.

Watkins, D., & Regmi, D. (1996). Toward the cross-cultural validation of a Western model of student approaches to learning. *Journal of Cross-Cultural Psychology, 27,* 547–560.

Weisfeld, C., Weisfeld, G., & Callaghan, J. (1982). Female inhibition in mixed-sex competition among young adolescents. *Ethology and Sociobiology, 3,* 29–42.

Weiss, B., & Parish, B. (1989). Culturally appropriate crisis counseling: Adapting an American method for use with Indochinese refugees. *Social Work, 34,* 252–254.

Weldon, D., Carlston, D., Rissman, A., Slobodin, L., & Triandis, H. (1975). A laboratory test of the effects of culture assimilator training. *Journal of Personality and Social Psychology, 32,* 300–310.

Werner, C., Brown, B., & Altman, I. (1997). Environmental psychology. In J. Berry, M. Segall, & C. Kagitcibasi (Eds.), *Behavior and applications: Vol. 3. Handbook of cross-cultural psychology* (2nd. ed., pp. 255–290). Boston: Allyn & Bacon.

Westermeyer, J. (1987). Cultural factors in clinical assessment. *Journal of Consulting and Clinical Psychology, 55,* 471–478.

Whiting, D. B. (1980). Culture and social behavior: A model for the development of social behavior, *Ethos, 8,* 95–116.

Whiting, R. (1989). *You gotta have wa.* New York: Macmillan.

Williams, J. (1987). *Eyes on the prize.* New York: Penguin.

Williams, J., & Best, D. (1982). *Measuring sex stereotypes: A thirty-nation study.* Beverly Hills, CA: Sage.

Williams, J., & Best, D. (1990a). *Measuring sex stereotypes: A multination study* (Rev. ed.). Newbury Park, CA: Sage.

Williams, J., & Best, D. (1990b). *Sex and psyche: Gender and self viewed cross-culturally.* Newbury Park, CA: Sage.

Wilson, E. (1998). *Consilience: The unity of knowledge.* New York: Knopf.

Wing, J., & Bebbington, P. (1985). Epidemiology of depression. In E. Beckman & W. Leber (Eds.), *Handbook of depression: Treatment, assessment, and research* (pp. 765–794). Homewood, IL: Dorsey Press.

Winikoff, B., & Laukaran, V. (1989). Breastfeeding and bottle feeding controversies in the developing world: Evidence from a study in four countries. *Social Science and Medicine, 29,* 859–868.

Witkin, H. (1967). A cognitive-style approach to cross-cultural research. *International Journal of Psychology, 2,* 233–250.

Witkin, H., Dyk, R. B., Faterson, H. F., Goodenough, D. R., & Karp, S. A. (1962). *Psychological differentiation.* New York: John Wiley.

Wober, M. (1974). Towards an understanding of the Kiganda concept of intelligence. In J. Berry & P. Dasen (Eds.), *Culture and cognition.* London: Methuen.

World Health Organization. (1979). *Schizophrenia: An international follow-up study.* New York: John Wiley.

World Health Organization. (1983). *Depressive disorders in different cultures: Report of the WHO collaborative study of standardized assessment of depressive disorders.* Geneva, Switzerland: Author.

World Health Organization. (1987). *World health statistics annual.* Geneva, Switzerland: Author.

Wright, S., Taylor, D., & Ruggiero, K. (1996). Examining the potential for academic achievement among Inuit children: Comparison of the Raven Coloured Progressive Matrices. *Journal of Cross-Cultural Psychology, 27,* 733–753.

Yamaguchi, S., Kuhlman, D., & Sugimori, S. (1995). Personality correlates of allocentric tendencies in individualist and collectivist cultures. *Journal of Cross-Cultural Psychology, 26,* 658–672.

Yan, W., & Gaier, E. (1994). Causal attributions for college success and failure: An Asian-American comparison. *Journal of Cross-Cultural Psychology, 25,* 146–158.

Yando, R., Seitz, V., & Zigler, E. (1979). *Intellectual and personality characteristics of children: Social-class and ethnic-group differences.* Hillsdale, NJ: Lawrence Erlbaum.

Yang, K. S. (1988). Will societal modernization eventually eliminate cross-cultural psychological differences? In M. Bond (Ed.), *The cross-cultural challenge to social psychology* (pp. 67–85). Newbury Park, CA: Sage.

Yao, F. K. (1990). The prevention of AIDS among African youths: Cultural constraints. *Hygie, 9*(4), 18–21.

Ying, Y.-W., & Liese, L. (1994). Initial adjustment of Taiwanese students to the United States: The impact of postarrival variables. *Journal of Cross-Cultural Psychology, 25,* 466–477.

Yoshida, Y., Sauer, L., Tidwell, R., Skager, R., & Sorenson, A. (1997). Life satisfaction among the Japanese living abroad. *International Journal of Intercultural Relations, 21,* 57–69.

Yuchtman-Yaar, E., & Gottlieb, A. (1985). Technological

development and the meaning of work: A cross-cultural perspective. *Human Relations, 38,* 603–621.

Zaidi, S. M. H. (1979). Applied cross-cultural psychology: Submission of a cross-cultural psychologist from the Third World. In L. Eckensberger, W. J. Lonner, & Y. H. Poortinga (Eds.), *Cross-cultural contributions to psychology* (pp. 236–243). Amsterdam: Swets & Zeitlinger.

Zajonc, R. (1998). Emotions. In D. Gilbert, S. Fiske, & G. Lindzey (Eds.), *The handbook of social psychology* (Vol. 1, 4th ed., pp. 591–632). New York: McGraw-Hill.

Zaldivar, R. (1998a, August 3). Mexican Americans pose a paradox. *The Seattle Times,* p. A2.

Zaldivar, R. (1998b, August 3). Statistics mask big differences among Asians. *The Seattle Times,* p. A2.

Zhang, J. (1996). Suicides in Beijing, China, 1992–1993. *Suicide and Life Threatening Behavior, 26,* 175–180.

Zhang, J., & Bond, M. (1998). Personality and filial piety among college students in two Chinese societies: The added value of indigenous constructs. *Journal of Cross-Cultural Psychology, 29,* 402–417.

Zimba, R. (1994). The understanding of morality, convention, and personal preference in an African setting: Findings from Zambia. *Journal of Cross-Cultural Psychology, 25,* 369–393.

Author Index

Subject Index